INSI

Indonesia

INSIGHT GUIDE
Indonesia

ABOUT THIS BOOK

Editorial
Managing Editor
Francis Dorai
Editorial Director
Brian Bell

Distribution
UK & Ireland
GeoCenter International Ltd
The Viables Centre, Harrow Way
Basingstoke, Hants RG22 4BJ
Fax: (44) 1256 817988

United States
Langenscheidt Publishers, Inc.
46-35 54th Road, Maspeth, NY 11378
Fax: (718) 784 0640

Canada
Thomas Allen & Son Ltd
390 Steelcase Road East
Markham, Ontario L34 1G2
Fax: (1) 905 475 6747

Australia
Universal Publishers
1 Waterloo Road
Macquarie Park, NSW 2113
Fax: (61) 2 9888 9074

New Zealand
Hema Maps New Zealand Ltd (HNZ)
Unit D, 24 Ra ORA Drive
East Tamaki, Auckland
Fax: (64) 9 273 6479

Worldwide
**Apa Publications GmbH & Co.
Verlag KG (Singapore branch)**
38 Joo Koon Road, Singapore 628990
Tel: (65) 6865 1600. Fax: (65) 6861 6438

Printing
Insight Print Services (Pte) Ltd
38 Joo Koon Road, Singapore 628990
Tel: (65) 6865 1600. Fax: (65) 6861 6438

©2004 Apa Publications GmbH & Co.
Verlag KG (Singapore branch)
All Rights Reserved

First Edition 1983
Fifth Edition 2001
Updated 2004

CONTACTING THE EDITORS
We would appreciate it if readers would alert us to errors or outdated information by writing to:
Insight Guides, P.O. Box 7910,
London SE1 1WE, England.
Fax: (44 20) 7403 0290.
insight@apaguide.co.uk

NO part of this book may be reproduced, stored in a retrieval system or transmitted in any form or means electronic, mechanical, photocopying, recording or otherwise, without prior written permission of *Apa Publications*. Brief text quotations with use of photographs are exempted for book review purposes only. Information has been obtained from sources believed to be reliable, but its accuracy and completeness, and the opinions based thereon, are not guaranteed.

www.insightguides.com

This guidebook combines the interests and enthusiasms of two of the world's best known information providers: Insight Guides, whose titles have set the standard for visual travel guides since 1970, and Discovery Channel, the world's premier source of non-fiction television programming.

Insight Guides' editors provide practical advice and general understanding about a country's history, culture and people. Discovery Channel and its web site, www.discovery.com, help millions of viewers explore the world from the comfort of their own homes, and also encourage them to explore it first hand.

This fully updated edition of

Insight Guide: Indonesia is structured to convey an understanding of the sprawling archipelago and its culture, as well as to guide readers through its sights and activities:

◆ The **Features** section, indicated by a yellow bar at the top of each page, covers the history and culture of the country in a series of essays.

◆ The **Places** section, indicated by a blue bar, is a complete guide to all the sights and areas worth visiting. Places of special interest are cross-referenced to maps by numbers.

◆ The **Travel Tips**, with an orange bar, provides a handy reference for information on travel, hotels, shops, restaurants and more.

ABOUT THIS BOOK

The contributors

The task of threading the 18,110 islands of the sprawling Indonesian archipelago into a palatable read was undertaken by **Francis Dorai**, Insight Guides' Singapore-based managing editor. He completely restructured this fifth edition, building upon an earlier book produced by **Scott Rutherford**.

Dorai assembled a team of Indonesia experts for the task. The update of modern history was the work of **Dan Murphy** a Jakarta-based writer for the *Far Eastern Economic Review*.

People was written by **Dr Leo Suryadinata**, an expert on Indonesian communal politics at the National University of Singapore. Bali-based writer **Dipika Rai** updated Cuisine, while Dance and Theatre was revised by **Garrett Kam**, a Bali-based Hawaiian-American trained in Javanese dance and Indonesian textiles. Gamelan Music was written by musicologist **Michael Tenzer**, who has a doctorate in music from USC, Berkeley. Textiles, Arts and Crafts, and the Insight On picture story on Batik were penned by American writer and Indonesian textiles hobbyist **Suzanne D'Angelo**, who also updated the Java and Sumatra chapters. **Linda Hoffman**, an American writer based in Yogyakarta, updated the Nusa Tenggara and Kalimantan chapters, plus the Geography feature and the Travel Tips section. Hoffman also played a key role in tracking down many of the writers for this edition.

Bali-based writer **Debe Campbell**, who wrote the Insight On picture story on World Heritage Sites, was a natural choice to update the Bali chapter, while Jakarta-based teacher and writer **Linda Hahn** – who spends part of her time on Papua – updated Papua with her Indonesian husband **Leksmono Santoso**. The Maluku chapter was updated by **Tanya** and **Mira Alwi**, Maluku natives from the Banda islands, while Sulawesi and the picture story on nature was the work of **Arnaz Mehta**, a Manado-based writer and diver.

In 2004, the guide was updated again by the aforementioned **Linda Hoffman**, together with help from **Jacky Djokosetio** (Jakarta and West Java); **Dian N. Gafar** (Bali); **Lucas Zwaal** (Kalimantan); **Rudolf V. Santana** and several other travel professionals from all corners of Indonesia.

This edition is indebted to the excellent foundations created by the writers of previous editions: **John Haseman, Joseph Yogerst, Julia Clerk, Genevieve Spicer, Dra. Asriati, Dave Heckman, Eric Oey, Satyawati Suleiman, Kathy MacKinnon, Peter Hutton, Made Wijaya, Kal Muller, Paramita Abdurachman, Michel Vatin, Bernard Suryabrata** and **Sodersano**.

Map Legend

— ·· —	International Boundary
– – – –	Province Boundary
—•—	National Park/Reserve
– – – –	Ferry Route
✈ ✈	Airport: International/Regional
🚌	Bus Station
❶	Tourist Information
✉	Post Office
† †	Church/Ruins
†	Monastery
☪	Mosque
✡	Synagogue
🏰	Castle/Ruins
∴	Archaeological Site
∩	Cave
▌	Statue/Monument
★	Place of Interest

The main places of interest in the Places section are coordinated by number with a full-colour map (e.g. ❶), and a symbol at the top of every right-hand page tells you where to find the map.

Insight Guide Indonesia

CONTENTS

Maps

Indonesia **114–5**
Java **118–9**
Jakarta **122**
Greater Jakarta **128**
Yogyakarta (Jogja) **142**
Sumatra **173**
Lake Toba **176**
Bukittinggi **184**
Bali **198**
Ubud & Environs **217**
Lombok **247**
Nusa Tenggara **256–7**
Kalimantan **281**
Sulawesi **302**
Maluku **324**
Papua **336**

Inside front cover: Indonesia
Inside back cover: Jakarta

Introduction

A Land of Many Lands **15**

History

Decisive Dates **18**
Birth of Empires **21**
The Rise of Islam **26**
Dutch Colonial Years **31**
Modern Indonesia **37**

People

People **51**
Religion **59**
Customs and Rituals **64**

Features

Spice-Islands Cuisine **69**
Dance and Theatre **75**
Gamelan Music **82**
Textiles **87**
Arts and Crafts **95**
Nature in the Raw **101**

Contents ◆ 5

Sculptured rice fields near Ubud in Bali.

Insight on …

Indonesian Batik **92**
World Heritage Sites **106**
Balinese Festivals **224**
Nature in Sulawesi **312**

Information panels

Separatist Provinces **45**
The Chinese Minority **57**
Indian Morality Epics **81**
Symbolic Keris **157**
The Matrilineal Minangkabau **189**
The Bali Bombing **211**
Orangutan: Fight for Survival **287**

Travel Tips

Getting Acquainted .. **346**
Planning the Trip **347**
Practical Tips **350**
Getting Around **352**
Java **353**
Sumatra **366**
Bali **372**
Nusa Tenggara **382**
Kalimantan **390**
Sulawesi **394**
Maluku **398**
Papua (Irian Jaya) ... **398**
Language **401**
Further Reading **403**

◆ **Full Travel Tips index is on page 345**

Places

General Introduction **114**
JAVA: Introduction **118**
Jakarta **121**
West Java **131**
Central Java **141**
East Java **159**
SUMATRA: Introduction **169**
North Sumatra **171**
West Sumatra **181**
South Sumatra & Riau **191**
BALI: Introduction **199**
South Bali **201**
Central Bali **213**
North & West Bali **227**
East Bali **233**
NUSA TENGGARA: Introduction **243**
Lombok **245**
Sumbawa **255**
Komodo & Rinca **259**
Flores **263**
Solor & Alor Archipelagos **268**
Sumba **270**
Roti, Savu & West Timor **272**
KALIMANTAN: Introduction **277**
East & South Kalimantan **279**
Central & West Kalimantan **289**
SULAWESI: Introduction **299**
South Sulawesi &
  Tana Toraja **301**
Central & Southeast Sulawesi **309**
North Sulawesi **315**
MALUKU & PAPUA **321**
Maluku **323**
Papua (Irian Jaya) **333**

A Land of Many Lands

It's the world's fourth most populous nation, encompassing an astonishing variety of peoples and cultures

Indonesia is one of the very few nations on earth to span such a broad spectrum of world history and human civilisation – from its ancient Hindu-Javanese temples to Bali's modern luxury resorts, and from the stone-age lifestyle in Papua (Irian Jaya) to the immense metropolis that is Jakarta. The country's motto, *Bhinneka Tunggal Ika*, or Unity in Diversity, is no mere slogan. The population of nearly 220 million people is derived from 300 ethnic groups who speak over 250 distinct languages. The common element is the national language of Bahasa Indonesia, very similar to Malay.

Almost 90 percent of the people are Muslims with a significant Christian population. There are also smaller numbers who claim Hindu and Buddhist beliefs. In most cases, at least in the rural areas, these beliefs are augmented by indigenous, centuries-old animistic traditions. The fourth most populous nation in the world, Indonesia straddles two geographically-defined racial groups, the Asians to the west and the Melanesians in the east. The majority are Asians, particularly in the western part of the archipelago. Over the centuries, mostly through commerce and trade, Indians, Arabs and Europeans have mingled with the indigenous people. The largest non-indigenous ethnic group is the Chinese, who control nearly three-quarters of the nation's wealth while comprising only 5 percent of the population. This has not gone unnoticed in the recent past, making them a favourite target of irate rioters.

Indonesia's people are unevenly distributed across the archipelago with more than half living in Java and Bali alone, which cover only 7 percent of the total land area. With more than 120 million people living in Java – approximately 60 percent of the Indonesian population – the demands on its land and resources are considerable. As a result, the government relocated landless people from Java to the more remote provinces. But the transmigration programme's success was elusive and it caused friction between the locals and migrants who were given free land. With East Timor having acquired its independence in 1999, some Acehnese, Papuans and Malukans await their turn.

As the old Suharto order is dismantled, the current leadership struggles to come to terms with the demands of a newly democratised system. However, it will take awhile before the government can get its act together. Political infighting, a weak presidency, the clamour for independence and a weak economy all conspire against an immediate recovery. ❑

PRECEDING PAGES: boys with *topeng* (masks) from Cirebon, West Java; a Balinese *kebyar* dancer in gilded finery; harvesting tea leaves in Puncak, Java; village elders at a pagan ritual in remote Sumba island, East Nusa Tenggara.
LEFT: *jaipongan* drummer at the highland town Bandung in West Java.

Decisive Dates

PREHISTORIC YEARS

1.7 million years ago *Homo erectus* live in Java.
250,000 years ago Solo Man, the distinct evolutionary descendant of *Homo erectus*, inhabit Central Java.
40,000 years ago Fossil records of modern humans *(Homo sapiens)* found in Indonesia.
5,000 BC Austronesian peoples begin moving into Indonesia from the Philippines.
3,000 BC Plain pottery pots, open bowls, shell bracelets and beads found in Sulawesi and Timor.
500 BC–AD 500 Dong Son bronze age. Characteristic

of the period are ceremonial bronze drums and axes, decorated with engraved geometric, animal and human motifs. This distinctive style, highly influential in many fields of Indonesian art, spread together with bronze casting techniques.

INDIANISED KINGDOMS

AD 400 Hindu kingdoms of Tarumanegara and Kutai emerge in West Java and East Kalimantan.
760 Construction of Shivaitic temples at Dieng and Buddhist Borobudur monument in Central Java.
850 Rakai Pikatan, a prince of the Sanjaya dynasty, seizes control of Central Java. The Sailendra flee to Srivijaya, blocking all Javanese shipping throughout the South China Sea for more than a century.
860–1000 The golden age of Srivijaya.
930 Political centre of Java moves to East Java; rise of Hindu kingdoms on Bali.
1019 Airlangga, King Dharmawangsa's nephew, succeeds to the throne after the Srivijayan forces depart.

SINGASARI AND MAJAPAHIT

1222 Ken Arok founds Singasari dynasty.
1275 Ken Arok sends first successful naval expeditions against Srivijaya to wrest control of the important maritime trade. Succeeded by Kertanagara.
1293 Kertanagara killed by Jayakatwang, one of his vassals. Civil war ensues in Singasari; and Mongol invasion joins Kertanagara's son-in-law Wijaya against Jayakatwang.
1294 Wijaya founds kingdom of Majapahit and rules as Kertarajasa.
1297 Sultan Malik Saleh of Pasai rules as first known Muslim king in the archipelago.
1330–50 Adityawarman rules Minangkabau.
1389 Majapahit's decline begins.
1403–06 Struggle for control erupts into civil war.
1429 The country is reunited; Majapahit loses control of the western Java Sea and the straits to Islamic Malacca.
15th century Majapahit and Kediri are conquered by new Islamic state of Demak on Java's north coast; the entire Hindu-Javanese aristocracy move to nearby Bali. All trading ports of the western archipelago brought within Malacca's orbit, including the important ports along the north coast of Java.
early 16th century Islamisation of coastal kingdoms of Java begins.
1511 The Portuguese seize control of Malacca.
1522 Portuguese build fort in Ternate.
1552–70 Banten rises as independent state under Sultan Hasanuddin.
1570 Revolt against the Portuguese in Ternate.

DUTCH COLONIAL YEARS

1596 First Dutch ships drop anchor in Banten.
1602 The Dutch form the influential United Dutch East Indies Company (VOC).
1605 Dutch seize Ambon.
1621 Dutch take control of the Banda Islands.
1641 Dutch capture Malacca from the Portuguese.
1646–67 Despotic reign of Amangkurat I in Java.
1666–69 Makassar wars.
1740–55 Great war in Java.
1799 Dutch financiers receive stunning news that the VOC is bankrupt.
1800 Dutch government assumes control of all former VOC possessions.

RESISTANCE AND REPRESSION
1811–16 Brief period of English rule under Thomas Stamford Raffles.
1811 Raffles authors monumental *History of Java*.
1825–30 Cataclysmic Java War against Dutch led by Diponegoro decimates population.
1830 In an attempt to remedy government debt, the Dutch introduce a land tax payable by labour or land use known as the "Cultivation System".
1821–38 Padri War between the Dutch and the Minangkabau of West Sumatra.

NATIONAL AWAKENING
1908 Indonesians attending Dutch schools begin to form regional student organisations; new national consciousness takes shape.
1910 Indonesian communist movement founded.
1910–30 Turbulent period of strikes, violence and organised rebellions.
1927 First major political party with Indonesian independence as its goal is founded by Sukarno.
1928 Second all-Indies student conference; "one nation, one language, one people" motto proclaimed.
1933 Crackdown ensues; Sukarno and all other student leaders exiled to distant islands for 10 years.

WORLD WAR II AND INDEPENDENCE
1942 Japanese invade Bali and Java.
1944 Japanese promise independence in an attempt to maintain faltering Indonesian support.
1945 Japan surrenders. Nationalist leaders Sukarno and Muhammad Hatta declare Indonesia's independence. Dutch return to resume control; war for independence breaks out.
1949 The Dutch acknowledge Indonesia's independence under UN pressure.
Late 1950s A communist insurgency prompts Sukarno to declare martial law. Sukarno resurrects the "revolutionary" constitution of 1945.

SUKARNO AND SUHARTO YEARS
1960 Sukarno dissolves parliament; his anti-colonial sentiments become more militant.
1963 Confrontation with newly-independent Malaysia reveals Sukarno's brand of militant nationalism.
1965 Blood-letting ensues after failed communist coup. The Chinese are the focus of anti-communist attacks. Up to 500,000 people are killed.
1966 Sukarno persuaded to sign over powers to his protégé, Suharto, who takes over presidency. Until 1998, he is re-elected six times.
1975 Indonesian troops invade East Timor after the Portuguese leave their former colony.
1976 Indonesia annexes East Timor.
1990s Indonesia joins Asia's "tiger" economies.
1996 Rioting in Jakarta sparked by government efforts to halt the rise of Sukarno's daughter Megawati Sukarnoputri. East Timor independence activists Jose Ramos Horta and Bishop Belo win Nobel Peace Prize.
1997 Asian economic crisis begins; Indonesia is the worst performer. Rupiah crashes, banks collapse and foreign debt surges.
1998 Suharto refuses to reform economy, riots over

rising prices and corruption mount. Suharto is forced to resign amidst mass student uprising; vice-president B.J. Habibie becomes Indonesia's third president.
1999 East Timor votes for independence; Christian-Muslim fighting erupts in Maluku; Indonesia's first democratic elections in 40 years are held; Abdurrahman Wahid becomes the fourth president.
2000 Slow reform of the military begins. Human rights and corruption investigations also launched.
2001 Wahid is impeached and resigns amidst charges of corruption and incompetence. Megawati Sukarnoputri becomes the fifth president. Economy continues to flounder and Jakarta's relations with separatist movements in Aceh and Papua worsen.
2004 First direct presidential election is held.

PRECEDING PAGES: Dutch map showing the prized Spice Islands of Maluku. **LEFT:** the 9th-century Hindu Candi Plaosan. **RIGHT:** Sukarno and his ministers, 1958.

BIRTH OF EMPIRES

Java Man, whose discovery shook off Southeast Asia's prehistoric backwater status, lived in a fertile region that later saw the rise of great maritime empires

Controversial excavations in northern Thailand have revealed that a metal-producing culture may have existed there much earlier than in China or India. Its discovery has overturned the notion of Southeast Asia as a prehistoric backwater, as some scholars now think that this region could have been one of the great prehistoric cradles of human development.

Such speculation, however, is still premature in the case of Indonesia, where relatively few neolithic sites have been dated with precision.

Java Man

Indonesian archaeological findings have contributed more than their share of controversy in the past. In 1891, a Dutch military physician discovered a fossilised primate jawbone in Central Java with human characteristics. The jawbone was at first discounted as belonging to an extinct species of apes. But in the following year, two more humanoid fossils were uncovered and thought to be the world's first evidence of Darwin's "missing link". But Darwin's evolutionary theories were still in dispute at the time and, the discovery, dubbed Java Man, was only vindicated with the discovery of similar fossils outside Beijing in 1921.

Java Man and Peking Man are now recognised as members of the species *Homo erectus*, a direct ancestor of people who inhabited the Old World from about 1.7 million to 250,000 years ago. The body skeleton of *Homo erectus* was essentially modern, but the skull was thick, long and low, possessing a massive face with strongly protruding brow ridges. Many fossils of this type have been discovered in Central Java, some more than a million years old. Replicas are on display at the Museum Geologi *(see page 136)* in Bandung, and at the Museum Trinil *(see pages 107 and 156)* at Sangiran, near Solo.

Research has shown that *Homo erectus* probably could not speak, but uttered sounds to communicate. They were omnivores and food gatherers who lived in caves as well as open campsites. They also produced an extensive stone tool kit that included flaked choppers, axes and adzes.

The classification of more recent humanoid fossils is still very much in doubt, particularly

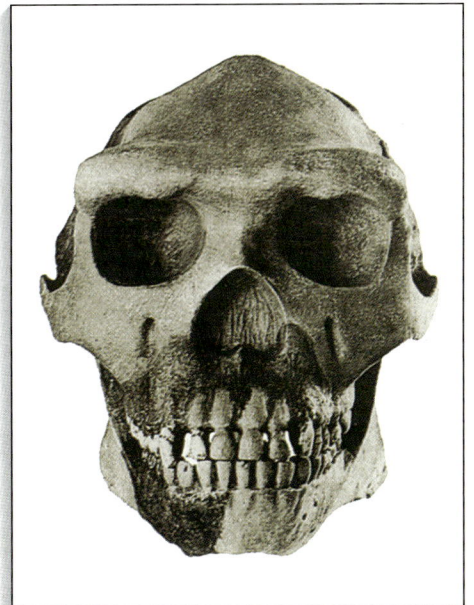

CONTROVERSIAL SOLO MAN

Controversy among archaeologists is centred on the dating and classification of the so-called Solo Man fossils, discovered between 1931 and 1933 next to the Solo River, at Ngandong, in Central Java. Some scholars classify Solo Man as an intermediate species, dating from perhaps 250,000 years ago, of distinct Southeast-Asian descent from *Homo erectus*. Others insist he was simply an advanced *Homo erectus* species who survived in isolation and then hit an evolutionary dead-end.

All Southeast Asian *Homo sapiens* fossils prior to about 5,000 BC are members of the Australoid group of people who survive today in isolated parts in the region.

LEFT: serene countenance of a *bodhisattva* at the 9th-century Candi Sari temple, Prambanan area, Java.
RIGHT: reconstructed skull of the Java Man.

for the transitional species between *Homo erectus* and modern humans. Central to the problem is the question of whether modern people evolved in a single place (thought by some to be sub-Saharan Africa) and then spread to other areas, or whether parallel evolutions occurred in various places and at different rates. Fossil records can be interpreted either way.

> **STRIKING MEGALITHS**
>
> The most striking megaliths in Indonesia are the carved statues of riding men and wrestling animals found on the Pasemah plateau in Sumatra. No definite date can be given for these.

Beginning about 20,000 years ago, there is evidence of human burials and partial cremations. Several cave paintings (mainly hand stencils, but also human and animal figures) found in south-western Sulawesi and New Guinea may be 10,000 or more years old.

The neolithic centuries – which appear to have begun soon after the end of the last Ice Age, around 10,000 BC – are characterised here, as elsewhere, by the advent of village settlements, domesticated animals, polished stone tools, pottery and food cultivation.

In northern Thailand, one recently discovered neolithic site has been reliably placed in the 7th millennium BC. For Indonesia, however, there is no evidence prior to the 3rd millennium BC, and most sites are of a more recent date. In Southwest Sulawesi and the East Timor plain for instance, pottery pots and open bowls dating from about 3,000 BC have been found, together with shell bracelets, discs, beads, adzes and the bones of pig and dog species that may have been domesticated.

The first agriculturalists in Indonesia probably grew yams before the introduction of rice. In fact, rice came to much of Indonesia only in recent centuries, and yams are still a staple crop on many eastern islands, together with bananas, taro (a root vegetable), breadfruit, coconuts and sugar cane. Bark clothing was produced with stone-pounding tools and pottery was shaped with the aid of a wooden paddle and a stone anvil tapper.

Neolithic Indonesians were undoubtedly experienced seafarers, like their Polynesian cousins who were spreading across the Pacific at this time. Today, the outrigger is commonly found throughout Indonesia and Oceania.

Dong Son bronze culture

It was once thought that Southeast Asia's Bronze Age began with the Chinese-influenced Dong Son bronze culture of northern Vietnam, in the 1st millennium BC. However, the discovery of 5,000-year-old copper and bronze tools in northern Thailand has raised the possibility of similar developments elsewhere. All early Indonesian bronzes known to date are clearly of the Dong Son type.

The finest Dong Son ceremonial bronze drums and axes are decorated with engraved geometric, animal and human motifs. This decorative style was highly influential in many fields of Indonesian art, and seems to have spread together with the bronze casting technique, as ancient stone moulds have been found in Indonesia. The sophisticated "lost-wax" technique of bronze casting was employed and such bronzes were found as far east as New Guinea.

Who were the Indonesian producers of Dong Son bronzes? It is difficult to say, but it seems small kingdoms based on wet-rice agriculture and foreign trade were flourishing in the archipelago during this period. Articles of Indian manufacture have been found at several prehistoric sites in Indonesia, and a panel from a bronze drum found on Sangeang island, near Sumbawa, depicts figures in ancient Chinese dress. Early Han texts mention the clove-producing islands of eastern Indonesia, and it is certain that by the 2nd century BC, trade was widespread in the archipelago.

Indianised kingdoms

Beginning in the 2nd century AD, a number of sophisticated civilisations emerged in Southeast Asia – civilisations whose cosmology, literature, architecture and political organisation were patterned on those of India. These kingdoms are known for the wonderful monuments which they created: Borobudur, Prambanan, Angkor, Pagan and others. Yet their creators remain largely an enigma. Who built these Indian monuments and how is it that Southeast Asians came to have such a profound knowledge of Indian culture in ancient times? It seems Southeast Asia was a thriving trade and cultural centre even in prehistoric times.

The most plausible theory is that Southeast Asian rulers Indianised their own kingdoms – either by employing Indian Brahmans or sending their own people to India to acquire knowledge. The motivation is clear: Sanskrit writing and texts, along with sophisticated Indian rituals and architectural techniques, afforded a ruler greater organisational control, wealth and social status. It also enabled him to participate in an expanding Indian trading network.

The first specific references to Indonesian rulers and kingdoms are found in written Chinese sources. Written in the south Indian *Pallava* script, the stone inscriptions were issued by Indonesian rulers in two different areas of the archipelago: Kutai on the eastern coast of Kalimantan, and Tarumanegara on the Citarum River, in West Java near Bogor. Both rulers were Hindus.

There is also the interesting figure of Fa Hsien, a Chinese Buddhist monk who journeyed to India in the early 5th century to obtain Buddhist scriptures and on his way home was shipwrecked and stranded on Java. Fa Hsien noted there were many Brahmans and heretics on Java and that the Buddhist Dharma there was not worth mentioning.

At the end of the 7th century, a Buddhist kingdom at Palembang took over the vital Malacca and Sunda straits. This was Srivijaya, which ruled throughout the next 600 years.

Srivijaya's maritime trade

The kingdom of Srivijaya relied for existence not on agriculture, but on control of maritime

LEFT: central Javanese neolithic stone tools.
ABOVE: Chinese-influenced Dong Son bronze-age ceremonial drum.

trade. Most of its citizens were sailors who lived on boats (as do many of the coastal Malay *orang laut*, or sea people, today).

It has been speculated that Srivijaya rose to prominence as a result of a substitution of Sumatran aromatics – the so-called *p'o-ssu* – for expensive Middle Eastern frankincense and myrrh. But Srivijaya was also located in a strategic position and is said to have had the largest ships in the world at the time, and appear to have achieved regular direct sailings to India and China by the late 8th century.

The nearest area suitable for wet-rice agriculture was in Central Java, where great Indianised kingdoms established themselves from the early 8th century onward. They first supplied Srivijaya with rice, and then later began to compete with it for a share of the trade.

Sanjaya and the Sailendra

The ever-present rivalry between Buddhist and Hindu ruling families in Central Java bore fruit with the surplanting of the Hindu rulers, Sanjaya and his descendants, by the Sailendra, a Buddhist line of kings from northern Java.

Both Buddhist, the Sailendra and Srivijaya maintained close relations and controlled Java for about a century. During this time, they constructed the magnificent Buddhist monuments of Borobudur, Mendut, Kalasan, Sewu and numerous others in the shadow of Gunung Merapi.

Meanwhile, the Sanjaya line continued to rule over outlying areas as vassals of the Sailendra, building Hindu temples in remote areas of Java – the Dieng Plateau and Gunung Ungaran. Around 850, the Sanjaya prince Rakai Pikatan married a Sailendra princess and seized control of Central Java. The Sailendra fled to Srivijaya, blocking all Javanese shipping throughout the South China Sea for more than a century.

Rakai Pikatan commemorated his victory by erecting the splendid Prambanan temple, the Hindu equivalent of Buddhist Borobudur.

A succession of Hindu kings followed, but the capital was suddenly transferred to East Java around 930. A number of factors might account for this. The Sailendra kings, who were installed at Srivijaya and had shut off the vital overseas trade from Java's north coast, may have threatened to return to Central Java. An eruption of Gunung Merapi may have closed the roads to the north coastal ports and covered Central Java in volcanic ash. There is also the possibility of an epidemic or of mass migration to the more fertile lands of East Java.

An eastern Javanese empire prospered in the 10th century and attacked and occupied Srivijaya for two years. Srivijaya retaliated later with a huge seaborne force that destroyed the Javanese capital, killed the ruler, King Dharmawangsa, and splintered the realm into numerous petty fiefdoms. It took nearly 20 years for the next great king, Airlangga, to restore the empire.

Airlangga was the dead king's nephew and he succeeded to the throne in 1019 after the Srivijayan forces departed. He is best known as a patron of the arts and an ascete who had Indian Sanskrit classics translated into Javanese. To appease his two ambitious sons, he divided the empire into equal halves, Kediri and Janggala (or Daha and Kahuripan). Kediri became the more powerful and is remembered today as the source of numerous works of old Javanese literature, mainly adaptations of the Indian epics in the poetic *kekawin* form.

Java prospered as never before under the rule of successive East Javan empires, which combined the benefits of a strong agricultural economy and a lucrative maritime trade. At this time, Javanese were the master shipbuilders and mariners of Southeast Asia. During the 14th century, at the height of the Majapahit empire, they controlled the sea lanes in the Indonesian archipelago, and to faraway India and China.

The Singasari dynasty was founded by Ken Arok in 1222. During his rule of Janggala, Ken Arok revolted against his sovereign, the ruler of Kediri, and set up his new capital at Singasari, near present-day Malang. The extraordinary Kertanagara, the last Singasari king, was a scholar and a statesman of the Tantric Bhairawa sect of Buddhism. In 1275 and 1291, he sent successful naval expeditions against Srivijaya and wrested control of the maritime trade.

Majapahit

Kertanagara's son-in-law Wijaya married four of Kertanagara's daughters and established a new capital in 1294 by the Sungai Brantas (near present-day Trowulan) in an area known for its *pahit* (bitter) maja fruits. The new kingdom became known as Majapahit. Its extensive system of canals were probably used to transport rice and other goods downriver to the seaports.

Majapahit was the first empire to embrace the entire Indonesian archipelago and reached its zenith in the mid-14th century under Wijaya's grandson, Hayam Wuruk, and his able prime minister Gajah Mada. Decline set in almost immediately after Hayam Wuruk's death in 1389. However, a smouldering struggle for supremacy erupted into civil war between 1403 and 1406, and although the country was reunited in 1429, Majapahit had lost control of the western Java Sea and the straits to a new Islamic power located at Malacca.

Towards the end of the 15th century, Majapahit and Kediri were conquered by the new Islamic state of Demak, on Java's north coast, and the entire Hindu-Javanese aristocracy then relocated to nearby Bali. ❏

KUBLAI KHAN SNUBBED

In the late 13th century, the Buddhist king Kertanagara's control of maritime trade was so complete that Kublai Khan, the great Mongol emperor from China, sent ambassadors to demand tribute from Java. Kertanagara not only refused but had the effrontery to disfigure the Mongol envoy, for which gesture the enraged Khan sent a powerful fleet in 1293 to Java.

The fleet landed only to discover that Kertanagara had been murdered by his vassal Jayakatwang. The Chinese, with an ally in Kertanagara's son-in-law, Wijaya, stayed in Java for about a year and defeated Jayakatwang. Wijaya later turned on the Mongol generals and drove them off.

LEFT: 5th-century Indian *Pallava* inscription and footprints of Hindu ruler of Tarumanegara in West Java.
RIGHT: sculpture of Ken Dedes, wife of Ken Arok.

THE RISE OF ISLAM

The growth of maritime trade was the conduit that brought Islam to the shores of Indonesia through its port towns of north-eastern Sumatra

Islam arrived in the Indonesian archipelago, not through a series of holy wars or armed rebellions, but rather atop the crest of a peaceful economic expansion along the trade routes of the East. Although Muslim traders had visited the region for centuries, it was not until the important Indian trading centre of Gujarat fell into Muslim hands in the 13th century that Indonesian rulers began to convert to the new faith. The trading ports of Samudra-Pasai and Perlak on the north-eastern coast of Sumatra became the first Islamic domains in Indonesia. Marco Polo mentions that Perlak was already Muslim at the time of his visit in 1292, and the tombstone of the first Islamic ruler of Samudra, Sultan Malik al Saleh, bears the date 1297.

Trade and Islam

Indonesia's conversion to Islam was not accomplished on the basis of faith alone; there were compelling worldly benefits to be obtained.

Islamic traders were becoming a dominant force on the international scene. They had controlled the overland trade from China and India to Europe, via Persia and the Levant. With the major textile producing ports of India in their hands, they began to dominate the maritime trade routes through South and East Asia as well. Conversion thus ensured that Indonesian rulers could participate in the growing international Islamic trade network. And equally important, Islam provided these rulers with protection against the encroachments of two aggressive regional powers – the Siamese (Thai) to the north, and the Javanese.

To understand the Islamisation of Indonesia, an understanding of the basic political and economic structure of the region is necessary.

There were essentially three important types of kingdoms. First, there were the coastal states around the Strait of Malacca who produced little food and few trade goods of their own, but relied on trade and control of the seas for their existence. Then there were the vast inland states on Java and Bali that produced surpluses of rice in irrigated paddies and possessed large populations. Finally, there were the tiny kingdoms on the eastern Maluku islands producing valuable cloves, nutmeg and mace – precious for trade – but little food.

These kingdoms imported luxury goods from abroad: textiles and porcelain, precious metals, medicines and gems. The coastal and spice-

PROPAGATION BY THEATRE

The traditional account of the Islamisation of Java is a fascinating one. According to Javanese chronicles, nine Islamic saints (*wali sanga*) propagated Islam through the Javanese shadow plays (*wayang kulit*) and *gamelan* music. They introduced the *kalimat shahadat*, or Islamic confession of faith and the reading of Koranic prayers, to performances of the Hindu *Ramayana* and *Mahabharata* epics. No better explanation could be given for the origins of Islamic syncretism in Java.

Today, Islam is the professed religion of 90 percent of all Indonesians and its traditions and rituals affect all aspects of their daily life.

producing states also needed to import rice. The trade was not only inter-island, but involved foreigners as well, principally Indians and Chinese, but also Arabs, Siamese and Burmese.

Islam received its greatest boost when, in 1436, the shrewd ruler of the port of Malacca converted to the Islamic faith upon returning from an extended stay in China. Up until now, Malacca had been a vassal of China ruled by descendants of the prestigious Hindu line of Palembang (Srivijaya) and peninsula kings who had been attacked and evicted by the Javanese and Siamese during the 14th century. China had proved a valuable patron of Malacca since its founding in 1402, but by 1436, China's influence in the region was on the wane, and the Siamese were again demanding tribute.

By embracing Islam, the ruler of Malacca gained protection against Siamese advances. As a port ruled by a dynasty with a long tradition of catering to overseas traders, Malacca was in an excellent position to capitalise upon the commercial successes of the Islamic world. By 1500, Malacca was to become a major trading port in the region and the greatest emporium in the East, a city comparable in size to the largest European cities then.

> **A TRADERS' FAITH**
>
> During the 16th century, Islam was the faith of traders and urban dwellers and firmly entrenched in the substantial maritime centres of the Southeast Asian region.

Conquest

During the 15th century, all of the trading ports of the western archipelago were brought within Malacca's orbit, including the important ports along the north coast of Java. Traditionally, these ports owed their allegiance to the great inland Hindu-Javanese kingdoms, acting in effect as import-export and shipping agents, exchanging Javanese-grown rice for spices, silks, gold, textiles, medicines, gems and other items in a complex series of value-added transactions. After about 1400, however, the power of the inland Javanese rulers was rapidly declining and the rulers of the coastal cities were seeking ways to assert their independence and retain the profits of the trade. Gradually, through intermarriage between leading Islamic traders and local aristocrats, relations were cemented with Malacca's Muslims.

LEFT: tombstone of first Islamic monarch, Sultan Malik al Saleh. **RIGHT:** Muslim traders helped spread Islam.

If Islamisation at first occurred peacefully in the coastal kingdoms of Java, a turning point was reached sometime in the early 16th century, when the newly-founded Islamic kingdom of Demak on the north-central coast attacked and conquered the last great Hindu-Buddhist kingdom of Majapahit on Java. They drove the Hindu rulers to the east and annexed the agriculturally rich Javanese hinterlands. Demak then consolidated its control over the entire north coast by subduing Tuban, Gresik, Madura, Surabaya,

Cirebon, Banten and Jayakarta – emerging as the master of Java by the 16th century.

During the 16th century, Islam continued to spread throughout the Indonesian archipelago, but the whole system of Islamic economic and political alliances was swiftly overturned in the dramatic conquest of Malacca by a small band of Portuguese in 1511.

Portuguese meddling

Although the Portuguese were never able to control more than a portion of the total trade in the region, the capture of Malacca itself had far-reaching consequences.

Never again was an Islamic state able to exert

the sort of regional influence once exercised by Malacca. Instead, a number of competing Islamic centres vied with each other – and with the Europeans – for the area's trade, with the end result that the Dutch were later able to divide and conquer almost all of them.

The Islamic kingdom of Aceh, at the northern tip of Sumatra, was best situated to benefit from the fall of Malacca. Islamic traders resorted increasingly to Aceh's harbour and a succession of aggressive Acehnese rulers slowly built an empire by conquering lesser ports all along the eastern coast of Sumatra.

Although repeated attacks on Portuguese Malacca and Islamic Johor to the east on the Malay Peninsula were unsuccessful, Aceh nevertheless established itself as the major sea power in the Indonesian archipelago. The Acehnese remained powerful and fiercely independent long after that golden age, resisting the Dutch into the 20th century. Today, Aceh is one of the most devoutly Muslim regions in the Indonesian archipelago.

During the second half of the 16th century, Java's centre of power abruptly shifted from the north coast to the southern part of Central Java. The new kingdom was called Mataram, the name of both the area and the classical

VASTLY GREEN CITIES

During the 16th century, Indonesia cities were physically different from cities in Europe, the Middle East, India or China. For the most part built without walls, Indonesian cities were located at river mouths or on wide plains, and relied upon surrounding villages for their defence. An official envoy from the Sultanate of Aceh to the Ottoman empire explained that Acehnese defences consisted not of walls, but of "stout hearts in fighting the enemy and a large number of elephants".

Indonesian cities tended also to be green. Coconut, banana and other fruit trees grew everywhere, and most of the widely-spaced wooden or bamboo houses had vegetable gardens. The royal compound was the centre for defence and might have walls and a moat. With perhaps no more than 5 million people in the entire archipelago, land had no intrinsic value except what people made of it. In 1613, when the English wanted some land to build a fortress in Makassar, they had to recompense the residents not for the space, but for the coconut palms.

With so few people and so much land, it is not surprising that the urban population of Indonesia in the 16th century at least equalled the agrarian population. Thus, the typical Indonesian of that period was not a peasant, but a town dweller engaged as an artisan, sailor, worker or trader.

Javanese kingdoms once located here. Mataram first conquered Demak; the eastern half of Java and other northern coastal ports were subdued by about 1625.

Makassar

Although the Mataram dynasty was Muslim, it patterned itself after the great Hindu-Buddhist empires of previous centuries. Court chroniclers traced the lineage of the Mataram line to the god-kings of Majapahit, rather than to the Islamic rulers of Demak. In fact, the fall of Majapahit to Demak was described in these chronicles as the "disappearance of the Light of the Universe", a rather odd viewpoint for a Muslim writer who narrated the demise of an infidel kingdom at the hands of an Islamic saint.

Clearly, identification with the prestigious Majapahit royal house was of greater importance than religious solidarity with the coastal powers. Indeed, the Islam of the central Javanese courts became an eccentric one – a potpourri of ancient mystical practices, European pomp and Islamic circumstance.

Islam came to the remaining islands of eastern Indonesia only sporadically. The trading port of Makassar in Sulawesi became an important Islamic centre, expanding rapidly towards the end of the 16th century. It captured a substantial share of the eastern spice trade for several decades, until it was forced to submit to the Dutch in 1667. Makassar was very cosmopolitan, with nobility who spoke Arabic and Portuguese and who were patrons of scholars.

Portuguese reports speak of the Islamic conversion of Makassar in the following way. Undecided whether to adopt Islam or Christianity, the Makassarese sent their emissaries to Aceh and to Portuguese Malacca, requesting that religious teachers be sent. The Acehnese, according to the account, simply arrived first.

In the Spice Islands of Maluku – Ternate, Tidore, Hitu, Ambon and Banda – most of the local rulers converted to Islam fairly early (some time in the 15th century) and maintained close ties with, first Malacca, then Makassar.

However, in the 16th and 17th centuries, these kingdoms were conquered by a succession of European powers; those who survived converted to Christianity. On other islands, Jesuit missionaries arrived before the Muslims, and together with late-arriving Dutch Calvinists, established Christian strongholds.

LEFT: Portuguese ships at Ternate in the Spice Islands of Maluku (Moluccas).
ABOVE: the historic mosque (Mesjid Agung) at Banten, one of the towns subdued by Demak.

The Dutch Colonial Years

The hunt for highly-prized spices drew the Western powers to the East where Indonesia's resource-rich islands were a star attraction

The saga of the Dutch in Indonesia began in 1596, when four small Dutch vessels, led by the incompetent and arrogant Cornelis de Houtman, dropped anchor in Banten, then the largest pepper port in the archipelago. Repeatedly blown off course and racked by disease and dissension, the de Houtman expedition was a disaster. In Banten, the sea-weary Dutch crew went on a drinking binge and had to be chased back to their ships by order of an angry prince, who then refused to do business. Hopping from port to port along the north coast of Java, de Houtman wisely confined his sailors to the ships and managed to purchase spices. On arrival in Bali, the entire crew jumped ship, and it was months before de Houtman could muster a quorum for the return voyage.

Back in Holland two years later, with only three lightly-laden ships and a third of the original crew, de Houtman's voyage was nonetheless hailed a success. So costly were spices in Europe that the sale of the meagre cargo sufficed to cover all expenses, even producing a modest profit. This touched off a veritable fever of speculation in Dutch commercial circles, and in the following year, five consortiums dispatched a total of 22 ships to the Indies.

Dutch East India Company

Since the 15th century, ports of the two Dutch coastal provinces in northern Europe, Holland and Zeeland, had served as entrepots for goods shipped to Germany and the Baltic states. Many Dutch merchants grew wealthy on this trade, and following the outbreak of war with Spain in 1568, they began to expand their shipping fleets rapidly, so that by the 1590s, they were trading directly with the Levant and Brazil.

Thus, when a Dutchman published his itinerary to the East Indies in 1596, it occasioned the immediate dispatch of de Houtman and later expeditions. Indeed, so keen was the interest in direct trade with the Indies that all Dutch traders soon came to recognise the need for cooperation, in order to minimise competition and maximise profits. In 1602, they formed the United Dutch East India Company (known by its Dutch initials, VOC), one of the world's first joint-stock corporations. It was empowered to

negotiate treaties, raise armies, build fortresses and wage war in Asia on behalf of Holland.

In its early years, the VOC met with only limited success. Several trading posts were opened, and Ambon was taken from the Portuguese in 1605. But Spanish and English, not to mention Muslim, competition kept spice prices high in Indonesia and low in Europe. Then, in 1614, a young accountant, Jan Pieterszoon Coen, convinced the directors that only a more forceful policy would make the company profitable. Coen was given command of VOC operations, and promptly embarked on a series of military adventures that were to set the pattern of Dutch behaviour in the region.

LEFT: Sultan Hamengkubuwono VIII of Yogyakarta arm-in-arm with the enemy – the Dutch resident.
RIGHT: Jan Pieterszoon Coen led the Dutch campaign.

Coen's first step was to establish a permanent headquarters at Jayakarta, on the northwestern coast of Java, close to the pepper-producing parts of Sumatra and the strategic Sunda Strait.

In 1618, he sought and received permission from Prince Wijayakrama of Jayakarta to expand the existing Dutch post, and proceeded to build a stone barricade mounted with cannons. The prince protested that fortifications were not part of their agreement; Coen responded by bombarding and destroying the palace. A siege of the fledgling Dutch fortress began, in which the powerful Bantenese and a

recently-arrived English fleet joined the Jayakartans. Meanwhile, Coen escaped to Ambon, leaving a few men in defence of the fort and its valuable contents.

Coen's cunning

Five months later, Coen returned to discover his men still in possession of their post. Although outnumbered 30 to one, they had rather unwittingly played one foe against another by agreeing to any and all demands, but never actually surrendering their position due to the mutual suspicion and timidity of the three opposing parties. Coen set his adversaries to flight in a series of dramatic attacks, undertaken with a small force of 1,000 men that included several score of Japanese mercenaries. Jayakarta was razed to the ground and construction of a new Dutch town begun, including canals, drawbridges, docks, warehouses, barracks, a central square, a city hall and a church – all protected by a high stone wall and a moat. In short, another Amsterdam.

Coen subsequently learned that during the darkest days of the siege, many of the Dutch defenders had behaved in a most unseemly manner: drinking, singing and fornicating. Worst of all, they had broken open the company storehouse and divided the contents among themselves. Those involved were immediately executed and memories of the infamous siege soon faded – save one. The defenders had dubbed their fortress Batavia; the name stuck.

Coen's next step was to secure control of the five tiny nutmeg- and mace-producing Banda Islands. He brought an expeditionary force there and, with the infamous Japanese *samurai*, rounded up and killed most of the 15,000 inhabitants within weeks. Three of the islands were transformed into spice plantations, managed by Dutch colonists and worked by slaves.

In the years that followed, the Dutch gradually tightened their grip on the spice trade. From Ambon, they attempted to negotiate a monopoly in cloves with the rulers of Ternate and Tidore. But the smuggling of cloves and clove trees continued. Traders obtained these and other goods at the new Islamic port of Makassar, in southern Sulawesi. The Dutch repeatedly blockaded Makassar and imposed treaties barring the Makassarese from trading with other nations, but were unable for many years to enforce them. Finally, in 1669, following three years of bitter fighting, the Makassarese surrendered to the superior Dutch forces.

Dutch control

The Dutch achieved effective control of the eastern archipelago and its lucrative spice trade by the end of the 17th century. In the western half of the archipelago, however, they became increasingly embroiled in fruitless intrigues and wars, particularly in Java. This came about largely because the Dutch presence at Batavia disturbed a delicate balance of power in Java.

Batavia came under Javanese attack as early as 1628. Sultan Agung, the third and greatest ruler of the Mataram kingdom, was aggressively expanding his domain and had concluded a successful five-year siege on Surabaya. He now controlled all of central and eastern Java, and intended to take western Java by pushing out the Dutch and conquering Banten.

Agung nearly succeeded. A large Javanese expeditionary force momentarily breached Batavia's defences, but was then driven back outside the walls in a last-ditch effort by Coen. The Javanese were not prepared for such resistance and withdrew for lack of provisions. A year later, Sultan Agung sent an even larger force of 10,000 provided with huge stockpiles of rice for a protracted siege. Coen, however,

The Makassar wars of 1666–69 and their aftermath created a diaspora of Makassarese and Buginese refugees. Many of them fled to East Java, where they united under the leadership of a Madurese prince, Trunajaya. Aided and abetted by the Mataram crown prince, Trunajaya successfully stormed through Central Java and plundered the Mataram capital in 1677. Amangkurat I died while on the retreat, fleeing from the enemy forces.

Once in control of Java, Trunajaya renounced his alliance with the young Mataram prince and declared himself king. The crown prince pleaded for Dutch support, promising to reim-

learned of the stockpiles and destroyed them before the Javanese even arrived. Poorly-led, starving and sick, the Javanese troops died by the thousands outside the walls of Batavia. Never again was Mataram a threat to the city.

Relations between the Dutch and the Javanese improved during the despotic reign of Amangkurat I (1646–77). They had common enemies – the *pasisir* trading kingdoms of the northern Java coast. Ironically, the Dutch conquest of Makassar later led to their ally's demise.

LEFT: built on the site of Jayakarta, the Dutch stronghold, Batavia, resembled Amsterdam.
ABOVE: Javanese troops were no match for the Dutch.

EXPLOITATIVE CULTIVATION

In reality, the pernicious effects of the cultivation system were apparent from the beginning. While in theory the system called for peasants to surrender only a portion of their land and labour, in practice certain lands were worked exclusively for the Dutch by forced labour. The island of Java, one of the richest pieces of real estate on earth, was transformed into a huge Dutch plantation, imposing unimaginable hardships and injustices upon the Javanese. Private plantations largely replaced government ones after 1870, but, in fact, some government coffee plantations continued to employ forced labour well into the 20th century.

burse all military expenses and to award the Dutch valuable trade concessions. The Dutch swallowed the bait and mounted a costly campaign to capture Trunajaya. This ended in 1680 with the crown prince, who styled himself Amangkurat II, being restored to the throne.

But the new king was in no position to fulfil his end of the bargain with the Dutch; his treasury had been looted and his kingdom was in ruins. All he had was territory, and although much of West Java was ceded to the Dutch, the VOC still suffered a heavy loss.

In 1799, Dutch financiers received stunning news: the VOC was bankrupt. During the 18th century, the spice trade had become less profitable, while the military involvement in Java had grown costly. It was a great war in Java (1740–55), however, that dealt the death blow to the already delicate Dutch finances. And once again, through a complex chain of events, it was the Dutch themselves who inadvertently precipitated the conflict. The details of the struggle are too convoluted to dissect here, but it began in 1740 with the massacre of the Chinese residents of Batavia, and ended 15 years later, after many bloody battles, broken alliances and shifts of fortune had exhausted almost everyone on the island.

Indeed, Java was never the same again, for Mataram had been cleft in two, with rival rulers occupying neighbouring capitals in Yogyakarta and Surakarta. Nor did the VOC ever recover from this drain on its resources.

In the traumatic aftermath of the VOC bankruptcy, there was great indecision in Holland as to the next course. In 1800, the Dutch government assumed control of VOC's former possessions, now renamed Netherlands Indies, but for many years no one could make them profitable.

> **RAFFLES' MANY HATS**
>
> Stamford Raffles was a brilliant scholar, naturalist, linguist, diplomat and strategist. He has been credited with rediscovering Borobudur and he also wrote the monumental *History of Java*.

Raffles renaissance

A brief period of English rule under Thomas Stamford Raffles (1811–16) soon followed. In 1811, he planned and led a successful invasion of Java and was then placed in charge of its government at the age of 32.

Raffles' active mind and free-trade philosophy led him to make reforms almost daily, but the result was bureaucratic anarchy. Essentially, he wanted to replace the old mercantile system (from which the colonial government derived its income through a monopoly on trade) with one in which income was derived from taxes and trade was unrestrained. This enormous task had barely begun when the order came from London, following Napoleon's defeat at Waterloo, to restore the Indies to the Dutch.

Nevertheless, many of his land-tax ideas were eventually levied by the Dutch, and they made possible the horrible exploitation of Java later. And this in turn led to the cataclysmic Java War of 1825–30.

Carnage to cultivation

So numerous were the abuses leading to the Java War, and so great were the atrocities committed by the Dutch, that the Javanese leader Pangeran Diponegoro (1785–1855) has been proclaimed a great hero even by Dutch historians. He was indeed a charismatic figure: crown prince, Muslim mystic and man of the people.

His guerrilla rebellion against the Dutch and his own rulers might have succeeded but for a Dutch trick: luring him out of hiding with the promise of negotiation, Diponegoro was captured and exiled to Sulawesi. The cost of the conflict in human terms was staggering: 200,000 Javanese and 8,000 Europeans lost their lives, many from starvation and cholera rather than from death on the battlefield.

By then, the Dutch were in desperate economic straits. All efforts at reform ended in disaster with the government debt reaching devastating amounts. New ideas were sought, and in 1829, Johannes van den Bosch submitted a proposal to the crown for what he called a *Cultuurstelsel* or cultivation system of fiscal administration in the colonies. His notion was to levy a tax of 20 percent (later raised to 33 percent) on all land in Java, but to demand payment not in rice but in labour or use of the land. This would permit the Dutch to grow crops that they could sell in Europe.

Van den Bosch soon assumed control of Netherlands Indies, and in the estimation of many, his system was an immediate, unqualified success. In the very first year, 1831, it produced a substantial profit. And within a decade, millions of guilders were flowing annually into Dutch coffers from the sale of coffee, tea, sugar, indigo, quinine, copra, palm oil and rubber.

FAR LEFT: Javanese soldier in full battle order. **LEFT:** Stamford Raffles led the English invasion of Java in 1811. **RIGHT:** Javanese leader Diponegoro.

With the windfall profits received from the sale of Indonesian products during the rest of the 19th century, the Dutch not only retired their debt, but built new waterways, dikes, roads and a national railway system.

Outside of Java, military campaigns throughout the 1800s extended Dutch control over areas still ruled by native kings. The most bitter battles were fought against the powerful Islamic kingdom of Aceh, in a 30-year war. Both sides sustained horrendous losses. In the earlier Padri War between the Dutch and the Minangkabau of West Sumatra (1821–38), the fighting was almost as bloody. In the east,

Flores and Sulawesi were repeatedly raided and finally occupied by the 1900s.

But the most shocking incidents occurred on Lombok and Bali, where on three occasions (1894, 1906 and 1908) Balinese rulers and their courtiers, armed only with ceremonial weapons, stormed headlong into Dutch gunfire after ritualistically purifying themselves for a *puputan* ("fight to the finish") and thus avoiding the humiliation of defeat.

In some ways, the tragic massacres symbolised the abrupt changes wrought by the Dutch: they had achieved the unification of the entire archipelago at the expense of indigenous kingdoms, sultans and tens of thousands of people. ❑

MODERN INDONESIA

After the heady feeling of freedom that followed the departure of the colonial powers, people began to realise that things were far from perfect

At the beginning of the 20th century, signs of change were everywhere in the Indies. Dutch military expeditions and private enterprises were making inroads into the hinterlands of Sumatra and the eastern islands. Steam shipping and the Suez Canal (opened in 1869) had brought Europe closer, and the European presence in Java's cities was growing steadily. Gracious new shops, clubs, hotels and homes added an air of cosmopolitan elegance to the towns, while newspapers, factories, gas lighting, trains, buses, electricity and cars imparted a distinct feeling of modernity.

The Dutch move in

Indeed, thousands of newly-arrived Dutch immigrants were moved to remark on the tolerable conditions in the colonies – that is to say, it was just like home, or even better.

In the Indies, nationalism was slow in developing but inevitable. A small but growing number of Indonesians living in cities were receiving Dutch education. The irony is that Dutch education provided much of the intellectual basis for Indonesian nationalism. As early as 1908, Indonesians attending Dutch schools began to form regional student organisations with political overtones. Small, aristocratic and idealistic, such organisations spawned an elite group of leaders and provided forums for a new national consciousness to take shape.

National awakening

In 1928, at the second all-Indies student conference, the concept of a single Indonesian nation (one people, one language, one nation) was proclaimed in the so-called *Sumpah Pemuda* (Youth Pledge). The nationalism and idealism of those students later spread through newspapers and the non-government Dutch- and Malay-language schools. But while the urban elite grew, the Dutch authorities were preoccupied with the nation's emerging pan-Islamic and communist movements.

The pan-Islamic movement's roots were in the steady and growing stream of pilgrims visiting Mecca and in the religious teachings of the *ulama* (Arabic scholars). What began in Java in 1909 as a small Islamic traders associ-

ation (*Sarekat Dagang Islam*) soon became a national confederation of Islamic labour unions (*Sarekat Islam*), with 2 million members in 1919. Mass rallies attracted tens of thousands, and many peasants came to see in the Islamic movement hope of relief from oppressive colonial conditions.

In 1910, the Indonesian communist movement was founded by small groups of Dutch and Indonesian radicals, with support from the working-class people. The movement soon embraced Islam, with many of its leaders gaining control of Islamic workers' unions and speaking at Islamic rallies. Following the Russian Revolution of 1917, they also maintained

LEFT: early oil exploration in Sumatra – where Indonesia's vital oil revenue was generated.
RIGHT: a 19th-century facet of colonialism.

ties with the Comintern and increasingly espoused Marxist-Leninist doctrine.

The period 1910–30 was a turbulent one. Strikes in cities frequently erupted into violence and the colonial government arrested many Indonesian leaders. Moderate Muslim leaders soon disassociated themselves from political activities. The rank-and-file deserted their unions, and while the communists fought on for several years in Java and Sumatra up through 1927, they too were crushed.

> **350 YEARS TOO LONG?**
>
> The Dutch governor-general claimed the Dutch had "been here for 350 years with stick and sword and will remain here for another 350 years with stick and sword". He had to eat his words.

Japanese Occupation

In the 12th-century, the Javanese King Jayabaya (sometimes spelled Joyoboyo), had prophesied that despotic white men would one day rule the Indonesian archipelago. But following the arrival of yellow men from the north (who would remain just as long as it takes the corn to ripen), Java would be freed forever from foreign oppressors and enter a millennial golden age. Therefore, when the Japanese invasion came, it was no surprise that many

Leadership of the anti-colonial movement then reverted to the student elite. In 1927, a recently-graduated engineer by the name of Sukarno, together with his Bandung Study Club, founded the first major political party with Indonesian independence as its goal. His *Partai Nasional Indonesia* (PNI) grew, and within three years, had over 10,000 members, Shortly thereafter, Sukarno was arrested for making "treasonous statements". Although publicly tried and imprisoned, he was later released. A general crackdown ensued and, after 1933, Sukarno and other student leaders were exiled to distant islands, where they remained for 10 years. The hope of independence seemed elusive.

Indonesians interpreted this as a sign of impending liberation from the Dutch.

The immediate effect of Japan's 1942 invasion was to show that Dutch military might was a bluff. The Japanese encountered little resistance and, within weeks, had rounded up all the Europeans and placed them in concentration camps. Initially, there was jubilation. But it quickly became apparent that, like the Dutch, the Japanese had come to exploit the Indies, not to free them. Escalating Japanese rice requisitions created famines and sparked peasant uprisings that were ruthlessly stomped out.

However, the Japanese found it necessary to rely on the Indonesians and to promote a sense of nationhood in order to extract their desired war materials. Indonesians were placed in many key positions held previously by Dutch nationals. The Dutch language was banned and replaced by Bahasa Indonesia. Nationalist leaders were freed and encouraged to cooperate with the Japanese. Most of them did.

When it became clear in late 1944 that Japan was losing the war, the Japanese promised independence to bolster faltering support. Indonesian leaders were brought in for discussions, and close to 200,000 young people were mobilised into paramilitary groups.

Merdeka

In 1945, on the same day that the second atomic bomb was dropped on Japan, three Indonesian leaders were flown to Saigon to meet with the Japanese military commander for Southeast Asia. The commander promised independence for all the former Dutch possessions in Asia and appointed Sukarno chairman of the preparatory committee and Mohammad Hatta the vice-chairman. They returned to Jakarta the day before Japan's unconditional surrender to the Allies. Following two days of debate, Sukarno and Hatta proclaimed *merdeka*, independence, on 17 August.

The following months were a chaotic struggle. News of the Japanese surrender spread like wildfire and millions of Indonesians echoed the call for *merdeka*. The Dutch tried to reclaim the islands, but Holland was in a shambles. Heroic sacrifices on the battlefield by tens of thousands of Indonesian youths placed them in an untenable position. Three Dutch "police actions" gave the returning colonial forces control of the cities but each time, the ragtag Indonesian army, under the inspired leadership of the youthful commander-in-chief, Gen. Sudirman, valiantly fought back.

Finally, in 1949, the United States ceased the transfer of Marshall Plan funds to the Netherlands, and the UN Security Council ordered the Dutch to withdraw from Indonesia and negotiate a settlement. Dutch influence crumbled, and on 17 August 1950 – the fifth anniversary of the *merdeka* proclamation – the new government of the Republic of Indonesia took charge.

Euphoria swept through the cities and towns of Indonesia following the withdrawal of Dutch forces. Mass rallies and processions were held; flag-waving crowds thronged the streets shouting *Merdeka, Merdeka* (Freedom, Freedom). Independence had come at last, and Indonesians were at last in control of their destiny.

The final chapters of early Indonesian nation-building were still to be written. The Dutch held on to the western half of New Guinea, called West Papua, after granting independence to the rest of Indonesia. Pressure from the United Nations and the threat of all-out war by Sukarno eventually resulted in the transfer of

the territory in 1962 and its integration as the country's 26th province, renamed Irian Jaya. In 1975, after Portugal abandoned its colony of East Timor, Indonesia invaded and annexed that territory. The East Timorese won their independence in 1999 while many residents of Papua (Irian Jaya) are still pressing for theirs.

Headaches of a new nation

In Jakarta, the slow and arduous process of constructing a peacetime government began. While the unifying power of the revolution had done much to forge a national identity, the fact of Indonesia's complex ethnic, religious and ideological diversity remained. Moreover, mas-

LEFT: opposition to the Dutch found a voice in the educated elite – such as these medical students.
RIGHT: a pro-independence march in progress.

sive economic and social problems faced the new nation – a legacy of colonialism and war. Factories and plantations were shut down, capital and skilled personnel were scarce, rice production was insufficient to meet demand, people were overwhelmingly poor and illiterate, and the population was growing at a spiralling rate. A Western-style parliamentary system was adopted to deal with the problems.

From the beginning, however, the existence of more than 30 rival parties paralysed the system. A string of weak coalition cabinets rose and fell at the rate of almost one a year, and attempts at cooperation were increasingly stymied by growing ideological polarisation and by parochial loyalties. Sukarno, whose powers as president had been limited by the provisional constitution of 1950 and the army leadership grew frustrated by the deadlock.

A series of separatist uprisings in Sumatra, North Sulawesi and West Java in the late 1950s gave Sukarno his cue. He declared martial law and gave the army a free hand to crush the rebels. In 1959, with the rebellions under control, Sukarno resurrected the "revolutionary" constitution of 1945 and declared a period of "Guided Democracy".

Under the new political system, power was

DEWI, SUKARNO'S FOIL

As his grip on power began to loosen and Indonesia's economy spun further out of control, Sukarno's behaviour became erratic and bizarre. He spent hours talking to spirits and ancestors and consulting seers. His usually flamboyant political speeches became filled with convoluted neo-colonialist plots. It was at this point that the ageing president found his perfect foil in the stunning young Japanese Naoko Nemoto.

Nemoto was under 20 when she married Sukarno in 1963, becoming Dewi Sukarno, the nation-builder's seventh and best remembered wife. After his death, she made herself known as an international socialite with a volatile reputation. In the early 1990s, she slashed a Filipino socialite at a Colorado cocktail reception with a broken champagne glass and served a month's jail. The 50-something Dewi went on to assault a Jakarta gossip columnist and released a book of mid-life nude photographs of herself that both titillated and shocked Indonesia.

She attended lectures by Indonesian politicians abroad and heckled them from the crowd. She also insisted Sukarno's ouster had been the direct result of a CIA plot. Nothing seemed to get her down. Upon emerging from the well-appointed Colorado prison, she had said: "I will treasure (memories of the jail) for the rest of my life."

focused in the hands of the president and the army leadership. Militant nationalism became Sukarno's recipe for national integration, and the blame for most of the economic and political problems was placed at the feet of foreign imperialism and colonialism.

In the early 1960s, Sukarno became more militant. The long and successful campaign to wrest control of western New Guinea from the Dutch was followed by military confrontation with newly-independent Malaysia in 1963. In 1965, he pulled Indonesia out of the UN, angry that Malaysia was made a member state. Domestically, however, it was Sukarno's nationalistic elan that helped create a nation out of disparate ethnic groups.

But Sukarno's reliance on charisma alone – he ignored day-to-day administration – created a vacuum in which the nation floundered. While he attempted to offset the growing influence of the military by courting the Partai Komunis Indonesia (PKI), the economy crashed. Foreign investments fled, deficits left the government bankrupt, and inflation skyrocketed to 700 percent. Discontentment was brewing and by 1965, Indonesia was a political tinderbox.

Bloodbath

In the early hours of 1 October 1965, a group of radical army officers kidnapped and brutally executed six leading generals. However, the rebel officers soon lost the initiative to General Suharto, then commander of the Army Strategic Reserve. In a few hours, Suharto assumed command of the army, crushed the attempted coup and declared the PKI to be the culprit.

The nation was shocked by news of the execution and vengeance was demanded against the communists. A purge ensued, in which the military and moderate Muslims sought to settle old scores. Hundreds of thousands were killed as long-simmering frustration erupted into mob violence, first in North Sumatra, then later in Java, Bali and Lombok. The blood-letting continued for months, and the period from 1965 to 1966 is remembered today as the darkest in the republic's history.

Meanwhile in Jakarta, Suharto was slowly pushing Sukarno out of power. On 11 March 1966, Sukarno was persuaded to sign a document bestowing wide powers on General Suharto that charted Indonesia's course for the next 32 years.

Change came quickly. Martial law was declared and order was restored. Marxist-Leninist teachings were outlawed and thousands of alleged communists, including the prominent novelist Pramoedya Ananta Toer, were jailed. Existing political parties were weakened, and in 1967, the new government granted itself the right to appoint a third of the representatives in the nation's highest legislative assembly. A major realignment in foreign

LEFT: Sukarno reads a statement to the press while his would-be successor Suharto looks on.
RIGHT: Sukarno and Suharto.

policy restored long-fractured relations with the US and the West, and severed ties with China and the Soviet Union. Building political legitimacy on promises to revive the moribund Indonesian economy, Suharto placed a team of American-trained economists in charge of cooling inflation and restarting the economy.

These so-called technocrats guided the rapid reintegration of Indonesia into the world economy, liberalised foreign investment laws, and imposed monetary controls. Western aid was sought – and received – to replenish the nation's exhausted foreign exchange reserves. By the early 1970s, results began to show. Investors – American, Japanese and Indonesian

Chinese – moved in to take advantage of Indonesia's vast copper, tin, timber and oil reserves and to set up factories.

Indonesia's mineral wealth made the job easier. In 1883, a Dutch planter sheltering from a storm in a northern Sumatran shed noticed a torch burning brightly. On inquiring, he was led to a nearby spring where a viscous black substance lay thick across the water. The discovery led to the formation of Royal Dutch Shell and, eventually, to Indonesia's position as the world's fifth-largest and Asia's sole OPEC producer. Though the dominance of oil fell as the economy matured, it and other natural

resources have remained Indonesia's primary source of foreign exchange.

The country made rapid gains in agricultural production and population control. An intensive family-planning campaign was considered a model for the developing world and Indonesia managed to reduce the birth rate to just over 1 percent annually. Still, Indonesia's main islands of Java and Bali are desperately overcrowded – representing only 7 percent of the total land area while housing more than half of its people. By 2000, Indonesia's population stood at almost 220 million. A programme to ship the landless of Java and Bali to West Papua (Irian Jaya), Kalimantan and other sparsely inhabited regions was abandoned after the fall of Suharto. The expensive programme had exacerbated ethnic tensions in the provinces.

The New Order

Even as he liberalised the economy, Suharto undermined Indonesia's political institutions and cut off dissenting voices. Suharto and his supporters liked to call their regime the "New Order", to stress its departure from the past: less populist, stridently anti-communist and more accommodating to international capital.

The new elite exerted total control through Golkar, the political vehicle of the new government. Newspapers were closed, dissidents were jailed and the military was given a free hand to deal brutally with opponents of the regime. For most of his reign, Suharto delivered on his promise of "Development yes, politics no!" He ensured political survival by stage-managing elections every five years and then ruled by fiat.

But politics had never gone away entirely. Many Muslims, despite being in the majority, felt marginalised. By the mid-1990s, gratitude to Suharto for the progress made since 1965 was increasingly being replaced by anger at rampant corruption – particularly the vast business empires carved out by his children and a close circle of cronies. Rioting and religious tension became more intense. In 1996, a ham-fisted effort to discredit Megawati Sukarnoputri, the daughter of Sukarno who had risen to lead the strongest opposition party, backfired and led to rioting in Jakarta that frightened off investors and exposed the strains in Suharto's consensus-based polity. After 32 years of creeping change, Indonesia seemed poised to lurch forward once more.

The eventual trigger echoed Sukarno's fall 33 years earlier. In July 1997, when Southeast Asia's financial crisis began, conventional wisdom had it that Indonesia, with its tradition of inflation control and restrained spending, would weather the storm better than its neighbours.

But as the rupiah fell alongside other regional currencies, it exposed massive fissures in the economy hidden by the glitter of the boom years. The foundations that the gleaming office towers, five-star hotels and state-of-the-art factories of the New Order rested on were riddled with debt. Corporations alone owed more than US$80 billion to foreign investors.

As banks collapsed and factories closed, prices for food and other basics soared. Millions lost their jobs, and even more saw their economic gains of the previous 30 years evaporate. By the end of October, Suharto – who in 1992 had proudly echoed Sukarno's defiant "to hell with your aid" cry to the US – was forced into the arms of the International Monetary Fund. The fund arranged a US$40 billion support package but at a price: the required economic reforms would strike at the monopolies and business groups of his friends and family.

While Suharto dragged his feet over the programme, the rupiah fell to one-seventh of its pre-crisis value, driving inflation and unemployment even higher. Students, the elite and disaffected officers began to move against him. In March 1998, after Suharto was elected to a new term, opposition groups kicked into gear.

University, providing the spark for the capital's worst rioting in a generation. Foreigners fled and Jakarta's commercial districts became ghost towns. As flames swept the capital and troops took charge, Suharto scrambled to hold on. But one by one, his most trusted lieutenants abandoned him. On the morning of 21 May, he resigned. Joyful students frolicked in the fountain at parliament as Suharto's vice-president and close friend B.J. Habibie was sworn in as his successor. During Habibie's short rule, he freed the press, allowed a referendum on East Timor and steered Indonesia to a democratic election that ended with his own October 1999

Reformasi

Student protests took on a new, more urgent tone with "*Reformasi!*" (Reform) as their rallying cry. On 12 May 1998, six student protestors were shot and killed at Jakarta's Trisakti

LEFT: Suharto poses for the press in the early 1990s.
ABOVE: grim-faced security personnel were helpless in the face of the May 1998 student riots in Jakarta.

STREET PROTESTS

With the lifting of censorship after the fall of Suharto, for the first time Indonesians are free to say whatever is on their minds without fear of retribution. Street protests are common throughout the country, particularly in larger cities and those with universities. Causes change daily and include escalating utility prices, corruption in the government, women's rights, protecting natural resources and international issues. Demonstrators can be students, housewives, religious groups or activists. Generally they are well-organised and non-violent. The traffic circle in front of Jakarta's Hotel Indonesia and university campuses are popular protest venues.

defeat – the first democratic political transition in Indonesian history.

The near-blind Abdurrahman Wahid, the former head of Nahdlatul Ulama (NU), a 35-million member Muslim social organisation, was Habibie's surprise successor. Though Wahid's National Awakening Party came in fourth in the general election, savvy politicking in the parliamentary assembly that selects the president won him his position over Megawati Sukarnoputri, whose Indonesian Democratic Party-Struggle (PDI-P) had run away with the general election.

Indonesia's fourth president was a study in contradiction. Gus Dur, as he is popularly

known, was devoted to a secular state. An avowed democrat, he was also a hereditary leader (NU leadership ran in the family).

The nearly blind Gus Dur was famous for his flip-flops, designed to confuse his opponents, some say. In the early 1990s, Gus Dur was a leader in the movement to oust Suharto, but as a crackdown loomed, he reconciled with the latter. This move cost Gus Dur many supporters – but kept him in the political fray, and ultimately helped him prevail.

Unfortunately, Gus Dur's brief time in office was racked by continued fighting among various political factions, a worsening economy and violent ethnic conflicts, among many other problems. He was charged with incompetence and implicated in several corruption scandals. In July 2001, parliament impeached him, despite violent threats of retaliation.

Vice-President Megawati replaced him as head of state amidst great rejoicing in the streets. With virtually no political experience but heir to a famous family name as daughter of Indonesia's first president Sukarno, the quiet housewife who owned not much more than a florist shop and petrol station selected a ministerial cabinet of capable advisors.

Unfortunately, Megawati has not lived up to expectations. As Indonesia's fifth president, she promised to eliminate corruption, rein in the military and reinvigorate the devastated economy. But rather than work on these pressing problems, parliament still seems more concerned with settling old political party rivalries and differences. Real reform remains stuck in the doldrums. In the meantime, ethnic and religious intolerance have flared violently across the archipelago, while separatist movements in both Aceh and Papua have been answered with harsh military responses – in spite of promises of greater autonomy. Thousands have died in these struggles, but Megawati remains determined to keep Indonesia's immense territories intact as a legacy from her late father Sukarno.

As a result, not much had changed for Indonesia as the economy continued to spiral downwards and the ranks of the poor increased. Indeed, the image of the country took a severe beating among foreign investors nervous about stability in the country. Tourism has taken a beating, particularly after the 2002 terrorist bombing in Bali in which more than 200 people, mainly Australians, were killed.

Nevertheless, Indonesia is continuing its journey towards democracy. Despite enormous odds, 140 million eligible voters – 25 percent of whom are uneducated, with 10 percent of the electoral districts in regions so remote that they have no electricity – demonstrated in the July 2004 elections that they would not support candidates tied to Islamic extremism. Because none of the top two contenders, incumbent Megawati of the PDI-P and former security minister Susilo Bambang Yudhoyono of the Democratic Party (PD) were able to secure more than 50 percent of the popular vote, on 20 September 2004, a second election will take place to decide on who will be Indonesia's new president. ❑

Separatist Provinces

National integrity has always been an obsession of the sprawling Indonesian archipelago. Its hundreds of cultures, languages and ways of life have always been a challenge to the national motto, *Bhinneka Tunggal Ika* (Unity in Diversity). In the 1950s, the young republic faced down separatist movements in West Java, Maluku and Sumatra.

In the post-Suharto era, separatist movements – and the fear of separatist movements – are having profound effects on national politics, and are reworking the traditional relationship between the strong centre in Java-Jakarta and the weak, often resource-rich outer provinces. In areas like Kalimantan, traditionally a bastion of nationalism, politicians are using the rhetoric of independence to extract concessions from the central government in the form of money and political control.

On 7 December 1975, the Indonesian navy attacked Dili, the sleepy seat of colonial Portuguese power in East Timor (now Timor Leste). Portugal was then pulling out of its neglected colony after 500 years. The invasion, in defiance of the United Nations, was designed to head off East Timor's independence movement and claim it as Indonesia's 27th province. Suharto's short-term objective was accomplished but at an enormous price, one that Indonesia might pay for years to come.

With just 700,000 people, few resources and poor soil, there was little to be gained materially. But to Suharto, and many other Indonesian leaders, an independent East Timor – sharing an island with the Indonesian West Timor – would be a blot on territorial integrity and an example to secessionist movements elsewhere in the archipelago.

As it happened, Indonesia's invasion of East Timor fuelled the very sentiments the government had hoped to suppress. In August 1999, after years of UN pressure, armed insurgency and international condemnation of the military's human rights abuses, East Timor won its freedom, with nearly 80 percent voting for independence.

The vote, which came during B.J. Habibie's brief presidency, gave the independence movements of Aceh and Papua (Irian Jaya) a shot in the arm. The two movements are very different. Papua, like East Timor, is predominantly Christian and its Melanesian people are both culturally and ethnically distinct from Indonesia's dominant Javanese. And like East Timor, Papua was added to the republic well after independence. The people did not participate in the independence struggle, and their alignment with Indonesian "nationhood" is tenuous at best. In 2000, the mostly peaceful "Free Papua" movement used the political freedoms of the new regime to organise a series of mass conferences in the capital Jayapura.

Aceh is a different story. Acehnese heroes fought in the independence struggle and were always a part of the modern Indonesian state. But

the fiercely independent Muslim population has long chafed at a central government that had always taken more than it had given. In the early 1990s, a brutal military campaign against rebels made victims of many average Acehnese, and clashes with the military were common. Though most Acehnese say they support independence, analysts expect that if perpetrators of human rights abuses were brought to justice and more of Aceh's natural wealth was returned to its people, the central government could win them back.

The Wahid government decentralised the central government in 2000, giving the provinces full autonomy. However, the usual problems of corruption and mismanagement remain in many areas. ❑

LEFT: Megawati Sukarnoputri, Indonesia's fifth president, is a daughter of Sukarno, the first president.
RIGHT: an East Timorese armed freedom fighter.

PEOPLE

Anyone travelling through the length of Indonesia will find the complexity and sheer diversity of peoples, languages and customs astounding

Indonesia consists of 18,110 islands, on which live 250–300 ethnic groups (*suku bangsa*) who make up its population of nearly 220 million. It is no easy task to identify all the different ethnic groups and the Dutch used language and tradition as two important criteria for ethnic definition. In practice, however, language has become the most important criterion in ethnic identity. There are more than a dozen major languages but many more are still to be studied. The major ones are Javanese, Sundanese, Madurese, Balinese, Minangkabau, Malay, Bugis (Buginese), Makassarese, Minahasan and Ambonese, spoken by groups of the same names. (In some cases, the ethnic name does not reflect the language; for example, the Torajan speak a Loinang dialect.)

The precise current proportion of the total population formed by each ethnic group is not known as post-1949 (Independence) population censuses have not factored in ethnicity. The closest guide is the last colonial census of 1930, which will be the basis in this chapter. All ethnic groups, with the exception of the Chinese, have their respective homelands in Indonesia.

Java

Central and East Java are the home turf of the Javanese, who form 60 percent of the population. The Javanese are proud of their long history which saw the rise of the great Majapahit empire. They believe it was the first kingdom to unite Indonesia in an empire which included territory beyond the republic's present boundaries. Due to their numbers and glorious past, the Javanese tend to dominate the country's bureaucracy, military and politics. To date, all the Indonesian presidents, except B.J. Habibie who had a brief stay in office, have been Javanese.

Although they form the majority, their language was not popular. It is a complex and hierarchical (considered undemocratic) language, unlike Malay, which had wider appeal. There are at least three levels of Javanese speech: formal, semi-formal and informal. Formal speech is further sub-divided into *ngoko*, *madya* and *krama*. *Ngoko* is used among close friends or to address someone either younger or lower in

social status, *krama* is employed when speaking to older people or those of a higher status, and *madya* is a combination of the two. In addition, Yogyakarta (Jogja) and Surakarta (Solo) have a palace language called *kedaton*, while villagers speak a kind of rural *krama*.

The majority of Javanese are Muslims, with a small number of Christians. The Muslims are comprised of *santri* (rigid) and *abangan* (liberal). *Abangan* themselves dislike the term (which means red) and prefer to be known as *agami kejawen*. In the past, most aristocrats were *abangan*. Generally speaking, those who live in the coastal areas have a greater adherence to Islam, while the interior dwellers tend

PRECEDING PAGES: Yogyakarta's Sultan Hamengkubuwono X and his wife; Balinese children let their feelings fly. **LEFT:** Sumatran bride in her wedding finery.
RIGHT: Javanese elder wearing a *blangkon* headwrap.

to embrace animistic or Hinduistic beliefs. Some *abangan* have developed a kind of Javanese mysticism known as *kebatinan*. Many Javanese, especially the *abangan*, are aficionados of *wayang*, shadow or puppet plays based on Hindu epics. Javanese-dubbed *wayang* are central to traditional culture.

There is segmentation also within the culture: coastal or court culture, and peasant or urban culture. Society is divided into *priyayi*, or the aristocrats, who are also termed *wong gedhe* (important people); while at the other end of the scale are *wong cilik* (little people), mainly peasants; and the in-between class is *wong sudagar* (the merchants and traders).

Another ethnic group on the island is the Sundanese, who dwell in West Java's Priangan area. The Sundanese, forming 17 percent of the population, are the second largest Indonesian group. Like the Javanese, they too have a long history; the Sundanese culture has borne Javanese influence (though this is not often recognised). The Sundanese, however, have a better established bureaucratic system. In social life, lineage is important; *menak* are descendants of aristocrats, while commoners are *cacah* or *somah*. The language is divided into three levels: refined (*lemes*), medium (*sedang*) and vulgar (*kasar*). Although most are Muslims, there are some Catholics and Christians.

There are another two small ethnic groups on Java which are insignificant in number but well-known abroad due to their unusual customs: the Hindu Tenggerese in East Java, and the animistic Badui in West Java.

Off the north-eastern coast of Java is an island called Madura. The Madurese, who form 7 percent of the Indonesian population, are well-known for their bravery and quick temper. Madura, administered with East Java, is likewise over-populated, and this has resulted in the people's transmigration to other parts of Indonesia. The Madurese language is also divided into refined, medium and vulgar categories. The people are pious Muslims who accord high status to Islamic preachers.

Sumatra

Although Islam penetrated Sumatra as early as the 13th century, pre-Islamic religious influence still has its place. The most Islamic inhabitants are the Acehnese, who constitute only 1 percent

> **MANNERED JAVANESE**
>
> Javanese society requires one to be *sopan santun* (well-mannered). *Rukun* (harmony) is the primary goal, achieved through knowing one's place in society and acting out one's assigned role.

of the Indonesian population. Fiercely independent, they have taken up arms against both the Dutch and the present government in Jakarta. Aceh was the last territory to be conquered by the Dutch at the beginning of the 20th century.

In the north are the clan-ruled, monogamous Batak, who form 2 percent of Indonesia. They comprise the Batak-Tapanuli, Batak-Toba, Batak-Karo and other sub-categories. Most of the Batak-Tapanuli are Muslims, while the Batak-Toba and Batak-Karo are Christians. The Batak have a large military presence and in early history, spawned many top officers such as A.H. Nasution and T.B. Simatupang.

Another well-known ethnic group in Sumatra is the matrilineal Minangkabau. These highly educated entrepreneurs practise the coming-of-age ritual for men of *merantau* (seeking a fortune abroad). They spawned the first group of Indonesian writers and many outstanding political leaders. Sutan Syahrir, the first prime minister, and M. Hatta, the first vice-president, were Minangkabau. Constituting 3.3 percent of the Indonesian population, the Minangkabau are pious Muslims. However, they also have their own *adat* (customary laws), which may not always be in accordance with Islamic laws.

The Malays, who form 1.6 percent (some sources have it as 7 percent) of the population, are an important minority in Southeast Sumatra and Riau. They established the Buddhist kingdom of Srivijaya in Palembang in the 7th century, but later converted to Islam after its demise. The Malays have spread beyond Indonesia to other parts of Southeast Asia, and their language, the *lingua franca* of the Indonesia archipelago, has become the national language.

Kalimantan

Dayak is a collective name for more than 200 tribes who live on the island of Borneo, which were divided into British and Dutch portions during the colonial era. Dutch Borneo was later named Kalimantan by the Indonesians. The Dayak are an important minority (less than 1 percent of the population) who are well-known as headhunters and animists. They are the true "people of the jungle" who used to live in long-houses and for the most part, have enjoyed a peaceful existence in relative isolation.

In the south-eastern part of Kalimantan live the Muslim Banjarese, who form about 1.5 percent of the population. They are closer to the Malays in terms of language and religion. The different ethnic groups used to live in cordial co-existence, but in 2001–2002, the Dayak were involved in bloody conflicts with the Banjarese, and with the immigrant Madurese.

Sulawesi

In the southern part of Sulawesi live two ethnic groups, the Buginese (2.6 percent) and the Makassarese (1.1 percent). Both ethnic groups

are Muslim seafaring people. They are known as good sailors and shrewd businessmen who are skilled in shipbuilding. In the past, they often migrated elsewhere to seek their fortunes and, at one time, almost controlled the trade of the region. In the 1950s, a number of them rebelled against the government in the hope of establishing an Islamic state. The movement, led by Kahar Muzakar, was soon quashed. Well-known Buginese in the Jakarta government are Gen. M. Yusuf (former defence minister) and ex-president B.J. Habibie.

Slightly north of South Sulawesi live half a million Torajan, who comprise mainly Christians. There are a small number of Muslims and ani-

FAR LEFT: plucking tea leaves in Bandung, West Java.
LEFT: demure Javanese girl with *selendang* scarf.
RIGHT: Dayak woman of Kalimantan.

mists, however. Outsiders find the pre-Christian birth and death traditions of the Torajan fascinating. Found in North Sulawesi are the Christian Minahasan, who number around 800,000.

Maluku

In southern Maluku live the Christian Ambonese. Maluku was the place which attracted the Portuguese to Indonesia during the 16th century. The Ambonese were later conquered by the Dutch and were subsequently Christianised.

During the colonial period, the Ambonese were recruited into the Dutch army and employed in the upkeeping of law and order. When Indonesia gained independence from the Dutch, the Ambonese tried to declare their own independence but were crushed. Following the demise of the iron-fisted rule of Suharto, a new separatist group – the Maluku Sovereignty Front (FKM) – emerged. Carrying on the cause of *Republik Maluku Selatan* (RMS), they are once again demanding independence.

Papua (Irian Jaya)

There is massive commercial exploitation in Papua because of its mineral wealth. Many of the tribes there still live in the Stone Age.

The province, now renamed Papua, was incor-

TRANSMIGRATION AND AUTONOMY

The aim of the controversial transmigration programme, started by the Dutch, continued by the new Indonesian government after independence and enhanced by Suharto, was aimed at relieving overcrowded conditions in Java and Bali by relocating entire communities to more sparsely-populated places like Sumatra, Kalimantan and Sulawesi. Conflicts – often confused with differences in religions and ethnicity, but more likely economic – naturally arose between the locals and the migrants, who were given free houses, land, seed and start-up funds upon arrival in their new areas. It was also thought that sending Jakarta-influenced Javanese to remote places would engender national cohesion.

The transmigration programme was discontinued when provinces were given full autonomy by the Wahid government in 2000. Under autonomy, taxation, budgeting, infrastructure and trade are now managed locally, with 70 percent of revenues earned remaining in the province and 30 percent – instead of 100 percent as in the past – going to Jakarta. This is good news for some provinces, such as resource-rich East Kalimantan, which has used its newly found wealth to improve infrastructure, education and health care. However, autonomy is not particularly beneficial for poorer areas, which must eke out their existence with loans, grants and other foreign aid.

porated into Indonesia in 1963, which paved the way for an influx of immigrants, including the Javanese, who settled into the urban areas. The Papuans, also called Irianese by some Indonesians, are traditionally animists and have largely remained so, although some have converted to Christianity and Islam. Feeling exploited and perceiving themselves as having a culture very different from the other Indonesians, some Papuans continue to demand independence.

Bali and Nusa Tenggara

Bali has become the main attraction for tourists since the end of World War II. Forming about 2 percent of the population, the Balinese have a unique culture and except for small groups in Java and Lombok are the last bastion of Hinduism in Indonesia. The islanders are not only gifted in the arts, but also live their lives by their religion, participating in the many rituals of life and agricultural cycles.

Balinese society is structured around a hereditary caste system that is far more relaxed than the Indian version. It does, however, carry certain rules of etiquette, as ordained in the Hindu scriptures. At the top is the Brahman caste; only Brahmans are allowed to be high priests. Satriya form the second strata of society; they are the descendants of warriors and rulers. The merchants, or Wesia, occupy the third rank, and at the bottom are the Sudra, the common people, who account for 90 percent of the population.

The Sudra are not deemed inferior nor denied access to specific professions; above all, a high-class background does not guarantee a high income or direct access to political power. In Bali, a university professor could be a Sudra or a waiter may turn out to be a Brahman.

Of the Nusa Tenggara islands, Lombok, which is located to the east of Bali, has a Hindu-Balinese community that comprises 10 percent of its population. But the majority of its inhabitants are Sasak Muslims. Further east is predominantly Muslim Sumbawa, and animistic Sumba, which are also the names of their inhabitants. Nearby Flores was formerly a Portuguese settlement acquired by the Dutch in the 19th century. Some 90 percent of Flores' population are Catholics, in contrast to Sumba and Sumbawa.

LEFT: young girls in Indonesia's large cities dress – and act – like youth everywhere.
RIGHT: young Balinese surfer "hanging loose".

"Unity in diversity"

Indonesia is the product of Dutch colonialism, a multi-ethnic and multi-religious society whose diverse population was formed by historical accident. Under Dutch rule (1619–1945), the different elites received Western education, were governed by the same economic and administrative system, and experienced similar, if not identical, problems. The Dutch provided a form of social cohesion, which enabled the various ethnic groups to come together. The Japanese Occupation, although lasting a brief 3½ years, was significant in that it provided Indonesians with military training

and further stoked their zeal for independence. To their own ends, the Japanese also actively promoted nationalism, a movement which eventually gained Indonesia its independence and created a nation based on the boundaries of the former Dutch East Indies.

Another factor that helped to unite the ethnic groups was language. Although the language of a minority group, Malay was used widely as a medium of communication in the marketplace between different ethnic groups. Campaigners used it to propagate the Indonesian nationalist movement throughout the diverse archipelago. When Independence was achieved in 1945, Malay was made *Bahasa Indonesia*.

The transmigration policy was not only used to redistribute population density, but was also used as a guise to promote national unity. Java only accounts for 6.5 percent of the Indonesian territory but 60 percent of the population live on the island. The policy put pressure on those who lived on Bali and Java, particularly the Javanese people, to migrate to the Outer Islands. However, the forced resettlement created much friction between locals and newcomers.

Java versus Outer Islands

Ethnic and religious conflicts have always occurred between Java and the Outer Islands, livelihood does not depend solely on agricultural products and trade is important for survival, people tend to be more individualistic.

Of course, the aristocratic nature of Javanese society and the entrepreneurial nature of non-Javanese society is also another difference influencing conflicting attitudes and behaviour.

Today, the Indonesian nationalism that was fanned in the run-up to Independence is still very much alive, though not evenly shared by all ethnic groups. Some Acehnese, Papuans and Malukans have strong separatist sentiments and a desire for outright independence. Not surprisingly, many such ethnic groups were

especially after Independence. The people of the two regions are not only ethnically different but also dissimilar in their approach to agriculture. The principal farming method in Java and Bali is that of *sawah*, or wet rice-paddy cultivation, while the main method employed in the Outer Islands is *ladang* agriculture, also known as slash-and-burn cultivation.

Until recently, Java and Bali had been collectively regarded as an agricultural society, in contrast to the Outer Islands, which were known as a maritime society. In an agricultural society, the need for close cooperation among villages is paramount, and people tend to be socialistic. In a maritime society, where the only added to the Indonesian nation-state in the last few decades. East Timor, which was annexed by Indonesia in 1976, a year after the Portuguese left, finally gained its independence in August 1999. The separatist Acehnese, Papuans and Malukans may be divided on their demands, but their desire for independence is a common goal that has been expressed through agitation and periodic riots. Clearly, the multi-ethnic Indonesian nation-state is facing a problem of disintegration. ❑

ABOVE: Jakarta's rambunctious street campaigners are more interested in partying than in political platforms.

The Chinese Minority

The ethnic Chinese only comprise 5 percent of the Indonesian population, but are often perceived as the group which controls the country's economy. This has been a perennial source of resentment in Indonesia, and something which has periodically spilled over into violence. The Chinese also differ from the Muslim majority in religion: although there are Chinese Muslims, most are Buddhist, Confucian or Christian.

As a non-indigenous minority, the Chinese are politically weak and vulnerable to acts of deep-seated prejudice. Dating back to the 1945 Indonesian revolution, in times of crisis, be it economic or political, they have often been the target of riots. The most recent example was the Jakarta riots in May 1998, in which many Chinese were killed and the women systematically raped.

Although most Chinese have become Indonesian citizens, in the eyes of many indigenous people, they are foreigners. In the past, policy towards ethnic Chinese had two thrusts – to integrate and assimilate them, and to reduce their economic strength. But since Abdurrahman Wahid's presidency, the policy has been relaxed.

The *Tionghoa*, as the Chinese are known, are not a homogeneous group but are divided broadly into the Indonesian-speaking *Peranakan* and the Chinese-speaking *Totok*, the latter of whom maintain their overseas ethnic network and are more business-savvy than their *Peranakan* counterparts. But the overwhelming majority of ethnic Chinese, especially in Java, is *Peranakan*.

From assimilation to integration

In the colonial days, the Dutch government divided society along ethnic lines. The Europeans formed the upper class; the natives were at the bottom; while the Chinese were placed in the middle. Intermarriages were rare, and in most cases, the pairings were of indigenous females and Chinese males (which led to the *Peranakan* culture).

The early *Totok*, who arrived at the turn of the 20th century and formed their own community, had been born and brought up in China and were thus culturally and politically China-oriented. These *Totok* were also known as the *singkeh*, or "new guests".

When Suharto came into power in October 1965, he put his assimilationist policy for the ethnic Chinese into practice. He banned the Chinese language press and Chinese socio-political associations; encouraged Chinese names be changed to Indonesian ones; closed Chinese schools; discouraged the use of the Chinese language; and restricted the public practice of Chinese customs and festivals. In short, he banned the use of anything related to the Chinese culture.

This had limited effect, however, undermined on one hand by Suharto's own policy of confining Chinese activity to the economic field – which ironically only strengthened Chinese economic position and further increased their alienation – and

RIGHT: Chinese youth praying with incense during a traditional ceremony.

on the other hand, by the state ideology of Pancasila, which guarantees religious freedom for all citizens.

Since Suharto's fall in 1998, some discriminatory regulations have been lifted. After three decades of suppression, Chinese-language newspapers, magazines and TV news reports are allowed; dragon and lion dance troops appear publicly, sometimes even at non-Chinese celebrations, and in 2002, the Chinese Lunar New Year was declared a national holiday. In the 2004 parliamentary elections, 172 Chinese candidates even vied for seats, adding a new dimension to Indonesia's political arena. While discriminatory practices are still in place, there is slow progress towards equality for Chinese-Indonesians. ❑

RELIGION

Muslim or Hindu, Buddhist or Christian – Indonesians are free to worship their own faith, provided they adhere to the Pancasila creed, aimed at preserving harmony

Although Indonesia has the world's largest Muslim population, it has stopped short of declaring itself an Islamic state. Nearly 90 percent of Indonesians is Muslim, with most of the remainder being Christian (primarily Protestant) or Buddhist. Pockets of Christianity are found among the Batak people of North Sumatra, the Ambonese, Florinese and a few tribes in Papua and Kalimantan. Indonesian Christians are few in number but well-represented within the educated military and political elite. Similarly, there is a small minority of Buddhist Indonesians who are overwhelmingly represented in the economic sector of the country.

As was the case with Buddhism, Hinduism was at one time a significant power in the archipelago, but its presence is now limited to Bali, East Java, and western Lombok.

Animism

The native religion, animism – essentially the worship of spirits believed to preside in all living or non-living things – is still practised on remote islands and is mixed freely with modern religions. Animism rests on the basis that trees, rivers, mountains, snakes, and even personal effects such as daggers are all inhabited by living spirits.

Offerings of food are sometimes found beside a tree or a river, placed there in appeasement of the nearby deity in the hope of being granted a safe passage, a rich harvest or a good day's fishing. There is usually a spirit medium or *dukun* in each village and who enjoys high status since he plays the all-important role of intermediary to the spirits.

Despite national statistics which claim high adherence to foreign religions, in everyday life, the form if not the spirit of animism continues to rule social behaviour. In everyday practical life, worship of a mainstream faith like Islam, Hinduism or even Christianity, does not rule out ingrained fundamental beliefs in the power of spirits nor preclude the enactment of rituals of appeasement. Each of the major religions, including those which embody a pantheon of gods, has managed to get around the Pancasila code for social harmony, which includes a requirement for monotheistic worship.

LEFT: a devout Muslim reading the Arabic script of the *Koran*, the Islamic holy book.
RIGHT: Muslim girls in religious garb.

PANCASILA: FIVE PILLARS

Pancasila is a social tool conceived by then president Sukarno in 1945 to encourage unity among Indonesians. In an echo of Islamic practice, Pancasila has five pillars or principles: a belief in a singular and omnipotent God, a civilised and fair humanitarianism, a united Indonesia, a democracy guided by wisdom and representation, and social justice for all Indonesians. A device intended to unify an extremely diverse people separated by vast distances, Sukarno's Pancasila was outlined so as to ensure that Indonesian identity was not defined in reference to Islam. It offered a common creed over and above the laws of each religion.

Islam

The most important of the major religions is Islam, which became the fulcrum for the region's development. By the late 13th century, Islam had gained a foothold in Sumatra and, within a few centuries, had became embedded in Southeast Asia, anchored by a powerful Islamic commercial and political centre in Malacca during the 15th century.

The history of Islam's development in Indonesia is one of cultural accommodation, essential from the first contact. The Indonesian islands are an affiliation of many ethnic and cultural groups, traditions, languages and religions.

For that reason, throughout Indonesia's history, there has often been a general inclination towards a convergence of basic social, cultural and political needs. In many ways, the traditional tolerance of Islam has permitted a give and take – although in the wake of the 11 September 2001 terrorist attacks in New York, this aspect has increasingly come under scrutiny.

Based upon the teachings of Muhammad, who is usually referred to as the Prophet, Islam's billion-strong believers extend from the Arab lands of the Middle East – where Islam originated and blossomed – and North Africa, west to southern Spain, and east through Turkey, Iran, Afghanistan, Pakistan, India and eventually into Southeast Asia, especially Indonesia, Malaysia and the Philippines. It is one of the world's most important religions and the second-largest religion in Europe.

Although Indonesia has an overwhelming majority of Muslims, a history of religious tolerance and freedom of religion is guaranteed by the constitution. Islam proposes how Muslims should live together with other Muslims, and with non-Muslims.

The faith is practised most traditionally in northern Sumatra, especially in Aceh, and in West Java, Southeast Kalimantan and in parts of Nusa Tenggara. Outside of these areas, Islam may be the professed religion, but the strict rituals of fasting and prayers, for example, are less strictly followed. On Java, perhaps one-third to half follow strict practices.

The rituals of the religion are intertwined with the basic needs and acts of daily life. Belief and practice of the religion define the nature and quality of life itself and of the community. Islamic beliefs and practices are based upon two important touchstones for the Muslim: the *Koran* and the *Sunna*. The *Koran* is considered to be the word of God, as spoken to Muhammad (c. AD 570–632) during the last 22 years of his life, through the angel Gabriel. And as it is considered the word of God, the *Koran* in all its 114 chapters is irrefutable and faultless.

The *Sunna*, less well-known to outsiders, reflects the traditional norms regarding assorted concerns and issues, based upon what Muhammad himself did or said regarding those concerns. Although secondary to the *Koran*, it is a fundamental component for most Muslims.

Cousin to Christianity

Little known among non-Muslims is that Islam accepts most Biblical miracles and prophets, in both the Old Testament and New Testament. Abraham, Moses and Jesus, for example, are important prophets for the Muslim. Adam was the first prophet, later forgiven by God for his sins. But they were early prophets. Muhammad came later as the last and final prophet, and thus revealed a more perfect word of God. The *Koran* itself is considered Muhammad's eclipsing miracle, as perfect as possible on earth. Islam regards all religions as essentially repre-

LEFT: a village mosque in Java. **RIGHT:** statue of Jesus draped in *ikat* cloths, in Waingapu, Sumba.

sentations of the same divine truth, except that Islam is closest to that truth.

The Islamic God is omnipotent and singular. One does find, however, permutations of this fundamental idea in some parts of Indonesia, where local and often polytheistic beliefs, and in some places, from Hinduism and Buddhism, have been melded with Islam. This modifying of practice and doctrine is not restricted to Islam, however; one finds assimilations and modifications among the Buddhist, Hindu and Christian believers within the archipelago.

Like Christianity, there is a heaven and a hell in Islam. The world's creation was an act of mercy by God; if God had not done so, there would be nothingness. Everything on earth has its function and form, defined towards making a harmonious world. Nature exists to be exploited by humanity, and as for humans, their purpose is simple: to be in the service of God.

But, unlike Christianity, which is more individualistic, Islam has it that humanity's responsibility includes the establishment of social systems that are pure and free from vice and corruption. God also judges societies and nations, which are subject to the same transgressions and weaknesses as people.

World history reflects the results of God's

CHRISTIANITY, COLONIALISM AND CONFLICT

The Portuguese arrived in Flores during the 16th century and converted the local community to Catholicism, which then spread eastwards to parts of Nusa Tenggara and Timor. Dutch missionaries brought Protestantism to a few parts of the archipelago in the early 19th century, especially Minahasa in north Sulawesi, Maluku and parts of Kalimantan and Papua. German Christian missionaries also converted the Batak in North Sumatra.

In most places, indigenous animist practices were integrated with Christianity. Indonesia's minority Christian population, however, have never been well received in this predominantly Muslim country. In recent years, parts of Maluku and Central Sulawesi have been ripped apart by violence between its Christian and Muslim communities. Several churches, even some in Jakarta, have been the target of attacks. Although Muslim and Christian religious leaders persistently denounce these attacks, observers blame the trouble on small sects of radical Muslim militants. Whipped into a frenzy, some Muslims reacted by declaring a *jihad* (holy war) on the Christians and sent armed paramilitary groups to Maluku, adding to the violence that has claimed thousands of lives since 1999. In April 2004 on the anniversary of the 1947 separatist movement, violence erupted again, raising fresh doubts about a fragile peace pact in the troubled region.

judgement regarding all nations. Those that are good, persist; those that are not, such as communists and colonialists, are eventually superseded by other states and cultures. (That colonialism was replaced by an independent state reinforces this view.)

Sharia

The basis of an Islamic society is the sustenance of the community of the faithful, guided by the Sharia, or Islamic law. This law defines a community's moral goals; in fact, in many

> **INDIAN TO INDONESIAN**
>
> Indonesia adapted Indian religion to its needs. Even the events and people recorded in Hindu epics like the *Ramayana* and the *Mahabharata* have been shifted out of India to Java.

Muslim countries, Islam defines all the laws, both moral and legal.

According to the *Koran*, people are proud, if not egotistical, and susceptible to selfishness and greed. (Satan is a significant factor in earthly affairs.) Belief in the *Koran* is said to assist people in rising above these inadequacies by establishing an inner ethical bearing called *taqwa*. Through this quality, good and evil, and right and wrong, are recognisable. In the end, a person is judged by *taqwa*, not by earthly deeds or accomplishments. The role of the Islamic prophets has been to show individuals, as well as whole societies and even nations, the way to *taqwa*.

Balinese Hinduism

Most of Indonesia's Hindus live on the island of Bali, where they form more than 90 percent of the population. Balinese Hinduism has developed local characteristics that distinguish it from Indian Hinduism.

Central to Balinese Hinduism – known as Agama Hindu Dharma – is the belief in the balance of two opposite forces: manifested as good and evil; light and dark; male and female; positive and negative; order and chaos, and so on. The two realms co-exist and are equally important.

Good, as represented by benevolent gods such as Dewa and Bhatara, is to be emulated, cultivated and esteemed. Worship of these gods is marked by celebrations, in the form of offerings of food, holy water and flowers, dancing and beautiful art pieces. Credit for a bountiful harvest, for example, is given to the popular goddess of rice and fertility, Dewi Sri.

The hierarchy of Balinese gods starts off with Sanghyang Widi Wasa — the supreme invisible being who is manifested through the three main gods: Brahma, Vishnu and Shiva. By emphasising the importance of Sanghyang Widi Wasa, Bali's Hindu Council managed to convince the central government of Hinduism's monotheism (a requirement under Pancasila), thereby gaining it official recognition.

The Balinese live for festive activities, which centre on the village temples, taking place once every 210 days or during a particular full moon in the lunar-solar year, when a communal birthday feast *(odalan)* is held on the anniversary of its consecration. In a typical celebration, delicately-carved idols are brought out, wrapped in sacred woven cloths and then infused with the protective spirits of the villages before being borne to the river or sea in a colourful procession. On return to the temple, mediums tell if the celebrations have been satisfactory to the god. If so, the villagers pray together and feast throughout the night — there is dancing, puppet theatre and *gamelan* performances.

Cleansing holy water

Evil forces, in the shape of earth demons, can cause ill fortune, such as natural calamity, a breach of human relations, or illness, and are to be placated with purification offerings and rituals, such as ritual cleansing. Uncleanliness is a state that anyone can stumble onto, for example, during menstruation, a long illness, a death in the family, or a natural disaster such as a volcanic eruption. Central to the cleansing ritual is the administration of holy water. To the Balinese, the mountains are holy because they are high and the source of the holy element of water. From this understanding has come the placement and orientation of physical structures; the sites of houses, temples and schools are aligned according to the direction of and proximity to sacred mountains and the sea.

Another form of Hinduism practised elsewhere in Indonesia is Shivaism, which takes a more ascetic path, in which destruction and fertility are intertwined. Shivaism is popular perhaps because it incorporates fertility worship and the idea of appeasing malevolent spirits.

Buddhism

Buddhism, that gentle, contemplative offshoot of Hinduism, penetrated China, and through the travels of wandering Buddhist pilgrims, subsequently entered Java and Sumatra. Buddhism is basically an offshoot of Hinduism that has cast off the notions of caste differences as well as the myriad array of gods. In its purest form, it offers a practical, moral way of life.

Buddhism's founder was an Indian prince named Siddhartha Gautama who lived during the 6th century BC. He came to realise that pain and sadness was caused by desire, in itself an illusion. He offered a solution. By rising above desire and human attachments, human beings can live a life free from suffering. He formed a spiritual recipe called the Eightfold Path that laid out steps to help an individual contain passion and emotion; by focusing on wisdom, thought, speech, conduct, livelihood, effort, attentiveness and concentration. Achievement is realised when one arrives at enlightenment and the bliss that comes with attaining non-attachment. One is then freed from the endless cycles of rebirth, and from human suffering.

Most Buddhists in Indonesia are Chinese. Although Chinese religion mixes Buddhism with ancestor worship, Taoism and Confucianism, most Chinese will tell you they are Buddhist, to satisfy the Pancasila's tenet of monotheism. Indonesian law once decreed that Chinese religion only be observed in the home. After the fall of Suharto in 1998, however, some of these discriminatory laws have been lifted. ❑

LEFT: image of Durgha at the ancient Hindu temple complex Prambanan, Central Java.
ABOVE: Pura (temple) Taman Ayun in Bali.

Customs and Rituals

Although observance of adat, or local custom, has ceased to be vital in today's society, it still has an important role to play in ensuring smooth relations

Indonesia has by far the world's largest Muslim population; almost 90 percent are believers. The remainder profess Christianity, Hinduism and Buddhism. In fact, Indonesians have an almost infinite variety in what they do and believe in spiritual matters – religious beliefs and practices are strongly affected by local traditions passed from generation to generation. These locally-defined beliefs form the fabric of each society, known as the *adat*, or custom, of an ethnic group or community.

The *adat* and religion of any given Indonesian group tend to be remarkably eclectic. The classic example is that of the average Javanese – a self-declared Muslim who firmly believes in the existence of Indian deities and in the indigenous folk heroes portrayed in the ever-popular *wayang kulit* shadow play, as well as in a host of deities, ghosts, spirits, demons and genies said to inhabit the worldly environment.

Typically, in addition to fulfilling the requirements of the Islamic faith, the Javanese will burn incense and leave small offerings to local spirits; hold frequent communal feasts (*selamatan*) to celebrate special occasions and to mitigate the disruptions of unsettling events; seek and heed the advice of a local *dukun* or mystic in times of distress; and trust the magical potency of an inherited *keris* dagger and a variety of other talismans.

Feasts

Central to the *adat* observances of most Indonesians is the ritual communal feast. In the Javanese *sesaji*, ceremonial foods are offered to the spirits in invitation, but are not eaten, whereas in Bali the food is an offering, publicly consumed to ensure well-being and to strengthen solidarity.

The most common example of such a feast is the Javanese *selamatan*, in which special foods are eaten (like *tumpeng*, an inverted cone of yellow-coloured rice with various dishes), incense is burned, Islamic prayers are intoned and announcements or requests are made. A *selamatan* may be given at any time and for almost any reason – to celebrate birth, marriage, circumcision, death or an anniversary, or to initiate a new project or a new building, or to dispel bad luck or invite good fortune.

In Bali, festive activities centre on the village temple, where a communal birthday feast (*odalan*) is held on the anniversary of its

---

SOCIETY'S GLUE

Adat is often viewed as the glue that binds society and allows it to function with minimal conflict. With it, all community members have the same perspective of right and wrong. Elders with intimate knowledge of *adat* are greatly respected. Some *adat* are of a superstitious nature: i.e. banishing twins of opposite sexes from villages because they are considered to bring bad luck. However, others are practical. In many forest communities, *adat* prohibits cutting certain trees or killing specific animals, thus promoting a balance between human needs and nature. Even in the 21st century, most Indonesians agree that *adat* is of vital importance to their daily lives.

consecration. Days beforehand, the entire village is engaged in the preparations of elaborate decorations and offerings.

Everyone, from young children to aged great-grandparents, gets involved with the preparations, for it is a time for socialising as well. Women trim and pin together palm leaves into containers and ritual ornaments, shape coloured rice-dough into symbolic shapes, and assemble countless offerings from a dazzling range of materials.

Meanwhile, the men of the village slaughter animals for meat offerings in addition to feeding those helping out in the *odalan*. They also construct temporary platforms and pavilions, repair shrines and climb trees to collect the necessary leaves, flowers and fruits that are used for the offerings.

When the offerings are presented, the deities and spirits consume the invisible essence of the offerings. The physical parts are considered to be "leftovers" and would be eaten by the worshippers at the temple or brought home for a family feast. Clearly, the Balinese have the best of both worlds.

LEFT: ceremonial foods are offered up to the spirits and blessed, and then shared by the community.
ABOVE: ritual birthday blessings in Solo, Java.

Jiwa

These and other types of communal feasts and rituals frequently have to do with enhancing the fertility and prosperity of the participants by strengthening, purifying or augmenting something known to many Indonesian peoples as *jiwa* – the spirit or soul thought to inhabit and animate not only humans but plants, animals, sacred objects and also entire villages or nations. These spirits bring bad as well as good consequences, and it is believed that by boosting their own life-giving *jiwa*, people are able to achieve and maintain a fragile balance.

The *jiwa* of human beings is thought by some

to be concentrated in the head and hair, and in the past, the Torajan of Sulawesi, the Dayak of Kalimantan and the Dani of Papua sought to promote their own *jiwa* at the expense of an adversary through head-hunting raids. Skull trophies were once regarded as powerful talismans that would enhance the prosperity of a community, and also ward off sickness, war, famine or ill fortune.

A ceremonial first haircut often serves to initiate an infant into human society. The exchange of snippets of hair is an integral part of some Indonesian marriage rites, while human hair curiously features in the costumes of many supernatural characters. Likewise, hair clippings are disposed of carefully (as are nail trimmings), lest they fall into the hands of an enemy sorcerer.

Blood, too, is thought to be infused with *jiwa*, which can be especially easily transmitted or conferred. On many islands, the pillars of a new house are anointed with the sacrificial blood of animals to render them strong and durable. And it used to be widely reported that, in many parts of the archipelago, victors in battle drank the blood of their slain enemies, or smeared it over themselves, to augment their own *jiwa* with that of the fallen.

Many Indonesians believe that this soul upright but bends to the ground with the weight. This is symbolic of a mature human soul (*jiwa*). The more educated one is, the more powerful and wiser. Therefore, like the rice, humans must humble themselves and give thanks to the origins that gave them life. If humans can take on the characteristic of mature rice plants, their *jiwa* (souls) will become wiser, calm and humble, capable of accepting inner peace and achieving balance.

This philosophical merit is not reserved for older people but is also desirable in young people. Certain rituals are performed before babies are born, for infants and for teenagers

substance is also found in plants such as banyan trees. An interesting metaphor for human life is the powerful but sensitive *jiwa* associated with the rice plant, which is symbolic of important philosophical values.

When still young, the rice grains are light because they are empty; thus the plant is straight, standing upright as if challenging the sky. This personifies the immature human soul (*jiwa*), which is unstable, arrogant and lacking life experience. It also represents the rice plant's ingratitude to the life-giving nutrients and water of the earth.

When the plant grows older, the grains become full and heavy and it no longer stands to ensure they will be powerful, humble and wise in the future, while remembering their heritage. The ceremonies attempt to imbue these children with good *jiwa* (soul).

All ancient and curious objects, mountains and bodies of water are likewise thought to be imbued with a special *jiwa*. Bezoar stones, mineral deposits found in animals and in the nodes of certain bamboos, are used for magic and healing, while more generally, any object that is designated a *pusaka* or sacred heirloom is credited with harbouring a vital spiritual essence that requires special veneration and care. Antique *keris* daggers, lances, spear heads, cannons, jewellery, textiles, ceramics, manuscripts, gravestones and masks can all become *pusaka* and may contain a soul of its own or that of a previous owner. Such objects are often in the custody of a king, priest, chief or an elder, a link between the living and the powerful ancestral spirits.

A place for souls

Much of a community's private and public ritual life often centres on the management of its human souls, both living and dead. In this, there are invariably certain individuals in the communities who possess specialised knowledge or skills in such matters. Special attention is always devoted to funerary rites, in which the dead are ritually venerated and can be transformed into protective clan or village deities.

It is commonly believed that the soul of a person may become detached during life, which can result in illness. Even under normal conditions, it is thought the soul wanders during sleep. Sorcery can entice unwitting souls away.

A distinction is made virtually everywhere between good and bad spirits, resulting respectively from good and bad deaths. A bad death, generally premature or violent, releases a vengeful ghost or *hantu* that may bring considerable misfortune on a household or community. The soul of a woman who dies at childbirth is pictured as a bird with long talons that jealously stabs and rents the stomachs of pregnant women. This so-called *kuntilanak* can also assume the shape of a beautiful maiden, who waits at night beneath a banyan tree to seduce and emasculate passing men. Elaborate rituals must then be performed by a shaman to mollify the *hantu* and banish it from the area.

Good deaths must also, of course, be attended by a lengthy sequence of elaborate

funerary rites. When a person dies, it is universally thought the soul is at first resentful and potentially harmful. Some rites are therefore designed to confuse the soul and dissuade it from returning. It is a widespread custom in Sumatra, Kalimantan, South Sulawesi and Halmahera, for instance, to send the corpse out of the house through a gap in the wall or floor of the house, which is then sealed.

Observers of rituals should respect local custom concerning dress and silence. No one who has witnessed a Balinese funeral procession and cremation, a Torajan funeral sacrifice, or a Dayak death ceremony will forget the dignity and colour of the events.   ❑

FAR LEFT: Balinese priestess in trance. **LEFT:** *keris* daggers are said to be endowed with supernatural powers. **ABOVE:** an elaborate cremation on Bali.

Spice-Islands Cuisine

Indonesian food is strong in flavours, with a delicious array of fish, unusual vegetables and fruits, and minimal meat. But only the brave should sample the chillies

The food of Indonesia is influenced by the culinary traditions of diverse nations such as China, India, the Middle East and Netherlands. In fact, Indonesian cuisine is so varied that travellers can be assured of finding at least one dish that becomes a lifelong favourite.

Mealtime for most Indonesians is a quick, private and non-social activity. In most Indonesian homes, the food is cooked in the morning to last the whole day. The prepared dishes are placed on the dining table at noon and again at dusk, and family members simply help themselves to a meal whenever they feel hungry. It is only on special occasions, such as on feast days or when having guests over, that the Indonesian family sits and eats together.

The Chinese influence in Indonesian cuisine is most evident in the use of stir-fried dishes cooked in a huge steaming wok, while Indonesia's popular curries can only have originated in India. Marinated meat on skewers, known locally as *sate*, owes its heritage to the Middle Eastern kebab, while the *rijstaffel* (rice table) traces its roots to Dutch colonial times. In today's Indonesia, all of these various culinary traditions have blended and adapted to form regional cuisines on nearly every major island.

Five pillars of the cuisine

Rice, coconut, banana, peanut and soya bean are the five pillars of Indonesian cuisine and it is almost impossible to find a meal that does not include at least one of these items. Rice is the staple food on most of the islands, particularly the more fertile Sumatra, Java and Bali.

There are several kinds of rice in Indonesia: *beras putih* (white rice), *ketan putih* (sticky white rice), *ketan hitam* (sticky black rice) and *beras merah* (red rice). Nearly every menu offers dishes prefixed with the word *nasi*, which means they come with rice. The most well-known of these is *nasi goreng*: fried rice with an assortment of vegetables and chicken, prawns or meat – or a combination of all three. If the word *istimewa* (special) appears, it means the dish comes with a fried egg on top. A cone shaped mould of *nasi kuning* (yellow rice) cooked with turmeric, coconut milk and spices is served on feast days on a banana leaf platter.

LEFT: mouth-watering array of spicy dishes from the Indonesian archipelago.
RIGHT: a multi-course *rijstaffel* feast.

RIJSTAFFEL

Much of the Dutch influence has long since faded away, but a remnant of it remains in the *rijstaffel*, a more elaborate form of the Sumatran *nasi padang*.

Rijstaffel (literally, rice table) is a series of meat and vegetable courses, served with rice and spicy condiments, presented at the table with much ceremony by a string of sarong-clad waitresses.

Expect about five to six courses in a typical *rijstaffel*, a far cry from Dutch colonial days when the serving might include as many as 350 separate dishes. Due to the elaborate nature of this meal, it is offered primarily at tourist restaurants and hotels.

Mi (noodles) made from rice or wheat flour is another staple. In *mi goreng* (fried noodles), the noodles are fried in coconut oil with meat, vegetables and perhaps fried egg, with hot chilli shrimp paste and lime on the side. Both *mi goreng* and *nasi goreng* are popular breakfast dishes. Other starches like maize, tapioca, millet and sago are eaten in the drier islands east of Bali and in smaller archipelagoes along the coast of Sumatra. In the islands of Roti and Savu, the staple food is sweet nutritious juice tapped from the *lontar* palm.

Coconut and coconut products are central to Indonesian cooking. Every meal includes this versatile palm nut prepared in a variety of ways. Coconut oil is the common cooking medium while *santan* (coconut milk) is used to thicken and add flavour to soups and curries and as a marinade for meats. Grated coconut is often added to various vegetable dishes to provide texture, flavour and an oil base. Fried shredded coconut is served as a condiment. Coconut is also a vital ingredient in Indonesian sweets.

There is an astonishing variety of bananas in Indonesia, ranging from the tiny *pisang mas* to the larger *pisang lembut* popular in Bali. Bananas can be eaten baked, fried or boiled, and are a popular snack. Even the banana

SPICE UP YOUR DAY

It is no small wonder that spices are so readily used in the food of the Spice Islands, and make all the difference to Indonesian food. Spices can be either wet or dry. The wet type has fresh ingredients like shallots, onions, ginger, garlic and turmeric root ground into a paste, whereas the dry type includes powdered peppercorns, coriander seeds, cinnamon, cummin seeds, candlenut and *terasi* (shrimp paste). *Terasi* is an acquired taste and can be overpowering.

Fresh spices are first ground in a stone mortar and pestle, then fried to release their aroma before being added to meat, poultry or vegetables. Different spices are used with different kinds of meat. Pre-packaged spices are becoming common, available in local *warung* and supermarkets. However, in the villages, the woman of the house still prepares spices the old-fashioned way.

No spice mixture is complete without chillies, for the Indonesians love their food *pedas* (hot). The varieties include the long red *tabia lombok* with its sweet flavour, the chunky red and yellow *tabia bali* and the dynamite bird's eye chillies. If you are unused to really spicy food, ask that it be prepared sans chillies. In addition to spicy, Indonesian food can be rather aromatic, as fresh bay leaves, lime leaves, basil and lemon grass are common ingredients. The best samplers are found in the Padang restaurants.

flower is eaten as a vegetable and the leaves are used as wrapping material for steamed meat, fish and vegetables.

Peanuts form an integral part of some meals in the form of a sweet and spicy sauce served with *sate*, *gado-gado* (steamed vegetables) and a host of other dishes. Much of the protein in Indonesian food comes from soya beans. They are eaten boiled or fermented to make *tempe* (soybean cake) and *tahu* (soybean curd). Peanuts are also fried and tossed together with *tempe*, either as a snack or served as a side dish to a main meal.

However, it is the fermented soya bean sauces, spinach). Other vegetables are grown in home gardens including different types of beans, young jackfruits, papayas and bananas, all varieties of squash and pumpkin, and carrots. Indonesians do not eat much meat for the most part, although it is common to find a few dried fish alongside a mound of white rice. Among other things, the choice of meat is determined by cultural and religious factors.

Typically, the Javanese eat chicken and fish, and the favourite dishes are *soto ayam* (chicken soup), *sop buntut* (oxtail soup) and *ayam goreng* (fried chicken). The Balinese favour duck and pork. Famous Balinese dishes include

kecap asin (salty) and *kecap manis* (sweet), that are important flavouring agents used with gusto in almost every dish. Most Indonesian restaurants tend to use liberal amounts of MSG (monosodium glutamate) in their cooking so let the waiter know beforehand if you prefer your food without this flavouring agent.

Indonesians eat a large variety of vegetables. Most greens are picked wild and include tender tapioca, papaya and soya bean leaves, *kangkung* (water spinach), and *bayam* (Asian

LEFT: wars were once fought in the famed Spice Islands of Maluku (Moluccas) for these ingredients.
ABOVE: charcoal-broiled *sate* is known the world over.

babi guling (roast suckling pig) and *bebek tutu* (spiced slow-cooked duck).

The Sumatrans eat a lot of beef. One of the most popular dishes introduced by the Sumatrans is *rendang* (beef chunks served in a rich and spicy sauce). South Sulawesi is known for seafood dishes that run the gamut from shrimp, lobster and crab, to carp, eel and sea slugs.

Exotic fare

Typically, the food of Java tends to be sweeter than the food of Sumatra and Bali, which is more spicy. The coastal Papuans are said to offer the best *ikan bakar* (grilled fish) in the whole country. Some of the Dayak tribes of

Kalimantan consider roast lizard a mouthwatering delicacy while mice and dogs are common fare in Minahasa kitchens.

As a general rule, the more rural the area, the higher are one's chances of having meals prepared with meat and animal parts that may not agree with the palate or conscience. Once you go off the beaten track, it is a good idea to check what type of meat has been cooked to avoid consuming animal innards.

Favourite vegetarian dishes include *gado-gado* (vegetable salad with peanut sauce) and *cap cai* (wok fried vegetables). Main dishes are often accompanied by freshly-made *sambal* (a thick chilli concoction), of which there are numerous varieties, ranging from a simple fried diced shallot, garlic and very hot chilli paste to a pungent fried version liberally laced with *terasi* (shrimp paste).

Indonesia sampler

One of the best ways to sample a wide variety of Indonesian food is to order *nasi rames* or *nasi campur*. This sampler is a plateful of steamed rice, chicken, fresh and preserved vegetables, fried egg, roasted peanuts, shredded coconut, fiery *sambal* sauce, and oversized crispy *krupuk* (fried prawn crackers).

The traditional Padang restaurant is Sumatra's great contribution to the national cuisine. It offers a bewildering array of tasty local dishes including *ayam* (chicken), *sapi* (beef), *kambing* (mutton), *sayur* (vegetables), *ikan goreng* (fried fish), various curries and maybe an assortment of entrails, plus a substantial serving of steamed rice.

Diners are charged only for the amount consumed, so depending on your budget, either try a variety of dishes or do as most locals do and choose only a few main dishes and then fill up with rice. As a general rule, vegetable dishes are the cheapest with beef the most expensive. It is a good idea to find out the price of each dish before you begin.

Fruits and sweets

The array of fresh tropical fruit available in Indonesia often astounds visitors. There are more than 40 varieties of bananas (*pisang*), pomelos (*jeruk Bali*), mangoes and pineapples (*nanas*), plus an array of lesser-known delicacies. Durians might best be described as spiky green bowling balls that smell rather strange but taste like caramel peach. Rambutans are bright red, have a hairy exterior and a flavour very similar to lychee. And the skin of the *salak* (which has a crisp texture and sharp flavour) closely resembles that of a snake. Passion fruit (*markisa*) is a delicious refreshing fruit full of tiny, edible seeds. Other delicious local fruits include thirst-quenching watermelons and rose apple (*jambu*). The local tart green apples are surprisingly juicy and excellent to eat, as are several varieties of oranges.

Coconut milk, rice, tapioca, mung bean and banana are common dessert ingredients. Each island has its version of tiny cakes stuffed with

COFFEE, TEA OR BINTANG?

Indonesians often drink sweetened hot tea with their meals, but iced tea (*es teh*), local coffee (*kopi*), and fruit juices and bottled sodas are usually available. Typically, most drinks come premixed and tend to be very sweet, so do ask to have the sugar on the side.

Fruit juices may be ordered fresh or bottled. Among the popular choices are watermelon, papaya, pineapple and avocado.

Local alcoholic beverages include Bintang beer (whose roots are traceable to the Dutch Heineken), *tuak* (palm wine), *brem* (rice wine), *badek* (rice liquor) and *arak*, the most potent of rice spirits.

sweetened mung bean, shaved coconut or banana, in a variety of colours made with sticky rice cooked in coconut milk. Indonesians mostly use dark brown palm sugar as a sweetener for desserts and other dishes.

Look for *kueh lapis*, the Indonesian version of a light layered cake made of rice flour and fragrant coconut palm sugar, and *bubur ketan hitam* (black rice porridge cooked in coconut milk and sweetened with palm sugar). Delicious pancakes of all sorts, filled with fruit or palm sugar and shredded coconut, are available in nearly every big city.

Perhaps the most popular dessert is *es campur*, the Indonesian equivalent of the ice cream sundae. *Es campur* does not have a nationally accepted set of ingredients, but shaved ice is usually the base. A number of things can be poured over the ice, including syrup and coconut milk, bits of fruits, cubes of brightly-coloured gelatin, palm fruit, fermented tapioca and various other sweet tidbits.

> **IN THE KITCHEN**
>
> The centrepiece of the traditional kitchen is a woodfired stove and rice steamer. Other utensils include a pestle and mortar, wok and banana leaves for wrapping.

Indonesians eat three meals a day, which are interspersed with snack times. Snacking is a way of life here. Children cannot resist *krupuk* or a plate of *rujak* (spicy fruit salad). Food vendors ply their trade in practically all the tiny bylanes, attracting customers by twanging a metal chime, beating a low wooden gong or a steam whistle. They serve *bakso* (meatballs), *bakpao* (steamed buns stuffed with meat) or simply a bowl of noodles.

People also get their meals and snacks at traditional Indonesian eating places known as *warung*, makeshift foodstalls set up on the pavements of busy streets and in marketplaces with rows of tables and rickety-looking benches. Not the most romantic setting, but here, most of Indonesia's favourite dishes can be enjoyed at ridiculously low prices. Standards of hygiene are low, however, and refrigeration virtually non-existent, so cast-iron stomachs are a pre-requisite for sampling street fare.

Western food and other speciality cuisines are available at the more popular tourist destinations and in major cities. In recent years, Indonesians have developed a taste for fast food and the popular chains are Kentucky Fried Chicken, McDonald's and Pizza Hut. ❑

LEFT: locally-brewed Bintang beer.
ABOVE: Indonesian desserts are invariably made from glutinous rice flour, palm sugar and coconut milk.

Dance and Theatre

The finest of Indonesian performing arts is found in Java and Bali, where they have evolved through the court as highly-stylised acts retelling the classics

There is such a variety of dance and dramatic tradition throughout the archipelago that it is impossible to speak of a single, unified tradition. Each Indonesian ethnic and linguistic group possesses its own unique performing arts. Nevertheless, there are certain shared features among the groups, and most have several things in common.

Dance, storytelling and theatre are ubiquitous in Indonesia, elements of a cultural life that is all-encompassing and fulfilling a wide variety of sacred and secular needs. Dancers, shamans, actors, puppeteers, storytellers, poets and musicians are members of the community performing vital roles in informing, entertaining, counselling and instructing their fellows in the well-worn ways of tradition.

Ritual dances

Dance and ritual life are inseparable among so-called primitive tribes in Indonesia, most of whom have their shaman dances performed by priests or priestesses for purposes of exorcism and spirit propitiation. The Batak *datuk* (magician) of highland Sumatra, for example, holds a magic staff as he treads with tiny steps over a design he has drawn on the ground. At the climax of this dance, he hops and skips, thrusting his staff into an egg on the ground.

Most tribes also have their ritual group dances, performed to mark rites of passage – births, funerals, weddings, puberty – and agricultural events, as well as to exorcise sickness or evil spirits, and, in the past, to prepare for battle or celebrate victory.

More refined ritual dances are performed by a select group, but often all the males or females in the community join in. Female movements are generally slow and deliberate, with tiny steps and graceful hand movements; men lift their knees high and use their hands as "weapons", often in imitation of martial arts movements (*pencak silat*). Accompaniment is provided by chanting, pounding of rice mortar (*lesung*), and bamboo chimes or flutes.

Group dances often involve the entrancement and possession of participants, best known of which is the Balinese *Barong*. The Barong-Rangda dance drama is a contest between the

Left: *legong* dancers in Bali are traditionally pre-pubescent females.
Right: lion-like *Barong* in the exorcist dance-drama.

Dancing to a Different Beat

To keep up with the times, traditional Indonesian dance and drama has managed to co-exist with modern forms of entertainment, even blending with them to suit contemporary tastes. Some of these new theatre genres are more like stage plays for re-enacting historical dramas or period pieces.

For example, in Javanese *kethoprak* and *ludruk* as well as Balinese *drama gong*, traditional music is used throughout for setting moods, but the actors perform only a few dance movements. The focus is on dialogue and risqué humor instead, which primarily attracts and entertains a younger audience.

opposing forces of good and evil in the universe, represented by a good lion-like beast called Barong and the evil witch Rangda. The battle, which ends in a temporary quelling rather than complete victory, often occurs within the context of the exorcist drama, *Calonarang*.

Men and even women armed with daggers (*keris*) attempt to kill Rangda, but she makes them turn their knives on themselves instead. They are saved thanks to the intervention of the Barong. Some of them are so deeply entranced that they must be awakened with sprinkles of holy water, and by inhaling the smoke of incense.

Another Balinese family of dances, the or more riders on hobby horses made of plaited bamboo, accompanied by musicians, masked clowns and perhaps also a masked lion, tiger or crocodile similar to the *Barong*.

Now rare, such hobbyhorse troupes were once commonly seen at weekly markets during festival days. However, some hotels are now promoting this art form for tourists. The riders would begin in an orderly fashion, trotting in a circle, then one of them would become entranced and start behaving like a horse, charging back and forth wildly, neighing and eating grass or straw. The others might follow his lead, and sometimes there might be a

sanghyang trance dances, also involve the possession of dancers by gods and animal spirits. The most famous of these is the *sanghyang dedari* or heavenly maidens dance, in which two young girls dressed in white enter a circle of 40 to 50 chanting men, the *kecak* chorus. The girls dance in unison with eyes shut, and when they are finally possessed by goddesses, they are clothed in glittering costumes and borne aloft on the shoulders of the men, touring the village to drive out evil.

On Islamic Java, the trance dance has developed into something of a commercial spectacle. It is variously known as *kuda kepang, kuda lumping, reog* and *jatilan*, and consists of one confrontation between the masked animal and the horsemen. Eventually, the riders would be brought out of the trance by their leader, and money would then be collected from the assembled crowd.

Court dances of Java

Before the turn of the 20th century, all traditional rulers of the coastal and inland kingdoms maintained palace dance-and-theatrical troupes. But following the Dutch conquests, most court traditions lapsed into obscurity. Only in Central Java are courtly performances and royal patronage of dancers, actors and musicians still found and appreciated.

Java has by far the oldest known dance and theatre traditions in Indonesia. Stone carvings dating from the 8th and 9th centuries depict dances and theatrical performances. The walls of the great central Javanese temples of this period – Borobudur, Prambanan and others – are adorned with numerous reliefs depicting dancers and entertainers, from market minstrels and roadside revellers to sensuous court concubines and prancing princesses.

The reliefs at these Central Javanese temples, illustrating popular dances and musical entertainment, suggest that dance once figured prominently in traditional Javanese life. However, outside of the palace courts, very little dancing remains in the area today.

Most of the dances in Central Java today are attributed to rulers of one of several Islamic dynasties, particularly those of the 16th to 18th centuries. Undoubtedly, the vocabulary of movements and the music employed are much older. Throughout the 19th century, rulers frequently were credited for dances choreographed for special occasions. Often it was the palace dance master who actually created the pieces, though a few rulers were also accomplished dancers and musicians.

Bedoyo and serimpi

The most famous of all Javanese court dances is the *bedoyo ketawang*, performed in the Surakarta palace on the anniversary of the Susuhunan's coronation. This is a sacred and private ritual dance said to have been instituted by Sultan Agung in the early 1600s, the greatest of the Mataram kings. It celebrates a reunion between the descendant of the dynasty's founder, Panembahan Senapati, and the powerful goddess of the South Seas, Ratu Kidul.

Nine female palace dancers perform the stately *bedoyo ketawang*, attired in royal wedding dress, and so sacred is it that they may rehearse only once every five weeks on a given day. Until recently, no outsiders were permitted to witness the performance, for it is claimed that Ratu Kidul herself attends and afterwards "weds" the king.

The other important Javanese court dance,

LEFT: in the Javanese *kuda kepang*, dancers often go into a state of trance.
RIGHT: Arjuna teaches archery to his wife Larasati in a traditional Javanese dance.

serimpi, was traditionally performed only by princesses or daughters of the ruling family. It portrays one or two duelling pairs of Amazons who move in unison, fighting with dainty daggers and tiny bows and arrows. Following the rise of dance schools in the early 1900s, the *serimpi* became the standard dance taught to all young women.

Balinese dance

There are clear indications that dance and drama, closely tied to religion, have played a central role in Balinese life since time immemorial. Following the demise of Balinese

CELEBRATING SEXUALITY

To promote the community's fertility, some dances are used primarily for the purpose of courtship. Young Dayak women in Kalimantan for instance perform graceful dances holding bunches of hornbill feathers as bachelors watch and attempt to approach them.

Many social dances are offshoots from such fertility rites, and usually women take the initiative. In *gandrung* from Lombok, a female dancer selects male partners for short dance duets by tapping them with her fan. In some places in Bali, a young man dressed as a woman performs *gandrung*, although it is more common for a woman to pick her partner in the popular *joged bumbung*.

kingdoms at the beginning of the 20th century, the focus for dance and drama shifted from the royal courts to the villages.

In Balinese dance, some Indian influence is evident in the facial expressions. Balinese dance costumes, with their glittering headdresses and elaborate jewellery, are clearly of Hindu-Javanese origin and, as in Java, Balinese dancers adopt the same basic stance.

> **CROSS-DRESSERS**
>
> Wonosobo in Central Java has its *lengger* dance, in which men dress as women. And the male Buginese *bissu* of South Sulawesi dances in trance as a woman.

throughout Bali. Traditionally, *legong* was performed by two young girls, introduced by a court attendant (*condong*) who performs a solo and then presents the dancers with fans. Sheathed in glittering gold costumes, with headdresses crowned by frangipani blossoms and fans twirling in a blur of colour, the two dancers then enact one of a dozen or so possible stories. Today, female performers need not be very young.

But unlike the Javanese in Central Java, who developed slow, controlled, continuous move-

The *baris* warrior dance, often performed in groups and with weapons, appears to have

ments performed with eyes downcast and limbs close to the body, the Balinese dancer is charged with energy, eyes wide, darting this way and that, high-stepping, arms up, moving with quick, cat-like bursts that would startle a Javanese. The Balinese distinguish between dances that are sacred (*wali*), ceremonial (*bebali*) and simply for watching (*bali-balihan*). The last category of dances appears to have developed exclusively among the nobility, but they are now performed by villagers as part of a ceremonial repertoire.

The *legong keraton* was originally a court dance developed for royal amusement, but it is now seen frequently at temple ceremonies

developed out of an old ritual battle dance. A solo *baris* performance is a true test of wits for the dancer and musicians, for they must respond to each other's signals to produce the quivering bursts of synchronised energy that are the essence of the dance.

Contemporary dances

New dances are being created all the time. The powerful *kecak* dance was adopted from the *sanghyang dedari* at the beginning of the 20th

ABOVE: now part of the standard tourist dance programme, *kecak* originated from Bedulu village on Bali.
RIGHT: shadow cast by Javanese *wayang kulit* puppet.

century, and is now performed by as many as a hundred chanting and swaying men, dressed only in loincloths. The *kecak* is by far Bali's most popular tourist spectacle.

In the 1920s, the legendary dancer and choreographer, Mario (I Ketut Marya), introduced a dance known as the *kebyar*, based upon a type of *gamelan* music that appeared in northern Bali around 1915. It is performed by a seated virtuoso soloist, who uses the face and upper parts of the body to interpret the capricious moods of this scintillating music. Mario's other creations include *Oleg Tambulillingan*, which depicts two bumblebees flitting about a garden.

Theatre

In Java, all theatre seems to have its roots in the *wayang* puppet tradition, among which the flat leather shadow puppet play, the *wayang kulit*, is pre-eminent in Central Java. This is evident from the fact that all Javanese theatre, whether performed by actors or by puppets, is referred to as *wayang*. Performed by actors on a stage, *wayang topeng* (mask drama) and *wayang orang* (dance-drama) are the best known, with many of the tales, ichnography and characters' movements borrowed from the shadow play.

Wayang topeng is the oldest form, dating back to 14th-century East Java. It enacts tales from the Panji cycle of epics concerning the founding of the 13th-century Singasari dynasty. In Bali, mask plays are still popular, as they are in the courts of Central Java, and in some villages in the east and west of the island.

Javanese *wayang orang* or *wayang wong* (literally, human *wayang*) dance-dramas are said to have been created in the 18th century by one or another of Central Java's rulers. This has become a partisan matter, in which Surakartans claim their Prince Mangkunegara I as the originator of the genre, while the Yogyakartans insist their Prince Hamengkubuwono I created it.

Neither ruler truly invented the *wayang orang*, for dance-dramas existed in Java from a much earlier time. But both rulers were extremely active in creating new pieces, and the strong rivalry intensified during the 19th century, when Javanese rulers became more and more concerned with matters of cultural

PUPPET THEATRE

Puppet theatre is limited to a few places in Indonesia and appears to be derived from ancestral worship.

The remarkable life-sized Batak *sigale-gale* puppet of North Sumatra is manipulated from below with cords and pulleys during funeral ceremonies. It was first created by a childless woman who made an image of her dead husband and animated it to communicate with his soul. Some figures have water-filled sponges at the eyes to make them weep. Traditionally, at the end of the funeral, spears and arrows were shot at the figure to drive away evil spirits.

In Central Java, *wayang kulit* uses flat leather puppets that are perforated and polychromed with moveable arms for *Ramayana* and *Mahabharata* stories. In Western Java, *wayang golek* (wooden rod puppets) performs tales from Indian epics and Islamic *Amir Hamzah* or *Menak* romances.

Balinese *wayang* refers to many types of shadow puppet theatre with different repertoires. *Wayang Ramayana* uses stories from the epic of the same name, while *wayang parwa* performs episodes from the *Mahabharata*. An 11th-century Javanese exorcist legend of black magic is used for *wayang Calonarang*.

In Lombok, *wayang Sasak* uses flat leather puppets for Islamic *Menak* romances, which were introduced from Java during the 17th century to spread the teachings of Islam.

prestige, and, fortunately, possessed the time and the means to devote to cultural pursuits.

Wayang orang became a part of the state ritual in these kingdoms, performed in an open pavilion to commemorate the founding of the dynasty and the coronation of the king, as well as at lavish royal weddings. The great age of *wayang orang* was during the 1920s and 1930s, when productions lasted days and would often employ 300 to 400 actors.

Today, three commercial *wayang orang* companies in Java hold nightly performances for the public: Sri Wedari in Surakarta, Ngesti Pandhawa in Semarang and Bharata in Jakarta.

Dancers of the *barong* in the village of Batubulan, for example, perform every morning for busloads of foreigners, then at night they may dance again in elaborate *topeng* or *arja* dramas before enthralled villagers.

A new generation of Indonesian choreographers, educated at the performing arts academies and familiar with Western classical and modern dance, is now at work. One result has been the *sendratari* (literally, art-drama-dance), which is essentially a traditional dance-drama minus the dialogue, but one that incorporates some modern movements and costumes.

The first *sendratari*, an adapted version of

Modern trends

Traditional Indonesian dance and drama is in great competition with modern entertainment. However, there's growing interest among educated Indonesians in keeping these arts alive.

The government has helped to remedy the situation by establishing performing arts academies in various cities. Tourism, in turn, provides commercial demand for traditional dances, albeit in non-traditional settings like hotel poolsides, and in shorter and quicker versions.

In Bali, every village has its own dance troupe, and these now have an impetus to improve and expand their repertoire for a steady schedule of tourist performances.

the Javanese *wayang orang*, was staged in the early 1960s for an international dance festival. Today, this *Ramayana* ballet spectacular, with a cast of over 200, is performed during the dry season months (May to October; check local listings for dates), on a large stage erected in front of the elegant 9th-century Prambanan temple complex in Java. Less enthusiastic dance aficionados may watch a condensed version performed at Yogyakarta's Dalem Pujokusuman Theatre *(see page 146)* throughout the year on Mondays and Fridays from 8–10pm. ❑

ABOVE: Balinese *gamelan* musicians prepare to accompany a dance.

Indian Morality Epics

The *Ramayana* and the *Mahabharata* are the basis of the most important *wayang* stories in Java and Bali. These gripping tales, one about a great love and the other about a great war, are products of India which entered Java with the propagation of Hinduism.

Filled with high drama and popular appeal, they are actually morality plays which over the ages have contributed largely to the establishment of traditional Indonesian values. Their fascination lies partly in the complex moral themes posed; life is never a case of absolutely black or absolutely white. Good heroes may have bad traits, and bad characters may have redeeming qualities. Although the forces of good do triumph over evil in the end, more often than not, the victory is incomplete; both sides suffer losses and though a king may win a righteous war, he may lose all his sons as well.

The *Ramayana* is a morality tale full of instructions and examples on how to lead a good and moral life. Written by the poet Valmiki about 2,000 years ago, it tells the story of Prince Rama. Long before he was born, the gods had determined that Rama's life would be that of a hero, but he would be put to the test on many occasions. Rama is actually an incarnation of the god Vishnu, and it is his destiny to kill the evil ogre king Ravana, also known as Dasamuka (Ten-Headed One).

Due to intrigues in the palace, Rama, his wife the beautiful Sita and his brother Laksamana are exiled to the forest. An ogre takes the form of a golden deer, luring Rama and Laksamana away. Ravana then carries off Sita to his island kingdom of Lanka. Rama's search for Sita is helped by the monkey god Hanuman and the monkey king Sugriva. Eventually, a full-scale assault is launched on the evil king and Sita is rescued. Sita, in turn, proves her chastity during captivity in a trial by fire before Rama accepts her.

The *Mahabharata*, which was written after the *Ramayana*, is a collection of stories that have great appeal to popular imagination. The epic centres on a long-standing feud between two family clans: the Pandava and the Korava. The feud culminates in an epic battle during which the five Pandava brothers come face to face with their 100 cousins from the Korava clan. After 18 days of fighting, the Pandava emerge victorious and the eldest brother becomes king. The plays usually focus on one or other of the five Pandava brothers, each of whom is a hero.

The great war portrayed in the *Mahabharata* is believed to have been fought in northern India in 13th-century BC. The war became a focus of legends, songs and poems and at some point, the vast collection accumulated over centuries was gathered into a narrative called the *Epic of the Bharata Nation* (India), or *Mahabharata*.

Important events that take place in the epic include the appearance of Krishna, an incarnation of Lord Vishnu, who becomes the adviser of the

Pandava; the marriage of Prince Arjuna of the Pandava to the Princess Drupadi; the Korava's attempt to kill the Pandava; and the division of the kingdom into two in an attempt to end the rivalry between the two groups.

In one scene during the great war, the Pandava warrior Arjuna becomes despondent at the thought of fighting his own flesh and blood. Krishna, his charioteer and adviser, then explains to him the duties and obligations of the warrior in a poem known as the *Bhagavad Gita*. Krishna explains that the soul is indestructible and that whoever dies shall be reborn and so there is no cause to be sad; it is the soldier's duty to fight as the outcome of the battle is already predetermined.

RIGHT: Javanese dancer plays a mythological queen in the Hindu *Mahabharata* epic.

GAMELAN MUSIC

The trance-like rhythms of the gamelan have earned it fame as a unique music form. The contemplative Javanese variety contrasts with Bali's sparkling sounds

Gamelan music is comparable to only two things: moonlight and flowing water. It is pure and mysterious like the first and ever-changing like the second. Since 1893, when Claude Debussy first heard a Javanese ensemble perform at the Paris International Exhibition, the haunting and hypnotic tones of the *gamelan* have fascinated the West. This music has been sensitively studied by scholars such as Jaap Kunst and Colin McPhee, and is now indisputably recognised as one of the world's most sophisticated musical arts. In Indonesia, *gamelan* music has always been the sound of everything civilised.

The term *gamelan* derives from *gamel*, an old Javanese word for handle or hammer, as most of the instruments in the orchestra are percussive. The interlocking rhythmic and melodic patterns found in *gamelan* music are said to originate in the rhythms of the *lesung* – the stone or wooden mortars used for husking rice. Others ascribe the patterns to the chanting of frogs in the rice fields after dusk or the cacophony of roosters crowing at dawn.

No one knows exactly when the first *gamelan* orchestra came into being. Metallophones (bronze, brass or iron percussion instruments) date from prehistoric times, and the manufacture of bronze gongs and drums is associated with the Dong Son bronze culture that is thought to have reached Indonesia from Indochina in the 3rd century BC. Since then, large bronze gongs have formed the heartbeat of this distinctive music, with a deep and penetrating sound that can be heard for miles on a quiet night.

Highest refinement

Gamelan ensembles most commonly perform in accompaniment to dance and theatre. *Karawitan* is the Indonesian term coined in the 1950s by Ki Sindusawarno, the first director of the music conservatory in Surakarta, for the entire range of Javanese and Balinese performing arts incorporating *gamelan* music.

In Java, *karawitan* and related arts reached the height of refinement in the Islamic courts of the 18th and 19th centuries. Renowned instrument sets supposedly date from the 14th-century Majapahit Kingdom in East Java, and there are references to the instruments from 1,000 years ago. The aristocratic refinement of the *gamelan* in Central Java has resulted in slow,

THE SOUNDS OF MUSIC

Aside from the classical beauty of *gamelan* music, Indonesia's other music forms have a part to play in the social scene: the popular *dangdut, keroncong, jaipongan,* the meditative *degung* and Sundanese and Batak pop. *Keroncong,* the first major folk music, was originally associated with the town's lowlife but later gained respectability when it was adopted by the film industry during the 1930s. The unmistakable to-and-fro beat of *dangdut* is heard all over the country. Essentially dance party music, it is usually accompanied by blasting ballad vocals. The percussion-based *jaipongan* started in Bandung in the 1960s and is also a popular dance music.

stately and mystical music, designed to be heard in the large audience hall of the aristocratic home and to convey a sense of awesome power and emotional control.

Five to 40 instruments make up a *gamelan* orchestra, and most of them are never played other than as part of an ensemble. In fact, the two instruments that see regular solo use – the *rebab* (a two-stringed bowed lute, probably of Middle Eastern origin) and the *suling* (bamboo flute) – are non-percussive and thought to have been later additions to the orchestra.

The basic principle underlying all *gamelan* music is that of stratification. It is essentially a technique of orchestration in which the density of notes played on each instrument is determined by its register; higher instruments play more notes than lower ones.

In addition, instruments are grouped according to their function. Gongs, for example, maintain the basic structure of the music, while mid-register metallophones carry the theme and other instruments provide ornamentation. The *kendhang* – wooden drums with skins stretched over both ends – lead the orchestra by controlling the tempo of the piece. Many Indonesian musicians metaphorically compare the structure of *gamelan* music to a tree. The roots, deep, sturdy and supportive, are the low registers; the trunk is the melody; and the branches, leaves and blossoms, the delicate complexity of the accompanied ornamentation.

In Central Java, the main *balungan* (skeleton) of a piece is played on the various *saron* (small- to medium-size metallophones, with six or seven bronze keys lying over a wooden trough resonator), and on the *slentem* (metallophones with bamboo resonators). Faster variations on the *balungan* are played simultaneously on the

elaborating instruments: the *bonang* (a set of small, horizontally-suspended gongs), *gender* (similar to the *slentem*), *gambang* (a wooden xylophone), and *celempung* (a zither with metal strings). Together with the *suling*, the *rebab* and the vocalists, they create the complex, rich and sensual sounds unique to *gamelan* music.

Vocals

Vocal parts in an ensemble became popular in Java only in the 19th century, but it is now common to have soloists as well as a chorus. Female (*pesinden*) singers seem to be more popular, but the sound of voices is regarded merely as another element in the overall tex-

LEFT: a Javanese *gamelan* ensemble at Jakarta's Hilton hotel. **ABOVE:** the *kendang* drummer leads the musicians in a *gamelan* orchestra.

ture of the orchestra, and the singing is not necessarily given prominence over the instrumental parts.

Lyrics are only rarely understood, as they were normally composed in an archaic or literary language. Also, they become lost as they are woven into the overall fabric of the music. For Westerners, appreciation of the music often requires concentration.

A common misconception of *gamelan* compositions is that they are improvised. This impression arises perhaps because scores are rarely used. Most compositions (*gendhing*) are in fact as rigidly determined as they are lucidly performed. There are literally thousands of pieces, and every region of Java has its favourites. Each *gendhing* has its own name and theme (*balungan*), usually corresponding to the specific character, dance or ritual for which the *gendhing* is played.

ticularly in contrast to the slow and measured *gamelan* performances of Java.

One of the most frequently encountered ensembles in Bali is the *gamelan gong kebyar*. *Kebyar* refers to a particularly flashy music style that originated in North Bali in 1915, but the ensembles that play it have since expanded their repertoire to include other styles. In the gong *kebyar*, four different gongs mark the musical phrase. They are, in order of descending size: the gong, *kempur*, *kempli* and *kemong*.

The melodic theme is carried by two pairs of large metallophones: the *jegogan* and *calung*. Several *gangsa* (high-pitched metallophones)

Balinese gamelan

In Bali, the *gamelan* exhibits overwhelming variety. Dozens of completely different types of ensembles exist, some of which are found all over the island, others of which are restricted to isolated areas. But on the whole, Balinese musical performances are noted for their capriciousness, stridency and rhythmic vitality – particularly

ornament the theme, and the *reyong* (Bali's version of the Javanese *bonang*) is played by four musicians producing a rippling stream of visceral, syncopated figurations. A pair of *kendhang* drums leads the group, interlocking with each other to produce spectacular rhythms. The drummer of the lower-pitched *kendhang* is generally also the leader, teacher and composer for the ensemble. A set of shimmering cymbals (*cengceng*) and several bamboo flutes (*suling*) complete the orchestra.

ABOVE: *saron* metallophones have six or seven keys fastened onto a wooden trough.
RIGHT: large bronze gongs punctuate *gamelan* melodies.

Gamelan musicians were traditionally trained by other musicians in their spare time, without any reference to written scores. In the central Javanese palaces, a system of notation was developed. Some court musicians began to teach outsiders at the beginning of the 20th century. Since independence, however, several government music academies have been founded and students now learn in a more formal setting.

At the village level, it is often difficult to distinguish amateurs from professionals. Many village artists are experts in the music of their region but no special status is assigned to them nor are they paid sizeable fees for their services.

Some *gamelan* musicians are itinerant, making the rounds of traditional performances, be they theatrical or ceremonial or both, including the ever-popular shadow play or *wayang kulit* circuit. There are many famous artists who lead this precarious lifestyle, which come with minimal financial rewards.

Court orchestras

The big orchestras are still royal heirlooms and the musical style of a royal house is considered to be a part of the orchestra. In Java, instrument sets are invariably a precious family possession, even in the villages, and are often highly decorative. Good examples of Javanese court *gamelan* can be seen in the Museum Sono Budoyo in Yogyakarta (Jogja), and the Keraton Mangkunegaran in Solo (Surakarta).

Once a year during the Sekaten festival celebrating the Prophet Mohammed's birthday, the court *gamelan sekaten* of Jogja and Solo perform in the mosque to an audience of thousands, in clear conflict to fundamental Islamic beliefs regarding music, but testimony to the enduring eclecticism of the Javanese culture.

Balinese *gamelan* are normally owned and maintained cooperatively by village music clubs (*sekaha*). The Balinese religious calendar prescribes a hectic schedule of performances for temple festivals, and the provincial government has taken an active role in preserving lesser-known musical styles that may be in danger of extinction.

Island-wide, inter-village musical competitions provide an impetus for Balinese composers and performers to constantly expand the expressive essence of the music. ❑

THE FAHNESTOCK EXPEDITION

The Fahnestock brothers, Bruce and Sheridan, sailed for Indonesia on the 137-ft schooner *Director II* in 1940 with state-of-the-art recording equipment and 15 scientists. They also had with them 3 km (2 miles) of insulated microphone cable to enable them to record on shore while the equipment remained safely on board. What was unknown to the public was that the Fahnestocks were at the same time spying for President Roosevelt, noting the sea defences of Java, under cover of making the recordings in Java, Bali, Madura and the South Seas.

The boat sank off Australia in 1941, but not before the discs had been taken back to New York. Bruce was killed in New Guinea during the war, while Sheridan later became a publisher. The original recordings were donated to the US Library of Congress after Margaret Fahnestock, Sheridan's wife, wrote to it in 1986 asking if the library was interested in some old recordings that had been gathering dust in her attic for 40 years. The library accepted them as part of its Endangered Music Project.

A selection of the recordings has been released by Rykodisc, on CD and cassette, as *Music for the Gods – The Fahnestock South Sea Expedition, Indonesia*. The most sophisticated and euphonious pieces are those from Bali, reproducing the *gamelan* orchestras of the temples.

TEXTILES

Indonesia's great variety of peoples has produced an equally wide array of lovely and intricate textiles that tell of identity and the rites of passage

Indonesia is one of the world's greatest producers of fine traditional textiles. One of the oldest expressions of traditional art, handmade cloth is a vital component of Indonesian culture. Textiles are not only mere articles of clothing, but are also important to the cultural heritage of the country, as spiritually-charged talismans, and symbols of wealth and status.

To understand the true value and meaning of Indonesian textiles, we have to examine their cultural context and the belief systems of the people who produce them. The materials, colours and motifs, along with rituals for their creation and use, all serve as powerful messages that convey wealth, social status, religious belief, the marriage contract and a connection to the spirit world.

Traditional textiles are works of art created by craftswomen who incorporate a medley of technical skills: weaving, dyeing and embroidery using any choice of natural fibres from bark, cotton and silk. Some are embellished with shells, beads and gold or silver threads but use methods and techniques that have changed very little over centuries.

Symbol of birth

The process of manufacturing textiles is interwoven with taboos that define gender-role responsibilities to ensure the harmony of the community. Spinning, dyeing and the weaving of yarn are regarded as symbolic of the process of creation, and of human birth in particular. Weaving is generally an exclusively female activity. Men are permitted to participate only in the dyeing of certain colours of the thread, analogous with their role in human conception. The dyeing process is carried out in the utmost privacy, behind partitions set up around the work area. Pregnant, menstruating or sick women are excluded from this work.

A traditional cloth produced with natural dyes used to take many years to complete. The main natural dyes used in traditional textiles are indigo (*Indigofera tinctoria*), *mengkudu* (*Morinda citrifolia*) and *soga* (a brown dye from root and bark). Today, because of time and economic constraints, many textiles are coloured by chemical dyes.

RECIPE FOR INDIGO DYE

Indigo dye is the most widely used natural blue dye in the world and it comes from the indigo plant (*Indigofera tinctoria*) native to Indonesia. The recipe for the dye was once a guarded secret, but today, it is known across the archipelago. The dye is prepared in a vat and goes through a fermentation and oxidation process. Indigo leaves are first soaked in earthenware jars of water. The leaves are then removed, lime is added and, days later, ash is mixed in. Cotton or silk threads are left overnight in the mixture, and then hung up to oxidise. This process is repeated till the desired colour intensity is achieved and the indigo threads deemed ready to be woven.

LEFT: Chinese-inspired cloud motifs are a hallmark of batik produced in Cirebon, Western Java.
RIGHT: Sumba women wearing *hinggi ikat* shawls.

In some areas, the mounting of threads on the loom is done on an auspicious day, otherwise the threads would break and bring bad luck. In several coastal villages, this means a full moon and a high tide. If a death occurs in the village, weaving stops at once to prevent the spirit of the departed from exacting vengeance by bringing sickness upon the weaver and causing the threads to lose their strength. Finished products are usually sanctified by metaphysical and psychological associations, and therefore regarded as powerful objects that can protect the weaver, cure illness, bring rain and are often necessary for life-cycle rituals.

Development

The first common material used for clothing was bark, as cotton and silk were traditionally reserved for the local aristocracy. As the spice trade developed, traders discovered they could obtain valuable spices in exchange for Indian cotton and silk. Indonesians in turn found they could barter their easily-gathered cloves, nutmeg, peppers and aromatic woods for fine textiles from the traders.

Many of the techniques and motifs in Indonesian textiles were adapted from foreign examples. As early as the 14th century, Indian fabrics were imported on a large scale, and the Indian textile revolution extended to fabrics that were considered rare and valuable, or even magical. The single most influential cloth is the Indian *patola*, a double-*ikat* silk fabric produced in Gujarat. Widely reproduced in Indonesia, it was incorporated into the ceremonial life of many Indonesians and formed part of the costumes of kings on many islands, including Java. As fewer *patola* were imported after 1800, many weavers in Indonesia set about producing replicas. Today, the eight-pointed-flower, or *jilamprang*, design is seen everywhere.

Indonesian textile methods fall into two categories: dye-resist and woven techniques. The dye-resist process of batik is produced in Java, Madura and in the Sumatran areas of Jambi and Palembang. Woven textiles have three main styles: warp *ikat*, weft *ikat* and double *ikat*. Warp and weft *ikat*, created on a backstrap loom, are produced by the Batak of North Sumatra, by people of the East Nusa Tenggara islands, East Java and South Sulawesi. Weft *ikat* is produced on a shaft loom in Bali, West Lombok, East Java, Palembang, Sumatra and Ujung Pandang in South Sulawesi, while double *ikat* is only produced in Bali.

Batik

Batik is Indonesia's renowned textile art, especially Javanese batik which is regarded as the world's finest. In the technique, dye-resist wax is applied to the cloth to prevent the dye from penetrating certain areas, thus resulting in a pattern in the negative. Finely-detailed batik *tulis* ("written" design) is made possible with a tool unique to the Javanese. The *canting*, a small copper cup with a spout through which melted wax flows, is mounted on a handle and wielded like a pen, allowing the artist to execute designs.

The first step is to draw a design on a piece of silk or cotton cloth. Areas not to be coloured in the first dyeing are covered with wax. This process alone can take hundreds of hours. The cloth is then immersed in dye and dried off. With natural dyes, repeated immersions and dryings are necessary, and a single dyeing can take months to complete.

For the second dyeing, the cloth has to be de-waxed and waxed again. The old wax is first removed by boiling water or wax from the unwanted areas is scraped off. Wax is then applied onto the desired areas. Dyeing and drying follow, and the process repeated as many times as there are number of colours on the cloth.

In Central Java, certain motifs were once reserved for the royal court, such as the *parang rusak barong*, a broken sword design that consists of diagonal rows of interlocking scrolls. Today, out of respect for the descendants of the royal family, many locals will choose not to wear batik printed with motifs that were originally regarded as sacred to the royal court.

Batik *cap* is produced with the use of a metal printing block. The *cap* stamps are built out of thin strips of copper and wire soldered to an open frame. The *cap* is dipped into heated wax before it is pressed firmly onto the cloth. The advent of batik *cap* revitalised the industry in the 1890s, making mass-produced cloths that were affordable to all and creating an export trade from Java to the Outer Islands.

Ikat

Warp *ikat* is a traditional method of weaving in which the warp threads (on the length) of a cloth are tie-dyed prior to weaving. The process of spinning cotton threads and preparing the dyes, tying the warp threads into a pattern that will resist the dye, and then repeatedly immersing and drying them to achieve the desired colour requires tremendous skill and patience. In the hands of a master weaver, the end result is intricate, detailed motifs executed in deep, rich colours. Weaving is done on a backstrap loom, with the warp threads affixed to beams. While one end is attached to a grounded object (tree or house post), the other end is secured to the weaver with the tension maintained by a strap placed around the weaver's back as she sits on the ground. String heddles are employed to create individual sheds and sometimes a bamboo comb is introduced to maintain the warp spacing.

The most famous warp *ikat* are the *hinggi* from East Sumba. These cloths are known for their rich colours, fine details and bold, horizontal fields of stylised human and animal figures. Normally produced in pairs, one to wrap around the body and one to drape over the shoulders, they have served as valuable trade goods for centuries and were exported extensively by the Dutch in the 19th century. *Hinggi* textiles are used in Sumba to seal a marriage

> **SACRED CLOTH**
>
> *Geringsing,* a sacred Balinese textile, is said to have protective powers. Kings once presented *geringsing* garments to warriors prior to battle.

LEFT: *ikat* cloth from West Timor is so intricately woven it resembles embroidery.
ABOVE: a weft *ikat* weaver in Gianyar, Bali.

contract and in funerals; it is not uncommon to wrap the body of a nobleman or woman in as many as 100 textile pieces.

The neighbouring island of West Timor is known for its brilliantly-coloured warp *ikat* embellished by special techniques such as *sotis*, a float weave using contrasting colours and usually woven into small panels. There is also the complex process of *buna*, which resembles heavy embroidery.

The predominant colour for men's textiles is red: a colour mostly associated with bravery, war and masculinity. In the past, using traditional means, it would take anything from seven to 10 years to achieve a desired shade of natural red.

Another well-known warp *ikat* is the brown-and-white *ulos ragidup* (pattern of life) cloth of the Sumatran Bataks. This is presented by the father of the bride to the mother of the groom, who later presents the cloth to her daughter-in-law when she is seven months' pregnant with her first child, as an *ulos ni tondi* or "soul cloth".

Weft *ikat* (resist-patterning of the crosswise threads) occurs primarily in Bali and the Islamic coastal trading areas of Gresik, East Java, Palembang and South Sumatra. Weft *ikat* is usually woven on a "fly shuttle" handloom.

FABRICS FOR ALL SEASONS

West Timor once comprised independent kingdoms that had a propensity for war. As such, the ability to ascertain friend or foe at a distance was imperative. Banners were thus woven with motifs and colours that revealed one's alliance to a particular village or clan. The *selimut*, a waist wrap worn by men that had folds in the front and was secured with a belt, bore designs which conveyed one's allegiance. It was this need for quick and easy identification that contributed to the large variety of textile patterns found within a relatively small area.

Textiles also play a nuptial role. They are an important part of the dowry given to a groom's family in return for the bride price. If a bride comes from a wealthy family, her family may be expected to present 100 textiles as part of her dowry, while the groom's family in return will present buffaloes or gold and silver. In some villages, the bride gives the groom a *selimut*, which demonstrates her weaving skill. This skill is an important criteria of a girl's maturity and determines whether she is ready for marriage.

The engagement period can last up to three years. During this time, special ceremonies are held in which textiles are hung up outside the girl's room. During the rituals, the husband-to-be makes payments as part of the bride price in order to have the textiles gradually removed.

The Palembang and Bangka weft *ikat* are extremely sophisticated, done on silk in rich tones of red, blue and yellow, often with supplementary gold threads in the weft. Indian, Javanese and Chinese motifs are all employed, sometimes simultaneously.

Today, weft *ikat* is a thriving cottage industry, with great amounts of cloth woven in bright colours and floral or geometric designs. A special weft *ikat* textile, *kain limar*, woven with gold threads, is worn by boys on the day of circumcision, a special rite among Muslim Palembang and Sumatran families.

Geringsing

The rare double *ikat*, known as *geringsing*, is made in Tenganan, a small village in eastern Bali, one of only three places in the world to produce this labour-intensive textile. The other two places are India and Japan. It can take several years just to complete a single *geringsing* piece. Both warp and weft threads are tied and dyed, then woven to produce an integrated motif on the finished fabric. Red being the predominant color in *geringsing*, the background is overdyed with indigo to produce a midnight black.

Considered by the Balinese to be sacred, *geringsing* is used in many important ceremonies throughout the island, including tooth filings. In Tenganan, wearers of the cloth are thought to be protected from evil and illness, as *geringsing* means "without sickness".

Songket

Songket – cloth of gold or silver – is an ornately brocaded textile that has gold or silver threads worked into it. On a silk or cotton base, "floating" metallic weft threads are woven in to create a raised pattern that almost resembles embroidery. Areas with the best *songket* are Bali and Palembang, and those produced by the Minangkabau are sought after as well.

Palembang *songket* features gold threads woven onto bright red silk to form a fine geometrical pattern that often covers the entire cloth, while the Minangkabau's silver-threaded *songket* has a background of wine-red or black silk. Wearing *songket* became a sign of physical and spiritual blessings.

Once a favoured cloth by the royal class, *songket*, also known as *tanuk*, is worn today in a formal headdress by the Minangkabau women of West Sumatra. It serves as a display of wealth and the way it is folded also indicates which village the wearer is from.

Bark cloth

Bark cloths found among upland tribes in Kalimantan, Sulawesi and Papua display a high degree of artistry, even though they date to the prehistoric era.

The Torajans boil and ferment the inner bark of pandanus, mulberry or other trees before

beating – with special wooden and stone mallets – the resultant pulp into extremely soft and pliable sheets. This cloth (*fuya*) is then dyed, painted or stamped using natural pigments.

Certain tribes in Kalimantan, Flores, Sulawesi and Timor produce warrior tunics from fibres by twining them, a simple process in which two weft fibres are alternately wrapped above and below a passive warp.

The sacred *maa* cloths of the Torajan of South Sulawesi are kept in special baskets, and are considered necessary for major rituals. Some *maa* are thought to be effective vessels for fertility spirits, and opening a powerful cloth is said to bring immediate rainfall. ❑

LEFT: symbolic *hinggi ikat* from Sumba are used as dowry gifts and in funeral rituals.
RIGHT: a Minangkabau headgear made of *songket*.

INDONESIAN BATIK: ART ON FABRIC

Batik is the great leveller in Indonesian society. It is both the formal attire of Jakarta urbanites as well as simple villagers working the paddy fields

Batik is one of the most prominent expressions of cultural identity in Indonesia. Nowhere in the world has the art of batik evolved into such high standards, finetuned over the centuries under the patronage of the Javanese royal courts. Today, the making and wearing of batik remains a source of national pride, a vital and unifying medium found in every conceivable form: sarong, dress, shirt, scarf, table-cover, wall hangings and more.

The Indonesian word batik (from "tik" meaning dot) was originally a term used to describe the dye-resist technique; today, the term is used for both the process and the decorated fabric. The value of each piece is determined by the method of creation, the most highly prized and expensive is the labour-intensive batik *tulis* (literally, to write) using a *canting* tool. The best pieces are created by small cottage industry workshops in Java. A cheaper alternative is the block-printed batik using a metal printing stamp called *cap*. Batik *cetak* is mass-produced screen-printed fabric imitating traditional designs.

Each area of Java has its own unique style of batik which comunicates ethnic identity and social status while the folds of the sarong convey one's gender. Special motifs with symbolic meaning, once reserved for the royal courts of Java, are today worn by all for ceremonies like weddings, circumcisions, childbirth and burials.

▷ **FOREIGN INFLUENCE**
Traditional batik *tulis* from Cirebon, Java, with stylised lions inspired by old Dutch coins and Chinese mythological winged creatures with elephant heads.

△ **BALI BEACH WRAP**
Created for the tourist market, bright floral batik beach wraps, or *sarong*, are inexpensive and can be found in most tourist destinations.

△ **VILLAGE DRESS**
Young boys in Tenganan, East Bali, clad in traditional batik wrap known as *kain panjang* or "long cloth", often mistaken for a *sarong*.

◁ **CLASSICAL DANCER**
Javanese dancer in batik costume: the red is inspired by Indian *patola* cloth while the brown and white *parang rusak* design is the pattern of the Javanese royal court.

▽ **BATIK TULIS ARTIST**
Expert skill and patience is employed in applying melted wax onto a white cloth base using a *canting* tool, a small copper reservoir with spout attached to a handle.

THE ART OF BATIK ◆ 93

THE EVOLUTION OF BATIK

Few of Indonesia's traditional arts can juxtapose the old and the new like batik. The above picture is an example of fine contemporary batik *tulis* by batik designer, Josephine Komara of Bin House, who almost single-handedly has imbued new life to the centuries-old art of batik *tulis*. Designers and batik artists have elevated batik to a higher art by adapting to changing fashion styles while incorporating traditional designs. Today, fashion models in Indonesia and Europe are clad in *haute couture* batik; with Iwan Tirta as Indonesia's first international designer to make the fashion headlines in this regard.

◁ **BAG IT**
Small bags made of fine detailed batik. An infinite supply of batik handicrafts are sold in tourist shops and traditional markets throughout Indonesia.

◁ **PUPPET-WEAR**
Decorative *wayang golek* puppets clad in traditional batik – used in the performances of Hindu epics – from West Java.

▷ **HIGH-FASHION**
Models wear contemporary designer apparel made with high-quality silk batik *tulis*.

ARTS AND CRAFTS

Art lovers are spoilt for choice. A spectrum of styles and forms include Dayak beak-nosed masks, Balinese paintings and rustic Lombok earthenware

As a crossroads for maritime trade, the Indonesian archipelago has for centuries been subject to foreign cultural influences, most notably Indian, Arab, Chinese and Dutch, as is evident in the art and culture of the Islamic coastal areas, the royal courts and in the architecture of ancient Hindu and Buddhist temples. In the remote interior and outer islands, many tribes lived in relative isolation until as recently as the 20th century, producing "primitive" art that was a medium of expression of their animistic beliefs.

Indonesian creative arts is primarily seen as a manifestation of the peoples' spiritual beliefs. As a result, traditional Indonesian art is surfeit with spiritually-charged talismans. Creative arts serve to establish social and cultural identity, and fulfil social rites of passage such as birth, puberty, marriage and death.

In Central Java, the *loro blonyo*, painted wood statues that represent Dewi Sri, the goddess of fertility, and her consort Sedono are placed in the home of newly-married couples. Many objects of art are produced as the bride's dowry, such as the *mamuli* of Sumba, a decorative metal object given by the groom's family to the bride's family in exchange for textiles and other goods. A *mamuli* will also be placed into the grave for wealth in the after-life.

Indonesia is a treasure trove of handcrafted items. Many artisans carry on the timeless tradition of fine craftsmanship using traditional iconography passed on from one generation to the next. In many villages and tourist destinations, the main streets and local *pasar* (markets) are full of artisans working at their trades in the open. Few other countries in the world offer the opportunity of direct encounters with so many craftsmen practising skills that are centuries old.

The production process is usually divided between what is considered male and female.

Male energy items use substances that are hard and strong or created with fire, as in the crafts of the ironsmith and woodcarver. Female energy is expressed through what is soft and flexible, as in the weaving of textiles, basketwork and beadwork. There is no power struggle or competition between the sexes but rather a

desire to maintain the balance between the two in a unified symbol of an ordered universe.

Puppets and masks

Indonesia is best known for its shadow puppets, or *wayang kulit*, flat puppets made of buffalo hide with finely chiselled, painted details, and rod puppets, or *wayang golek*, with carved and painted wooden faces. Puppets are typically used for performances of the *Ramayana* and *Mahabharata* Hindu epics, which impart complex yet subtle lessons in social behaviour. The oldest and best-known puppet makers are found in the environs of Yogyakarta (Jogja) and Surakarta (Solo), Central Java.

LEFT: these colourful conical hats also double up as tourist souvenirs.
RIGHT: demonic wooden faces from Bali.

Ceremonial masks are found on many of the islands and believed to access the spiritual essence of the wearer's soul. The island of Bali is famed for elaborately decorated and highly expressive *topeng*, carved soft wood masks used in sacred temple ceremonial dramas. Cirebon masks from Java are used in theatrical pageants. Central and East Javanese masks celebrate the lives of past Javanese royalty. The Dayak of Kalimantan make oversized wooden masks, *hudog*, with bulging eyes and large beaked noses, that are used in a ceremonial dance to keep maleficent spirits from taking over the "soul" of the rice. The Batak of Lake Toba make carved masks and wooden hands that are symbols of their ethnic identity, copied from the *si gale-gale*, a life-sized puppet used in pre-Christian funeral ceremonies as artificial mourners for those who died childless.

Woodcarvings

Prized by museums and collectors throughout the world, many of Indonesia's woodcarvings are masterpieces of primitive art. Every island maintains a unique tradition and today most produce countless "copies" of traditional sculptures, usually out of tropical hardwood. The woodcarvings of the Asmat of Papua are some of the most impressive of Indonesian primitive art. Decorative carved shields serve as vessels for ancestral spirits, and large spirit poles are the homes of the spirits of departed ancestors. In Sumatra, Batak ancestor statues called *si baso nabolon* are placed in the loft of a traditional house and serve as protectors against evil spirits. Kalimantan's Dayak produce large carved wooden guardian poles, *hampatong*, with a stylised crouching ancestor figure usually with an outstretched tongue; they are placed at the front of a Dayak longhouse for protection against evil spirits.

The Javanese are known for their refined furniture-making skills, while the Balinese are known for their highly ornamental motifs found on doors, windows and posts. Expert chip wood carving is also evident in furniture, which in the past was ceremonial rather than utilitarian and limited to storage chests.

From the 1600s, European and Chinese influences appeared in the form of enormous frame beds used for wedding ceremonies and embellished with carved panels of flowers and birds and painted in the style of Chinese wedding beds. Today, furniture shops are filled with cabinets, beds, tables, chairs, chests and wall panels made of tropical woods.

Stone and metal

Religious stone statues of Hindu gods and Buddha have been carved for centuries in Java and Sumatra (excellent examples are found in Jakarta's National Museum). Newly-made copies of these masterpieces are still produced in Central and East Java as well as Bali. The village of Batubulan on Bali is dedicated to the creation of stone statues. Working in *paras*, a soft ashy stone, Hindu gods are produced alongside fanciful garden statues. On other islands such as Nias, stone statues of ancestors are found.

Metalwork was introduced to Indonesia during the Dong Son Bronze Age around the 3rd century BC. To this day, metal items are produced either by forging or by wax-casting. One of the most revered examples of metal art is the ornamental dagger, *keris*, decorated with silver, gold or precious stones and thought to possess magical powers. Unfortunately, there are few *empu* or master smiths left today, and this dying art form is the preserve of a few ironsmiths in Central and West Java as well as in Kusamba, Bali, where a new *keris* can be commissioned.

Kalimantan and Nusa Tenggara islands produce a functional cutlass, or *parang*, which usually has an ornate hilt of carved wood. The scabbard is sometimes decorated with old Dutch coins, rattan trim and the teeth of wild boar. At one time, *parang ilang* or *mandau* were used for headhunting by Dayak. Today, the finest *parang* are used ceremonially. Swordsmiths forge *parang* from scrap metal and employ bellows; the blade is repeatedly beaten, folded and hardened in cold river water.

Gold and silver smithery have a long history in Indonesia. Early travellers were impressed by the riches and quality workmanship of the royal courts: parasol fittings, the bejewelled golden *keris* and exquisite ornate boxes fashioned of gold. Traditional jewellery is an important part of the bride price and each island produces its own distinctive style, ranging from the delicate filigree work of Bali and Java to the bold and expressive beaten gold of the Outer Islands. A symbol of social rank and a link to ancestors, Indonesian gold and silversmiths are masters of several decorative and labour intensive techniques such as repousse or embossing. For centuries, the royal courts of Bali have expressed sacred and temporal power through art.

Kamasan village is still a centre for Balinese court arts, producing objects of silver and gold for ceremonial use. Statues of Hindu deities, offering bowls and containers for holy water are embellished with intricate designs and mythological figures. The use of simple equipment and skills have been handed down to the children from the family elders. A thriving business is modern silverwork for the tourist market. Celuk village in Bali is lined with rows of homes and shops producing silver rings,

LEFT: artisan creating furniture from bamboo.
ABOVE: Balinese craftsman carving a statue from a soft volcanic stone called *paras*.

DAYAK BABY CARRIER

Several ethnic groups, known collectively as Dayak or jungle people, inhabit the Kalimantan interior on the island of Borneo, producing powerful and expressive art which maintain balance and harmony with the spirits of the supernatural world. The ornate Kenyah and Kayan Dayak baby carrier is an important charm designed to protect the young soul and indicate social stature. Many are highly decorative works of traditional art. Carved out of wood with spiritually protective designs or out of rattan and embellished with ancient sacred beads and coins, they bear the claws and teeth of wild jungle animals and serve to protect the young child carried within.

bracelets, necklaces, pins and utilitarian objects, while in Java, the silver centre is Kota Gede near Yogyakarta. Most pieces are made with 90–95 percent pure silver, some set with imported semi-precious stones.

Basketry and pottery

Indonesia has an inexhaustible supply of useful plant products derived from bamboo, coconut palms, rattan, *pandan* (screw pine), breadfruit trees, reed and grass. Basketry serves as a functional craft; fishing traps, baskets, backpacks, hats and all manner of useful containers are made in every shape and size. Men help to gather the materials but it is the women who work the weaving or plaiting, usually with great speed and aesthetic and technical refinement.

In Lombok, bark and rattan boxes are used to transport wedding clothes while large rectangle or round boxes made of palm leaf are decorated with split shells and used for storing rice. The baskets of Sumatra are embellished with fine gold leaf and lacquer while those made on Kalimantan island display superb rattan palm-weaving skills.

Pottery has been made since neolithic times. Earthenware vessels such as bowls and *kendi* (water pitchers), decorative roof gables, animals and figures of Hindu deities serve both a functional and decorative purpose. Terracotta pottery is usually only produced in villages that specialise in the craft and only by women who make the clay vessels. In recent years, Lombok pottery has entered the limelight, with entire villages now producing high-quality earthenware that is sold locally or exported.

Textiles

The making of high-quality handloom textiles (*see page 95*) such as batik *tulis* or handwoven *ikat* is the work of women and a skilled art. Today, machine-made mass-produced "copies" of traditional work is made for the tourist market using quick chemical dyes. Each has its own appeal with hand-made cloth found in most hotel shops and markets. Prices vary according to quality from inexpensive ones to thousands of dollars for collectors pieces.

Beadwork is associated with agricultural fertility and femininity; and except for the Toraja of Sulawesi, all beadwork is done by women.

LOMBOK POTTERY

Lombok island is well known for many of its traditional handicrafts, in particular earthenware pottery.

In 1988, the governments of Indonesia and New Zealand jointly launched the Lombok Crafts Project. Three villages received funds to build workplaces, warehouses and showrooms, along with receiving technical and design advice and marketing and business ideas. The result is a thriving cottage industry producing high-quality decorative as well as functional pottery.

The clay used for the pots is obtained locally from riverbeds by women who then work the grey-brown clay by hand, using a round stone and wooden paddle. This method, which dispenses with the need for a potter's wheel, has changed little over the centuries.

Geometric patterns are incised with a sharp bamboo stick, set in the sun till sufficiently dry, and then fired. The stack is covered with a fast-burning, ash-forming fuel of rice straw and rice husks that will burn out quickly and leave a thick ash cover that holds the heat for the final stages of firing. A second firing using coconut husks, dung and wood turns the pottery jet black. After cooling the finished product turns a rich red-brown.

Many women of Banyumulek, Masbagik and Penunjak villages now have their own thriving pottery business.

The Dayak regard beads as having magical power and use them in the necklaces worn by shamans and to embellish ritual objects such as baby carriers. Antique beads came from as far away as Venice, introduced by the Portuguese and Dutch, while today, most of the beads are from Europe and Japan.

New art

In Java, one of the first modern painters of note was Raden Saleh (1816–80) who spent 20 years in the courts of Europe, and later painted some memorable portraits of the royal families of Central Java. In later years, Yogyakarta and Bonnet. Based in Ubud, they promoted painting as an art form and donated materials to the local Balinese, who began to paint naturalistic scenes of everyday life for the first time. Prior to this, most Balinese paintings were of religious objects and primarily commissioned as decorations for its numerous palaces and temples. Various artist associations promoting local art developed in Bali, including the famous Pita Maha Artists of Ubud (1936–42).

In the 1960s, under the influence of Dutch artist Arie Smit, the Young Artists group developed, and began depicting different aspects of Balinese life in vivid and strong oil colours.

Bandung became the two crucibles of modern Indonesian art, and many accomplished artists appeared on the scene. Soedjojono (1913–86), Hendra Gunawan (1918–83) and Affandi (1907–88) for instance were strongly united in expression through their desire for independence from colonial rule and in their propagation of a strong national awareness.

A fresh approach to painting was introduced during the early 20th century in Bali by the Western artists like Walter Spies and Rudolph

LEFT: an oversized water jar from Lombok.
ABOVE: brilliant colours and bold brushwork are the defining features of artist Hendra Gunawan (1918–83).

Today, contemporary art has evolved and gained many adherents among Indonesian artists – mostly from Java and Bali – who are highly acclaimed in international art circles. Although there is nothing apart from subject matter to make the works specifically Indonesian, artistic cross-pollination, particularly in the government art academies and colleges, has resulted in new styles that have given way to foreign influence without surrendering personal and compelling visions.

While you can pick up decent works of art in Bali and Java for a song, well-known names are known to command prices which run up to hundreds of thousands of US dollars. ❑

NATURE IN THE RAW

Volcanoes dot the extensive landscapes of this vast archipelago and provide a rich ground on which thrive tens of thousands of plant and animal species

The Indonesian archipelago is by far the world's largest. It has 18,110 islands strewn across 5,120 km (3,200 miles) of tropical seas, straddling the equator. When superimposed on a map of North America, Indonesia stretches from Seattle to Bermuda. On a map of Europe, it extends east from Ireland to the Caspian Sea, and beyond.

Of course, four-fifths of the area is occupied by ocean, and many of the islands are tiny – no more than rocky outcrops populated, perhaps, by a few seabirds. Fewer than 10 percent are large enough to be inhabited, and New Guinea and Borneo (of which Indonesia claims two-thirds) rank as the second- and third-largest islands in the world (after Greenland). Of the other major islands, Sumatra is slightly larger than Sweden, Sulawesi is roughly the size of Great Britain, and Java is as large as California. With a total land area of 2 million sq km (780,000 sq miles), Indonesia is the world's 14th-largest nation.

Befitting its reputation as the celebrated Spice Islands of the East, this archipelago also constitutes one of the most diverse and biologically intriguing areas. Unique geologic and climatic conditions have created spectacularly varied tropical habitats – from the exceptionally fertile rice lands of Java and Bali to the luxuriant rainforests of Sumatra, Kalimantan, Sulawesi and Maluku, and the savannah grasslands of Nusa Tenggara to the jungle-laced, snowcapped peaks of Papua (Irian Jaya).

The geological history of the region is complex. All of the islands are relatively young; the earliest dates only from the end of the Miocene 15 million years ago – just yesterday on the geological time scale. Since then, the archipelago has been the scene of violent tectonic activity, as islands were torn from jostling super-continents or pushed up by colliding tectonic plates, and then enlarged in earth-wrenching volcanic explosions. The process continues today – Australia is drifting slowly northward, as the immense Pacific plate presses south and west to meet it and the Asian mainland. The islands of Indonesia lie along the lines of impact, a fact reflected in their geography and in the region's seismic instability.

RAINFOREST PRODUCTS

Products from Indonesian forests have been exported for centuries. Rattan was sold to China, where it was made into cordage. "Dragon's blood", a red resin from rattan, was used for medicine and to stain Dayak basketry. Other resins included camphor, highly prized for incense and medicine; *damar*, for varnish and sealing wax; and benzoin, a balsamic resin used in perfume and medicines. Birds contributed plumage, which appeared on the hats of European elite, and hornbill "ivory" is still carved into ornaments or ground up by the Chinese as an aphrodisiac. Rainforests also yield beeswax and honey, as well as lac, insect secretions used in making shellac.

LEFT: Anak Krakatau emerged from the sea 44 years after the catastrophic Krakatau eruption of 1883.
RIGHT: one of Sulawesi's rare endemic butterflies.

In fact, some of the Indonesian islands were connected to each other and to the mainland during the Ice Age, when sea levels receded as much as 200 metres (656 ft) and the entire Sunda shelf was exposed as a huge subcontinent. Today, the islands fringed with broad plains, expanding as alluvial deposits collect.

Volcanoes

Not only do volcanoes dominate the landscape of many Indonesian islands with their majestic smoking cones, they also fundamentally alter the size and soil by spewing forth millions of tonnes of ash and debris at irregular intervals. Eventually, much of this is washed down to form gently-sloping alluvial plains. Where the ejecta is acidic, the land is infertile and practically useless. But where it is basic, as on Java and Bali and in a few scattered locations on other islands, it has produced spectacularly fertile soil.

Of the hundreds of volcanoes in Indonesia, over 70 remain active, and hardly a year passes without a major eruption. On a densely-populated island like Java, eruptions inevitably bring death and destruction. When Krakatau, off Java's west coast, erupted in 1883 with a force equivalent to that of 10,000 Hiroshima atomic

ILLEGAL LOGGING

Indonesia's rainforests cover approximately 140 million hectares (350 million acres) or 70 percent of the country's land territory – the largest tropical forest area in Asia. Following devastating fires in 1997–98, international attention began focusing on Indonesia's woodlands.

Illegal logging, particularly in national parks, is a hot topic in recent years. About two-thirds of Indonesia's deforestation is caused by illegal logging activities. Environmental experts and activists both at home and abroad point to several compelling reasons to take action: depletion of biodiversity and animal habitats, dwindling water supplies due to loss of catchment areas, and landslides that cost lives and loss of livelihood for about 30 million of the poorest Indonesians who live in and around forests. However, loss of state revenues is more likely to spur the government into action.

With some groups calling for the total cessation of logging of any kind, others are trying to find a workable compromise. Alliances with foreign aid and environmental groups are being formed. Strengthening archaic laws to enable prosecution, and labelling exported timber as "legal" are on the agenda.

It is hoped that by working together, international pressure and a new generation of concerned Indonesian activists will succeed in convincing law makers to take action.

bombs, it created tidal waves that killed more than 35,000 people on Java. The eruption was heard as far away as Sri Lanka and Sydney, and the great quantities of debris hurled into the atmosphere caused vivid sunsets all over the world for three years afterwards.

But the Krakatau explosion was dwarfed by the cataclysmic 1815 eruption of Mount Tambora, on Sumbawa, the largest in recorded history. Around 90,000 people were killed and over 80 cu km (20 cu miles) of ejected material blocked the sun for many months, producing a universal "year without summer" in 1816.

Arboreal canopies

The archipelago's vegetation varies greatly according to rainfall, soil and altitude. On the wetter islands, the luxuriance of the rainforests is overwhelming. The main canopy of interlocking tree crowns may be 40 metres (130 ft) above ground, with individual trees as high as 70 metres (230 ft). Beneath this grows a tangle of palms, epiphytic ferns, rattans and bamboos, with gingers and other plants needing little light on the forest floor.

One would imagine that in order to support such growth, the soils would have to be very rich, but this is generally not so. The rainforests of Sumatra, Kalimantan, Sulawesi and Papua (Irian Jaya) typically thrive on very poor and thin soils that have been heavily leached of minerals by incessant rains. The rainforest flourishes due to an eco-system that essentially holds most of its minerals and nutrients in the form of living tissues. As these die and fall to the ground, they immediately decompose and are absorbed in a self-fertilising system largely independent of the soil.

Lowland rainforests display the greatest diversity. Areas dominated by stands of a single tree are rare; rather, the lowland forest is an extravagant mosaic of different species. In Kalimantan alone, for example, 3,000 different tree species have been recorded.

In remote and diverse Papua, more than 2,500 species of wild orchids are found in the rainforest, including the world's largest, the tiger orchid with its three-metre-long spray of yellow-orange blooms.

LEFT: mountains and volcanoes are a defining feature of Indonesia's landscape.
RIGHT: river rafting in West Java.

Alpine forests and swamps

At high altitudes, temperatures drop and cloud cover increases, resulting in slower growth, fewer species and a less-complex ecology. Rainforests give way to more specialised montane forests dominated by chestnuts, laurels and oaks. Higher up are rhododendrons and stunted moss forests – dwarf trees draped in lichens. Higher still, there are alpine meadows with giant edelweiss and other plants more reminiscent of Switzerland than the tropics. This unexpected habitat can be seen at Gunung Gede-Pangrango National Park, 100 km (60 miles) south of Jakarta. On Indonesia's highest

peaks – the Lorentz mountains of Papua that rise to over 5,000 metres (16,000 ft) – are found the only ice fields in the eastern tropics.

In the vast tidal zones of East Sumatra, Kalimantan and Southern Papua, mangrove trees with looping roots and air-breathing nodules flourish. Mangrove swamps are inhabited by fish that skip out of the water and in Kalimantan by the web-toed proboscis monkey.

Moving east from Central Lombok into Nusa Tenggara, the climate becomes drier and lowland jungles are replaced by deciduous monsoon forests and open savannah. Depending on how dry the climate is, these forests are partly or wholly deciduous, with fewer species but many broadleaf trees like teak, which shed their leaves during the dry season. This renders them vulnerable to forest fires; most of the forests on Sumbawa, Sumba, Flores and Timor have been either cut or burned off in recent centuries by people. The exposed land is then devoured by voracious *alang-alang* (elephant grasses); today, there are only useless grasslands where once stood valuable hardwood forests.

Not only are Java and Bali among the few islands where volcanic ejecta is basic and not from Sumatra; petroleum, copper and bauxite from Sumatra and Bangka; copper and gold from Papua and Sumbawa; and oil and timber from Kalimantan.

ECO-TOURISM

Managed tourism can help conservation. Human presence deters illegal poachers and loggers, and tourist revenues can go to maintain park security.

National parks

For some time, Java has suffered from soil exhaustion and pollution. Now as the nation's export resources are increasingly called upon to support a burgeoning population, massive deforestation has led to soil erosion and the depletion of rainforest flora and fauna.

acidic – so that frequent volcanic eruptions have, in fact, continually improved the soils by adding mineral-rich nutrients – but they are also areas that achieve something of a golden mean in climate, with plentiful rainfall and sunshine during alternating dry and wet seasons, each lasting half of the year.

Whereas Java and Bali have been characterised for centuries by their high population densities and labour-intensive irrigated agriculture, the other large islands are home, traditionally, to rainforests, thinly-spread farming communities and riverine trading networks. Today, the large Outer Islands are also the source of valuable exports: rubber and palm oil

These problems have been recognised by the Indonesian government, which is taking slow steps towards encouraging selective cutting and reforestation; 6 percent of the nation's land has been set aside as nature reserves and national parks. These do not just protect the many endangered animals; they also safeguard a genetic treasure trove of many plant species, as well as providing watershed population and recreational facilities. Although human impact on the environment has been severe in the more heavily-populated areas of Sumatra, Java, Bali and Kalimantan, much of Indonesia remains pristine wilderness.

Of particular interest to tourists is the extensive system of nature reserves and protected forests, now numbering over 300 and comprising altogether some 120,000 sq km (46,000 sq miles) of land. Over 40 of these are national parks being developed for recreational use, and many of the smaller reserves and protected forests are accessible and worth visiting. The national parks vary greatly in size, habitat, wildlife and visitor facilities. Some are quite remote and require several days to visit, while others are quite accessible. Several parks also have special marine areas with excellent snorkelling and scuba diving, where one can observe coral reef life, or swim with larger fish.

All national parks and nature reserves come under the jurisdiction of the Department of Forest Protection and Nature Conservation (PHPA) based in Bogor. Most can be entered by paying a small entrance fee and with a permit acquired from the regional PHPA office nearest the park or nature reserve.

Flora and fauna

The most interesting plant life of Indonesia originates almost exclusively from the Asian mainland, and it is abundant and incredibly diverse – almost 40,000 different species belong to 3,000 different families, with 10 percent of all plant species in the world. Most of these are natives of the varied equatorial rainforest, with its thousands of varieties of wild orchids, ferns, fruits, spice trees, and the world's largest flower, the Rafflesia.

The animals of Indonesia are just as diverse, having come from two quite different sources at opposite ends of the archipelago. From the west came the Asian mammals, and from the east came the marsupial species and plumaged birds so typical of Australia. More than 500 mammals are found in Indonesia, from the tigers, orangutan and elephants of Sumatra to the freshwater dolphins of Kalimantan, and the tree kangaroos and wallabies of Papua.

About 1,500 species of birds are known in the archipelago, many of them rare Australasian plumage species, like the cockatoo, flightless cassowary, numerous parrots and more than 40 species of birds-of-paradise. In addition, reptiles, amphibians and invertebrates populate the seas and coasts, including giant turtles and the huge, carnivorous monitor lizards of Komodo.

The boundaries of the Asian and Australasian faunal regions are far from clear; the islands of Sulawesi, Maluku and Nusa Tenggara lying between the two regions are, in fact, transitional areas and therefore of great interest to zoologists. Here are found both Asian and Australasian species, as well as endemic species found nowhere else in the world. Today, this area is known as Wallacea, in honour of the great 19th-century naturalist, Sir Alfred Russel Wallace, who was the first to recognise the geographical separation in floral and faunal types that occurs here.

Of all the islands of Wallacea, Sulawesi is the most biologically interesting. Most of the island's mammals, including deer, civets and tarsiers, are of obvious Asian origin; however, the two types of cuscus found here are marsupial and typically Australasian. But Sulawesi has many curious animals uniquely its own – including the *anoa* dwarf buffalo; the babirusa, a "deer" pig with curved tusks growing from its snout; the giant palm civet; and four species of macaques, including the heavy black macaque. Sulawesi's bird life includes hornbills, kingfishers, babblers, cockatoos and the maleo bird, which buries its eggs in warm sandy areas, leaving its young to hatch on their own.   ❑

LEFT: amethystine python in Papua, an island which is host to an amazing biodiversity of flora and fauna.
RIGHT: Maluku's brilliantly-coloured black-capped lory.

INDONESIA'S WORLD HERITAGE SITES

Indonesia is unique in that it is the only country in Southeast Asia that has six of its landmarks declared as UNESCO World Heritage Sites

In 1991, the UN listed six architectural and natural wonders in Indonesia as United Nations Educational, Scientific and Cultural Organisation (UNESCO) World Heritage sites. Five are listed here and the sixth, on the opposite side bar.

The Buddhist Borobudur monument in Central Java, built from around 788 AD, was "rediscovered" in 1814 buried in volcanic ash. Its restoration was completed by UNESCO and Indonesia between 1973 and 1983.

Prambanan, also in Central Java, is the largest Hindu temple complex in Indonesia. Completed in 856 AD, some 244 temple remains are still found in the outer compound.

Ujung Kulon National Park, West Java, has less than 50 endangered white Javanese rhinoceros and Java's largest lowland rainforests housing hornbills, deer, wild boar, black panthers and green turtles. The offshore Krakatau island is part of the park.

Komodo National Park in Nusa Tenggara is primarily the home of the protected 2,500 carnivorous monitor lizards known as the Komodo dragons.

Lorentz National Park, Papua (Irian Jaya), is the largest protected area in Southeast Asia and one of the few areas in the world with snow-capped mountains in a tropical environment. Its amazing biodiversity breeds rare animals like the spotted cuscus (pictured above).

△ **UJUNG KULON PARK**
Green turtles only became a protected species in Indonesia in 1999. Adults return to the islands and shores within the park to lay their eggs, sometimes 100 at a time.

▷ **LORENTZ NATIONAL PARK**
Isolated and primitive tribes residing within the park are: Amungme, Western Dani, Nduga, Ngalik, Asmat (Sempan, Komoro, Mimika and Somohai.

WORLD HERITAGE SITES ♦ 107

◁ **BOROBUDUR TEMPLE**
Six lower terraces are carved with Buddhist scenes. Three upper tiers with 72 lattice-work stupas each contain a Buddha image.

△ **PRAMBANAN TEMPLE**
Niches within temples house statues while exterior walls are decorated in reliefs from the *Ramayana* epic. Pictured here is the Candi Plaosan.

SANGIRAN'S JAVA MAN

The earliest Java fossil finds, by Dutchman Eugene Dubois in 1891, were the "missing link" proving Darwin's evolution theory. And later finds proved that *Homo erectus* (upright man) existed on Java about the same time that he also evolved in Africa.

German palaeo-anthropologist G.H.R. Von Koenigswald began his Sangiran research in 1930. Excavations between 1936 and 1941 uncovered hominid fossils, proving that Java was inhabited for 1.5 million years and was a birthplace of man. The largest artefacts were found in 1979, with animal remains and femur fossils.

UNESCO proclaimed Sangiran, near Solo in Central Java, as a World Heritage Site in 1996, declaring this one of the most important places in the world for understanding human evolution.

Pictured above is the sandy Sangiran geological structural dome, about 8 km (5 miles) long and 4 km (2½ miles) wide and located above sea level.

◁ **KRAKATAU CRATER**
In 1883, Krakatau exploded and sunk, re-emerging in 1927 as Anak Krakatau, "Child of Krakatau". It remains active with frequent eruptions, and is part of Ujung Kulon park.

▽ **UJUNG KULON PARK**
Lowland rainforest like Ujung Kulon's may contain 200 species of trees in a single hectare, with every second or third tree a different species.

▽ **LORENTZ NATIONAL PARK**
The park contains 10 globally threatened bird species. Pictured here is the Victoria Crowned Pigeon (*Govra Victoria*), which is not endangered – yet.

△ **KOMODO NATIONAL PARK**
The prehistoric monitor lizards called Komodo dragons can grow up to 3 metres (10 ft) long, and average 70 kg (154 lbs). They have been known to kill and eat humans.

▷ **JAVA MAN**
The first *Pithecanthropus erectus* (ape-man) samples – a skull and femur – became known as "Java Man". The skull is displayed at Jakarta's National Museum.

PLACES

A detailed guide to Indonesia's principal sites, cross-referenced by number to the maps

While the aeroplane increasingly makes exploring this vast country reasonably certain and tidy, Indonesia is one of those lands that – if the imagination is permitted to ramble – is best explored on the ground and over the water. It is a country of 18,110 islands, large and small, which wraps itself around one-eighth of the world's circumference – and begs to be travelled by boat.

Indonesia's capital city, Jakarta, is unquestionably the only true metropolis in the country. Nestled on Java's north-western coast, it is not especially beautiful by day, but at night, its electrified skyline can be elegant. To many Indonesians, it is the city of hope, the one place that best exemplifies a prosperous and united Indonesia.

Java is home to nearly half of the nation's population, no mystery considering the land's lush volcanic landscape. Here, one finds some of the country's most elegant aesthetic endeavours: music, dance and drama, textiles and architecture.

Sumatra is where spice traders and Islam first anchored after passage from India, and later, from Europe. The soil is not especially good for farming, although volcanoes exist here as well. But there are

verdant jungles, wondrous gatherings of wildlife, and perhaps Indonesia's most independent ethnic groups.

East of Java lies Bali, which needs little introduction since most foreign visitors seem to head there directly. Beyond Bali is Lombok, and then Nusa Tenggara, or what the colonial Europeans called the Lesser Sundas. From here eastward, the islands are tiny, at least until one reaches New Guinea, the western half of which belongs to Indonesia. Called Papua (formerly Irian Jaya), it was a land of unknown peoples and mountain valleys until early in the 20th century.

Due north of Java is Kalimantan, Indonesia's portion of the mystical island of Borneo. Kalimantan was once synonymous with remoteness, inaccessibility and headhunters; today it suggests timber wealth and oil frontiers.

This leaves Sulawesi and Maluku, the original Spice Islands. At one time, only in Maluku did nutmeg, cloves and mace grow, making these islands an obsession of European nations. In recent years, however, it is ethnic and political unrest that have kept the eyes of the world trained here and on isolated spots in Indonesia.

Although the country remains for the large part a safe and desirable tourist destination, visitors would do well to stay informed about the trouble spots and to avoid them. Take along, too, large doses of common sense, which will probably stand you in good stead. ❑

PRECEDING PAGES: Java's breathtaking Gunung Bromo at dawn; the magnificent Hindu temples at Prambanan; Bali's paddy fields are a photographer's delight.

JAVA

Although it covers only 6 percent of the total area, Java is Indonesia's heartland, and its political and economic centre

Java (Jawa) island, the nation's cultural and political capital, is a varied landscape of small villages and dazzling modern cites. In 1817, Sir Thomas Stamford Raffles, then Lieutenant-Governor of Java, wrote of the island's attributes as being "... the most romantic and highly diversified in the world ...," words that hold true even today. Java is an island of contrasts: nightly activity is divided between enchanting *wayang kulit* puppet performances and all-night dancing at discos in the nation's capital. Courtly dance and *gamelan* is performed with a subtle passion while others pour their energy into working the rice fields and scratching out a living. At its heart is a strong spiritual foundation mixed with *adat*, or tradition.

For most visitors, the first introduction to Java is Jakarta, the sprawling capital city and nucleus of Indonesia, centre for business, finance, politics and the arts. A bustling metropolis, the population of roughly 15 million people live among glittering skyscrapers and Mercedes cars that stand alongside historical enclaves and pockets of shanty communities. The pulse of the country's tumultuous economic and political climate is gauged here.

The drama of Jakarta gives way to larger Java, a patchwork landscape of rice-fields, jungle and volcanic peaks spread over 50,000 sq km (132,000 sq miles), roughly the size of England or Florida. Almost half the inhabitants are farmers, living in traditional villages and working the most productive land area in the world. Ideal for irrigation cultivation, Java is endowed with fertile soil from nutrient-rich ash deposits from any one of the 30 active volcanoes that run along the island's spine.

The island's long history dates back one million years to man's early ancestor, "Java Man", or *homo erectus*. Central Java is home to 8th- and 9th-century Buddhist and Hindu temples, most notably the Borobudur. Java's golden age occurred during the time of the Hindu Majapahit kingdom in the 14th century. Conversion to Islam took place during the 16th century, while the 17th century brought in the Dutch who remained as colonisers for the next 350 years.

The matrix of modern Java is influenced by a fusion of foreign, religious and cultural ideas. Javanese, the main ethnic group, maintain a highly-developed culture rich in language, social behaviour and performing arts, while the west-dwelling Sundanese are more earthy and devotedly Islamic. Proud Madurese occupy the northeast, and small pockets of Badui and Tengger people live in remote regions. Coastal cities are a melting pot of outer islanders, Indians, Chinese and Arabs. ❑

PRECEDING PAGES: Jakarta's Jalan Thamrin – the heart of its urban sprawl.

JAKARTA

Don't look for rustic charm in the huge sprawling metropolis of the capital city. Jakarta dwellers themselves are proud of the cultural and intellectual life in this ever-changing, chaotic capital

Maps:
Area 118–9
City 122

For the majority of its residents, **Jakarta** ❶ is a city of promise. This hope for a better life has caused the city's population to more than double in the past two decades – over 15 million people live in the greater metropolitan area. The city has grown tremendously in recent years, with the addition of new skyscrapers, motorways and middle-class suburbs.

Capital to the world's fourth most populous nation, Jakarta is a metropolis that verges on the chaotic. The busy Jalan Thamrin-Sudirman corridor, in the heart of the city, is a wall of glimmering glass and steel with some of the most interesting high-rise architecture in Southeast Asia. A whole new Central Business District (CBD) in the Senayan area has sprung up, and the bustling Glodok and Blok M districts throb with neon signs and modern shopping centres. Tanjung Priok is the nation's busiest port, and nearby Ancol and Pluit have developed into waterfront resort communities. In fact, much of Jakarta is hardly recognisable from a decade ago.

Yet there are other parts of the city that seem frozen in time. Little residential districts with market gardens and makeshift *kampung* (village) dwellings impart something of a village atmosphere to many back alleys.

Jakarta's attractions are abundant. Ask the locals. Those with an interest in Indonesian history and culture will talk about the city's fine museums, colonial architecture, performing arts and rich intellectual life.

Batavia

Starting out as a simple spice trade harbour in the 14th century, under the Hindu Pajajaran kingdom, the waterfront grew into a major seaport as the lucrative maritime trade expanded with Indian, Chinese and Arab traders. In 1522, the Portuguese arrived in search of the legendary Spice Islands, followed later by the English and Dutch. The seaport was conquered in 1527, by the combined forces of the Javanese Islamic kingdoms of Banten and Demak, re-naming the area Jayakarta or "City of Victory".

But it was the Dutch that had bigger designs, taking Jayakarta by force in 1618, and claiming the land in the name of the VOC (East India Company). From here, the colonial Dutch ruled for the next 350 years.

In 1618, the architect of the Dutch empire in the Indies, Jan Pieterszoon Coen, moved his headquarters here from Banten and ordered construction of a new town: Batavia. Under the VOC, Batavia's fortunes rose and fell. It had grown rich during the 17th century on an entrepôt trade in sugar, pepper, cloves, nutmeg, tea, textiles, porcelain, hardwoods and rice.

At the beginning of the 19th century, however, the city was demolished to provide building materials for

LEFT: modern office towers along Jalan Sudirman, Jakarta.
BELOW: modern Jakarta children flock to McDonald's.

a new city to the south, around what are now Medan Merdeka and Lapangan Banteng. The fashionable architectural styles of the period blended with newly laid out tree-lined boulevards and extensive gardens. By the turn of the century, Batavia's homes, hotels and clubs were in no way inferior to those of Europe.

During the brief Japanese Occupation of World War II, Batavia was renamed Jakarta. Following the nation's independence in 1945, hundreds of thousands of Indonesians flooded in from the countryside and outer islands, and Jakarta quickly outstripped all other Indonesian cities in size and importance, becoming what scholars term a primate city: the unrivalled political, cultural and economic centre of the new nation.

Map on page 122

Colonial beginnings

Hail a taxi and start your tour where the city's history began, the old spice trading seaport **Sunda Kelapa Harbour** Ⓐ. Early morning is the best time to walk along the 2-km (1¼-mile) wharf among the ships' prows and gangways and witness one of the world's last remaining commercial sailing fleets. Filled with the romance of a bygone era, watch the unloading of cargo from the majestic wooden *pinisi* schooners built by the seafaring Bugis people of South Sulawesi.

The area around Sunda Kelapa is rich in history and the best way to survey the area is on foot. Near the river stands a 19th-century **Dutch lookout tower** Ⓑ (Uitkik), constructed upon the site of the original customs house of Jayakarta. Behind the lookout stands a long two-storey structure dating from VOC times, now the **Museum Bahari** Ⓒ (Jalan Pasar Ikan No. 1; open daily 9am–3pm except Fri 9am–noon; entrance fee). This warehouse, now a maritime museum, was built by the Dutch in 1646 and was used to store coffee, tea and Indian

Sunda Kelapa's graceful Bugis schooners are being fast supplanted by modern freighters.

BELOW: Sunda Kelapa's old-world schooners.

The Jakarta History Museum at Taman Fatahillah is a fine example of Dutch colonial architecture. Built in 1710, it was formerly the site of the Dutch City Hall.

BELOW: Ancol's Dunia Fantasi is a Disneyland of sorts.

cloth. Inside are displays of traditional sailing craft from all corners of the Indonesian archipelago, as well as some old maps of Batavia. Down a narrow lane and around a corner behind the museum lies the **Pasar Ikan** ❿ (fish market), beyond which are numerous stalls selling nautical gear.

Further east along the waterfront is a giant seaside recreation area, **Ancol Dreamland** ❺. Once swampland, it now features beachfront hotels, a golf course, bowling alley and an arts and crafts market. There are also several theme parks, including **Sea World** (open Sun–Fri and public holidays 9am–8pm; Sat 9am–9pm; entrance fee) which has a tropical oceanarium, an underwater acrylic tunnel which allows you to view sharks, stingrays and a variety of fish native to local waters. In the same area is **Dunia Fantasi**, an amusement park with a roller coaster and ferris wheel, very crowded on weekends and school holidays. Close by is the **Ancol Marina** ❻, where you can embark a seacraft for any one of the **Kepulauan Seribu** (Thousand Islands).

The old city

Take the new Trans-Jakarta bus *(see Travel Tips, page 354)* to the area known as **Kota**, in the old town of Batavia that came to life in the 1620s as a tiny, walled town modelled after Amsterdam. Most of the original settlement – Old Batavia – was demolished at the beginning of the 19th century. Only the town square area survived and has been restored and renamed **Taman Fatahillah** ❼ (Fatahillah Square). Three of the surrounding colonial edifices have been converted into museums.

Start at the **Museum Sejarah Jakarta** ❽ (Jakarta HistoryMuseum; open Tues–Fri and Sun 9am–4pm; Sat 9am–3pm; entrance fee). It was formerly the city hall (Stadhuis) of Batavia completed in 1710 and used by successive governments, right up to the 1960s. It now houses fascinating memorabilia from the colonial period, notably 18th-century furnishings and portraits of the VOC governors, along with many prehistoric, classical and Portuguese period artefacts. Dungeons visible from the back of the building were used as holding cells, where prisoners were made to stand waist-deep in sewage for weeks awaiting their trials. Executions and torture were once commonplace in the main square as judges watched from the balcony above the main entrance.

The **Museum Wayang** ❶ (Puppet Museum; open Tues–Fri and Sun 9am–4pm; Sat 9am–3pm; entrance fee) is on the western side of the square. It has many puppets and masks, some of them rare buffalo-hide shadow puppets (*wayang kulit*), along with a collection of *topeng* masks, and tombstones of several early Dutch governors.

Museum Seni Rupa ❷ (Fine Arts Museum; open Tues–Fri and Sun 9am–4pm; Sat 9am–3pm; entrance fee) is the former Court of Justice building that was completed in 1879. The museum has collections of paintings and sculptures by modern Indonesian artists, and an important exhibition of rare porcelain, including many Sung celadon pieces from the Adam Malik collection, ancient Javanese water jugs (*kendhi*) and terracotta pieces dating from the 14th century.

Fertility symbol

Before leaving the area, walk over to the old 16th-century Portuguese cannon mounted on the north side of Taman Fatahillah. **Si Jagur**, "The Robust One", as it is called, is regarded by many as a fertility symbol, perhaps because of the fist that is cast into the butt end of the cannon, with a thumb protruding between its index and middle fingers (regarded as an obscene gesture in Indonesia). Occasionally, young couples are seen approaching it bearing offerings. Nearby is a trendy restaurant called **Café Batavia**, once an old warehouse, with window tables that offer excellent views of the square.

Next, walk behind the Museum Wayang to view two Dutch houses dating from the 18th century. Across the canal and to the left stands a solid red brick town house (Jl. Kali Besar Barat No. 11) that was built around 1730 by the then soon-to-be governor-general. The design, and particularly the fine Chinese-style woodwork, are typical of old Batavian residences. Three doors to the left is another house from the same period.

Jakarta's **Chinatown** is immediately adjacent to the old European centre just to the south of the old city in an area now known as **Glodok** ❸. Unlike Chinatowns elsewhere, you will see no signs in Chinese here, except in the two Buddhist temples deep within the convoluted back alleys. The public use of Chinese characters was banned decades ago during the failed but bloody Communist insurgency.

Begin at bustling Pasar Glodok shopping centre or the City Hotel across the street (Jl. Pancoran) and walk through the maze of narrow lanes winding past shop fronts. During the demonstrations of 1998, much of this area was set ablaze and some of the damage is still visible, but for many living and working in the area, life has returned to business as usual.

Map on page 122

Si Jagur is regarded as a fertility symbol by childless couples. Note that the clenched fist is commonly perceived as an obscene gesture in Indonesia.

BELOW: a Chinese worshipper in the Glodok area.

The phallic Monas monument in Central Jakarta – which critics say was built to satisfy Sukarno's over-inflated ego.

BELOW: Jakarta's neo-Gothic Catholic Cathedral.

Freedom Square

A circumnavigation of Central Jakarta begins at the top of the **Monas** ⓛ (National Monument; open Tues–Fri and Sun 9am–4pm; Sat 9am–3pm; entrance fee). A 137-metre (450-ft) tall marble obelisk is set in the centre of **Medan Merdeka** (Freedom Square). An observation deck surmounts the monument and a 14-metre (45-ft) bronze flame sheathed in 33 kg (73 lbs) of gold. It was commissioned by Sukarno and completed in 1961 – a combination Olympic Flame-Washington Monument with the phallic overtones of an ancient Hindu-Javanese *lingga*. In the basement are dioramas depicting historical scenes from a nationalistic viewpoint. A high-speed elevator rises to the observation deck, where on a clear day there is a fabulous 360-degree view of Jakarta.

From Monas, travel north along Jalan Gajah Mada to the splendid villa that now houses the **National Archives**. This is the last of scores of 18th-century mansions built by rich Dutch officials of the East India Company. Unfortunately, special permission is needed to tour the building, but even from the street, the beautiful woodwork and manicured gardens that were once the hallmark of old Batavia town are visible.

Double back to Medan Merdeka and pass behind the **Presidential Palace**, situated between Jalan Medan Merdeka Utara and Jalan Veteran. The palace building consists of two 19th-century neo-classical villas situated back to back. The older of the two, the **Istana Negara**, faces north and was built by a wealthy Dutch merchant around 1800. It was taken over some years later to serve as the town residence of the governor (whose official residence was then located in Bogor). The south-facing **Istana Merdeka** was added in 1879 as a reception area. President Sukarno resided in the palace and frequently gave lavish banquets in the central courtyard.

Mosques and churches

Head eastwards about 1,000 metres (3,280 ft) to the imposing white marble **Mesjid Istiqlal** Ⓜ (Istiqlal Mosque) on Jalan Veteran. The largest mosque in Southeast Asia, it was built on the former site of the Dutch Benteng (Fort) Noordwijk. During the Islamic fasting month Ramadan, the mosque is filled to capacity. Tours of the mosque are available.

Lapangan Banteng (Wild Ox Field) lies just to the east, bounded on the north by the neo-Gothic **Catholic Cathedral** Ⓝ on Jalan Katedral, completed in 1901; note the rather interesting spires on the east by the Supreme Court (1848) and the Department of Finance (1982), and on the south by the Borobudur Hotel with its lush gardens.

In the centre of the square stands a muscle-bound giant bursting from his shackles. This is the **Irian Jaya Freedom Memorial** – placed here in 1963 by Sukarno to commemorate the annexation of Irian Jaya. When the statue was first erected, Jakartans joked that the giant was crying "empty" – referring to the Department of Finance behind.

Returning to the eastern side of Medan Merdeka, one passes two more colonial structures: the 1830 **Gedung Pancasila** on Jalan Taman Pejambon where Sukarno unveiled the five principles of the Indonesian state, and the small **Immanuel Church** on Jalan Medan Merdeka Timur, built in 1835, resembling a Greek temple.

On the west side of Medan Merdeka lies one of Indonesia's great cultural treasures, the **National Museum** ⓞ, on Jalan Medan Merdeka Barat (open Tues–Thur and Sun 8.30am–2.30pm; Fri 8.30–1.30am; Sat 8.30am–1.30pm; entrance fee). Opened in 1868 by the Batavian Society for Arts and Sciences – the first scholarly organisation in colonial Asia that was founded in 1778 – the museum houses extremely valuable collections of antiquities, books and ethnographic artefacts acquired by the Dutch during the 19th and early 20th centuries. The objects exhibited are fascinating: Hindu-Javanese stone statuary, prehistoric bronze wares and Chinese porcelains are among the exhibits that will need hours to be viewed properly. The star collection, however, is housed in the Treasure Room – a stupendous hoard of royal Indonesian heirlooms. The newest feature is the Ceramics Room featuring the largest collection of Southeast Asia ceramics under one roof.

Southeast of the square, a short ride down Jalan Cikini, are two other noteworthy attractions. **Taman Ismail Marzuki** ⓟ is a multi-faceted cultural centre that presents a continuing bill of drama, dance and music from around Indonesia. Nearby, **Jalan Surabaya** ⓠ is the city's famous so-called "antique street", with dozens of shops selling everything from *wayang* puppets to ship fittings, most of it brand new.

South Jakarta

Hail a taxi and cruise west across the upper-class residential area of **Menteng** to the **Welcome Statue**, a busy roundabout with a statue of two waving youths

Map on page 122

TIP

Members of the Indonesian Heritage Society conduct free guided tours of the Museum National in English, French and Japanese. Call ahead (tel: 021-381 1551) for the schedule.

BELOW: the bronze Welcome Statue is one of several grand monuments which dot the city.

Motorized three-wheelers, known as bajaj, are a convenient means of getting around in Jakarta but note that they are banned from main thoroughfares.

and a fountain. **Jalan Thamrin** runs north and south here, turning into Jalan Sudirman a few more blocks south. The roundabout fountain is an urban anchor of Jakarta, built by Sukarno in the early 1960s.

Surrounding the roundabout are the Hotel Indonesia, the nation's first international-class hotel, and the **Grand Hyatt**, a wonderful place for afternoon tea, a ceiling-to-floor bay window lets you look out to the heart of the city. The hotel is perched atop Jakarta's finest shopping mall, **Plaza Indonesia** ®, offering numerous food outlets and a Western-style market stocked with imported goods.

Shops and more shops

Adjacent to the Hilton Hotel is the **Jakarta Convention Centre** ⓢ. Everything from art exhibits and cultural events to rock concerts are held here. Close by is the **Taman Ria**, an amusement park with arcade games, nightclubs and fashionable eateries very popular with Jakarta's young crowd. Further south on Jalan Sudirman, behind the Senyan sports field, home to the national soccer games, is the **Senayan Plaza** ⓣ, one of the newest shopping malls.

Blok M ⓤ is where Jakarta's middle-class does much of its shopping. The area bustles with street stalls, hundreds of shops and at least seven modern shopping malls, including two giant shopping centres: Blok M Plaza and Blok M Mall. This is also the home of the famous **Pasaraya** department store.

Take a drive through Jakarta's southern suburb of **Pondok Indah** where wealthy Indonesians and many of the city's expatriates live. This is a large housing estate comprising Western-style homes, mansions and country clubs. The **Pondak Indah Mall** ⓥ is one of Jakarta's busiest malls, a water slide park is contained in the same complex.

BELOW: Senayan Plaza is where Jakarta's upper class shops.

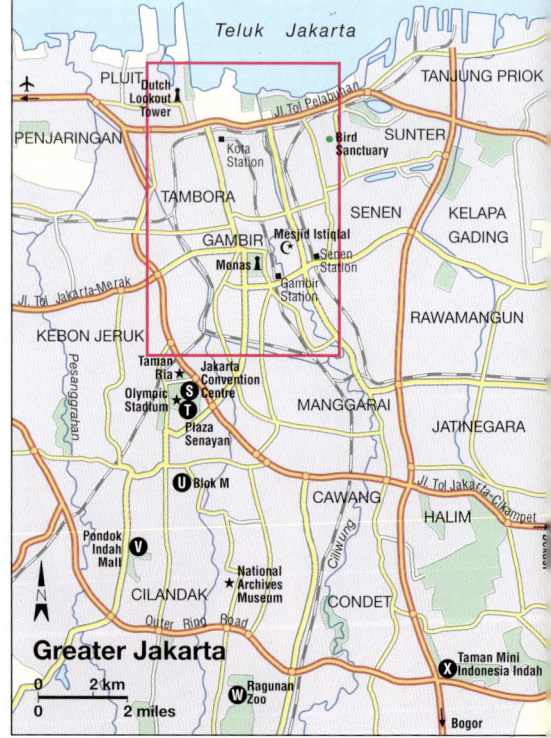

Still heading south about 15 km (9 miles) from the centre of the city is the **Ragunan Zoo** W (open daily 9am–6pm; entrance fee). With a pleasant relaxed atmosphere set in a tropical garden park, there are over 3,000 animals indigenous to Indonesia. This may be your only chance to see the infamous Komodo dragon, along with orangutan and Sumatran tigers.

Taman Mini Indonesia X (Indonesia in Miniature Park; open daily except Mon 9am–5pm; entrance fee) covers nearly 100 hectares (250 acres) of land near Kampung Rambutan. While not entirely successful in compressing the entire archipelago into a single attraction, the park nonetheless permits you a glimpse of the many thousands of Indonesian islands you will probably not visit. Taman Mini has 27 main pavilions – one for each of Indonesia's provinces – constructed in the traditional architectural style of each province and using only authentic materials. Housed inside each pavilion are interesting displays of handicrafts, traditional costumes, musical instruments and other artefacts for which each region is known.

In addition, there are at least 30 other attractions here, including a tropical bird park, orchid garden, IMAX cinema, cable car ride, transport museum, swimming pool, and the splendid **Museum Indonesia** (open daily except Mon 9am–5pm; entrance fee) – a three-storey Balinese palace filled with traditional textiles, houses, boats, puppets, jewellery and wedding costumes.

The most recent addition is the **Museum Purna Bhakti Pertiwi** (Presidential Palace Museum; open daily except Mon 9am–4pm; entrance fee) established by the late First Lady Ibu Tien Suharto as a showcase for the family's private collection of antiques and art along with the many diplomatic gifts Indonesia received while the family was in office. ❏

Map on page 128

TIP

The best stop for souvenir shopping is Pasaraya department store, packed with items from every corner of Indonesia, from Javanese batik to Dayak wood carvings and Balinese art.

BELOW: a *jamu* vendor in Jakarta's suburbs; one of the herbal concoctions is a purported cure-all for ailments.

WEST JAVA

This most populous region of Indonesia, home of the earthy Sundanese, offers majestic volcanoes, the university town of Bandung, a wild and rugged coast, and the gentle Bogor gardens

Map on pages 118–9

In the early 1800s, Java had about 3½ million inhabitants, a number that had been relatively stable since the time of the great Hindu-Buddhist empires a millennium earlier. Wet-rice cultivation was the basis of civilisation, and as long as the population was fairly small, the Javanese produced vast surpluses.

All of this changed dramatically following the intervention of the Dutch in Javanese economic and political affairs, culminating with the institution, from 1830 to 1870, of the infamous cultivation system (*Cultuurstelsel*) of forced labour and land-use taxes. Under this system, Javanese land was cleared for cultivation, the products of which the Dutch sold for a handsome profit overseas. An unforeseen side effect of the policy was a spiralling birthrate. By 1900, Java's population had soared by 28 million and today stands at 120 million.

The inhabitants of West Java are mainly Sundanese, whose culture has remained alive despite continual border incursions and sporadic warfare. Unlike the refined Javanese, the earthy Sundanese value individualism, and possess a strong sense of humour that is easy to enjoy. Casually dismissed as "mountain Javanese" by the people of the heartland, the Sundanese have developed a strong culture of their own that actually predates the great empires to the East. However, cultural performances – mainly *gamelan* and *angklung* music, popular *jaipongan* dances, and lively *wayang golek* performances – are often mostly confined to remote villages.

West Java or Tanah Sunda (Sunda Lands) may be roughly divided into two distinct regions: the volcanic highlands centred on the provincial capital of Bandung, and the northern coastal plain.

Island getaways

One of the best ways to unwind and recapture a taste of the tropics after the bustle of **Jakarta ❶** is to escape to clear blue waters and white-sand beaches at any one of the 600 small islands off the north coast of Jakarta, known as **Kepulauan Seribu ❷** (Thousand Islands).

Day trips can be taken to Bidadari, Kelor and Kahyangan islands near the coast. On Onrust Island, explore the ruins of an old Dutch fort, which has remains of an 18th-century shipyard. Bokor and Rambut islands are home to bird sanctuaries; you need a permit from the national park office, PHPA, in Jakarta. Ferries depart every day from Jakarta's Ancol Marina to various islands at 7am and return at 2.30pm.

Continuing further out about 100 km (65 miles) is a group of islands that have been developed into resorts: Pelangi, Putri, Matahari, Kotok, Ayer and Pantara. Each has fully-equipped hotels with hot water, beachfront bungalows and restaurants. All bookings to island resorts have to be made in Jakarta through a travel agent. Activities include scuba diving,

LEFT: Dutch colonial house in Banten, Western Java.
BELOW: Mr. Muscles at Kepulauan Seribu.

In 1770, Captain Cook repaired his ship – the HMS Endeavour – at the shipyards on the small island of Onrust, north of Jakarta, and praised the carpenters as being "the best in the East".

snorkelling, swimming and fishing. Diving gear can be rented on most of the islands but check with your travel agent first.

Banten

Heading west from Jakarta on the Jakarta-Merak toll road for about 1½ hours is historical **Banten** ❸. During the 16th and 17th centuries, this was one of Asia's largest and most cosmopolitan trading emporiums. Once a grand walled city, it was laid to ruin as trade was shifted to Jayakarta (Jakarta).

Today, it is a tiny fishing village with interesting historical sites. There are the ruins of a large palace Surosowan, and a Dutch fortress, Speel Wijk, along with the ruins of Kaibon Palace and the 16th-century **Mesjid Agung** (Grand Mosque). Standing at its centre is the five-tiered red-tiled roof of early Javanese Hindu-Islamic style. Climb the staircase to the top for a view. A small museum (entrance fee) offers a glimpse into the seaport's great past.

Across the bridge is the Chinese Wan-De Yuan temple, one of the oldest in Java. The ruins of Banten are 10 km (6 miles) from the main road. It is best to go by hired car from Jakarta, or take the Jakarta-Serang bus, alight in Serang and then switch to a public mini-van to the site.

West coast beaches

A quick getaway from Jakarta by car or public bus takes you to Java's sandy and secluded west coast beaches. You can enjoy a swim and cool ocean breezes within 2½ hours, or a distance of about 110 km (70 miles), west from Jakarta. At the town of Cilegon, the road branches off to the right and continues 13 km (8 miles) to **Merak**, where ferries depart for Bakauheni on Sumatra.

BELOW: Banten's 16th-century Mesjid Agung.

Branching south towards the beaches, there are pretty bays and long stretches of deserted white-sand beach lined with coconut palms. At **Anyer** ❹, however, several large resorts now grace the coastline; taking central spot however is the Dutch-built Anyer Lighthouse. Continuing another 6 km (3½ miles) takes you to **Karang Bolong**, a huge rock forming a natural archway to the sea. This has become a popular weekend swimming spot for Jakartans. There are hotels, bungalows, restaurants and occasional fishermen selling fresh prawns.

Another 10 km (6 miles) south is **Carita**, with its sandy beaches situated in a lovely cove. The area is well-served by luxury beachside accommodation, a marina and operators offering sailing, jet-skiing, scuba-diving and snorkelling.

In addition to sun, sea, sand and solitude, this palm-fringed coast is famous for its sunset views of the uninhabited volcanic islands off **Krakatau** (also claimed by Sumatra as part of its territory). Although dormant for centuries, this volcano achieved instant and lasting infamy in 1883, when it erupted with cataclysmic force, ripping out a huge chunk of the earth's crust to form a monstrous 40-sq km (16-sq mile) submarine caldera. The sea rushed in, and tidal waves up to 30 metres (100 ft) high swept the coast, claiming more than 35,000 lives.

In the decades that followed, undersea activity continued and a new active crater has emerged from the sea in 1927: **Anak Krakatau** (Child of Krakatau). Boats can be chartered for day trips out to the volcano's rim. It is 4 hours each way and another 3 hours to climb the peak. Many "guides" walk the beach promoting the excursion, but it is best to make prior arrangements with your hotel or tour agent, and do check that the vessel is adequate before departure.

Ujung Kulon National Park ❺ is located on the south-west tip of Java, a 420-sq km (260-sq mile) reserve that is the last refuge for the shy and rarely-

Map on pages 118–9

There have been reports of tourists injuring themselves on the hike up Anak Krakatau or inhaling poisonous fumes, so excercise caution.

BELOW: boatman along the Carita coast.

Bogor's cooler temperatures have attracted a resident community of wealthy Indonesians – who commute to Jakarta when they have to.

sighted Javan rhino. The park has other interesting animals including leopards, macaques, leaf monkeys, mouse deer, crocodiles and wild oxen. Much of the area is dense lowland rainforest with beaches in the north and south.

The best time of the year to visit is during the dry season, from April–September. A permit is required from the PHPA (national park) office in Labuhan (15 minutes south of Carita). Here, they will arrange accommodation, guide and transport (usually a 5-hour boat ride each way). You need to take your own food and water. Or make arrangements through a travel agent in Jakarta.

Highland garden towns

The most scenic of West Java's escape routes is the ascent to the dramatic **Parahyangan Highlands** south of Jakarta. First stop is **Bogor** ❻ – an hour's drive from central Jakarta via the Jagorawi Expressway. Situated about 80 km (50 miles) above sea level, Bogor is appreciably cooler (and wetter) than the coast. The main attraction here is the glorious **Kebun Raya** (Botanical Gardens; open daily; entrance fee), started by the British in 1817 and world-renowned during the 19th century for its range of tropical botanical specimens and research into cash crops such as tea, cassava, tobacco and cinchona. The vast park with its rolling lawns, lily ponds and forest groves contains 15,000 species of trees and plants (including 400 types of palms) and orchid nurseries.

The elegant white Presidential Palace called **Istana Bogor**, constructed by the Dutch in 1856 as the official residence for the governors-general of the Dutch East Indies, stands at the northern end of the gardens. The palace was a favorite hideaway of President Sukarno and contains a selection of paintings and sculpture from his vast collection. In fact Sukarno lived here while he was under "house arrest" from 1967 until his death three years later.

BELOW: harvesting tea at the Puncak Pass area.

East of Bogor is a favourite getaway for Jakartans. **Puncak Pass**, which offers a welcome relief with its cool, clean mountain air, is very crowded on weekends because of its accessibility. The main road is lined with small hotels and restaurants, while further on are manicured landscapes of tea plantations and the 168-hectare (400-acre) **Taman Safari** (Safari Park; open daily 9am–5pm; entrance fee). This is an open-air zoo where lions, tigers, bears and giraffes forage in the open. The most recent addition is the **Night Safari**, where visitors travel by tram or on foot to view nocturnal animals feed and play in natural settings (open Fri, Sat and daily during the school holidays; 7–9pm; entrance fee). Day excursions can be booked in Jakarta.

Beyond Puncak Pass, a turn-off to the right leads to **Cibodas Botanical Gardens**, an extension of Bogor's Kebun Raya, and famous for its collection of montane and temperate flora from around the world. Next to the main gate of the gardens is the entrance to the **Gunung Gede-Pangrango National Park**, the oldest park in Indonesia (since 1889) spread across the upper incline of two volcanoes. The 15,000-hectare (37,000-acre) park is home to the rare Javan gibbon and leaf monkeys, both of which are often spotted, and a variety of bird species. Obtain a permit at the PHPA office at the park's entrance; maps of the trails are also available.

Once inside the park, **Cibeureum waterfall** is a 90-minute walk away, and a climb will take you to one of the many hot springs in the area. For the serious trekker, there are two options: Gunung Gede at 2,960 metres (9,600 ft) requires a 7-hour climb, or Gunung Pangrango (3,020 metres, or 9,800 ft) which needs an 8-hour hike. Both excursions require an overnight stay and should be done with a local guide. Be prepared as it gets chilly at the summit.

Excellent accommodation and food are also available in the nearby mountain resort of **Cipanas**, a lovely place to spend a few days hiking through the highland forests and tea estates and relaxing in the natural hot springs whose sulphurous waters are believed to cure skin problems and other ailments.

Beaches and highlands

Head south 2½ hours from Bogor – a good road winds south from Ciawi over the pass between Gunung Pangrango and Gunung Salak – to the fishing village of **Pelabuhan Ratu** ❼. Here, the ragged, wind-lashed Indian Ocean foams and crashes onto smooth black-sand beaches. The village is unspoiled and vital – when the boats moor in the morning, the fish market does a roaring trade in fresh tuna fish, prawns, whitebait, sharks, stingrays and other delicacies. A number of good swimming beaches and hotels line the coast for several kilometres past the town, but be warned that the surf and undertow can be treacherous. Visit the bat cave about 1 km (½ mile) out of town; every evening at sunset thousands of these winged creatures take to the sky.

The highland city of **Bandung** ❽ offers a cool alternative to the capital's oppressive heat. Located in a huge basin 700 metres (2,300 ft) above sea level and surrounded on all sides by lofty volcanic peaks, it is a burgeoning city with

Map on pages 118–9

TIP

In Puncak, stop by the historic Puncak Pass Hotel and Restaurant, built in 1928, to enjoy spectacular views. Specialities are delicious pancakes and a refreshing drink, *wedang jahe* (hot ginger tea).

BELOW:
surf-lashed beach of Pelabuhan Ratu.

At Pelabuhan Ratu, head to the harbour and select from the fishermens' fresh catch of the day. Most small restaurants in town will clean, cook and serve the fish at your table.

over 2 million inhabitants. Before World War II, it was a quaint Dutch administrative and university town of about 150,000 and called the Paris of Java for its broad, shady boulevards and elegant homes. Although it is now a rapidly-growing industrial city, Bandung is still green and attractive, and is often called Kota Kembang (City of Flowers).

University town

Bandung's foremost industry is education, with over 27 colleges and universities and thousands of students. But there is plenty for travellers, with an abundance of Dutch-colonial art-deco architecture, including the magnificent **Gedung Sate**. You can also browse in factory outlet shops along **Jalan Cihampelas**, a feast for the eye as well as the pocket book. Many of the shops have quirky facades fashioned from papier mâché, chrome or plywood. One even has King Kong peering down; another, a dinosaur crashing through a roof.

The **Museum Geologi** (Geological Museum) on Jalan Diponegoro (open daily; entrance fee) is definitely worth a visit for its extraordinary array of rocks, maps and fossils – including replicas of the famous Java Man or *homo erectus* skulls found in Central Java. The campus of Bandung's **Institute of Technology** (ITB), Indonesia's oldest and finest university established by the Dutch, is also worth a visit. It has an interesting library built in the 1920s.

Spend some time, too, wandering around the old Dutch shopping district downtown around **Jalan Braga**, and take a look into the remodelled art-deco Savoy Homann Bida Kara Hotel on Jalan Asia-Afrika. The site of the 1955 Non-Aligned Conference is across the street. The town's large flower market is also nearby on Jalan Wastukencana. In the evenings, many theatres and clubs put up Sundanese dance performances; check with your hotel or tour office for details.

An accessible volcano

Southeast of Bandung are the Parahyangan Highlands (roughly translated as "Abode of the Gods") with endless vistas of manicured tea plantations, hot springs, waterfalls and the easiest-to-visit volcano in all of Java, 30 km (20 miles) north of the city: **Gunung Tangkuban Perahu** (Mountain of the Overturned Boat). Stay in the old Dutch resort town of **Lembang**, famous for its fruit, vegetables and flowers.

From here, head east 9 km (5½ miles) to the park entrance and another 4 km (2½ miles) to the crater's rim. Morning clouds mix with sulphurous fumes, rising from a perfect bowl-shaped centre to create a spectacular scene. This accessible tourist spot is well-served by souvenir shops and restaurants. The area offers a whole series of smaller craters to hike around and exploration is best carried out during the dry season from April to September. Some 7 km (4 miles) beyond Tangkuban Perahu is **Ciater**, where hot springs offer a soothing soak amid tea and clove estates.

Northern coast

The northern coastal ports of Java were once the busiest and richest towns on the island; they served as exporters of agricultural produce from the fertile

BELOW: mist-shrouded Gunung Tangkuban Perahu.

Javanese hinterland, as builders and outfitters of large spice trading fleets, and as trading entrepôts frequented by merchants from all corners of the globe. Between the 15th and 17th centuries, when Islam was a new and growing force in the archipelago, these ports flourished as political and religious centres.

First port of call along the northern route east of Jakarta, 4 hours by car or Cirebon Utara express train, is the ancient sultanate of **Cirebon** ❾ – a intriguing potpourri of Sundanese, Javanese, Chinese, Islamic and European influences. With a small harbour and a sizeable fishing industry, Cirebon is famous for its seafood, notably its delicious prawns. Most sites in the city are within walking distance, though a nice way to get around is by *becak* (pedicab).

Cirebon's two major palaces were both built in 1678, so that each of two princes could have his own court. The **Keraton Kesepuhan** (belonging to the elder brother) sits on the site of the 15th-century Pakungwati Palace of Cirebon's earlier Hindu rulers. The palace, Javanese in design with a Romanesque archway framed by mystical Chinese rocks, is a spacious, pillared *pendopo* furnished with French period pieces. And the walls of the Dalem Ageng (ceremonial chamber) behind it are inlaid with blue-and-white tiles exhibiting biblical scenes. The adjoining museum has a coach in the shape of a winged and horned elephant grasping a trident in its trunk – a glorious fusion of Javanese, Hindu, Islamic, Persian, Greek and Chinese mythological elements.

Right next to the Kesepuhan palace stands the **Mesjid Agung** (Grand Mosque) constructed around AD 1500. Its two-tiered *meru* roof rests on an elaborate wooden scaffolding, and the interior contains imported sandstone portals and a teakwood *kala*-head pulpit. Together with the Demak and Banten mosques, it is one of the oldest remaining landmarks of Islam on Java.

Map on pages 118–9

TIP

Cirebon is famous for its distinctive hand-painted batik; the best places to shop are in Trusmi village, 12 km (7 miles) west out of town.

BELOW: fishing boats at Cirebon harbour.

> **TIP**
>
> Some 4 km (3 miles) south-west of Cirebon is Gua (cave) Sunyarangi, an uncanny assembly of of rocks, bricks and plaster, with secret staircases and chambers. It is said to be the 18th-century water palace of a Cirebon sultan.

BELOW: batik artisan in Pekalongan handrawing designs using a *canting* tool.

Keraton Kanoman (palace of the younger brother) is nearby, reached via a busy marketplace. Large banyan trees shade the peaceful courtyard within, and as at Kesepuhan, the furnishings are European and the walls are studded with tiles and porcelain from Holland and China. The museum has a collection of stakes still used to pierce the flesh of Muslim believers on Mohammed's birthday (*seni debus*), as well as relics from Cirebon's past.

Taman Arum Sunyaragi, about 4 km (2½ miles) out of town on the southwestern bypass, was originally built as a fortress in 1702 and used as a base for resistance against the Dutch. It was cast in its present form in 1852 by a Chinese architect to serve as a pleasure palace for Cirebon's sultans. About 5 km (3 miles) north of the city along the main Jakarta road sits the hilltop **Tomb of Sunan Gunung Jati**, a 16th-century ruler of Cirebon and one of the nine legendary *wali* who helped to propagate Islam on Java.

Heading east

About 220 km (140 miles) and 4 hours east of Cirebon is **Pekalongan**, which announces itself on roadside pillars as **Kota Batik** (Batik City). Quite apart from the many factories and retail shops lining its streets, Pekalongan justifies this sobriquet by producing some of the finest and most highly-prized batik on Java. The Pekalongan style, like Cirebon's, is unique – a blending of Islamic, Javanese, Chinese and European motifs.

Another 90 km (55 miles) and 2 hours to the east, the city of **Semarang** ❿ rises out across a narrow coastal plain and up onto steep foothills. Known during Islamic times for its skilled shipwrights and abundant supplies of hardwood, it is today the commercial hub and provincial capital of Central Java. The old Dutch Church, **Gereja Blenduk**, on Jalan Suprapto downtown, with its copper-clad dome and Greek cross-floor plan, was consecrated in 1753 and stands at the centre of the 18th-century European commercial district.

Semarang's most interesting district is its **Kampung Cina** (Chinatown) – a grid of narrow lanes tucked away in the centre of the city, reached by walking due south from the old church from Jalan Suari to Jalan Pekojan. Here, some old townhouses retain the distinctive Nanyang style of elaborately-carved doors and shutters and delicately-wrought iron balustrades.

Half a dozen colourful Chinese temples and clan houses cluster in the space of a few blocks, the largest and oldest of which is on tiny Gang Lombok (turn right by the bridge from Jalan Pekojan). This is the **Thay Kak Sie temple**, built in 1772, which houses more than a dozen major deities. Those with time and an interest in things Chinese should visit **Gedung Batu**, the famous grotto of Ming Admiral Cheng Ho, sited on the western outskirts. Cheng Ho arrived in Java in 1405 and is credited with helping to spread Islam.

Teakwood carvings

From Semarang, there are several towns to the east that may be visited as day trips. During the early 16th century, a Muslim kingdom centred on **Demak** was the undisputed nonpareil among the coastal states of Java; now, only the mosque remains. The city has become a place of pilgrimage; seven visits here is equal to a single pilgrimage to Mecca. The introduction of Islam to Java is credited to Sunan Kalijaga, a spiritual adviser to the royal court of Demak. He used *wayang kulit* puppet shows to teach the illiterate masses about the new religion. His grave lies 2 km (1½ mile) south-east of the city. Another focal point is Demak's **Mesjid Besar** (Grand Mosque), considered the oldest and holiest mosque in Java. Built in 1466, its architecture combines Hindu and Arabic elements.

Neighbouring **Kudus** is famous for beautiful hand-carved teakwood houses that grace the narrow lanes surrounding the Kauman area along its early 16th-century mosque and Muslim quarter. (At the entrance to the Kudus Bar in the Hilton Hotel Jakarta is a beautifully-carved antique teakwood door from this area.) Kudus is also known as "Kota Kretek", or clove cigarette capital, as several *kretek* companies are found here.

The village of **Jepara**, 35 km (20 miles) north of Kudus, has long been famous for its teakwood carvings, catering to strong demand for finely-detailed panels depicting scenes from the *Ramayana* and other Hindu-Javanese tales. Today, more than 4,000 carpenters work in the 500 shops here.

About 20 km (12½ miles) south from Semarang is the mountain resort of **Bandungan**, with its cool air and a flower market. It is 3 km (1½ miles) away from the **Gedung Songo** temples – among the oldest and certainly the most spectacularly-situated antiquities in Java. The nine Sivaitic shrines were built in the 8th century and are perched on a series of collines overlooking the lofty peaks and verdant valleys of Central Java. Arrive at sunrise and spend the day exploring the temples and soaking in the hot springs. You can hike or ride on horseback around the inspiring landscape. ❑

The brilliant colours of a north coast fishing boat.

BELOW: teakwood house in Kudus.

CENTRAL JAVA

From ancient times, this fertile region has been the focal point of human activity. Its glorious past still lives today in the immense Borobudur and myriad other examples of divine craftsmanship

The green crescent of fertile rice fields that blankets Gunung Merapi's southern flanks – with historic **Yogyakarta (Jogja)** ⓫ as its focal point – is today inhabited by about 11 million Javanese. Rural population densities here are high, with over 1,000 people per square kilometre; in some areas, labour-intensive farming goes to feed 2,000 people for every 1 sq km. The cultural attractions are many: the sombre stillness of beautiful Hindu and Buddhist temples – from the 8th, 9th and 10th centuries – is found again in the sequestered courtyards of its 18th-century Islamic palaces, where the liquid cadences of Central Java's *gamelan* provide a measured counterpoint to the boisterous clamour of colourful city streets and village markets.

Much of interest is concentrated in and around the twin court cities of Yogyakarta (familiarly called Jogja) and Surakarta (or Solo). It was here, on the well-irrigated banks of several adjacent rivers, that Central Java's two great Mataram empires – one ancient and one modern – flourished. The role of the Javanese courts as cultural centres has long been recognised, but their vast catalogue of artistic wealth has only begun to be explored.

Ancient Mataram

Although it was founded only in 1755, the sprawling city of Yogyakarta is situated at the very core of an ancient region known as Mataram, site of the first great Central Javanese empires. From the 8th to the early 10th century, this fertile plain was ruled by a succession of Indianised kings – the builders of Borobudur, Prambanan and dozens of other elaborate stone monuments. Around the AD 900s, however, these rulers suddenly and inexplicably shifted their capital to East Java, and for more than six centuries, Mataram was deserted.

At the end of the 16th century, the area was revived by a new Islamic power based at Kota Gede, east of present-day Yogyakarta. This second Mataram dynasty was founded around 1580 by King Panembahan Senapati, and his descendants have ruled Central Java (Jawa Tengah) up until the present day, although with widely varying degrees of power and influence over the centuries.

The history of the Yogyakarta sultanate is one of resistance to increasing colonial influence in Central Java. The court was twice invaded for failure to comply with colonial instructions – once by the Dutch in 1810 and again by the British in 1812. Later, it was swept into the Great Java War (1825–30), led by the charismatic crown prince of the ruling family, Pangeran Diponegoro.

In more recent times, Yogyakarta served as the capital of the troubled Indonesian republic for four

LEFT: *serimpi* dancers from Yogyakarta.
BELOW: *bedoyo* dancers at the Sultan's Palace in Yogyakarta, circa 1860.

TIP

The best way to explore Yogyakarta is by *becak*, a three-wheeled man-powered pedicab. Confirm fare upfront, then climb in and enjoy the ride through scenic back streets.

long years during the fight against the Dutch, until 1949. This was a time of extraordinary social ferment. Six million refugees, more than a million young fighters and an enlightened young sultan (Hamengkubuwono IX) transformed the venerable court city into a hotbed of revolutionary idealism.

The Sultan's Palace

Today, it is primarily Jogja's traditional attractions that travellers come to see – ancient temples, palaces, batik, *gamelan*, dances and *wayang* puppet performances. Growing in popularity are nature-related activities. A mere 1 hour from Jakarta by plane or 9 hours by the Bima Express train brings you here. And from Bali, it is 1½ hours by air or 12 hours by bus. Jogja is an easy city to get around; there are plenty of taxis, mini-vans or man-powered *becak* (pedicab). *Andong* pony carts are used both inside the city and the countryside.

The first stop is the **Keraton** Ⓐ (Sultan's Palace; open Sat–Thur 8am–1pm; Fri 8–11am; entrance fee), a two-century-old palace complex that stands at the heart of the city. According to traditional cosmological beliefs, the Yogyanese ruler is literally the "navel" or central "spike" of the universe – anchoring the temporal world and communicating with the mystical realm of powerful deities. In this scheme of things, the Keraton is both the capital of the kingdom and the hub of the cosmos, bringing the two together through the application of certain elaborate design principles.

It houses not only the sultan and his family, but also the dynastic regalia (*pusaka*), private meditation and ceremonial chambers, a magnificent throne hall, several audience and performance pavilions, a mosque, an immense royal garden, stables, barracks, an armaments foundry and two expansive parade grounds planted with sacred banyan trees – all laid out in a carefully-conceived complex of walled compounds, narrow lanes and massive gateways, and bounded by a fortified outer wall measuring 2 km (1½ mile) on every side.

Construction of the Keraton began in 1755 and continued for almost 40 years, throughout the long reign of Hamengkubuwono I. Structurally, very little has been added since his death in 1792. Today, only the innermost compound is considered the Keraton proper, while the maze of lanes and lesser compounds, the mosque and the two vast squares, have been integrated into the city. Long sections of the outermost wall (*benteng*) still stand, however, and many of the residences inside are still owned and occupied by members of the royal family.

A different world

To step within the massive inner walls is to enter a patrician world of grace and elegance. In the first half of the 20th century, the interior was remodelled along European lines, incorporating Italian marble, cast-iron columns, crystal

Maps:
Area 118–9
City 142

Demonic wooden face at the entrance of Yogyakarta's Keraton is said to scare off evil spirits.

BELOW: the Sultan's Palace or Keraton of Yogyakarta.

chandeliers and rococo furnishings into a classical Javanese setting. The "Golden Pavilion" or **Bangsal Kencana** (central throne hall) is its most striking feature – a *pendopo* or open pavilion consisting of an ornate sloping roof supported at the centre by four massive wooden columns.

There is much else to see within the Keraton, including a museum, ancient *gamelan* sets, two great *kala*-head gateways and several spacious courtyards.

Taman Sari

TIP

Dance aficionados should visit the Keraton palace on a Sunday when court dancers rehearse to *gamelan* music in the central throne hall.

Behind the Keraton stand the ruins of the royal pleasure garden called **Taman Sari** ⓑ (open Sat–Thur 8am–1pm; Fri 8–11am; entrance fee). It was constructed over many years by Hamengkubuwono I and then abruptly abandoned after his death. Dutch representatives to the sultan's court marvelled at its large artificial lake, underground and underwater passageways, meditation retreats, a series of sunken bathing pools, and an imposing mansion of European design.

The ruins of the mansion, also called the Water Castle, occupies high ground at the northern end of the huge Taman Sari complex, overlooking a crowded bird market and a colony of batik painters. Although its stairways have collapsed, one can still scramble atop the crumbling walls to gain a commanding vista of Yogyakarta's downtown and beyond. A tunnel behind the castle leads to a complex of three partially-restored bathing pools. The large central pool with a *naga*-head fountain was designed for the use of queens, concubines and princesses, while the small southernmost pool was reserved for the sultan.

Farther south, tucked amid a crowded *kampung* (village), lies the interesting **Pesarean Pertapaan**, a royal retreat reached by passing through an ornate archway west of the bathing area, then following a winding path to the left. The main structure, a small Chinese-style temple with a forecourt and galleries, is said to be where the sultan and his sons meditated for seven days and nights at a time.

BELOW: a Yogyakarta palace guard.

The most remarkable structure at Taman Sari is the **Sumur Gumuling** (circular well), commonly referred to by locals as the *mesjid* (mosque), but more likely intended as a trysting place for the sultan and Ratu Kidul, the powerful Goddess of the South Sea, to whom all rulers of Mataram had been promised in marriage by the dynasty's founder (and from whom they are said to derive their mystical powers). Access is by an underground passageway, whose entrance lies to the west of the Water Castle. The "well" is in fact a sunken atrium, with circular galleries facing onto a small, round pool.

Before leaving the area, stroll through the **Pasar Ngasem** ⓒ (Bird Market), where bird lovers browse and haggle over a multitude of parrots, cockatoos, macaws, parakeets and more. Birds purchased here are prized for their singing voices.

Next to the bird market and water garden is a batik painters' colony, home to scores of young and unsung artists of the cloth. Motifs here fall into two distinct categories: traditional *Ramayana* scenes (in non-traditional colours) and attempts at primitive expressionism. Most of it is kitsch, even if of a rather exotic variety, as talented artists who succeed quickly move out to set up their own studios. Bargain hard if you intend to make a purchase here.

Jalan Malioboro

Yogyakarta's main thoroughfare, **Jalan Malioboro** D, begins in front of the royal audience pavilion, at the front of the palace, and ends at a *tugu* shrine – dedicated to the guardian serpent spirit Kyai Jaga – some 2 km (1¼ miles) to the north. Jalan Malioboro derives its name from the Sanskrit words *malya bhara*, meaning "garland bearing" (rather than the British Duke Malborough), as the royal processional route was always adorned with bouquets in the past.

Today, Jalan Malioboro is primarily a shopping district, though it is also an area of historical and cultural interest. Begin at the northern square (*alun-alun*) and stroll up the street, stopping first at the **Museum Sono Budoyo** E on the north-western side of the square. This was opened in 1935 by the Java Institute, a cultural foundation of wealthy Javanese and Dutch art patrons, and today houses important collections of prehistoric artefacts, Hindu-Buddhist bronzes, *wayang* puppets, dance costumes and traditional Javanese weapons.

Visit also the nearby **Mesjid Ageng** F (Grand Mosque), built in 1773, and notice the two fenced-off banyan trees standing on either side of the road in the centre of the square. They symbolise the balance of opposing forces within the Javanese kingdom.

Proceed northward from the square through the main gates and out across Jogja's main intersection. Immediately ahead on the right stands the old Dutch garrison, **Benteng Budaya** G (Fort Vredeburg), a cultural centre complete with exhibition and performance halls. Opposite it, on the left, stands the governor's residence. It was first the Dutch Resident's mansion and, during the revolution, was also used as the presidential palace. Farther along on the right, past the fort, is the huge central market, **Pasar Beringharjo**, a rabbit warren of small stalls.

Map on page 142

Jalan Malioboro is a hive of activity at night. Apart from a string of souvenir and handicraft shops, many students – Yogyakarta has a large university population – converge in this area for spirited intellectual discussions.

BELOW: *becak trishaws lined up along a street in Yogyakarta.*

Several schools in Yogyakarta offer short and long term Indonesian language courses. Among them is Realia, Jl. Pandega Marta V/6, tel: (0274) 583-229; fax: 581-053; e-mail: realiajogja@yahoo.com. Teaching "formal" Indonesian, their students are primarily diplomats, researchers and aid volunteers.

BELOW: reprising the roles of Rama and Sita in a classical dance-drama.

Back out on Malioboro, both sides of the street are lined with handicraft shops selling a great range of batik, leather goods, baskets, tortoise shell, jewellery and endless knick-knacks. Many restaurants here cater especially to foreign tourists, serving refreshing iced-fruit juices, and Chinese, Indonesian and Western fare. In early evening, the sidewalks explode into an incredible street market of handicraft stalls and food and drink stands.

Performing arts

Of the many art forms, *wayang kulit* or shadow-puppet play lies closest to the heart of the Central Java Javanese. All-night performances for *selamatan* ritual feasts, weddings or circumstances occur regularly, often in village compounds. There is an 8-hour presentation of *wayang kulit* on the second Saturday of every month at the **Sasano Higgil** ❽ (open daily 9pm–5am; entrance fee), near the Keraton.

Court dances are also taught outside the Keraton, at a number of private schools and government art academies in the city. The weekly rehearsal within the Keraton itself should not be missed, but the schools also present regular evening performances, and are open to visitors who wish to observe their dance classes. **Dalem Pujokusuman Theatre** ❶ (Jalan Brigjen Katamso No. 45) holds dance classes for young students (Mon, Tues, Thur 4–6pm; free), dance performances by students (Mon and Fri 8–10pm; entrance fee), as well as one-day classes for tourists.

Perhaps the ultimate in Javanese dance spectaculars is the Ramayana Sendratari Ballet. A modernised version of the lavish *wayang orang* dance-drama productions, it is performed monthly over four consecutive nights during the dry season (May–October), under the full moon in front of the elegant 9th-century Roro Jonggrang temple at Prambanan *(see page 152)*. (Check with your hotel or tourist office for dates.)

The villages around Yogyakarta specialise in different traditional crafts. **Kasongan** makes earthenware pottery, **Kota Gede** is famous for its delicate filigree silverwork, and yet others produce leather bags, weaving, baskets, wooden masks, cane furniture, *wayang* puppets or hand-forged ceremonial *keris* blades.

Batik town

Jogja's most famous handicraft is still batik. Visit the **Balai Penyelidikan Batik** ❶ (Batik Research Centre), located on Jalan Kusumanegara. An individually-guided tour costs nothing, and is an excellent introduction to the craft's painstaking manufacturing process, as well as to the staggering variety of patterns and colours to be found throughout Java. Intensive personalised courses are offered at the centre and several galleries. Batik courses are taught here and at other centres in the city.

Batik cloth is produced and sold all over Jogja, but especially in the south of the city on **Jalan Tirtodipuran** ❶, a street with over 25 batik factories and showrooms, most of which are happy to let visitors observe production. Many of the city's better-known artists, and a number of aspiring ones, also produce batik paintings made with the same resist-dye method, but specifically designed for framing and hanging.

The Indian Ocean is less than an hour's drive south of central Yogyakarta. **Parangtritis** is a wonderful stretch of black sand backed by towering bluffs, both a popular recreation spot and a place of worship, where the legendary Ratu Kidul, Queen of the South Seas, is said to live. The rip tides are dangerous here, so be careful if venturing into the water. This can be a day trip from Jogja, but lodgings are available.

Java's ancient past

For the Central Javanese, the *candi* or ancient stone monuments are tangible evidence of the great energy and artistry of their ancestors. For the foreign visitor, communion with one of these 1,000-year-old shrines provides an opportunity to ponder the achievements of a magnificent culture.

A great deal of effort has been expended since 1900 to excavate, reconstruct and restore their reliefs, study their iconography and decipher their inscriptions. Still, we know little more than the most basic symbolism of these structures. Fundamental questions as to their stylistic affinities with Indian art, and with their function within ancient Indonesian society, remain unanswered. Even their chronology is in doubt. What is known is that they are among the most technically-accomplished structures produced in ancient times; and that the awe inspired by their presence has formed a substantial part of their message.

Borobudur

A leisurely 1-hour drive across river beds and rice fields leads to the steps of fabled **Borobudur** ⓬, 40 km (25 miles) north-west of Yogyakarta (open daily, 6am–sunset; entrance fee; licensed guides available). Allow yourself a minium of 2 hours to tour the temple, though you could easily spend half a day here. This huge stupa, the world's largest Buddhist monument, was built sometime during

Map on page 142

One of the best batik courses in Jogja is at Brahma Tirta Sari. Not only does it teach the process of batik, it also explains the philosophical meanings behind the traditional patterns. Contact Nia or Ismoyo at tel: 274-377 881; e-mail: isniabts@yahoo.com.

BELOW: Buddhist *stupa* at Borobudur.

This image of a Buddhist deity was carved from a single block of stone.

BELOW: Buddha statue at Borobudur – seated in the so-called lotus position.

the relatively short Sailendra dynasty in Central Java, between AD 778 and AD 856 – 300 years before Angkor Wat and 200 years before Notre Dame. Yet, within little more than a century of its completion, Borobudur and the other structures in Central Java were mysteriously abandoned. At about this time, too, neighbouring Gunung Merapi erupted violently, covering Borobudur in volcanic ash and concealing it for centuries.

Restoration

In 1900, the Dutch government responded to cries of outrage from within its own ranks and established a committee for the restoration of Borobudur. The huge task was accomplished between 1907 and 1911 by a Dutch military engineer with a keen interest in Javanese antiquities.

At this time, Borobudur was discovered to be a fragile mantle of stone blocks that had been built upon a natural mound of earth. Rainwater was seeping through the stone mantle and eroding the soft foundation from within, while mineral salts were collecting on the monument's surface, where they acted in conjunction with sun, wind, rain and fungus to destroy it. Grandiose plans for a permanent restoration were never realised, due to the intervention of two world wars and an economic depression.

During the 1950s and 1960s, it became increasingly evident that Borobudur was structurally endangered. UNESCO was called to direct a rescue operation. Technical assistance and financing became available, and the project officially got underway in 1973. The scale of the project was spectacular. It took 10 long years to dismantle, catalogue, photograph, clean, treat and reassemble a total of 1,300,232 stone blocks. Each stone had to be individually inspected, scrubbed and chemi-

REDISCOVERY OF BORODUDUR

The story of Borobudur's "rediscovery" began in 1814, when the British governor of Java, Thomas Stamford Raffles (who later founded Singapore in 1819), visited Semarang and heard rumours of "a mountain of Buddhist sculptures in stone" near the town of Magelang. Raffles dispatched his military engineer, H.C.C. Cornelius, to investigate. Cornelius found a hillock overgrown with trees, but curiously scattered with hundreds of andesite blocks.

For two months, Raffles directed a massive clearing operation, removing vegetation and layers of earth, until it became clear that an elaborate structure lay beneath. He dug no further, for fear of damaging the unknown monument. In the years that followed, Borobudur was laid bare, and subsequently suffered almost a century of decay, plunder and abuse; thousands of stones were "borrowed" by villagers and priceless sculptures ended up as decorations in the homes of the rich and powerful.

In 1896, the Dutch gave away eight cart loads of Borobudur souvenirs to visiting King Chulalongkorn of Siam, including 30 relief panels, five Buddha statues, two lions and a guardian sculpture. Many of these and other irreplaceable works of Indo-Javanese art ended up in private collections, and now reside in museums around the world.

cally treated before being replaced. In addition, a new infrastructure of reinforced concrete, tar, asphalt, epoxy and tin was constructed to support the entire monument, and a system of drainage pipes installed to prevent further seepage.

In the end, the work was completed at a cost of US$25 million, or more than three times the original estimate. It is unlikely that we shall ever know the full import of Borobudur as a religious monument. An estimated 30,000 stonecutters and sculptors, 15,000 labourers and thousands more masons worked anywhere from 20 to 75 years to rebuild the monument. At a time when the entire population of Central Java numbered less than 1 million, this represented perhaps 10 percent of the available work force to a single effort.

Spiritual significance

Seen from the air, Borobudur forms a mandala, or geometric aid for meditation. Seen from a distance on the ground, Borobudur is a stupa, a model of the cosmos in three vertical parts: a square base supporting a hemispheric body and a crowning spire. As one approaches the traditional pilgrimage route from the east, and then ascends the terraced monument, circumambulating each terrace clockwise in succession, every relief and carving contributes to the whole.

There were originally 10 levels at Borobudur, each falling within one of the three divisions of the Mahayana Buddhist universe: *khamadhatu*, the lower spheres of human life; *rupadhatu*, the middle sphere of "form"; and *arupadhatu*, the higher sphere of detachment from the world. The lowest gallery of reliefs, now covered, depicts the delights of this world and the damnations of the next.

The next five levels (the processional terrace and four concentric galleries) show, in their reliefs (beginning at the eastern staircase and going around each gallery clockwise), the life of Prince Siddhartha on his way to becoming the Buddha, scenes from the Jataka folktales about his previous incarnations, and the life of the Bodhisattva Sudhana (from the *Gandavyuha*). These tales are illustrated in stone by a parade of commoners, princes, musicians, dancing girls and saints, with many interesting ethnographic details about daily life in ancient Java. Placed in niches above the galleries are 432 stone Buddhas, each displaying one of five *mudra* or hand positions, alternately calling upon the earth as witness and embodying charity, meditation, fearlessness and reason.

Above the square galleries, three circular terraces support 72 perforated *dagob* (miniature stupa), which are unique in Buddhist art. Most contain a statue of the meditating *dhyani* Buddha. Two statues have been left uncovered to gaze over the nearby Menoreh mountains, where a series of knobs and knolls is said to represent Gunadharma, the temple's divine architect. These three terraces are, in fact, transitional steps leading to the 10th and highest level, the realm of formlessness and abstraction (*arupadhatu*), embodied in the huge crowning stupa.

Pawon and Mendut

Two smaller, subsidiary *candi* lie along a straight line directly east of Borobudur. The closer of the two is tiny **Candi Pawon** (meaning "kitchen" or "cremato-

Map on pages 118–9

Every year, thousands of Buddhists walk in procession to Borobudur in celebration of Waisak, the holiest day of the year for Buddhists.

BELOW: mythical creature adorning the foot of a staircase.

The 3-metre (10-ft) tall Sakyamuni Buddha statue at Candi Mendut is regarded as one of the finest in the world.

rium"; open daily 6am–sunset; entrance fee), situated in a shady clearing 1.7 km (1 mile) from the temple's main entrance. It is often referred to as Borobudur's "porch temple" because of its proximity, and may well have been the last stop on a brick-paved pilgrimage route.

Just 1 km (½ mile) farther east, across the confluence of two holy rivers (the Progo and the Elo), lies beautiful **Candi Mendut** (open daily 6am–sunset; entrance fee). Unlike most other central Javanese monuments that face east, Mendut opens to the north-west.

The base and both sides of the staircase are decorated with scenes from moralistic fables and folktales, many of which concern animals. The main body of Mendut contains superbly-carved panels depicting *bodhisattva* and Buddhist goddesses. These are the largest reliefs found on any Indonesian temple.

The walls of the Candi Mendut antechamber are decorated with money trees and celestial beings, and contain two beautiful panels of a man and a woman amid swarms of playful children. It is thought that these two panels represent child-eating ogres who converted to Buddhism and became protectors instead of devourers.

The Mendut contains three of the finest Buddhist statues in the world: a magnificent 3-metre (10-ft) tall figure of the seated Sakyamuni Buddha, flanked on his left and right by Bodhisattva Vajrapani and Bodhisattva Avalokitesvara, each about 2.5 metres (8 ft) high. The central or Sakyamuni statue symbolises the first sermon of the Buddha at the Deer Park near Benares, India, as shown by the position of his hands (*dharmacakra mudra*) and by the small relief of a wheel between two deer. The two *bodhisattva*, or buddhas-to-be, have elected to stay behind in the world to help all of Buddha's followers.

BELOW: a bird's-eye view of Borobudur's grandeur.

Valley of the Kings

East of Yogyakarta, past the airport, the main Jogja-Solo highway slices across a volcanic plain littered with ancient ruins. Because these *candi* are considered by the Javanese of Central Java to be royal mausoleums, this region is known by them as the Valley of the Kings or the Valley of the Dead.

In the centre of the plain, 17 km (10 miles) from Jogja, lies the Hindu temple complex of **Prambanan**  (open daily 6am–sunset; entrance fee). Completed sometime around AD 856 to commemorate the victory of Sanjaya's Sivaitic descendant, Rakai Pikatan, over the last Sailendran ruler of Central Java, Balaputra (who fled to Sumatra and became the ruler of Srivijaya), it was deserted within a few years of its completion, however, and eventually collapsed. Preparations for the restoration of the central temple began in 1918, work started in 1937, and it was completed in 1953. The Indonesian government is conducting a long-term restoration project on the other temples and buildings in the Prambanan courtyard, several of which have been completed.

Prambanan complex

The central courtyard of the main complex contains eight buildings. The three largest are arrayed north-to-south: the magnificent 47-metre (155-ft) tall main **Candi Siva Mahadeva** flanked on either side by the slightly smaller shrines of **Candi Vishnu** (to the north) and **Candi Brahma** (to the south). Standing opposite these, to the east, are three smaller temples that once contained the "vehicles" of each god: Siva's bull (*nandi*), Brahma's gander (*hamsa*) and Vishnu's sun-bird (*garuda*). Of these, only *nandi* remains. By the northern and southern gates of the central compound are two identical court temples, standing 16 metres (50 ft) high.

TIP

Trams run between the main Prambanan temple complex and the Candi Sewu temple, about 1 km to the north. You can alight and rejoin at any time.

LEFT: Candi Siva Mahadeva, main temple at the Prambanan complex.
BELOW: stone figures on the grounds of the Prambanan temple.

Apart from the main Prambanan temples comprising Candi Siva Mahadeva (Roro Jonggrang) and the smaller Candi Brahma and Candi Vishnu, and Candi Sewu 1 km north, there are several other temple clusters in the Prambanan plain.

BELOW: wall reliefs of Hindu deities at Candi Roro Jonggrang.

Candi Siva Mahadeva, the largest of the temples and dedicated to Siva, is also known as **Roro Jonggrang** (often incorrectly spelled Loro) (Slender Maiden), a folk name sometimes given to the temple complex as a whole. Local legend has it that Roro Jonggrang was a princess wooed by an unwanted suitor. She commanded the man to build a temple in one night, and then frustrated his nearly successful effort by pounding the rice mortar prematurely – announcing the dawn. Enraged, he turned the maiden to stone, and according to the tale, she remains here in the northern chamber of the temple – as a statue of Siva's consort, Durga. In the other three chambers are statues of Agastya, the "Divine Teacher" (facing south); Ganesha, Siva's elephant-headed son (facing west); and a 3-metre (10-ft) Siva (central chamber, facing east).

One aspect of Roro Jonggrang's appeal is the symmetry and graceful proportions. Another is its wealth of sculptural detail. On the inner walls of the balustrade, beginning from the eastern gate and proceeding clockwise, the wonderfully vital and engrossing tale of the *Ramayana* is told in bas-relief (and completed on the balustrade of the Brahma temple).

Prambanan's beauty and variety demand more than a single visit. One of the most romantic ways to view the temple is by moonlight, during an open-air performance of the *Ramayana*, staged on moonlit nights between May and October. During the rest of the year, abridged performances of the epic are held in the adjacent **Trimurti Theatre**.

Dieng Plateau

Around 100 km (60 miles) and 3 hours north-east of Borobudur are arguably the oldest temples in Central Java, dating back to the late 7th century. Eight small

temples stand on an isolated plateau 2,000 metres (6,500 ft) high that is usually shrouded in mist. The temples are simple in detail but it is the unique mystery of the location and the close proximity to volcanic activity with brightly-coloured sulphur springs and bubbling mud-holes that are of interest. For most, there is an eerie quality to this site, which ancient Javanese of Central Java felt to be a centre of supernatural powers. The remains of other temples (originally 400 structures stood here) and several wooden pavilions, indicating perhaps a palace or monastery, are spread among the sulphur lakes.

The main temples are named after the heroes of the *Mahabharata* and all are Hindu in design. To the east of Candi Bima is the **Telaga Warna** (Coloured Lake), with fluorescent hues caused by sulphur vents. Close by are meditation caves. A visit to the plateau is a full-day trip. There are basic accommodations as well as a lovely four-star hotel in nearby **Wonosobo**. Visit Dieng Plateau early before the afternoon clouds roll in.

Solo

Located just 60 km (40 miles) east of Yogyakarta is noble **Surakarta**, also known as **Solo** , only an hour away by car or train. Start early for a one day visit to the palace or, if time permits, stay longer and enjoy a batik course, *gamelan* lesson or join one of the many meditation centres. Solo can also be reached by air from Jakarta and Bali.

Although larger than Yogyakarta, Solo is more sedate and refined. The two can be distinguished by certain cultural characteristics, such as customs. Solo was the original seat of the great Mataram empire before it was separated from Yogyakarta in 1755, a consequence of a Dutch-negotiated peace treaty.

Keraton Kasunanan

The **Keraton Kasunanan** (open Sat–Thur 8.30am– 1pm; entrance fee) was constructed between 1743 and 1746 on the banks of the mighty Bengawan Solo, Java's longest river. As with the Yogyakarta palace, Surakarta's Keraton simultaneously defines the centre of the town and the kingdom, as well as, metaphysically, the hub of the cosmos. Indeed, the similarities between the two courts, built within 10 years of each other, are striking. Both have a thick outer wall enclosing a network of narrow lanes and smaller compounds, two large squares, a mosque and a central or inner royal residential complex. Perhaps the major difference is that Surakarta has no north-south processional boulevard or pleasure palace.

Enter the Keraton at the east gate and pay a small fee for a guided tour of the museum and the inner sanctum. Here, shaded by groves of leafy trees, between which flit the bare-shouldered *abdidalem* or female attendants, is the large throne hall of the Susuhunan – a titular Muslim prince. Most of the original structure was destroyed by a fire in 1985, The inner columns supporting the roof are richly carved and gilded. Crystal chandeliers hang from the rafters and marble statues and cast-iron columns and Chinese blue-and-white vases line the walkways. Remove your shoes and refrain from taking photographs.

> **Map on pages 118–9**
>
> **TIP**
>
> Kalilurang, 25 km (16 miles) north of Yogyakarta, is the main access point for hikes up Gunung Merapi (Fire Mountain), which stands a 2,911 metres (9,550 ft). Highly volatile, Merapi constantly belches lava and steam, so check with the authorities first before planning an ascent.

BELOW: scenic Dieng Plateau.

TIP

When the Mataram empire split in 1755, Surakarta and Yogyakarta were formed. The present Sultan of Yogyakarta is descended from one of two Yogyakarta royal families, thus two palaces in Jogja. From the original Surakarta line, there are also two families and two palaces, Kasunanan and Mangkunegaran.

Below: the throne hall at the Keraton Kasunanan, Solo.

Notice the royal meditation tower to one side – if it looks familiar, that is because it is essentially a Dutch windmill without the arms.

Ugly giant

The Keraton museum was established in 1963 and contains ancient Hindu-Javanese bronzes, traditional Javanese weapons and three marvellous coaches. The oldest coach – a lumbering, deep-bodied carriage built around 1740 – was a gift from the Dutch East India Company to Pakubuwono II. The museum also displays some remarkable figureheads from the old royal barges, including Kyai Rajamala, a giant of surpassing ugliness, who once adorned the bow of the Susuhunan's private boat and is said even now to emit a fishy odour when daily offerings are not forthcoming.

After visiting the Keraton, stroll through the narrow lanes outside and be sure to pay a visit to nearby **Sasana Mulya** – the music and dance pavilion of the **Indonesian Arts College** (STSI), located just to the west of the main or north palace gate. This is an art school with an illustrious history, for it was here that the first musical notation for *gamelan* was devised at the turn of the 20th century. Visitors are welcome to listen and observe as long as they do it unobtrusively.

Keraton Mangkunegaran

About 1 km (½ mile) to the west and north of the main Keraton Kasunanan, a branch of the Surakarta royal family has constructed its own smaller, more intimate palace. Begun by Mangkunegara II at the end of the 18th century and completed in 1866, the **Keraton Mangkunegaran** is also open to the public (open Sat–Thur 9am–2pm; Fri 9am–12.30pm; entrance fee).

Map on pages 118–9

The outer *pendopo* or audience pavilion of the Mangkunegaran is said to be the largest in Java – built of solid teakwood, and jointed and fitted in the traditional manner, without the use of nails. Note the brightly-painted ceiling, with the eight mystical Javanese colours in the centre, highlighted by a flame motif and bordered by symbols of the Javanese zodiac. The *gamelan* set in the southwest corner of the *pendopo* is known as Kyai Kanyut Mesem ("Kyai Kanyut Smiles"). Try to visit the palace on Wednesday mornings, when it is used to accompany an informal dance rehearsal before noon.

The museum is in the ceremonial hall of the palace, directly behind the *pendopo*, and it mainly houses the private collections of Mangkunegara IV: dance ornaments, *topeng* masks, jewellery (including two silver chastity belts), ancient Javanese and Chinese coins, bronze figures and a superb set of *keris*.

Antiques and batik

Solo, with its sizeable "antique industry", where many dealers collect and restore old European, Javanese and Chinese furniture and bric-a-brac, is excellent for the unhurried shopper who likes to explore out of the way places in hopes of finding hidden treasures. The starting point for any treasure hunt is **Pasar Triwindu**, just south of the Mangkunegaran palace. Solo is also the home of Indonesia's largest batik manufacturers, three of whom have showrooms in town with reasonable fixed prices for superb yard goods, shirts and dresses. Many smaller batik shops also line the main streets. To see why Surakarta calls itself the City of Batik, visit the huge textile market called **Klewer**, beside the Grand Mosque and near the Keraton. Just be sure to know what you are doing if making a purchase here – batik can sell for as little as US$1 or as much as US$100 a yard.

Brass kenong or small gongs are one of the instruments that make up a gamelan.

BELOW: Solo's aristocracy paying their repects to the Surakarta royalty.

> Map on pages 118–9

Just 18 km (11 miles) north of Solo is Sangiran, where the remains of the prehistoric "Java Man" were first unearthed in 1891 (see also page 107). The small Museum Trinil (open Mon–Sat 9am–6pm) in nearby Krikilan village, has a collection of bones and other fossil remains.

BELOW: a *gamelan* musician hitting the right notes on a *saron* metallaphone.

As is Jogja, Solo is renowned as a centre for traditional Javanese performing arts. It is one of the best places to see an evening *wayang orang* dance performance or *wayang kulit* shadow play, or listen to live *gamelan* music. Here, you can buy ornately-carved and painted leather puppets, contorted wooden masks, gilded headdresses and even monstrous bronze gongs for highly distinctive gifts or house decorations. Solo is also a major centre for meditation and there are a few places which hold yoga courses specially for foreigners.

Central Java's new attractions

The countryside around Jogja and Solo are vast expanses of volcanic mountain ranges riddled with caves and lava formations that attract climbers and spelunkers from around the world. Small, family-run homestays now offer forest treks for bird watching, and traditional Javanese villages are opening their doors to travellers who seek a more intimate look at life at its simplest. New hillside resorts offer upscale options. Sunset cocktails at the luxury **Amanjiwo** resort overlooking Borobudur, near Magelang, is a rare pleasure, while the newly opened **Losari Coffee Plantation Resort & Spa** further north is an oasis of cool, fresh air combined with old world charm.

In and near Jogja are a growing number of spas featuring massage and body treatments using *jamu*, the herbal concoctions favoured by royal Javanese princesses, golf courses and fine dining. Thanks to a large student population – young intellectuals grown weary of economic and political instability – new ventures are popping up, including natural fibre handicrafts and coffee shops by the scores. Cultural appreciation is on the rise too, often resulting in new twists to traditional themes in dance, music, painting and fashion design. ❑

Symbolic Keris

Neatly tucked into the waist band of the traditional attire of the Indonesian man is the ceremonial dagger, or *keris*. No longer a weapon of defence, this ornate blade is rather an indication of social ranking, a source of cultural pride and a symbol of masculinity. An old Javanese proverb states that "Happy is the man owner of horse, wife, bird and *keris*." In many parts of Java, the *keris* is considered to be the most important item a man can own.

The traditional *keris* is a lightweight elongated dagger with a blade that is either straight or wavy, resembling a flame or serpent; coupled with a hilt and sheath. Originally worn for protection and used as a thrusting weapon, today, it is an essential part of the groom's wedding ceremonial attire in parts of Indonesia. So revered is the dagger that a man's *keris* can be a substitute in his absence at his own wedding.

Thought to possess a life of its own and endowed with magical powers, the *keris* is treated with great respect and reverence. There are many *keris* legends, including stories about wilful and bloodthirsty daggers that are capable of flying, turning into snakes, fathering children and taking human lives.

Stored in a place of honour, treated with perfumed oils and wrapped in silk and velvet, *keris* are passed down as sacred family heirlooms. Every year on the first day of the Javanese calendar, the sultan of Yogyakarta cleanses with holy water the palace *pusaka* (heirlooms with spiritual powers), which include an assortment of sacred *keris*. Believing the objects to be magically endowed, crowds wait outside for the chance of receiving just a drop of the holy water used in the cleaning ritual, while the *keris* is carried from the palace in a coach.

The *keris* were crafted by *empu* (master craftsmen), esteemed ironworkers imbued with divine status and who were so revered that they came under the patronage of the court and were often considered members of the royal household.

Before beginning his work, the *empu* would make offerings, fast, meditate or ask for divine inspiration. The blade is forged from several layers of nickel and meteoric iron, using a damascening technique which in turn produces the desired shades of light and dark patterns on the blade, the *pamor*. This pattern becomes visble after the blade has been polished and treated with citrus juice and arsenic. Each pattern has a name and meaning. *Wos wutah* (scattered rice grains), for example, represents prosperity.

Keris are distinguished by the number of curves (always uneven) they support. One wave represents god and king, while three, fire and passion. Each of these qualities is believed to have an effect on the life of the owner. If a man is not suitably matched to his *keris*, it can affect his life in a negative way. The hilt can be plain or carved with a mythical figure – believed to be capable of warding off evil spirits – in wood, bone or ivory and inlaid with precious metals and stones. The scabbard is usually wooden and encased in richly-embossed brass, silver or gold. ❑

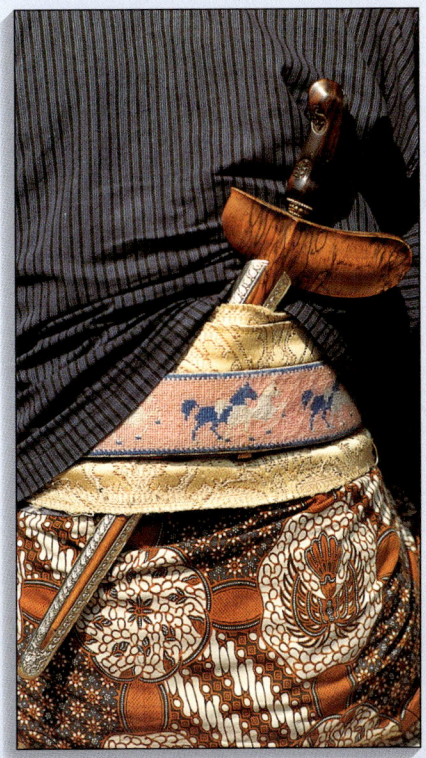

RIGHT: a *keris* dagger is supposedly imbued with magical powers.

EAST JAVA

Like Central Java, the eastern region is rich in archaeological interest and stunning volcanic scenery. Highlights are the traditions of ancient Surabaya, and the splendour of Gunung Bromo

Geographically and historically, East Java (Jawa Timur) may be divided into three regions: the north coast (including the island of Madura) with its old Islamic trading ports, the Brantas River Valley with its ancient monuments and colonial hill stations, and the eastern salient (known to history as Blambangan) with its spectacular volcanoes, secluded nature reserves and unparalleled scenic beauty nearly everywhere. The broad **Sungai Brantas** traces a circular path through the ancient and fertile rice lands of eastern Central Java, and around several adjacent peaks – Arjuna, Kawi and Kelud. For five centuries after AD 930, this valley was the undisputed locus of power and civilisation on the island. The great kingdoms of this period – Kediri, Singasari and Majapahit – have bequeathed a rich heritage of art, literature and music.

With the arrival of Islam as a political force in the 16th century, and with the great fluorescence of the spice and textile trade, a struggle arose between the rice-growing kingdoms of the interior and the new Islamic trading powers of the coast. Muslim forces conquered the Brantas Valley around 1530, and many Hindus then fled eastward to Blambangan and Bali.

LEFT: inaccessible wind-lashed East Java coastline.
BELOW: Surabaya is the birthplace of the Indonesian independence movement.

City of heroes

Up until the 1900s, the East Java provincial capital of **Surabaya**  was the largest and most important seaport in the archipelago. It still ranks second (after Jakarta's Tanjung Priok) with more than 400 years of colourful history behind it.

Dutch descriptions of the city in 1620 paint it as a formidable adversary surrounded by a canal, and with heavily-fortified bastions measuring some 40 km (25 miles) in circumference. And its army is said to have numbered 30,000 warriors. In the end, Surabaya succumbed to the powerful Mataram rulers of Central Java in 1625, but only after Sultan Agung's armies had devastated its rice lands and diverted its mighty river.

In the mid-18th century, Surabaya was ceded to the Dutch and developed into the greatest commercial city of the Indies – the chief sugar port and rail head on Java. Immortalised in many of Joseph Conrad's novels, this era was characterised by square-riggers in full sail, wealthy Chinese and Arab traders, eccentric German hoteliers, and lusty seamen brawling over the likes of Surabaya Sue (who really existed).

Today's reality is different. Surabaya is Indonesia's second-largest city, with 4 million people. It is known as a city of heroes because of the momentous first battle of the revolution in November 1945. Although the local rebels were driven out by the better-equipped British troops, they inflicted heavy casualties and proved that independence could be fought for.

Arab and Chinese quarters

The most interesting areas of Surabaya are the old Arab and Chinese quarters at the northern end of the city, not far from the harbour. Spend some time wandering the narrow lanes east of Jalan K.H. Mas Mansyur, around the mosque and the **Tomb of Sunan Ampel**, one of the nine legendary *wali* saints who propagated Islam on the island. There is a bazaar that leads up to the mosque, with scores of stalls selling perfumes and handmade textiles from all over Java.

Hail a taxi and travel south to Jalan Dukuh II/2, to the **Hong Tik Hian Temple**, with its daily Chinese hand-puppet (*potehi*) performances for the assembled deities. And just across Jalan Kembang Jepun, on Jalan Selompretan, stands Surabaya's oldest Chinese shrine, the 18th-century **Hok An Kiong Temple**, built entirely of wood by native Chinese craftsmen. The temple's central deity is the goddess Ma Co, the protector of waterlogged sailors. From the Chinese quarter, walk westward along Jalan Kembang Jepun to the famous **Red Bridge** straddling Kali Mas canal. Nearby is **House of Sampoerna**, a recently-restored Dutch building housing a museum, gift shop and café. Visitors can view the rolling, cutting, packing and wrapping of hand-rolled *kretek* (clove cigarettes).

Climb into a taxi and travel south from here, parallel to the river past the **Heroes Monument**, to see how Surabaya has expanded in recent times. On Jalan Tunjungan is the old-world **Mandarin Oriental Hotel Majapahit**, built in 1910 and wonderfully refurbished. From Jalan Tunjungan, the main shopping street with several shopping centres, turn left down Jalan Pemuda to the former Dutch **Governor's Mansion**. Constructed after the turn of the 20th century, this stood at what was then the new centre of colonial Surabaya, and which now is a major hotel district. **Joko Dolog**, a centuries-old statue of King

Experience old world charm at the historic Mandarin Oriental Majapahit. The hoisting of the Dutch flag here in 1945 sparked the war for independence.

BELOW: Surabaya's Kali Mas canal.

SURABAYA SUE

Surabaya Sue was a Scottish national who was best known for her role as an Indonesian freedom fighter during the Japanese invasion. Born as Muriel Pearson in 1908, she travelled to Bali as a curious young girl in her 20s and fell in love with Indonesia. Known to the locals as K'tut Tantri, she seized the world's imagination as a brave spirit after she was captured, cast in solitary confinement and tortured for two years by the Japanese during their occupation of Surabaya.

She recounted her ordeal in the autobiographical and highly-colourful (some would say "coloured") book, *Revolt in Paradise*. After she was set free, this foreigner joined the Independence movement and fought alongside the Indonesians, smuggling arms and supplies between islands. She operated an underground radio station and broadcast news reports to gain the world's attention.

In this, she succeeded handsomely, and in the process earned the nickname "Surabaya Sue" given her by the foreign media. After achieving Independence, the gratified Indonesian government put her up in a hotel in Jakarta.

Surabaya Sue lived a long and eventful life – she was closely associated with the raja of Bangli in Bali – before dying at age 89 in an old folk's home in Australia.

Kertanegara, the last king of the Singasari dynasty (who died in 1292), is enshrined in a small, hidden park directly opposite.

A 20-minute drive south from the city centre is **Kebun Binatang** (open daily 8am–5pm; entrance fee), one of the largest and oldest zoos in Southeast Asia, housing Komodo dragons, orangutan and other fauna of Indonesia. In the same area is the **Centre Culturel Francais** on Jalan Darmokali, periodically featuring exhibits and dance performances.

Map on pages 118–9

Bull races

A 30-minute ferry ride from the Kamal seaport and you are in neighbouring **Madura** ⓰ island, a major destination particularly during August or September – the time of the exciting annual bull races (*karapan sapi*). According to the Madurese, it began long ago when plow team was pitted against plow team over the length of a rice field.

Today's racing bulls are never used for plowing, but are specially bred; they represent a considerable source of regional pride. Only bulls of a high standard (condition, weight, colour) may be entered and are judged on appearance as well as speed. District and regency heats are held all over Madura and East Java, building up to the finale in September in **Pamekasan**, the island's capital.

The main event is a thundering sprint down a 100-metre (328-ft) long field lined by throngs of screaming spectators. These huge and normally slow-moving creatures attain speeds of over 50 km per hour (30 mph).

The Madurese have long enjoyed a reputation for toughness, and Madura's dry limestone terrain may account for this. The major industries here are fishing, tobacco growing and salt panning. The southern coastal fishing villages

Madurese prized racing bulls are fed on a special diet of honey, eggs, beer and chillies. To make them run even faster, pins are sometimes stuck into their posteriors.

BELOW:
Madura's bull races attract a frenzied crowd every year.

Remains of the Hindu-Buddhist temple of Candi Jawi near Tretes, East Java.

exude a solid but slightly jaded Mediterranean air and has some good beaches. To the east is a modest but interesting palace at **Sumenep**, a beautiful 18th-century mosque, **Mesjid Jamiq**. Close by is a small museum with examples of wonderfully-carved wooden furniture, a skill that Madurese craftsmen are famous for, and an adjacent library with important manuscripts.

Mountain retreat

The delightful mountain resort of **Tretes**, just 55 km (35 miles) south of Surabaya, offers fresh air, cool nights and superb mountain scenery. Walk or ride on horseback in the morning to one of three valley waterfalls in the vicinity. Then spend the afternoon by a bracing spring-fed swimming pool, or curl up with a good book and a huge pot of tea or coffee, or take in a round of golf.

More active souls will perhaps want to hike up **Gunung Arjuna** (3,339 metres, 10,950 ft), located behind Tretes, through lush montane casuarina forests, or across the Lalijiwa Plateau along a well-worn path to neighbouring **Gunung Welirang**, where sulphur is collected by villagers from hissing fumaroles. The area is also studded with ancient monuments, beginning with **Candi Jawi**, just by the main road 7 km (4 miles) below Tretes. This slender Hindu-Buddhist shrine was completed around 1300, and is one of several funerary temples dedicated to King Kertanegara of the Singasari dynasty.

Candi Jawi overlooks **Gunung Penanggungan** to the north – a perfect cone surrounded on all sides by smaller peaks and regarded, because of its shape, as a replica of the holy mountain Mahameru. Penanggungan is littered with dozens of terraced sanctuaries, meditation grottoes and sacred pools – about 80 sites in all, most of which are on the mountain's northern and western faces. The most accessible and charming of these is **Belahan**, a bathing pool situated at Penanggungan's eastern foot. It is thought to be the burial site of King Airlangga, who died in 1049. The pool is reached by a dirt road from the main Surabaya highway, only a few minutes' drive north of Pandaan.

BELOW: statuary at the Belahan bathing pools.

Traces of the past

From Tretes or Surabaya, it is about an hour to the village of **Trowulan** near Mojokerto, once the seat of Java's greatest empire, 14th-century Majapahit. Unfortunately, most of Majapahit's monuments were built of wood and soft redbrick, so that only the foundations and a few gateways remain. The **Museum Trowulan** by the main road nevertheless has a fascinating collection of terracotta figures and fragments and a useful table-top map of the area. From here, seek out nearby ruins: **Candi Tikus** (a royal bathing complex), **Candi Bajang Ratu** (a tall brick entry way) and **Wringin Lawang** (a palace gate). Also visit the cemetery of **Tralaya**, 2 km (1¼ mile) south of Trowulan, site of the oldest Muslim graves on Java.

Malang and environs

Malang ⑰ is a pleasant highland town with a cool climate and a colonial atmosphere that is a 2-hour drive south of Surabaya. Through the centre of town runs the Sungai Brantas; the residential area lies to the north and the busy commercial hub to the south. A superb collection of Javanese and Chinese antiques and art is displayed in **Hotel Tugu Malang**. Even if not staying at this fascinating 44-room hotel, visit it to see the collection of Dutch- and Indonesian-inspired heirlooms acquired by the hotel owners from around the region. Room rates are high but worth every cent for their atmosphere.

There are three interesting temples outside of Malang. **Candi Singosari** is on the west side of the main highway from Surabaya, at the town of Singosari. From the village of Blimbing, north of Malang, take the road to Tumpang, about 20 km (12 miles) away. Just before the Tumpang market, a small road to the left leads to **Candi Jago**, begun in 1268 as a memorial to the Singasari king, Wisnuwardhana. All around the terraces are reliefs in the distinctive *wayang* or Javanese shadow puppet style of scenes from the *Mahabharata*, and a frightening procession of underworld demons.

East Java's only sizeable temple complex is **Candi Panataran**, located 80 km (50 miles) west of Malang, just north of the city of Blitar (best reached by taking the longer but more scenic route over the mountains via Kediri). This was apparently the state temple of Majapahit, assembled over a period of some 250 years, between 1197 and 1454. A series of shrines and pavilions arranged before a broad platform, it is assumed that the pavilions were originally roofed with wood and thatch, as was the body of the main temple.

Near Panataran (on the road to Blitar) stands **Sukarno's mausoleum**, the final resting place of the "father of Indonesian independence" who died in 1970. And on the way to or from Blitar via the scenic Malang-Kediri high road, make a detour north from Batu to the mountain resort of **Selekta** – famous for its colonial bungalows, swimming pools and apple orchards.

Map on pages 118–9

BELOW: Malang town tykes.

Tengger highlands

The steep slopes of the active volcanoes Gunung Semeru and Gunung Bromo in **Bromo-Tengger-Semeru National Park** have been the home of the Tenggerese people for several hundred years. The only group of people on the island who remained Hindu, they are believed to be descendants of the Hindu-Buddhist Majapahit kingdom that fell in the 16th century. As Islam swept through Java, Hindu priests and aristocrats fled to Bali, Blambangan (in South Java) and the Tengger highlands. Today, the Tenggerese maintain a unique form of Hinduism mixed with animism and live as farmers working the fertile farmland on the slopes of Bromo. The region is a major vegetable-growing area and the spectacular gardens and high-altitude pine trees are a lovely sight. But the main attraction of the area is a visit to the rim of Bromo's smouldering crater at sunrise.

Gunung Bromo ⓲ (Mount Bromo) is an ancient caldera 10 km (6 miles) across, with four smaller peaks rising in the centre, ranging from between 300 and 400 metres (1,000 and 1,300 ft). Surrounding these peaks on the crater floor is sand and lush vegetation; every few years cinder and ash pour forth in eruptions to carpet the countryside with nutrient-rich deposits.

There are two ways to take in the view: either from the crater's edge or a panoramic view of the entire caldera from afar (if time permits, watch the sunrise from both vistas). For the first, make the trek across the sand-sea floor, either by pony or by foot. Once at the base of the crater, climb up an incline of 250 concrete steps. At the top is a narrow lip from where you can look into the belly of the belching sulphurous centre of the crater and take in the 360-degree view of the entire caldera and the majestic **Gunung Semeru**, Java's highest peak at 3,676 metres (12,060 ft). Temperatures can drop to freezing before dawn, so be

The Kasodo festival is held every year during which thousands of Hindu Tenggerese take part in a midnight procession to toss offerings into the centre of Gunung Bromo.

BELOW: tortured lavascape of Gunung Bromo.

RIGHT: morning mist rises over Bromo.

sure to dress warmly and bring a flashlight. For the panoramic view, hire a jeep to **Gunung Penanjakan**, about 3 km (2 miles) to the west, then it is a short hike along a paved road to the summit. Usually less crowded here, the view is just as amazing. All arrangements need to be made the night before. Both walks can be done in the pre-dawn period; if time is limited, enjoy sunrise at Gunung Penanjakan and after breakfast take a pony ride for the view of Bromo's navel.

There are several ways to reach the Tengger highlands and transport can be arranged in Surabaya, Malang or even Bali. Public buses and the train go as far as Probolinggo; from here, there are tour companies with mini-vans to take you the rest of the way. There is modest accommodation in both **Ngadisari** and **Cemara Lawang** (closer to the rim) and the better rooms come with hot water. As Gunung Bromo is inside a nature park, a small entrance fee is required.

Other national parks

There are three coastal game reserves in East Java that can be visited on the way to or from Bali (by the Ketapang–Gilimanuk ferry). The most accessible of these is the **Baluran National Park** at Java's north-eastern tip. The park is spread over 50,000 hectares (124,000 acres) inside an old eroded volcano cone. This is a chance to see dry-terrain wildlife not seen in other areas of Java.

To experience the park, go on long walks with a guide. Sightings include deer, feral buffalo and the rare Javanese wild dog called *ajag* and 150 bird species. Obtain a permit at the park entrance. Simple lodgings are available inside the park (bring food, water and mosquito net). More comfortable hotels are found in Ketapang, south of the Bali-Java ferry point. The best time to visit is the dry season (June–Nov) when animals congregate at the waterholes.

South-west of Baluran is **Ijen National Park**. Gunung Ijen's attraction is its haunting sulphuric crater lake. Miners carry 80 kg (176 lbs) or more of sulphur from the bottom of the crater in bamboo baskets on shoulder poles. Hikes to the summit of Gunung Ijen take about 90 minutes on a shaded path. Also available are treks through rainforest to mountain springs, coffee plantations and breathtaking scenery.

The south-eastern tip of Java has also been designated as **Alas Purwo National Park**, and though there are no main roads leading into it, surfers have constructed bamboo shacks on the western shore, and often charter boats from Bali for the excellent waves here. The park can be visited throughout the year. First collect a permit at the PHPA office in Tegaldelima, drive 4 km (2½ miles) to Sadengan, park your vehicle, then begin an easy walk to a watchtower for views of grazing cattle, peacocks, wild hen and boar.

The journey to **Meru Betiri National Park** on the southern coast requires a tough vehicle. Take the main road from Banyuwangi to Genteng and turn south to the village of Sukamade. The 35-km (21-mile) trip to the park centre can take from 1 to 3 hours (the dry season is the best time to visit). The main attractions are its sea turtle conservation area, splendid hornbills, Java warty pigs and giant owls. Unconfirmed rumours of Java tiger sightings are probably proliferated for the benefit of tourists. Accommodations are basic. ❑

Sulphur mining is a profitable livelihood at Gunung Ijen.

BELOW: *banteng* bull at Baluran National Park.

SUMATRA

The extraordinary wealth of natural resources on this large island helps fill the national coffers

Exotic Sumatra (Sumatera) is one of the world's last frontiers – an island of lush tropical rainforests, extraordinary flora and fauna, and active volcanoes. Home to the Sumatran tiger and a host of diverse and dynamic ethnic groups, it is the third largest island in Indonesia and the fifth largest in the world (roughly the size of Spain). Vastly rich in natural resources, over half of the country's exports come from the treasure trove of Sumatra's bounty of oil, natural gas, hardwoods, rubber, palm oil, coffee and sugar.

The people maintain their strong cultural identity while embracing the future. On the east coast, oil companies work some of the world's most productive oil fields, and the small islands of the Riau archipelago are building world-class luxury resorts as part of a so-called "golden triangle" – a three-way venture with Singapore and Malaysia. In spite of this evolution, Sumatra still maintains strong and well-established traditions that are rooted in their colourful past.

Situated at the western rim in the archipelago along the Strait of Malacca, for centuries the region was the gateway for maritime trade through Southeast Asia, receiving merchants from China, India, the Middle East and Europe. The early coastal seaport kingdoms were the entry points for the influx of foreign influence that has left a lasting imprint on the very fibre of Indonesia's culture. The first wave started in the 2nd century with the Hindu-Buddhist Indian civilisation; later in the 13th century, Islam entered by peaceful means.

Sumatra is a tapestry of ethnic groups mostly living in rural communities: in the north are the independent and devout Muslim people of Aceh; in the northern highlands, the proud Christian Batak; and in the west, the business-savvy Minangkabau, a matrilineal society. The Kubu in the south live as did their nomadic stone-age ancestors while the Orang Laut (sea people) live aboard boats and ply the seas among the hundreds of islands off the east coast.

Sumatra is a travel haven for nature-lovers, with its pristine environment, white water rafting, unspoiled beaches, elephants and orangutan. Add the memorable sights of Danau Toba, Asia's largest lake, along with impressive architecture, graceful mosques and Stone Age cultures. Allowing yourself enough time is the challenge; most people are overwhelmed by the sheer size, and nothing less than two weeks would do justice to the rugged terrain. The best time to visit is the dry season in the months of June and July. For the intrepid traveller, the rewards are worthwhile while an added bonus is the warmth and friendliness of the Sumatran people. ❑

PRECEDING PAGES: traditional Minangkabau architecture near Padang features upturned rooflines which resemble buffalo horns.
LEFT: blues and greens as far as the eye can see at Danau Toba, North Sumatra.

NORTH SUMATRA

This engrossing region is best known for its great cultures in the Muslim Acehnese and the proud Batak, once fearsome cannibals. Yet they are not primitive, and live by complex ancient mores

From the booming industrial metropolis of Medan to the forested Sungai Alas Valley to the fiercely-independent Islamic stronghold of Aceh, Sumatra's northernmost segment is easily its most diverse. North Sumatra has historically been the Indonesian archipelago's first point of contact with external influences from as early as the 2nd century, when Hinduism and Buddhism were brought in by Indian traders. Later, Islam reacted its shores through Arab and Indian Muslims in the 13th century.

Early north-coast kingdoms took advantage of sea trade passing through the nearby straits. During the Golden Age under Sultan Iskandar Muda (1604–37), Aceh expanded to include all the major ports of eastern Sumatra and several on the Malay peninsula. The Dutch declared war on Aceh in 1873 and it took more than 10,000 troops – the largest military force the Dutch ever mustered in the East Indies before the eventual defeat of the sultanate in 1878. Guerrilla activities then spread inland to Gayo territories, where the rebel-controlled pepper trade financed the purchase and smuggling of arms from the British.

The Acehnese are still fiercely independent; a strong Islamic movement and extremist separatist activity are thorns in the side of the central government. Since 1999 there has been a resurgence of guerrilla activity by the Free Aceh Movement (GAM). Although the province has been granted the status of *Daerah Istimewa* (Special Autonomous District), the GAM continues to push for full independence. Today, Aceh's economy relies largely on trade and vast reserves of natural gas and oil at Lhokseumawe.

Note: Though Aceh is open to foreigners at this writing (2004), check with a local travel agent for restrictions before planning travel to Aceh.

Banda Aceh

Banda Aceh ❶, capital of the province, is located along the shores of two rivers, Sungai Krong Aceh and Sungai Krong Daroy. The original fortress and palace of the Sultan of Aceh were destroyed along with the great mosque when the Dutch invaded in 1874, but vestiges of Aceh's glorious past can still be found around **Jalan Teuku Umar**. The **Gunongan** is a royal water pleasure garden built by Sultan Iskandar Muda in the 17th century for his Malay princess wife. Opposite this is the Pintu (door) Aceh, used only by the royal family.

On Jalan Keraton are the tombs of 15th- and 16th-century sultans of Aceh, while another series of royal tombs on Jalan Mansur Sjah includes that of Sultan Iskandar Muda. They in turn surround the **Museum Negeri Aceh** (Aceh State Museum; open daily; entrance fee). **Museum Rumah Aceh Awe Gentah**, a

LEFT: GAM freedom fighter in Banda Aceh addressing a crowd.
BELOW: Acehnese wedding couple.

An armed struggle has been raging for years between the central government and GAM freedom fighters in Aceh. Check with a local travel agent on restrictions in Aceh.

BELOW:
Moghul-inspired Baiturrahman Mesjid Raya.

former aristocrat's house displaying daggers, textiles and jewellery, has a 15th-century bronze bell at its front door that was a gift to the Sultan of Pasari from a Chinese emperor.

Most of the Dutchmen killed in the Aceh War, including a number of generals and other senior officers, are buried at the Christian cemetery on Jalan Iskandar Muda. With wrought-iron art-nouveau gates, the entrance stands between two marble plates on which are engraved the names of all the soldiers.

At the centre of Aceh is the beautiful **Baiturrahman Mesjid Raya.** Designed by an Italian architect in the Moghul Indian style, it was built by the Dutch between 1879–81 to replace the destroyed grand mosque. At night, the huge white structure and its black domes are illuminated. The marble interior may be visited by non-Muslims, except during prayer times. Behind, and to the west, are the market and the Chinese quarter along Jalan Perdagangan.

The nearby village, **Kampung Kuala Aceh**, is a place of pilgrimage where lies the grave of Teungku Sheikh Shaj Kuala (1615–93), a holy man who translated the Koran into Malay. Aceh's university bears his name.

Banda Aceh is not Indonesia's Land's End. That distinction belongs to remote **Pulau Weh** (Weh island), reached by plane or a 2½-hour ferry ride. There have been reports of malaria so preventive medication is advised.

The island's main town, **Sabang**, flourished throughout the 1970s as a duty-free port linked to Calcutta, Malacca, Penang and Singapore. Today, the quiet island offers beautiful white-sand beaches with aquamarine water excellent for snorkelling and scuba diving and hot water springs at Senekai. The Iboih National Park on its north-west coast and 20 km (12½ miles) from Sabang, is home to monkeys, flying foxes and the rare Nicobar pigeon.

Gayo highlands

A scenic Japanese-built track constructed by slave labour during World War II connects Blangkejeren to **Takengon**, the Gayo capital that lies 1,100 metres (3,600 ft) up. Takengon is built on the banks of **Danau Laut Tawar** (Lake Tawar). The water is clean, cool and refreshing, but local people do not swim in it. Fearing they may be pulled into the underwater realm of a seductive fairy, they opt instead for the public baths and hot springs at **Kampong Balik**. A paved road follows the west side of the lake, affording spectacular views of rice paddies and pine-clad mountain slopes. The east coast town of **Bireuen** is the chief marketplace for Gayo coffee, cinnamon, cloves and tobacco.

A distance of 110 km (60 miles) from Medan is **Sigli**, known as Padri when it was the principal port from which Acehnese *haji* (pilgrims) departed to Mecca. The tragic Padri War started here in 1804; the Dutch took the town and completely destroyed it in the process. Remains of the *padri kraton* (fortress) can be seen on the outskirts of town, along the road to Banda Aceh. At nearby Kam-

Coffee beans grown in the rich volcanic soil of the Gayo highlands are considered to be the best in Indonesia – full-bodied and flavourful.

pong Kibet is the grave of Sultan Maarif Syah, the first Islamic sultan of Aceh, who died in 1511. Some 60 km (40 miles) down the coast and a short distance inland is the village of **Lamno**. Its inhabitants, said to be descended from Portuguese stranded there three centuries ago after a shipwreck, do indeed have green eyes and faces that are recognisably Iberian.

Medan

Most visitors enter northern Sumatra via **Medan** ❷, a sprawling and crowded city of about 2½ million and with one of the strongest economic growth rates and highest per capita incomes in Indonesia. Once the marshy suburb of a small court centre, Medan developed into a commercial city after the Dutch overran the Deli Sultanate in 1872, and 14 years later, became the regional capital.

Medan has retained architectural gems from its colonial days. The largest concentration of such examples is found along **Jalan Jendral A. Yani** and around **Merdeka Square**: General Post Office, former White Societet (now Bank Negara), Hotel de Boer (now Hotel Dharma Bhakti), Grand Hotel Medan (now the Granada Medan), and the estate offices of Harrison & Crossfield's (now P.T. London Sumatra Indonesia).

Chinese shops line Jalan A. Yani. Here also is the mansion of millionaire Tjong A. Fie. Despite enormous wealth acquired from modest beginnings as a horse trader, he died of malnutrition in a concentration camp during the Japanese Occupation. His mausoleum stands in the Pulau Bryan cemetery.

The central market district is just adjacent to the downtown area, and an ever increasing flow of buses, cars, motorcycles and pedicabs converges around the main markets of Pasar Kampung Keling, Pasar Ramas, Pasar Hong Kong and the Central Market.

BELOW: Chinese worshipper at Vihara Gunung Timur temple.

At the southern end of Medan's longest street, Jalan Sisingamangaraja, stands the imposing **Mesjid Raya** (Grand Mosque), built in a rococo style in 1906 to match **Istana Maimoon**, the nearby sultan's palace. Constructed by an Italian architect in 1888, it is the largest mosque in the city. The nearby palace is still the residence of the sultan's descendants and may be visited during the day. Cultural performances can be arranged, such as the colourful Malay and tribal dances of the many peoples of northern Sumatra.

Across the Sungai Deli, on the west side of Medan, is the old European plantation town. Its wide avenues, flanked by huge colonial villas, are planted with flowering trees. The art-deco **Immanuel Protestant Church**, erected in 1921, is on Jalan Diponegoro, while on Jalan Hang Tuah is **Vihara Gunung Timur**, Indonesia's largest Chinese temple. It is said to be such a powerful place that photographs taken within will remain unexposed. Nevertheless, cameras are not permitted. A Hindu temple, **Sri Mariaman**, off Jalan Arifin, is the spiritual centre for Medan's sizeable Indian community.

In south Medan, the **Taman Margasatwa** zoo (open daily; entrance fee) has a varied collection of native Sumatran wildlife, including Sumatran tigers. The **Medan Fair** has permanent cultural and agricultural exhibits, and an amusement park. The **Museum**

Sumatera Utara on Jalan Joni (open Tues–Sun 8.30am–5pm; entrance fee) houses rare Buddhist and Hindu statues, Islamic gravestones and Batak artefacts.

Gunung Leuser National Park

North-west from Medan, or some three hours by road, a narrow road winds up the Alas River Valley to **Gunung Leuser National Park**, an 8,000-sq km (5,000-sq mile) park covered in dense jungle that is home to elephants, rhinos, sun bears, tigers, 500 bird species and orangutan. Surrounding sputtering **Gunung Leuser**, at 3,404 metres (11,167 ft) high and Sumatra's second-highest peak, the park reaches all the way to the west coast and is probably one of the most accessible in Indonesia.

On the eastern edge of the Mount Leuser reserve is **Bukit Lawang**, where the **Bohorok Orangutan Rehabilitation Centre** is located. Established in 1973, the center takes in orangutan that have been kept as pets and trains them – in the skills of tree climbing, nest building and food foraging – to become self sufficient in the wild. So far, more than 200 of these primates have been successfully returned to their natural habitat.

A 1-hour hike through the jungle brings you to the platforms used for early-morning and afternoon feeding of orangutan. Permits are required from the PHPA office (take a photocopy of your passport with you). The well-run Bukit Lawang station provides comfortable lodging, decent food along with a superb visitor centre complete with slide shows and information concerning local wildlife. The centre also arranges treks to Mount Leuser, ranging from a couple of hours to several days. This type of trekking through jungle is not for the uninitiated: leeches, malaria and protection from dampness is a major concern.

Map on page 173

TIP

In November 2003, a flash flood swept through Bukit Lawang, levelling the village. The Bohorok Orangutan Rehabilitation Centre is currently closed and tourists are advised not to visit for the time being. The future of the center is unclear. For more information see www.sumatranorangutan.org.

BELOW: orangutan and gamekeeper at Bohorok.

Marco Polo, the renowned 13th-century explorer, lingered in Sumatra for months waiting for the winds to change before sailing on. His writings acknowledge a fear of exploring the area because of the headhunting Batak.

BELOW:
Batak architecture overlooking Danau Toba.

The park's centre in **Kutacane**, situated in the heart of the Alas Valley, a 3–4 day hike north, is the jumping off point for white-water rafting on the Sungai Alas and the base camp for other activities in the national park, which is also reachable in 6–8 hours from Medan.

Medan to Danau Toba

The main route from Medan to **Danau Toba** ❸ (Lake Toba) runs east and south along the coast through the market towns of Tebingtinggi and Pematangsiantar. Side roads along the first 50 km (30 miles) offer access to fine beaches such as **Cermin** and **Sialangbuah**, renowned for its mudskipper amphibians that swim like fish and climb trees.

Pematangsiantar, 130 km (80 miles) from Medan, is the second-largest city in North Sumatra. This cool highland rubber and palm-oil centre is notable for its **Museum Simalungun** Ⓐ (open daily; entrance fee) on Jalan Ahmand Yani, which contains an excellent display of Batak artefacts including *pustaha laklad* which are bark-leafed books containing sacred formulas in Batak script used by ancient shamans. From here, continue west to Prapat and Lake Toba.

A longer, more westerly Medan–Prapat route runs through the hill resort and market town of **Berastagi** – famous for its Dutch-built villas and cool climate – and the Karo Batak highlands. Only a short bus trip from **Kabanjahe** is a spectacular viewpoint near the northern tip of Danau Toba that overlooks the remote **Tongging Valley** and **Sipisopiso Waterfall**. In the surrounding area are the traditional Karo Batak villages of **Barus Jahe** and the area's most popular village, **Lingga**, with its massive, pyramid-roofed *rumah adat* (traditional clan houses), some over 250 years old. A lucky visitor might witness a Karo Batak wedding or

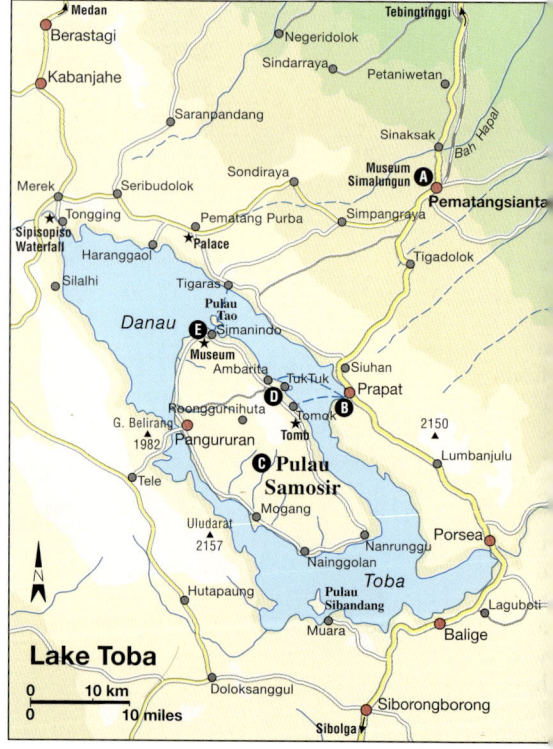

rice harvest festival. From here, the road skirts Toba's eastern shore, passes through the Monday-market village of Haranggaol, and continues to Prapat.

The Batak, one of the great highland peoples of Sumatra, inhabit a fertile volcanic plateau, south of Medan, that covers much of northern Central Sumatra. In the middle lies the lovely Danau Toba, a vast crater lake containing the lush Samosir island, (nearly the size of Singapore). Danau Toba, the result of a great prehistoric eruption, is today one of the highest (900 metres/2,900 ft) and deepest lakes (450 metres/1,480 ft) on earth.

More than 3 million members of six distinct Batak tribes make their homes in the high country, which stretches 500 km (300 miles) north-south and 150 km (90 miles) east-west around Lake Toba. Each of these groups – the Toba, Karo, Pakpak, Simalungun, Angkola and Mandailing Batak – has its own dialect, customs and architectural style.

The Batak migrated from the Himalayan foothills of upper Burma and Thailand over 1,500 years ago, settling in these mountains so similar to their ancestral homelands. Contact with coastal peoples led to the adoption of wet-rice agriculture, the plow and water buffalo, cotton and the spinning wheel, Sanskrit vocabulary and writing, and a pantheistic religion.

Not primitive after all

Wedged between two fervently Muslim peoples, the Minangkabau and the Acehnese, the Batak somehow remained isolated, animistic and cannibalistic until the middle of the 19th century, when German and Dutch missionaries converted many to a mystical sort of Christianity. Northern Batak are largely Protestant Christians, while southern Batak, especially the Mandailing, are Muslim. But traditional *adat* and bygone customs are still practised. Cemeteries display stone sculptures of dead ancestors, shamans communicate with spirits, and priests consult astrological tables to make decisions for their clans.

When first discovered by the Dutch, the Batak were viewed as primitive cannibals isolated for centuries from the rest of the world. They seemed to be constantly warring with their neighbours; headhunting and cannibalism were common. But the Batak were anything but primitive. In fact, they were sophisticated and settled agriculturalists, possessing elaborate crafts, calendars and cosmological texts written in an Indic alphabet. Buddhist stupas and statues dating from between the 11th–14th centuries, and perhaps even earlier, have been discovered on the southern edges of the plateau. It appeared that the Batak were in close contact with the ancient Hindu empires of Sumatra and Java.

As with the Minang and other highland Indonesian tribes, Batak houses are massive multi-family wooden dwellings raised on stilts, with tall thatched roofs that recall the shape of a boat or a sail. Typically, dwellings are about 18 metres (60 ft) long. Built with rope and wooden pegs, without nails, these sturdy structures have withstood a century of wear. Corrugated iron is increasingly used for the roofs, requiring less-frequent replacement. Mosaics and woodcarvings of mystical

Maps:
Area 173
Site 176

Traditional Batak houses are built on stilts and have thatched roofs which resemble the shape of a boat.

BELOW: Batak woman winnowing rice grains.

Batak people are skilled musicians and famous for their emotive and powerful singing of Lutheran hymns. Apart from their gongs and drums, there is also a two-stringed mandolin and a wind instrument that sounds like a clarinet.

BELOW: sunset paddle over Danau Toba to Samosir island.

patterns and mythical creatures decorate gable ends. Between 10 and 12 families live in separate areas surrounding a central corridor and four fireplaces, where people work, play, cook and visit.

A Batak *marga* (clan) consists of several *huta* (communities) tracing descent from a single male ancestor. Kinship and clan loyalties are especially strong – in some cases fiercely defended – and weddings and funerals can draw kinsfolk in the thousands. Genealogies, some of which go back five centuries, are carefully kept as they determine status in personal relations and formal ceremonies.

Samosir island

Around 170 km (110 miles) from Medan, on the eastern shore of Danau Toba is **Prapat** ❺. A tourist resort since colonial times, today it offers deluxe hotels, golf courses, watersports and a refreshingly brisk climate. Prapat is nestled on the lake's eastern shore, and is a favourite weekend getaway for Medan residents. For most visitors, Batak sights are the main attractions.

The best place to experience Danau Toba's spell is **Samosir** ❻, a 1,000-sq km (380-sq mile) island located near the centre of the lake. Boats depart Prapat for Samosir daily, taking visitors directly to the dozens of *losmen* accommodations scattered in Tomok, Ambarita and on the Tuk Tuk peninsula.

Most lakeside *losmen* have both electricity and hot water, and visitors do not lack for comfortable accommodations. Samosir is regarded as the original home of the Batak in Sumatra, and the Toba Batak, the "purest" Batak tribe.

The main entry point for boats from Prapat is **Tomok**, a 30-minute ride across quiet water. The carved boat-like tomb of animistic King Sidabutar is here. In an enclosure opposite the tomb are ritual statues of a buffalo sacrifice. A small museum in the royal house nearby is kept by a dignified old aristocrat. At the end of an avenue of souvenir booths leading from the jetty are dozens of stands selling *kain ulos* (a beautiful woven fabric), two-stringed mandolins, ornate woodcarvings, Batak calendars and many other items of cultural interest.

Tuk Tuk ❼ is a tourist village composed largely of small hotels. On the peninsula is a new community hall for Batak dances and a few traditional houses, as well as inexpensive *losmen*. With the arrival of Christianity on Samosir in 1848, Toba Batak took enthusiastically to Lutheran hymnals. Sunday church services are fine entertainment, though there are many other opportunities to hear *ture ture* (tribal ballads) in village *warung* (cafés).

Grisly breakfast

Ambarita, an hour's walk from Tuk Tuk, has three megalithic complexes. The first is just up from the jetty and is notable for its 300-year-old stone seats and the tomb of Laga Siallagan, the first *raja* of Ambarita. If an enemy was captured in Ambarita, neighbouring *raja* were invited to this first hilltop complex for an initial conference, before moving on to the second, a cluster of stone chairs where the fate of the prisoner was decided. The third complex is located south of Ambarita and includes a unique breakfast table. Here, the prisoner was beaten to death,

decapitated and chopped up on a flat stone, cooked with buffalo meat, and eaten by the *raja*, who washed his meal down with blood.

Simanindo E, at Samosir's northern tip and a half-day walk from Tuk Tuk, is 16 km (10 miles) from Ambarita. Ferries run to Simanindo from Tigaras on the eastern shore north of Prapat. The village has a huge former king's house, which has been restored and is now a traditional Batak **museum**. Look for the buffalo horns in front, one for each generation. A 10-minute boat ride off Simanindo is little **Tao** island, where a few tiny bungalows offer escape to those who find even Samosir hectic.

Although **Pangururan**, on Samosir's west coast, can be reached in half a day by the coastal path from Simanindo, a hike across the island's forested central plateau offers unforgettable views. From Tomok, one can climb past the king's tomb to the plateau above in about 3 hours. Pangururan is another 13 km (8 miles) beyond and can be reached in less than 10 hours. Stay the night at one of the villages before pressing on to Ronggurnihuta and its swimming lake. It may be necessary to frequently ask directions from locals. In the wet season, this climb is extremely muddy and slippery. It is easier to take a ferry to Pangururan and then hike back to Tuk Tuk.

Pangururan lies close to the Sumatran mainland and is connected by a short stone bridge. Its main attraction is an hour's walk away – the *air panas*, or hot springs, halfway up the hill which command a fine view of the lake. Every Sunday, a round-island cruise lasting most of the day departs from several villages, stopping at many of the islands and villages. Or take a stroll along the island's only road and listen to the glorious hymns at the many churches, an uplifting way to spend the morning. ❑

Map on page 176

BELOW: Ambarita village was once the scene of grisly beheadings.

WEST SUMATRA

This is Minangkabau territory, a lush wonderland of flora and fauna, amid which a unique people live by a matrilineal social structure that runs counter to most other cultures of the world

The terrain of West Sumatra with its fertile valleys, lush rainforests and majestic peaks offer some of the most spectacular landscape in all of Sumatra. It is dominated by Bukit Barisan, a mountain range that is home to the island's highest peak, Gunung Kerinci. The country's largest national park, Kerinci Seblat, spreading over 345 sq km (210 sq miles), is here too. The region is also graced with two large crater lakes while just off the west coast seaboard lie a string of islands where the inhabitants existed in isolation for centuries.

The pristine environs are rich with wildlife and unique flora. While the attractions are limitless, the number one destination remains the Minang Highlands, home to the Minangkabau people – who despite their staunch Islamic devotion, make up the largest matrilineal society on earth. Property and wealth are inherited through the female line, and both men and women trace their lineage through their mothers and retain loyalty to the clan houses of their grandmothers.

The distinctive traditional *rumah gadang* (clan house) of the Minangkabau dot the countryside of the highlands, with upturned rooflines that resemble the horns of a water buffalo. (See Minangkabau feature on page 189.)

LEFT AND BELOW: both the headdress and the architecture of the Minangkabau people are inspired by the horns of the buffalo.

It all started with two buffaloes

Tradition has it that the Minangkabau derived their name – *minang* (victory) and *kabau* (buffalo) – from an ancient battle between the two water buffaloes. When the Javanese arrived ready for battle one day, the people of Sumatra tried to avoid bloodshed by proposing a contest between two water buffaloes. The Javanese agreed and brought to the arena a strong male water buffalo, while the Sumatrans entered an infant nursing calf that had been starved for days and had spikes affixed to its horns. The small calf quickly went in search of milk only to impale the underside of the large animal and bring about its death. The Javanese returned home and left the Minangkabau in peace.

The Minangkabau are also skilled rice farmers and craftsmen, and savvy merchants. Their business skills are evident in the numerous Padang restaurants found across the country. And because of their high rate of literacy and formidable managerial skills, they have played a vital role in Indonesia's political, economic and intellectual development. Many famous Indonesian leaders and writers have been of Minang descent, including two former prime ministers.

Padang

The capital of and gateway to West Sumatra is Padang ④, a thriving commercial centre. It is the island's third largest city and the fastest growing, with a population of more than 500,000, 90 percent of

Sumatra once produced half of the world's pepper output.

BELOW: typical spicy Padang-style *dishes*.

whom are ethnic Minangkabau. It is home to the largest seaport on the western coast, **Teluk Bayur**, located 6 km (4½ miles) south of the city centre. The harbour came into existence in the 18th century after the discovery of gold in the highlands and to accommodate the lucrative pepper trade. At one time, Sumatra supplied over half of the world's pepper needs. Today, the busy seaport loads ships with cargoes of coffee, tea, cinnamon, coal and wood.

Most travellers regard Padang as a stopover to the Minang Highlands or west coast islands. But the city does have some semblance of old-world charm, in the Dutch-built colonial homes and shophouses lining the wide avenues in the area around **Kampung Cina** (Chinatown) and the **Pasar Raya** (Central Market) area. Best explored by walking or by horse-drawn cart, the route starts at **Jalan Hiligoo** and continues south along **Jalan Pondak** and onto **Jalan Niaga** to the old colonial waterfront. Here, both banks of the Sungai Muara are filled with hand-painted fishing boats and ferries. Cross over for a view of the Chinese cemetery before proceeding 4 km (2½ miles) south to the fishing village of **Air Manis**.

This city offers few sights other than the **Museum Adityawarman** (open daily; entrance fee) which houses Minangkabau artefacts in a traditional *rumah gadang*. Regular cultural dance performances take place nearby. (Check the schedule with the tourist office or museum.) In the evening, head to the waterfront for a spicy Padang meal, cool ocean breezes and a view of the sunset over the Indian Ocean.

Bukittinggi

A 3-hour ride from Padang through the lush tropical Anai Valley delivers you to the picturesque hill-top town of **Bukittinggi** ❺, the heart of Minangkabau culture. Blessed with a friendly people, a relaxed atmosphere and cool mountain air, Bukittinggi is the best base for visiting the surrounding Minang Highlands.

Bukittinggi, which means "Tall Hill", stands at 930 metres (3,050 ft) and is surrounded by the volcanic peaks of Gunung Agam, Gunung Singgalang and Gunung Merapi. It is a pleasant town to stroll through. The highly-educated townsfolk, who have the highest literacy rate in the nation, are friendly and eager to practise their English. The cool mountain air also enhances touring on foot. In the centre of town, a clock tower with a stylised roof stands as the city's landmark; nearby is the busy **Pasar Raya** (Central Market).

Taman Dundo Kanduang Ⓐ (Rumah Adat Baandjuang Museum; open daily 7.30am–5pm; entrance fee), a 140-year-old *rumah gadang*, marks the city's highest point. Exhibits include wedding and dance costumes, musical instruments, weaponry and other cultural artefacts.

Crossing a foot bridge takes you to the remains of **Benteng de Kock**, built by the Dutch in 1825. The fortress itself does not hold much interest, but it provides a good vantage point to view farmland and the smouldering **Gunung Merapi** (2,891 metres/9,484 ft) and **Ngarai Sianok Canyon** Ⓑ.

Better views of the spectacular canyon, sometimes referred to as the Grand Canyon of Indonesia, can be had at the lookout point in Panorama Park, a favourite leisure spot for locals. A pleasant hike through the 4-km (2½-mile) canyon is possible along a footpath that starts through rice fields. At the half-way point is a bridge; head up a flight of steps (slippery in the rainy season) to the silversmith village **Kota Gadang** Ⓒ. Here, delicate silver filigree jewellery and hand-embroidered shawls (based on Flemish laces) are made. From here, you can take public transport back to Bukittinggi.

Maps:
Area 173
City 184

BELOW: Bukittinggi is ringed by lofty volcanic peaks.

Indonesia has the largest number of endangered species in the world. Increasingly, local activist groups are forcing the government to crack down on the illegal trade of animals and birds.

A day trip north

An easy 12 km (7½ miles) north of Bukittinggi is the 3,100-hectare (750-acre) **Rimba Panti Nature Reserve**, which contains the **Rafflesia Sanctuary D**, named for the world's largest flower, which can grow up to a metre (3 ft) in diameter. The foul-smelling *Rafflesia arnoldii* only blooms between August and September. It may be necessary to hike over muddy paths in search of the bloom.

Continuing north another 15 km (9 miles) takes you to **Ngalau Kamang**, a limestone cave with stalactites and stalagmites. It also houses a small lake. **Payakumbuh**, 40 km (25 miles) east, is the gateway to the cliffs and waterfalls of **Harau Canyon E**, a lush reserve surrounded by 100-metre (330-ft) high granite walls and home to monkeys, deer, honey bears, leopards and tigers. To get there from the main highway, head north past Payakumbuh for 10 km (6 miles) to the village of Lamaksari. Turn left and proceed for another 3 km (2 miles). Permits are sold at the entrance.

Heading west and south

Heading west from Bukittinggi brings you to the deep crater lake, **Danau Maninjau F**, renowned for its serenity and beauty. There is a wide range of accommodation and eateries there, along with canoes and motorboats for hire. For a day trip, the lake can reached within 2 hours by bus from Bukittinggi. Even better, spend a few days relaxing and swimming in the cool, clear water. From the lookout point of Embun Pagi, the road winds and zigzags an amazing 44 turns before arriving at the lake.

Just 12 km (7½ miles) south of Bukittinggi is the weavers' village, **Pandai Sikat G**. Here, weaving has been a major business since the late 18th century.

BELOW: a deer does a double take at Harau Canyon.

Women and girls create by hand *kain songket* (cotton or silk base worked through with heavy gold or silver threads). These beautiful textiles make up the traditional attire of *sarong*, shoulder band and headcloth. The rich *kain songket* are popular with Jakarta women for formal events. Good *sarong* can be expensive and are sometimes just rented for the evening.

Continue south-east to the plains of **Tanah Datar**, where the ancient Minangkabau kingdom existed for half a millennium before succumbing in the Paderi wars of the early 1800s. The area has the finest examples of traditional Minangkabau architecture: *rumah gadang* with roofs turned up to resemble the horns of a water buffalo. The first stop in the village of **Batipuh** ❸ is the traditional *surau* or men's house, built entirely of wood in the Koto Piliang style.

A side road from here, heading east for 5 km (3 miles) and skirting Gunung Merapi, delivers you to the village of **Pariangan** ❹, believed to be the original first village of the Minangkabau. Set in a beautiful valley, the village has steps leading to the traditional clan houses and a royal tomb. Take a leisurely stroll here and view one of the last *surau* of its kind still in use. Back on the main road, the village of **Tabek** has fine examples of traditional clan houses and the oldest building in West Sumatra.

Continuing east, the area between Bukittinggi and Batusangkar is arguably among the most scenic. Fertile lands grow many varieties of fruits and vegetables, as well as irrigated highland rice. Some 20 km (12 miles) east of Padangpanjang is **Batusangkar** ❺, once a residence of the Minangkabau kings. Today, the main attraction is the reconstructed royal palace, with ornately-carved and brightly-painted wooden panels. South from Batipuh is the lovely **Danau Singkarak** ❻, larger than Danau Maninjau and easily accessible by rail or

Map on page 184

TIP

West Sumatra is a good place to buy exquisite *songket* cloth – gold and silver brocade on silk or cotton. You will see many Minangkabau women dressed in traditional outfits made from *songket*.

BELOW: lone fisherman on Danau Maninjau.

road, though not as developed, and **Solok**, a mountain town famous for its picturesque high-roofed houses and woodcarvings.

Kerinci Seblat National Park

About 10 hours south of Padang is Indonesia's largest park, **Kerinci Seblat National Park**, which covers an amazing 1.4-million hectare (3.5-million acre) stretch of jungle and mountains. It is dominated by the dormant volcanic cone of **Gunung Kerinci** that rises 3,800 metres (12,500 ft), making it Indonesia's second-highest peak after Gunung Puncak Jaya in Irian Jaya. Travelling along the Trans-Sumatran Highway, turn off the coast road at Tapan and proceed inland (in a four-wheel-drive vehicle) to **Sungaipenuh**, the main town at the heart of the reserve, where limited lodgings are available.

Footpaths lead in all directions from here to **Gunung Tujuh** and its beautiful crater lake; to the high-altitude marsh-surrounding **Danau Bentu** (Lake Bentu); and to the wild rainforests around Gunung Seblat, the last such woodlands in southern Sumatra. Here, elephants, rhinos, tigers, tapirs, leopards and sun bears still roam. There are no orangutan, but occasionally, sightings have been reported of the mysterious *orang pendek*, a hairy, squat "man", and the mythical *cigau*, an animal that is half-lion and half-tiger.

West coast islands

Running parallel to Sumatra's west coast, about 100 km (60 miles) offshore, is a string of ancient islands – peaks of an undersea non-volcanic ridge separated from mainland Sumatra by a deep trench. Simeulue, Nias, the Mentawai group, and Enggano were first "discovered" in the 17th century by the Dutch. In the

One of the best, and most novel, ways of getting around in the towns of Sumatra is by dokar, or horse-drawn cart.

BELOW: surfing in Nias island is top-class.

19th century, missionaries arrived, and today 80 percent of the islanders are Christian but still retain strong animistic beliefs. The most-visited island, Nias, is famous for its stone jumping rituals. Travelling from Medan or Padang will require an overnight's stay in **Sibolga** ❻.

Nias island

There are daily flights, which are provided by the Merpati and SMAC charter airlines, from Medan to Gunung Sitoli on **Nias** ❼ island. Or travel more leisurely by ferry. Private ferries are available while the government-owned PELNI ferry operates a twice-weekly service from Sibolga to Gunung Sitoli.

The main points of interest – the traditional villages and surfing beaches (considered to have the best surf breaks in the world) – are located in the south, a 4- to 7-hour journey on poor roads. Lodgings are simple *losmen* or stilted huts on the beach in **Lagundi**. Recently, a new luxury resort opened and there are plans for further development.

Nias island, the largest of the west coast islands at 100 km (60 miles) long by 50 km (30 miles) wide, is home to one of Southeast Asia's most unusual ancient cultures. The Niasan culture revolves around stone: in architectural style, stone sculptures and rituals. Traditional dances are still performed, mostly at the request of paying tourists. *Fahombe* is the most memorable: acrobatic Niasan tribesmen leap feet first over stone columns several metres high. *Tutotolo* is a warrior dance performed by young men leaping in combat.

Niasan villages are veritable fortresses, with great stone-paved central "runways". Stilt houses stand in parallel rows on hillsides, shielded by a bamboo barricade from foreign attack. Northern Nias, raided by Acehnese slave traders for centuries, has few cultural remnants, although the capital, Gunung Sitoli, is found here. The remote centre of the island holds cultural interest however. Amid jungle are the ruins of abandoned villages with huge *menhir*, single standing stones.

Southern villages

All of the major tourist attractions are located in southern Nias. **Telukdalem** is the largest city and offers simple *losmen*. Most visitors head for the beautiful white-sand beaches and aquamarine waves of **Lagundi**, proclaimed to be one of the best surf spots in the world. Here, simple *losmen* or stilted beach huts and a resort offering bungalow accommodation are available.

The attractions of southern Nias begin with **Bawomataluwo**, 15 km (9 miles) from Telukdalem, a village turned touristy because of its easy accessibility. Built more than 100 years ago on a summit in protection from Dutch attacks, it is now reachable by a wide stone staircase of 480 steps along a stone-paved alley between two rows of houses. The central "square" is the venue for stone-jumping performances, while nearby is the ornate chief's house. There are stone statues and around 300 megaliths.

Hillisimaetano village was built in the past 70 years, a quiet village where the livelihood of raising chickens and pigs goes on at a traditional pace. All 140 traditional houses in the village face the chief's

The best surfing in Nias takes place from June to October. Sorake beach in fact holds a leg of the World Qualifying series in June/July each year.

BELOW:
a stone-leaping Nias tribesman.

Map on page 173

house located in the centre. **Gomo Lahusa** (40 km, or 24 miles, north-east of Teluk Dalem) and **Gomo** are both worth a visit to view fine old *menhir* stones.

Note: An expedition to Nias island is for the experienced traveller. Travel is rough, and lodgings and food are basic. Malaria and cholera are widespread, so exercise caution.

Siberut island

The Mentawai chain of non-volcanic islands runs parallel to the west coast of Sumatra. **Siberut** ❽, the largest and most visited of the group, is covered in dense tropical rainforest with isolated farming settlements. Until a short time ago, the people lived by archaic traditions.

Siberut island measures about 110 km by 50 km (70 miles by 30 miles); the port of entry is in the south at Muara Siberut, reached by ferry from Padang. There are no hotels or *losmen* and travellers have to rely on the generosity of locals. The main attraction is the trek inland to visit remote villages where people live in traditional longhouses. **Rodok**, a 4- to 5-hour boat ride away, is a government village. Another 2 hours' journey brings you to **Madobat**. Both are ideal locations from which to begin a trek inland.

The people of the interior live in small villages or in *uma* (longhouses) and are well-known for the tattoos they incise over large sections of their bodies, and for their *puliajiat* rituals which purify houses in order to ensure harmony.

Siberut is home to a unique collection of flora and fauna. In no other part of the world is there such a variety of animals within such a small area, most notably primates such as monkeys. There are also tree squirrels, civets, flying squirrels, gibbons and langur. ❑

TIP

In remote inland villages on Siberut island, the preferred "currency" is barter, particularly food and tobacco.

BELOW: Nias warrior in ceremonial garb.

The Matrilineal Minangkabau

The fertile highlands of West Sumatra are home to one of Indonesia's most interesting ethnic groups, the Minangkabau. With a reputation for being intellectuals, Minangkabau men feature prominently in the national government. They are also known for their keen business sense. All over Indonesia are restaurants run by Minangkabau men who serve up spicy Padang food.

However, what makes the Minangkabau so interesting is that while they are devout Muslims, they also belong to a matrilineal society, tracing social identity and inheritance through the female line. In fact, the Minangkabau are one of the few remaining matrilineal societies that still exist in the modern world.

Minangkabau can trace their descent to a *rumah gadang* (clan house), to which they pledge allegiance and maintain a social obligation to throughout their lives. Each *rumah gadang* has descendants who can be traced back to a single grandmother.

All valuable property, land and house are owned in common by the clan and cannot be sold without group consent. The leaders are the grandmother and all of her female heirs, including her eldest brother. The men are involved in the management of the communal property, but it is the women who maintain the rights of use; this includes land ownership. Minangkabau women thus have a high economic status in society.

When a woman marries, she pays a groom price to her husband's female family members. After the wedding, the man goes to "visit" his wife in her home, but in the morning, he returns to the home of his mother to work the fields and to raise his sisters' children. His nieces and nephews are his responsibility; his own children are in turn raised by his wife's brothers.

Men spend most of their time in the fields, while young boys spend their nights in the *surau*, an Islamic study hall. Young men are encouraged to travel, in what is known as *merantau* ("to know about being without"), to seek their fortunes and experience the world. This rite of passage has enabled the development of keen trading skills and an entrepreneurial spirit. When the seasoned wayfarer returns home with his wealth, he is deemed ready for marriage.

Households are the domain of the women, while husbands, sons and brothers live elsewhere. The women are actively involved in the day-to-day affairs of the longhouse. The men travel but their hearts are always with the village. Money is sent home for the building of mosques, ceremonies and for the maintenance of the family's longhouse that remains a source of cultural pride.

The longhouse is a large wooden rectangular structure with a roof that resembles buffalo horns. Elaborately-carved exterior panels are the pride of local woodcarvers. Other examples of the tribe's excellent craftsmanship are beautiful hand-woven *kain songket* textiles, fine silver filigree jewellery, lively music and unique *silat* dance, which combines martial arts movements with dance. ❑

RIGHT: Minangkabau women believe in taking the bull by the horns.

South Sumatra and Riau

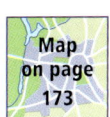

South from oil-town Palembang, Indonesia's richest city, is Way Kambas National Park, where Sumatran elephants go to school. On Bintan island, a venerable temple rests in a giant banyan tree

South Sumatra is made up of the provinces of Lampung, Bengkulu, Jambi and the Riau archipelago. Nearly all of Jambi and the eastern two-thirds of Lampung is made up of broad alluvial lowlands no more than 30 metres (100 ft) above sea level. The entire area is drained by numerous meandering rivers, including the Sungai Batanghari, navigable for nearly 500 km (300 miles) inland, and the Musi, Sumatra's longest river. Western Lampung province is mountainous, rising to volcanic peaks of more than 3,000 metres (10,000 ft) before dropping sharply to the Indian Ocean at the former British colonial outpost of Bengkulu. Sitting off the eastern coast are the Riau and Lingga island groups, the former being developed as part of a "golden triangle" project between Indonesia, Singapore and Malaysia.

Jambi

Jambi ❾, the site of the ancient Melayu Kingdom, is today a modern city. It is home to around 250,000 people of mixed heritage, with a growing economy based on logging, rubber, palm oil, coffee and tea exports. The surrounding forests are home to the Kubu people, the original inhabitants of the area who live as hunters and gatherers. The government tried to bring them into the 20th century, only to have them reject the lifestyle and return to the forest. Clad in loincloths, they can sometimes be seen walking along the roadside.

Exploration of the city starts along the river where a large number of people live on floating rafts or in houses built on stilts over the Sungai Batanghari. You can walk or ride on a *dokar* (horse-drawn cart), and visit the **Pasar Raya** (Central Market).

The Hindu temple complex of **Candi Muara**, 25 km (15 miles) north-east of the city, is an hour by car or 30 minutes by speedboat. Reachable by four-wheel drive along the Sungai Sengering are the 10 stalactite **Tiangko Caves**. From Jambi to Kerinci-Seblat National Park *(see page 186)* is a distance of 500 km (300 miles), accessible also by four-wheel drive.

Palembang

The booming oil town of **Palembang** ❿ is the second-largest city in Sumatra, located on the banks of the Sungai Musi, about 200 km (125 miles) from the coast. A major port for well over 1,200 years, Palembang, up until the 13th century, was the major focus of trade in Indonesia and a great international bazaar. It was also a spiritual centre where Mahayana Buddhist monks studied and translated texts.

LEFT: majestic Sumatran elephant at Way Kambas National Park.
BELOW: oil refinery near Palembang.

TIP

In Palembang, Jalan Sudirman is the best street for shopping, while Jalan Veteran is the best for dining.

Palembang was nurtured during the Dutch era as a riverine entrepôt, servicing the tin mines on Bangka island. Rubber and coffee plantations contribute to the city's economy today, but it is oil that has turned it into Indonesia's richest city. There is a US$200-million petrochemical complex at **Plaju** and a refinery with a daily capacity of 75,000 barrels at **Sungaigerong**.

Palembang has houses and shops raised on piles above the Musi, with river merchants plying their trade from boats. The region produces fine woven fabrics and has unique dances, including the Gending Srivijaya, dating from the 7th century. The **Museum Rumah Bari** (open Tues–Sat 8am–4pm; Sun 8am–noon; closed Mon; entrance fee), occupying several buildings, contains important megalithic statuary, Hindu and Buddhist sculptures, primitive ethnic crafts, weaponry and Chinese porcelain.

West of Palembang is **Lahat**, gateway to the Pasemah Highlands. Dotting this mountain plateau are carved megaliths, tombs, pillars and other stone ruins thought to date from about AD 100. These are considered the best examples of prehistoric stone sculptures in Indonesia. Oddly-shaped rocks have been fashioned into figures of armed warriors either riding elephants, wrestling buffaloes or fighting snakes. There are dolmens, sanctuaries, collared paintings and other works of art in the area of volcanic **Gunung Dempo**.

Bengkulu

The seaport town **Bengkulu** ⓫, formerly known as Bencoolen, was founded in 1685 by the British. **Benteng Marlborough** was constructed in 1762 as a castle with a gate house that contains old gravestones with English inscriptions. Sir Thomas Stamford Raffles, who later founded Singapore, was lieutenant-

BELOW: Palembang couple in their wedding finery.

governor of Bengkulu from 1818 to 1823. He introduced coffee and sugar cultivation, established schools and fought a royal decision to hand control of Sumatra over to the Dutch in 1824. His scientific zeal (as first president of the Zoological Society of London) led to the naming of the giant Rafflesia flower in his honour. This can be found at the **Dendam Taksuda Botanical Gardens**.

Bandar Lampung

Crossing the Sunda Strait from West Java, the Sumatran port of entry is **Bakauhuni**, the harbour for **Bandar Lampung** ⑫. The ferry passes within view of **Anak Krakatau**, which sits on the site of the former enormous island volcano of Krakatau that erupted in 1883, killing 30,000 people and altering global climate for a year *(see also page 133)*.

Revitalise yourself with a soak in hot sulphur springs at **Kalianda**, 38 km (23 miles) north of the ferry terminal. Nearby are the remains of an old Dutch fort. The **Museum Provincial Lampung** on Jalan Teuku Umar (open daily; entrance fee) has Chinese ceramics, Dongson bronze kettledrums, *kain tapis* (handwoven ceremonial cloth) and archaeological finds from Labuan Meringgai.

About two-thirds of the residents of central and southern Lampung province are Javanese farmers who migrated here – either voluntarily or government-assisted – to relieve overcrowded conditions on Java. The effectiveness of the policy is debatable: the Javanese still tend to overpopulate the rice land on which they live and work. The South Sumatran railway, which has its terminus at Telukbetung's twin city of **Tanjung Karang**, wends its way north as far as Palembang, with a western branch to Lubuklinggau.

Way Kambas National Park ⑬ comprises estuaries, marshes and open

Map on page 173

If there is one thing you should try while in Indonesia, it is sate. *This is where the real McCoy comes from.*

BELOW: Benteng Marlborough in Bengkulu.

TIP

Boats can be hired in Canti Village, near Bandar Lampung, to make the choppy 3-hour crossing to Anak Krakatau volcano. Krakatau can also be accessed from West Java, leading to some dispute as to whether it is part of Java or Sumatra.

grassland along the south-east coast and is the best place to see wild elephants. Tigers and wild boars are also plentiful, and birdwatching is a delight.

Conserving the natural riches of this coastal land is an uphill battle. Migrant farmers, loggers, Jakarta-based developers and other entrepreneurs have claimed tens of thousands of hectares of land; three disastrous fires nearly eliminated a substantial forest; and tigers were legally hunted until 1974.

Park authorities in Tanjung Karang can arrange for visitors to take a 4-hour (one-way) boat trip from **Labuhan Meringgi**, 12 km (7 miles) south of the reserve, to the Way Kambus estuary, navigable for 25 km (16 miles) inland from the coast. You can enter the park by car from Tridatu, 10 km (6 miles) north of Jepera and a 2-hour drive from Bandar Lampung and 3 hours from the Java–Sumatra ferry terminal. There is a simple guesthouse at Way Kanan, 13 km (8 miles) past the park entrance. Elephant training classes can be viewed daily at 8am and 3pm.

Strategic Riau archipelago

Between the swampy shores of Sumatra and the Malay Peninsula lies a chain of more than 3,000 small islands. These and the eastern Sumatran lowlands comprise the province of **Riau**, one of the fastest-growing parts of Indonesia in terms of economics, population and tourist expansion.

Pekanbaru ⑭, the provincial capital and the largest city in mainland Riau, is a thriving oil-production centre. This friendly Caltex oil town, with a large foreign population, is a good base for exploring nearby jungle abodes of the durian-loving Sumatran rhinoceros, as well as tigers, elephants and birds. Four hours downriver at **Siak Sri Indrapura Village**, stands a palace that was built in 1723.

BELOW: swanky pool at the Angsana Resort & Spa, Bintan island.

Elsewhere in Riau, fishing and timber are still the mainstays of the local economy. Riau is considered one of the heartlands of Southeast Asia culture and was the centre of Malay civilisation from the 16th to 18th century. Mainland Riau is inhabited by coastal Malays, while island populations include Malays, Bugis Orang Laut (sea gypsies), Chinese, Arabs and Indians. The Orang Laut are renowned seamen in self-imposed exile from their Sulawesi homeland, living aboard wooden *pinisi* sailing boats and trading throughout the archipelago.

Map on page 173

Batam and Bintan islands

While most of Riau remains untouched, change has come swiftly to Batam and Bintan islands. **Batam** 🅕 island has been developed into a major industrial satellite of Singapore and is popular with weekend visitors from there, who come for its golf courses, beaches, duty-free shopping and seafood. Ferries and hydrofoils ply nearly hourly, from sunrise to sundown, to and from Singapore. **Nagoya**, the largest town, has hotels, restaurants and karaoke bars to cater to businessmen and construction workers.

Bintan 🅖 is the largest of all the Riau islands. For years, it remained largely undisturbed, an expanse of jungle, swamp and mountains. But like neighbouring Batam, it is changing fast. The entire northern shore is being developed into a mega resort with dozens of hotels and other tourist facilities. Industrial zones have sprung up like mushrooms.

The energetic **Tanjung Pinang** port town, situated on the south-eastern coast of Bintan, is a quick 2-hour ferry ride from Singapore. The town is also a jumping-off spot to nearby tiny islands as well as the Lingga Archipelago.

Good hotels are available in Tanjung Pinang and attractions include the small but interesting **Museum Riau** situated on Jalan B.G. Katamso in the eastern suburbs. You can catch a speedboat to **Senggarang**, a Chinese village on the far side of the Sungai Riau. Its four shrines include the **Banyan Temple**, a 200-year-old clan house suspended in a giant banyan tree.

Just across from Tanjung Pinang is **Penyengat**, the home base of the sultans of Riau, with a lavish court and royal city that encompassed nearly 10,000 citizens. A book called *Bustanul Katibin*, the first Malay grammar text, was published on Penyengat in 1857, laying the foundation for Bahasa Indonesia, the lingua franca of the entire country.

Just beyond the main ferry pier is the old **Mesjid Sultan**, built in 1818 and the most important place of worship in Riau. A path leads across the island – past the **Istana Raja Ali Marhum** with its faded yellow facade and red-tiled roof – to the southern shore, where there are several ruins. On a hill is the 18th-century **Benteng Bukit Kursi**, one of three forts built as defence against the Dutch.

Trikora beach on Bintan's east coast is a stretch of white sand and turquoise water, with several thatched-roof restaurants and modest accommodations. Spanning 14 km (9 miles) along the north coast is **Pasir Panjang** beach, which has been transformed into the Bintan Beach International Resort – a sprawling complex of deluxe hotels, golf courses and condos. ❑

Both Batam and Bintan islands are easily accessible from Singapore. High-speed catamarans can whisk you to the resort islands in under an hour, and numerous travel agents in Singapore sell room and ferry packages.

BELOW: sunset over Bintan.

BALI

It's been defiled by tourism, some veteran travellers claim. But millions of visitors have found it far from spoiled

The name Bali evokes mystical images which have lured travellers for centuries. Warm and naturally hospitable islanders with quick smiles, the Balinese remain unfazed by continued waves of intruders. Bali's culture is as much a lure to visitors as are its exquisite arts, stunning landscape, beautiful beaches and literally thousands of temples.

Balinese culture has survived intact, despite colonial domination, war-time occupation and unrelenting tourism. The temples and the unique Hindu-Dharma religion have endured earthquakes, volcanic eruptions and the wave of Islam; not to mention divergent cultures and practices brought by foreign tourists. The Balinese accept what they want and ignore the rest, continuing their spirit-filled life.

The Balinese social cohesion traditionally centres on agriculture. Rice cultivation defines the collection of communities that make up Bali. The social structure is cooperative, in everything from preparation for elaborate festivals, to political, economic and social decisions, even solving problems for individual members. The *banjar*, an aggregate of family units, extended family members and neighbours, executes most life activities. The critically important communal *subak* units coordinate shared irrigation water and farming tasks, while the *banjar* organises everything else. Rice, water and religion are the foundations of Balinese life.

Situated almost smack in the middle of the Indonesian archipelago, Bali is approximately 5,620 sq km (2,170 sq miles) in size with a population of approximately 3 million. The international airport is on the island's extreme south, in Badung. One of eight regencies, Badung is the urban and commercial centre. Here, most tourists spend their holidays at the beach, playing and partying, most often in the tourist enclaves of Nusa Dua, Sanur or Kuta/Legian. But even here, despite blatant commercialism, traditional undercurrents remain.

Inland and north – Tabanan, Gianyar and Bangli regencies – the island's contours soften, villages shrink and the culture is more unfettered. Eastward, Klungkung and Karangasem regencies once held Bali's power base. Central Bali is the heart of the artistic community.

Spiritually, culturally and geographically, three volcanic peaks anchor the island: Batur, Batukau and the most sacred Agung, the centre of the Balinese universe. The holy mountains are also the source of water. Bali's northern coast, the regency of Buleleng, is dry and agricultural, growing everything from coffee and cinnamon to grapes. Western Bali – Jembrana and part of Buleleng – is sometimes dry, sometimes lush, but typically ignored by travellers. A national park, refuge of endangered species, graces the west. ❑

PRECEDING PAGES: *kecak* dance performed against the backdrop of Kusamba beach.

SOUTH BALI

Many visitors do not venture beyond the tourist belt of Kuta, Sanur and Nusa Dua. Here, hotels jostle with endless bars, shops and restaurants, and entertainment of every persuasion abounds

Balinese cosmology considers south the most impure direction. Yet southern Bali attracts most travellers, where the infrastructure and commercialism are most developed. While the ambience of Denpasar is that of a city, the mood changes in the tourist centres of Sanur, Nusa Dua and Kuta. Office-block facades give way to signs advertising hotels, tours and shops.

Southern Bali's growth continues to generate endless squabbles about overdevelopment, yet new hotels, restaurants and retail shophouses, *ruko*, proliferate. Bali caters to every imaginable persuasion, whether it means being pampered in a five-star hotel spa or hurtling through the air on the end of a bungy cord. The area's beaches bustle by day and non-stop bar-hopping and dancing after hours can prove frenetic. South Bali is without doubt an intoxicating chameleon.

Throughout the island's history, southern Bali has been the first to welcome or repel outsiders. At Belanjong, at the turn-off to the Raddin Sanur Hotel, an inscription engraved on a short pillar commemorates the victories of Bali's first king Sri Kesari Warmadewa over his enemies in AD 913. In later times, famous priests from Java trod these shores. Empu Kuturan came to Bali in the 10th century and introduced the *meru*, or roofed shrine. The three best-known temples of the area – Pura Sakenan, Pura Luhur Uluwatu and Pura Petitenget at Kerobokan – are associated with the itinerant 16th-century priest Danghyang Nirartha, also known as Pedanda Sakti Wawu Rauh. This eminent teacher brought the concept of the lotus throne, or *padmasana*, for the worship of Sanghyang Widi Wasa, the Balinese Hindu supreme deity.

It was at about this time that Bali's exposure to the West began. Many sailors from Dutch explorer Cornelis de Houtman's fleet were so entranced by the island that they jumped ship to stay forever, beginning a trend that has continued to this day.

LEFT: multi-hued flags at Sanur beach.
BELOW: Denpasar's Lapangan Puputan Memorial.

Denpasar

A growing metropolis, **Denpasar ❶**, originally called Badung, is a busy city of winding alleys, illogical one-way streets, pungent smells, and home to more cars per capita than Jakarta. If your mind has been unwinding on the beach, it may well be wound back up on an excursion into Denpasar. Once a parking spot is located, most of the city's main sights are within walking distance from each other.

Central to the city is **Lapangan Puputan** (Puputan Field or Alun-Alun Puputan), a large, grassy open space commemorating the battle between the *raja* of Badung and the Dutch militia in 1906, when thousands of Balinese warriors, dressed in their finest regalia and armed only with *keris* daggers and spears, hurled

Carved toothy crow head frightens away evil at Denpasar's Pura Jagatnata.

themselves against the line of Dutch soldiers in a heroic sacrifice, dying either by their own hands or by Dutch bullets in ritual suicide known as *puputan* (literally, "end"). Today, the slaughter of the estimated 600 to 2,000 is memorialised by a bronze statue. North of the square is the former governor's residence, where the *raja*'s palace once stood.

Catur Mukha, the great statue with four faces and eight arms at Denpasar's main intersection (at the north-western corner of Taman Puputan), represents Brahma manifested as lord of the four directions.

Museum Bali

East of the square is **Museum Bali** (open Tues–Sun 8am–5pm; entrance fee). Built in the early 1930s by the Dutch, it presents a comprehensive history of Bali's social and cultural development from prehistoric times to the early 20th century. Items are well presented, although no specific dates of origin are given, but knowledgeable English-speaking guides are on hand. The museum is notable for its fine architecture, combining the two principal edifices of Balinese temples (*pura*) and palaces (*puri*): split gate with outer and inner courtyards, and the *kulkul* (wooden signal drum) tower.

The museum is representative of the entire island. The main building, with its wide-pillared verandah, resembles the Karangasem palaces of east Bali, with a porch used by officials in audience with the *raja*. The windowless building to its north reflects the Tabanan palace style of western Bali. The brick building belongs to the northern palace style of Singaraja; inside this **Gedung Buleleng** are beautiful examples of wedding costumes and items used in religious rituals.

Next to the museum is **Pura Jagatnata**, dedicated to Sanghyang Widi Wasa, the supreme god (manifested in Bali's numerous local deities and ancestral spirits). The modern state temple is used for worship every full and new moon. The tall *padmasana*, made of white coral, symbolises universal order. The turtle Bedawangnala and two *naga* serpents represent the foundations of the world, while the throne signifies the cosmic mountain.

BELOW: colourful produce at Pasar Badung.

Denpasar means "north of the market". The centre of town is the **Pasar Badung**, a four-storey building housing Bali's largest traditional market. Locals shop for fruit and vegetables, meat and seafood, clothing, spices, baskets, ritual paraphernalia and everything else. Women wait outside, offering market tours for a negotiable fee, with stops at shops where they earn a commission. Politely decline their assistance and stroll on your own. Across the Tukad Badung canal is **Pasar Kumbasari**, a market with stalls jammed with clothes and handicrafts and small eateries.

There are no grand hotels; rather, Denpasar has numerous small hotels to cater to a largely domestic tourist market. Of historical note is **Hotel Puri Pemecutan**, a palace-turned-hotel (albeit a little shabby) on Jalan Thamrin. Much of it was destroyed in battles with the Dutch at the turn of the 20th century, during which the palace's royalty committed suicide (*puputan*). **Natour Bali Hotel** on Jalan Veteran retains its Dutch colonial charm.

Pura Maospahit, on Jalan Sutomo, is the oldest

temple in the city. It dates from the 14th century, when Majapahit empire emissaries arrived from Java. Extensive earthquake damage early in the 20th century resulted in much of the temple being rebuilt; the section at the back is the only part that has remained unaltered for 600 years.

Denpasar's arts

A permanent exhibition of traditional and contemporary Balinese visual arts is at the **Werdi Budaya Art Centre** (open Tue–Sun 8am–5pm; entrance fee), east of downtown, on Jalan Nusa Indah. Bali's numerous art disciplines are represented at this large complex, including painting, woodcarving, shadow puppetry, silverwork, weaving, dance costumes and even ivory carving. Works by Bali's foreign artists are displayed in the museum.

The art centre was established in 1973 to showcase Balinese culture and includes teaching facilities, a restaurant, craft shop and an outdoor arena for traditional dances. The grounds are also home to the annual Bali Art Festival.

Next to the centre is **Sekolah Tinggi Seni Indonesia** (STSI), the College of Indonesian Arts, founded in 1967. Students study traditional dance, music and puppetry, and classical and contemporary choreography.

For serious study, the **Pusat Dokumentasi** (Documentation Centre) in Renon offers a collection of works in all languages on Balinese life and culture. Documents may not be removed, but can be photocopied on the premises.

Sanur

Local tradition maintained that shipwrecks held bounty from Baruna, god of the sea, and thus anyone had rights to them. In 1904, a Chinese schooner was

The name Walter Spies crops up repeatedly in books on Balinese art. The shy German artist, who settled in Campuhan, Ubud, in 1927, together with Dutch artist Rudolf Bonnet had a profound effect on the development of Balinese painting.

BELOW: battle scene by artist Hendra Gunawan (1918–83) at the Werdi Budaya Art Centre.

TIP

Bali Hyatt, Sanur, is noted for its fabulous gardens, the work of Australian Michael White, aka Made Wijaya, who "jumped ship" and over the decades became a renowned garden developer for hotels in Bali. Garden tours at Bali Hyatt are held on Tuesday and Friday at 10am.

wrecked off the shores of **Sanur** ❷. This breeched a previous treaty between the Balinese and the Dutch, and pillaging shipwrecks was just the excuse the Dutch needed to wage war against the Badung *raja*. Rather than continue fighting against the better-equipped Dutch forces, the king and his entire entourage, dressed in white and carrying daggers, walked straight into Dutch gunfire, in what is known as *puputan* (royal suicide). Only one child survived the massacre.

Sanur became an enclave for artists around the world in the 1930s. By the 1950s, the first cluster of bungalows in Sanur was built, attracting international travellers. The Bali Beach Hotel opened in 1966, built with Japanese reparation money for World War II. When the 10-storey hotel first opened, it was a source of wonder to the Balinese with its running water, electricity and elevators. Bali's only high-rise structure at the time, and something of an eyesore, it was gutted by a mysterious fire in 1993 but was rebuilt and reopened less than one year later as the **Grand Bali Beach Hotel**. It has Bali's first golf course, a rather mundane nine-hole field.

Today, Sanur beach has all levels of accommodation, with access roads lined with shops and restaurants. Amid the development and tourism frenzy, Sanur has managed, remarkably, to retain much of its quaint heritage as a Brahman-dominated village, where trance performances are still staged during local temple festivals. Sanur's seas are calm and shallow, disappearing altogether at low tide, leaving little more than great swathes of sandy mud and coral stretching for hundreds of metres out along the reef. When the tides are high, however, Sanur offers windsurfing and sailing.

One of the few historical sites in Sanur is the home of Belgian painter Jean Le Mayeur de Mepres. He moved to Bali in 1932, where he lived till his death in

BELOW: kite vendor at Sanur beach.

1958. **Museum Le Mayeur** (open Sun–Fri 8am–2pm; entrance fee), just north of Grand Bali Beach Hotel, has gardens full of statues, luxuriant gold and crimson carvings, and Le Mayeur's own paintings, all of which depict his late wife, Ni Polok, a renowned *legong* dancer.

At the southern end of Sanur is the **Pura Belanjong**, notable for the island's oldest example of writing, the Prasasti Belanjong, an inscribed pillar dating from AD 913 and discovered in the early 1930s. The 177-cm (70-inch) tall stone column is not much to look at, but close inspection reveals two forms of writing, ancient Balinese and Sanskrit.

The highly unusual **Pura Segara** temple has mounds of black rock and coral and brightly-painted statues made of coral.

Kuta and surroundings

Few visitors to **Kuta** ❸ pause to consider that in former times it was both a leper colony and slave station with poor soil. Cynics might draw a parallel with the hordes who flock here for the combination of sun, sand, sea and various other s-words. The original Kuta villagers were farmers, fishermen and metalsmiths. At the genesis of mass tourism, they looked askance at foreigners frolicking along the ocean – the Balinese idea of the underworld. But they soon saw there were profits to be made and invited travellers into their homes for clean, simple and cheap accommodation.

For many, Kuta is Bali, while others decry its plunge into rampant commercialism. As long as the pleasure seekers are happy and villagers continue to leave *canang* – little offering trays – at the high-tide mark each day to pacify the spirits, Kuta beach seems to embrace both worlds. Both Balinese and foreign-

Map on page 198

Parasailing at Sanur beach is fun but accidents have been reported in the past.

BELOW: surfboards for rent at Kuta beach.

...ers are found along its golden sands day after day, surfing, sunbathing, strutting and selling. Kuta's surf break is among the best for learners. However, it is said that Kuta's god of the sea claims at least one victim a year here. In reality, the notorious undertow and rip tides claim many lives each year, so be sure to swim in places marked by flags. When one stares out to sea, leaving behind the commercial swirl, the sunset seems just as glorious as always.

Inland from the beach, Kuta is packed with a dazzling array of pubs, bars, souvenir shops, tattoo parlours, travel offices, accommodation and fast-food joints. Street hawkers remain an annoyance in Kuta, despite government efforts to control them. Handicrafts abound in Kuta, the export of which is big business here. Nestled amid it all are a number of superb restaurants, bungalows and even temples, somehow retaining their dignity. Crime has escalated in Kuta, and this once peaceful village is now punctuated by drugs, prostitution and muggings. Don't get too starry-eyed on the dark beach at night.

Kuta's **Tourist Office**, at Jalan Bakung Sari and Jalan Kuta Raya, is open until 8pm. Inside is the Bali Hotel Reservation Service for those without accommodation. **Matahari Department Stores**, in Legian, Kuta and on Jalan Bypass Ngurah Rai, are a great attraction for local and foreign shoppers. The **Kuta Art Market** (undeniably a generous moniker for two long stretches of stalls) sells all the usual things of interest only to tourists. Sharpen your bargaining skills.

South of Kuta, down Jalan Kartika Plaza, quieter **Tuban** village offers a respite from Kuta's frenzy. **Waterbom Park** (open daily 9am–6pm; entrance fee) has water slides, restaurants and spa treatments.

Along Jalan Melasti and north to Jalan Legian, retail shops continue unabated for several kilometres. As the chaos of Kuta evaporates, it is replaced by a more cultivated scene with strong leanings towards New Age spiritualism. **Legian** ❹ may be more sedate than Kuta but don't expect to be completely free of beach hawkers. The area is preferred by Bali's expatriate population and their influence can be seen throughout Legian in boutiques and a number of excellent restaurants, cafés and bars.

Further north is the decidedly hip **Seminyak**. This once distant Kuta suburb now merges with Legian, and is home to exclusive hotels such as The Legian and The Oberoi and trendy beachside restaurants like Ku de Ta and La Luciolla. Seminyak has the same wide sandy beach and thundering surf as Kuta but without the heaving crowds. **Jalan Laksmana** and **Jalan Dhyna Pura** in this area are also fast making a name for themselves: the former has a clutch of hip restaurants and the latter to equally trendy bars and clubs.

Bukit Badung

Aircraft from all parts of the world swoop low over the sea here, bound for **Ngurah Rai International Airport**, attractively designed along Balinese lines. Fixed-price taxis are plentiful, and you will soon be heading out to wherever you are staying past a gigantic statue depicting a mythological battle between a flying hero and his enemy in a chariot.

An exclusive resort area is found along the coast south of **Jimbaran** ❺. Housing hotel bigwigs like

---

Danish trader Mads Lange came to Kuta in 1839 and soon monopolised commodity trading and currency exchange. He died two decades later, perhaps of poisoning. He is buried in a Kuta cemetery where his home and palm oil factory once stood.

BELOW:
a slew of shades for sunseekers.

The Ritz-Carlton, the Four Seasons and the Inter-Continental, all of them face white-sand beaches and are within easy reach of Jimbaran village and its justly celebrated seafood restaurants.

Connected to the mainland by a low, narrow isthmus, the limestone tableland of **Bukit Badung**, a peninsula rising to 200 metres (660 ft) above sea level, is a striking contrast to the lush Bali mainland. Surfaced roads meander across the hill. Vantage spots along the road afford breathtaking northern vistas rising to the peaks of distant volcanoes; an ideal place to catch beautiful sunsets.

A temple of the world

At the western tip of Bukit Badung, where rocky precipices drop almost 100 metres (330 ft) to the ocean, is **Pura Luhur Uluwatu** ❻, 70 metres (230 ft) up on a dramatic promontory. Originally dating from around the 16th century, it is one of the Sad Kahyangan, or Six Temples of the World, revered by all Balinese. The famous Balinese priest Danghyang Nirartha established this temple, and it is said he achieved enlightenment here. The innermost sanctuary, *jeroan*, is off limits to non-worshippers but can be viewed from the side. South of the temple and car park, a panoramic short path leads along the cliff top. Uluwatu beach is a popular surf site but difficult to access.

The road to Uluwatu temple passes the **Garuda Wisnu Kencana** cultural complex, which is an on-going project scheduled to be finalized in 2005 (www.gwk-bali.com). The giant statue of Wisnu riding the *garuda* sunbird will be one of the tallest statues in the world. The complex houses several restaurants, an art museum and a venue for cultural performances.

Nusa Dua ❼, on the east coast of Bukit Badung, is a slightly sterile paradise

Map on page 198

The aim of the Garuda Wisnu Kencana monument is to "symbolise humankind's journey into the new millennium, much as the Statue of Liberty signifies freedom for those arriving in America and the Eiffel Tower is testament to Europe's entry into the Industrial Age."

BELOW:
the surf- and wind-battered coastline of Bukit Badung.

A stone warrior guards the split gate entrance to the swanky resort area of Nusa Dua.

BELOW: Balinese-style swimming pool at Nusa Dua's Hilton resort.

in a ribbon-wrapped package. A purpose-built, luxury hotel enclave, sprawling in the middle of a coconut grove and alongside a white-sand beach, Nusa Dua caters decidedly to the upscale traveller. In many ways, Nusa Dua is thin on local ambience, having been built on unused land in a concerted government effort to prevent tourism from affecting the island's cultural sanctity. A dozen luxury hotels wrap around the beach, among which are several international chains like the Grand Hyatt, Hilton, Sheraton and Meliá. Watersports available here include spectacular parasailing and jetskis. The well-regarded **Bali Golf & Country Club** boasts a championship golf course, with nine holes seaside and nine holes inland. At least seven temples are within Nusa Dua's bounds.

Galeria Nusa Dua is an upscale shopping centre. **Tragia**, outside the estate gates, is a retail complex with souvenir shops, banks, photo developing, a grocery shop and restaurants. Shuttle buses make the rounds to all Nusa Dua hotels and both shopping centres. **Bualu** village, also outside Nusa Dua, has a strip of restaurants serving a range of international and local fare.

Fishing village with five-star hotels

For many years, the fishing village of **Tanjung Benoa** ❽, on a long peninsula off the north-east of Bukit Badung, was overlooked by hotel developers blinded by the obvious potential of Sanur, Kuta and Nusa Dua. The peninsula is now lined with four- and five-star hotels, as well as lower-end accommodation and restaurants. Novotel's Coralia Benoa Beach and Conrad Hotel are leading anchors here. Benoa offers an attractive stretch of white-sand beach which, like Sanur, is susceptible to the tides. A walk north up the peninsula reveals a bustling morning market and a multi-cultural community, evolved from decades as a trading centre, reflected in Chinese and Muslim cemeteries, and Chinese, Muslim and Hindu temples.

A new development between Jimbaran and Nusa Dua, **Pecatu** was launched with the building of Bali Cliff Resort and Nikko Bali Resort & Spa, along the southernmost cliffs. However, the economic crisis in the late 1990s put other hotel projects on hold.

Tanah Lot

One of Bali's most noted sites, in Tabanan just across the boundary of Badung regency, is easily reached from Bali's southern tourist centres. From the Kerobokan junction, turn west towards **Canggu**. Follow the signs to Le Meridien Nirwana Golf & Spa Resort, which sits adjacent to Bali's most famous and most photographed temple, **Pura Tanah Lot** ❾.

Set apart from the land on a stone pedestal carved by incoming tides, Tanah Lot's solitary black towers and tufts of foliage spilling over the cliffs recall the delicacy of a Chinese painting, although the gauntlet of souvenir stalls and hawkers on the temple approach may diminish this image. In caves surrounding the temple dwell striped sacred snakes, discreetly left undisturbed by Balinese. Only worshippers are allowed inside the temple, but visitors get a dramatic view from the adjacent hill, especially at sunset.

Tanah Lot is attributed to the 16th-century priest Danghyang Nirartha. During his travels, Nirartha saw a light emanating from a point on the west coast and came to this spot to meditate. The disciple of a local spiritual leader became fascinated by Nirartha and began to study with him. This angered the local priest, who filled with jealousy, challenged Nirartha. The unflappable Nirartha simply moved his meditation spot into the ocean, and this point became known as Tanah Lot, or "Land in the Sea".

Tabanan and Mengwi

Tabanan and Mengwi were once powerful and warring regencies, until the Dutch conquest of southern Bali in 1906. Unlike the *raja* of Karangasem to the east, the Tabanan *raja* had no agreement with the Dutch and lost rights to his lands, which were then distributed among the councils of individual villages. With their own land, the communities thrived. Together with the other southern regencies, Badung, Gianyar and Tabanan form the island's most prosperous region, an extension of the rice belt.

Tabanan became a separate and powerful kingdom during the 17th century. It has long been home to some of the most admired *gamelan* orchestras and dancers. Tabanan's coast is sprouting tourist resorts, even though its coastal waters are rather rough and dangerous, with little reef as buffer. At the end of every side road to the coast lies a long and deserted, often black sand beach, with surf that sometimes breaks over 3 metres (10 ft) high. The undertow and currents are treacherous, and drownings are common.

In **Kerambitan** ❿, the Tabanan royal family has two palaces – **Puri Anyar** and **Puri Agung** – and showcase their *tektekan gamelan* ensemble of bamboo drums and wooden cow-bells. For a fair amount, anyone can charter a "royal"

Map on page 198

TIP

There are venomous sea-snakes living in the caves and rocks surrounding Pura Tanah Lot – said to be guarding the temple against intruders – so be careful if you cross over. Most people are content with the view from across the beach.

BELOW: spectacular sunset vista of Pura Tanah Lot.

evening, including either a *joget* (flirtation dance accompanied by a bamboo *gamelan*) or a *Calonarang* (trance performance), complete with a dinner. If it is just the surroundings you are interested in, you could rent a room in Puri Anyar.

North from Denpasar and about 6 km (4 miles) south of Mengwi, **Kapal** ⓫ shelters the most important temple in the area, **Pura Sada**, an ancestral sanctuary honouring the deified spirit of Ratu Sakti Jayaningrat, whose identity remains uncertain. The temple's original foundations may be as old as the 12th century, but the temple itself was rebuilt during the 16th century. The oldest of the Mengwi state shrines, Pura Sada was destroyed in the great earthquake of 1917 and restored in 1950.

Mengwi ⓬ principality was, until 1891, the centre of a powerful kingdom dating from the Gelgel dynasty. **Pura Taman Ayun**, founded in the 17th century, has a surrounding moat, giving the impression of a garden sanctuary, explaining the name *taman*, or garden. The temple is a *penyawangan*, or a place to worship other sacred sites. Here are shrines to Bali's mountain peaks of Agung, Batukau and Batur, as well as to Pura Sada mentioned above.

Marga

North from Taman Ayun is the historically important village of **Marga**. In 1946, the commander of Indonesian troops in Bali, Lt. Col. I Gusti Ngurah Rai, and his company of guerrilla fighters were killed in battle at Marga. Surrounded and outnumbered by Dutch forces and under air bombardment, Ngurah Rai's 94 men refused to surrender. Instead, they attacked the Dutch and died to the last man – a suicidal assault reminiscent of the royal *puputan* 40 years earlier. A Margarana monument honours these valiant soldiers.

Topeng masked dancer from the Tabanan area.

BELOW: Pura Taman Ayun dates back to the 18th century.

The Bali Bombing

The evening of 12 October 2002 will long be remembered by all Balinese. A high-powered bomb and a second, smaller one were set to detonate at 11.15pm on a busy Saturday night at Kuta. Carried inside the vest of a suicide bomber, the smaller bomb exploded inside Paddy's Pub. Panic-stricken patrons ran into the street. Then the bigger bomb detonated with a mighty blast in front of the well-known Sari Club.

More than 200 people were killed by the bombs, mainly foreigners, a large number of whom were Australians. Many more were injured and crippled, some for life. Some of the bodies and body parts were never found. All the plate-glass windows of shops, bars and cafés as far away as 600 metres (¼ mile) were shattered. Cars, motorcycles and trees were either set on fire from the heat of the blast or were blown away. Electricity failed as utility transformers melted. Away from the epicenter of the fire, people stumbled in total darkness, crying for help.

Today there's a memorial monument at the bomb site in front of the ill-fated Sari Club's location. It is visited by many travellers, as well as by friends and relatives of those who lost their loved ones in the tragedy. Within months of the bombing, three masterminds of the scheme – Muslim terrorists from Java – were taken into custody by the police, and have since been sentenced to death. Twelve other men received prison terms ranging from five to 15 years.

In the wake of the tragedy the Indonesian government acted swiftly to aid the Balinese and help restore Bali's economy, which is heavily dependent on tourism. President Megawati Sukarnoputri immediately declared that all national holidays falling mid-week would be moved to a Friday or Monday and enhanced with an extra day, creating long weekends to encourage Indonesians to holiday in Bali. The tourism industry contributed by offering discounted packages that included airfares, accommodation and tours. It was hoped that if the world saw Indonesians going back to Bali, international travellers would follow suit.

The plan took awhile but it worked; Indonesians who may have spent their leisure time abroad holidayed domestically. Many of them included Bali in their travel plans, and their enthusiasm for travelling at home spilled over to other local cities, which had also experienced dramatic downturns in tourism after the Bali bombing. Many hotels and restaurants also took the opportunity to renovate their premises in expectation of better things to come. New hotels, spas and restaurants were also built during this lull.

Unfortunately, the years following the bombing haven't been kind. Wracked by the SARS epidemic, the Iraqi war, and other economic and security concerns, enthusiasm for travel in the region has dampened. Today the Balinese have taken this terrible tragedy in their stride. They conducted elaborate purification ceremonies to re-balance the island's harmony. The Balinese are ready to welcome visitors back to their paradise and the gods must have listened, as already there are positive signs that the tourists are returning.

RIGHT: floral offerings and mementoes at the Bali bomb site.

CENTRAL BALI

Beyond the tourist centres lie a series of craft villages, a timeless affirmation of the spirit of Bali – where art, as material culture, is an authentic part of everyday life

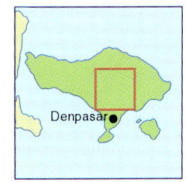

Map on page 198

North of Denpasar, Ubud is the first major and most popular point outside southern Bali. It is the artistic heart of Bali, surrounded by culture, sites and sounds of the Bali that remains unchanged by time. Ubud can be the hub for excursions into Gianyar regency to the east, the mountain highlands in Bangli and Buleleng regencies to the north, and the island's rice bowl regency, Tabanan, to the west.

North from Denpasar

The first "village" outside Denpasar is **Batubulan** ⓭, stretching for about 2 km (1¼ miles) and distinguished by stone-carving shops lining the roadside. Soft *paras* stone, found in nearby ravines, is used to create deities and demons for temples, households and, now, tourists. Humid tropical weather quickly wears down the porous stone, so temple carvings have to be renewed periodically. Males carve in groups at roadside "factories", reproducing designs formed by their ancestors, and, increasingly, those which appeal to visitors.

Batubulan holds daily performances of the Barong dance on a stage near Pura Puseh temple. The drama depicts the age-old struggle between good and righteousness – the path of *dharma*, or right-doing – and the negative forces which seek to destroy them. Barong, the benevolent, is a mystical lion-dragon creature played in the dance-drama by two men. The hairs of Barong's beard are said to hold healing powers. His adversary Rangda, queen of the underworld, is equally feared and respected by the Balinese. In the dance-drama, Rangda is never destroyed, for the balance between positive and negative must be maintained. To kill Rangda on stage would destroy half of the life force. To an outsider, this may be just a play, but to the Balinese it is a serious portrayal of the struggle of life.

Taman Burung Bali Bird Park (open daily 9am–6pm; entrance fee), houses over 1,000 specimens of 250 exotic bird species in a well-designed aviary and is dedicated to the conservation of rare and endangered birds from Indonesia and elsewhere. Endangered Bali starlings (*Leucopsar rothschildi*), the first-ever born in captivity in Bali, are examples of the programme's success. Paved paths lead through 2 hectares (5 acres) of gardens representing deserts, rainforests and marshlands. The park has an attractive open-air restaurant and gift shop.

At **Singapadu**, a row of woodcarving shops and a few stone carvers, can be found highly-skilled mask carvers. Continue north for about 1 km to a junction with a huge banyan tree on the left and the Pura Desa (village temple), just beyond Taman Burung Bali Bird Park. Next to the temple, the main *puri* or palace of

LEFT: nightmare-inducing Rangda represents evil in the Barong dance-drama.
BELOW: lotus-covered pond at Ubud's Café Lotus.

Batubulan is a centre for craftsmen producing stone sculptures made of malleable paras stone.

BELOW: *gamelan music is essential for ceremonies.*

Singapadu, is a place where Barong masks are made. Further down the road is the home and workshop of I Wayan Tangguh, a prominent mask artist. The main prototypes of *topeng* dance masks in his collection are some of Bali's finest specimens. Singapadu, also stages a Barong dance performance, and some of the finest Barong "legs" (men who play the front legs of Barong) hail from here. This tiny village also produces some of the best *arja* singers and dancers on the island. *Arja* is a genre of dance-drama similar to the Western operetta.

Celuk to Gianyar

At the main junction before the bird park, the route turns eastwards to Gianyar. **Celuk** ⓮, some 4 km (2½ miles) from Batubulan, beckons visitors with sterling silver and gold brooches, gem-studded bracelets and earrings of all descriptions. The intricacy and detail achieved with simple hand tools is amazing. Craftsmen use a tree stump with a protruding metal spike as an anvil, a bamboo stem to catch the filings, and a manually operated gas pump for heat. As with most Balinese crafts, smithing is an art passed down in families. Visitors can observe the workshops, often small rooms or areas containing 5 to 20 workers, some not even in their teens. Don't miss the shops on the road north and perpendicular to the main road, as many fine jewellers dwell off the beaten track.

Across the Wos River, **Sukawati** ⓯ anchored an extremely powerful kingdom in the 18th century. The town now sports an art market and is home to some of the best *dalang* (shadow puppeteers) on Bali. *Wayang kulit* – shadow puppetry – is a difficult art. Aside from manipulating different puppet characters, memorising hundreds of stories, singing, cuing the musicians, and creating a variety of voices, a *dalang* must be clean in mind, body and soul. He is akin to a priest in many respects and can even make the holy water so necessary for Balinese rituals (an honour usually reserved for Brahman priests). *Wayang kulit* stories are imbued with innuendo and impart the values of daily life to the audience.

Many *dalang* make their own puppets, delicately carved out of buffalo hide and then painted. A number of *dalang* live in the *banjar* (neighbourhood association) behind the Sukawati wet market, where they can be observed at work. Cowhide also is made into dance accoutrements in Puaya village, north of Sukawati. Here, production of traditional dance costumes – ornamented filigree leather headdresses, colourful gilded clothes and beaded epaulets – are seen. If shopping for dance costumes, it's best to go with someone who knows the quality of the handiwork.

Sukawati's **Pasar Seni** or Art Market is a two-storey building filled with woodcarvings, clothing and knick-knacks, ceremonial umbrellas, statues, bamboo flutes and basketry. If passing Sukawati early in the morning, look through the **pasar pagi** or morning market, about a block behind the Pasar Seni. In this steaming, packed, warehouse-like barn is every trinket that is on sale in Kuta, but for half the price. The market closes in the mid-morning.

The **Pura Puseh** (village temple) in **Batuan** (north-west of Sukawati) dates from the 11th century, with fine examples of temple carvings. Head west at the bend in the road. The temple is located directly across an open-air pavilion.

Mas ⓰ (located north of the "Fat Baby Statue" T-junction to Sakah), is best known for its intricate woodcarvings and masks. At Tilem Art Gallery, on the main road, are highest-quality woodcarvings (at some of the highest prices). Carvings and masks can be found along the street and in side alleys. Take along a photograph or design you would like reproduced to place a special order. The

Map on page 198

In the 1930s, fearful of tourism's effect on the quality of art, Ubud artists established the Pita Maha association. Painters, sculptors and others joined, seeking to make all artists aware of the need to maintain aesthetic quality and to exhibit work outside of Bali.

BELOW: skilled woodcarvers at work in Mas.

Bamboo is a member of the grass family, with nearly 500 species worldwide, but mostly in Asia. "Bamboo" is derived from the Malay word bambu. *At Bona, bamboo is turned into sturdy utilitarian furniture.*

BELOW:
dyed threads ready for weaving *kain endek* cloth.

inhabitants of Mas are primarily Brahmans, the priestly caste, who trace their roots to Danghyang Nirartha, the founder of Pura Taman Pule temple, which is just behind the soccer field. This great Brahman sage created the system of the traditional village (*desa adat*) as a microcosm of the larger cosmos.

At the *gamelan* factory in Banjar Babakan, **Blahbatuh**, barefoot men pump bellows to stir up the heat for forging. They squat with large hammers, bending bronze alloys into the desired shape for the metallophones and knobbed kettles used in *gamelan*. After they are cooled, the master adjusts the instruments' tuning with a bamboo tuning fork. *Gamelan* casings are assembled and painted here, and instruments for entire orchestras (worth well over US$10,000) may be purchased. Orders should be placed well in advance.

Between Blahbatuh and Gianyar, **Bona** specialises in quality bamboo furniture. Plain or fantastically carved, virgin or varnished, chairs, beds, and tables are available. Bona is also an important centre for dance, and offers three forms of trance dancing – *sanghyang dedari*, *sanghyang jaran* and *kecak* – performed every night for tourists.

Gianyar

This richly cultural region is part of the old Gianyar kingdom, extending from the centre of Bali down south to the coast. It is this region that has given Bali much of its reputation as a focus of creativity – literally born from the high fertility of the spring-fed, lava-enriched soil. With such bountiful fields and harvests, the people have had ample time to cultivate artistic talents, applying these to their daily tasks and religious duties. The result is an island where aesthetic excellence takes pride of place in everything – carving, painting, weaving, along with music and dance.

Once the capital of a powerful kingdom of the same name, **Gianyar** ⓱ is now a sleepy and overgrown, but contemporary, village. During Dutch confrontations, the Gianyar regency was sympathetic to the colonists and thus suffered considerably less violence than other southern regencies. The last *raja* maintained his figurehead position until his death in 1999. The former palace, Puri Agung Gianyar, is opposite Gianyar field.

The speciality of the area is woven *kain endek* (weft *ikat*) cloth used in traditional wear. Numerous factories conduct informal tours, and it is intriguing to watch the process in which bundles of tied-off white threads are passed through a complex dyeing process before they are woven into cloth. Good quality *kain endek* can be found at the Klungkung or Denpasar's Kumbasari market.

Ubud

North-west of Gianyar is **Ubud** ⓲. Named after *ubad*, or medicine, it refers to the healing powers of priests living in the area, many of whom are still renowned for their healing powers. Ubud was also the seat of a 19th-century aristocratic family. Even after the dissolution of their royal status, Ubud's royalty still continue to command great respect among the locals.

It was inevitable that Ubud should be subjected to outside influences. The first few foreigners to settle here, from Europe in the 1920s, were artists seeking inspiration within their surroundings. The masses that followed in subsequent decades brought commercialisation, which in turn benefited growth of the arts.

Almost alone among Balinese communities, Ubud has a tourism foundation, **Yayasan Bina Wisata** (www.ubudvillage.com), aimed at preserving the area's natural and cultural beauty. Instead of encouraging tourism on a grand scale, the foundation unifies the needs of both visitors and locals. Visitors are asked to respect local ceremonies, wear traditional clothing when appropriate, and learn about the area's people. At the office, located west of the main market, the staff is helpful in answering questions and plotting journeys, and a message board carries details of festivals, ceremonies and cremations in the area.

The arts quarter

West of the Ubud market on Jalan Raya Ubud is **Museum Puri Lukisan** A (open daily 8am–4pm; entrance fee). It was founded in 1956 to preserve the rich traditional heritage of Balinese visual arts created by local artists both past and present. The main building exhibits a collection of older works, a second displays paintings by the spirited Young Artists of the 1960s, and a third houses temporary exhibits. Further west is the **Antonio Blanco Museum** (open daily 9am–5pm; entrance fee), which sits at the top of a steep driveway, just past Campuhan Bridge. The ornately decorated museum displays the works of the late self-professed Spanish-Filipino "maestro" – mainly erotic paintings of his favourite models, his Balinese wife and their daughter.

To better understand Balinese art, a visit to **Museum Neka** B (open daily 9am–5pm; entrance fee) beyond Campuhan is essential. This wonderful display

Maps:
Area 198
City 217

> **TIP**
>
> In Campuhan, drop by the Hotel Tjampuhan and pay a small fee for a quick dip in its swimming pool. This hotel was once Ubud's top place to stay, and its rustic charms linger. In the 1930s, famous German artist Walter Spies lived here.

BELOW: ornate door detail at the Museum Neka.

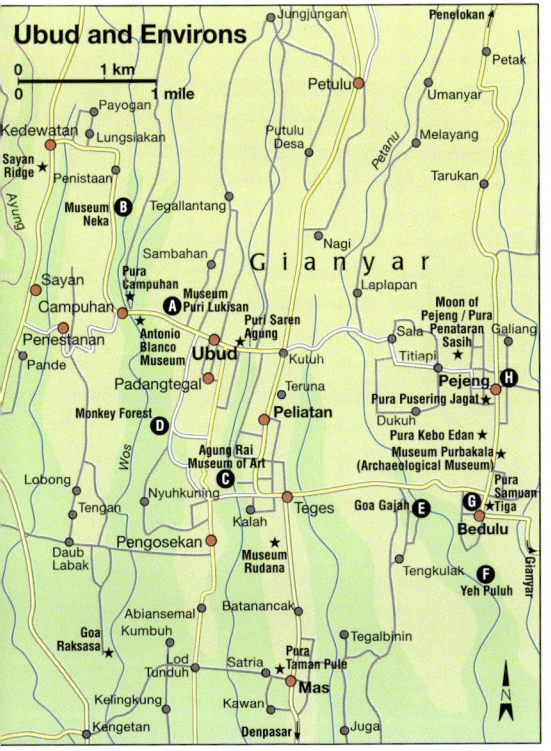

Many Balinese artists are extremely versatile and have a natural ability to paint in many different styles.

BELOW: one of Ubud's numerous "tourist art" shops.

of paintings was assembled by former school teacher Suteja Neka, one of Bali's best art dealers. Opened in 1976, the museum's collection is displayed chronologically and well documented, providing an excellent background to the history of Balinese art and culture. The museum also has a research library, well-stocked bookstore and souvenir shop, and a café with panoramic views.

East of Ubud's market, on Jalan Raya Ubud, is **Puri Lempad** (open daily 8am–6pm; free), with a small selection of drawings and paintings on display by Bali's most renowned artist, I Gusti Nyoman Lempad (1862–1978). Lempad had a broad range of talents in many media, including painting, sculpture and architecture. With his fluid and concise lines, he created formal classical scenes that gained international recognition.

Further east along the same street is **Seniwati Gallery** (open daily 10am–5pm; free), established in 1991 by British expatriate Mary Northmore. The gallery represents local women artists from Bali along with works by female Indonesians and foreigners.

South of Ubud in the direction of Pengosekan village lies **Agung Rai Museum of Art (ARMA)** ❻ (open daily 8am–6pm; entrance fee) with an extensive collection of works by Balinese, Indonesian and foreign artists. A side room features a small painting attributed to German artist Walter Spies. Works are titled in English, Indonesian and Japanese. ARMA also promotes Balinese performing arts and has a bookshop and library.

Continue south on the main road towards Denpasar to **Museum Rudana** (open daily 8am–5pm; entrance fee). Its massive building shows works in the Kamasan, Ubud and Batuan styles, along with paintings by well-known contemporary Indonesian artists and a display of wooden sculptures.

Central Ubud

Like all Balinese markets, **Pasar Ubud** is a great place to begin one's walkabout. At the junction of Jalan Raya Ubud and Jalan Wanara Wana, the morning market is open daily; on *pasah*, which occurs every three days, it is packed. Across the market, on the north-east corner of the intersection, is **Puri Saren Agung**, from where Ubud was ruled from the late 1800s until World War II. The buildings were erected following a devastating 1917 earthquake. Evenings here see traditional dance performances.

An excursion popular with first-time visitors is the **Monkey Forest** ᗰ (open daylight hours; entrance fee). Its attraction is perhaps due more to tradition than to any intrinsic value. This has led the 2-km (1¼-mile) Jalan Wanara Wana (commonly referred to as Monkey Forest Road) to become lined with tourist-related establishments. In the forest, walk through beautiful and dense tropical jungle. Like all "monkey forests" in Bali, the experience is punctuated by roving gangs of mischievous, annoying and fearless macaques, which ostensibly protect the temple. They are amusing up to a point, usually breached when one of them pinches keys, sunglasses or any other shiny object, and runs off with it. This walk is best done in the cooler early morning or late afternoon. A temple in the forest, **Pura Dalem Agung Padangtegal**, is dedicated to Durga, the goddess of death, who often takes the form of Rangda, the queen of the underworld.

Around Ubud

West from downtown beyond Campuhan, the road turns north to **Kedewatan**, a village blessed with outstanding views. Upscale accommodation is available along the ridge here in all ranges, from the Kedewatan intersection further north

Map on page 217

BELOW: mischievious macaques at the Monkey Forest.

Gilded fans are often used by Balinese dancers to accentuate their dynamic movements.

toward Payangan. South from Kedewatan is **Sayan**, a small Ubud "suburb" that teeters on the edge of the devastatingly beautiful Sayan ridge, with the Sungai Ayung tumbling along the bottom. The scenery here is undoubtedly some of Bali's most dramatic. The Ayung is a popular spot for whitewater rafting trips. The 2-hour journey floats through 25, Class II rapids, giving an adrenaline rush without too much danger.

Penestanan, between Sayan and Ubud, grew from obscurity when Dutch-born Arie Smit, a naturalised Indonesian citizen who still lives and works in Ubud as a respected artist, established a small art group here during the early 1960s. With Smit's encouragement and enormous freedom on subject matter and style of expression, young painters produced imaginative, naive-style scenes of village life and rituals. From these experimental beginnings emerged the lively Young Artists style.

East of Ubud, **Peliatan** gained fame in the 1950s for its *legong* dancers, who took New York by storm while on tour. Today, their descendants continue the tradition. Each Friday night, in Banjar Teruna, some of Peliatan's finest exponents of music and dance perform as the *Gamelan Tirta Sari*.

Beyond Ubud

North-west of Ubud is another noted monkey forest. Sangeh's legendary history can be traced to the Hindu *Ramayana* epic, in which the monkey-general Hanuman went to search for magical healing herbs that grew on a mountain. Unable to find the plants, he broke off the peak, but part of the mountain fell to the earth in **Sangeh**, along with a group of monkeys from his army, whose descendants remain there to this day to pester travellers. There is a cluster of

BELOW: rafting on Ayung river is most exciting during the rainy season.

unique towering nutmeg trees. A moss-covered 17th-century temple, **Pura Bukit Sari**, lies in the heart of the woods. The resident monkeys are tourist-savvy, intelligent and expect considerable remuneration, if not protection money, for their annoying antics and thievery.

An "elephant cave" lies off the Ubud–Gianyar road, east of Peliatan in Bedulu. **Goa Gajah** E (open during daylight hours; entrance fee) is mentioned in the 1365 *lontar* (palm-leaf manuscript) *Nagarakertagama* as a Balinese place called Lwa Gajah (Elephant Water, or River), a Buddhist priest's dwelling. Elephant Water may refer to the Petanu River, near the cave. Goa Gajah, dating from at least the 11th century, was excavated in 1922.

The entrance is actually a carved head of a monster with a gaping mouth and hands which look as if they are trying to pull apart an opening for people to enter. All around the entrance are fantastically carved leaves, animals, waves and humans. Inside is a 13-metre (43-ft) long passage stopping at a T-junction 15 metres (50 ft) wide. At one end of the passage is a four-armed statue of elephant-headed deity Ganesha. At the opposite end is a set of three *lingga* (phalluses). One might conclude Goa Gajah is a Hindu temple. However, sleeping niches and Buddhist ruins outside the cave suggest religious syncretism. To the side of the entrance is a 1,000-year-old statue of Hariti, a Buddhist demoness-cum-goddess. Large male and female figures spout water from their stomachs in a bathing place in front of the cave.

Continue down the road and turn south at a statue to see rarely-visited 14th-century reliefs at **Yeh Puluh** F (open daily during daylight hours; entrance fee). This 25-metre (80-ft) long, 2-metre (7-ft) high rock wall is carved in high relief. Aside from Ganesha, there are no religious themes, only scenes from daily life. The sequence begins with a *kayon*, the first puppet used in the *wayang kulit*.

Bedulu and northward

Bedulu G village was once the site of the early Mahayana Buddhist Warmadewa dynasty dating from the 5th century. By the late 10th century, Balinese religion lacked cohesion due to conflicts between the different sects. Several holy men gathered with the king at **Pura Samuan Tiga** (Temple of the Tripartite Meeting). Out of this exceptional meeting emerged the fusion of Balinese religion as practised today, with the three elements of animism-ancestor worship, Buddhism and Hinduism.

North of Bedulu is the archaeology museum, **Museum Purbakala** (open daily 8am–noon; entrance fee) that contains dimly lit and poorly explained displays of megalithic and Bronze Age remains found in this area, including huge stone sarcophagi.

The **Pejeng** H area has a cluster of important old shrines and sacred springs. Across the road in the rice fields of Pejeng is **Pelinggih Arjuna Metapa** (Shrine of the Meditating Arjuna). Loincloth clad statues of Arjuna, warrior-hero from the Hindu *Mahabharata* epic, along with two servants are displayed in a small pavilion with a few other relics.

Just up the road on the same side is **Pura Kebo Edan** (Crazy Water Buffalo Temple). The site is

There are elements of both Hinduism and Buddhism found at Goa Gajah. The cave may be an early precursor to the Hindu-Buddhist character which to a large degree defines Bali today.

BELOW: worshipper with baskets of offerings at Goa Gajah.

The 11th-century Gunung Kawi monuments are believed to have been carved on a solid rock wall by the supernatural hand of Kebo Iwa

BELOW: sacred temple offerings of coloured rice.

remarkable for its more than 3-metre (11-ft) tall statue called the Pejeng Giant. Restored in 1952, it shows a masked male figure dancing upon a wide-eyed figure, perhaps a corpse. His huge penis, its tip adorned with balls, swings to the left and indicates the more sinister aspects of Balinese worship. Scholars believe that the figure symbolises Bhairava, a Tantric manifestation of the Hindu god Shiva.

Still further north is **Pura Pusering Jagat** (Navel of the World Temple). It has a shrine with large and unusually realistic stone figures of a *lingga* (phallus) and *yoni* (vagina). Childless couples bring offerings, pray, and touch the shrine to ask for offspring. The temple also houses the Pejeng Vessel, called Naragiri (Mountain of Man), an unusual cylindrical vessel carved with a scene of the gods and demons churning the ocean of milk to produce the elixir of immortality.

One of the most impressive antiquities in this area – in all of Indonesia, for that matter – is the **Moon of Pejeng** at **Pura Penataran Sasih**, on the main road to the north of Bedulu. This temple was probably the religious centre of the old Pejeng-Bedulu kingdom.

A large 190-cm (75-inch) bronze kettledrum, the Moon of Pejeng dates back to Indonesia's Bronze Age, which began in 300BC. It is the largest metal drum in the world cast as a single piece. Shaped like an hourglass, the rare drum is decorated with eight stylised faces displaying wide-open eyes and earlobes distended by big rings. Other ornamentation suggests that it probably originated in northern Vietnam during the Dong Son era.

Legend says that the drum was a moon (or the moon's earring) that fell from the heavens one night and landed in a tree. The brilliant light disturbed a nocturnal thief, so he climbed up the tree and urinated on it. The moon exploded and killed him, cracking and losing its shine as a result (thus explaining its present

OFFERINGS AND INCENSE

Consecrated offerings of food, flowers and palm-leaf figures are essential to the religious rituals of Bali. The island's Hindu-Dharma religion is a fusion of Hinduism, animism and ancestor worship. Ancestors and deities of fertility and nature are worshipped along with the Hindu Trinity – Brahma, Vishnu and Shiva – and the Buddha.

The divine god is Sanghyang Widi Wasa, and all gods are considered mere manifestations of him. Hindu-Dharma is founded on the Balinese system of cosmology that strives to maintain the harmony between the cosmos, its divine principles and human existence. Gods and demons are worshipped equally and daily rituals are performed to maintain this balance. Religious life revolves around sacrifices, offerings and purification ceremonies.

The common daily offering, *canang*, is a small palm-leaf tray of flowers and cooked rice, sprinkled with holy water and anointed with incense. Offerings presented to the gods are made from gifts of nature and left to decay naturally or, if containing food, are later taken home to be eaten by the family who made them. Offerings made to demons or evil spirits are left on the ground, while those to gods are put on high altars, with incense used to carry the essence of it upwards to heaven.

condition). Today, no one dares touch the drum, not even the temple priests.

Continuing north to **Pura Gunung Kawi** ⓳, a complex of rock-hewn temples and monks' meditation niches overlooks the Pakerisan River in a valley near **Tampaksiring**. There are 10 temple facades here, grouped in three locations. Legend says that Kebo Iwa, powerful prime minister of Bedulu, used magic to carve the monuments in just one night just by using his fingernails. This 11th-century "Mountain of Poets Temple" complex is remarkably preserved. Mistakenly called tombs, research indicates that the temple facades are monuments commemorating the Warmadewa dynasty. Royal funeral cults – in which kings, queens and consorts were deified after death – began in Bali around this time.

Further up the road is **Pura Mengening** (Clear Water Temple). In a newly built temple on a hillside is a free-standing structure similar in form to those hewn from rock at Pura Gunung Kawi. This temple has a spring of pure water as indicated by its name and feeds into the Pakerisan River. It might be the commemorative temple of the Warmadewa king Udayana.

Just to the east, the sacred **Pura Tirta Empul** ⓴ (Bubbling Water Temple) spring at Tampaksiring was created by the god Indra when he pierced the earth to create the elixir of immortality to revive his fallen warriors. The bathing place was built in the 10th century and its waters are said to have curative powers. Balinese from all over the island come to purify themselves here – after presenting a small offering to the spring's deity, men and women go to different sides to bathe. The waters have a common source but each spout has a different ritual function.

Further inland up the slopes of the volcano, the weather turns cooler. Bamboo forests line the roads, and plots abound with sweet potatoes, peanuts, corn and spices on the way to **Bangli** ㉑, capital of an 18th-century kingdom of rulers descended from the Klungkung royal house. The largest and most sacred temple of the district is **Pura Kehen**, an ancient terraced mountain sanctuary and state temple of Bangli.

Below the foot of the stairway is an old temple that houses a collection of bronze plate inscriptions. Statues of mythological figures line the first terrace to Pura Kehen, from which steps lead to a magnificent gate that the local people call "the great exit". Above the gate looms the frightening face and splayed hands of Bhoma, the demonic son of the earth who prevents harmful spirits from entering the temple. On both sides of the opening are figures of villagers gesturing in welcome.

An enormous banyan with a *kulkul* (large log bells) tree-house nestled in its branches shades the first courtyard, where the upper walls are inlaid with Chinese porcelain plates. An 11-tiered meru (pagoda) dedicated to the god Shiva dominates the inner sanctuary. In the northeast corner of the courtyard is a high throne with three compartments for the Hindu trinity of Brahma, Vishnu and Shiva.

Just 3 km (2 miles) west out of Bangli is a road to **Bukit Demulih**. It is well worth to climb this "Hill of No Return" for superb views of Central Bali on a clear day. To reach the volcanoes of Batur and Agung, continue north from either Bangli or Tampaksiring. (*See the North & West Bali chapter on page 227.*) ❏

Map on page 198

On the full moon of the 4th Balinese month (Sep–Oct), villagers bring a sacred stone for ritual cleansing at Pura Tirta Empul. Dated 962AD, the inscription on the stone – deciphered in the early 1900s and which describes the bathing of the stone – was something the villagers had unwittingly been carrying out for over 1,000 years.

BELOW:
Pura Tirta Empul

BALINESE CEREMONIES AND FESTIVALS

The frequency of Balinese ceremonies and festivals means that most visitors will be able to attend at least one celebration during their stay

The Balinese believe in the eternal cycle of reincarnation and view their life on earth as just one stage in their continued existence. As part of these beliefs, a person's life is marked by rites of passage that are celebrated by the whole community.

The first important ritual is performed at birth when the baby's placenta is buried in a coconut shell near the entrance to the family house. Babies are regarded as being the reincarnation of ancestors. They are therefore thought of as being holy and are treated with reverence. At puberty the tooth-filing ceremony takes place, although this expensive custom is often delayed until marriage to save money.

The final and most important rite in the cycle of life is cremation. Cremation rituals are seen by the Balinese as joyous occasions as they release the soul from the body of the departed.

TEMPLE FESTIVALS

An *odalan* takes place every 210 days or once a year during a particular full moon to mark the "birthday" or dedication of a temple. It can be a brief one-day affair or an elaborate event that goes on for weeks and involving months of preparation.

The most important of Balinese festivals is Galungan. During this time, the deified ancestors descend from heaven and take up residence in their family temples, where they are worshipped by their descendants for five days. As part of the festivities, all over the island, streets are lined with *penjor*, tall bamboo poles decorated with palm leaf ornaments, fruits and biscuits.

△ **TOOTH FILING**
At puberty, the incisors and canine teeth are filed to symbolically eliminate any demonic characteristics and to temper passions.

◁ **CHILDHOOD**
A baby ritually receives a name after 105 days. The child first touches the ground and its hair is cut only when it is 210 days old.

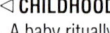

◁ **GETTING HITCHED**
A wedding takes place after the groom's family sends a delegation of villagers to the bride's home to officially ask for her hand. In the past, there were prearranged marriages or a mock (sometimes even forced) abduction of the woman, but such practices are rare today. The couple dresses in their finest garments for the ceremony, which is traditionally performed at the groom's house.

▽ **CREMATION CEREMONY**
At the village cemetery, the body of the deceased, or its exhumed remains, will be placed in an animal-shaped sarcophagus made of wood, bamboo, cloth and paper, and then set on fire. Afterwards, the ashes of the bones are gathered, placed in a coconut, and then tossed into a river or at sea.

◁ **MELASTI RITUALS**
A few days before the end of the lunar-solar year in March or April, villagers take their temple artefacts to the sea for ritual cleansing. New year begins with Nyepi, the "Day of Silence", when no one is allowed outside. Fires and lights are extinguished, and noise is forbidden so that evil forces leave in the belief that the island is deserted.

DAYS OF HONOUR

Tumpek are days set aside to honour physical things that make life possible. On Tumpek Landep, *keris* (daggers) are ritually cleansed and presented with offerings to fortify their protective powers. Other metal objects, especially cars and motorcycles, also are treated with respect.

Small packets of rice cake are tied around trees on Tumpek Wariga, or Uduh, to thank them for their fruits, flowers and wood. Songbirds and *gamelan* instruments are honoured on Tumpek Krulut because of the beautiful sounds that they make. Domesticated animals such as cattle, water-buffalos and pigs are fed better food on the special days set aside for them, called Tumpek Uye or Kandang.

Sacred masks and dance costumes along with *wayang kulit* (leather puppets) used for ceremonies are presented with offerings on Tumpek Wayang. A special day honours Betari Dewi Saraswati, Goddess of Learning and Knowledge. Offerings are given to *lontar* (palm leaf manuscripts) and books. No reading and writing are allowed, and students pray to Saraswati to ask for her blessings.

NORTH AND WEST BALI

Map on page 198

For a slower pace and more intimate encounter with nature, head to the mountains of the west or to the quieter north where you can lie on deserted black sand beaches and watch dolphins dance

In contrast to the verdant hues of the south, the colours of Bali turn green and gold in its northern lands, due to the lower rainfall and a drier climate. You can circumnavigate the north and west, from Danau Bratan to Singaraja, along the northern coastline and around the western horn of Bali, before returning to the populous southern region.

Gunung Batur

Less than an hour north of Bangli is the crater lake **Danau Batur** ㉒, Bali's largest lake and cradled within the caldera of **Gunung Batur**. An active volcano, Gunung Batur is 1,717 metres (5,635 ft) above sea level and is considered to be the female element next to Gunung Agung's male. The crater itself is 11 km (7 miles) in diameter and 180 metres (115 ft) deep. Try to arrive in the early morning, before the mist descends.

Penelokan ㉓, at 1,450 metres (4,800 ft) above sea level, is a spectacular point to take in views of Gunung Batur and its nearby lake. A steep, winding road descends to lakeside **Kedisan** – where boats can be hired – but does not go around the lake. On the volcano's flank at **Toya Bungkah** are hot springs reputed to have medicinal qualities. Travellers who climb Batur use Toya Bungkah as a staging point, which also has an art centre.

Trunyan ㉔, the best known Bali Aga village across the lake, is inhabited by the original Balinese, who rejected changes brought by Majapahit invaders in the 14th century. The villagers have kept their unusual burial customs. The dead are left in the open air for nature to eliminate, and are covered only by a cloth and a bamboo roof. The name Trunyan comes from the *taru menyan* (fragrant tree) that grows in the cemetery. Isolated for centuries from mainstream Bali, Trunyanese keep under wraps – in a pagoda – Bali's largest traditional statue, a 4-metre (13-ft) high patron guardian they believe is the "God of the World's Centre".

Gunung Batur intermittently spews lava, ash and steam. The last major activity was in 1994, but nothing drastic has occurred since 1926. It is the site of Bali's second-most important temple after Besakih – **Pura Ulun Danu Batur** ㉕. As a major *subak* (irrigation) temple, rituals here are linked with the veneration of the Goddess of the Lake, Dewi Danu.

Inscriptions from the 10th century indicate that nearby **Kintamani** – a mountainous area taking its name from the windy town at 1,500 metres (4,920 ft) up – was one of Bali's earliest kingdoms. A paved road at Sukawana leads to Pinggan on the crater's north side, with a flight of 300 steps rising to the mountain sanctuary, **Pura Tegeh Koripan**, the highest temple in Bali, at 1,745 metres (5,725 ft).

LEFT: worshipper brings an offering piled with fruits and rice cakes to Pura Ulun Danu Batur.
BELOW: Danau Batur with Gunung Batur in the background.

TIP

Most tourists avoid visiting Trunyan village – a rare example of Bali's pre-Hindu culture – as it is neither a pleasant excursion nor a welcoming village. The people are known to "beg" aggressively and some tourists have been charged to be allowed to leave.

BELOW:
boats for hire at Danau Bratan.

The lakes

From the southern plains at Tabanan and Gianyar, heading northward to the central mountains, the landscape changes from rice terraces to agrarian patches in the cooler highlands. **Bedugul** 26, 1,300 metres (4,300 ft) above sea level, is the name of both a small town and a mountain-lake resort area which Balinese have long used for weekend retreats. At the mountain crest dividing north and south Bali lies **Danau Bratan**, a lake filling the long-extinct, often mist-veiled Gunung Catur crater. The lake is an essential water source for surrounding farmlands, and Bedugul people honour Dewi Danu, the lake goddess, at **Pura Ulun Danu Bratan**, a temple on a small lake-shore promontory.

North of Bedugul proper is Bukit Munggu market, popularly called **Candi Kuning**, where wild orchids and brilliant lilies are sold alongside vegetables. Adjacent to the market is **Kebun Raya Eka Karya Bali** (Bali Botanical Gardens; open daily 8am–5pm; entrance fee). This refreshing 130-hectare (320-acre) park is sliced by hiking trails through towering forests, and the sprawling grounds are home to more than 650 tree and 400 orchid species.

South of this area along the winding artery skirting the mountains is one of Bali's most venerated temples – **Pura Luhur Batukau** 27, near Batukau on the slopes of Gunung Batukau, 2,278 metres (7,474 ft) high. The western highlands of Batukau are famed for its magnificent landscapes and the view from the mountain village of **Jatiluwih** takes in the whole landscape of southern Bali. Nearby **Yeh Panas** surges hot water from the riverbank, graced by a small temple for prayer and offering. The springs are part of a modest resort and are open to visitors for a fee.

North of Bedugul, the highway descends north towards **Danau Buyan**, a quiet lake embraced by cozy hillsides of coffee. Beyond the lake, a westward turn follows the lake's northern shore and passes **Danau Tamblingan**, the smallest of three mountain lakes. Continue on to Munduk, which has simple lodgings in cool climes, and here, the road joins the north coast drive near Lovina, the black-sand beach resort area.

Buleleng and the north coast

Buleleng regency and the north are a contrast from the south in landscape and history. Orchards of citrus fruit, tomatoes, vanilla, coffee, cacao, grapes and cloves replace the familiar rice paddies. About 10 km (6 miles) before the road from Danau Bratan ends at Singaraja, the **Air Terjun Gitgit** ㉘ waterfalls flow vigorously during the rainy season. The soft pink sandstone which gives northern Bali's temples their distinctive character were quarried near Singaraja. Temple offerings are also generally more modest in the north.

Singaraja ㉙ has a cosmopolitan flavour, derived from centuries as an important trading port. Bali's second-largest city after Denpasar, its population comprises many ethnic and religious groups: Muslim, Christian, Buddhist, Arabic and Indian. The **Gedong Kirtya** (open Tues–Thurs 8am–2pm; Fri 8–11am; Sat 8am–1pm; free) historical library on Jalan Veteran is a repository of some 3,000 Balinese manuscripts, established by the Dutch in the late 1920s. It has the world's finest collection of *lontar* – traditional books inscribed on palm-leaf strips and preserved between two pieces of wood or bamboo. The ancient volumes cover subjects such as literature, mythology, history and religion.

Singaraja to Air Sanih – East

East from Singaraja, the land is dry and agricultural diversity along the coast is evidenced by the cultivation of grapes, cocoa, cloves and vanilla. In **Sangsit** ㉚, a 15th-century *subak* (irrigation cooperative) temple, **Pura Beji**, dedicated to rice goddess Dewi Sri, sports many *naga*, serpents that symbolise earth and fertility.

About 15 km (10 miles) south-east of Singaraja at **Jagaraga** is **Pura Dalem** ㉛ (Temple of the Dead). Reliefs portray life before and after the arrival of the Dutch, including scenes such as two Europeans in a Model T Ford attacked by armed bandits and a Dutch steamer under attack by a sea monster. Southward is **Sawan**, a village with *gamelan* makers and a talented *gamelan angklung* orchestra.

The road from Danau Batur and Kintamani meets the northern coastal road at Kubutambahan. Further east on the coastal road is **Pura Meduwe Karang** ㉜, a dry-land agriculture temple. Just as *subak* temples ensure irrigated crop harvests, this 1890 temple gives "blessings" for plants grown on unirrigated land. It has many fertility themes, including numerous portrayals of erotic acts. Carvings in this "Temple of the Land Owner" show ghouls, domestics, lovers, noblemen and even a bicycle-riding Westerner, believed to be Dutchman W.O.J. Nieuwenkamp, who travelled all over Bali by bicycle at the beginning of the 20th century.

Further east, 17 km (11 miles) from Singaraja, is **Air Sanih** ㉝ (Yeh Sanih), where for a small fee,

Map on page 198

Sun-ripened tomatoes from Bali's north coast plantations.

BELOW: a banana balancing act.

TIP

Dolphin-watching, a popular activity in Lovina, is increasingly controversial. Convoys of early-morning boats carrying dolphin-seeking tourists go on a chase which very likely disturbs the dolphins' morning reveries.

travellers can dip in a cool, spring-fed swimming pool. Facilities include lodgings and restaurants. Continuing east, the road and villages become simpler, the land grows drier and the number of tourists dwindles.

Singaraja to Gilimanuk – west

Six km (4 miles) west of Singaraja is an 8-km (5-mile) long stretch of black-sand beach encompassing Anturan, Tukad Mungga, Kalibukbuk, Kalisasem and Temukus villages, collectively called **Lovina** ㉞. Accommodation here ranges from simple *losmen* to upmarket resorts. The pace of life is slower here than at other beach resorts, but tourist interest is picking up. **Air Panas** (Hot Springs) near Banjar village is a public bathing area with changing rooms and a restaurant.

At **Pengastulan**, a road leads south, climbing the mountains through rice fields and clove plantations before descending to the coast. Several routes are possible, among which is one of Bali's most beautiful but meandering drives that goes through **Asahduren** and **Manggisari** villages. An eastward turn at Mayong continues to the lake regions of Tamblingan, Buyun and Bratan in Bedugul. A more direct southern route heads south to Tabanan and Denpasar.

Continuing west on the coast road, **Pulaki** has a sacred rock-hewn temple which overlooks the ocean and is guarded by monkeys. Further west, **Pemuteran** has bungalows, hotels and exquisite luxury villas catering to divers, snorkellers and nature lovers.

In **Labuan Lalang** ㉟ on Teluk Terima (Reception Bay), guided hikes into the West Bali National Park or scuba diving off **Menjangan** ㊱ (Deer Island) can be arranged. Menjangan, an uninhabited island about 10 km (6 miles) offshore, offers deep coral reef walls and is one of Bali's best diving sites. Near Labuan

BELOW: grapes bound for the market at Lovina.

Lalang and still within the park is **Makam Jayaprana**, a local hero's tomb and temple, worth the hike for the view.

West Bali National Park

In order to visit **West Bali National Park** ❸❼ (Taman Nasional Bali Barat), first obtain the essential hiking permit from the Forestry Department in Denpasar or from Park headquarters (open Mon–Fri 9am–3pm) in Cekik.

Official guides, who usually speak English, are a requirement within the park, much of which is off-limits. The 760-sq km (300-sq mile) park is home to deer, civets, monkeys, rare wild Javan buffalo and the nearly extinct Bali starling or Rothschild's mynah (*Leucopsar rothschildi*), a small white-crested bird with brilliant blue streaks around its eyes and black-tipped wings. Many wild birds live on the gentle slopes of **Gunung Prapat Agung**, which anchors Bali's western tip of Bali. An interesting 24-km (15-mile) trail encircles Prapat Agung.

The endangered Bali Starling is a protected species.

Gilimanuk to Medewi

The north and south-west coast roads meet at **Cekik**, where a short spur road continues a few kilometres north to Gilimanuk, the access point for a 30-minute ferry journey (but much longer wait), operating 24 hours a day across the Bali–Java Strait. Accommodation in Gilimanuk is limited to homestays.

The Bali–Java Strait is just 3 km (2 miles) wide, but its waters are treacherous. From Gilimanuk, the road south through Jembrana regency parallels the south-western coast through coconut palms and rice fields. The national park occupies much of this regency, extended by the Batukau Nature Reserve running up Bali's central mountain spine – long ago the home of tigers. Today, deer, crocodile and wild pigs roam the dense bushlands.

A kilometre south of Negara is **Loloan Timor** ❸❽. Its residents are Muslim Buginese who originated from Sulawesi, and they continue to build their homes in the Buginese style on stilts. The bamboo musical instruments they play, *gamelan jegog*, are an ensemble that sounds like thunder. Instruments may be seen at the Sangkar Agung museum, 3 km (2 miles) east of Negara, off the main road near Dangin Tukaddaya.

Perancak is 2½ km (1.5 miles) south-west of Negara, at the mouth of Sungai Perancak. **Taman Rekreasi Perancak** has a modest zoo with monkeys, lions, Bali eagles and wallabies.

Continuing southwards takes you to **Medewi**, an ordinary beach that is a popular surf spot. Nearby is the tranquil **Pura Rambut Siwi** ❸❾ (Lock of Hair Temple) that was founded by Danghyang Nirartha in the 16th century. The famous priest left behind a lock of hair, thus the temple's name.

At **Pekutatan**, a spur road heads north up the mountain slopes, climbs over the mountain and descends to the northern coast at Pengastulan. This narrow paved road is among Bali's most beautiful routes, and driving 10 km (6 miles) up the road through rainforest and coffee and clove plantations is an exquisite experience. The road passes directly through an old *bunut* tree which has aerial roots wrapped around both sides of the road. ❑

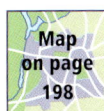

Map on page 198

BELOW: colourful north coast outrigger.

East Bali

The inland east is for those seeking relaxation and reflection. Slow and steady does it, in a realm where timeless rice terraces, palaces and temples dot a countryside laced by black-sand beaches

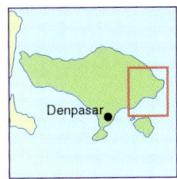

Map on page 198

ast is the most auspicious of compass points in the Balinese worldview, and an excursion among the temples, palace ruins and black-sand beaches of this area reveals why. Less developed and simpler than the island's south, eastern Bali has a different ambience, defined by archaic rituals, lava-strewn landscapes, and high, bare hills ribbed with ancient terracing. The eastern coast is primarily coconut and banana groves, although it is a tourist destination in its own right. (Unfortunately, coral gathering – ground into lime and used in local construction – has irreparably eroded some of the beaches.) Partly hidden by the eastern coastal ranges is the colossal cone of Gunung Agung, Bali's highest peak at 3,142 metres (10,308 ft), which on clear days soars high above the countryside.

From Gianyar, follow the main road to Klungkung (also called Semarapura) regency. East of Klungkung, the landscapes remain blackened by lava streams from Gunung Agung's 1963 eruption, which isolated this area for several years. To see the east, plan a night or two in Manggis or Candidasa. Explore the area in two or three days: the first to Klungkung and Besakih, and the second to Tenganan and Amlapura.

Klungkung

As the seat of the Dewa Agung, nominally the highest of the old Balinese *rajas*, **Klungkung** ⑩ holds a special place in the island's history and culture. As artistic centres, the palaces of Klungkung's *raja* and noblemen supported and developed the styles of music, drama and the arts that flourish today in Bali.

The regency capital was moved to Klungkung from nearby Gelgel in 1710 and here a new palace was built. Today, the remains of the old palace, **Puri Semarapura**, razed in 1908, are within the grounds of **Taman Gili** (open daily 7am–6pm; entrance fee).

Probably towards the end of the 18th century, the original Kerta Gosa (Hall of Justice) was erected at the town's main intersection within Taman Gili. Disputes were heard here only if they could not be settled among families or individual villages. The Kerta Gosa was the island's highest court, and by far the strictest.

The **Kerta Gosa** is an open *bale* (pavilion) beautifully decorated with exquisite examples of Kamasan paintings and Klungkung architecture. Ceiling murals depict *Bima Swarga* (Bima in Heaven) from the *Mahabharata* tale. As subscribers to reincarnation, Balinese strongly believe in *karma phala*, punishment or reward for past actions, either in the present lifetime or the next.

These two-dimensional Kamasan-style paintings, dating back to the 18th century, show in frightening characterisations, the good and bad consequences of deeds.

LEFT: Kamasan-style paintings adorn the ceiling of Bale Kambang.
BELOW: remnants of Puri Semarapura.

The most common offering to the gods you'll see is the canang sari, *a small palm-leaf tray of flowers and rice.*

Artisans from Kamasan directed the last restoration of these paintings in 1960.

Kamasan village remains the singular home of this painting tradition. The **Bale Kambang** (Floating Pavilion), surrounded by a moat, is similarly decorated and was used by the royal family as a place to rest and be entertained. Most of the old palace was destroyed after a battle with the Dutch in 1908.

Kamasan ㊶ village lies 2 km (1¼ miles) south. Painting themes are drawn from old Javanese classic literature and the figures look like *wayang kulit* shadow puppets. In 1973, Nyoman Mandra began a painting school here so young artists could imitate the master's strokes. Kamasan is also a thriving gold and silver centre. Shops retail modern and antique Kamasan-style *wayang* paintings, carvings and silks.

About 5 km (3 miles) west of Klungkung, near Takmung, is the **Museum Seni Lukis Klasik Bali** (open Tues–Sun 9am–5pm; entrance fee). Housing both traditional Balinese art and historical artefacts, it also includes the contemporary works of renowned painter Nyoman Gunarsa, the museum's founder.

Mountain villages

From Klungkung, turn north, passing through Bukit Jambul's astonishing landscapes. In **Sidemen**, every household is engaged in some aspect of textile weaving. This is one of the centres of *ikat* weaving, and from the road, one can hear the clack-clack-clack of looms. *Songket* cloth – cotton or silk with an overweft of silver or gold threads – is also produced here.

There are several *losmen* in Sideman. If you are seeking an isolated place to stay, to stroll through serene rice fields and soak in the view, this is it. There is a school of traditional arts, where the young study literature, painting, dance,

BELOW: serene rice fields at Sidemen.

music and the Balinese language, in addition to the regular school curriculum.

In **Muncan**, an unusual ritual occurs on the last day of the lunar-solar year in March or April. Two crudely made wood figures of a man and woman with oversized genitals are used in an old fertility ritual. After they have been made to copulate in public, the figures are taken to a river and discarded. The surrounding rice fields are then irrigated by the water from this river.

Pura Besakih and Gunung Agung

Folklore has it that when the deities made mountains for their thrones, they set the highest peak in the east, the direction of honour to the Balinese. In every temple, a shrine is dedicated to the spirit of **Gunung Agung**. The tapering form of cremation towers, pagodas, and even temple offerings bear the shape of a mountain, mirroring reverence for this holy volcano.

On the slopes of Agung lies **Pura Besakih**, the Mother Temple (open daily 8am–6pm; entrance fee). Easily accessed from Besakih village, the temple houses ancestral shrines for all Hindu Balinese, who regard Pura Besakih as the pinnacle of sanctity. Non-worshippers are not allowed into the inner temple unless they wish to pray, but one can see the layout quite easily from the open gates. Do not enter the grounds unless invited, and be sure to be dressed in *sarong* and a temple sash.

In 1963, devotees of Pura Besakih were completing preparations for the Eka Dasa Rudra, the greatest of Balinese sacrifices that occurs only once a century. Suddenly, a glow of fire shone from the crater and Gunung Agung began to rumble. A priestess interpreted the ashes of the volcano as a sacred portent sent to purify Besakih, and the devotees continued with the festival arrangements.

Map on page 198

If you've forgotten to bring a sarong and temple sash, they can be "rented" outside Pura Besakih, or purchased from the numerous vendors there as a souvenir.

BELOW: worshippers on their way to Pura Besakih.

If smoking aromatic clove cigarettes for the first time, don't be alarmed by the crackle and pop the clove-tobacco mixture makes as it burns.

BELOW: the most revered of all Balinese temples, Pura Besakih.

By the time the great sacrifice was held in March, thick columns of dark smoke had started surging from the summit. Shortly after, Agung erupted, killing more than 1,500 people. To the Balinese, the eruption did not occur by chance, but was a chastisement for offending the gods. The volcanic ash destroyed most crops on the island. The sacrifice ceremony was held again in 1979 to properly mark the end of a Balinese century.

Besakih's main annual festival takes place during the tenth lunar month of the Balinese calendar (March or April), in a ritual called Bhatara Turun Kabeh (All Gods Descend Together). Balinese island-wide come to pay homage to their gods and deified ancestors during this month-long festival. Don't expect serenity and solitude outside of the temple during this time.

Besakih originated in the 8th century as a terraced sanctuary honouring Gunung Agung's gods. Over a period of 1,000 years or more, it was enlarged and today, it comprises 22 main complexes with more than 200 structures.

Pura Penataran Agung is the paramount sanctuary in the Besakih complex. Steps ascend in a long perspective to split gates. Inside the main courtyard is a triple-throned shrine for three aspects of god: Shiva, as creator; Pramashiva, god without form; and Sadashiva, god as half male and half female. Others interpret this trinity to be Vishnu, Brahma and Shiva. Only worshippers may enter, but visitors can circle the outer walls for a view of the courtyard.

During festivals, the shrines are wrapped in coloured cloth. Three sacred colours are used in the shrine: red, symbolising the earth as lava and associated with Brahma; white, as light, associated with Shiva; and black, as both water and heaven, and associated with Vishnu. Yellow cloth – a colour symbolising compassion – is also used to cover the shrines during festivals.

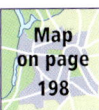

Map on page 198

East coast

Gelgel, the former capital, is a 4-km (2½-mile) long side trip south from Klungkung. In the 1400s and 1500s, Gelgel's Dewa Agung (a title of the time given to the current king and literally meaning "Great God") held immense power. The dynasty's influence declined in the 17th century as it lost battles and allegiances. This misfortune was attributed to a curse which had fallen on the palace. Consequently, the palace was moved to Klungkung. But there was no improvement in fortune. Small conflicts and jealousies broke out among the kings and the result was the creation of numerous minor kingdoms.

Bali's eight regencies today are based upon the last eight kingdoms. Pura Jero Agung, Great Palace Temple, is the local palace's ancestral shrine. To the east is another temple, Pura Dasar. Families from across Bali come here for the temple festival each year.

Colourful outrigger *prahu* line the black-sand shores of **Kusamba** ⓭, a fishing village where salt is panned from the sea. The thatched huts lining the sands are tiny salt-making factories. To make salt, sea water is splashed onto sandy plots. After drying, the sand is dumped into large bins inside the huts, where more sea water is drained through the sands. The residue is then poured into bamboo troughs and left to evaporate in the sun's heat, leaving behind salt crystals. In good weather, the process takes about two days, and the salt panner can make 5 kg (11 lbs) of salt.

Nusa Penida lies directly across from Kusamba on a dry, sparsely-cultivated island of around 40,000 people. Fishermen who set out for Nusa Penida with cargoes of peanuts, fruit and rice also carry passengers wishing to visit its coral gardens and white-sand shores. **Nusa Lembongan**, north-west of Nusa Penida, has professional dive centres and is a popular watersports and relaxation stop for sailing trips from the mainland. The road east from Kusamba parallels lovely seascapes in full view of Nusa Penida. It passes near **Goa Lawah** ⓮ (open daily 7am–6pm; entrance fee), a cave filled with thousands of bats – their bodies packed so close together that the upper wall surface resembles undulating mud. Goa Lawah is a holy temple and surrounding shrines protect the entrance. The cave is said to extend all the way to Pura Besakih and may link to an underground lava tube that emerges, it is said, at Pura Goa in the Besakih complex.

Eastward, a perfectly-shaped bay is cradled by the hills. **Padang Bai** harbour is a transit port to neighbouring islands Lombok and Nusa Penida, with passenger and cargo vessels departing each morning. International shipping lines stop over in Padang Bai, anchoring to the north; visitors and cargoes are ferried to the pier. There are a few *losmen* here and the beach is ideal for a quiet escape. Named after the delectable *mangosteen* fruit, nearby **Manggis** is a fishing village. Some of the island's best *prahu* are made here. Nearby Balina beach has a few upscale hotels, along with lower budget *losmen*.

Candidasa and environs

Candidasa ⓯ has developed as a resort area over recent decades, but in a much simpler fashion than in

BELOW: blazing sunset at Candidasa.

Geringsing cloth, also known as double ikat, is painstaking work. A single piece can take up to five years of daily effort.

BELOW: colorful cloths on display for sale at Tenganan village.

Bali's south. Most accommodation here is at the low end, although there are a few upscale hotels. Candidasa beach is blighted by jetties protruding into the water, intended to stop the erosion caused from years of coral blasting. These structures make it impossible to walk more than 50 metres (164 ft) on the beach, once a truly lovely landscape. The beach is now only visible at low tide.

Those interested in culture should visit Ibu Gedong's **Gandhi Ashram** (tel: 0363-41108). Started in the 1970s as a self-sufficient community based on Gandhian principles, the *ashram* was once the only structure along this isolated beach. Founder Gedong Bagoes Oka has worked courageously to support the environment and help young people learn useful trades. Volunteer workers can rent bungalows or stay in simple lodgings. Note: a strict code of conduct governs behaviour of residents here.

East of Candidasa lies **Bugbug**, a Bali Aga (aboriginal) village in structure. Every two years on the full moon of the fourth month (October), the Perang Dewa (War of the Gods) festival takes place on a hilltop. Balinese from four surrounding villages carry offerings of suckling pigs to hang in the trees.

Tenganan

West of Candidasa is a turn-off northwards to the Bali Aga village of **Tenganan** ㊻. While there are numerous such villages scattered around northern Bali, the most famous is Tenganan. Within its bastions, all living compounds are arranged in identical rows on either side of wide, stone-paved lanes running the length of the village. There is evidence the villagers originated from Bedulu.

Tenganan communally owns large tracts of well-cultivated land and is one of the island's richest villages. Traditionally, the *krama desa*, or elder men's association members, were not permitted to work with their hands in the fields. The aristocratic Tenganan people instead rented out their land to neighbouring villagers and only went to tap *tuak*, palm wine.

The women still weave the famous *kain geringsing*, a shimmering cloth which they say has the power to immunise the wearer against evil and sickness. To make a single piece in the intricate double *ikat* process of dyeing and weaving takes up to five years. Only the finest *geringsing* pieces are worn by the Tenganan people as ceremonial dress. Imperfect ones are sold off, and even these fetch high prices on the market.

Amlapura (Karangasem)

By crossing an area once ravaged by the 1963 eruption, (a wide, solidified lava flow field slowly being returned to cultivation), the road enters **Amlapura** ❹, the main town of Karangasem regency. The former kingdom, founded while the Gelgel dynasty waned in the late 1600s, turned into the most powerful state in Bali during the late 18th and early 19th centuries.

Puri Agung Karangasem long served as the residence of these kings, who extended their domain across the eastern straits to Lombok. During the Dutch conflict at the turn of the 20th century, the Raja of Karangasem cooperated with the conquering army and was allowed to retain his title and powers.

Puri Kanginan, the palace where the last *raja* was born, is a 20th-century amalgam of European, Chinese and Balinese design. The main building is called *Bale* London; its furniture bears the royal crest of Britain. The wooden panelling seems Chinese, while *Ramayana* reliefs on a pavilion remain Balinese.

A photograph over the entrance to Bale London portrays the late king, Anak Agung Anglurah Ketut, who delighted in building fantastic moats and bathing pools. Some 8 km (5 miles) south, near the beach at **Ujung**, lies the ruins of a water palace with a moat which the monarch helped design in 1921. Unfortunately, earthquakes in 1963 and 1978 destroyed most of the structures. Still, it is an interesting site.

Tirtagangga (open daily 7am–6pm; entrance fee), which lies 6 km (4 miles) north on the road to Culik, was built by the same late king in the late 1940s. It is a water retreat with a series of pools decorated by unusual statuary. With its isolation and a commanding hilltop view of the surrounding rice fields, Tirtagangga is a wonderful place to spend a few days. Lodgings and fare are simple here and the air and pools, wonderfully refreshing.

Remote excursions

At Culik, one can continue east through **Amed** ❹ or north to **Tulamben**, with the scenery changing drastically to dry hills covered with scrub. A World War II *Liberty* cargo shipwreck, off Tulamben, is Bali's – if not Indonesia's – most noted diving site. Reef walls off Amed have abundant and varied marine life.

One can drive completely around the eastern coast to Singaraja. Village life here is simple and rustic, and there are occasional views of the ocean. Experiencing this unfettered part of Bali is pure adventure. ❑

Map on page 198

It has long been thought that double ikat were made only in Gujarat, India, a few islands off the coast of Japan, and in Tenganan, Bali. With the recent discoveries of double ikat in Palembang and Bangka (Sumatra), now some textile experts believe there may be other previously unnoticed areas producing it.

BELOW: salt extraction at Amed beach.

NUSA TENGGARA

These little known remote islands, bearing a tenuous link to Jakarta, seem to exist in another age

In Old Javanese, Nusa Tenggara means "South-eastern Islands". This sparsely-inhabited archipelago extending eastwards from Lombok to West Timor is formed by the protruding peaks of a giant submarine mountain range that links Sumatra. Nusa Tenggara is organised into two provinces: West Nusa Tenggara (comprising Lombok and Sumbawa) and East Nusa Tenggara (made up of Sumba, Flores, West Timor and the adjacent islands).

The coastal areas of Nusa Tenggara have been involved in regional trade since very early times. Although the islands produce no spices, the sandalwood trade in Timor and Sumba depleted forests centuries ago. Small kingdoms dominated the region until the 14th century, when the Majapahit empire claimed the entire Nusa Tenggara chain. Islam arrived in the 15th and 16th centuries, via Java and Ternate in Maluku.

The first Portuguese ships reached the area in 1512 and, by the end of the century, they had hijacked the Timorese sandalwood trade and established fortresses on Flores and Solor. The Dutch wrestled much of the spice trade away from their rivals in the 17th century, but what remained of the area's sandalwood was nearly depleted by then.

Today, Nusa Tenggara is among the poorest and least-fertile regions of Indonesia. Most of its 10 million inhabitants – who make up only 4 percent of the Indonesian population – are subsistence farmers or fishermen. Until the end of the 20th century, fish, livestock and some agricultural products (coffee, copra, rice, beans, onions) were the major exports to other islands, and even today, manufactured goods, fuel and some food products are imported, mainly from Java. But that situation is changing with the discovery of possibly Indonesia's second largest gold reserves on Sumbawa. During his presidency, Suharto's government invested in improvements to communications, education and health care, bringing rapid change to some urban areas. Yet, because the population is so scattered, many villages remain remote and relatively untouched by modern civilisation.

Worship of nature and ancestral spirits is still common in many places, and in areas where animism is not practised openly, ancient beliefs are often disguised by a thin veneer of Islam or Christianity. Supernatural beings are thought to control harvests and bring disease and guard against disaster. Chickens, pigs and water buffalo are frequently sacrificed to the spirits and human blood often flows in ritualised contests – boxing matches, whip duels or cavalry bouts – associated with planting, harvesting and marriage.

Nusa Tenggara continues to receive relatively few foreign visitors. Therefore, modest dress and politeness out of respect for ancient cultures and religions are imperative. ❑

PRECEDING PAGES: striking low-sided but high-peaked thatched houses of Sumba.
LEFT: a Lombok aristocrat in his traditional finery.

LOMBOK

Some visitors prefer Bali's eastern neighbour for its quieter and more laid-back island experience. Listen to men vocalise gamelan or buy the globally-recognised Lombok pottery at its source

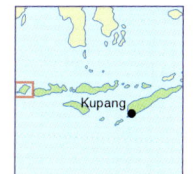

Map on page 247

Lombok is often called Indonesia's island of 1,000 mosques. Yet it is culturally diverse. Buginese dominate the coasts and there is a Javanese-style aristocracy, while Arabs and Chinese are the merchants. The Sasak, the majority ethnic group, comprise about 95 percent of Lombok's population of more than 2½ million, with Balinese, Buginese, Chinese, Javanese and Arabs making up the remainder. Lombok's predominantly Muslim Sasak race is divided into two distinct groups: the Wetu Telu – whose customs are still basically pagan with some Muslim and even Balinese-Hindu influences – and the Wetu Lima, who inhabit the lowlands and the coasts, and are orthodox Sunni Muslims. In the western part of Lombok are Balinese-Hindu communities, remnants of the Karangasem Balinese who conquered Lombok in pre-Islam times.

Lombok, which means "chilli pepper" in Javanese, is roughly 4,700 sq km (1,840 sq miles). Dominating its landscape is a mountain range of 13 peaks anchored by the volcanic Gunung Rinjani – at 3,726 metres (12,224 ft) the third-highest peak in Indonesia. The Wallace Line, named for naturalist Sir Alfred Russel Wallace, runs between Bali and Lombok, demarcating climatic, zoological and botanical distinctions within the region.

Most of western Lombok is green and lush, but to the east and south, the island becomes progressively drier, until wet-rice agriculture turns to dry-rice cultivation. The main tourist hub, Senggigi Beach, is on the west coast, home to accommodations ranging from basic backpacker lodgings to five-star hotels. To the north-west are three small islands, Gili Trawangan, Gili Meno and Gili Air, popular with divers and snorkellers. Other dive resorts have sprung up on Lombok's southwestern peninsula and on the southern beach, Kuta (also spelled Kute). Mataram, the island's main city, is the provincial seat of West Nusa Tenggara, which includes its eastern neighbour, Sumbawa.

While there are several world-class hotels on the island, Lombok does not have the overwhelming commercialism of Bali. And if its cultural experience is more restrained, the flipside is that it does possess a greater sense of adventure.

Western Lombok

Three main towns in western Lombok – Ampenan, Mataram and Cakranegara – meld together to create what is, for Lombok, an urban sprawl. **Mataram ❶** is the administrative centre of political and cultural life, with provincial government offices, banks, mosques, bookstores, the general post office and Mataram University.

In Mataram, the **Museum Nusa Tenggara Barat** (open Tues–Sun 8am–4pm; entrance fee) houses

LEFT: the distinctive pottery of Lombok is made without a potter's wheel.
BELOW: bountiful rice harvest.

It is these red-hot chilli peppers that give Lombok its name.

artefacts from Lombok and Sumbawa, and occasionally hosts special exhibitions. Displays include exhibits on geology, history and culture. The **Pusat Budaya** cultural centre on Jalan Pariwisata presents traditional music and dance nightly. The provincial tourist office is on Jalan Langko.

The **Gunung Pengsong Temple**, south of Mataram, sits atop a peak with vistas of rice fields, Gunung Rinjani and the sea. Populated with monkeys, this is the hill the Balinese had aimed for in the mythical account of their initial arrival in western Lombok. Today, it is an area populated by a significant community of Balinese Hindus. In March or April, a buffalo is sacrificed here to ensure a rich harvest. At that time of the year, houses are repainted and the entire village spruced up to honour the rice goddess Dewi Sri.

Just west of Mataram is **Ampenan**. With its numerous shops, cheap hotels, dusty roads, plentiful horse-drawn carts called *cidomo*, Islamic bookstores and an Arab quarter, it is easily the island's most colourful town. Early Arab traders were drawn to Ampenan when it was the only harbour for incoming and outgoing ships. Nowadays, it is used only for fishing and shipping cattle. On special holidays, the beach is a venue for performances of the *gandrung* social dance or for the *wayang Sasak* shadow play.

Most of the goods shipped to Lombok today arrives at **Gerung** ❷, near **Labuan Lembar**. Gerung is the village of the *cepung*, a men's social dance in which they read and sing from the *lontar monyet* (monkey manuscript), drink *tuak* (palm wine), dance and imitate *gamelan* instruments vocally. The road southwards continues to the westernmost point of the island – a sheer cliff standing above Bangko-Bangko beach. Turning on the road to **Sekotong** ❸ just after Lembar, you will eventually skirt the coastline for a beautiful, scenic

BELOW: entrance to the Balinese Pura Meru.

BEASTS OF WALLACEA

Although 19th century biologist Alfred Russel Wallace simultaneously developed the theory of evolution with Charles Darwin, he is best known as the identifier of the deep oceanic trench that runs between Bali and Lombok. He theorized that the trench, now known as the Wallace Line, distinctly separated the flora and fauna of mainland Asia from that of the islands to the east.

Apprenticed as a surveyor, Wallace spent eight years travelling through the "Malay archipelago" – now part of Indonesia – collecting over 125,000 insect, bird and mammal specimens. During that time he noticed a marked difference between the mammals, banyan trees and hornbills of the western islands and the marsupials, eucalyptus and birds of paradise in the east.

Over the years Wallace's theory has been refined. It is now clear that many Asian species were able to migrate into the eastern islands and many Australian species are found towards the west, depending on their abilities to float, swim or fly.

The islands from Lombok to Timor are known as Wallacea in his honour, and this area is recognised as a transitional zone between the flora and fauna of the two land masses.

drive. The route ends at **Bangko-Bangko** ❹, with a stunning forest and a white-sand beach surrounding Lombok's best surfing area. Off the northern coast of the peninsula is **Gili Nanggu**, where there are cottages and good snorkelling.

Market town

Cakranegara ❺, to the east of Mataram, is Lombok's main market centre. It is also home to many Chinese and Balinese, who make up more than 50 per cent of the town's population. Many weaving and basketry industries are located in Cakranegara – items of which are sold in Bali at many times the Lombok price.

Several important Balinese temples are in Cakranegara and the surrounding area. **Pura Meru**, built in 1720 by Balinese prince Anak Agung Made Karang, is the island's largest temple. Its giant *meru* (pagoda) for the Hindu trinity – Siwa (Shiva), Wisnu (Vishnu) and Brahma – is the "centre of the universe" for the Balinese here, and its annual festival, held over five days during the September or October full moon, is the largest Balinese Hindu event on Lombok. The outer courtyard hall has drums that call the devout to ceremonies and festivals. Two buildings with raised offering platforms are in the centre courtyard, while the interior enclosure holds 33 shrines and three multi-tiered *meru*.

Across the street stands **Pura Mayura**, built in 1744 as the court temple of the last Balinese kingdom in Lombok. A large artificial lake holds a *bale kambang* (floating pavilion) that was once used as a platform where justice was dispensed and meetings held. Today, the palace grounds are filled with grazing livestock and playing children. The temple sits behind sedate water gardens.

The structures and pool at **Pura Narmada**, 10 km (6 miles) east of Cakranegara, were reportedly built in 1805 as a replica of Gunung Rinjani and Segara

Map on page 247

TIP

A festival held at Pura Lingsar temple *(see next page)* during the November or December full moon presents sacred Hindu Balinese and Islamic Sasak performing arts. This is the only event on the island that unites the two groups.

TIP

The Reefseekers Dive Centre & Turtle Nursery on Gili Air island operates a turtle hatchery, concentrating on the conservation of Hawksbills, Greens and Olive Ridleys. Since 1999, they have released hundreds of hatchlings into the sea.

BELOW: door carving at Pura Lingsar, which attracts both Hindus and Wetu Telu Muslims.

Anak, the lake within Rinjani's caldera. When the elderly king Anak Gede Karangasem of Mataram could no longer make the trek to Segara Anak, he built Pura Narmada. The annual pilgrimage and offering at Rinjani's crater lake continues today, and the festival at Pura Narmada coincides with it during the full moon of either October or November. The Narmada gardens are splendid, with traditional dances performed on special occasions. Some of the pools are open to swimmers (modest attire, please) and are popular with local kids.

In nearby **Lingsar** ❻ is the temple complex of **Pura Lingsar**. Originally built in 1714, this main temple of Lombok, not only for Hindus but also for the Wetu Telu, an unorthodox Islamic sect which prays three times a day rather than five. Even Buddhists, Christians and occasionally Wetu Lima (traditional Muslims) come here to pray for prosperity, rain, fertility, health and general success.

Located a few kilometres north of Narmada in **Suranadi** ❼ is the oldest and holiest of the Balinese temples in Lombok, **Pura Suranadi**, a complex of three temples founded by a priest, Pedanda Wawu Rauh. Chilly spring water bubbles up into restored baths, which are open to swimmers, but be sure to be modestly dressed. Beyond Suranadi is **Hutan Wisata Suranadi**, literally the Suranadi Tourist Forest. Stroll through the botanical garden, where specimens are labelled, to see birds, monkeys and butterflies. The little market town of **Sesaot** ❽, 5 km (3 miles) beyond Suranadi, and **Air Nyet** village, another 3 km (2 miles) up the road, are good spots for river swimming and picnicking.

Northern Lombok

North of Ampenan is **Pura Segara**. Following cremations, the Balinese come to the temple to scatter the ashes of their loved ones into the sea. About 10 km (6 miles) north of Ampenan is **Senggigi** ❾, the main tourist area of Lombok. With its beautiful beaches, picturesque views of Bali's Gunung Agung to the west, good coral for snorkelling and diving, and millions of dollars invested for tourism, Senggigi is an attractive place to stay, with several deluxe hotels as well as budget accommodation.

Batulayar, near Senggigi, has an important *makam* (ancestral grave) where nominal Muslims come to picnic and to pray for health and success. Nearby is **Pura Batu Bolong**, an interesting Hindu temple on a cliff facing Bali. It sits beside a large rock with a hole, from which the temple takes its name. This is a great sunset point with fantastic vistas encompassing Bali.

North of Senggigi, towards Bayan along the hilly coastal road, is a variety of terrain and villages. First, is **Pemenang**, followed westwards by **Bangsal** ❿, which has an attractive beach. Boats depart here for the three islands with the best diving and snorkelling in Lombok: Gili Air, Gili Meno, and Gili Trawangan. The crystal-clear waters that surround the islands are extremely bountiful, with over 3,500 species of fish, more than twice the 1,500 varieties found in Australia's Great Barrier Reef.

Gili Trawangan ⓫, the largest and most distant of the three islands, was once filled with backpackers who slept on the beach, but with the addition of The Vila Ombak, an upscale boutique resort equipped with

a three-tier swimming pool, spa and dive centre, the island is certain to attract more sophisticated guests. Similarly, **Gili Meno** ⓬ once had a desert-island atmosphere, but now has a resort, Bounty Beach Bungalows, and is serviced daily by Bounty Cruises hydrofoil runs from Bali. **Gili Air** ⓭, closest to the mainland, has the largest local population and a range of dive shops that service all the needs of divers. It has basic as well as upscale accommodation.

There is no fresh water on the Gili islands. Problems with cholera during the dry season (May–October) and malaria and dengue fever during the wet season (November–March) have been recorded in the past. Drink only bottled water, eat only cooked food, and choose accommodation with mosquito nets.

Back on the mainland, the south-facing beach at **Sira**, along the peninsula north of Bangsal, is beautiful with stunning land and seascapes. There is a new golf course and associated facilities nearby. The white-sand beach is a good launch spot for snorkelling on the offshore coral reef. Around the point, in Medana Bay, is the luxury Oberoi resort.

West of **Gondang**, up the coast, is **Tiu Pupas** waterfall, a 20-minute walk beyond the end of a poorly-marked, rocky road. While the spring-fed falls may be disappointing during the dry season, they flow into a deep pool suitable for swimming. Trekking through a traditional Sasak village, **Kerurak**, makes the effort worthwhile. Dusty **Segenter** village, about 35 km (20 miles) north of Bangsal on the road to Anyer, provides a glimpse into the harsh reality of life on the island's dry side. The 300 villagers in this northern interior village eke out a living growing corn and beans, yet they welcome visitors with smiles.

Bayan ⓮ maintains old dance and poetic traditions, as well as *kemidi rudat*, a theatre form based on the *Thousand and One Nights* fables. One of the most

Meyer's Butterfly fish is a shy and retiring species that is difficult to approach.

BELOW: gin-clear waters of Gili Air island.

> **TIP**
>
> In addition to guides and maps, Rinjani Trek Centre also offers tourist information and village walks to see hand-loom weavers, panoramas, wildflowers and waterfalls. Even if you're not a mountain climber, there's good reason to stop by the centre. See www.lombok sumbawa.com for more information.

important Wetu Telu mosques is in Bayan. In nearby **Sedang Gile**, the waterfalls are among the island's most spectacular and are worth the effort of descending 200 vertical steps to view them.

One can reach the summit of **Gunung Rinjani** from the east via Sembalun Lawang, or from the north, via Bayan through **Batu Koq** to **Senaru** ⓯. At Senaru is the **Rinjani Trek Centre**, a unique partnership of the National Park, tourism industry and local communities, who manage and protect the mountain environment. There's an Information Centre at Sembalun Lawang. Inside the Gunung Rinjani caldera is a crater lake, **Danau Segara Anak** ⓰ (Child Sea Lake), with a second steaming volcano growing at the edge. It is a difficult climb; do go with a local guide and wear warm clothing.

Eastern and central Lombok

Southward and further inland are **Sembalun Bumbung** ⓱ and neighbouring **Sembalun Lawang** ⓲ located in a valley on the slopes of Gunung Rinjani. There are many *haji* (Muslims who have gone to Mecca) in both villages, but Sembalun Bumbung has retained the older traditions of dance and theatre. (In contrast, Sembalun Lawang has become an orthodox village banning most arts.) Sembalun Bumbung has an old tomb that holds the remains of a Majapahit ancestor. It is also the site of the phenomenal *alip* festival held once every three years.

Well-known as a source of traditional Sasak music and dance, **Lenek** also offers *tari pakon*, a medicinal trance dance. A local cultural patron of the arts has established an organisation to re-invigorate the performing arts, and visitors are welcomed for a rustic stay here.

Other villages in eastern Lombok are strongly Islamic. Although transport

BELOW: crater lake at Gunung Rinjani.

and lodgings are not easily available, it is worthwhile to visit **Labuan Lombok**, a friendly harbour with ferries running to Sumbawa, and **Labuan Haji**, which has an appealing beach.

Tetebatu ⓭, at the southern foot of Gunung Rinjani, is a cool mountain retreat with views of beautiful rice terraces. The area is wet and misty during the rainy season. The waterfall at **Jukut** ⓮, to the north-east of Tetebatu, is found in a monkey-filled trekking forest. (Be advised to stay well away from the mischievous monkeys, who are known to nip tourists, and steal food, bags and jewellery.) **Bonjeruk**, in central Lombok, is a village of *dalang*, or puppeteers, for the *wayang Sasak* shadow play; many of the puppets are made here. Near **Lendang Nangka** ⓯ is Jojang spring with great vistas and a forest inhabited by black monkeys. In August, Sasak boxing takes place in the village.

To the south

South-east of Cakranegara, and on the road to Praya, is **Getap**, where blacksmiths forge by hand window grating, horseshoes, machetes and sickles for harvesting rice. The older folk in the village fan the flames by using plungers in bamboo tubes. **Praya** ⓰ is a crossroads and the hub of the south. Home of the Saturday market, it is central to many of the area's handicraft villages.

South-west of Praya is **Penujak** ⓱, one of three pottery-making villages sponsored by the New Zealand government. The other two are Banyumulek, south of Mataram, and Masbagik Timur, in East Lombok. The project aims to improve the standard of living of the locals by lending technical and marketing assistance for the unique earthenware they produce.

The women of all three villages have been making pottery since the early

Map on page 247

TIP

Rare today, traditional Sasak rites occur occasionally in Bayan, Lenek and Sembalun Bumbung villages. Bayan is also the site for traditional Hindu dances.

BELOW: a Penujak village potter.

Lumbung rice barns, found in all Sasak villages in Lombok, store the rice needs of virtually the entire village.

BELOW: weaver at Rambitan village.

16th century, with skills being passed from one generation to the other. Although there are only minor differences in the processes used, the designs vary. Gecko motifs originated in Penujak; Banyumulek traditionally decorated its jars and vases with rattan and old coins; and Masbagik is the source of a starfish motif.

In Penujak, as in the other two villages, visitors can watch as a greyish-brown clay that comes from local riverbeds is manipulated into shape by hand, sometimes using a wooden paddle. Instead of a potter's wheel, female craftsmen walk around the jar, building up and scraping the walls as they go. After drying in the sun, the earthenware is baked in pits or ovens fuelled by firewood and coconut husks, then covered with rice straw. The clay turns a rich reddish-brown in the process. Although pottery making has always been done by village women, today, the men are also involved in the decorating and firing stages.

In addition to traditional Sasak motifs, new designs have appeared. Magnificent giant water pots, incense boxes, cooking pots, tableware, lamp bases and garden lanterns have joined the line of *kendi* (drinking vessels), also produced in Java. Lombok pottery centres in the three villages (plus one in Mataram) provide a packing and shipping service to Bali and Java. Container shipments to any destination can be arranged through shipping agents in these cities.

On the road leading south from Praya to the coast are two traditional Sasak villages sandwiched between the main road and rice fields. On the east side of the road is **Sade** ㉔, a village with clusters of thatched *lumbung*, or rice barns that is open to tourists. On the west side of the road is **Rambitan** ㉕, a more authentic hilltop village with the oldest mosque in Lombok, **Mesjid Kuno**. Only Muslims may enter this thatched-roof house of worship. An interesting walk through the village is encouraged by residents, who act as guides for a small fee.

Kuta ㉖, 45 km (30 miles) south of Cakranegara, is several steps behind Senggigi in development. Yet Kuta is fronted by an expansive and beautiful white-sand beach. The architecturally interesting Novotel Coralia hotel is moderately priced, and the homestays in the area are cheap. Kuta's market (open early on Wednesday and Sunday mornings) is a lively cacophony of chickens and local chatter and is brightened by colourful fruits and woven baskets.

A few minutes east of Kuta village, is **Mandalika**, the site of the annual Putri Nyale festival commemorating the legend of the beautiful Putri (Princess) Mandalika, who long ago was sought as the bride of every Lombok *raja*. When she could not choose between the suitors, she threw herself into the sea from a headland, saying, "*Kuta*", or "Wait for me here". When she jumped, hundreds of *nyale* sea worms floated to the surface. Thus, every year on the anniversary of her fateful demise, the *nyale* worms return to the site. Thousands of residents – including young people who flirt and strut while watching the sea worms spawn – gather for the festival. Associated with fertility, the *nyale* are ground up, and the resulting mixture is either placed in irrigation channels to ensure farmers will have a good harvest, or fried and eaten in the manner of a love potion.

Astonishing landscape

West of Kuta village, the beach at **Mawun** ㉗ runs the length of a perfect half-moon bay, flanked by massive headlands. This deserted spot off the beaten track is barren of trees, a fact which accentuates the spectacular scenery and the sound of the sea. Apart from the occasional fisherman or young girls selling *sarong*, it is possible to have this fine beach all to oneself. It can also be reached by bicycle from Kuta, although the road is a bit steep.

A dirty little fishing village lies on the fringe of the wide, sweeping **Selong Blanak** ㉘ beach, west of Mawun. Colourful, small fishing *prahu* (boats) rock in gentle waves at the eastern end of the bay. The livelihood of these industrious people, who originate from eastern Lombok, is fishing, especially for squid. What sets this site apart from other beaches is the scale of the surrounding landscape, which is of continental, not islandic, proportions. The sand, sea and distant hills are painted in an astonishing palate of colours, making this an ideal place to bask in nature's beauty.

East of Kuta lies a series of beautiful, untouched beaches. **Tanjung Aan** has spectacular scenery off the peninsula, just a few vendor shacks and a virtually undisturbed beach. Another 3 km (2 miles) east is **Gerupuk**, where there is a weekly market on Thursday. Local fishermen harvest seaweed in the nearby bay. It is also an ideal spot for wind or body surfing.

Further east, beyond **Batu Nampar**, is the infrequently-visited **Batu Rintang**. With its traditional thatched-rice barns and huts, this village offers a realistic look at local life. Outside Batu Nampar are salt works and floating seaweed frames, farmed by migrants from South Sulawesi and Madura. South and east, respectively, are found the coastal settlements **Ekas** ㉙ and **Tanjung Luar**, inhabited by Bugis fishermen from Sulawesi, who arrived here during the early 1600s. ❑

Map on page 247

TIP

Buying direct from the artist in villages where handicrafts are produced ensures that the artisan – and not a middleman – reaps the full benefits.

BELOW: few visitors make it to Selong Blanak beach because of the distance.

SUMBAWA

Some of the best surf in the world can be found here. For something less energetic, visit an all-wooden palace on 99 stilts, view ancient stone sarcophagi, or just stroll around the colourful towns

Larger than Bali and Lombok combined, Sumbawa's contorted form is the result of violent volcanic explosions. It is divided into four administrative regencies: Sumbawa Besar in the west; West Sumbawa; Bima in the east; and Dompu, the home of Gunung Tambora, in the middle. It was Tambora that isolated the people of the west from the Bimanese for centuries. So separate are they that the native language of the Sumbawanese is more akin to the Balinese and the Lombok Sasaks, while the Bima language is more like those of Flores and Sumba. When islanders say "Sumbawa", they mean the Western part of the island. The east is simply called "Bima".

Gold towns

Most of Sumbawa's 800,000 inhabitants farm or fish. Its exports are almost entirely agricultural: rice, peanuts, beans and cattle. The most recent development to hit the island, though, is the discovery of gold. Sumbawa's mines are projected to be second in production to the great Freeport mine in West Papua (Irian Jaya). Thousands of workers are already in place in the few sites currently under exploration, with tens of thousands more expected when the 150 potential locations are fully exploited. The accompanying influx of expatriate management and labourers has already begun to change the face of Sumbawa, with even greater adjustments expected for the future.

The people of Sumbawa are devout Muslims. The *kerundang* or orthodox Islamic dress for women is very much in evidence in Bima and Sape, and powerful loudspeakers amplify the *muezzin*'s pre-dawn call to prayer in all major towns on the island. Yet there is also a strong undercurrent of ancient customs and beliefs. One tradition is the *dukun* or shaman, who can cure diseases or make water buffaloes run faster.

Most visitors speed through Sumbawa Besar and Bima, the island's two main settlements. Nevertheless, both towns are worth a sojourn. The main attraction here is history and culture, particularly since it is the first island east of Lombok which has never been influenced by Javanese Hinduism. And marine activity is booming in the west, with good surfing.

In **Sumbawa Besar** ❶ is the **Dalam Loka**, the former sultan's palace. Made entirely of wood, it is raised on 99 stilts to remind followers of the 99 names given to their god. The reconstructed palace was meant to be a museum, but due to a lack of security, the sultan's heirlooms are kept in the **Balai Kuning** (Yellow House) where the late sultan's daughter lives, and can only been seen by appointment.

The hills east of Sumbawa Besar contain large stone sarcophagi, carved in low relief with human forms

LEFT: orthodox Muslim practice in parts of Sumbawa demands that women cover exposed skin.
BELOW: ancient megalith.

and crocodiles. **Batutering** ❷ is about 18 km (11 miles) from Sumbawa Besar on the main road to Semamung and has megaliths said to be the royal tombs of a Neolithic culture that thrived about 2,000 years ago. Continuing on the road towards Lunyuk, about 12 km (7 miles) further are the waterfalls of **Ai Beling**, an idyllic setting for a picnic and a swim.

World-class surfing

Maluk, on the west coast, is enjoying the benefits of the new mining industry. Once a sleepy fishing village, it and **Benete** have become bustling centres of goods and services. Bars, restaurants, small hotels (several with live music on weekends) and a health club have sprung up to satisfy the needs of mine employees. The main road in the area has been widened and paved.

Nearby, there is world-class surfing at Scar Reef near **Jereweh** and at Supersucks, Yoyo's and Townsite beaches.

Travelling in the opposite direction is **Moyo** ❸ island. Two-thirds of the island is a game reserve to protect the island's deer, wild boar and other animals. Hunting is allowed, but only with a police permit. For non-hunters, there is excellent snorkelling and scuba diving. Travel agents in Sumbawa Besar (*see Travel Tips*) can arrange safari adventure tours and scuba diving to Moyo Island. It takes about 45 minutes by speed boat from Kencana Beach Safari Resort. Alternatively, fishing boats can be hired from **Ai Bari** for the voyage to Moyo. Simple accommodation is available at **Tanjung Pasir** on the mainland. The luxurious Amanwana resort, with modified villas using canvas tent toppings, is also on Moyo. It's totally isolated, and bookings have to be made in advance.

Heading east from Sumbawa Besar, a stop at **Poto** village might be

TIP

Sumbawa is known throughout Indonesia for its wild honey, reputed to have special powers that enhance the sexual prowess of men. Ask for *madu Sumbawa* at any local market.

worthwhile. Using backstrap looms, the women here weave *songket* using silver threads. From here, fertile river valleys with shimmering velvet-green rice fields are replaced by the monotony of rolling scorched brown hills. Picturesque bays and harbours shelter *bagan*, fishing platforms. Along the coasts, families line the shores damming up sea water to make salt.

Serious climbers may want to ascend **Gunung Tambora** ❹. In 1815, some 100 cubic km (25 cubic miles) of debris were ejected into the atmosphere with a force equivalent to that of several hydrogen bombs, creating "the year without summer" the following year. Located on the northern peninsula of Sumbawa, the gaping, 2,820-metre (9,250-ft) high caldera offers spectacular views on a clear day. The ascent begins at **Calabai** ❺, a small logging town on the coast. It is a very difficult climb and a guide is imperative.

Due south of Dompu is **Hu'u** ❻, where the intrepid can catch some really big waves, said to be among the best in the world. It was discovered in 1988 by Australians and prime season is June–August, with the best surf at the beginning of the month and at full moon. A good variety of accommodation has sprung up since the early 1980s along the white-sand Lakey's beach for surfers and holiday-makers though you may want to bring along a tent during peak season.

Continuing on to **Bima** ❼, the royal palace is not much to look at. The sultan's heirlooms are kept at the home of one of his descendants and can only be seen with permission, which is difficult to arrange. If there is a festival going on, visitors may catch *pencak silat* (martial arts) and other dance performances.

Most visitors simply pass through Bima on the way to **Sape** ❽ to catch a boat to Komodo. The road that connects the two towns is hilly and winding. Look for rice storage barns near **Maria** village and plantations of little purple shallots. ❑

Map on pages 256–7

TIP

Sumbawa is at its best from April–November because during the rainy season (December–March) country roads may be impassable and the sea can be rough.

BELOW: young Sumbawa dancer.

KOMODO AND RINCA

The main attraction of these inhospitable islands is their famous resident, the extant Jurassic-like Komodo Dragon, the largest lizard in the world

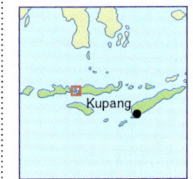

In the island-strewn strait between Sumbawa and Flores lies **Komodo National Park**, home of the world's largest reptile, *Varanus komodoensis*, the Komodo dragon. This giant monitor lizard (called *ora* by the locals) is one of the world's oldest species, a close relative of the dinosaurs that roamed the earth 100 million years ago. The park's three largest islands are Komodo, Rinca (pronounced *ren-cha*) and Padar, and it includes numerous smaller islands. Encompassing nearly 2,000 hectares (4,940 acres) of water and land, the park was designated a UNESCO Man and Biosphere Reserve and World Heritage Site in 1986.

Komodo ❾ island lies 500 km (300 miles) east of Bali, and is 30 km (20 miles) long on its north-south axis and 16 km (10 miles) at its widest point. One of the driest areas in all of Indonesia, its forests are covered with scrub brush, *gebang* (*Corypha elata*) and acacia trees while drought-resistant *lontar* palms dot its parched hills.

In the one village on Komodo, a population of about 1,000 people clings precariously to the shore. Requested by the government to abandon their inland homes inside the new park boundaries, most of its inhabitants make their living fishing by night from graceful outrigger canoes. There is not much to see in Komodo village except the daily routines of some very poor people.

But visitors are welcome, particularly if they are interested in buying one of the locally-carved Komodo dragon statues (the quality is uneven, so you have to choose carefully), a handful of seed pearls or souvenirs from elsewhere in Indonesia.

Unique species

A 1999 study by Italian scientist Claudio Ciofi estimated that there are about 3,000 dragons on Komodo, Rinca, Gili Montang (south-east of Rinca) and a coastal area of western Flores, though there are believed to be small isolated populations in northern Flores and on Gili Dasami, south of Rinca. The research determined that there are genetic similarities between the dragons of Flores and Rinca, while the populations of Komodo and Gili Montang showed a clear pattern of genetic divergence.

Komodo dragons can reach 3 metres (10 ft) or more and weigh an average of 70 kg (154 lbs). Females usually attain only two-thirds of this size and lay up to 30 eggs at a time. Komodo dragons are carnivores and their favourite diet is rotting meat, which they track by flicking their yellow, forked tongues into the air and inserting them into the so-called Jacobson's organ in the roof of the mouth to identify the odour.

But they can hunt, and do so when there is no carrion available. They are able to lift their enormous bodies up on muscular legs and sprint briefly at 20

LEFT: Komodo island is one of the most arid parts of Indonesia.
BELOW: a pack of hungry Komodo dragons.

TIP

During the mating season (May to August) Komodo dragons prefer to attend to the business at hand in seclusion, making them more difficult to spot.

BELOW: the saliva produced by the Komodo dragon is highly septic.

km per hour. They are stealth predators, lying in wait to make an ambush, then using weapon-like claws or their mighty tails to knock a victim senseless as it passes by. If the lizard has managed to sink its serrated teeth into the victim's flesh, even if the victim escapes, it will usually die from septicaemia due to the toxic bacteria in the dragon's saliva.

Threats to survival

The greatest threat to the monitors is from deer poachers, who kill off the animals upon which they feed. Dogs abandoned on the island also compete with the dragons, and eat their eggs. The waters around the park are also in jeopardy, thanks to the cyanide bombing by fishermen; the Nature Conservancy (TNC) and the park director have been working to contain the problem, with some success. TNC reports show a slow but steady regrowth of coral since studies began in 1996, which indicates an enormous slowing down of dynamite fishing.

The highlight of a visit to the national park is seeing the dragons in their natural habitat. On Komodo, the most popular trek is a 2-km (1¼-mile) walk to **Banunggulung**. With prior arrangement, the intrepid can continue past Banunggulung to **Poreng**, in the north-eastern part of the island, or as far as **Sebita** on the coast. Short walks are also possible, from the Ranger Station at **Loh Liang** (where tourist accommodations are sited) to the island's one village to the southwest, or from the Ranger Station to Pantai Merah on the south-east.

There are several other trails to choose from, and park regulations require that all visitors be accompanied by a ranger (whose fee is nominal). The most frequented long-haul trek is to **Gunung Ara** (730 metres, or 2,390 ft), one of a chain of mountains which extends along the northern part of Komodo. It is an all-day excursion, and from the summit you can take in great panoramas of the islands, their craggy peaks, sandy bays and the sparkling turquoise sea. Similar views can be enjoyed from **Gunung Satalibo**, at 740 metres (2,420 ft) high, the island's tallest peak. The trails are those used by foraging animals, bordered by tall grasses concealing large stones, so sturdy walking shoes and trousers are recommended. There are basic tourist bungalows at the Ranger Station in Loh Liang, but watch out for the rats.

Scuba diving and snorkelling in the park waters are reputed to be some of the best in the Asia Pacific region. The 260 species of reef-building coral, sheer drop walls and around 1,000 species of fish and marine mammals, including manta rays, sharks, sea turtles, dolphins and whales, are a diver's delight. With the marine area constituting 67 percent of the park, diving brings a significant number of tourists. The waters to the south of the park are cooler than those to the north, creating an ideal habitat for corals and reef fish, while to the north, rich plankton and nutrients attract a wide variety of temperate marine life. For snorkellers, **Pantai Merah** (Red Beach) offers butterfly, parrot and trigger fish, giant clams and colourful corals at close range. The gorgeous beach is pink due to an abundance of red coral in the region.

As Komodo National Park is in the transition zone described by 19th century naturalist Sir Alfred Russel Wallace *(see page 246)*, birdwatchers will find a mixture of Asian and Australian species. Squawking cockatoos and noisy friarbirds flock in tropical *kapok* and gnarled tamarind trees, disturbing green Imperial pigeons, black-naped orioles, sunbirds and flowerpeckers. On the forest floor, there are jungle fowl, the forebears of domesticated chickens, quails scratching for insects, and mound-building megapodes.

Map on pages 256–7

Pantai Merah beach on Komodo island gets its name from the presence of red coral in the area.

BELOW: delicate shrimp resting on bubble coral.

Rinca

Rinca ❿ island has only been open to tourists within the last few years and is not as crowded as Komodo can be in the high season (July and August), and therefore, provides a far more natural experience.

On Rinca, there are two moderately easy treks (2–3 hours each) from the Ranger Station at **Loh Buaya**. One, to the east of the compound, is up and across a ridge where there is a breathtaking view of the Komodo group of islands, with Flores rising from the sea at one point. Watch for herds of wild horses, which are absent from Komodo. The other trail goes in the opposite direction through monsoon forest, where wild buffaloes wallow in streams.

There is a shortage of park rangers in July and August, the busiest tourist season. Those wishing longer treks requiring a ranger may be happier visiting during the off-season. It is best to leave on expeditions in the early mornings when the animals are at their most active, avoiding the extreme mid-day heat.

When visiting Komodo, whether arriving by government ferry or by a private boat chartered on Sumbawa or Flores, be aware that the currents around Komodo are very strong and the seas usually rough. When swimming, keep an eye out for sea snakes, which are plentiful in these waters, and always be mindful of currents and riptides. ❑

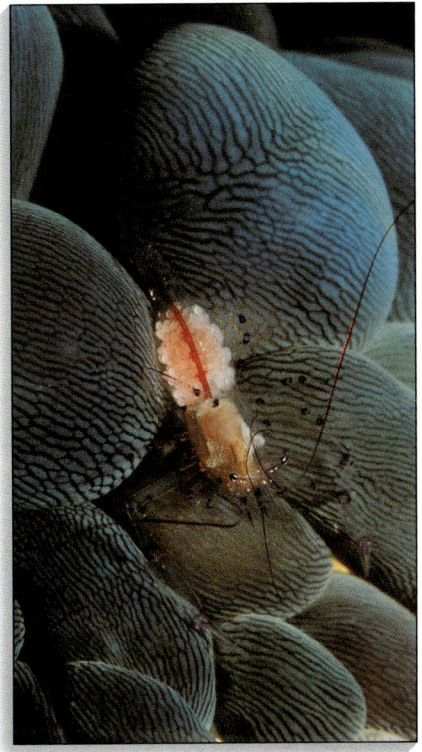

FLORES

Named for its untamed verdant beauty, the island includes the beguiling Gunung Kelimutu, with three crater lakes that constantly change colour. Here too, high-quality ikat is woven

The largest island in the East Nusa Tenggara chain, **Flores** received its name in 1512 from passing Portuguese explorers who christened it *Cabo das Flores* (Cape of Flowers). Before that time, it was known to traders as the unimaginatively-named Stone Island. Flores has absorbed foreign influence from many quarters. Its ports once formed a vital link in inter-island trade and, during the 1400s, it was drawn into the commercial and political sphere of the Hindu-Javanese Majapahit empire. Some coastal communities began to convert to Islam in the 15th and 16th centuries as a result of contact with the far-flung trading sultanate of clove-producing Ternate.

In the mid-16th century, the Portuguese arrived. They established a mission at Larantuka and built a fort on Solor island, east of Flores, primarily to protect their trading interests in Timor. By the 1570s, there was already a seminary in Larantuka, and Catholicism was spreading quickly to other areas.

In 1664, Muslim invaders from Goa in South Sulawesi took control of Ende, ostensibly to stem the tide of Catholic conversions. Subsequent Makassarese immigrations created a strong Islamic community, and the Endenese raided Sumba for slaves and traded sandalwood from Timor. The Dutch acquired the Portuguese settlements on Flores in 1859, with a proviso that the Catholic church be encouraged. They also bombarded Muslim Ende twice and exercised increasing authority there, but fully controlled the island only after subduing a bloody rebellion in 1907–08. Thereafter, Catholic missionaries flooded Flores, sparking a new wave of conversions that continues today.

Catholicism mixed with animism

Catholicism claims 90 percent of Flores' 1 million inhabitants. The church has put heavy emphasis on improving living conditions through its schools, health services and agricultural programmes. And although the clergy in Flores is well aware of the continued existence of many traditional beliefs and customs, they make no systematic efforts to eliminate them. The ancient traditions that have survived are many and varied, and constitute much of the island's fascination for the visitor.

Many islanders still worship their ancestral spirits. They also believe in Dewa, a god who lives in the sky, and Nitu, a goddess who lives beneath the earth, in the water, in large trees, and in the ocean. Pythons were once worshipped in Flores, lending the island its former name, Snake Island.

A 670-km (420-mile) road, paved for about half the distance, runs the length of the island in a series of curves and switchbacks from Labuhanbajo in the west to Larantuka in the east. To travel the entire route is

LEFT: the majority of Flores' islanders profess to be Catholics.
BELOW: Catholic missionary in Flores, circa 1920.

TIP

When travelling throughout Flores, buy toilet tissue and soap at local shops, as none is provided in simple *losmen*. A *sarong* makes a good bath towel or a makeshift top sheet at night.

long and exhausting, and often involves dodging landslides in the rainy season. It is definitely not recommended for those who suffer from car sickness. But the changes in scenery along the way are spectacular: from mountains to rice fields and coastal views, plantations of cocoa, vanilla, coffee and pineapples, and the corresponding differences in village life.

The western third of Flores is called **Manggarai** and contains almost half the island's population. Manggarai is self-sufficient in rice, and exports fine coffee and livestock. **Labuhanbajo** ⑪ sits on a beautiful harbour filled with the outriggers of local fishermen. Its primary importance from a tourist's perspective is its proximity to the Komodo National Park. Tours to Komodo and boat charters can be arranged through *losmen*, and the sail to the national park is far more scenic and the waters calmer than the crossing from Sape (Sumbawa) to Komodo. For those who wish to linger on, there is accommodation on isolated islands (in addition to the row of simple *losmen* on the main street of town), snorkelling and some fairly good scuba diving. You can also explore **Batu Cermin** (Mirror Rock), a series of caves and canyons about 4 km (2½ miles) outside town.

From Labuhanbajo, the road winds up to **Ruteng** ⑫, a pleasantly cool town situated up in the western hills. Watch for the traditional *lingko*, spider web-shaped rice fields near **Cancar** before reaching Ruteng.

Ruteng is primarily a government centre and a good stopping-off place to break up the long overland trip. The top of **Golo Curu** (Welcome Mountain) has great sunset views and an old Dutch church (5 minutes by *bemo* or a 45-minute walk). Rainforest-covered **Gunung Ranaka** (2,140 metres or 7,021 ft) looms over Ruteng – it is a 3-hour walk to the summit – and is a good venue for birdwatching.

BELOW: cacao plantation near Labuhanbajo.

Traditional villages

Kampung Ruteng, with a stone ancestral altar, is just outside of Ruteng. **Todo** village is 21 km (13 miles) from Ruteng and features megalithic stones and a drum whose head is reputedly covered by a woman's skin. From Todo, it is a 30-minute walk to **Welo** village, which holds a sacrificial ceremony at every New Year celebration. Some of the oldest houses in Manggarai are in **Dintor**, a 3-hour mountain trek from Ruteng. A 15-minute boat ride from Dintor leads to the white-sand beaches of Mules island and nearby Wae Rebo, a cultural centre, hot springs and a bird conservation area. The Trans-Flores road passes **Rana Mese** (Big Lake), a crater lake surrounded by forest, near Mborong.

While in Manggarai, travellers may see a spectacular *caci* whip duel, held as part of a wedding or other important ceremonies. Combatants are outfitted with buffalo-hide shields, and attack each other with long rattan whips. The aim is to overcome the physical and spiritual defence of one's opponent. Welts and scars are admired, and blood drawn is offered to the ancestral spirits.

The next stop is **Bajawa** ⓭, where the Manggarai district ends and **Ngada** begins. Bajawa's attraction is its cool, mountain air. Exquisite yellow-on-black supplementary warp *sarong* are produced in the area. Accommodation and food are basic here, and dog meat is a local delicacy. You have been warned.

Bena, **Langa**, **Watujaji**, **Warusoba**, **Likowali**, **Boloji** and **Boripo** are examples of Ngada's ancient villages. All have *ngadhu* shrines with carved tree-trunk bases and *bhaga*, small houses in the village center. The *ngadhu* and *bhaga* symbolise male and female tribal ancestors who live in the village. There are interesting megalithic stones in every village, but these are easiest to find at Bena and also at nearby **Wogo Tua** (Old Wogo). The week-long Reba festival

Ngadhu shrine in Langa with a human figure on its rooftop.

BELOW: traditional thatched houses in Bajawa.

begins in Bena in late December, then moves to other villages according to dates selected by their *adat* (traditional customs) leaders. Wearing their traditional *ikat*, the people dance around the village, and the ceremony concludes with them forming a circle around several men who begin to sing. The entire village responds to the song in chorus.

A deer hunt in **So'a** ⓮ follows the mass and is a fertility ritual associated with puberty rites: circumcision for the boys and tooth filing for the girls. Strong taboos against sex are enforced throughout the hunt, including a prohibition against the consummation of recent marriages. After the hunt, young women dip their hands into the blood of slain deer to enhance their fertility.

Langa and Bena lie in the shadows of the perfectly-coned volcano, **Gunung Inerie** (2,230 metres or 7,316 ft). It can be climbed in 2–5 hours, depending on your level of physical fitness. **Gunung Ebulobo**, one of Flores' most magnificent volcanoes, can be climbed from Mulakoli village, off the main road to Ende.

From Bajawa, it is a 3-hour drive to the northern coastal village **Riung** ⓯, an excellent side trip for those with time to spare and who are interested in snorkelling in the **Seventeen Islands Nature Reserve**. Riung is also the only site inhabited by Komodo dragons outside of Komodo and Rinca islands.

On the main road from Bajawa, it is 125 km (80 miles) and about 5 hours to **Ende** ⓰, one of Flores' two major towns. In contrast to the other, Maumere, Ende has a distinctly Islamic flavour; it was an important Islamic trading port from the late 17th century to the 19th century. During the Japanese Occupation, the city was the regional capital for the eastern archipelago. Sukarno was exiled here for a time, and Ende was later bombed by the Allies. Today, commerce is largely in Chinese hands.

BELOW: the curious coloured lakes at Kelimutu.

Map on pages 256–7

Sorcerers, sinners, virgins

A couple of hours north-east of Ende are three adjacent volcanic crater lakes on **Gunung Kelimutu**, the island's main tourist attraction. The lakes, at an altitude of 1,640 metres (5,380 ft), are separated only by low ridges and, curiously, are of different colours: blue, turquoise, and dark burgundy. Like chameleons, their colours constantly change. No scientific study of the lakes has been made, but one possible explanation is that the coloration results from dissolved minerals, the water eating through mineral layers at varying rates, perhaps due to changes in acidity. The natives of this area say that one lake holds the souls of sorcerers, another the souls of sinners, while the third lake cradles the souls of infants and virgins.

The best time for viewing is at sunrise. Be forewarned that the road to the lakes is often impassable in the rainy season (October–April). Hotels in Ende can arrange pre-dawn departures, or stop at the road junction and hire a truck for the ride to the summit. Alternatively, stay overnight in one of the many *losmen* in **Moni** ⓱ at the foot of the mountain.

Around Ende is the beginning of the *ikat* weaving area, exquisitely-woven material in which intricate designs are tie-dyed onto the threads before weaving begins. In Ende *ikat*, the designs are of a solid colour, usually reddish brown. Some 12 km (7½ miles) east of Kelimutu, at **Wolowaru**, turn south to **Nggela** coastal village via **Japo** to see superb material being woven. From Ende to Maumere, the road cuts diagonally across the island towards the north coast. The distance is 150 km (90 miles), but the winding, scenic drive can take 7 hours.

Maumere ⓲ is benefiting from increased copra and coffee exports. The Catholic Church, with its large coconut and coffee holdings, is behind much of the development. Although the town and nearby Catholic seminary were severely damaged in a 1992 earthquake and tidal wave that killed thousands along the north coast of Flores, little evidence remains of the tragedy. Visit Maumere's market to see local ladies with swept-up hairdos dressed in traditional *sarong*, bright green or yellow blouses and heirloom ivory bracelets. While made in the same manner as Ende's, the *ikat* material of Maumere sport a greater variety of colours. Watch weavers at work in nearby villages **Watublapi**, **Sikka** or **Nita**. Snorkelling and diving off Maumere's fine beaches have suffered from dynamite fishing.

Unlike the people in the rest of Flores who eat rice, the staple food in Maumere is ubi, a sweet potato-like tuber from the cassava family.

BELOW: Flores girl with carved ivory and silver bangles.

A slice of Iberia

A 140-km (80-mile) road journey takes you to **Larantuka** ⓳ on the eastern tip of Flores. It was a Portuguese colony for about 300 years and the Catholic rituals reflect that Iberian influence. Men dressed in white hoods carry the coffin of Jesus through the streets during Good Friday processions, stopping along the way for prayers and hymns in a version of the *Via Dolorosa*. But local beliefs creep in. A statue of the Virgin Mary is bathed – said to have been found on the beach by a local man, who reported to the king that he met a beautiful lady. But when the king reached the beach, the lady was not there. Instead, they found a statue and a message in the sand that said: "Renha Rosari". Larantuka is a departure point for excursions to the small islands to the east. ❑

SOLOR AND ALOR ARCHIPELAGOS

Visit the primitive whaling village of Lamalera where the hunt begins with a harpoon, or ascend the volcano Ile Ape for an other-world experience atop its smoky yellow-sulphur interior

East of Flores lie the archipelagos of Solor (comprising Solor, Adonara and Lembata) and Alor (including Pantar and Alor). While their inhabitants have been in contact with each other since ancient times, they have remained relatively isolated from the rest of the world. Larantuka (on east coast of Flores) is the gateway to the Solor group of islands, and boats frequently ply the waters between the two. To get to Alor, hop on a fairly reliable ferry in Kupang (in West Timor).

Solor [20] has an old Portuguese fort, constructed in 1566 and still in good shape. Massive stone walls, some 2 metres (6½ ft) thick and 4 metres (13 ft) high, encircle a rectangular interior. The entrance is covered by an impressive arch and, in one corner, rusting cannons have survived and stand guard over approaches from the sea. In Solor, too, are woven *ikat* cloths that have a brilliant red background instead of the dark indigo used in other parts of the region.

Lembata [21] (formerly known as Lomblen) is noted for its primitive whaling industry centred on the town of **Lamalera** on the south coast. Shallow-draught, sail and oar-propelled wooden boats are used. When a whale is sighted, a harpooner balances precariously on a narrow plank extending from the bow of the boat and then jumps off with his harpoon, thrusting it accurately into the whale's back.

BELOW: cannon at abandoned Portuguese fort in Lohayong, Solor.

Lembata women still weave ceremonial *ikat* cloth from homespun threads made from cotton grown in local gardens. A good "bride wealth" sarong sells for hundreds of dollars due to their importance in weddings. While the groom's family is expected to give the bride's family ivory tusks – first brought to the area in the 14th century as payment for slaves – the bride's family has to reciprocate with something of equal value, usually *ikat*. The most frequently found pieces are from Ile Ape in the north, Lamalera in the south, and Atadei in the south-east. When they are sold the money is often for medical expenses or children's school fees. *Ikat* sold at the market and worn daily are made from rayon or cotton using bright colours from synthetic dyes, and thus less expensive.

Ile Ape volcano

Lewoleba, 3–4 hours away from Lamalera, is renowned for its Monday market. Buyers and sellers from throughout the region descend on the town on that day. Chickens and pigs, betel nuts, cigarettes, plastic buckets, small cakes, dried fish and fresh vegetables all find their way to the Lewoleba market.

Towering over the island is **Gunung Ile Ape**, revered by Lembata people who retain animistic beliefs. Although most of the island is outwardly

Catholic, small shrines bearing simple offerings are prevalent on the slopes of the volcano. Ili Api can be climbed from its northern slope in 4 hours of fairly easy walking, but take a guide and go early, before the clouds cover the sulphurous crater. Excursions usually start from Atawatung or Mawa villages. There is good snorkelling in the bay on the eastern side of the volcano.

Further east is **Pantar** ㉒, which is not exactly a favourite tourist destination. But for those seeking an out-of-the-way experience, **Gunung Sirung** awaits. Catch a ferry from Kalabahi (Alor) to **Baranusa** where it is possible to access Gunung Sirung. Adventurers who make it to Sirung's summit will be rewarded with views of the bright yellow crater and the aroma of sulphurous fumes.

Alor ㉓ is known for its bronze kettledrums, replicas of those from the 2,000-year-old Dong Son era of northern Vietnam. Hundreds and perhaps thousands of these drums, called *moko* by the local residents, are still kept as heirlooms and are an essential part of the bride price. Although the *moko* found on Alor were cast in either Java or China, how they ended up on this island, which was not part of traditional trade routes, remains unknown.

Unlike their neighbours on either side, the Alorese have the dark skin and frizzy hair of the Papuans. Eight distinct languages – not dialects – have evolved on this relatively small island.

In the market at Alor's major town of **Kalabahi** is the village "popcorn popper", a cannon-like affair which announces with a huge "bang" that the taste treat – coated with sugar rather than salt – is ready. For a fee, too, dances can be arranged, such as one depicting a trip to the forest to cut trees to build traditional houses. Weavers also sell traditional indigo cloths bearing *ikat* borders, hand-plaited baskets and embroidered bark cloth. ❑

The presence of ancient bronze kettle drums called moko in Alor is a mystery as they were not cast on the island.

BELOW:
Lembata fisherman harpooning a whale.

SUMBA

Free of the usual tourist hordes, Sumba has stayed untouched. Its two distinct halves – one lush, the other sparse – make up this fascinating island of full-moon festivals and warp-dyed ikat cloths

Well to the south of the main Nusa Tenggara chain, **Sumba** has always been a major backwater region of the archipelago. Barren throughout the long dry season and with few tourist facilities, the island teems with remnants of an ancient pagan culture. Because it never had much historical significance and few resources, Sumba escaped the waves of Hindu, Muslim and Christian influence that washed over neighbouring islands.

Known in past centuries as a source of sandalwood, slaves and horses – and as a land of cannibal tribes – Sumba is today famous for its sculptured megalithic tombs, war game rituals and intricate *hinggi ikat* textiles. The island is almost oval-shaped, about 300 km (180 miles) long and 80 km (50 miles) wide, and is divided politically and climatically into two distinct halves.

West Sumba, with a population of 350,000, is the more prosperous half, higher and thus lush and green during the rainy season. It is also more culturally diverse, with two separate linguistic groups speaking at least eight dialects. West Sumbans live in huts with high peaked roofs. Agricultural communities flourish and ancestral and land worship are still strong.

East Sumba is dry, rocky and inhospitable, with 250,000 inhabitants who speak one language. Most people live near or on the coast, and an extensive hand-loom industry has flourished for several centuries, producing distinctive, high-quality woven *ikat*.

Uncommon megaliths

Traditional villages with elaborate megalithic tombs are scattered throughout West Sumba. The small district capital, **Waikabubak** ㉔, boasts a number of ancient mausoleums. **Tarung** village, an important hilltop ceremonial centre just west of Waikabubak, has tombs and houses decorated with water buffalo horns and souvenirs of sacrificial feasts.

There is another tomb with unusual carvings at **Pasunga** in Anakalang district, 20 km (14 miles) east of Waikabubak on the main road to Waingapu. A bit further east and a few minutes off the road, the Resi Moni grave – one of the largest megaliths on the island – is the burial site of a former *raja* of Anakalang. Nearby **Lai Tarung** has many old graves and an important ceremony called *purunga ta kadonga*. **Wanokaka** district, 18 km (12 miles) south of Waikabubak, has the oldest megaliths in the area, the *batu kajiwa* (spirit stones) at **Prai Goli**.

Sodan is perhaps the most interesting traditional village in West Sumba, located 25 km (16 miles) south-west of Waikabubak. The area is steeped in magic and taboos and an important new year ceremony takes place each October at full moon. Sodan once possessed a sacred drum reportedly covered with

BELOW: some of Indonesia's most distinctive *ikat* cloth is produced on Sumba.

the skin of a human being. This was destroyed in a fire about 10 years ago.

The Pasola is West Sumba's most exciting ritual, with scores of colourfully-arrayed horsemen on bareback, battling with spears. Held during February in **Lamboya** and **Kodi** (on the western tip of the island) and during March in **Gaura** and **Wanokaka**, it begins after the full moon and coincides with the yearly arrival of multi-hued sea worms, called *nyale*, to the shore. Riders charge one another and fling spears, which modern law now requires to be blunt.

To relax in West Sumba while waiting for the Pasola or other rituals, swim at the white-sand beach at **Rua**, 21 km (13 miles) south of Waikabubak, or at the spring-fed pools at **Waikelo Sawah**, 10 km (6 miles) west of the town. A small luxury hotel has opened on the lovely beach south of Waikabubak.

East Sumba ikat

East Sumba has been known for centuries for its distinctive *hinggi ikat*, patterned by dyeing designs on the warp threads before the weft is introduced. The tedious process takes several months. Traditionally, homespun threads were used, but today factory-made ones are more prevalent. The threads are stretched on a frame and tied with dye-resistant fibres to create the pattern before being immersed in dye and sun-dried. Subsequent re-binding and re-dyeing create the final design, usually blue and red with bold animal and human figures.

To see the process, set out for **Prailiu**, just outside of **Waingapu** ㉕. Some 70 km (40 miles) from Waingapu is **Rende**, which is known for good *ikat* as well as for megalithic tombs with unusual carvings. In the vicinity of **Ngallu** and **Baing**, 125 km (80 miles) from Waingapu, whole villages produce the famous *kombu* woven cloths. Bargaining is expected.

A common motif in Sumba's hinggi ikat is the skull tree or andung, which draws upon the former practice of hanging the heads of vanquished enemies on a tree to scare away evil spirits.

BELOW:
East Sumba village.

Map on pages 256–7

ROTI, SAVU AND WEST TIMOR

This remote region holds many surprises. Savu is known for its beautiful women, Roti men are prized for their oratorical skills, while Timor's fragrant timber is a centuries-old draw

Roti and Savu are two seldom-visited islands off the west coast of Timor. With little rainfall to encourage rice-growing, both learnt centuries ago to rely on a sturdy drought-resistant palm, the *lontar* (*Borassus sundaicus*), for sustenance when there was no other food available. *Lontar* is also used for building materials and household tools. The palms are often farmed plantation-style. Twice daily, a tapper climbs to the towering fronds to make a slice in the inflorescence before it flowers, with a basket put in place to catch the sweet juice. The liquid from two or three trees is enough to support a family during times of drought, or can be fermented into a wine known as *tuak*, or reduced to a treacle and stored for later use.

Savu ❷⓺ (also spelled Sawu) has a reputation for some of the most beautiful women in Indonesia. Ask any seaman about Savunese women and wait for the swoon. Equally beautiful are the island's *ikat* weavings, which are coveted by women as far away as Flores. Historians will more likely remember Savu as one of the islands visited by Captain Cook in 1770 on his expeditions aboard the *Endeavour*. Other explorers may have called at the remote little island, too, as evidenced by the etching of a sailing ship on a rock near **Namata** village.

Savu is also known for its small "sandalwood" horses, similar to those found on Sumba. Much stronger than they look, the little horses are used for transport and are ridden bareback in mock battles and dances recreating the ousting of a plague of locusts that threatened crops long ago.

Immaculate beaches

Roti ❷⓻ (also spelt as Rote), a land of dazzling white-sand beaches and rolling plains, is about one-fifth the size of Bali, yet it shelters 18 different ethnic groups, each of which was formerly ruled by its own *raja*. Rotinese men are known throughout Indonesia for their debating skills, and many attorneys and administrators throughout the archipelago are Rotinese.

One of the *ikat*-producing islands, Roti's cloths are colourful – with a good deal of red – compared to the textiles of its neighbours. Unique to the island is the *sasando*, a mandolin-like bamboo instrument with a resonator of *lontar* leaves, which produces soft lyrical sounds. Souvenir collectors may like one of the *lontar* hats worn by Rotinese men. Also sought after is silver jewellery from neighbouring **Ndao** ❷⓼ island.

For many centuries, **Timor** has been known as a source of fragrant sandalwood, a draw for Chinese, Javanese and Islamic traders. The Portuguese and the Dutch later fought to control the trade and subsequently divided the island into Dutch West Timor and Portuguese East Timor. After Indonesia's independence, the East remained a Portuguese possession

BELOW:
Savu native astride a miniature "sandlewood" horse.

until 1975. Politics overtook the island the following year, when a left-wing movement threatened to gain control. Indonesia retaliated by seizing the territory using military force, and in 1999, after a long and bloody struggle, **East Timor** (now called **Timor Leste**) gained its independence from Indonesia.

Note: Despite foreign government travel warnings still in place after the turmoil in 1999–2000, currently both West Timor and Timor Leste are calm and trouble-free, and very welcoming of visitors.

West Timor

The capital of East Nusa Tenggara province, **Kupang** ㉙ has regular air and ferry services to and from the rest of Indonesia. There are numerous hotels and shops for replenishing supplies before sailing to outlying islands. Kupang's attractions include the town market and the **Museum Negeri Kupang** (Museum of East Nusa Tenggara; open Mon–Thur 8am–2pm, Fri 8–11am, Sat 8am–12.30pm, Sun 10am–2pm; free, but a small donation is appreciated.) Here, one can ask about cultural performances.

West Timor offers bustling markets, traditional villages, World War II relics, good snorkelling and a great variety of fine textiles which are regionally-specific in their designs and techniques. There are three major towns on the main road between Kupang and Dili: **So'e**, **Kefamenanu** and **Atambua**. Each has reasonable-quality hotels, restaurants and tourist information and are good bases for exploring outlying villages and countryside with the help of local guides.

Now that Timor Leste is a separate country, visitors often travel by road from Kupang to Dili to get new visas for Indonesia, or as a point of transit on their way to Australia. ❑

Cotton used for West Timor ikat is locally spun and dyed by hand. Selimut blankets are an especially good buy.

BELOW: Roti island beachcombers.

KALIMANTAN

This vast, wild territory used to be known for its headhunters. Today orangutan head the list of attractions

Kalimantan is Indonesia's name for its two-thirds of Borneo, the world's third-largest island (after Greenland and New Guinea). The rest of Borneo, on the north coast, is formed by the East Malaysian provinces of Sarawak and Sabah, and the tiny independent oil-rich sultanate of Brunei. Kalimantan, with an area of 540,000 sq km (200,000 sq miles), represents nearly 30 percent of the nation's land area, but with less than 5 percent of the population.

The centre of Kalimantan is made up of mountain ranges, whose summits seldom exceed 1,500 metres (5,000 ft). Great rivers cascade down from the highlands, and are often navigable for hundreds of kilometres, serving as crucial channels of communication between the communities of the coast and the interior. The river highways attract tourists who want to travel deep into jungle regions to visit the Dayak tribes, once headhunters who still dwell in communal houses.

Geology is the key to Kalimantan's economy. The eastern coastal region produces petroleum and natural gas. Diamonds have been mined in the west and south since pre-colonial times; an area near Banjarmasin still yields substantial gemstones. Mining firms have tapped into gold reserves far inland, while locals still pan the rivers. Large-scale coal mining started in the 1800s and continues unabated. Deposits of uranium and other minerals await exploitation.

Logging has been a major industry since the 1960s. Mills have been developed on the lower reaches of many rivers, notably near Samarinda and Banjarmasin. Logs are floated downstream to be processed into planks, plywood and other wood products. There are other cash crops – pepper, rubber and palm oil – but most people survive on subsistence farming, hunting and fishing.

Kalimantan's coast features mangrove swamps and low-grade forest. An inland belt of gentle hills and alluvial plains marks the start of the jungle. The main canopy is about 25 metres (80 ft) above the ground, occasionally punctured by towering *Dipterocarpus* trees with crowns reaching 70 metres (230 ft). Valuable ebony and ironwood trees are scattered throughout. In the colder reaches of the central highlands, trunks are often draped in moss and lichen.

The wildlife is just as exotic. Orangutan, found only in Sumatra and Borneo, head the list, along with the endemic proboscis monkey. Other forest denizens include the clouded leopard, leaf monkey, crab-eating macaque, the pangolin anteater and the tiny tarsier, with its huge eyes and an ability to swivel its head 180 degrees. There are about 600 species of birds, among them magnificent Argus pheasants and hornbills, considered sacred by the Dayak peoples. ❑

PRECEDING PAGES: river adventure on Sungai Sekonyer, in Tanjung Puting National Park.
LEFT: orangutan, or "forest man" are a protected species.

EAST AND SOUTH KALIMANTAN

Stay close to the earth, where white water rapids, montane forests and wildlife rule. Overnight stays in longhouses allow glimpses of a simple existence led by Borneo's myriad river-fed villages

Kalimantan Timur (East Kalimantan), or Kaltim for short, is one of the two most popular destinations in Indonesian Borneo. The province is huge, embracing the Sungai Mahakam and its various tributaries as well as several river basins to the north. With over 200,000 sq km (77,000 sq miles), the district covers an area the size of England and Scotland combined. Yet it holds only 1½ million people, many of whom are farmers from Java who arrived during the government's transmigration scheme.

Much of the land is uninhabited jungle, and the population is primarily concentrated in the coastal areas. In addition to oil, Kaltim also produces natural gas, processed into methanol at Bontang. However, most jobs are in the timber industry, which has been booming since the early 1970s. The province also exports gold, coal, shrimp, pepper and other agricultural products.

Balikpapan ❶ is the usual port of entry to Kaltim. This busy oil and timber town, with a population of nearly 500,000, holds little interest for travellers unless they are on business. One can take in the hilltop view of Pertamina's sprawling oil installations, do some souvenir shopping and sample local nightlife in the company of burly oil workers. But that is all. Independent travellers head straight to Samarinda by air or via the 115-km (70-mile) paved road to begin their journeys up the great Sungai Mahakam.

Samarinda ❷, with about 300,000 people, is the jumping-off point for visits to Dayak country and the capital of Kaltim province. There is not much to see here. To soak in local culture, an interesting activity is to hire a boat and observe activity along the waterfront: freighters loading or discharging, coal barges being shoved around, rafts of logs under tow to nearby lumber mills. Early morning or late afternoon hours are best for these jaunts. Half a day is enough in Samarinda, giving you enough time to check out schedules for planes or boats heading inland.

Sungai Mahakam trips

Tour packages, which can be arranged in Balikpapan or Samarinda, are the easiest way to traverse the Mahakam in search of Dayak folk, with some offering overnight stays either on houseboats outfitted for tourists or in longhouses set up for such visitors. The houseboats are large and comfortable. Some of them provide amenities such as air-conditioning, fresh water showers, modern toilets and satellite television.

For all river boats, the first major stop out of Samarinda is **Tenggarong ❸**, the former sultan's capital about 2–2½ hours away. Along the way, look out

LEFT: Dayak villages flanking a tributary of Sungai Mahakam.
BELOW: a 17th-century Dutch lithograph of Borneo tribes.

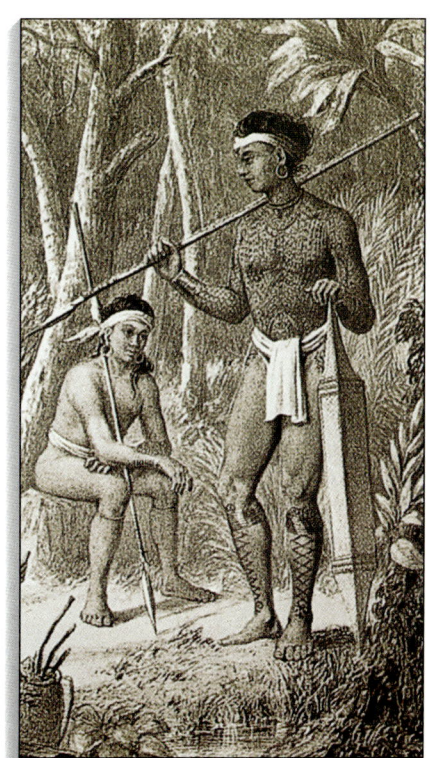

> **TIP**
>
> Tanjung Isuy is one of the last places in Kalimantan where a traditional fibre cloth called *ulop doyo* is still woven. To see a demonstration, ask your guide or the villagers.

for sawmills and barges laden with coal – evidence of two of Kaltim's major industries – and daily activities in riverside villages. There is a **museum** housing Ming dynasty ceramics and Dayak handicrafts that is worth a visit.

Alternatively, a new toll road links Samarinda to Tenggarong. The drive takes about 30 minutes, and the tour allows travellers to visit Tenggarong's museum and then join a cruise boat for short trips on the Mahakam or longer cruises upriver. One of the Mahakam islands, **Pulau Kumala**, is also under development. A resort, a sky tower and lift are already operating on the island. Dayak longhouses, other cultural attractions and a lake containing freshwater dolphins will open soon on the island.

Tenggarong is also home to the Erau festival, held every 22–28 September, which celebrates the founding of the town and honours former royalty. Dayak come from miles away to perform traditional dances and recreate pagan rituals such as funeral ceremonies, contrasting greatly to the more sedate dances of the Muslims from Kutai who don their best ceremonial costumes for the occasion.

The next major stop, **Kota Bangun** ❹, lies 6 hours upstream from Tenggarong and is the last chance to experience accommodation with modern conveniences. It is also the last place that can be reached by road. From here, travellers can hire a motorised canoe into the hinterland of Kalimantan upstream.

The riverside town **Muara Muntai**, 2–3 hours from Kota Bangun, is home to both Kubai Dayak and transmigrants from Java and other places in the archipelago. It is also the point of departure for exploring the mid-Mahakam lakes region, the beginning of Dayak country. Small motorised canoes can be rented here for the 2-hour run to **Tanjung Isuy** ❺, a Dayak village on **Danau Jempang**, often called Green Lake due to massive amounts of a rampant water

BELOW: Dayak longhouse at Tanjung Isuy.

weed. Welcome rituals and dances are often put on for tourists here by the locals, the most popular destination in the Kaltim area. At the village of **Mancong**, a rebuilt *lamin* (longhouse) with 24 doors – the only two-storey longhouse in Kalimantan – gives an idea of past splendours. There has been a communal house on this site for more than 300 years.

Dayak country

Melak ❻, 3 hours away, either by air, foot or motorised canoe, marks the first stop within Dayak-dominated areas. Travellers to the village are served by several *losmen* and foodstalls which offer simple meals.

There is a local road system out of Melak with transport (usually jeeps or motorcycles) for visiting the **Kersik Luwai** orchid reserve, and its 100-plus species of orchids, including the famous "black" variety, as well as nearby Dayak villages with lived-in longhouses. Ask around if you wish to witness a funeral ceremony in progress; the rituals feature the sacrifice of a water buffalo performed with spears.

Upriver from Melak is **Barong Tongkok**, where the nearest authentic longhouses are located. Beneath the T-shirts and shorts worn by most villagers in the area beat the hearts of followers of the traditional religion, Kaharingan. Influenced by Hinduism, Kaharingan focuses on the supernatural world of spirits. There is a *losmen* in Barong Tongkok, or ask the *kepala desa* (village chief) for permission to stay in a longhouse.

Six hours upstream from Melak, year-round river navigation stops at **Long Iram**, a week or so out of Samarinda and more than 400 km (250 miles) from the coast. Some of the larger passenger boats make the Samarinda–Long Iram

Purple Vanda Hookerinia blooms at Kersik Luwai orchid reserve.

TIP

When entering a new inland town or village, stop in at the police office, if there is one, or call on the *kepala desa* (village chief) to show your passport. This formality will make your visit a smoother one.

run in about 36 hours, have bunks and mattresses for a small surcharge, and kitchens serving simple meals. Several larger riverside towns offer basic accommodation and their restaurants serve rice-based meals. Beyond Long Iram, there is only the hospitality of the Dayak or government officials. Many of the Dayak in this area, and also further upstream, belong to the Roman Catholic church, which tolerates and even encourages some traditional rituals.

If the river level is not too low – or too high, in the event of a flood – cargo and passenger boats can reach **Long Bagun** in a matter of 4–6 hours from Long Iram. Several Dayak groups are settled along this stretch of the Mahakam, including the Kenyah, who are known for their huge sculptures and paintings in communal buildings.

Beyond Long Bagun, logistics may be a problem because a series of rapids choke off most river travel, with only an occasional powerful twin-outboard longboat roaring through. Chartering a boat may entail a long wait. It is a great experience, but unless one has plenty of time, the best way to reach the uppermost areas of the Mahakam is to fly from Samarinda to **Data Dawai**, a landing strip near Long Lunuk village. From Data Dawai, it is possible to charter a boat to go upriver to Long Ampari, the last village on the Mahakam.

For Kaltim's **Apokayan** ❼ region, near the border of Sarawak and homeland of the Kenyah Dayak, air travel is the only means of access, other than weeks of trekking. Be warned that flights are often delayed or cancelled, and it is advisable to avoid this scenario if time schedules are tight.

Located on the uppermost reaches of the Sungai Kayan, a dozen villages are strung out on either side of the landing strip at **Long Ampung**. Due to its isolation and difficulty in obtaining essentials (soap, medicines, cooking oil),

BELOW:
colourful river life along Long Bagun.

most of the Apokayan's inhabitants have migrated to more accessible locations. Those who remain usually live in longhouses, and the prolific artwork of the Kenyah is still in evidence. There are good trails for trekking and distances between villages can be covered in a few hours.

Among the highlights are **Long Uro**, a 2-hour walk from Long Ampung, where there are Dayak carvings in front of the village and a cemetery. An easy hour's walk away is **Long Lindung Payau** with its ancient stone relics.

The last human settlement on the Sungai Kenyah, **Long Sungai Barang**, is a demanding 4-hour walk over hills and through jungles. On a lake surrounded by mountains, Long Sungai Barang is an excellent place to rest for a few days and gather new strength for the trip back to "civilisation".

Although the chances of spotting wildlife are fairly good on hikes in the Apokayan and the upper Mahakam areas, your best option is the **Kutai National Park** on the east coast.

To get there, travel either by road from Samarinda, or fly from Balikpapan to **Bontang** ❽, a natural gas plant on the coast. At Bontang, contact the park office so that they will radio ahead to the rangers. From Bontang, take a motorised canoe to Sengatta for the best wildlife viewing, which is along the river. The principal attraction there is the orangutan, but there are also 60 species of mammals and 300 species of birds, including proboscis monkeys, deer and hornbills – a symbol of the upperworld to the Dayak people – as well as monitor lizards, crocodiles, pythons, mangroves and orchids. The park offers only the most basic and essential of facilities.

Dayak-inspired Catholic church. Although a significant portion of Dayak are Christian, animist practices are a part of daily life.

South Kalimantan

Kalimantan Selatan (South Kalimantan), or Kalsel, often called the "Land of A Thousand Rivers", is a small, swampy province on the south-east coast. There are frequent flights to the capital city, **Banjarmasin** ❾, famous for its colourful floating markets and bustling canals. The majority of Kalsel's people are Banjarese. Largely Muslim, with a sprinkling of Protestants and Catholics, the Banjarese are strict adherents to their religion, with thousands making the pilgrimage to Mecca each year. Modest dress is required while travelling in the region.

Kalsel grows a surplus of rice, which is exported to other areas of Indonesia, but its timber is the major export. It also produces rubber and rattan, which is processed into furniture and *lampit* (hand-plaited carpets) and exported overseas. Kalsel also produces and exports diamonds, gold, coal, granite and oil, along with resins and birds' nests – the latter of which is prized by the Chinese.

Crisscrossed by rivers and tributaries, Banjarmasin teeters at the brink of sea level, dipping below that when the tide is in. Perched on the banks of the intersection of the Martapura and Barito rivers, *lanting* (floating houses) line the waterways, water taxis ply the riverine "highways" and *jukung* (dugout canoes) replace streetside shops.

There are a couple of places (under the Yani bridge and at Kuin Pertamina) where travellers can rent

BELOW: menacing crocodile at Kutai National Park.

TIP

Each year in mid-April, the Bugis of Banjarmasin make offerings to the sea. Week-long festivities, which include traditional dances, surround the event.

BELOW: boat vendor selling fresh produce at Pasar Terapung.

klotok (motorised canoes) to tour Banjarmasin and the Sungai Barito. Start early for one of the floating markets. **Pasar Terapung**, 30 minutes from town, is the most famous and has been bobbing along the Sungai Kuin for 400 years. It gets underway before dawn and the activity peters out a couple of hours after sunrise. Produce is brought from villages in small boats and sold to female vendors paddling canoes. The women then glide through the canals to sell fruit, vegetables and fish to housewives whose front (or back) doors open onto the water. There are also little boats serving light refreshments, such as coffee, tea and snacks for those who require a quick breakfast.

Worth a look further upstream on Sungai Barito are traditional lumber mills; the modern mills are located downstream. On the mighty Barito, which is navigable 500 km (310 miles) inland and is more than a kilometre (¾-mile) wide in places, is **Kembang** island, 10 minutes away by *klotok*. It houses a Chinese shrine believed to have the ability to bring good health and prosperity, as well as scores of sacred long-tailed macaques.

Closer to town, the Martapura or the Barito are good places to experience riverside life at its bustling best. Take a *klotok* or a *bis air* (water bus) up a branch of the Sungai Martapura just beyond the Trisakti docks – which are for large ships – to see a modern lumber mill, where cranes lift enormous felled trees out of the river.

A short way up the Martapura, open-fronted stores sell brightly-coloured plastic items to water-borne shoppers. Housewives gossip and exchange pleasantries as they handle laundry chores, while naked children bathe. Such scenes are part of the daily comings and goings of the Banjarese.

A bit further, graceful Bugis-style schooners are constructed from sturdy ironwood along the riverbank. Just beyond, there is an all-night fish market and a red-light district. Sunsets on the rivers can be bewitching.

The ultra-modern **Mesjid Raya Sabilal Muhtadin** (Grand Mosque) rests on land formerly occupied by a Dutch fortress and is one of Asia's largest places of worship. Its metallic flying saucer-shaped dome is clearly visible from the river, and a visit inside is very rewarding. Beautifully-finished stone panels with copper inlaid inscriptions from the Koran line an open space for praying. Doors and windows are decorated with reliefs taken from traditional Banjarese designs. As when visiting any mosque, dress modestly (women should have their knees and arms covered) and remove footwear before entering.

Gemstones and gold panning

At **Cempaka**, about 45 km (28 miles) from Banjarmasin, workers dig shafts 10–15 metres (33–49 ft) deep, shored up with bamboo scaffolding outfitted with steps where men – usually family members – wait down-hole to pass baskets of soil, clay and gravel to the surface. The search is for precious and semi-precious gems, and they hope to duplicate the 1965 find of the 100-plus carat Trisakti Diamond. Attentive women puddle the dirt, sift it through a screen, then pan it, watching with experienced eyes for even the smallest diamonds, sapphires, amethysts, garnets and gold. In the nearby town of **Martapura** ❿, the gems, called *galuh* (princess), are cut and polished. Some stones purchased in this area have been appraised in the West at a higher value than what was paid, but nevertheless, prospective buyers should shop with reputable dealers, paying particular attention to quality.

For another look at mining, 65 km (40 miles) south-east of Banjarmasin in **Pelaihari** is a gold mining region started by Chinese settlers at the request of the king of Banjar six centuries ago.

While Banjarmasin may be the only city in Kalimantan worth visiting for its own merits, adventure is another reason for stopping over in Kalsel. Unless relatively fluent in Bahasa Indonesia, the national language, an organised tour with an English-speaking guide is recommended.

Travel agents in Banjarmasin have some outstanding itineraries. Ranging from two-day trips to 10-day expeditions, participants can build their own traditional bamboo rafts (under experienced supervision, of course) and pole downriver from Loksado through white-water rapids past scenic mountains on the Sungai Amandit, which originates in Gunung Meratus, flows through Loksado and meets the Barito further downstream.

The Amandit can be navigated in two segments: from Loksado to **Muara Hatip**, near Kandagan (Class 1–2.5 rapids), including a night's stay at a simple lodge at Muara Hatip. Stage two is from Muara Hatip to **Batu Laki**, where the rapids increase to Class 3 at the mouth of the Sungai Muara Harang.

Getting to **Loksado** – a small village on the slopes of Gunung Meratus – and Dayak country, involves long, hard jungle trekking for 8 hours or more on trails through forests overlooking valleys, crossing hanging bamboo bridges, and

Map on page 281

Kalimantan is the only place in Indonesia where diamonds are found. As early as the 1500s, Kalimantan's diamonds had earned a reputation for their brilliance and purity.

BELOW: panning for gold and diamonds at Cempaka.

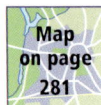

Map on page 281

revelling in cool mountain air. Starting from **Pagat** or **Batu Tangga**, the journey to Loksado can take several days.

The longhouses in the area do not have the long verandas seen in other parts of Kalimantan. Nevertheless the idea is the same, with one particular *balai* housing more than 150 residents under its roof. En route, visit Miulan Dayak and Kedayang Dayak longhouses, stay overnight in one owned by the Papangkaan Dayak, and return to Banjarmasin via bamboo raft, passing fishermen plying their craft and riverside villages. Shorter treks to the **Kentawan Nature Reserve** can also be arranged.

"Live" in the forest

For more challenging adventure, take the 10-day "Tropical Rainforest and Bukit Dayak Expedition" to the summit of **Gunung Tiranggang Hulu** and down through the forest to the Sungai Batang Alai. Trek through dense jungles that are alive with hornbills and gibbons. Experience setting up camp and learn to establish bivouacs, fish and hunt, cook, find water and learn to recognise edible tropical plants (and more to the point, avoid poisonous ones). An occasional night's stay in a longhouse is a unique opportunity to experience the daily life of the inland farmers.

An alternative jungle expedition begins by crossing the waters of **Danau Riam Kanan** in the **Pelaihari Martapura Nature Reserve** ⓫. At the outset, trek tropical rainforest over narrow, winding paths and, after gingerly crossing a river filled with rapids, re-appear in montane forest with its thorny, mossy trees. Descend into the **Kahung Valley** and across open grassland, then cross Riam Kanan Lake once again to return to Banjarmasin. ❑

BELOW: war shields in these post-headhunting days are purely ceremonial.

Orangutan: The Fight for Survival

In the wild, an infant orangutan stays with its mother for the first seven to eight years of its life. During this time, it learns to distribute its weight while moving through the trees, build a fresh sleeping nest each night and to identify edible forest foods. To capture an infant, poachers must first kill the mother, thus halting the learning process dead in its tracks. Logging, of course, creates access to areas that were formerly havens for orangutan and other animals.

Most of the orangutan who reach rehabilitation centres were caught by poachers and sold to individuals, who keep them as pets. The centres' jobs are to teach the orangutan survival skills so they can survive in their jungle habitats.

In 1971, Dutch zoologist Dr. Herman Rijksen established the first rehabilitation project while studying orangutan in Sumatra. Two years later, the Bohorok centre in Gunung Leuser National Park was started with support from the Frankfurt Zoological Society (FZS). In 1980, Bohorok was handed over to the Indonesian government. The heavy influx of tourists and over-saturation of surrounding forest encouraged FZS, a Swiss NGO, and the Indonesian government to form a partnership to find a new re-introduction site at Bukit Tigapuluh National Park in Jambi in 1999. Learning from mistakes made at Bohorok, tourist visits are not encouraged.

Arguably, Indonesia's most famous former rehabilitation centre is in Tanjung Puting National Park, Central Kalimantan, where Birute Galdikas established Camp Leakey for research in 1971 until the Indonesian government took over management in 1991. The Tanjung Puting forest is also considered to be saturated, and releases are no longer made there. While visitors are welcome and can see daily "staged shows" of feedings of milk and bananas to ex-captive orangutans, do not expect to see any research or rehabilitation going on there.

Wanariset centre, in East Kalimantan, was established in 1991. It is managed by Dutch tropical forest ecologist Dr. Willie Smits and is not open to the public. It is the only rehabilitation centre in Indonesia that keeps and re-introduces orangutan into the wild under new IUCN (International Union for Conservation of Nature and Natural Resources) guidelines for species reintroduction. Contrary to Galdikas' controversial surrogate mothering technique, Smits' approach is based on Rijksen's, whereby orphaned infants are bonded with their peers, and feeding and care during rehabilitation is done as mechanically as possible to reduce human impact. Once released, the orangutan are taken deep into jungle areas not inhabited by wild populations to reduce the risks of spreading human disease. The orangutan lifestyle – breaking off branches to build nests and seed dispersal – helps to regenerate forests.

Despite the small success of these groups, saving the orangutan and other endangered species rests with the government's ability to save the forests and stop illegal poaching. ❏

RIGHT: baby orangutan from Tanjung Puting National Park in Central Kalimantan.

CENTRAL AND WEST KALIMANTAN

The Dayak peoples, once headhunters, live in isolation from the rest of humanity – fishing, hunting and gathering crops. Sharing their jungle world are the human-like orangutan

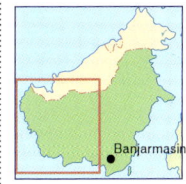

Kalimantan Tengah (Central Kalimantan), or Kalteng, is the Dayak province par excellence. For centuries dominated by the Muslim Banjarmasin, the local Dayak – led by war hero Tjilik Riwut – fought a short guerrilla conflict to obtain separate provincial status, which was granted them by former President Sukarno in 1957.

The Ngaju Dayak predominate among the province's several groups. Many were converted to the Protestant faith and became aware of their cultural identity, thanks to German missionaries in the late 19th century. Many other Ngaju, along with their more isolated cousins, retained their belief in Kaharingan, the ancient Dayak faith. One of the demands of the autonomy movement was to obtain official recognition for this traditional religion, finally acknowledged as part of the sanctioned "Hindu Bali" religion in 1980.

The *tiwah*, or funerary ritual, is Kaharingan's most spectacular feature. This series of rites cleanses the bones of the deceased and guides the soul to paradise. Structures are erected for the ceremonies, including a carved ironwood coffin and a totem-like pole used to tie up animals for sacrifice. A properly-conducted *tiwah* ensures the spirit's intervention with the supernatural in helping to produce abundant harvests and good health for descendants.

The *tiwah* set of ceremonies lasts up to one month and is expensive for the relatives of the deceased. Unless the family is wealthy, several groups get together for a collective ceremony, during which dozens of souls can be dispatched simultaneously.

Palangkaraya

The capital of Kalteng, **Palangkaraya** ⑫, has a population of less than 100,000. Most of the commercial and business activities are concentrated in the Pahandut district, where a village once existed on the Sungai Kahayan before the place was selected as the provincial capital. Newer and larger hotels are located in the centre of the new city.

There are two docks on the river: Rambang, the lower one, serves boats heading downriver. Flamboyant is for upstream passengers. While in Palangkaraya, see Dayak artefacts at **Museum Negeri Probinsi Kalimantan Tengeh Balanga**, or Museum Balanga for short (open Tues–Thur 8am–1pm; Fri 8–10am; Sat–Sun 8am–noon; free). It is located near the Pasar Kahayan market at the 2.5-km mark, just off the paved road running parallel to the river.

Dayak country is found up the **Sungai Kahayan**. There are daily passenger boats heading upriver as

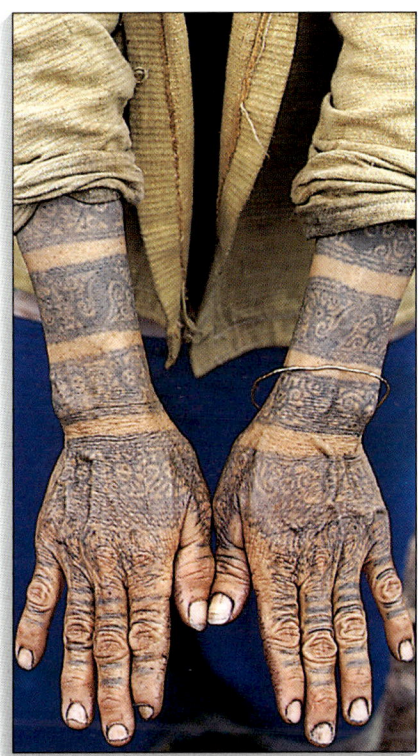

LEFT: Dayak child tucked into a carrier adorned with animal teeth.
BELOW: every Dayak tattoo tells a story.

Dayak babies suspended in sarong cradles that hang from the ceiling sleep in minutes – despite the apparent discomfort of its position.

BELOW: hunting by blowpipe.

far as **Tewah**. One can also charter a speedboat that allows stops along the way. From Tewah, where regular river traffic usually stops, hire a motorised canoe to **Tumbang Mire** and beyond, to the traditional Ot Danum Dayak land with longhouses and funerary structures. Travel here depends essentially on water levels. Try to reach Tumbang Korik, on a tributary, or **Tumbang Maharoi**, the last village on the river.

Alternatively, let a tour operator do all the logistical work, difficult without a basic knowledge of the Indonesian language. Or from Palangkaraya, arrange boats on the Katigan (Rangkan) River for two full days, camping or staying overnight in village homes in **Tumbang Samba** and **Penda Tangaring**. It is a 3-hour hike from Penda Tangaring to a Dayak longhouse built in 1870 by a member of the Kahayan Dayak tribe. In front of the longhouse is a mausoleum where the bones of ancestors were placed following the customary *tiwah* ceremony. *Sepundu* poles, carved to represent humans, were used in days gone by to tie up sacrificial animals (and slaves) awaiting their fate.

Guided orangutan-watching tours are available through adventure travel agents in Jakarta and in Kalimantan. The starting point is **Pangkalanbun**, which is accessible by air with at least five arrivals and departures daily, and unlike in the past, the flights are quite reliable. Scheduled arrivals and departures ply routes to and from Pontianak, Banjarmasin, Palangkaraya (Kalimantan), Jakarta, Semarang and Yogyakarta (Java).

Once in Pangkalanbun, it is necessary to obtain an entry permit at the park office. From there hire a taxi for the 20-minute drive to **Kumai** ⓭, a riverside village that is the entry point to **Tanjung Puting National Park** ⓮. At the harbour, either hire a *klotok* (local motorised boat) or a speedboat to go upriver.

DAYAK OF KALIMANTAN

The term "Dayak" is an amorphous one. Although its origin is unclear, "Dayak" distinguishes the 200 or more ethnic groups living in the interior of Kalimantan from the coastal-dwelling Malays. While Malays make their living through trade, sea fishing and farming settled areas, the Dayak prefer to fish the rivers, hunt and gather forest produce.

The Dayak were romanticised in the past – and with good reason. They were noted headhunting jungle warriors, lived in massive longhouses and practised strange rituals. One of the more novel practices of Dayak men was the *palung*, the practice of inserting objects into the foreskin of the penis as sexual enhancers. One British explorer wrote of this practice in the 19th century: "One lively range of objects can be so employed – from pigs' bristles and bamboo shavings to pieces of metal, seeds and beads…"

While the *palung* – mostly used by the Kenyah and Kayan – never hurt a man's chances with women, there was however the bride price to come up with. Back in the old days, no suitor needed to apply to marry the chief's daughter unless he could produce several freshly-severed heads. These heads were believed to be essential for the spiritual and material welfare of the village. Thankfully, for most, heaadhunting is now outlawed.

(Note: Speedboats are faster but the noise they generate may nullify whatever chances there are for birdwatching or quiet enjoyment of the *nipah* and mangrove eco-systems up the muddy jungle river.)

There are two lodges on the river, both with basic amenities and food service, or serious adventurers can elect to sleep aboard the *klotok*. If choosing the latter, buy supplies in Kumai (include enough for a two-man boat crew), and one of the crew will be able to prepare simple meals of rice and vegetables. However, if rooms are available in the small Sekonyer River Ecolodge, take pleasure in knowing that they employ staff from neighbouring Tanjung Harapan village.

Friends of the National Parks Foundation (FNPF) runs a small guest house at the Tanjung Harapan post. The FNPF can also arrange boats for upriver expeditions and homestays in Tanjung Harapan village. All money received helps support FNPF's conservation and village projects.

Watch orangutan feed

The highlight of the Tanjung Puting National Park experience is the orangutan feeding sessions (check times upon arrival) at one of the three park outposts. The first, **Tanjung Harapan** – directly opposite the Sekonyer River Ecolodge – cares for orphaned infants and new arrivals and has a Visitor Information Centre. By far the most famous of the three, **Camp Leakey** can be somewhat of a circus during high season (June–August), with visitors who are less conservation-oriented clamouring to walk down jungle paths to see the red apes in action. Older orangutan, sometimes with their offspring, can be found at **Pondok Tanggui**. During the feeding sessions at all three posts, orangutan that hover near the stations are offered bananas and milk to supplement seasonal lack of food in the

Map on page 281

Mercury from illegal gold mining pollutes the Sekonyer River, endangering not only flora and fauna, but also people. The once beautiful mahogany-coloured water leading to Camp Leakey is now a muddy brown.

BELOW: ape play at Camp Leakey.

Fresh green coconuts are the ultimate thirst quenchers in the tropics. Have the top sliced off, stick in a straw and drink its juice. When you're done, scoop up the silky soft flesh with a spoon. Pure bliss.

BELOW: besides orangutan, Tanjung Puting has rich birdlife as well.

forest. Allowing tourists to experience the feeding sessions achieves an additional benefit: that of raising awareness of the plight of orangutan and the shrinking forests. It is a joy to sit quietly and watch as semi-habituated orangutan, lumbering hand over heavy hand through the trees, arrive at the feeding platforms. Their gregarious antics can be amusing.

Former centre for research

Camp Leakey was established by Birute Galdikas in 1971 as a centre for research into orangutan behaviour. A disciple of Louis Leakey, whose life's work was to establish a link between humans and apes, Galdikas was the only scientist among his protégés which included Jane Goodall and Dian Fossey. In the early 1970s, as is happening now, forest trees were felled at an alarming pace to make room for transmigrant rice fields. As forests shrank, orangutan habitats became overcrowded. Some animals fell into the hands of poachers, who sold them to zoos, circuses and the wives of important men, who liked to dress the infant apes in baby clothes. The forestry department began to confiscate such pets, and Galdikas took them in. Although she continued her research for another 20 years, today the PHPA manages all three ranger stations. New releases of ex-captive orangutan are no longer made at Tanjung Puting *(see also page 287)* and substantive research no longer carried out here.

Local guides at all three stations can be hired for a small fee to conduct treks through Tanjung Puting's peat swamp forest. While it is difficult to spot wild orangutan as they live solitary lives high in the treetops, you may be lucky; besides them, there is interesting fauna such as pitcher plants, ironwood trees, insect nests and plants used for medicinal purposes.

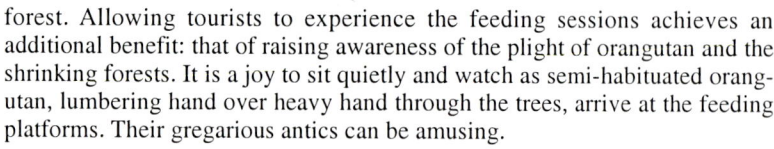

The best wildlife viewing is done from the river. At sunrise, the monkeys begin their day's foraging. Occasionally, one will belly-flop into the river, his lightly-webbed toes enabling him to swim against the currents. During these times, the birds are particularly active. Azure-hued kingfishers, greater coucals and three species of hornbills are among the 220 species recorded in the park. Along the riverbanks, watch for mudskippers and archerfish, pythons sunning themselves on branches and, rarely, an estuarine crocodile. In the late afternoons, the groups of proboscis monkeys, one male and his female harem per tree, settle in for the night and are easy to spot, with their long straight tails hanging down from their branch roosts. For a sublime jungle river experience, ask the boatman to stop the engine for a while to allow the boat to drift quietly. Sunsets can be spectacular.

West Kalimantan

Kalimantan Barat (West Kalimantan), or Kalbar, covers another huge area, enveloping essentially the Sungai Kapuas Basin. In the 1600s, diamond fields attracted the attention of the Dutch – who had been busy defending Java and the spice trade in Maluku – and these were quickly depleted. In the 1700s, the Sultan of Sambas imported Chinese coolies to work alluvial gold deposits; this went on till the beginning of the 19th century. The 18th century also saw

Pontianak established as the resistance headquarters for Dutch efforts to stave off advances from Englishman James Brooke, the "White Raja", who ruled the neighbouring territory now known as Sarawak.

Dominated by the Kapuas, the longest river in Indonesia, Kalbar's transport, communications and economy revolve around its waterways. However, unlike the Sungai Mahakam, there has been little tourism development in the province. Consequently, there are fewer English speakers and limited tourist facilities.

The provincial capital, **Pontianak** ⓯, lies near the sea at the juncture of a branch of the Kapuas and the Landak rivers, their bridges giving views of riverborne markets and *bandung* (floating houses) below. Sprouting up alongside a working port filled with freighters and Bugis schooners, there are ample photo opportunities for those who stop to watch the loading and unloading.

While the city's **Museum Negeri** (State Museum; open Tues–Sun 8am–noon; entrance fee) housing prehistoric and historic artefacts as well as ceramics might be worth a visit if there is time, the old wooden **Keraton Kadriah** or Istana Qadriah (Sultan's Palace) on the far side of the Kapuas from downtown, is excellent. The main entrance to the palace is in the shape of a Portuguese gate. The *istana* belongs to the descendants of Syarif Abdul Rahman, an Arab rover who founded the city in the late 18th century with Dutch backing. The city's name – Pontianak – refers to evil spirits who inhabited the area before Syarif Rahman scattered them with a sustained cannon barrage. Nearby is the 250-year-old **Mesjid Jami** (Abdurrahman Mosque).

The coastal road heading north from Pontianak passes a strange-looking monument called **Tugu Khatulistiwa** (Equator Monument), which marks the equator. Having become somewhat symbolic of Pontianak, miniatures of the

Map on page 281

Proboscis monkeys have sacculated stomachs that break down fibre and toxins, enabling them to eat leaves avoided by other primates. Ripe fruits can make them "blow up".

BELOW: floating logs on the Kapuas; Kalimantan timber is a major export.

> **TIP**
>
> Generally, the further upriver you go, the longer the delays and the more rudimentary the facilities. Take with you a good sense of humour, and be flexible.

monument are available in local shops. About 120 km (75 miles) north-west of Pontianak on the road to Singkawang is **Kampung Saham**, a longhouse settlement of the Kendayan tribe with a beauty all its own. At **Mempawah** is the **Amantubillah Palace**, built in 1780, and the **Juang Mandor Cemetery** commemorating the 21,000 people killed in Japanese skirmishes and buried in mass graves.

Just outside **Singkawang** ⓰ are a couple of huge ceramic kilns turning out vases and jars. The large Chinese population in this area descended from the miners who arrived here to work during the gold rush at the beginning of the 19th century. Setting up independent, self-sufficient enclaves around the gold fields, the output of the industrious miners in this area reached one-seventh of the yearly world gold production in the early 1800s. But by the mid-19th century, the gold reserves were dwindling and the Dutch put an end to local independence. Most of the Chinese miners remained and intermarried with locals. Their progeny represents one of the largest ethnic Chinese enclaves in Indonesia. There are several striking Buddhist temples in the area.

Near Singkawang is **Pasir Panjang** beach, ideal for swimming. Also in the vicinity is the **Gunung Poteng** hill resort, a great place for nature lovers with its cool, fresh air. **Raya Pasi** is home to a variety of flora and fauna, including the parasitic Rafflesia, the largest flower in the world. Singkawang is also near the Lo Fat Fun, Nuit and Prinsen nature reserves.

North of Pontianak (5 hours by car) is **Sambas** ⓱, a former sultanate and pirate's lair. There is not a lot to see in Sambas, but if one is interested in watching weavers at work, the town is a centre for the production of a fine textile interwoven with gold and silver threads called *kain sambas*. Many of the

BELOW: intricate Dayak embroidery.

homes have simple weaving looms where women turn out the material in their spare time or as essential income. Similar to the Malay *songket* and those from Palembang (Sumatra), the cloth is sold at a much lower price by the weavers than in Pontianak shops.

The **Istana Sambas**, a palace remnant of the former kingdom, is still in good condition and houses many antiques. Adjacent to the palace is a mosque. Both are similar to the ones in Pontianak, though not as grand.

Deep into Dayak land

For trips inland to Dayak country, riverboats are the generally accepted mode of transport, but facilities are geared for local travellers and it takes two to three days to reach Sintang and five to six days to Putussibau. Riverboats depart from downtown Pontianak, near the ferry landing. Be prepared for poor onboard toilet facilities (a simple hole, no paper) and nothing but basic meals.

East of Pontianak, on the way to Sintang is **Sanggau**, which has an abundance of hot springs, lakes, waterfalls, caves and forests for jungle trekking. There are basic overnight facilities in Sanggau.

Sintang ⓲, the home of some of West Kalimantan's most traditional Dayak groups, is situated in the middle portion of the Kapuas Basin. It can be reached by road (12 hours by bus), small plane (about 45 minutes via a DAS nine-seater aircraft) or boat (two days by house boat) up the Sungai Kapuas from Pontianak. There is a small museum in Sintang that is worth a visit and it is possible to visit some of the area's longhouses.

Nearby, **Gunung Kelam** (Dark Mountain) looms over the countryside. This superb sheer-walled rock is a challenge to even the best of climbers. For traditional Dayak country, head up the Sungai Melawi, which flows into the Kapuas at Sintang. Take either the Sungai Kayan, a tributary of the Melawi close to Sintang, or else head up the main stream of the Melawi, past **Nanga Pinoh** and to Gunung Schwaner. In the far upriver villages, there are carved funerary structures.

Putussibau ⓳, the last town in West Kalimantan on the Sungai Kapuas, can be reached by plane, boat, or via bus from Sintang (about 6 hours) on a good, new road. From here, visit traditional Dayak villages such as those of the Kayan on the Sungai Mendalam or the Maloh longhouses a short way upstream on the Kapuas. Further inland, in Gunung Muller, most Dayak have been proselytised by American fundamentalist missionaries who frown on just about all aspects of traditional life. For the adventurous, it is possible to make the week-long trek from upper Kapuas to upper Mahakam.

South of Pontianak is **Ketapang** ⓴ and the **Gunung Palung National Park**, home to orangutan, tarsiers and gibbons. The trip here is not for the casual traveller, involving roads, ferries and more roads, with no tourist accommodation in the park. However, a place to sleep might be negotiated at the ranger station or in one of the huts utilised by orangutan researchers from Harvard University who have worked in the park since 1994. ❑

Map on page 281

TIP

In Sintang, Father Jacques Maessen and the Ford Foundation are helping Dayak women revive weaving traditions. Their warp *ikat* story cloths are some of the finest examples of contemporary *ikat* weaving in Indonesia.

BELOW: misty river crossing.

SULAWESI

This strangely shaped island with unusual jagged contours contains an astonishing variety of animal life

Primarily known as the home of two flamboyant ethnic groups – the highland Torajan and the seafaring Bugis – the oddly-shaped island of Sulawesi offers a startling array of landscapes: steep mountains, deep gorges, fast flowing rivers, highland lakes, lush rainforest, *lontar* palm savannahs, rich coral reefs and white-sand beaches. The island also tenders a fascinating range of mostly endemic fauna, including black macaque monkeys, *babirusa* deer-pig, *anoa* dwarf buffalo, the eccentric *maleo* bird, the saucer-eyed tarsier and many beautiful butterflies. The population of over 15 million is equally diverse, made up of peoples who speak more than 40 languages. Sulawesi, meaning Island (*sula*) of Iron (*wesi*), is aptly named for its rich deposits of nickel-iron, copper and gold.

The island's astonishing diversity is partially a product of its tortured geography. Its four outstretched arms rise from a deep seabed formed by contiguous folds in the earth's crust, isolated from one another by steep ravines, dense forests and forbidding peaks. Unlike other Indonesian islands, only Sulawesi's north-eastern Minahasa and south-western Makassar extremities are volcanic. And instead of gently sloping contours and broad plains, most of the island is jagged uplands and rugged plateaus lying 500 metres (1,600 ft) or more above sea level. Sulawesi is 227,000 sq km (87,645 sq miles) and is divided into five provinces: South (including Tana Toraja); Southeast; Central; Gorontalo and North Sulawesi with a population mainly comprising Bugis and Torajan but also Makassarese and Minahasan.

A neolithic settlement, cave stencils, megaliths, sarcophagi and other artefacts reveal mankind's long presence on the island. For two millennia, Sulawesi was a key stop on international trading routes due to its natural harbours and central position within the archipelago. When its Islamic conversion began in the late 1500s, it already had a dozen major ports, where Chinese, Indian, Siamese, Malay and Portuguese traders exchanged fine textiles and metals for precious metals, cloves, nutmeg, pearls and camphor.

The first Western visitors were the Portuguese, seeking fresh territory after they conquered Malacca in 1511. They called their new discovery Celebes, a corruption of Ponto dos Celebres (Cape of the Infamous) on the Minahasa coast. Spanish missionaries followed but in the early 1600s, the Dutch arrived and drove out all competition. In 1667, after failing to impose monopolistic treaties on the southern sultanates, the Dutch sailed into Makassar, halted free trading and enforced an external monopoly. Much later, in the early 20th century, they finally secured political control over Sulawesi. ❑

PRECEDING PAGES: the fertile rice lands of South Sulawesi.
LEFT: burial caves in Tana Toraja with galleries for effigies of the dead.

South Sulawesi and Tana Toraja

Two groups with rich cultural interest co-exist in this sphere: The once-powerful seafaring Buginese with their textured history and the highland Torajan with their elaborate death rituals

Striking landscapes and remarkable people are the hallmarks of **Sulawesi Selatan** (South Sulawesi) – a province gaining notoriety as a unique travel destination. The coastal and lowland regions of South Sulawesi are inhabited mainly by the proud and outspoken Buginese. These Mongolian descendants are believed to have settled along these shores well over 1,000 years ago and have since had one of the more colourful histories of any Indonesian people.

The Buginese have always been great seafarers and shipbuilders. It is thought that in ancient times, they sailed from here in their hand-built *prahu* (boats) to as far afield as Madagascar and northern Australia, leaving behind artefacts and loan words, and returning with foreign goods as well as treasures from the sea.

LEFT: traditional Bugis house on stilts.
BELOW: a reminder of Sulawesi's Portuguese past.

Bugis glory days

Buginese settlers from Hindu-period maritime capitals such as Sumatra's Srivijaya (7th–13th century) and East Java's Kediri, Daha and Majapahit (11th–14th century) are thought to have returned here with new beliefs and practices culled from their sojourns abroad. These influences lasted for many centuries. As a result, various Bugis kingdoms – Luwu (Palopo), Bone, Soppeng, Goa, Supa and Mandar – rose to power in South Sulawesi between the 12th and 15th centuries. After 1500, trade relations with the Islamic sultanates on Java's north coast were strong, and with the emergence of the Makassarese kingdom of Goa-Tallo as the pre-eminent power in the early 17th century, South Sulawesi officially converted to Islam.

Though the Bugis kingdoms were later subdued and dominated by the Dutch, even in the 18th and 19th centuries, Bugis groups continued to found new sultanates on the Malay peninsula and in the Riau archipelago. Today, there is hardly a bay or estuary without a Bugis settlement on it.

The Bugis courtly heritage is preserved only in South Sulawesi villages today, and imperfectly so. Cultural performances seem to be limited to displays of fire-breathing and *takaro* ball manoeuvres. Most tourists are wont to bypass the Bugis homelands en route to the highland Toraja in the north although there is much history and natural beauty in the south.

Today, **Makassar** ❶ is a big modern city of about 1.5 million people – the business centre for eastern Indonesia and the capital of South Sulawesi province. Following Independence, the city was renamed Ujung Pandang (meaning Lookout Point). In 1999, however, the city reverted to its colonial name of Makassar, which had been coined by the Dutch after they con-

The Sulawesi coastline is longer than that of the entire continental United States, and any given location on the island is no more than 100 km (60 miles) from the sea.

quered the kingdom of Goa and established a fortified trading post there in 1667.

The town flourished as the port and trading centre for the mediaeval kingdom of Goa. The old fort (*benteng*) of Makassar was one of the 11 Goanese strongholds when it was first erected in 1545. The Dutch conquered and reconstructed it in 1667, renaming it **Benteng Rotterdam**. With its interior church and trading offices, it stands as an excellent example of 17th-century Dutch fortress architecture. The fort now houses the **Museum Provincial Makassar** (open Tues–Thur 8am–12.30pm; entrance fee), with displays of old ceramics, manuscripts, coins, musical instruments and ethnic costumes.

And there is a famous dungeon – in the south-west corner of the fort – where one of Indonesia's national heroes, Prince Diponegoro of Yogyakarta (1785–1855), was imprisoned for 27 years after defying both the Dutch and his own family by leading a series of popular uprisings in Central Java between 1825 and 1830. Outside the fort is a statue of the hero on horseback. The **Tomb of Diponegoro** is located in the middle of town on a street which carries his name.

Another interesting stop is the residence of Dutchman **C.L. Bundt**, at No. 15, Jalan Mochtar Lufti. Bundt's house, with its spacious gardens, contains a private collection of rare orchids, seashells and coral.

In the late afternoon, **Pelabuhan Paotere** on the north end of the city is a pleasant place to stroll and watch the bustling activity aboard the many *pinisi* schooners. **Pantai Losari**, a sand-free seafront promenade and cruising strip, is a popular sunset gathering place lined by numerous food and drink stalls. A nearby getaway, **Samalona** island offers good snorkelling and sandy beaches.

Just south of Makassar lies **Sungguminasa**, the former capital of the sultanate of Tallo. Today, the wooden palace houses the **Museum Ballompoa** and contains many weapons, royal costumes and a gem-studded gold crown weighing 15.4 kg (34 lb) that may be viewed on request. Near Sungguminassa are tombs of the Goa kings, of whom Sultan Hasanuddin (1629–70) is the most famous for his brave leadership in the struggle against the Dutch. Just outside the cemetery, a small fenced-off plot holds **Batu Tomanurung**, the stone upon which the kings of Goa were once crowned. On a side road nearby lies the tomb of Aru Palakka, the king of Bone and arch enemy of Sultan Hasanuddin.

Southern round-trip

To escape the lowland heat of Makassar, travel 70 km (45 miles) to **Malino** ❷, lying on the slopes of Gunung Bawakaraeng, about 760 metres (2,500 ft) above sea level. This cool, quiet pine forest resort area is noted for its *markisa* (passion fruit) orchards. The seedy fruit produces a refreshing drink. The lovely **Takapala Waterfall** is an easy 4-km (6½-mile) walk south of the town.

A road from Malino leads east to **Sinjai** on the southern coast of the penin-

Make a special request to see the gem-studded crown at Sungguminasa's Ballompoa Museum.

BELOW: remains of Benteng (Fort) Rotterdam, built by the Dutch in 1545.

Pare Pare is the hometown of Indonesia's third president, Bacharuddin Jusuf Habibie, who took over the reins after Suharto's ousting. Habibie served a disastrous short term from 1998–99.

sula. From there, a coastal road – breathtaking for its steep precipices and spectacular views – leads east to **Tana Beru** ❸, heart of the Bugis shipbuilding industry. Round-bellied *prahu* are still fashioned here with simple hand tools and without the use of metal or nails. Teak cords are hewn into planks, then fastened with wooden pegs according to an ancient design retained in the communal memory. Sails were once made of plaited banana and pineapple fibres, then later of woven cotton and silk. Rituals are employed in all phases of construction, from the selection of the tree to the final launching, to ensure that the craft will be seaworthy. The finished 200-tonne *pinisi* or a lighter vessel called *bago* appear to be unstable till fully loaded with copra or timber – then they are among the best cargo ships afloat today.

Further down the south-east tip of the peninsula lies **Bira** ❹, a relaxed white-sand beach resort area featuring caves, reefs for snorkelling and diving, boat-building and traditional weaving crafts. Turning westward along the southern **Bulukumba Coast**, the road returns to Makassar through small towns like Bantaeng, Jeneponto and Takalar, names found in a Chinese text six centuries ago.

Ancient caves

A mountainous 180-km (110-mile) road heads north-east from Makassar towards Watampone, the former capital and port city of the Bugis kingdom Bone. En route, it passes a series of gushing waterfalls at **Bantimurung** ❺. This rocky karst area is famed for the variety of common and rare butterflies. Nearby are **Gua Leang-Leang** caves, which contain 5,000-year-old red-henna hand stencils. To the east is the brisk mountain resort of **Camba**, where the views are superb and there are many mysterious caves.

BELOW:
the Buginese are well known for their shipbuilding skills.

The once-bustling port town of **Watampone** ❻ (or Bone) is quiet now, but retains its former dignity. The **Museum Lapawawoi** houses the regalia of the kings of Bone, as well as a copy of the 1667 Treaty of Bonggaya that ended the Dutch economic dominance over the area; both may be seen on request. Watampone's harbour is still a centre for inter-island shipping, and a ferry leaves here for Kolaka in South-east Sulawesi. Boat building and fishing are the principal industries although beautiful cotton and silk *sarong* are still woven here, as well as unusual orchid-fibre plaiting. South Sulawesi's largest cave system, **Gua Mampu**, is about 30 km (20 miles) away. Stalactites and stalagmites here resemble animals and humans, and give rise to local legends.

On the mountain plateau north-west of Watampone, nestled on the shores of Danau Tempe, lies **Sengkang**, seat of another feudal kingdom of old. It is best known today for its hand-loomed silk weavings. South of Sengkang in the hill country is the town's twin-court centre, **Watangsoppeng**.

From Watangsoppeng, a road leads north-west to the coast and port town of **Pare Pare**. This was once the site of the powerful trading kingdom of Supa that connected Makassar to the highlands and the ports of the Mandar Kingdom. In the days of *pinisi* and Portuguese galleons, Pare Pare's deep natural harbour was favoured over Makassar's. Farther to the north and west, the kingdom of Mandar once stretched all along the coast of what is now Mandar Bay. The Mandarese are distinct from the Bugis, yet, as great sailors, are often confused with them. Their shipbuilding tradition still rivals that of their southern neighbours and is centred on **Balangnipa**, between Polewali and Majene. On the eastern coast lies the Bugis kingdom of Luwu – with its harbour, **Palopo** – deemed the oldest of all Bugis kingdoms, and today, an important gateway to South Sulawesi.

Map on page 302

The tympanum-like triangles over the doorways of Bugis homes are composed of three, five, seven, or nine parts, indicating the social rank of the inhabitants. Nine parts are reserved for royalty.

BELOW: distinctive Torajan *tongkonan* houses.

Highland Toraja tribes

Tucked amid the rugged peaks and fertile plateaus of inland South Sulawesi live many isolated tribes known collectively as the Torajan. According to traditional accounts, the Torajan left Pongko island, located to the south-west, some 25 generations ago and crossed the ocean in canoes (*lembang*). Arriving in Sulawesi, they made their way up the Sungai Sa'dan, which now cuts diagonally across **Tana Toraja** ❼, and settled on its banks.

The Torajan remained in this landlocked region, growing rice and vegetables. Cloves and coffee were later introduced as cash crops. Traders and missionaries exerted a certain degree of influence but for the most part Torajan animistic customs and social structures endure as before.

The Torajan traditionally live in small settlements perched on hilltops surrounded by stone walls. Several extended families inhabit a series of *tongkonan* houses in each village, which are arranged in a circle around an open field. In the middle stands a sacred stone or banyan tree used for ritual offerings. Granaries (*lumbung*) face the dwellings. The roofs of *tongkonan* rise at both ends like the bow and stern of a boat; ritual chants compare these dwellings to the vessels that carried their ancestors here. House panels are exquis-

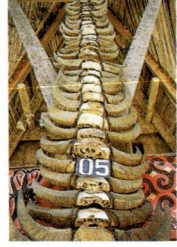

Buffaloes are the most highly prized animals in Torajan society. These rows of buffalo horn represent the honour bestowed on the deceased.

BELOW:
tau tau effigies at Ke'te – not for the weak-kneed.

itely carved with symbolic geometric and animal motifs executed in the sacred colours of white, red, yellow and black. The roof represents the heavens, and the house – representing the universe – is always oriented north-east to south-west, the directions of the two ancestral realms, according to Torajan cosmology.

In the early 20th century, Dutch missionaries penetrated the highlands of Tana Toraja and in 1905, many Torajan villages were brought under direct Dutch control. To facilitate their administration, they were ordered to move from their hilltop perches and settle in more accessible valleys and plateaus. Instead of stone walls, hedges now ring these villages.

The road from Makassar to Tana Toraja passes Pare Pare and Enrekang, the inland river town. From here, the road enters a land of steep terraced slopes, tall bamboo forests and high mountain peaks. Across the Sungai Sa'dan from Salubarani, the road passes under a large boat-shaped arch, marking the entrance to Tana Toraja. The road continues through Bambapuang Valley and past the shapely **Buntu Kabobong** (Erotic Hills).

Some 18 km (11 miles) past Makale lies **Rantepao** ❶, the centre of the Toraja tourist trade. In nearby *tongkonan* villages, Torajan practise weaving and woodcarving. Interspersing rice paddies are several cave tombs (*liang*) where rows of wooden effigies (*tau tau*) stare eerily from suspended balconies like sentries of their stony graves. The best-known gravesite is at **Londa**, about 2 km (1.2 miles) off the main road connecting Makale with Rantepao. Here, the effigies are those of noblemen and other high-ranking community leaders. Similar tombs can be seen at **Lemo**, where the burial chambers are carved out of a sheer rock face. On a hillside behind **Ke'te**, coffins are guarded by life-sized statues.

Especially beautiful *tongkonan* grace **Palawa**, a village on a small hill about

TERRIFYING TAU TAU

Torajan death rituals are enthralling and is one of the main reasons why Tana Toraja is such a popular destination for tourists. After undergoing elaborate funeral rituals (*see opposite page*), the coffins of the dead are entombed in the deep recesses of hillside caves. Carved into the cliff face outside the caves are galleries where the *tau tau* – life-sized wooden effigies of the dead hewn from the wood of the jackfruit tree – are displayed. If there is no appropriate cliff face to be found, the *tau tau* are placed in hanging galleries close to the burial caves. As the *tau tau* is meant to be a "living" representation of the dead, much effort is spent making sure the effigy resembles the likeness of the deceased, although in earlier times, the statues were more crudely made and only indicated the person's gender. Because of the immense cost involved, *tau tau* images are only commissioned by the wealthy. As most *tau tau* are exposed to the elements, they appear to be quite weatherbeaten; statues are repaired once every 25 years, and in a ceremony known as *ma'nene*, performed between July and September, the clothing of the *tau tau* is replaced. Over the years, many burial sites have been plundered by grave robbers, as genuine *tau tau* effigies are highly prized by collectors in the West.

9 km (5½ miles) from Rantepao. Other traditional villages are located north and east of Rantepao. A journey from Makale to **Sangalla** is worth the effort as older *tongkonan* houses here provide a more traditional atmosphere. And the 80-km (50-mile) trek west through the mountains to **Mamasa**, or 120 km (75 miles) north to Rongkong, introduces other facets of Toraja life.

The south-western area of Mamasa is accessible by a paved road up from the Mandar coast west of Pare Pare. The mountainous road winds its way between and up river valleys, and is one of the most scenic drives in all Sulawesi. Mamasa's spectacular villages rest on rugged tracks, but several are accessible with a jeep and a guide. This is the only place in Sulawesi where copper is worked and a dazzling array of jewellery with unique designs produced.

Feasts for the dead

The Torajan are perhaps best known for their elaborate funerary feasts, offered to ensure that souls of the dead may pass to the after-world (*puya*) in a manner appropriate to their living status. Only when the rites have been performed, it is believed, will the ancestors bestow their blessings upon the living, thus maintaining the fragile balance between the various realms of the cosmos.

The week-long feasts require an enormous outlay of material wealth – kin groups save and work for many years to ensure a suitably elaborate funeral is held between July and September, following harvest. A man is considered dead only when his funeral feast has been held. Before that, the deceased is regarded as merely "sick" and the body is embalmed and kept in the south-west end of the *tongkonan*, where it is fed and visited as if still alive, for weeks, sometimes months.

When enough money has been saved, the ceremonies are performed in two stages, presided over by a *tombablu* (death specialist). Buffaloes and pigs are slaughtered, and offerings of betel nut, fruit and *tuak* (palm wine) made. The body is moved to face north-east; at this point he is regarded officially as dead. This is followed by the *ma'bolong* ceremony, in which a pig and a buffalo are again slaughtered. The body is placed in a sandalwood coffin in the shape of a *tongkonan*, then brought out of the house draped in a glittering death shroud and placed on an open platform beneath the granary. Meanwhile, an effigy (*tau tau*) and funeral tower (*lakkian*) are prepared, and a large stone is placed in the village ceremonial field (*rante*).

The second phase takes place on the *rante*, decorated for the occasion with banners and the *lakkian*. The coffin is then borne from the house to the field and suspended in the *lakkian*. Feasting, chanting and dancing continue all night, with buffalo fights and boxing matches during the day. The rites culminate in the slaughter of water buffaloes, ranging from one to more than 100, depending on the wealth and status of the deceased. The blood is collected, cooked with the meat, and distributed among the guests. On the last day of the feast, the coffin is lowered from the *lakkian* and carried to the mountainside family gravesite. From here, the soul of the deceased ascends to the realm of the deified ancestors (*deata*) and its *tau tau* is installed on a high balcony overlooking the green valleys. ❑

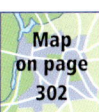
Map on page 302

TIP

The best time to photograph the *tau-tau* effigies at Lemo is when they are facing the morning sun, before 10am.

BELOW: *tongkonan* houses face north-east, the direction the Torajan ancestors came from.

CENTRAL AND SOUTHEAST SULAWESI

Travel is challenging in this land of remote people and great mountain ranges, but the reward is unequalled: wild natural beauty, rare animals and ancient megaliths amid vibrant tranquillity

The island's central and south-eastern provinces (**Sulawesi Tengah** and **Sulawesi Tenggara**) are still considerably off the beaten track and are bypassed by most visitors because of relatively challenging travel. Both these regions have some of the lowest densities of people in all of Indonesia and some of the largest tracts of wilderness, but also some of the least-developed infrastructure for tourism and travel. They are potentially the most exciting and rewarding areas for exploration, but not without a lot of patience and a willingness to forego comfort. There are, however, a number of places with cultural, historical and natural interest that are not particularly difficult to reach, but require a taste for adventure, knowledge of a few key Indonesian phrases, and a flexible time schedule.

Central Sulawesi

Central Sulawesi is the largest province in Sulawesi with about 60 percent of its terrain swathed in rainforest. The majority of the province's 2.2 million people live along the coastlines while the rest inhabit rifts and valleys of the mountainous landscape. Extensive mountain ranges have proved formidable barriers to migration and many of the inland dwellers remain relatively isolated. Twelve ethnic groups and 24 languages are officially recognised, making Central Sulawesi one of the most multicultural regions in Indonesia.

The capital of Central Sulawesi is **Palu** ❾, a pleasant port town surrounded by grassy hills and located at a bottleneck of land between Tomini Bay and the Makassar Strait. A visit to the **Museum Negeri Propinsi Sulawesi Tengah** gives a preview of Indian-inspired silk woven by the indigenous Kaili people called *kain Donggala*, as well as displays of arts and crafts, traditional bark cloth, and megalith replicas from the valleys around Lore Lindu.

An hour's drive north of Palu lies **Donggala** ❿, a sleepy town with a picturesque bay that was once a key trading route stop between Sulawesi, Borneo and India. The Dutch had turned Donggala into an administrative centre for the region, until the Japanese gave the role to Palu. Amid hillsides of coconuts and vegetable gardens, Donggala is a relaxing place for walks. The weavers' village of **Towale** is located just south of town, and lovely beaches and watersports are found just north at **Tanjung Karang**.

Arguably one of the country's most important biological refuges, **Lore Lindu National Park** ⓫ hosts incredibly diverse plant and animal life within its

LEFT:
Napu valley mother and son pose for the camera.
BELOW: boat travel.

TIP

Ongoing sectarian violence between Christians and Muslims has claimed many victims in the Poso and Palu areas since 2001. Exercise extreme caution if you are travelling in these areas.

BELOW: ancient stone megaliths from Napu valley.

rugged geography. Hornbills and eye-catching butterflies abound, and three of Sulawesi's strangest and most illusive mammals, the *anoa* (dwarf buffalo), *babirusa* (deer-pig) and nocturnal Sulawesi palm civet reside in the park. Patience and a bit of luck will reveal tarsiers, the Tonkean macaque, *maleo* fowls and the bear-like *cuscus*. A total of 50,000 people – a mixture of indigenous people, Bugis and transmigrants placed by the Indonesian government from over-crowded regions of Bali and Java – live in 117 villages near the park.

Rainforests and megaliths

Megalithic statues estimated between 700 and 5,000 years old dot the valleys of **Napu**, **Besoa**, and **Bada** in Lore Lindu. The origin of these carvings is unknown although they almost certainly related to ancestor worship. While the smaller stones are just 50 cm (20 inches) high, the decidedly phallic-inspired stone images of humans are up to 4 metres (13 ft) high.

A rough 80-km (50-mile) jeep track from the town of **Gintu** ⓬ in Bada Valley leads east to **Tentena** ⓭, situated on crystal-clear **Danau Poso**. Restaurants serve eels, up to 2 metres (6½ ft) long, harvested from Danau Poso. The lake is surrounded by dense rainforest, rice terraces, and lush clove and coffee plantations. Cool breezes make boat trips a pleasant way to explore the stunning environs and lakeside villages. The **Taman Angerek Bancea** on the western shore displays about 45 species of orchids that bloom three times yearly.

Further along the eastern peninsula, the land becomes increasingly infertile and isolated, but no less captivating. The administrative centre of **Poso** is the usual hub to **Morawali Nature Reserve** ⓮ and Kepulauan Togian, two infrequently visited but remarkable areas. **Kolonodale**, a tiny town on spectacular

Teluk Towori, is the most convenient starting point into Morawali. Transport and guides can be arranged in Kolonedale to visit the Wana people who still hunt wild boar and other Sulawesi fauna with poisoned-dart rattan pipes.

Towards the north, the remote forest-capped **Kepulauan Togian** ⓯ islands cluster in the huge, calm azure Bay of Tomini. Sheer limestone cliffs, secluded white-sand beaches, and wonderful snorkelling and diving can be found despite extensive damage to the northern reefs from dynamite fishing. The beautiful setting and relaxed pace often lulls travellers into extending their stay. Here, the once-nomadic sea gypsies, or Bajo people, live in stilt houses over the water. **Una-una**, a volcano island with spectacular coral reefs, violently erupted and blew its cone off in 1983, causing extensive damage but, fortunately, no human lives.

Southeast Sulawesi

Southeast Sulawesi is a rugged province with impassable mountains to the north, savannah to the east, and a chain of fragmented islands to the south. Although isolated from the rest of the island by land, air and sea links are quite good. The majority of the 1.8-million population live in the south. The settlers include the Tolaki and Tomekongga people, the Buginese and Makassarese from South Sulawesi, and government-sponsored transmigrants from Java and Bali.

The capital of Southeast Sulawesi is **Kendari** ⓰, a port town whose craftsmen are renowned for their intricate silver filigree work. Outside of town, fine beaches and snorkelling are located at **Hari** island. In **Morame** ⓱, spectacular seven-tiered waterfalls canopied under lush foliage are wonderful to visit for a day of soaking and swimming. **Rawa Aopa National Park** ⓲, about 70 km (43¾ miles) west of Kendari, has a number of ecological habitats to explore with the assistance of guides arranged by the Kendari tourist office. Deer and macaques are often seen in the savannah and rainforest, and a paddle in a dugout along mangrove forests and peat swamps is a good way to catch sight of rare birdlife.

On the larger islands south of the mainland, the area around **Raha** ⓳ on **Muna** island is famous for horse fighting while red-ochre cave depictions can be seen at **Goa Mabolu**; but the highlight is the incredibly scenic of **Napabale Lagoon**. Although Muna is largely deforested, the neighbouring **Buton** – the largest island in Sulawesi and former seat of the powerful Sultan of Wolio – is still cloaked in impenetrable virgin rainforest. However, more accessible secondary rainforest in Buton, such as **Kakanawue Nature Reserve** ⓴, offers a good chance to see macaques, tarsiers and hornbills. **Benteng Keraton** near **Bau Bau** ㉑, Buton's main settlement, was a fortress built from 3 km (1¾ miles) of stone around a hill overlooking the Buton Strait to protect the sultanate. During the Dutch era in the 17th century, Bau Bau was an important stop between Makassar and the Spice Islands of Maluku to the east.

The remote islands of **Kepulauan Tukang Besi** ㉒, also known as Wakatobi, is Indonesia's newest marine park. Enthusiasts have discovered spectacular diving off the many atolls and uplifted limestone islands that string out into the deep Banda Sea. ❑

Sulawesi's distilled tuak liquor – stored in bamboo containers like these – can leave you with a nasty hangover, so go easy on it.

BELOW: colourful hornbill.

SULAWESI: A REAL NATURALIST'S NIRVANA

Thanks to its diverse ecological zones, Sulawesi has a range of fauna and underwater life that is quite unlike anything else seen on this planet

It is little wonder that nature lovers regard Sulawesi as paradise on earth. Sulawesi's terrestrial fauna is a mosaic of Asian and Australian animals that has evolved into new species found nowhere else on the planet. The predecessors of these new species first came together when land rafts fragmented from the Asian and Australian continents and collided to form the distorted Sulawesi landmass.

After centuries of isolation from the rest of the archipelago, Sulawesi has become a natural laboratory in species evolution. Of the 127 mammal species that inhabit the island, nearly two-thirds are exclusive to Sulawesi. And, if all of its bat species are taken into account, an astonishing 98 percent of its mammals are endemic to Sulawesi alone.

JEWELS OF THE SEA

Warm, clean, plankton-rich seas that sweep the fringes of Sulawesi have created an ideal environment for some of the most biologically diverse coral reefs in the world. The reefs – some of which have escaped the more destructive practices of man – swirl in a kaleidoscope of thousands of fish species and hundreds of corals species, unrivalled by the Caribbean or Red Sea.

△ **TURN TURTLE**
Bunaken Marine National Park offers world-class diving and close encounters with marine creatures such as this Hawksbill Turtle.

▽ **UNDERCOVER FISH**
Nearly indistinguishable from a sponge at a distance, this frog fish waits in ambush for prey on the muddy bottom of Lembeh Strait.

◁ **OH DEER**
Timor deer, found throughout eastern Indonesia, was introduced to Sulawesi by man and thrive in areas such as Bogani Nani Wartabone National Park.

▷ **MONKEYING AROUND**
Sulawesi is home to four endemic, fruit-eating black macaque species; the *Macaca tonkeana* is most commonly found in Central Sulawesi.

▽ EXQUISITE ORCHIDS
Thick sprays of wild orchids like this one – the Phaius Tankervilliae from Lore Lindu National Park – cling to branches of large trees throughout Sulawesi's forests.

▽ TREE DWARF
Dwarf cuscus, an arboreal marsupial of Australian origins, is endemic to Sulawesi. Its diminutive size and nocturnal behaviour is a mystery to researchers.

◁ CORAL COLOURS
Colonial ascidians, which are invertebrate coral reef animals, take on a dazzling array of shapes and colours. Many of such coral are still unnamed by science.

▷ BIRDWATCHER'S HAVEN
Altogether some 382 species of birds have been identified in Sulawesi, like this Eclectus Parrot, 88 of which are endemic to the island.

THE OLDEST FISH IN THE WORLD

In 1998, shark net fishermen from Manado Tua, North Sulawesi, shocked the scientific world with their catch of a living coelacanth (pictured above). This extremely rare and endangered fish was assumed extinct for 70 million years until a fishing trawler accidentally dragged one up in South Africa in 1938. Since then, a small population of the prehistoric fish, dating back 400 million years, was thought to exist exclusively off an isolated island group in eastern Africa.

Coelacanths inhabit underwater lava caves between 200–600 metres (656–1,968 ft) depth during the day and drift-hunt during the night. Their fleshy, lobbed fins resemble legs, which places them at the base of four-legged animal evolution.

The Manado Tua coelacanth, hailed as a new species, *Latimeria menadoensis*, was found an amazing 10,000 km (6,200 miles) from its African counterparts. The specimen can be seen preserved in the Museum Zoologicum Bogoriense in Cibinong, Java.

NORTH SULAWESI

The residents of Manado have the best of both worlds: the comforts of urban life but yet surrounded by spectacular underwater scenery and the primaeval beauty of the Minahasan Highlands

Something of an anomaly, **Sulawesi Utara** (North Sulawesi) is a fertile, snake-like volcanic peninsula outstretched in the middle of the vast Maluku Sea. World-class diving surrounds the province and a menagerie of endemic wildlife resides in its national parks and reserves. Dubbed *Nyiur Melambai* (Land of Swaying Coconuts), North Sulawesi is also the "bible belt" of Indonesia – with 95 percent of its populace being Christians.

Over 2½ million people make their homes here and about 10 percent of them reside in **Manado** ㉓, the pleasant provincial capital. The city lies at the foot of the lovely mountainous Minahasa region, which is dotted with active volcanoes, clear highland lakes and hot water springs. Coconut plantations stretch for miles along the coasts (18,000 tonnes of copra are produced in North Sulawesi every month) that teem with fish and coral, and inland there are bountiful clove and coffee plantations, terraced rice fields and vegetable and flower gardens. The crops grown and exported from North Sulawesi afford a relatively high standard of living for its people, who survived relatively unscathed during the financial crisis that devastated most of Indonesia in the late 1990s.

All the way from Mongolia

The fair-skinned Minahasans of North Sulawesi have had a long history of hunting and farming since their arrival from mainland Asia several thousand years ago. Over the centuries, large numbers of Chinese and Europeans have settled here and intermarried with them. The islanders, on the other hand, are accomplished fishermen and farmers sharing ethnic roots with the Filipino to the north, and cultural ties with the people of Maluku to the east.

Portuguese traders arrived in Manado early in the 16th century and were followed by Spanish missionaries from Manila, who persuaded many Minahasans to convert to Catholicism. Dutch Calvinist missionaries later converted most of them to Protestantism.

Although most of the traditional crafts of Minahasa have been lost, traditional music has endured. Ensembles of *musik bambu*, bamboo and homemade brass wind instruments, play at weddings. Local marimbas called *kolintang* can often be heard as background music at restaurants and hotels. And the *cakalele* war dancers, adorned with macaque skull necklaces and hornbill headdresses, sometimes give performances.

In agricultural areas, various seasonal events are worth watching for. At the beginning of the planting season and at harvest time, villagers march to the fields singing songs in a festival known as Mapalus. Following the harvest, thanksgiving feasts last for several days and nights. They are inaugurated with reli-

LEFT: preparing for a dive at Manado's Bunaken National Park.
BELOW: coconuts are a thriving economy in North Sulawesi.

Face to face with a vibrantly-coloured boxfish at Bunaken.

gious convocation but consist mainly of eating, *saguer* (palm toddy) drinking and dancing, often held outdoors on an open coconut-palm clearing or sandy beach.

Seaside city

Alfred Russel Wallace called Manado "one of the prettiest towns in the East" but the city has since lost its initial lustre. An influx of people from other parts of Indonesia seeking solace in North Sulawesi from unrest in their home regions since 1999 has resulted in problems associated with an over-burgeoned city. Manado itself offers little in the way of urban attractions apart from the 19th-century **Bin Hun Kiong** Buddhist temple and the **Museum Negeri Propinsi Sulawesi Utara** which displays ethnographic artefacts from Minahasa. The real attractions, however, are the nearby mountains, coral reefs and rainforests.

Manado is an excellent staging point for scuba diving and snorkelling trips to **Bunaken National Marine Park** ㉔, 15 km (10 miles) offshore. The coral reefs teem with thousands of different species of colourful tropical fishes along steep drop-offs that plunge thousands of metres into the abyss. Sea turtles, sharks, pods of dolphins and dugongs make their way around the park, and there is also a World War II-era wreck to explore. In fact, Bunaken is rated one of the best dive spots in Asia. Further to the north, the 70-odd islands in the Sangihe-Talaud island chain offer white-sand beaches and spectacular diving.

An excellent road network radiates from Manado. One interesting route runs 55 km (35 miles) east to **Bitung** ㉕ on the eastern coast of the peninsula. Bitung is situated along **Lembeh Strait**, which has recently become a diver's Mecca for unusual muck-dwelling creatures such as hairy frog fish and mimic octopus. Along the way, the road passes through **Airmadidi** (Boiling Water) and the main road continues east to the coastal town of **Kema**, populated by *burghers* (Minahasan-Dutch settlers) who all have Dutch surnames. South of Kema there is a stretch of coastline ideal for watersports, with coral gardens in the neighbourhood of **Nona** island.

BELOW:
a clump of colourful coral at Bunaken.

From Bitung, a fairly bumpy northern road winds through to the **Tangkoko-Dua Saudara Nature Reserve** ㉖, home to spectral tarsiers (one of the world's smallest primates), troops of endangered crested black macaques, marsupial cuscus and endemic red-knobbed hornbills. Local guides are available at **Batu Putih** village at the entrance of the reserve.

Minahasan hills

A road south from Airmadidi winds up through the **Minahasan Highlands** to the lovely lake district of **Tondano** ㉗, an attractive town surrounded by rice fields and forested hills. On the way to Tondano is the open-air museum in **Sawangan** displaying *waruga* – stone sarcophagi hewn from boulders with engraved depictions of the deceased's prior occupation. Dating from the 1st century, Minahasans once encased their dead in sarcophagi in a crouching fetal position (to facilitate re-birth) together with their most valued possessions. Traditionally, they were placed around the family house but now they are gathered in one place to best preserve them.

On a hill outside Tondano lies the mausoleum of

Kyai Maja, a Javanese leader who fought with Diponegoro during the Java Wars (1825–30) and was exiled here by the Dutch. His **Kampung Java** is a Muslim enclave in a Christian region. There are a number of interesting towns around **Danau Tondano**, including **Ranopaso** and **Remboken** (noted for hot springs and ceramics). At the southern end of the lake is the **Kolongan Kawangkoan**, site of *kolintang* performances, bullock cart races and an underground Japanese fortress. Bukit Temboan Rurukan offers a panoramic vantage point.

West from Tondano, the road cuts through more hills on the way to **Tomohon**, a busy centre for market, education and missionary activities. There are hot springs nearby at **Lahendong** amidst a clove tree plantation, and at **Langowan**. An impressive waterfall is a short walk from **Tincep**, and construction of made-to-order Minahasan houses can be seen at **Woloan**. An easy hour's hike up a wide path on the active volcano **Gunung Mahawu** is rewarded by a 360-degree view of Minahasa and the surrounding islands around a steaming crater. From here, the road descends to the north coast.

The small harbour town **Amurang**, located 80 km (50 miles) south-west of Manado, has a thriving trade with East Kalimantan across the Sulawesi Sea. Surrounded by lovely hills, this is the gateway to southern Minahasa and the colonial town **Gorontalo** ❷❽ (a day's drive west) via the Trans-Sulawesi Highway. A scenic inland road heads east to the **Kotamobagu** coffee plantation region. Nearby is **Gunung Ambang Nature Reserve** ❷❾, an active nesting site for the unusual mound-building maleo bird. Further west lies **Bogani Nani Wartabone National Park** ❸⓪, a vast mountainous rainforest rich in fruit-bearing trees such as durian, nutmeg and figs, and home to a collection of endemic Sulawesi animals including *babirusa* and the shy *anoa*. ❑

Map on page 302

TIP

Tomohon market offers a cornucopia of Minahasan-grown produce – and also features an extensive selection of barbecued dogs, fruit bats, wild boar and forest rats for the Minahasan dinner table.

BELOW: Minahasan war dance, *cakalele*.

MALUKU AND PAPUA

The mysterious Papua, Indonesia's last frontier, remains largely unexplored, unlike its more famous neighbour, Maluku

Like Papua (formerly Irian Jaya), Maluku is seen as a backwater by most Indonesians. Meaning "Land of the Kings", the name Maluku (or the Moluccas) originally applied only to five tiny clove-producing islands off the west coast of Halmahera: Ternate, Tidore, Moti, Makian and Bacan. Today, Maluku refers to more than 1,000 islands spread over a huge area spanning 1.5 million sq km (580,000 sq miles), only 10 percent of which is land. Forests and active volcanoes cover the northern and central islands, while the southern isles are ringed by mangrove swamps.

Ambon, in central Maluku, is the provincial capital. Halmahera, the second largest island in Maluku, is in the north. South-east of Ambon is the Banda archipelago, nine small islands that supplied the world's demands for nutmeg and mace for more than 200 years.

The early part of 1999 saw Ambon ripped apart by violence, caused by religious differences between Christians and Muslims. The unabated upheaval spread to Halmahera, Seram, Saparua and Banda, and a state of civil emergency was declared in mid-2000. The troubles continue till today, and Maluku's population of 2 million is fast depleting; either killed in violent skirmishes or fleeing elsewhere to seek safe refuge.

Papua (Irian Jaya)

Headhunters and cannibals, penis sheaths and grass skirts, poisonous birds and water-spitting fish. Papua, the western half of New Guinea, the second-largest island in the world (after Greenland) is captivating, diverse and remote. Annexed as part of Indonesia in 1969 after a disputed vote, Papua is currently petitioning the Indonesian government for another vote for independence. The island has a population of more than 2 million on a land mass almost twice the size of Britain, representing 22 percent of Indonesia's total area. The Freeport-McMoRan mine outside of Timika is one of the world's richest copper and gold mines. Yet, more than anywhere else in Indonesia, the generated wealth flows out to non-locals.

Many of the locals – the Dani, Lani and Yali of Baliem Valley and the south coast's Asmat, Amungme and Kamoro – are indigenous tribespeople who have long been marginalised by the government. Pro-independence Papuans are especially targeting transmigrants from other parts of Indonesia, as well as security forces from Java.

It remains to be seen when or how the state of flux in both Maluku and Papua will be resolved, but until such time, travellers are advised to proceed with caution and common sense. ❑

PRECEDING PAGES: tribesman sporting a penis sheath against panoramic Danau Habbena in Papua (Irian Jaya).
LEFT: village elder from the remote Tanimbar islands in Southeast Maluku.

MALUKU

The fabled Spice Islands, once a prize coveted by European powers, are a sleepy backwater today. Aside from remnant shipwrecks and such, there are immaculate beaches and good diving spots

Known as the Spice Islands, Maluku was zealously sought for many years before it was happened upon by Portuguese mariners in the 1500s. Men like Christopher Columbus, Vasco da Gama, Ferdinand Magellan and Sir Francis Drake all dreamed of finding their wealth there. In fact, one of the main incentives for Europe's Age of Discovery was the avid search for spices, easily worth their weight in gold then. Spices like cloves, nutmeg and mace were used to camouflage the taste of spoiled meat in the days before refrigeration, and for medicine. As far back as the 3rd century BC, the Chinese knew of cloves, calling them "odoriferous nails". By the 4th century AD, fragrant cloves had reached Europe. Yet for hundreds of years, the world's total clove production poured forth only from five little islands off the west coast of Halmahera.

While its current production of nutmeg and mace is negligible, for centuries the tiny Banda islands supplied every last ounce of both, their origin a well-kept secret by Arab traders in Venetian markets prior to the arrival of the Portuguese. Control of the spice-producing islands assured vast fortunes, and countless lives were lost in the quest for them. But the introduction of refrigeration and British success in propagating nutmegs and cloves in Sri Lanka was to end the spice wars forever.

Most Malukans today live on fishing and subsistence farming of vegetables, bananas, yam, cassava and sweet potatoes. Although cloves, nutmeg and mace retain a measure of importance, the cash economy is mainly based on copra, or dried coconut flesh. In addition, large companies exploit timber resources for the Japanese market, processing logs into sawn planks and plywood. The seas also yield important harvests of tuna, shrimp, sea cucumber, mother-of-pearl shells and pearls.

Except for about 10,000 people in the interior of the large islands of Seram, Buru and Halmahera, who still adhere to ancestral beliefs, the rest of the 1.2 million Malukans are almost evenly divided between Christianity (mostly Protestant) and Islam. In early 1999, war broke out between the two rival groups. Thousands were killed, tens of thousands more fled, and cities destroyed as the struggle continues. It is believed that outside instigators are responsible for the conflict and that religion is merely a scapegoat; the real cause of the violence being political and economic differences.

Flora and fauna

The ecology of Maluku is one of feast and famine. There are only a dozen or so species of land mammals, the placental ones probably introduced by people, with most restricted to the eastern portion of the archipelago. The indigenous marsupials include the squirrel-like flying opossum; three kinds of wide-

LEFT: Benteng Kayu Merah (Red Wood Fort) on Ternate island.
BELOW: nutmeg seeds with red membrane called mace.

Dried salted fish is a food staple in many remote islands where modern appliances like refrigerators are non-existent.

eyed, prehensile-tailed furry cuscus; a tree-climbing kangaroo; and the wallaby. There are also over 25 species of bats.

The 300-odd species of birdlife include over 40 different kinds of birds-of-paradise, which are concentrated in the Aru archipelago; a couple of dozen species of parrot, headed by the large, handsome red-crested Palm cockatoo; and beautiful crimson lories. These strange megapods, using large feet and strong claws, build immense mounds of vegetable matter up to 10 metres (33 ft) in diameter and over 3 metres (10 ft) high. Large eggs laid inside the nests hatch from the heat generated by decomposing plants.

Ambon

Ambon ❶ has nearly 250,000 inhabitants and is the metropolitan focus of Maluku. By the 19th century, because of the Dutch, about half of Ambon's population had converted to Christianity. The newly-baptised Ambonese availed themselves of educational opportunities, forming the backbone of the Dutch colonial army. Not even World War II could shake their loyalty to Holland. Maluku was overrun by superior Japanese forces in spite of heroic Australian resistance in Ambon and the area became a central Japanese base. After the war, the Dutch returned to a rousing welcome in Ambon. When Indonesia became independent later, Ambon resisted; thousands fled to Holland while others fought a guerrilla war against the Indonesian military.

Ambon city's architecture, functional but nondescript due to bombing in 1944, was almost entirely destroyed during the 1999–2000 upheaval. Fortunately, the entrance to the 18th-century **Benteng Victoria**, Ambon's only worthwhile colonial relic, still stands. However, it is difficult to find, and is forbidden to photographs unless one has a permit from military security in Jakarta. At the end of Ambon's main street, Jalan Patty, is the **Mesjid Al Fatah** mosque next to the handsome old **Mesjid Jame**.

The **Museum Siwalima** is located on a hill just beyond the urban area. (Off the paved road on the way up, see the impressive Japanese shore battery, still protected by its concrete bunker.) The museum displays aspects of Maluku's natural history and geology, but the emphasis is on ethnography, with many fine objects, including ancestral carvings from the southern islands. Unlike many other museums in Indonesia, most of the showcases have an English description. The summit of **Gunung Nona** has the best view of the bay and Ambon town. The bay looks better from a distance than it does while you are underwater. The once-beautiful coral banks and marine life have been destroyed, the ecological price paid for the town's growth.

On the outskirts of town, in the opposite direction from the museum, the large, well-trimmed **Australian War Cemetery** holds the remains of Australian

Map on page 324

Some 2km north-east of town in Karang Panjang is the statue of Martha Tiahahu, a local heroine who took up arms against the Dutch when her father was captured by the colonial forces. When caught and exiled to Java on a ship in 1818, she starved herself to death.

BELOW: a conch orchestra in Ambon.

and other Allied troops who died during World War II. Maintained by the Australian government, many of those buried here were prisoners of war who perished in spite of the heroic aid given to them by the Ambonese.

Beyond the city

Soya Atas village is less than halfway up the slopes of 950-metre (3,100-ft) tall **Gunung Sirimau** ❷. There is a fine church there, but be sure to also check out the *baileo* – a ritual meeting place with sacred megaliths. From Soya Atas, a path leads up to a sacred hilltop site with more megaliths and a water container that never dries out. Drinking this water is said to bring health, love and prosperity. Footpaths from Soya Atas descend to some of Ambon's most traditional villages. A guide is recommended. Beware of the local Luhu ghost in the area, the beautiful daughter of a former *raja* with a predilection for handsome foreign men.

A couple of popular beaches lie to the west of town. **Amahusu** ❸ is 7 km (4 miles) away on the bay side, while **Namalatu** ❹, 16 km (10 miles) out, faces the island's south-western shore. In the other direction, east of Ambon, the beach at **Natsepa** offers protected, shallow water. Beyond Natsepa, the road leads to Tulehu village and on to **Waai** ❺, which has sacred eels living in a spring-fed cave whose waters flow into a crystal-clear pool. Their keeper entices the eels to slither out of the cave by flicking his fingers on the water's surface, then cracking open raw eggs. Near **Honimua** village at Liang, there is a long, deserted beach and a pier from which dolphins and skipjacks can be spotted. The best swimming and snorkelling is off **Pombo** ❻ island, accessible by boat from either Tulehu or Honimua.

Rounding the bay out of Ambon city, a paved road cuts across Hitu to the

National hero Thomas Matulessy, known as Pattimura, was a native of Saparua island. He fought Dutch oppression but was defeated in Saparua – and subsequently hanged in Ambon in 1817.

BELOW: pristine Namalatu beach is a big draw.

island's north coast. On either side of this road are clove plantations, occasional stands of nutmeg and – with some luck – you can see the processing of sago tree trunks into a starchy paste, the staple for many people. On the north coast, the road swings to the west. At **Hila** village is **Immanuel Church** and the **Mesjid Wapauwe**, whose foundations were laid in 1414. A short stroll away are the seaside ruins of the majestic but neglected **Benteng Amsterdam**.

Diving, magic and the Naulu

Among the islands near Ambon, **Saparua** ❼ offers the most attractions. The 2-hour boat run from Tulehu to Saparua reveals lush tropical islands emerging from shallow seas. There are many clove spreads on Saparua, along with stands of sago palms and the occasional nutmeg tree. **Ouw** village produces pottery – simple, elegant and functional – for use in this area and for sale in Ambon. Dominating a turquoise bay, **Benteng Duurstede** has been restored and bristles with cannons. Look for the keeper of Thomas Matulessy's (better known as Thomas Pattimura) war paraphernalia, said to have acquired a sacred character because of the hero's prowess in fighting the Dutch. Several spots off Saparua, as well as nearby **Nusa Laut**, are world-class diving spots.

Seram, the largest and among the least-known islands in Maluku, hovers over Ambon, Saparua and lots of sea. Not connected to either Asia or Australia, Seram lies within the Wallacea transitional zone and is a key area for global studies on species evolution. The **Manusela National Park**, which is home to 2,000 species of butterflies and moths and 120 species of birds, covers an area of 186,000 hectares (460,000 acres) in the centre of the island. **Wahai** village is the northern entrance to the park, and **Sanulo** village, overlooking the Bay of Teluti, is the southern gateway.

Many of Ambon's traditions are said to have originated in Seram, including the division into two sets of customs, the *patasiwa* and the *patalima*, as well as the *pela* alliances between two villages, often located far apart. Seram is also steeped in magic, for the Ambonese anyway, with many anecdotes of men who can fly, kill at a distance and change their shape at will. While the western part of the island has lost its mystery, thanks to a thriving lumber industry, the remote eastern mountains is where the magic is concentrated. **Gesser**, on the eastern tip of Seram, has excellent coral reef dropoffs and the exotic Bati hill-tribe, known to have exceptional supernatural powers. They remain secluded from civilisation by choice.

Another group of mountain people – the Naulu – live fairly close to **Masohi** ❽. Of the few remaining tribes in Maluku who closely adhere to ancient traditions without the veneer of a foreign religion, the paganistic coastal Naulu are the easiest to reach. The men's distinctive red headbands, first worn after initiation rituals, distinguish the Naulu from their Malukan neighbours. The initiation requires a five-day trek in the mountains of their ancestral homeland, where they must kill a deer and a boar with a spear and a tree-dwelling cuscus with a single arrow. Explorations further into Naulu lands require hiking (with a guide) inland to the mountainous Manusela National Park.

The Nicobar pigeon of Maluku feeds on the fruit of the nutmeg tree.

BELOW: a Maluku islander bearing fruit.

Banda and beyond

South of Seram and Ambon is **Kepulauan Banda** ❾, or the Banda archipelago. "Founded" by the Portuguese in 1512, it was the Dutch who arrived a century later to set up a spice monopoly. The English, who came later, undercut the Dutch efforts of price control by shipping nutmeg and mace to Europe from Run island, in the Bandas. The Dutch monopoly was restored when Manhattan was traded for Run, but as spices were increasingly produced elsewhere, the nine Banda islands faded into obscurity.

The Bandas importance in the English-Dutch struggle to control the spice trade is evidenced in its remaining forts. A military headquarters until 1860, **Benteng Belgica** was restored in the early 20th century and dominates **Bandaneira** ❿, the major island of the archipelago. Closer to the sea, **Benteng Nassau**, important during VOC Governor-General Jan Pieterszoon Coen's efforts to control Banda in 1621, crumbles in neglect. The string of forts continues on neighbouring **Banda Besar** ⓫ island with Benteng Concordia and Benteng Hollandia, built by Coen high on a ridge to command the surrounding seas, and destroyed by earthquake in 1743. Benteng Revingil (Revenge) rises from the ocean on **Ai** island. On both islands, old nutmeg smokehouses line trails through fragrant nutmeg groves, dotted with huge mango and *kanari* (tropical almond) trees, coffee and other exotic plants as tropical birds fly overhead.

Energetic souls may want to climb **Gunung Api** ⓬, an active volcano directly opposite Bandaneira. It last erupted in 1988, but fortunately almost all of the lava and ash fell on the side away from the town. The view from the summit is spectacular. Attempt this with a guide and get an early start to beat the heat of the day. In Bandaneira, the **Museum Rumah Budaya** holds many historical artefacts.

In 1621, troups under the VOC Governor-General Jan Pieterszoon Coen massacred nearly every Bandanese male over 15 years of age. Banda's leaders were decapitated at Benteng Nassau, with their heads placed on spikes as an example to those opposing Dutch rule.

BELOW: active Gunung Api is an ever-present threat.

Other sites include a church dating from 1852, its interior stone slab graves inscribed with the names of Dutch colonialists, and the **Mesjid Hatta-Syahrir**. The **Istana Mini**, the old governor's mansion, has the former resident's suicide note carved on one of the window panes. Next door is the former **VOC headquarters**, which has a statue of King Williem III, the great-grandfather of the present Dutch queen. The **Museum Mohammed Hatta** and the **Museum Sjahrir** contain memorabilia of Indonesia's top nationalist leaders who were exiled in Bandaneira in the mid-1930s. The **Museum Captain Cole** was named for the British leader who captured Banda from the Dutch in 1811.

The Bandas is the primary tourism destination in Maluku because of its excellent diving and snorkelling. Barracuda, rays and wrasses swim in deep waters while butterfly fish dart among the corals in shallow depths. Steep vertical walls lead to caves where lobster and moray eels lurk about. In April and October, the seas are calm and visibility is excellent. The Bandas also have seasonal fishing, primarily for tuna, marlin and snapper.

East or south-east from Banda islands, travel becomes more difficult. Yet both Tual in the Kepulauan Kai archipelago as well as Saumlaki in the Kepulauan Tanimbar offer attractions. The airstrip near Tual was built by the Japanese during World War II. Nearby, on the grounds of the Roman Catholic mission, a relief-sculpture depicts the history of Catholicism in the area, starting with the arrival of Jesuits in the late 19th century. During the war, the Japanese invaded the Kai islands, murdering the bishop and 13 foreign priests.

Tual ⓭ on **Dullah** island is the capital of the Maluku Tenggara (South-east Maluku) district and the transportation hub for an extensive network of roads and sea lanes. A half-hour ride away is Dullah village, where the **Museum Belawang** displays a splendid ceremonial canoe, complete with carved decorations. Close to Tual is **Pasir Panjang**, a powder-white beach that stretches for 3 km (2 miles). From Tual, motorised canoes depart for the mountainous **Kai Besar** ⓮ island. Occasional boats from Tual also head for **Dobo** ⓯, Maluku's pearl capital and the largest town of the Kepulauan Aru archipelago. Comprising 25 islands, the coastlines of the Aru islands are mangrove swamps, housing an abundance of pearl oysters, shrimp, lobsters and other fish. Its low-lying palm forest holds unusual butterflies, flocks of several species of birds-of-paradise and wallabies. Aru is also significant as a turtle nesting ground. Rare dugongs are still easily spotted in the seagrass beds found throughout Aru.

Japanese air base

South of the Kai islands is the **Kepulauan Tanimbar** ⓰ group of islands. The area only went under Dutch control in the first years of the 19th century, during the final phase of Holland's colonial expansion in Indonesia. **Saumlaki** on **Yamdena** island was a Japanese air base during World War II. Tanimbar artists carve small strange statues of humans with big heads and tiny arms and legs.

At **Sanglia Dol** ⓱, on north-east Yamdena, there is a megalithic staircase that leads to the village ceremonial ground featuring a huge stone boat with a

Map on page 324

TIP

To catch the sunrise atop Gunung Api and the breathtaking views before early morning cloud cover forms, start your ascent at 5.30am. The climb should take 1½ hours but check on conditions first as the volcano last erupted in 1988.

BELOW: Banda's underwater life is unrivalled.

Abandoned cannon at the 17th-century Benteng (Fort) Oranje.

BELOW: Benteng (Fort) Toloko at Dufa-Dufa village.

carved prow. The local people believe that their ancestors arrived in this sacred craft. Near Saumlaki is an island known for its rare species of orchids.

Ternate and Halmahera

The administrative and geographical district of the northern third of Maluku, north of Seram, is dominated on maps by Halmahera, but tiny **Ternate** ⑱ island is the real centre of power and communications as it is the capital of North Maluku province. Two-thirds of the island's 80,000 people live in Ternate town, the business and market centre of the region.

One of the major clove-producing islands of Maluku, Ternate sultans had been trading with Chinese, Arab and Javanese merchants hundreds of years before the first European arrival. The Portuguese were there in the early 1500s, followed by the Dutch at the start of the 17th century. **Benteng Oranje** was built by the Dutch in 1667 and is currently used by the Indonesian police and military. There are many ancient cannons in the large complex. On the outskirts of town, in the direction of the airport, there is a mosque whose foundations date back to the 15th century. Its multi-tiered roof covers an airy space, beautifully designed for prayer and meditation.

A bit further out on the road to the airport, the **Kedaton**, or Sultan's Palace, houses a museum. Prior arrangements can be made through the local tourism office to see the museum's jewel: the magical crown, reputed to be a personal gift from Allah to the first sultan who submitted to Islam. Some hair attached to the crown is said to be growing, requiring periodic trimming. A few years ago, when Gunung Gamalama threatened to erupt, the son of the last officially-recognised sultan took the crown on a boat ride around Ternate to calm the impending eruption. It worked. Three times a week the crown and the resident spirits receive offerings of flowers, holy water and betel nuts.

A 45-km (30-mile) paved road encircles Ternate, never wandering far from the coastline and the volcanic slopes of the 1,720-metre (5,640-ft) **Gunung Gamalama**. At **Dufa-Dufa** village, the Portuguese **Benteng Toloko** fort stands on a seaside cliff, in surprisingly good shape and with a still-legible seal on its main entrance. **Batu Angus** (Burnt Rock) is a former lava flow, now jagged rock, which continues underwater for quite a distance. On the north-east coast, the steep slopes of **Hiri** ⓲ island pop into view. Nearby, there are two crater lakes, both called **Danau Tolire**. The smaller one is near the sea, while the other is a short distance inland.

After rounding the north of Ternate, the crumbling Portuguese **Benteng Kastella** fort comes into view. From here, there is a path to the sacred royal springs of Akerica and to the huge old Afo clove tree. Past Kastella and just before the village of Ngade is **Danau Laguna**. This lake, partially covered with lotus plants, is home to sacred crocodiles who, it is believed, trace their ancestry to a princess. Seeing one of them is said to lead to a lifetime of good luck. A path along one side of the lake rises to give a splendid view of Danau Laguna, with Maitara and Tidore islands in the background. The last stop, **Benteng Kayu Merah** fort, offers a sea-level view of the same islands.

Tidore ⓴ island, a bit larger than Ternate, is for the less energetic, belying its history as a former rival of Ternate's clove production in the 17th century. Frequent boats leave Bastion for **Run**, where there is a weekly market. Tidore is dominated by the volcano, **Gunung Kiematubu**. A paved road goes around most of the island, but beyond the main town of **Soa Siu**, the surface degenerates considerably.

Battle sites and bases

At one time governed by the sultanates of Tidore and Ternate, **Halmahera** ㉑ island was badly damaged in the recent Maluku conflict. The main town is **Tobelo**, which lies on the eastern shore of Halmahera's northern peninsula. **Daru** village is south of Tobelo while further south, near the bottom of the bay, is **Kao** ㉒, which hosted some 80,000 Japanese troops during World War II, earning itself the name of Little Tokyo. Prior to landing on Morotai below, Allied planes bombed the installations here. A few anti-aircraft guns still guard the landing strip. Offshore, superstructures of Japanese shipwrecks protrude above the surface of the water.

Morotai ㉓ island was the site of a major battle during World War II. The task force led by Gen. Douglas MacArthur swept ashore after destroying the light Japanese defence there, as well as the concentration of power at Kao Bay. Morotai was vital to MacArthur's island-hopping strategy towards the Philippines and onward to Japan. Although many of the relics from the war were carted off to a steel mill in Java, there are still remnants of war machinery. In 1973, a Japanese soldier came out of the jungle, nearly three decades after Japan surrendered. And it is rumoured that there may still be Japanese survivors on the island. ❑

The clove is not a seed or fruit but the unopened flower bud of the clove tree. A single tree will yield about 2 kg of cloves, best picked between the months of August and September.

BELOW: dried cloves from Ternate.

PAPUA (IRIAN JAYA)

As one of the world's last great wildernesses, this territory offers great promise to explorers, but advance planning is essential. Allow lots of time to take in the beautiful Baliem Valley

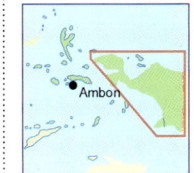

The capital of the province of Papua (Irian Jaya – formerly the Dutch City of Hollandia) has replaced Biak as the gateway for travel to interior destinations. **Jayapura** ❶, a city of 250,000, lies on Yos Sudarso Bay. Its city's constricted site along several indented, steep-walled coves is the most gorgeous of any provincial capital in Indonesia. There is a splendid view of Jayapura from the base of a communications tower, on a steep hill just at the back of the harbour. This stupendous view is the city's most recommended feature.

Those wanting to visit Papua's interior must stop in one of three places to have their *surat jalan* (travel letter) processed: Jayapura, Biak or Sorong, of which Jayapura is easily the most developed and modern. It has good infrastructure in roads, transport services and communications. The post office even has an Internet cafe and the city offers a good selection of hotels and restaurants. Jayapura also has Papua's largest university.

Travellers coming to the area by plane are often surprised to find that they have not landed in Jayapura, but in **Sentani** ❷, a town about a 45-minute drive from Jayapura. This creates an inconvenience because the *surat jalan* must be processed in Jayapura, not in Sentani, necessitating the renting of a car and a day spent in the area waiting for the documents to be processed. Jayapura and Sentani were unheard of by the outside world until MacArthur and the Allies landed in the area in 1944, turning it into a giant military base.

Hamadi, a coastal suburb about 4 km (3 miles) south of Jayapura, is the spot where the Americans landed in their quest to drive the Japanese out of New Guinea. Jayapura saw the biggest amphibious operation of the war in the south-western Pacific, involving 80,000 Allied troops. Rusting tanks and airplanes still rest half-buried in the sand. **Tanjung Ria** beach, known as Base G during World War II, lies to the west. The beach is pleasant and a popular weekend spot. There is also a view of Yotefa Bay and Engrus village, where all the homes, and a church, sit on stilts.

Hamadi has an interesting and colourful market, as well as a number of shops selling souvenirs from all over Papua. There is a good selection of carvings by the Asmat, as well as by the local Sentani.

Museums and a crocodile farm

In the suburb of **Abepura**, between Jayapura and Sentani, a stop at the **Museum Loka Budaya** (open Mon–Fri 7.30am–4pm; entrance fee), on the Cendrawashih University grounds, is a must. It has a good collection of ethnographic pieces, as well as an impressive collection of Asmat art donated by the Rockefeller Foundation. On the same road, the **Museum Negeri**, houses an interesting collection of

LEFT: boy warrior from Biak island on Papua's northern coast.
BELOW: view of Jayapura bay.

TIP

Danau Sentani is home to one of Papua's largest freshwater fish – the sawfish. It can reach some 5 metres (16 ft) long and weigh half a tonne. The Sentani believe their ancestral spirits live in the sawfish and refuse to consume it.

BELOW:
Dani tribespeople crossing Baliem river.

both natural history exhibits and ethnographic pieces. A small shop sells books and souvenirs (open Tues–Sat 8am–4pm, Sun 10am–4pm; entrance fee). In the same area is a **crocodile farm**, displaying several thousand crocodiles in varying stages of development waiting to become purses and shoes – give it a miss.

Danau Sentani is the third largest lake in Papua and has one of the best restaurants on the lake. Boats can be rented here for about US$10 to **Apayo** island, where the residents still produce Sentani bark paintings. A visit can also be made to the island village of **Doyo Lama**, famous for its large woodcarvings and unexplained rock paintings.

The remains of General McArthur's World War II headquarters can be seen on top of **Gunung Ifar**, 6 km (3¾ miles) outside of Sentani. This is one of the best places in the area to view the sunset over the lake. As the hill is on a military base, visitors have to report to the local military office to deposit their passports. An excursion may be arranged by most tour operators to see birds-of-paradise, often found after a two-day drive from Sentani.

Secret valley

The fertile **Baliem Valley** lies in Papua's highlands, a 45-minute flight from Jayapura. At 1,500 metres (4,900 ft), the valley is cool, especially at night. But the mid-day sun can still burn. The fertile, heavily-cultivated 525-sq km (200-sq mile) valley floor is surrounded by the steep Sudirman mountain range (previously Snow Mountain). Early morning clouds and mist often hide the surrounding heights, creating a timeless and mystical ambience that slowly dissipates with the sun's rays. These clouds kept the valley hidden from Western eyes until 1938 when American explorer Richard Archbold flew his seaplane over the mountains and sighted through a gap in the clouds a lush valley dotted with the thatched roofs of Dani huts. The *National Geographic* reported the discovery in its March issue of 1941, but it was not until 1945, when the first missionaries made contact with the estimated 95,000 tribespeople, that the world was made aware of the valley and its inhabitants. The creamy brown **Sungai Baliem** 55 km (34 miles) long and 15 km (9¼ miles) wide, snakes through the valley before pouring out through a southern gorge to the Arafura Sea.

The Dutch established **Wamena** ❸, the only urban centre in the Baliem Valley, in 1958. A town of about 7,000 inhabitants, mostly immigrants, Wamena was a boom town until the late 1990s. Businessmen from the other islands anxiously await the completion of the Trans-Irian highway, which was put on hold after the 1998 economic crisis. The town still has two banks, two telecommunications offices, a very busy post office and about 15 main street businesses. Increased activity by locals in favour of independence has made foreign investors nervous, and many have adopted a wait-and-see attitude.

The indigenous people of the Baliem Valley – Dani, Lani and Yali – are a Neolithic race with unknown origins. Until the 1960s when steel was introduced to them, they were using wood, flint and stone for weapons and tools.

Although foreign influence continues to chip away at their beliefs and traditions, the tribal people live basically as they have done for centuries, following tribal laws and time-honoured customs. In the villages, men still wear *koteka* (penis gourds) while women wear fibre skirts and carry babies or piglets in their fibre bags, known as *noken*. Men routinely carry bows and arrows. Disputes, which occur over land, pigs or women, are settled by fines and payment in pigs.

Different cultures, different habits

The Dani and Lani are closely related – speaking different dialects of the same language but able to understand each other. The Yali, however, speak an entirely different language, and are separated from the other two tribes by great distances and a rugged terrain. The Dani and Lani share the land in the lower highlands, while the Yali live a five-day's trek from Wamena.

The three groups are easily distinguished by their choice of dress. Dani men use a short, thin penis gourd; their single women wear knee-length bark skirts, while the married women don orchid fibre skirts. Lani men use a longer, thicker penis gourd, which also carries tobacco or other treasures, while the women wear knee-length grass skirts. Yali men sport cage-like rattan hoops and very long, thin penis gourds and the women wear tiny grass coverings.

In the past, the three tribes were staunch enemies, often meeting in orchestrated warfare. Minor skirmishes have been reported in more recent times, but none after June 1998. To show their respect for a Javanese tour company owner who had been bringing visitors into the valley for the past 15 years, 1,500 Dani, Lani and Yali tribespeople gathered in peace to attend a two-day ceremony in honour of the Javanese and his American schoolteacher bride. There have been no reported instances of tribal fighting since.

There is much to see and do in the Baliem Valley.

Map on page 336

The Indonesian government has long campaigned to get penis sheaths outlawed, without success.

BELOW: Dani native of Baliem Valley with nosebone.

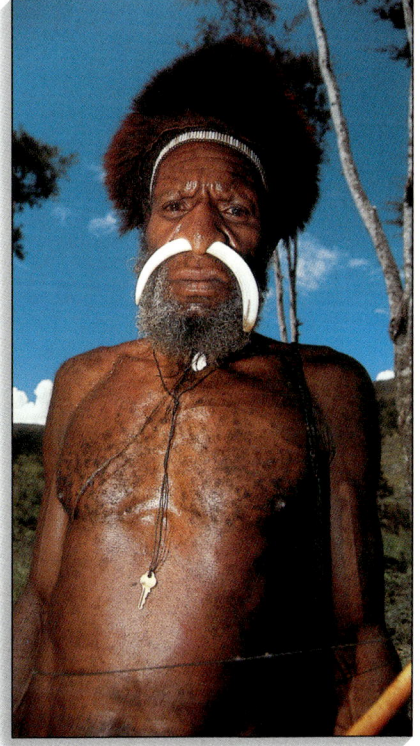

Travellers with only a few days usually arrange to have a Dani village perform a mock war and pig feast. **Amomoge** village, a 45-minute drive north-west of Wamena, is the most popular choice, and for good reason. Chief Yali is a traditionalist who believes that exposing outsiders to the Dani culture is one way to help preserve the culture. Yali's father, Papa Myok, is a respected Dani who will gladly show the seven arrowheads embedded in his body, attesting to his wartime bravery.

A 15-minute walk from Chief Yali's village is **Jiwika**, famous for its blackened, mummified warrior. In the past, important Dani were preserved with the use of herbs and a process of smoking in a secret ritual known only to a select few. Although it is still handed down to one couple in every village each generation, it has not been used for over 250 years. There is also a mummy at **Akima**, a 10-minute drive from Jiwika.

It is possible to spend an interesting day around Wamena. To visit its small **Museum Wamena** (free, but a donation is welcome), ask for it to be opened for you. It showcases the daily life and ceremonial items of the Dani, Lani and Yali tribes. Behind the building is a suspension bridge over the Sungai Baliem, leading to a small Dani compound which welcomes visitors. You will be expected to pay to take photographs; 5,000 rupiah per shot should suffice.

The large, local market, **Pasar G. B. Wenas**, is a 15-minute drive from the museum. Previously called the Nayak Market in downtown Wamena it has since been moved and renamed. Although the new market does not have the flavour of the old one, it is still colourful and worth a visit. There are several stalls selling interesting local handicrafts.

In the early 1990s, the government opened the **Balai Latihan Kerja**, a coop-

Wizened black mummies, like this one in Jiwika, are a ghoulish sight. Expect to pay in order to photograph them.

erative to teach the Dani and Lani skills in pottery making, rattan weaving and leather working. This facility is located near the police station and visitors are welcome. There is no admission charge.

One of the reasons to visit the Baliem Valley is to experience the excellent trekking. The treks into the highlands begin south of Wamena. A one- or two-day jaunt takes trekkers into the Baliem Gorge through sweet potato fields and over stone fences surrounding Dani villages. A five-day trek will take those in good shape to Yali country. It is easy to negotiate a night's stay in a traditional hut or a local schoolteacher's house.

Although many older Dani and Lani are still very traditional in their customs, beliefs and dress, the influence of over 50 years of missionaries, immigrants, schools and, within the last 10 years, the influx of satellite dishes into Wamena, have certainly brought change to the Baliem Valley and its inhabitants. In Wamena, as well as in many of the villages, the youth no longer choose to dress in the traditional style. Women are selling their orchid fibre skirts and men are finding ways to get Indonesian currency to buy their children and wives western clothes, watches and even rice instead of traditional sweet potatoes. At what rate or to what extent these changes will continue is impossible to predict. But if current trends persist, even greater change seems inevitable.

To express grief over the loss of a loved one, a young Dani woman uses a small stone to chop off her finger at the first joint. This tradition has persisted despite constant discouraging by missionaries and the government.

Timika – gateway to the Asmat

Timika ❹ has a mostly immigrant population of approximately 45,000. The main indigenous peoples in this area, the Amungme, Kamoro and Dani, complain that Timika is basically run by the administration of the **Freeport-McMoRan Mine**, the richest copper and gold mine in the world. Freeport, officially opened in March 1973 by then President Suharto, is Indonesia's fourth largest taxpayer.

The developers of the mine have also enhanced many aspects of the infrastructure, especially roads, which have made it easier for immigrants to reach the area and compete for jobs. Until recently, Freeport and the government seemed to have the situation under control. But in the mid-1990s, the area turned into a hotbed of discontent. After the death of several demonstrators, the local tribespeople began a steady stream of complaints – alleging human rights violations by the Indonesian military in support of Freeport.

Environmental groups have also become more vocal. As the independence movement gains momentum throughout Papua, demonstrations against Freeport and the Indonesian government have become more frequent and more violent, but so far the targets have always been specific. No incident involving tourists has been reported.

BELOW: Freeport's copper mines are a a subject of great controversy.

Headhunters, cannibals and artists

Timika is the jump-off point for travel to **Agats** ❺, the only town in **Asmat** (the land as well as the people share this name). The Asmat, once feared headhunters and cannibals and now fishermen and carvers, live in the harsh environment of an alluvial swamp on the south coast of Papua. Their first recorded encounter with Europeans occurred in 1770 when

Close-up of design work on an Asmat war shield made from mangrove wood.

English explorer James Cook stopped in Asmat territory near the Casuarina Coast in search of fresh water. As Cook and his men approached the jungle, a group of Asmat appeared. Cook, fearing danger, fired at the group and returned to his ship. In 1913, this place was named **Cook's Bay**.

Some 64,000 Asmat live in this swampy area bordered on the north by the towering central highlands of New Guinea and on the south by the Arafura Sea, making travel and exploration in this area extremely difficult. Throughout the 16th century, Spanish explorers continued to stop on the island, hoping to find gold. In the 17th and 18th centuries, the Dutch East Indies Company (VOC) established a foothold in what was then referred to as the "Papuan Islands". When the company went bankrupt at the end of the 18th century, the Dutch government inherited their "holdings", including the Asmat area.

During the Napoleonic Wars (1811–16) the British managed the Dutch colonies. After this period the Dutch strengthened their claims, fearing renewed British interest. The 1872 treaty with the sultan of Tidore stipulated that the Dutch government could take over direct rule of the feudal state of New Guinea whenever it desired. In 1898, due to constant complaints by British subjects of headhunting raids across the 141st meridian into British New Guinea, the Dutch established the first formal administrative posts. Explorations were conducted to the most remote upriver villages in 1904, and military and scientific expeditions were sent from 1907 to 1915. The first pieces of Asmat carvings were taken to Holland during this time. Thus began the art world's interest in these "primitive" carvers.

Although experts in the area of primitive art recognised the carvings of the Asmat as unique, the objects had no value to the Indonesian government. The

BELOW: an Asmat armada in the Agats area.

Map on page 336

Dutch gave up control of Papua in 1962, and the first thing the government did when it arrived in Asmat in 1963 was to order the destruction of the statues and to put an indefinite ban on carving and on feast ceremonies. (The ceremonies and carving were for use in rituals surrounding headhunting, cannibalism and warfare.) The ban proved effective. The combined efforts of the missionaries and the government did indeed bring headhunting and cannibalism under control.

Fortunately, the ban on carving and ceremonies was lifted five years later when the Indonesian government, in consultation with the United Nations, decided to open up the Asmat area to outside visitors.

Two important events happened at this time to ensure the preservation of Asmat art: the arrival in Agats of Catholic missionaries, and the arrival and death of Michael Rockefeller, son of American billionaire Nelson Rockefeller.

As the Indonesian government went about systematically destroying the art of the Asmat, Bishop Alphonse Sowanda and Father F. Trenkenschug worked hard to collect as many pieces as their funds would allow. Bishop Sowanda believed that Asmat art objects were "essentially vital religious expression in art". As a result, the **Asmat Museum of Culture and Progress** (open Mon–Sat 9am–noon, afternoons by appointment; entrance fee), housing the finest collection of Asmat art in the world, opened in Agats in 1973.

In November 1961, Michael Rockefeller was on his second trip to Asmat collecting art for museums in the United States. His boat overturned at the mouth of the Sungai Betsj and his body was never recovered. His frantic father mounted an extensive search of the area, prompting journalists from all over the world to descend on Asmat. Newspapers speculated that Michael had been "eaten by cannibals". These rumours gave the Asmat unfair negative publicity, but they also gave the world an awareness of their art.

The Asmat creation story centres on Fumeripitsj, who carved figures out of wood as he sat alone in the forest. These figures became the first Asmat man and woman.

BELOW: war shields at the Asmat Museum of Culture and Progress.

Animism

Even today, when many Asmat profess to be Christian, animism pervades their world. In the past, as the villagers searched for answers to the indiscriminate deaths of its members by illnesses such as malaria and dysentery, they looked to the world of magic and spirits for answers.

Misfortunes were thought to have been brought on by an unhappy or offended ancestral spirit. The spirit thus had to be placated. In this way, ancestral spirits came to demand fulfilment of obligations, especially in the case of revenge for the loss of life in warfare. In this way, many rituals and ceremonies evolved.

When a family member died, the spirit could not be released from the world of the living until an enemy had been killed by a close relative. Until then, the spirit of the ancestor would remain in the village, causing misfortune. Carving objects and naming them after the ancestor while waiting to kill an enemy became one way to appease the spirit. Village carvers began to acquire a high social status. A member of the family of the deceased would commission a carver for an appropriate piece – perhaps a canoe prow or a war shield. The carver would then meditate until he

The Asmat only use three colours for their art – white, black and red. The white comes from the residue of burnt and crushed mussel shells, the black from fire ash, and the red from mud found upriver.

BELOW:
a traditional Asmat dwelling on stilts.

felt the time was right to begin. During this time, the deceased's family paid for the daily living expenses of the carver's family.

It is rare to find an old, high-quality piece of Asmat art today. In the past, the tools used by the Asmat only worked on soft woods. Many of these carvings were used for a specific ceremony and then discarded. The recent introduction of metal tools now allows the Asmat to use hard woods such as ironwood.

The best way to proceed upon arrival in Agats is to go to one of the two hotels in town and ask around for an Asmat guide who speaks English. There are two villages near Agats – **Syuru Kecil** (small) and **Syuru Besar** (large). Syuru Kecil can be reached by elevated boardwalk, Syuru Besar by longboat. Either of these villages can be "hired" for several hours to don their traditional dress and perform dances and perhaps even a ceremony. A motorised longboat can provide transport to either upriver or downriver villages more removed from Agats. However, the villages within only a one-day longboat journey are very similar to those near Agats.

On a longer trip, it is often possible to negotiate to spend a night in the *jeu* or men's house. The Asmat speak their own language, but there is usually at least one person in each village who speaks Bahasa Indonesia, so the guide can act as translator. An introduction to the chief is the first order of business. The Asmat are usually quite happy to assemble their members in the men's house and answer questions. It is not considered impolite to ask if there are any former headhunters who wish to be interviewed. Having visitors is an exciting time for the Asmat and they enjoy talking about the past. Often they will conclude such a session with drum-playing and chanting. In 1998, a tourist who spent seven weeks travelling in Asmat interviewed three former headhunters.

Coastal Papua

Boot-shaped **Biak** ❻ island, lying one degree off the equator on Papua's north coast, is known today for its marvellous diving spots. The island is 50 km (31 miles) long and 18 km (11¼ miles) wide. Because of its proximity to the equator, Biak is extremely hot and humid. Travellers go to Biak for diving or snorkelling or because of an interest in the World War II battles fought there.

Biak, together with Supiori, Numfor and the Padaido islands, form the **Kabupaton Biak Numfor**, one of Papua's nine administrative districts. The total population of the Biak district is around 80,000, with 65,000 living on Biak island. Its economy is stable, thanks to the timber and tuna fishing industries. Biak also exports dried sea cucumber and shark's fin to Taiwan and Hong Kong.

All of these islands are essentially uplifted coral limestone. The area's heavy rainfall has eroded the limestone to form caves, which played a major role in World War II as a hideout for Japanese soldiers. Today, Biak is the site of an Indonesian naval base, but during World War II it was the location of some of the worst battles fought between the Allies and the Japanese over control of New Guinea. Divers can explore shipwrecks sunk from these battles. The **Japanese Caves** are also of interest. Near the entrance to the caves, on Jl. Sisingamangarja, is the **Museum Cenderawasih** with interesting war relics – one half for the Allied memorabilia and the other for the Japanese.

Kota Biak is the place to organise diving or birdwatching excursions between Sorong and Jayapura. It is also a good place to pick up souvenirs; there are two markets selling batik and carvings, including some Asmat and Dani handicrafts. Much of the town closes between 1 pm and 4pm due to the intense heat.

Biak and the islands scattered around it are truly a diver's paradise. **Yapen**

Map on page 336

TIP

Firewalking, once forbidden, is now performed in the Adoki Village, 11 km (7 miles) west of Biak. Men accused of adultery can prove their innocence by walking over burning hot coals.

BELOW: daring freefall on Biak island.

KAROWAI, TREE PEOPLE

Papua's Karowai people are often referred to as "tree people". Their homes can be as high as 45 metres (150 ft) above the ground. They live in the dense jungles of eastern Papua, a three-day journey by boat, charter plane and foot from Asmat on the south coast. They may also be reached from the highlands of the Baliem Valley. An extended family or two small families might share a treehouse, which consists of one large room with no room dividers, but with separate male and female areas which are obvious. (Intimate relations are never allowed inside.) Hunting dogs and baby pigs live alongside.

The Karowai women spend their days caring for the children, cooking and sometimes making a foray into the jungle to collect *sago* (the food staple) and *sago* worms (larvae of the scarab beetle). The men make bows and arrows, discuss the next hunt and clear land for growing *sago*. They also organise ceremonies, such as the yearly *sago* worm ceremony.

The Karowai have seen people from the outside, primarily missionaries but also some tourists. A related group, the Karowai Batu, rejects any contact with outsiders. They are one of the few peoples left in the world today who choose to remain totally isolated.

Cenderawasih or birds-of-paradise, although protected, are hunted till this day. Their magnificent feathers were much sought after by Western milliners in the 19th century.

BELOW: traditional hunting weaponry.

island, long and mountainous, has birds-of-paradise, a decent little hotel and daily flights from Biak. A permit is required to visit Yapen; this can be obtained at the police office in Kota Biak. The island has about 10,000 inhabitants, most of whom are Protestants. The north coast of Yapen is the best place to look for birds-of-paradise. There are several *losmen* in **Serui**, the district capital and only town on the island. Neighbouring **Arumbai** island is purported to have the best diving, featuring great coral reefs and dolphins.

Smaller **Numfor** island, flat with a couple of deep lagoons, also receives flights from Biak but holds no commercial facilities for travellers. Numfor lies just 100 km (65 miles) west of Supiori, between Biak and Manokwari. It is an undeveloped island with many beautiful beaches and friendly villages. Accommodation with a family may be arranged. Located north-west of Biak, **Supiori** is separated from the former by a tiny channel. Most of the island comprises the **Palau Supiori Reserve**, with endemic species of cockatoos and parrots, and mangrove swamps.

Pristine islands

The **Padaido** islands are a cluster of 30 islands, mostly uninhabited. The only way to see these pristine islands is to charter a boat from Bosnik. The best time to do so is on market days – Wednesday and Saturday – when the few inhabitants from **Owi** and **Auki** islands make their way to **Bosnik**. Arranging to return from these islands may cost more than it does to go there.

The **Bird's Head Peninsula** (Jaizerah Doberai), located on the western tip of Papua, is so called because, on the map, it resembles the head of a huge westward-flying bird. **Manokwari** ❼ and Sorong are the principal towns on the peninsula. Manokwari was the site of the first European settlement and the first permanent Christian mission. Today, it remains a strong missionary centre. **Gereja Koawi**, a monument to the first missionaries, is located just past the hospital and behind the church. Manokwari is also the site of a **Japanese War Memorial**.

Manokwari is host to over 30 separate language groups. The three main ethnic groups in the area are the Wamesa in the south, the Arfak in the Arfak mountains, and the Doreri along the coast.

The best reason to visit Manokwari is to take a side trip to **Danau Unggi** in the Arfak Mountains. Those interested can either fly there, or hike the distance in four days. The panorama is truly spectacular. The area is home to the endemic Arfak butterfly, famous for its shimmering wings.

The Sougb people make their home in the Unggi region. The Sougb, although Christian, still believe in black magic. The men wear red, the women black, and they have retained their traditional huts and customs.

Sorong ❽, the other large town in this area, survives mainly from the oil, timber and mining industries. The town has two World War II memorials to the Japanese who died here. Sorong is also the jumping off place to the **Raja Ampat** islands – **Batanta**, **Salawati** and **Waigeo** – to the west, and the best place to view birds-of-paradise. Sorong also has good beaches and reefs and has recently begun to attract dive charters.

Merauke, the easternmost town in Indonesia, is the entry point to southern Papua. It was founded in 1904 by the Dutch in answer to complaints from British citizens concerning Asmat headhunting raids on their side of the border. Today, it is virtually one long street – Jalan Raya Mandala. There is a bank and a police station, where permits for Wasur National Park may be processed.

Wasur National Park

Nearly 80 percent of Papua is covered with primary rainforest. Its coastal and marine habitats, with their spectacular mangrove swamps and exquisite coral reefs, are largely intact, and the province's freshwater swamps and peat bogs are some of the most extensive and undisturbed in Indonesia.

Wasur National Park ❾, located in the Merauke district in the south-east of the province, is a 400,000-hectare (990,000-acre) natural treasure trove. The park contains very diverse habitats – extensive open water swamplands (Rawa Biru), vast tidal mudflats, dry savannah grasslands, luxuriant mangroves, lowland forest and *Melaleuca-Eucalyptus* woodlands. Its wetlands attract huge numbers of the waders and waterfowl that migrate between northern Asia and Australia. The World Wide Fund for Nature (WWF) has documented 74 unique species of birdlife.

Wasur National Park is a joint project of the WWF and the 2,500 Kanum, Marori, Marind and Yei people who inhabit the park's 14 villages. These people have traditionally supported themselves through the sustainable hunting of animals such as deer, wallabies and wild pigs. They are the only ones permitted to hunt and sell game from the park, and they actively participate in protecting the park from poachers and uncontrolled hunting. ❑

Lorentz National Park, comprising more than two million hectares of wilderness, is located in south-west Papua. Because of its incredible biodiversity, this area has been classified as a World Heritage Site by UNESCO.

BELOW: Victoria crowned pigeons from Wasur National Park.

Insight Guides
Travel Tips

✻ INSIGHT GUIDES Phonecard

One global card to keep travellers in touch. Easy. Convenient. Saves you time and money.

It's a global phonecard

Save up to 70%* on international calls from over 55 countries

Free 24 hour global customer service

Recharge your card at any time via customer service or online

It's a message service

Family and friends can send you voice messages for free.

Listen to these messages using the phone* or online

Free email service - you can even listen to your email over the phone*

It's a travel assistance service

24 hour emergency travel assistance – if and when you need it.

Store important travel documents online in your own secure vault

For more information, call rates, and all Access Numbers in over 55 countries, (check your destination is covered) go to www.insightguides.ekit.com or call Customer Service.

JOIN now and receive US$ 5 bonus when you join for US$ 20 or more.

Join today at
www.insightguides.ekit.com

When requested use ref code: **INSAD0103**

**OR SIMPLY FREE CALL
24 HOUR CUSTOMER SERVICE**

UK	0800 376 1705
USA	1800 706 1333
Canada	1800 808 5773
Australia	1800 11 44 78
South Africa	0800 997 285

THEN PRESS ⓪

For all other countries please go to "Access Numbers" at www.insightguides.ekit.com

* Retrieval rates apply for listening to messages. Savings based on using a hotel or payphone and calling to a landline. Correct at time of printing 01.03

(INS001)

powered by ekit

"The easiest way to make calls and receive messages around the world"

Contents

Getting Acquainted
The Place 346
Climate 346
Public Holidays............346
Government 346
Economy 347

Planning the Trip
Visas & Passports........347
Embassies &
   Consulates 347
Customs.....................348
Health 348
Money Matters 348
What to Bring 349
What to Wear 349
Photography...............349
Business Hours 349
Tourist Offices 349
Getting There 349

Practical Tips
Accommodation 350
Food..........................350
Media........................350
Postal Services............350
Telecommunications ..350
Women Travellers........351
Travelling with Kids 351
Business Travellers......351
Gay Travellers.............351
Travellers with
   Disabilities 351
Tipping.......................351
Medical Services/
   Treatment..................351
Security & Crime 351
Etiquette 352

Getting Around
By Road 352
By Air 352
By Sea 352
By Train 352

Java
Jakarta.......................353
Around Jakarta............358
West Java 358
Central Java...............361
East Java 364

Sumatra
North Sumatra 366
West Sumatra 368
South Sumatra & Riau 370

Bali
General 372
South Bali 376
Central Bali 379
East Bali....................381
North Bali..................381
West Bali 382

Nusa Tenggara
Lombok 382
Sumbawa..................385
Komodo & Rinca.........386
Flores........................387
Solor &
   Alor Archipelagos 388
Sumba 388
West Timor, Roti &
   Savu.........................389

Kalimantan
East Kalimantan 390
South Kalimantan 391
Central Kalimantan......392
West Kalimantan 393

Sulawesi
South Sulawesi 394
Central Sulawesi 395
Southeast Sulawesi 396
North Sulawesi...........397

Maluku
Travel Advisory 398

Papua (Irian Jaya)
Jayapura/Sentani 398
Wamena.....................399
Timika 400
Agats 400
Biak 400
Merauke.....................401

Language
General 401

Further Reading
History 403
Geography &
   Natural History 403
Society & Religion 403
Textiles......................403
The Arts 403

Getting Acquainted

The Place

Area: Indonesia comprises 18,110 islands of various sizes – only 6,000 of which are inhabited. The five main islands are: Sumatra (473,606 sq km/182,861 sq miles), Java (132,107 sq km/51,007 sq miles), Kalimantan (539,460 sq km/208,287 sq miles), Sulawesi (189,216 sq km/73,057 sq miles) and Papua (formerly Irian Jaya, 421,981 sq km/162,928 sq miles). In comparison, Bali is tiny at 5,620 sq km (2,170 sq miles). The islands stretch about 5,280 km (3,200 miles) across water, and when superimposed onto a map of North America, it covers the width from California to Bermuda; on a map of Western Europe, it extends from eastern Ireland to the Caspian Sea. Indonesia's territory covers a total area of 9.8 million sq km, of which 81 percent (or 7.9 million sq km) is sea.

Situation: The Indonesian archipelago is bisected by the equator, which passes through Sumatra, Kalimantan, Sulawesi, and Halmahera. Geographically, it is situated between latitude 6° north and 11° south and longitude 94° west to 141° east. It lies between mainland Asia and Australia, bounded by the Indian and Pacific oceans. Located at the point where two of the world's greatest volcanic ranges collide, the physiography and geomorphology of the archipelago are strongly influenced by this.

Population: The official census from an extensive survey carried out by the government in 2000 tallied just over 206 million people. However it is thought that a more realistic number might be in the 220 million range, with 60 percent of Indonesia's people concentrated on Java and Bali, which cover only 7 percent of the total land area. Indonesia is the fourth most populated nation after China, India and the United States, and comprises 300 ethnic groups. Life expectancy is 62 years.

Language: The official language is Bahasa Indonesia, adapted from Malay, the lingua franca of a minority group in Sumatra. Over 350 other languages and dialects are spoken.

Religion: An estimated 87 percent of the population is Muslim, 6 percent Protestant, 3 percent Catholic, 2 percent Hindu, 1 percent Buddhist, and 1 percent animist. Religious freedom is protected by the Indonesian Constitution.

Time zones: Indonesia's considerable spread covers three time zones. Java, Sumatra and West and Central Kalimantan are on Western Indonesia Standard Time, 7 hours ahead of Greenwich Mean Time (GMT). Bali, Lombok, East and South Kalimantan, Sulawesi, Nusa Tenggara and West Timor are on Central Indonesian Standard Time, 8 hours ahead of GMT (the same time zone as Singapore and Hong Kong). Maluku and Papua (Irian Jaya) are on Eastern Indonesia Standard Time, at GMT plus 9 hours.

Weights and measures: Indonesia uses the metric system. 1 km is 0.6 miles; 1 metre is 3.3 feet; 1 kg is 2.2 lbs; 1 litre is 0.3 US gallons or 0.2 imperial gallons. To convert Celsius to Fahrenheit, multiply by 1.8 and add 32.

Electricity: Most hotels use 220 volts, 50 cycles and round two-pronged plugs. However, it is not uncommon to find some using 110 volts, particularly in remote areas. Check before using an appliance. Some hotels supply adaptors on request.

Climate

Indonesia's climate is fairly even all year round, roughly divided into two seasons, wet and dry. The north-east monsoon brings drenching rain to the western islands between November and April, and the tropical sun and the oceans combine to produce continuously high humidity (between 75–100 percent) everywhere. The dry season kicks in from May to October when high humidity levels are lessened by the cool dry air blowing in from the Australian land mass in the west. The further east you move, the shorter the rainy season is, making the dry season longer.

The transitional period between the two seasons alternates between sun-filled days and occasional thunderstorms. Even amid the wet season, temperatures range from 21–33 degrees Celsius (70–90 degrees Fahrenheit), except at higher altitudes, which can be much cooler, and warm clothes are required. The heaviest rainfalls are usually in December, January and February. The seas surrounding the eastern islands can be very rough during these months.

Government

The democratic republic is run by a president and a parliament, the People's Consultative Assembly (MPR). In the past, the president was named by parliament. But in 2004 the president was chosen by the people in Indonesia's first direct presidential election. Administratively, Indonesia has 30 provinces and special territories, led by an appointed governor. Each province is divided into *kabupaten* (regencies) or *kotamadya* (municipalities). *Kabupaten* are usually capital towns headed by a *bupati* (regent), and *kotamadya* are generally large cities and their suburbs, led by a *walikota* (mayor).

Within the regencies and municipalities are *kecamatan* (districts), over which is a *camat* (district chief), further divided into *desa* or *kelurahan* (villages), led by *kepala desa* or *lurah* (village chief). These are the lowest levels of governmental organisation, but within villages there are voluntary leaders which oversee the activities of hamlets or neighbourhoods.

Public Holidays

January 1	New Year's Day (Tahun Baru)
*January/February	Chinese Lunar New Year (Imlek)
	Muslim Day of Sacrifice (Idul Adha)
	Islamic New Year (Tahun Baru Hijriyah)
*February/March	Hindu New Year or Seclusion Day (Nyepi)
*March/April	Good Friday (Jumat Agung)
*April/May	Birthday of Prophet Muhammad (Ma'ulud)
	Ascension Day of Jesus Christ (Kenaikan Isa Al Masih)
*May/June	Birth, Enlightenment and Death of Buddha (Waisak)
August 17	National Independence Day (Hari Kemerdekaan)
*August/September	Ascension of Prophet Muhammad (Isra Mi'raj)
*October/November	End of the Muslim Fasting Month (Idul Fitri)
December 25	Christmas Day (Hari Natal)

*Variable dates

Planning the Trip

Economy

Until the economic crisis hit Southeast Asia at the end of 1997, Indonesia's rise in average per capita income – from only US$50 in 1966 to just over US$1,000 – was impressive. The number of people living below the poverty line had dropped from around 50 percent at the end of World War II to just 15 percent in 1996. Nearly all children attended primary school, compared with about half in the last three decades. However, in the 21st century, thanks to recent political upheavels, the days of food shortages and double-digit inflation have returned. In 2004, the average per capita income was around US$700.

In recent years, the export of shoes, wooden furniture, textiles, handicrafts, tea, tobacco, precious metals and fertilisers, and revenues from tourism are rapidly replacing foreign-exchange earnings from oil and gas as production falls and domestic consumption rises.

Even if the Indonesian economy can recover in the years ahead, there are issues bubbling under the surface that need attention. The main grouse among the middle classes is the lack of political transparency and accountability to match the country's economic and financial liberalisation. Adding to this is unrest in places like Aceh (Sumatra), Maluku, Sulawesi and Papua (Irian Jaya). Often blamed on differences in religion or ethnicity, it can be more accurately described as dissatisfaction between the haves and the have-nots. Apart from these social issues, there is a need to institute a more up-to-date legal system in place for business and law enforcement.

Most analysts agree that Indonesia must accelerate economic reform, continue to upgrade its physical infrastructure and foster a pool of managerial talent if growth is to be stabilised and sustained in the long term. The country's endemic corruption and cumbersome bureaucracy – it has a reputation for the highest hidden business costs in Asia – is also of concern to foreign investors.

Visas & Passports

All travellers to Indonesia must be in possession of a passport valid for at least six months after arrival and with proof (tickets) of onward passage. In 1 February 2004, Indonesia started a new visa policy. Free 30-day visas instead of the old 60-day ones are given only to citizens of Brunei, Chile, Hong Kong, Macao, Malaysia, Morocco, Peru, the Philippines, Singapore, Thailand and Vietnam.

Visa-on-arrival (VOA) is given to citizens of 21 other countries. The cost is US$10 for a 3-day stay and US$25 for a 30-day stay. Countries which fall under this category are: Argentina, Australia, Brazil, Canada, Denmark, Finland, France, Germany, Hungary, Italy, Japan, New Zealand, Norway, Poland, South Africa, South Korea, Switzerland, Taiwan, United Arab Emirates, United Kingdom and the USA.

All other nationals must apply to the nearest Indonesian embassy or consulate in their home country and make sure they possess a valid visa before arrival. Check with any Indonesian embassy or consulate for current regulations, which are in a state of flux.

In 2000, an extendable one-year visa became available to foreigners over age 55 who wish to retire in Indonesia. Certain restrictions apply. Check with an embassy or consulate for details.

A *surat jalan*, or travel permit, is required for visits to certain destinations. Check with a local travel agent or with an Indonesian embassy or consulate for details.

Embassies & Consulates

Embassies are found only in the capital Jakarta. In Bali, Medan (Sumatra) and Surabaya (Java), a few countries maintain small consular offices. Only addresses in Jakarta and Bali are given in the next column.

JAKARTA
(telephone area code 021)

Australia: Jl. H.R. Rasuna Said Kav. 15-16. Tel: 2550-5555, Fax: 522-7101, e-mail: public.affairsjakt@dfat.gov.au.
Britain: Jl. M.H. Thamrin 75, Menteng. Tel: 315-6264, 310-4229, Fax: 390-7484, e-mail: britemb@attglobal.net.
Canada: Jl. Jend. Sudirman Kav. 29, World Trade Center. Tel: 2550-7800, Fax: 2550-7811, e-mail: jkrta@dfait-maeci.gc.ca.
China: Jl. Mega Kuningan 2 Karet, Kuningan. Tel: 576-1039, Fax: 576-1034.
Denmark: Menara Rajawali 25th floor, Mega Kuningan. Tel: 576-1478, Fax: 576-1535, e-mail: jktamb@um.dk.
Finland: Menara Rajawali 9th floor, Mega Kuningan. Tel: 576-1650, Fax: 576-1631, e-mail: finemb@dnet.net.id.
France: Jl. M.H. Thamrin 20. Tel: 213-2807, Fax: 314-3338.
Germany: Jl. M.H. Thamrin 1. Tel: 390-1750, Fax: 390-1757, e-mail: germany@rad.net.id.
Italy: Jl. Diponegoro 45. Tel: 337-445, Fax: 337-422, e-mail: embitaly@italambjkt.or.id.
Japan: Jl. M.H. Thamrin 24. Tel: 324-308, Fax: 325-460.
Malaysia: Jl. H.R. Rasuna Said Kav. X-6, Jakarta Selatan. Tel: 522-4947, Fax: 522-4974, e-mail: kbmjkt@indosat.net.id.
Netherlands: Jl. H.R. Rasuna Said Kav. S-3, Kuningan. Tel: 525-1515, Fax: 570-0734, e-mail: nlgovjak@attglobal.net.
New Zealand: Gedung BRI II 23rd floor, Jl. Jend. Sudirman 44–46, Jakarta Pusat. Tel: 570-9460, Fax: 570-9457, e-mail: nzembjak@cbn.net.id
Norway: Menara Rajawali 25th floor, Mega Kuningan. Tel: 576-1523, Fax: 576-1537, e-mail: emb.jakarta@mfa.no.
Philippines: Jl. Imam Bonjol 6–8, Menteng. Tel: 310-0206, 315-5118, Fax: 315-1167, e-mail: phjkt@indo.net.id
Singapore: Jl. H.R. Rasuna Said, Kav. X-4 No. 2, Kuningan. Tel: 520-1489, Fax: 520-1416, e-mail: denpasar@pacific.net.id.
Spain: Jl. Agus Salim 61, Menteng. Tel: 335-771/940, Fax: 325-996, e-mail: embespid@mail.mae.es.
Sweden: Menara Rajawali 9th floor, Mega Kuningan. Tel: 2553-5900, Fax: 576-2691, e-mail: sweden@cbn.net.id.
Switzerland: Jl. H.R. Rasuna Said Kav. X/3-2, Kuningan. Tel: 520-7451,

525-6061, Fax: 520-3389,
e-mail: swiemjak@rad.net.id
Thailand: Jl. Imam Bonjol 74, Menteng. Tel: 390-4052, Fax: 390-4055, e-mail: thaijkt@indo.net.id.
United States: Jl. Medan Merdeka Selatan 5, Jakarta Pusat. Tel: 344-2211, Fax: 386-2269, e-mail: jakconsul@state.gov.

BALI

(telephone area code 0361)

Australia: Jl. Prof. Moch Yamin 51, Renon, Denpasar. Tel: 235-092, 235-093, Fax: 235-146, e-mail: ausconbali@denpasar.wasantara.net.id.
France: Jl. Mertasari Gg. II / 8, Sanur, Denpasar. Tel: 285-485, Fax: 286-406,
e-mail: consul@dps.centrin.net.id.
Germany (Honorary): Jl. Pantai Karang No. 17A, Sanur. Tel: 288-535, Fax: 288-826, e-mail: dtkonsbali@denpasar.wasantara.net.id.
Italy (Honorary): Lotus Tours, Jl. Bypass Ngurah Rai, Jimbaran. Tel: 701-005,
e-mail: italconsbali@italconsbali.com.
Japan: Jl. Raya Puputan 170, Renon, Denpasar. Tel: 227-628.
Netherlands (Honorary): KCB Travel, Jl. Raya Kuta 127, Kuta. Tel: 761-506, Fax: 752-777, e-mail: purwa@denpasar.wasantara.net.id.
Norway & Denmark: Mimpi Resort Jimbaran, Jimbaran. Tel: 701-070, e-mail: mimpi@mimpi.com.
Sweden & Finland: Segara Village Hotel, Jl. Segara Ayu, Sanu. Tel: 288-407, Fax: 287-242, e-mail: segara1@denpasar.wasantara.net.id.
Switzerland & Austria: c/o Swiss Restaurant, Jl. Werkudara, Legian Kelod. Tel: 751-735
Fax: 754-457, e-mail: swisscon@denpasar.wasantara.net.id.
United States (Consular): Jl. Hayam Wuruk 188, Denpasar. Tel: 233-605, Fax: 222-426, e-mail: amcobali@indo.net.id

Customs

Each adult is permitted to bring a maximum of 2 litres of alcoholic beverages, 200 cigarettes, 50 cigars, or 100 grammes of tobacco, and a reasonable quantity of perfume. Photographic equipment and computers must be declared and are admitted, provided they are taken out on departure. Prohibited from entry are the following: narcotics, arms and ammunition, TVs, radios and cassette recorders, pornography and fresh fruit. All movie films and video cassettes must be deposited for review by the Film Censor Board. There is no restriction on import and export of foreign currencies and travellers cheques; however import or export of Indonesian currency exceeding Rp 5 million is prohibited.

Health

Yellow fever vaccinations are required if arriving within six days of leaving or passing through an infected area. Check with your home physician regarding vaccinations for other ailments like typhoid, cholera and hepatitis A and B.

Diarrhoea and stomach upsets may be a problem, often a reaction to a change in food and environment. Tablets such as Lomotil and Imodium are invaluable, but offer only a temporary solution, best taken only when toilet facilities are lacking. A fever accompanying cramps and diarrhoea may require doctor-prescribed antibiotics.

Probably more stomach upsets are due to dehydration than anything else, as most people simply don't drink enough water. Drink more than you think you need, particularly if taking part in outdoor activities. Take precautions against the sun and the heat. Wear a hat as protection. Tanning oils and creams are expensive in Indonesia and difficult to find outside of big cities. Bring them from home.

Malaria is carried by night-biting mosquitoes. Prophylactics are increasingly questionable; strains are developing in Southeast Asia that are resistant to most medications; some like Larium can cause dizziness, stomach upset, even hallucinations. Before consulting a physician, first determine if you will be travelling in a malaria-infected area (not all of Indonesia is). Upon arrival, minimise contact with mosquitoes by using repellent; and as mosquitoes are most active around dawn and dusk, wear long-sleeved shirts and long pants during those times. Sleep under a mosquito net in infected areas. All bites, cuts and abrasions can easily become infected in the tropics; treat them immediately.

Dengue fever, carried by daytime mosquitoes, is far more prevalent in Indonesia than malaria. There is no prophylactic; take the precautions described above if travelling in an infected area.

All water must be made safe before consumption. Bottled purified water is readily available in even the smallest villages, but if caught in a bind, bringing water to a rolling boil for 20 minutes is an effective method of sterilisation. All fruit should be peeled before eaten; avoid raw vegetables.

AIDS and other sexually transmitted diseases are increasing in Indonesia. Local sex workers have multiple partners from around the world. Act responsibly and use condoms, available over the counter at *apotik* (pharmacies).

Money Matters

Rupiah (Rp) come in bank note denominations of 100,000; 50,000; 20,000; 10,000; 5,000; 1,000; 500 and 100. Coins come in 1,000, 500, 200, 100 and 50 rupiah.

Change is often not available in smaller shops. Carry a variety of coins and small notes, especially when travelling outside cities.

Changing money: Bring only new notes (no coins), as practically no one will change dirty or marred bank notes. The best exchange rate is usually obtained at money-changers, found at the airports of all major cities. Hotels usually offer a lower rate, and banks often offer even worse rates.

Particularly in Bali, where illegal money-changers know every scam in the book, stick to those advertising themselves as "Authorised". Count your money before leaving the counter and get a receipt. It is advisable to convert most of your money in the cities before moving towards the interior. Leftover rupiah is easily changed back into foreign currency at departure. At time of press, US$1 was roughly equivalent to Rp 9,100.

Travellers' cheques: These are a mixed blessing. Major hotels, banks and a few shops will accept them, but their exchange rates are slightly lower. (Most small towns won't accept them at all.) US-dollar travellers' cheques are more widely accepted. Credit cards are accepted in big hotels, international airline offices, city restaurants and shops. Don't count on using plastic in the hinterlands.

Credit cards: MasterCard and Visa are accepted in most large hotels and shops. Diner's Club and American Express are less prevalent. Don't be surprised if an additional 3–5 percent "handling charge" is added to the bill; this is an accepted practice.

Let it Be

Indonesia is a vast country. The best advice for travel in Indonesia is to remain free of deadlines, expect delays, and relax. Just enjoy being somewhere different from home. (Refer to the individual island entries for specific tips to help you navigate your way.)

Automatic teller machines: ATMS are found everywhere in the larger cities. Look for those affiliated with your international ATM network.

What to Bring

Travel as lightly as possible, as there are many good buys to be found in Indonesia and never enough luggage space for them. Essentials are insect repellent, sunscreen, prescription medicines and perhaps an extra set of spectacles. Always hand-carry medicines, as checked-in luggage can get delayed or lost. Make sure all luggage is locked.

What to Wear

Indonesians are concerned with how they present themselves, and are particularly mindful of modesty. As most Indonesians are Muslim, it is polite for women to keep their knees, midriffs and armpits covered. Singlets, halter tops, shorts and miniskirts are frowned upon, as are swimsuits anywhere else other than on the beach or at the pool.

As it is humid, bring all-cotton clothing or the synthetic quick-dry variety for sale in camping stores throughout the world. Sandals or footwear that can be slipped off easily are a good idea, especially if planning to visit mosques or homes, as shoes are always removed before entering. Hiking boots may be required for trekking.

Suits and party dresses are rarely worn. For formal occasions, men wear batik shirts and tailored pants; women, modest dresses, or ethnic outfits. A light jacket or sweater is welcome in mountain areas.

Photography

Most Indonesians love to be photographed, especially if they have children, but it's still nice to ask before shooting. Practically everyone understands "*Foto*?". Just point at the camera and, if you get a nod or a smile, click away. Older people may be shy; if they indicate "no", politely move on. It isn't polite to photograph people praying.

Regular print film is available in larger towns, though developing them can be problematic. Slide film and fancy camera batteries are not easily available.

Business Hours

In most places, government offices are generally open from Monday to Thursday, 8am–3pm, and close at 11.30am on Friday. On Saturday, they close at around 2pm. Business offices are open from Monday to Friday, 8 or 9am until 4 or 5pm. A few companies work on Saturday mornings as well. Banks are open 8am–3pm on weekdays.

Tourist Offices

During the economic crisis, the Indonesia Tourism Promotion Board closed its overseas offices, but plans are underway to reinstate a few of them.

There is plenty of information available on the Web, much of it conflicting, and a lot of it just plain wrong. A good test for reliability is this: if a site shows Indonesia as having anything less than 17,508 islands (the number has only recently increased to 18,110), it hasn't been updated in a while.

Although listed in each of the geographical sections of this book are offices of the Provincial Tourist Services in the district capitals, they are difficult to reach by telephone. The best bet is to drop by their offices before noon.

Useful Websites

www.asitajakarta.com
www.expat.or.id
www.indonesiaone.net
www.indonesiatourism.com
www.indonesia.com
www.asiatravel.com/indonesia
www.tourismindonesia.com
www.worldtravelguide.net/data/idn/idn.asp

Getting There

BY AIR

Until recently, international flights arrived either at **Sukarno-Hatta International Airport** (also spelled Soekarno-Hatta), 20 km (13 miles) west of Jakarta on Java, or **Ngurah Rai Airport**, near Denpasar, Bali. However, now there are international arrivals using smaller aircraft throughout the country. For example, Yogyakarta (Jogja) now has direct flights to Singapore and Kuala Lumpur.

Garuda Indonesia is the national carrier, covering both international and domestic routes. In addition to the government-owned Merpati Nusantara, which primarily focuses on domestic routes, there are a growing number of new, privately-owned airlines, making travelling to and from as well as within Indonesia easier than ever before.

Check with a reliable travel agent, as new airlines and routes are frequently added. Also ask about the new "no-frills" airlines that are cropping up in Asia, such as **Air Asia** (Malaysia-based) and **Lion Air** (Indonesia-based), which have arrival points in several Indonesia cities.

Singapore is a major hub in the region with a number of flights to various Indonesian destinations. The Singapore-based **SilkAir** (a sister company of Singapore Airlines), for instance, operates flights to Lombok, Jakarta and Solo in Java, Medan, Padang and Pekanbaru in Sumatra, and Manado and Makassar in Sulawesi direct from Singapore. There are also direct flights from Singapore, Malaysia, Bangkok and Hong Kong to Surabaya, the second largest city in Java.

Departing Indonesia: If required by your carrier (not all do), reconfirm international airline reservations at least 24 hours prior to departure. Arrive at the airport 2 hours prior to departure. International departure varies from one airport to another and must be paid in rupiah. Average is about Rp. 100,000.

BY SEA

If you're one of the lucky ones with plenty of time (and money), an ocean cruise to Indonesia should not be missed. Luxury cruise lines offer fly/cruise arrangements that allow you to fly to Bali and other ports, then catch a ship on the way home, or vice versa. Contact a travel agent in your home country to see which cruise operator is presently offering Indonesia as part of its itinerary.

Batam and Bintan islands, part of the Riau archipelago in Sumatra, are serviced by high-speed ferries which connect to Singapore.

There are also ferry connections from Penang and Malacca in Malaysia to Medan and Dumai in Sumatra respectively.

BY LAND

The only access by road is at Entikong between Kalimantan and Sarawak, Malaysia. Entry point is at the Pontianak–Kuching expressway.

(See individual island entries for more information on all of the above.)

Practical Tips

Accommodation

In Bali and the major business centres in Java, hotels range from five- to one-star and below, catering to every budget and taste. In more remote regions, anticipate only the basics, and take heart that you can delight in Indonesian hospitality. With the decline in tourist arrivals, bargains are to be found outside of the high season (June–August, Christmas and New Year), with even the fanciest rooms going at reduced rates.

The price guidelines shown are just that – guidelines – using the highest possible rate in high season. Note that the "Under US$30" category includes budget *losmen* for $4–5 per night, while the "Above US$150" category can also mean $800-per-night luxury villas. Check with individual hotels for current rates during the time of your visit.

HOTEL PRICE GUIDE

In the following chapters on individual islands, these price categories are used for standard rooms, usually without breakfast:
$$$$$ = above US$150
$$$$ = US$101–150
$$$ = US$51–100
$$ = US$30–50
$ = under US$30

Food

The staple for the majority of Indonesians is rice, although in the eastern islands, it's corn, sago, cassava or sweet potatoes. Coconut milk and hot chilli peppers are popular cooking ingredients nationwide. Dishes range from very spicy meat, fish and vegetables to those which are quite sweet. The most popular are *nasi goreng* (fried rice), *sate* or *satay* (grilled meat or chicken on skewers), and *gado-gado* (cold, steamed vegetables served with a peanut sauce). In the main tourist centres, many restaurants cater to visitors and serve a wide variety of cuisines. Chinese restaurants are found in almost every town. Bottled drinking water can be purchased everywhere.

The price guidelines shown are per person for an Asian meal that includes a meat dish and two vegetables or a western three-course meal. While the local beer, Bintang, is reasonably priced, imported beers, cocktails and wine (only available in larger cities) are expensive and can equal the price of a meal.

RESTAURANT PRICE GUIDE

In the following chapters on individual islands, these price categories are used for a three-course meal (Asian or Western), without drinks:
Inexpensive = under US$10
Moderate = US$11–25
Expensive = US$26–50

Media

The Jakarta Post is the major English-language newspaper. In addition, a few international newspapers – English-language and others – are available at the newsstands of large hotels and major airports. *Tempo* magazine is published in Indonesian and in English and is a good source of political and business news.

Television is available everywhere, even in the most remote locations. Larger hotels have cable TV, so in addition to Indonesian channels, they receive CNN, HBO, MTV and the like.

Postal Services

There are post offices in every major town and village. Hours are generally as follows: from Monday to Thursday 8am–2pm; Friday 8am–noon; and Saturday 8am–1pm.

Telecommunications

Telephone service is rapidly being modernised and overhauled throughout the country, meaning telephone numbers and area codes change frequently. If a number listed in this guide doesn't work, it has probably been upgraded.

Establishments such as hotels may have several telephone numbers, which may come in five to eight digits. Thus, listings never seem to match. Major hotels offer **International Direct Dial** (IDD). Dial 001, 007, 008 and 017 for an international line. Outside hotels, public telephones are at *wartel* (*warung telekomnikasi*) offices, which sell telephone cards, often offer fax services and, recently, Internet services as well. Numerous cyber cafés called *warnet*, also provide Internet access.

AREA CODES

Indonesia	62
Java	
Bandung	022
Jakarta	021
Yogyakarta (Jogja)	0274
Surakarta (Solo)	0271
Semarang	024
Surabaya	031
Malang	0341
Sumatra	
Medan	061
Banda Aceh	0651
Prapat, Samosir	0625
Padang	0751
Bukittinggi	0752
Palembang	0711
Bengkulu	0736
Bandar Lampung, Pekanbaru	0761
Batam	0778
Bintan	0770
Bali	
Denpasar, Badung, Tabanan	0361
Kuta, Sanur, Nusa Dua	0361
Gianyar, Ubud	0361
Klungkung (Semarapura)	0366
Bangli, Kintamani	0366
Buleleng, Singaraja, Lovina	0362
Karangasem (Amlapura)	0363
Candi Dasa	0363
Jembrana	0365
Bedugul	0368
Lombok	0370
Sumbawa	
Sumbawa Besar	0371
Bima	0374
Flores	
Labuhanbajo	0385
Maumere	0382
Ende	0381
Sumba	
Waikabubak	0387
Waingapu	0386
West Timor	
Kupang	0380
Kalimantan	
Balikpapan	0542
Samarinda	0541
Banjarmasin	0511
Palangkaraya	0536
Pontianak	0561
Sulawesi	
Makassar (Ujung Padang)	0411
Rantepao	0423
Palu	0451
Manado	0431

Calling Tips

If calling Indonesia from overseas, dial the country code 62 followed by the area code (without the zero) then the telephone number. When calling from one province to another in Indonesia, dial the area code with a zero in front of it. Domestic area codes are also given in the geographical listings in this chapter.

Maluku	
Ambon	0911
Bandaneira	0910
Ternate, Tidore	0921
Papua	
Jayapura	0967
Wamena	0969
Biak	0981

Women Travellers

It is highly unusual for a young woman to travel alone in Indonesia and solo females may have to put up with being pestered by gregarious Indonesian men; young local women almost always move around in company. However, you will be quite safe as long as you dress and behave modestly; women with bare legs and minimal tops are considered disrespectful.

Take the usual precautions: don't walk down dark alleys or beaches alone at night. In Bali and Jakarta, be wary of gigolos and "cowboys" offering free rides.

Travelling with Kids

All Indonesians love children. Reliable babysitters are available at all major hotels, and even small inn owners are happy to look after youngsters. Many hotels have kids' clubs and children's programmes. Disposable diapers and baby food are scarce outside major cities.

Business Travellers

Big hotels in cities and towns have conference rooms and business centres that are WiFi, Internet and e-mail friendly can send and receive faxes, make appointments and handle typing, photocopying and other administrative chores. In larger cities, Internet and e-mail is available.

Business etiquette: The correct protocol is of the utmost importance when doing business in Indonesia. Apprise yourself of the rules by reading books on the subject. Here are a few pointers.

The terms *bapak* or *pak* and *ibu*, meaning Sir and Madam, are universally applicable in Indonesia and used to address business counterparts. Both men and women shake hands on introduction. If drinks are served, don't reach for yours until your host has gestured for you to do so. Observe the formalities until your Indonesian counterpart gives the lead to be more relaxed. At first meetings, business may not be discussed at all, paving the way for subsequent consultations.

Meetings usually begin with the conversation centring on social or predictable topics. Specific or personal enquiries are avoided. The best way to air a grievance is to talk politely around the subject until your business partner sees your point of view. Do not be too direct; rather than saying "no" directly, most Indonesians would say "*belum*", meaning "not yet". Consensus is fundamental to all relationships.

Business with Indonesians requires endurance, and most deals negotiations will take far longer than hoped or planned.

Know the Hierarchy

Doing business in Indonesia is a lot about connections. Wherever possible, try to start at the top and work your way down through the rest of the business groups. Tied to the concept of hierarchy are a number of face-giving contortions. Senior levels of the hierarchy demand respect and it would not do for them to deal directly with a person of a lower hierarchy or a foreigner. Use a go-between in such negotiations.

Gay Travellers

Although homosexuals are broadly accepted in Indonesia, note that overt displays of romance are not. Such behaviour is considered distasteful – whether exhibited by homosexuals or heterosexuals. Indonesians, however, are wont to show open affection among one's own sex rather than between the sexes. It is common, for instance, to see two men hugging or holding hands, or girls walking with hands intertwined.

In Bali and Jakarta, there are gay communities and the clubs that cater to them. Bali also has a gay support group, Yayasam Usada Bhakti, which is based on Jalan Blimbing in Denpasar.

Travellers with Disabilities

There is little awareness in Indonesia for the special needs of the disabled, and anyone looking other than "normal" will certainly draw stares, maybe even laughter. Wheelchair ramps and van lifts are not the norm, though large international chains may have handicap facilities. Ask your tour operator in advance for extra assistance.

Tipping

Major hotels add a 10 percent service charge to bills. If it is not included in upscale restaurants, a tip of 5–10 percent is appropriate if the service has been satisfactory.

In small town eateries, tipping is not expected. Airport and hotel porterage is Rp 1,000 per piece for small bags and Rp 2,000 for large ones. Tipping taxi and hired-car drivers is not mandatory, but rounding up the fare to the nearest Rp 1,000 is standard. However, if you are travelling with a hired-car driver and/or a guide, a tip is a good idea.

Medical Services/ Treatment

Most drugs are available at pharmacies (*apotik*) in Jakarta and major cities without prescription, but if you need special medication, bring adequate supplies with you. International-standard medical treatment and specialist care is available in Jakarta and Bali at hospitals and clinics.

If you are finicky, fly to Singapore where the medical facilities are among the best in the world. For visitors in eastern Indonesia, Darwin, Australia, may be easier to get to. It goes without saying that you should not leave your country without comprehensive medical insurance.

Security & Crime

Indonesia is certainly safer, on the whole, than most Western cities. As with everywhere watch out for pickpockets in crowded areas, thieves in cheap hotels, and the occasional scam artist. Take the usual precautions. Don't leave valuables unattended, be careful of your purse, wallet and backpacks in crowded areas. Don't lend money if you expect it to be returned. Report any theft immediately to police or security

Important: Avoid Trouble Spots

Although Indonesia is largely a safe country for travellers, recent incidents of prolonged political unrest among the locals in some areas are reason enough to exercise caution.

Keep yourself informed of current situations and avoid travel to trouble spots such as Maluku, Aceh (North Sumatra), Poso (Central Sulawesi) and Papua (Irian Jaya). Certain foreign commissions, such as the US and Britain, have warned their nationals to avoid travelling to some parts of Indonesia for the time being.

officers. (Without a police report, new passports and travel documents are difficult to obtain.)

Exercise caution by carrying photocopies of your passport, tickets and travel documents, and keep the originals in hotel safes.

All narcotics are illegal in Indonesia and prosecution means a long prison term – perhaps even death – and/or huge fines.

Etiquette

Indonesians are remarkably friendly and courteous, but they are also staunchly conservative. Travellers who observe a few basic rules of etiquette will be assured of a warm welcome.

• Using the left hand to give or to receive anything is taboo (the left hand is reserved for hygiene acts), as is pointing or crooking a finger to call someone.

• Don't make any offers to purchase unless you intend to buy. When bargaining, start at half the asking price and then work out a compromise. Rp 1,000 can mean the difference of a day's meal, so avoid quibbling over small sums. Many Indonesians are still very poor, so be prudent and don't display large sums of money.

• Begging is not a tradition. However, a small contribution at a temple, a village or a cultural conservation centre is appropriate and will be appreciated.

• Hands on the hips indicates defiance or arrogance, especially when also standing with legs apart.

• When sitting, feet should be tucked away, not propped up with the soles facing another person.

• When visiting mosques and other places of worship, dress modestly and remove shoes.

Temple Taboos in Bali

Visitors to a *pura* (temple) in Bali should dress properly for a festival in a long hip-cloth, sash and sleeved shirt, with men adding a folded head-cloth and short overskirt. If visiting a temple on non-festival days, sleeved shirts and long trousers or skirts are sufficient, but a sash is required. Many temples will loan a sash for a fee, but it's easier to carry one with you. Don't climb on any structure, even a wall, to take photographs and avoid using a flash as it distracts the worshippers. Menstruating women and anyone with an open wound are forbidden to enter temples because of a taboo associated with blood.

Getting Around

By Road

Every city, town and village has inexpensive public transport: buses, mini-vans (*bemo*), horse-drawn carts (*andong, cidomo, dokar*), *becak* (pedicabs) or *ojek* (motorcycles). All except buses can be flagged down anywhere on the street. Negotiate fares before getting in. Between towns on all islands, public buses run frequently. A few are safer than others, but all except the air-con express varieties (most with reclining seats, videos and toilets) are noisy and crowded.

The alternative is to hire a car or mini-van, which would allow stops along the way. The hire of a car and driver can be arranged at even the smallest *losmen* (homestay) at rates by the day. Negotiate better rates if you are booking a vehicle for a week or longer but note that you are responsible for the driver's food and lodging, and for the petrol.

The quality of the roads vary greatly and distances in kilometres are irrelevant when calculating time over mountainous roads. Don't bother driving as the experience is not worth the bother of having to deal with near-manic drivers.

By Air

The domestic airline industry is growing by leaps and bounds, thanks to government licensing of several new carriers. **Adam Air, Batavia Air, City Link** (a Garuda subsidiary), **Lion Air** and **Star Air** are among the most recent. Lion Air and Adam Air have departures from Malaysia. Other airlines servicing domestic routes are **Garuda, Bouraq, Mandala** and **Pelita**. It's best to arrange all domestic flights once you are in Indonesia.

Note that in remote areas, flights are not connected to a central reservations system, so it's best to purchase tickets in the town itself rather than pre-book them from a larger city. Reconfirm all domestic flights to be sure they are on schedule. Be sure to get a computer printout with a confirmation number on it. Seats are not always assigned in advance. **Domestic departure tax** is set locally, so varies from airport to airport. The average is about Rp 12,000.

By Sea

PELNI (Pelayaran Nasional Indonesia), the state-owned shipping company, serves about 30 ports, with each ferry accommodating 1,000–1,500 passengers in four classes. They are basic and often dangerously overloaded.

PELNI tickets can be purchased at their local offices or at travel agencies. Or check www.pelni.co.id for more information. In bad weather, the seas can be quite rough, particularly between Sumatra and Java, between Bali and Lombok, and around Komodo.

By Train

There is an adequate train service in Java, a more limited one in Sumatra, but virtually non-existent elsewhere.

In Java, the railway extends from the west (which connects with a ferry to Sumatra) and to the east (this connects with a ferry to Bali).

In Sumatra, there are three rail systems, none of which is linked to one another. In northern Sumatra, a line runs from Medan north to Banda Aceh and south to Rantauprapat. In West Sumatra, a line from Padang runs north to Bukittinggi and Payakumbuh and south to Solok and Lunt. In South Sumatra, the line begins at Tanjung Karang and runs north to Parabumulih, east to Palembang and west to Lubulkinggau.

(See individual island entries for more information on "Getting Around".)

Java

Jakarta

Note: The telecommunications system in Jakarta has reached its limit for 7-digit numbers. All new telephone numbers have 8 digits. Therefore, it's not unusual for some businesses to have both 7- and 8-digit numbers if they have recently added a new telephone line.

GETTING THERE

By Air

Jakarta, the capital of Indonesia on Java island, is one of the two main entry points into Indonesia; the other is Denpasar in Bali.

From either point, there are numerous daily flights to major cities in Indonesia. Elsewhere in Java, large domestic airports are found in Yogyakarta (Jogja), Surakarta (Solo) and Surabaya.

Several new airlines operate both domestic and international flights. Check with ticketing offices or an Indonesian travel agent for the latest details.

Airline Offices
Adam Air: Jl. Gedong Panjang Raya No. 128. Tel: (021) 691-7540/1, Fax: 690-8650, 690-2911, www.adamair.com.
Air Asia: Tel: (021) 8089-9000, www.airasia.com. Accepts reservations via the Internet and payments by credit card only.
Air New Zealand: Chase Plaza, Jl. Jendral Sudirman Kav. 21, Jakarta Selatan. Tel: (021) 391-5501, Fax: 570-3439, www.airnewzealand.com.
Batavia Air: Jl. Ir. H. Juanda No. 15. Tel: (021) 691-7540/1, Fax: 421-2723.
Bouraq Airlines: Jl. Angkasa 1–3, Kemayoran. Tel: (021) 628-8815, 629-5364, www.bouraq.com.
British Airways: Menara Bank Mandiri, 11th floor, Jl. M.H. Thamrin 5, Jakarta Pusat. Tel: (021) 230-0655/0277, Fax: 230-2671, www.ba.com.
Cathay Pacific: Gedung Bursa Efek Jakarta, Tower 1, 26th floor,
Jl. Jendral Sudirman Kav. 52/53, Jakarta Selatan. Tel: 515-0777/ 1747/2747, Fax: 380-6533, www.cathaypacific.com.
Deraya Air: Halim Perdana Kusuma Airport, Tel: (021) 8089-9505/515, Fax: 801-6699, www.boedihardjogroup.com.
Eva Air: 10th floor, Price Waterhouse Coopers, Jl. H.R. Rasuna Said Kav. C3, Kuningan, Jakarta Selatan. Tel: (021) 520-5363, Fax: 521-2630, www.evaair.com.
Garuda Indonesia: Main office: Gedung Garuda Indonesia, Jl. Merdeka Selatan No. 13. Tel: (021) 231-0082, 231-1817, 231-1801, www.garuda-indonesia.com.
Japan Airlines: Ground floor, Kyoei Price Building, Jl. Jend. Sudirman Kav. 3–4, Jakarta Pusat. Tel: (021) 572-3211/3226, 570-3169, Fax: 572-3231, www.jal.com.
KLM Royal Dutch Airways: Sumitmas III, 17th floor, Jl. Jend. Sudirman, Kav. 61/62, Jakarta Selatan. Tel: (021) 252-6730/6735, Fax: 252-6750, www.klm.com.

From Jakarta's Airport

The Sukarno-Hatta (also spelled Soekarno-Hatta) International Airport is 18 km (11 miles) from the city centre, or 45 minutes to 2 hours away – depending on traffic. Terminal 1 is for domestic travel; Terminal 2 handles all international flights, along with all Garuda and Lion Air flights – both domestic and international.

The airport is modern with facilities such as fast-food joints, hotel and domestic air ticket reservation counters, and an efficient coupon-based taxi service. Taxi fares to Jakarta town are usually about US$10–15. Purchase a coupon from the taxi counter for door-to-door service. This is the best hassle-free option, ensuring English-speaking personnel, fixed prices and an air-conditioned ride. Or take your chances with metered taxis cruising the streets; avoid those touts who urge new arrivals into unmetered vehicles.

You could also hop aboard one of the many DAMRI airport buses which run from 3am–10pm servicing strategic stops in the city. The air-con buses run every ½ hour between the city and the airport for a US$1.50 fare. Budget travellers heading for the Jalan Jaksa/Kebon Sirih area should alight at Gambir train station.

For information on airport departures and arrivals, call (021) 550-5307/8/9.

Lion Air: Komplek Harmoni Plaza Blok B/5. Tel: (021) 633-7272, 638-6383, Fax: 533-1045.
Lufthansa: 2nd floor, Panin Centre Building, Jl. Jend. Sudirman 1, Jakarta Pusat. Tel: 570-2005, 739-6767, Fax: 571-1476, www.lufthansa.com.
Mandala Airlines: Jl. Garuda No. 76, Kemayoran, Jakarta Pusat. Tel: (021) 422-2455, 420-6646.
Malaysia Airlines: World Trade Centre, Jl. Jend. Sudirman, Jakarta Pusat. Tel: (021) 522-9682, Fax: 522-9815.
Merpati Nusantara Airlines: Jl. Angkasa, Blok B15 Kav. 2–3, Kemayoran. Tel: (021) 654-8888, www.merpati.co.id.
Qantas Airways: Menara Bank Mandiri, 11th floor, Jl. M.H. Thamrin 5, Jakarta Pusat. Tel: (021) 230-0655, 230-0277, Fax: 315-4636, www.qantas.com.au.
Singapore Airlines: Menara Kadin Indonesia 8F, Jl. H.R. Rasuna Said, Blok X5, Kav. 2-3, Jakarta. Tel: (021) 579-03828, Fax: 579-03886/7, www.singaporeair.com.
Star Air: Jl. Gunung Sahari Raya 57 A-B. Tel: (021) 422-2622, 422-2878, e-mail: starair@cbn.net.id.
Thai Airways International: Menara Bank Mandiri, Jl. M.H. Thamrin No. 5, Jakarta Pusat. Tel: (021) 233-2551/2, Fax: 230-3105, www.thaiairways.com.

For **Air Niugini**, **Ethopian**, **Saudi Arabian** and **Variq**, contact GSA PT Ayuberga, Menara Imperium, Mezzanine floor, Metropolitan Kuningan Superblok Kav. 1, Jl. H.R. Rasuna Said. Tel: (021) 835-6201, Fax: 835-6223, www.ayuberga.co.id.

By Sea

The national ferry passenger line, PELNI has fixed schedules for service from Java to destinations throughout Indonesia. There are four ports in Java: Jakarta, Cirebon, Semarang and Surabaya. Ticketing office: Jl. Angkasa 18. Tel: (021) 420-9193, Fax: 6385-9130, www.pelni.co.id.

By Train

Java's train network offers services to all its major cities. Trains run from the west to the east, connecting many major cities. In the east, it connects with the ferry to Bali, and in the west, with the ferry to Sumatra. The trains may be slow but are inexpensive and a nice way to see the countryside.

There are two basic routes: (north) Jakarta–Cirebon–Semarang–Surabaya; and (south) Jakarta–Bandung–Yogyakarta–Surakarta–Surabaya.

First-class usually ensures a reserved seat and is comfortable; a few have air-conditioning and a dining

car. Second-class can be hot, crowded and dirty. Javanese trains are often late, sometimes by many hours. For night travel, it is best to purchase tickets the day before; for day travel, buy tickets 1–2 hours ahead or through a travel agent. Train tickets can be purchased on the day of your departure at the station (allow 1 hour or more before departure) or two days beforehand from **Carnation Travel**, Jl. AM Sangaji (tel: (021) 231 3713) or any travel agent.
Gambir Station: Jl. Medan Merdeka. Tel: (021) 386-2362. Serves south- and east-bound train routes, including Bogor and Bandung.
Kota Station: Jl. Stasiun Kota. Tel: (021) 692-8515. Serves south- and east-bound trains.
Senen Station: Jl. Stasiun Senen. Tel: (021) 421-0006. Serves east-bound and Cirebon trains.
Tanan Abang Station: Jl. Jatibaru. Tel: (021) 384-0048. Serves west-bound trains, including the Sumatra ferry connection.

By Road
Inside the large cities, there are good road systems, with modern toll roads in Jakarta, Surabaya, Bandung and Yogyakarta. Once in the countryside, potholes and poor road conditions are common.

Bus
Most Indonesians travel by long-distance express buses – the least expensive way to travel. Many operate at night, leaving major cities at one end of Java and arriving at the other end in the early morning. Note that local bus drivers are generally reckless and accidents are common. Beware of pickpockets.
Seats are narrow – six across where buses in other countries only seat four. Some have air-con and screen videos. Bring along water and snacks, although there will usually be stops along the way for food and personal needs.
Long-distance buses operate from three terminals in Jakarta. All can be reached by taxi and are connected by local city buses.
Grogol Terminal (west Jakarta) has services to Sumatra and West Java; **Kampung Rambutan Terminal** (in north-east Jakarta, near the old Halim Airport) has buses that go to Bandung, Bogor and southwards; while **Pulo Gadung Terminal** (Jl. Bekasi Timur Raya) has services heading for Central and East Java.

Car/Mini-van
Probably the most comfortable and practical way to go on a limited budget. For trips out of town or across the island, the only extra you need pay for is the driver's food and lodgings, and maybe some or all of the petrol. Still, with a group of four or five people, you can go from Jakarta all the way to Yogyakarta via Bandung and the north coast for about the same cost as flying. Be sure the agreement is all worked out clearly in advance, including the amount you will give the driver every day for food and lodgings (tips are not expected, though they would be appreciated). You may have difficulty finding a driver who speaks some English, so expect to pay a premium for this. Count on an extra day's rental and a full tank of petrol for the driver to get home.

TOURIST OFFICES

Association of Indonesia Travel Agencies-Jakarta (ASITA): Wisma Nugra Santa, 4th floor, Jl. Jend. Sudirman Kav. 7-8, Jakarta Pusat. Tel: (021) 670-0455, 671-1706, Fax: 571-1703, e-mail: www.asitajakarta.com.
Directorate General of Tourism: Jl. Merdeka Barat 17–19. Tel: (021) 383-8231/4, Fax: 386-0828.
Jakarta City Tourist Office: Jl. Kuningan Barat No. 2. Tel: (021) 520-5455/9671, 525-0738, Fax: 520-9677, 522-9136.
PHPA: Jl. Merdeka Selatan 8–9, Blok G, 21st floor. The place to obtain information and permits for Indonesia's national parks.
Provincial Tourist Services: Jl. Abdurrohim No. 2, Kuningan Barat. Tel: (021) 525-0738/1073, 520-9677/89, Fax: 522-9136, 526-3923/6.
Tourism Promotion Board: Wisma Nugra Santana 9F, Jl. Jenderal Sudirman No. 8, Jakarta 10220. Tel: (021) 570-4879/4917, Fax: 570-4855.
Visitor Information Centre: Jakarta Theatre Bldg. (across from Sarinah), Jl. M.H. Thamrin. Tel: (021) 315-4094.

MEDICAL SERVICES

The following clinics are of international standard and are popular with expatriates living in Indonesia. Both have staff that can handle problems in English.
SOS Medika (AEA International Clinic): Jl. Puri Sakti No. 10, Cipete, Jakarta. Tel: (021) 750-6001, Fax: 750-6002/3.
Medical Scheme: Setiabudi Bldg. 11, Jl. H.R. Rasuna Said, Jakarta. Tel: (021) 525-5367, Fax: 520-2524.

CITY TRANSPORT

Car
Chauffeur-driven cars are highly recommended as a way to get around. Offered by many companies, the use of such cars can be arranged through your hotel.
Hourly or daily rates are charged within the city; trips out of town are charged on a round-trip basis. The most reputable companies are: **Avis** (tel: (021) 314-2900), **Hertz** (tel: (021) 550-5773), and **Bluebird** (tel: (021) 314-1307). Self-drive car rental is available, but are not recommended.

Taxi
One of the most practical ways to get around the city is by taxi. The fares are reasonable. Check that the meter is working and that your driver knows the location of your destination before getting in; alternatively, book a taxi from **Bluebird** (tel: (021) 798-1001), or its sister company, **Silverbird** (tel: (021) 798-1001). Otherwise, taxis are easily available at large hotels and shopping malls, or by flagging one down on major streets.

Bus
Regular city buses are cheap but are hot and crowded – an adventure for the intrepid traveller. They can be dangerous, as they tend not to stop completely when picking up or discharging passengers. Beware of pickpockets, especially during peak hours – the orange "Metro Mini" buses have a particularly bad reputation.
The **Trans-Jakarta bus** (also known as the "busway") is Jakarta's newest transportation system, linking South Jakarta (Blok M) to North Jakarta (Kota). Forty air-conditioned buses ply special car-free lanes for US30 cents one way. Convenient stops along the way are: Kebayoran, Thamrin, Majapahit, Gajahmada and Pintu Besar Selatan and vice versa. The busway is the fastest way to get from one end of town to the other. Visitors can alight at the Kota bus terminal and begin their walking tours of old Batavia (Kota) from there.

TOUR OPERATORS

Banten World Travel: Jl. Pintu Air Raya No. 7, Blok A4. Tel: (021) 384-3630, Fax: 344-2377, e-mail: katamsi@bantenworld.com. Small tour operator specialising in tours of coastal Banten province.
Karash Adventure & Training: Jl. Ciomas No. 6 Keborayan Baru.

Tel: (021) 723-4443, 7278-9730, mobile tel: 081-693-2245, Fax: 720-2445, e-mail: vickra@indosat.net.id, www.karashadventure.com. Karash specialises in introducing Indonesia's nature and culture to travellers who want to go off the beaten path. Organises trekking, mountain climbing and visits to see endangered animals and ethnic groups.

Universal Tour & Travel: Head office: 82C, Jalan Pintu Besar Selatan. Tel: (021) 690-1669, Fax: 690-0983, e-mail: unitour@cbn.net.id. Also has branches in Denpasar (Bali) and Yogyakarta (Java). Specialises in overland tours to Java but also does airline tickets, hotel reservations and tour packages.

WHERE TO STAY

If you arrive at the Jakarta International Airport, you can book a hotel room at a discount at the **Indotel** counter (located next to the baggage claim). Jakarta has a wide selection of first-class luxury hotels – most are found along the city centre of Jl. Sudirman-Thamrin.

Moderately priced hotels are a taxi ride away, while backpackers' guesthouses and *losmen* are found in the Jl. Jaksa and Jl. Kebon Sirih Dalam area near Monas/Medan Merdeka (Freedom Square).

Crowne Plaza Jakarta: Jl. Gatot Subroto. Tel: (021) 526-8833, Fax: 526-8832, www.crowneplaza.com. A five-star hotel in the "Golden Triangle" area with the excellent Spanish restaurant, Plaza de Espuma. Includes a 24-hour café and 24-hour business centre. $$$$$

The Dharmawangsa: Jl. Brawijaya Raya, No. 26. Tel: (021) 725-8181, Fax: 725-8383, www.dharmawangsa.com. Intimate boutique-style hotel with only 100 rooms, a third of which are suites. A haven of understated luxury, with expensive artworks throughout. The dramatic Sriwijaya restaurant combines Western flair and presentation with local ingredients and traditional Indonesian flavours. $$$$$

Grand Hyatt Jakarta: Jl. Jend M.H. Thamrin. Tel: (021) 390-1234, Fax: 390-6426, www.hyatt.com. Considered to be the best in Jakarta, this sophisticated hotel sits above the Plaza Indonesia mall. Excellent service. $$$$$

Gran Meliá Jakarta: Jl. Rasuna Said. Tel: (021) 527-3747, Fax: 526-4321, www.granmelia.co.id. One of the city's newer five-star hotels and part of the Spanish-run Melia Sol chain. An elegant 428-room hotel with beautiful landscaped gardens. Known for its good Sunday brunch. $$$$$

Gran Mahakam: Jl. Mahakam I No. 6, Blok M. Tel: (021) 720-9966, Fax: 725-2011, e-mail: reservation@granmahakam.com, www.granmahakam.com. As the name suggests, this is a grand (almost ostentatious) boutique-style hotel located away from the city centre in one of Jakarta's prime shopping districts. $$$$$

Hilton: Jl. Gatot Subroto. Tel: (021) 570-3600, Fax: 573-3089, www.hiltonindonesia.com. The largest five-star hotel in the city sits adjacent to the Jakarta Convention Centre. More than 200 apartments in separate wings cater to long-term guests. The hotel serves a great Sunday brunch, and offers monthly cooking classes. $$$$$

J.W. Marriott: Jl. Lingkar Mega Kuningan, Kav. E 1-2, No. 122. Tel: (021) 5798-8888, Fax: 5798-8883, www.marriott.com. Located in the golden triangle business district, its restaurant is popular with businessmen at lunch time. Rooms are comfortable and spacious. $$$$$

Mandarin Oriental: Jl. M.H. Thamrin. Tel: (021) 3983-8888, Fax: 3983-8899, www.mandarin-oriental.com. A 5-star hotel centrally located near the prestigious business area, along Jl. Sudirman, facing the Welcome Statue. Excellent service and complete range of restaurants and facilities. $$$$$

Mid Plaza Intercontinental: Jl. Sudirman, Kav. 10-11. Tel: (021) 251-0888, Fax: 251-1777, www.ichhotelsgroup.com. Jakarta's new five-star Intercontinental hotel features lots of wood and black marble and has easy access to the central business district. $$$$$

Mulia Senayan: Jl. Asia Afrika Selatan (South Jakarta). Tel: (021) 574-7777, Fax: 574-7888, www.hotelmulia.com. Located in the shopping district near Blok M, this hotel features spacious and luxurious rooms and all the mod cons you expect from a five-star hotel. $$$$$

Regent: Jl. Rasuna Said. Tel: (021) 252-3456, Fax: 252-4480, www.regenthotels.com. Situated in the Merdeka Monument area, this upscale hotel has all the facilities one expects from a Regent property. Very popular with business people. $$$$$

Shangri-La: BNI City, Jl. Jend. Sudirman Kav. 1. Tel: (021) 570-7440, Fax: 570-3530, www.shangri-la.com. One of the more popular luxury hotels, this 32-storey hotel is centrally located and offers free morning shuttle services to major office addresses. An excellent Chinese restaurant serves *dim sum* on Sundays, while the popular B.A.T.S. bar is on the first level. $$$$$

Sheraton Bandara Jakarta: Bandara Sukarno-Hatta. Tel: (021) 559-7777, Fax: 559-7770, www.starwood.com/sheraton. This five-star hotel is 3 km (2 miles) from the airport and 25 minutes to downtown. Pluses are an Internet service in every room, and an 18-hole golf course. It's also one of the few places in Jakarta that has a sea breeze. $$$$$

Alila Jakarta: Jl. Pecenongan, Kav. 7-17. Tel: (021) 231-6008, Fax: 231-6007, www.alilahotels.com. Trendy 4-star boutique hotel with cutting-edge design and large rooms with high-speed Internet access. Excellent fitness centre on site. $$$$

Batavia Hotel: Jl. Kali Besar Barat No. 44. Tel: (021) 690-4118, Fax: 690-4092, e-mail: bataviaadm@dnet.net.id. A hotel with a colonial feel, it is located in the Glodok business district, a 30-minute taxi ride from the city business centre. There is a baby-sitting service, a clinic and a business centre. $$$$

Hotel Ciputra: Jl. Letnan Jen. Parman. Tel: (021) 560-6006, Fax: 566-9655, www.hotelciputra.com. This four-star hotel sits above the Ciputra Mall, close to the toll road. Comfortable rooms. $$$$

Hotel Nikko: Jl. Thamrin No. 59. Tel: (021) 230-1122, Fax: 314-3631, www.nikkohotels.com. This comparatively older but well-run hotel is located in the heart of the city. $$$$

Sari Pan Pacific: Jl. M.H. Thamrin. Tel: (021) 390-2707, Fax: 323-650, e-mail: Jakarta@panpacific.com, www.panpacific.com. The only Pan Pacific hotel in Indonesia. Located within walking distance of Sarinah Shopping Complex, with Hard Rock Café at its top. $$$$

Arcadia: Jl. Wahid Hasyim No. 114. Tel: (021) 230-0050, Fax: 230-0995, e-mail: arcadia@indosat.net.id. This small and interesting hotel of art-deco design is well located and has a good range of services. $$$

Atlet Century Park: Jl. Pintu Satu Senayan 1. Tel: (021) 571-2041, Fax: 571-2191, www.centuryhotels.com. Originally built as the athlete's village

Hotel Price Guide

Price categories for standard rooms, usually without breakfast:

$$$$$	= above US$150
$$$$	= US$101–150
$$$	= US$51–100
$$	= US$30–50
$	= under US$30

for the Senayan Sports Complex, and situated in the south-west of the city near the Central Business District. **$$$**

Betawi Sofyan: Jl. Cut Mutiah. Tel: (021) 390-5011, Fax: 390-2747, www.sofyanhotel.com. A centrally-located, recently-opened small hotel with comfortable rooms. Excellent value. **$$$**

Quality Bandara: Terminal 2E, Sukarno-Hatta Airport. Tel: (021) 559-0008, Fax: 559-0018, www.qualityinn.com. The only hotel located inside the airport. Day use room (minimum stay 6 hours), restaurant and swimming pool are available. Guests can check flight schedules on monitors inside every room or in the lobby. **$$$**

Raddin Ancol: Ancol Dreamland Complex. Tel: (021) 640-5641, Fax: 640-5645, e-mail: radancol@indosat.net.id. One of Jakarta's few beach resorts, near Sea World and Fantasy Land. **$$$**

Sofyan Cikini: Jl. Cikini Raya 79. Tel: (021) 314-0695, Fax: 310-0432, www.sofyanhotel.com. A small, comfortable hotel that's a taxi ride away from the city centre. The staff is friendly and there is a good range of services. **$$**

Djody: Jl. Jaksa 35. Tel: (021) 390-5976, Fax: 314-2368. Situated close to the Medan Merdeka (Freedom Square) and the Gambir train station, this hotel has several small restaurants within walking distance. The rooms are very basic, with fan or air-con but no hot water. Breakfast and afternoon tea are included in the price. **$**

Yannie International Guest House: Jl. Raden Saleh Raya 35. Tel: (021) 314-0012, Fax: 327-005. A simple and charming guesthouse located near the TIM Culture Centre. It has 15 rooms with fan or air-con and hot water. Breakfast is included in the price. **$**

Restaurant Price Guide

Price categories for a three-course meal (Asian or Western), without drinks:
Expensive	= US$26–50
Moderate	= US$11–25
Inexpensive	= under US$10

WHERE TO EAT

Jakarta eateries offer something for everyone: from fine dining to Western-style fast-food joints in shopping malls, and very simple local fare at *warung* (roadside food stalls). An addition to the scene is the fancier *warung*, a few owned by Indonesian film stars; the permanent street-side eateries are clean and inexpensive. Try places like **Tenda Semanggi** and **Warung Kemang**.

Ah Yat Abalone: Mid Plaza 2 Building, Jl. Sudirman, Kav. 10-11. Tel: (021) 570-7333. A new Chinese restaurant offering a set menu for a minimum of 10 persons, but a la carte is also available. Specialities are abalone and almond pudding for dessert. *Expensive*.

Café Batavia: Jl. Pintu Besar Utara 14. Tel: (021) 691-5531. A stylish restaurant housed in a 19th-century Dutch heritage building. Good Indonesian and international dishes served amid charming atmosphere. *Expensive*

Nippon-Kan: Hilton Hotel. Tel: (021) 570-3600. One of Jakarta's best Japanese restaurants, it has nice views of a lake with gliding swans. *Expensive*

Oasis: Jl. Raden Saleh No. 47. Tel: (021) 315-0646. A landmark restaurant reminiscent of old-world colonial elegance. The speciality is *rijstafel*, served by waitresses in traditional dress, each carrying a separate dish. *Expensive*

Palm Beach: Jl. Wisma BNI 46, Jl. Sudirman. Tel: (021) 574-2188. Seafood prepared Singapore style. *Expensive*.

Sriwijaya: The Dharmawangsa, Jl. Brawijaya No. 26. Tel: (021) 725-8181. Very elegant restaurant located in the upmarket **Dharmawangsa Hotel**. The menu features a blend of European and Indonesian dishes like smoked forest mushrooms, spiced coconut soup and coriander roasted lamb. Save this for a special night out. *Expensive*

Bengawan Solo: Sahid Jaya Hotel. Tel: (021) 570-4444. The elegant Javanese décor goes with the speciality food from Central Java. *Moderate*

Dragon City: Lippo Plaza Podium, Jl. Sudirman. Tel: (021) 522-1933. This popular business-lunch meeting point serves Szechuan seafood delicacies. *Moderate*

Hazara: Jl. Wahid Hasyim No. 112. Tel: (021) 315-0424. Good North Indian food amid curios and antiques in an interesting setting. *Moderate*

Kafe Museum: Jakarta History Museum, Jl. Taman Fatahillah I. Tel: (021) 693-0140, Fax: 693-0141. Located in the west wing of Jakarta History Museum, a good spot for lunch while touring the exhibits. *Moderate*

Koi Gallery: Jl. Mahakam 1 No. 2. Tel: (021) 722-2864. The menu changes regularly to complement the exhibits in this gallery-cum-eatery. *Moderate*

Nelayan: Gedung Manggala Wanabhakti, Jl. Gatot Subroto. Tel: (021) 570-0248. One of the best places for seafood, which you can enjoy in a comfortable local setting. *Moderate*

Planet Hollywood: Jl. Gatot Subroto. This is American food with all the fanfare – the bar has a simulated volcano that "erupts" every hour. It's not just the best place in town for a burger or salad, the desserts are also excellent. *Moderate*

Payon: Jl. Kemang Raya 17. Tel: (021) 719-4826. Exquisite Javanese cuisine – from West, Central and East Java – served in a typical Yogyakarta-style house. Gamelan music tinkles in the background while you partake of your food. *Moderate*

Raja Laut: Jl. Jend. A. Yani 72-73. Tel: (021) 425-2173. A seafood restaurant featuring prawns, lobster and fish, selected from large aquariums. Spacious dining room and parking. *Moderate*

VOC Galangan Café & Restaurant: Jl. Kakap No. 1. Tel: (021) 667-0981, Fax: 667-8501. In an old Dutch warehouse located just opposite the Pasar Ikan and Bahari Museum. *Moderate*

Chopstix: Plaza Indonesia, Jl. Thamrin. Tel: (021) 3983-8792. Chinese food, primarily noodle dishes, prepared in small portions for individual diners. Very simple and quick. Rice is also available. *Inexpensive*

Sari Bundo: Jl. H. Juanda 27. Tel: (021) 380-6909. One of the best places to try spicy-hot Padang food where several dishes have been pre-laid out and the diner just has to sit and eat. You pay only for the amount consumed. *Inexpensive*

Senayan Sate Khas: Jl. Cokroaminoto, Jl. Kebon Sirih (Menteng) and Jl. Pakubuwono VI (Kebayoran). A place to sample inexpensive Indonesian fare in a casual atmosphere. The house speciality is *sate* (or *satay*). *Inexpensive*

CULTURE

For culture in any form, the first place to check is **Taman Ismail Marzuki** (TIM; tel: (021) 315-4087) at Jl. Cikini Raya, Jakarta's centre of cultural and performing arts. TIM hosts a variety of Indonesian dance performances, *wayang kulit* and *wayang orang*, modern and traditional theatre productions, as well as visiting performances of ballet, modern dance, classical and jazz music, and international film festivals.

Visit the **Museum Wayang** for traditional *wayang kulit* shadow puppet shows (tel: (021) 692-9560; Sunday 10am; free). **Gedung Kesenian** on Jl. Kesenian is a restored Dutch *Schouwburg* playhouse, and offers dance and musical performances (tel: (021) 380-8283; entrance fee). **Bharata Theatre** on Jl. Pasar Senen No. 15 puts on traditional Javanese performances of *wayang orang* (dance drama) and *ketoprak* (folk drama) (tel: 421-4937; daily 8pm).

Dome of Sarbini (Balal Sarbini), Plaza Semanggi, South Jakarta. www.theplazasemanggi.com. Built around totally renovated historic buildings, Jakarta's first "opera house" – opened in 2004 – has top-notch acoustics, a spacious stage and high-tech multimedia, sound and lighting systems, designed by consultants from Germany and Singapore. Home to the Nusantara Symphony Orchestra, it is also used as a venue for art and cultural performances.

NIGHTLIFE

Nightlife in Jakarta pulsates. As the sun sets and temperatures drop, the skyline lights up, as does the energy of crowds unwinding in the city's myriad pubs, bars, nightclubs and karaoke dens. The range is endless with something on the menu for everyone. There are relaxing elegant pubs or bars in most of all the major hotels.

Nightclubs are located near the downtown business centre, while the karaoke bars are in the Blok M shopping complex. The crowds usually start to gather at 11pm and continue streaming in up to the early morning hours.

Most of the major hotels have comfortable upmarket bars. Local favourites are **O'Reiley's** in the Grand Hyatt Hotel, with great pub lunches, while **Kudus** in the Hilton Hotel is good for a business get-together, or just for relaxing. Shangri-La's **B.A.T.S** bar is another popular hangout.

A few of Jakarta's long-established pubs and favourite expat waterholes are **Pete's Tavern** in the ATD Plaza basement and **Jaya Pub** in the Jaya Building, Jl. M.H. Thamrin, which has darts, pool and live music and is always lively and crowded. **The Tavern** in the Aryaduta Hotel serves grilled food and the **Green Pub** in the Jakarta Theatre Building prepares Mexican food, along with live country-and-Western music on the weekends.

Hard Rock Café, at Sarinah Bldg., Jl. Thamrin, is a popular restaurant and club with live music on the weekends. It is always crowded. **Planet Hollywood**, at Jl. Gatot Subroto, along with serving great food, has live music. The 24-hour **Café Batavia** at Taman Fatahilla serves food upstairs, while downstairs, there is live music – anything from African, South American, blues or jazz in a stylish art décor atmosphere. **Salsa Restaurant & Bar** in Kemang serves Italian and Mexican food and has a DJ nightly as well as live music to a Latin beat. Check schedules for Latin dance lessons.

For discotheques, try **Zanzibar Café** at Jl. Sultan Hasanuddin and the **D Bar** in Kemang or **CJ** in Hotel Mulia. The city's favourite is **Retro** in the Hotel Crowne Plaza.

Widely touted as the No. 1 nightspot is the hugely popular **Mata Bar**, which plays a mix of R&B, disco and retro music. **Diva**, at the Senayan driving range, shares the No. 2 ranking with **BC Bar** on Jl. Thamrin.

Techno music can be found at **M Club** at Blok M Plaza. **Parkit** on Jl. Wahid Hasyim hosts a young crowd while long-time favourite **Jamz Jazz Club** at Jl. Panglima Polim Raya has the best live funk jazz. **JJ**, next to Tanamour, is always crowded.

For untiring party animals, there is **Tanamur**, at Jl. Tanah Abang, which closes at 4am on weekends. There is no place like it elsewhere in Jakarta; it is always packed with people from every walk of life. For the true nightbirds, there is **Stadium** in old Kota, which opens 24 hours. Or try **Jalan Jalan**, Menara Imperium, 36th floor, Jl. Rasuna Said (Kuningan), with a restaurant with panoramic views of Jakarta, and a separate disco and music room. Another option is **Bugils Café**, Taman Ria Senayan recreation park, Jl. Gerbang Pemuda 3. "Bugils" is short for *bule gila*, or crazy foreigner. Clientele is primarily expatriates. Need more be said?

WHERE TO SHOP

Handicrafts

Pasar Raya at Blok M is the best one-stop shop for the full gamut of Indonesian products. Good, but smaller, are **Sarinah** on Jl. Thamrin and **Keris Gallery** in Menteng. These stores stock everything from baskets, cane chairs, and leather sandals to placemats, paintings, carvings, clothes, toys, and batik.

At the **Jakarta Handicraft Centre**, Jl. Pekalongan No. 12A, there is a large collection of high-quality handicrafts. As most of the merchandise is manufactured for export, the wood will have been treated for climatic changes.

Many of the antique and art shops along **Jl. Kebon Sirih Timur Dalam**, **Jl. Majapahit** and **Jl. Paletehan (Kebayoran)** also sell handicrafts.

Antiques

Although some copies are difficult to detect, there's a better chance of getting a genuine article at reputable dealers who offer refunds.

Gallery 50B: Jl. Ciputat Raya No. 50B. Tel: (021) 749-2850. This place provides a free hotel pickup service for serious buyers.

Cony Art: Jl. Melawai Raya No. 189E (near Blok M). Tel: (021) 720-2844. There are two floors of antique ceramic collections, mainly from Sulawesi.

Johan Art Curio: Jl. Salim No. 59A. Tel: (021) 336 023. It has one of the largest collections of old Chinese porcelains and statues.

Other shops are scattered throughout the city, but especially on **Jl. Kebon Sirih Timur Dalam**, where there are several tiny shops. **Bali**, **Bima**, **Djody** and **Nasrun** are all stocked with old furniture, weavings, masks, puppets and porcelains. Djody is especially well-respected.

The so-called "antique" market on **Jl. Surabaya**, near Embassy Row (Jl. Diponegoro), consists of numerous stalls selling porcelain, puppets, tiles, brass and silver bric-a-brac. Most of it is new but has been made to look old.

Ciputat Village, at Jl. Ciputat Raya, is a little outside of town, but it's well worth a visit for those interested in larger pieces, such as furniture.

ACTIVITIES

Golf Courses

For comprehensive information on golfing in Indonesia, see www.indogolf.com and www.golfinindonesia.com.

Jakarta Golf Club Rawamangun: Tel: (021) 475-4739. Located in East Jakarta, the city's oldest golf club, established in 1972. Former President Suharto's favourite club.

Klub Golf Cengkareng: Tel: (021) 559-1111. Designed by Walter Raleigh Stewart, Klub Golf Cengkareng is located at Sukarno-Hatta airport.

Klub Golf Senayan: Tel: (021) 5711-0181, 573-2508. This is one of the oldest clubs in Jakarta, and the only golf course centrally located in the heart of the capital.

Padang Golf Jaya Ancol: Ancol Dreamland. Tel: (021) 681-5112.

Located inside the Ancol Dreamland beach resort in north Jakarta. Has 18 holes and is open to the public.
Pantai Indah Kapuk Golf Course: Tel: (021) 588-2388. In north Jakarta, Pantai Indah Kapuk was designed by Robert Trent Jones. Facilities include golf carts, pro shop, driving range and club rental. 18 holes, par 72.

Around Jakarta

KEPULAUAN SERIBU

Most of the so-called Thousand Islands are uninhabited, though more than 30 have been developed into pleasant beach resorts. Several of the islands contain bird and marine sanctuaries, and the entire northern section has been declared a marine national park.

Getting There

Motorboat launches may be hired to all the islands from the Ancol Marina, located within the vast Ancol amusement park on Jakarta's north shore. The islands closest to the mainland are only 20 to 30 minutes away, making this an easy beach escape from the city. The furthest islands are about 2 hours away. The resorts will arrange the boat transfer when you make your booking with them.

Where to Stay

Alam Kotok: Kotok Island. Jl. Saraswati No. 48A, Cipete Utara. Tel: (021) 725-6302, 720-9625, Fax: 726-5765, e-mail: kotok@indosat.net.id, www.alamresorts.com. Offers comfortable bungalows, both air-conditioned and fan-cooled. Restaurant, bar and a range of watersports. Ask for packages which include meals and transfers. **$$$**
Matahari Island Resort: Macan Besar Island. PT Pantara Wisata Jaya, Jl. Pangeran Jayakarta 115 Ruko, Blok B No. 13-14. Tel: (021) 626-2629, Fax: 626-2627. Matahari Island Resort is 1½ hours by speed boat from Marina Pier and it also has a helipad. The resort occupies the entire 6-hectare (15-acre) island. Its air-con cottages come with bathrooms and television, and there is a swimming pool on the grounds. The price includes all meals and ferry transport. **$$$**
Pulau Ayer: Ayer Island. Jl. Mangga Besar VIII/21. Tel: (021) 625-3670, 629-8019, Fax: 624-3183. The closest resort to Jakarta, 30 minutes from Marina Pier. Day trips, including boat transfer, lunch and water activities are offered. **$$$**
Pulau Pelangi: Pelangi Island. PT Pulau Seribu Paradise, Jl. Sultan Agung No. 21. Tel: (021) 828-1093, 630-5877, Fax: 829-9002. Reachable in 1½ hours from Jakarta's Marina Pier. All bungalows face the sea. Watersports centre, floating restaurant, dive shop, tennis court and clinic are among the facilities. **$$$**
Pulau Putri: Putri Island. PT Pulau Seribu Paridise, Jl. Sultan Agung No. 21. Tel: (021) 828-1093, 830-5877, Fax: 829-9002. Reachable in 1½ hours from Marina Pier. In addition to the usual facilities, it also has an aquarium housing a collection of tropical fish and corals. **$$$**
Pulau Seribu Marine Resort: Pantara Island. PT Pantara Wisata Jaya, Jl. Pangeran Jayakarta 115 Ruko, Blok B No. 13-14. Tel: (021) 626-2629, Fax: 626-2627. Reachable in two hours by high speed cruiser from Marina Pier. Facilities include air conditioning, seaside restaurant, meeting room and watersports such as banana boat, jetski and yacht cruises.

West Java

West Java has recently been divided into two provinces: **Banten**, from the west coast to Jakarta and **West Java** province, from Jakarta east to Cirebon. Since tourism information offices are now regionalised, information on one province may not be available in the office of the other. See www.dispardabanten.com and www.westjava.com for help navigating through this area.

WEST COAST

Most of West Java and its nearby beach resorts at Anyer and Carita are easily accessible from Jakarta, connected by modern express toll roads or by improved high-speed trains. Good tourist accommodation is readily available.

Newly developed and just 28 km (17 miles) south of Carita is Tanjung Lesung Beach Resort. Located about one hour from Carita/Labuan, the resort offers 1, 2 and 4-bedroom villas, a private beach club with jetski, snorkelling, diving and yachting. Five minutes away by rented bike is the undeveloped and remote Bodur beach, an excellent place to see stunning sunsets.

Side trips to Krakatau and the Ujung Kulon National Park are best made from Carita. The Krakatau volcano achieved lasting infamy in 1883 when it erupted with cataclysmic force. In its place today is Anak Krakatau (Child of Krakatau) which rose from the sea in 1928.

At the Ujung Kulon National Park, you can tramp through pristine tropical rainforest for a first-hand look at some of Java's rare wildlife species, including the Javan rhinoceros. There is a scenic road that skirts the highland home of the Badui people.

While Krakatau can be done on a day trip, the national park is not really worth seeing unless you have at least four days to spare.

Tour Operators

Visits to Ujung Kulon National Park and Krakatau can be arranged with these Jakarta-based tour companies specialising in these areas.
Banten World Travel: Jl. Pintu Air Raya No. 7, Blok A4. Jakarta 10710. Tel: (021) 384-3630, Fax: 344-2377, e-mail: katamsi_nurrasa@yahoo.com. Specialty tours include Kratakau, old Banten, Ujung Kulon and Badui villages. The Badui area, isolated traditional villages in the Kendeng hills, is where the people still live simple lives in the ways of their ancestors without electricity.
Ujung Kulon Tours & Travel: Jl. Sultan Agung Tirtayasa No. 102, Simpang Tiga, Cilegon. Tel/Fax: (0254) 384-159, e-mail: asrori@ujungkulon-travel.co.id.
Wanawisata Alam Hayati: Gedung Manggala Wanabakti, Blok-IV, Lantai-2, Wing-3, Jl. Jend. Gatot Subroto, Jakarta. Tel: (021) 570-0238, Fax: 570-1141, e-mail: wanatrvl@pacific.net.id, www.advecoindonesia.com. This agency has the newest and fastest speed boats that can reach Ujung Kulon in 2 hours from Lippo Marina Pier at Carita.

Hotel Price Guide

Price categories for standard rooms, usually without breakfast:
$$$$$ = above US$150
$$$$ = US$101–150
$$$ = US$51–100
$$ = US$30–50
$ = under US$30

Where to Stay

Banten Beach Resort: Jl. Raya Sirih, Km. 15, Anyer. Tel: (0254) 600-982, www.thebantenresort.com. Villa-style beach hotel set in landscaped gardens and with views of the ocean. Swimming pool, restaurant and bar. **$$$$$**
Sol Elite Marbella: Jl. Raya Karang Bolong, Anyer. Tel: (254) 602-345, Fax: 602-346, www.solmelia.com. This Spanish-run hotel located right on the beach has swimming pools, shops and restaurants and organises a full range of activities. **$$$$**

Tanjung Lesung Beach Resort: Jakarta Reservations Office: Tel: (021) 572-7270, Fax: 572-7271, e-mail: resorthotel@tanjunglesung.com, www.tanjunglesung.com. 61 cottages (114 rooms), beach front restaurant, bar, ocean view swimming pool, beach club, children's play ground, kids club and meeting room. $$$$

Jayakarta Hotel: Jl. Raya Karang Bolong, Anyer. Tel: (0254) 601-781/2, Fax: 601-783. A beach resort with 103 rooms, restaurant, swimming pool, meeting room and karaoke. $$$

Lippo Carita Resort: Jl. Raya Carita Km. 9, Labuan. Tel: (0253) 801-900, 801-930, Fax: 801-929. This condominium-style accommodation has its own pier and water recreation, such as jetski, wind surfing and parasailing. Also has a large swimming pool and a good restaurant. $$$

Hotel Mambruk Anyer: Jl. Raya Karang Bolong, Anyer. Tel: (0254) 601-602, Fax: 601-723, www.mambruk.co.id. A deluxe beachfront resort with a watersports centre, children's playground, pool and a view of Krakatau. $$$

Resor Pantai Carita: Jl. Raya Carita, Labuan. Tel: (0253) 801-127/8, Fax: 801-863. A comfortable resort set in a peaceful cove on Anyer beach. The rooms have private patios, the staff is friendly and relaxed. $$$

Sunda Jaya Home Stay: At the border of Ujung Kulon National Park, Tamanjaya 42283, Sumur, Pandeglang. Tel: (0253) 803-221. $

Where to Eat

Jimbaran: Jl. Raya Carita (opposite Lippo Carita Resort), Labuan. Huge restaurant and spacious parking. Serves Indonesian, Asian and Western food. *Inexpensive*

Sambolo Sea Food Barbeque & Grill: Jl. Raya Bandulu, Anyer. Tel: (0254) 601-234. Specialises in barbequed and grilled saltwater fish such as red snapper. *Inexpensive*

Valentine de Mar: Jl. Raya Sirih (opposite Sol Elite Marbella Hotel), Anyer. Tel/Fax: (0254) 601-403. The best Chinese restaurant in Anyer. Serves Hong Kong dishes. Try the udang (prawns) a la Hong Kong. *Inexpensive*

Outdoor Activities

Diving

Tinjil Island is one of the best dive areas in the area, with many dive choices. Its multitudes of coral species are different from those seen in other places in Indonesia. In some seasons, visibility is very clear and the sea is calm, ideal for diving. For other dive sites in the area, *see text box*.

Dive Sites in Sunda Strait

Karang Care. A drop-off dive with visibility around 10–20 metres. Several varieties of soft corals and sea fans.

Karang Copong. A small island within sight of the northwest tip of Peucang Island, off Ujung Kulon Park's coast. The highlights of shallow (to 12 meters) dives are tunnels in the rock leading to caves in the island. Visibility is to 20 metres.

Karang Serang. Visibility is fair to good at 10–20 metres. Underwater scenery includes large blocks of volcanic rock seemingly sheared off by eruptions of Anak Krakatau. Schools of the Moorish idols and other reef fish inhabit the area. White tip sharks occasionally spotted.

Rakata. A nice drift dive, gentle current at a depth of 25 metres. Underwater scenery includes volcanic rock wall thanks to nearby Anak Krakatau.

Deep Sea Fishing

The waters of **Ujung Kulon National Park** and **Krakatau** in the Sunda Strait are top fishing sites. The area offers year-round fishing including blue marlin, yellow fin tuna, dogtooth tuna, wahoo, dorado and sailfish. Contact a local travel agent for details.

Birding

Ujung Kulon National Park offers a full complement of open woodlands, wetlands and lowland rainforest habitats, ideal for birdwatching. Pulau Dua, once a haven for migratory birds, has been damaged by poachers. But another island, **Pamojan Besar**, to the north in the bay of Banten, is reachable in one hour by boat. Between April and August each year, migratory birds flock to Pamojan Besar by the hundreds.

BANDUNG

The capital of West Java and the centre of the Sundanese culture, Bandung enjoys a cool climate, thanks to its 755-m (2,477-ft) high elevation. It is also a bustling industrial and technical metropolis.

Bandung is a good area to use as a base because of the numerous highland attractions in its environs. Tangkuban Prahu volcano, Ciater hot springs, Lembang and the waterfall at Maribaya are all less than an hour by vehicle to the north. The highlands to the south are even more spectacular, and anyone seriously interested in exploring them should get a copy of *Bandung and Beyond*, by Richard and Shila Bennett, available from Bandung Man (Jl. Cihampelas No. 120). This little booklet has detailed instructions on how to get to a wide variety of destinations.

Getting There

From Jakarta to Bandung, take the **Parahiangan Express** train or the faster **Argo Gede Executive Express**, which arrives in Bandung in 2 hours and has comfortable reclining seats, videos and offers a seat-side meal service. Or you can travel by express bus from Jakarta.

Tourist Office

Provincial Tourist Services: Jl. Sukarno-Hatta Km. 11. Tel: (022) 780-5741/2, Fax: 780-5739.

Where to Stay

Grand Preanger: Jl. Asia Afrika No. 81. Tel: (022) 423-1631, Fax: 423-0034. Bandung's best, this charming colonial-style five-star hotel is located in the centre of town. The traditional dance performances at the weekend are a treat. $$$$

Hyatt Regency Bandung, Jl. Sumatera No. 51. Tel: (022) 421-1234, Fax: 421-0380, www.hyatt.com. Deluxe hotel within walking distance of Bandung Indah Plaza and food stalls on crowded Jl. Merdeka. Also has a café, restaurants (Chinese and Indonesian) and a pub. $$$$

Malya Bandung: Jl. Ranca Bentang 56-58. Tel: (022) 203-0333, Fax: 203-0633, www.malyabandung.com. A four-star hotel built with local stone and timber that offers a unique relaxing ambience. All rooms overlook the valley, as does its cliffside pool. There is a brasserie-style restaurant and a health spa. $$$$

Sheraton Bandung, Jl. Ir. H. Juanda 390. Tel: (022) 250-0303, Fax: 250-8612, www.sheraton.com/bandung. Located 6 km (4 miles) from the city centre on the slopes of the Dago area. Surrounded by mountains, the hotel is conveniently located just a few minutes from the main business district. 157 spacious guest rooms. $$$$

Jayakarta Bandung, Jl. Ir. H. Juanda 381A. Tel: (022) 250-888, Fax: 250-5388, e-mail: jhrbdg@indo.net.id. Comfortable and reasonably priced hotel with a good location. Restaurant serving Western and Sundanese food. Large freeform pool. $$$

Savoy Homann Bidakara: Jl. Asia Afrika No. 112. Tel: (022) 432-244, Fax: 436-187, www.savoyhomann-hotel.com. This four-star 1939 hotel was refurbished in the early '90s with stylish art deco detailing. Live music pulsates nightly while dinner can be enjoyed in an interesting garden atrium restaurant. **$$$**

Restaurant Price Guide

Price categories for a three-course meal (Asian or Western), without drinks:
- Expensive = US$26–50
- Moderate = US$11–25
- Inexpensive = under US$10

Where to Eat

Most hotels offer Sundanese dishes on their menus or buffet tables. A few popular ones are *ikan mas bakar* (grilled carp) and *ayam panggang* (barbecued chicken in sweet soya sauce).

Bamboo Kafe: Jl. Cihampelas No. 222. Staffed by Bandung's Hotel School students, offering tasty food, low prices and friendly service, all in a relaxing bamboo setting. *Moderate*

Gambrinus Curry Kitchen: Jl. Sury Sumantri. Authentic North Indian food served in a beautiful setting. *Moderate*

Handyani: Jl. Sukajadi. Sample Sundanese food amid live traditional music. *Moderate*

Queen, Jl. Dalem Kaum 79. Tel: (022) 420-4561, 423-1659. Around since 1954, the best Chinese (Cantonese) dishes in Bandung. Within walking distance of Grand Preanger and Savoy Bidakara hotels. *Inexpensive*

Sindang Reret, Jl. Surapati 53. Tel: (022) 250-1474, Fax: 253-1216. The best authentic Sundanese food in town. Spacious restaurant and ample parking. *Inexpensive*

Where to Shop

Bandung is known for its handwoven baskets and mats from nearby Tasikmalaya, bamboo *angklung* instruments, and *wayang golek* puppets.

High-quality ceramics – including reproductions of Chinese antiques – are produced in nearby Plered village and sold in Bandung. If you visit the **Balai Penelitian Keramik** research office (Jl. A. Yani No. 390) in the mornings, you can watch the ceramic-making process. You can also buy the finished product here. There is also a textile institute in the same complex.

Batik Semar (Jl. Dalem Kaum No. 40) has a selection of paintings, batik, embroidered textiles, *angklung* instruments and ceramics, while **Sanggar Awi Wulung** (Jl. Raya Cibeureum No. 31) retails lampshades and bamboo furniture as well as paintings.

Bandung is the jeans-producing capital of Indonesia. Head to the **Cihampelas Jeans Shop** along Jl. Cihampelas for good bargains. Shoes are also a good buy at the **Cibaduyut Shoe Industry** at Jl. Cibaduyut.

Factory outlet shops along Jl. Cihampelas, Jl. Juanda (Dago area) and Jl. Riau (R.E. Martadinata) are popular with local people and bargain hunters from Jakarta.

Culture

There are frequent *wayang golek* (wooden puppet) performances at **Yayasan Pusat Kebudayaan** (Cultural Centre; Jl. Naripan; open daily 7am–9pm; entrance fee). Check out performance details from the tourist office. *Angklung* (bamboo rattle music) performances are held regularly in the afternoons at **Pak Ujo's Saung Angklung** (Jl. Padasuka No. 118). This is both an *angklung* school and a workshop. *Wayang golek* and dance performances are put on by request. Daily 3.30–5.30pm (entrance fee).

CIREBON

The ancient town of Cirebon (pronounced cheer-i-bon) was once an Islamic sultanate. Visitors come here to see its *keraton* (palaces) as well as shop in the batik villages around it.

Getting There

Cirebon is about 4 hours (260 km/160 miles) from Jakarta or 3 hours from Bandung. There is a small airport but trains and mini-buses are more convenient.

Tourist Office

Provincial Tourist Services: Jl. Brigien Darsono No. 5. Tel: (0231) 208-856.

Where to Stay

Cirebon Penta: Jl. Syarif Abdurakhman No. 159. Tel: (0231) 203-328, Fax: 204-491. The pluses of this cosy, centrally-located hotel are its roof-top garden and health centre. **$$$**

Hotel Prima: Jl. Siliwangi No. 107. Tel: (0231) 205-411, Fax: 205-407. A good-value hotel that has some style in its Islamic architecture. There is also an in-house restaurant. **$$$**

Puri Santika: Jl. Dr Wahidin No. 32. Tel: (0231) 200-662, Fax: 200-482, www.santika.com. Part of the Santika group known for its excellent service, this hotel is of a decent standard and has extensive facilities. **$$$**

Hotel Bentani, Jl. Siliwangi No. 69. Tel: (0231) 203-246, Fax: 207-527. Popular with business travellers. **$$**

Kharisma: Jl. R.A. Kartini No. 60. Tel: (0231) 200-645, Fax: 200-646. Well-located on the edge of the town centre, the hotel has rooms that are built around a pool with a sunken bar. **$$**

What to Eat

The local speciality is *nasi lengko*, a dish of rice with bits of fried *tempe* (fermented soy beans), *tahu* (soy bean cake), vegetables and sambal. Otherwise, the city is known for its good prawns and fresh seafood, said to be among the best in Java.

Jumbo: Jl. Siliwangi No. 191. The seafood here is cooked according to Sundanese and Chinese recipes. Good grilled dishes. *Moderate*

Maxim's: Jl. Bahagia No. 45–7. The best Chinese seafood place in town that's just a short walk from Thay Kak Sie Buddhist temple. Its specialities are steamed giant crabs and prawns. *Inexpensive*

Where to Shop

For Cirebon's famous distinctive hand-painted batik, there are many fine studios in Trusmi village, 12 km (7 miles) west of town. **Ibu Masina's** studio and **Ibu Ega Sugeng's** workshop are recommended. For Cirebonese *topeng* masks, visit **Pak Kandeg** at Suranenggala Lor village, about 5 km north of Cirebon on the road to Gunung Jati.

Four hours by road from Cirebon is **Pekalongan**, also known as Kota Batik (Batik Town) and is a must-stop for batik enthusiasts. For average-quality batik, look in the shops along **Jl. Hayam Wuruk** and **Jl. Hasanuddin**. Or seek out individual batik makers, such as **Tobal Batik** at Jl. Teratai No. 24, and **Klego**, which specialises in export clothing. **Ahmad Yahya**, whose batik sells in New York and Europe, is at Jl. Pesindon No. 221. Another well-known batik producer, under the Zaky label, is **Achmad Said**, Jl. Bandung No. 53.

For higher-quality, hand-drawn *tulis* work, visit **Jane Hendromartono**, Jl. Blimbing No. 36. Her superb batiks are part of the permanent collection in the Textiles Museum in Washington D.C.

Pekalongan's most famous batik artist is **Oey Soe Tjoen**, who continued many of the designs of the talented Eliza Van Zuylen, an Indo-Dutch woman whose rare batik pieces, produced in the 1920–30s, now fetch thousands of dollars. Oey's works are available south of town in the village of Kedungwuni at Jl. Raya No. 104. You can watch the manufacturing process everyday except Friday.

Central Java

Central Java and **Yogyakarta Special Province** are two separate administrative districts. Since autonomy was established in 2000, many services formerly provided by the central government in Jakarta have been regionalised.

Some websites that might be useful in finding your way around are Central Java: www.boroburpark.com, Yogyakarta: www.tasteofjogja.com, www.djoglo.or.id and www.jogjacraftcouncil.com.

Visitors who only stay one or two days to take in Borobudur, Prambanan and the royal palaces of Solo and Jogja only see one side of the region. But those who stay longer are discovering limitless nature opportunities in its beaches and coastlines, and forests and mountains. As Central Java is currently developing at a rapid pace, up-market resorts, golf courses, spas and fine dining restaurants have appeared on the scene.

YOGYAKARTA (JOGJA)

Yogyakarta – or Jogja as the city is fondly called – is Indonesia's second largest tourist destination after Bali. Its majestic temples and palaces, traditional crafts and performing arts provide a captivating counterpoint to those of Bali. Many who have spent time in both places profess to prefer this laid-back city.

Attracting the more adventurous are volcano climbing, bird watching and river rafting to the north and rugged shorelines and caving to the south. As a result of this modest tourist boom, the venerable Javanese court centre now has a wide variety of hotels and restaurants.

Getting There
By Air
With the opening up of the aviation industry, airlines and schedules are changing so rapidly that it's best to check with a travel agent who is familiar with local itineraries before booking. **Garuda** operates flights direct from Kuala Lumpur (Malaysia) and Singapore three times a week.

From Jakarta options include **Adam Air**, **Bouraq**, **Citilink**, **Garuda**, **Lion Air** or **Merpati**, all offering direct flights. **Garuda** also has direct flights to Yogyakarta from Bali.

By Train and Land
There are five executive-class trains plying the Jakarta-Jogja route: **Argo Dwipangga**, **Argo Lawu**, **Bima**, and **Taksaka I** and **II**. The second-rate **Senja Utama** and **Senja Jogja** trains cost much less, are slower and are not air-conditioned. Express buses also make the same journey.

From Solo
Silk Air has direct flights from Singapore to Solo. From Solo to Jogja it's 65 km or 1 hour by car on a newly-completed highway.

Tour Operator
Angsa Indonesia Tours and Travel: Jl. Sekardwijan 19A. Tel: (0274) 520-949, 561-402, Fax: 520-940, e-mail: angsa@yogya.wasantara.net.id, www.angsatour.com. Angsa is one of the few travel agencies in Yogyakarta that, in addition to city and temple tours, also offers cycling, trekking, caving and other opportunities to experience nature, village life and countryside. Also does air ticketing and hotel reservations.

Tourist Office
Provincial Tourist Services: Jl. Malioboro No. 14. Tel: (0274) 566-000.

Where to Stay
As the centre of Javanese arts and culture, Yogyakarta matches its reputation with a wide range of accommodation – from luxurious presidential suites to simple *losmen* in the Pasar Kembang area near the train station and guest-houses along Jl. Prawirotaman.

Rumah Sleman: Jl. Purboyo No. 111, Warak Kidul, Sumberadi, Mlati, Sleman. Tel: (0274) 866-611, 866-622, Fax: 866-633, www.rumahsleman.com. A villa located in a village outside the busy city centre, this is a fine example of traditional *joglo* architecture. Rental of one of two wings, one furnished in classical Javanese style and the other Western, entitle guests to use of the entire villa, staff and gardens. $$$$$
Melia Purosani: Jl. Suryotomo No. 31. Tel: (0274) 589-521, Fax: 588-070, www.solmelia.com. This five-star hotel in the centre of the city is just a short walk from Jl. Malioboro and the Keraton palace. Set amid beautiful landscaped gardens and resort-style swimming pool. $$$$
Dusun Jogja Village Inn: Jl. Menukan 5. Tel: (0274) 373-031, Fax: 382-202, www.jvidusun.co.id. This small, tranquil boutique hotel offers a unique and artistic atmosphere where intimacy, luxury, comfort and style come together. Recently renovated rooms have terraces or balconies with views of the gardens. Salt water swimming pool, restaurant, bar. $$$

Hotel Price Guide

Price categories for standard rooms, usually without breakfast:
$$$$$	= above US$150
$$$$	= US$101–150
$$$	= US$51–100
$$	= US$30–50
$	= under US$30

Hyatt Regency Yogyakarta: Jl. Palagan Tentara Pelajar. Tel: (0274) 869-123, Fax: 869-580, www.yogyakarta.regency.hyatt.com. An idyllic resort designed to symbolise Borobudur. Offers spa, golf course, Camp Hyatt for kids, excellent restaurants, tiered swimming pool and 5-star pampering. $$$
Ibis Malioboro Yogyakarta: Jl. Malioboro No. 52-58. Tel: (0274) 516-974, Fax: 416-977, www.accorhotels-asia.com. Located in the heart of the well known shopping district, Jl. Malioboro, the Ibis also connects to the largest shopping mall in town. Within a short walk to the Keraton, or explore nearby historical Jogja by *becak* (pedicab) or *andong* (horse cart). $$$
Novotel Yogyakarta: Jl. Jend. Sudirman No. 89. Tel: (0274) 580-930, Fax: 580-931, www.accorhotels-asia.com. Only 30 minutes from the airport and 15 minutes from the train station, the Novotel is modern and clean. Restaurants, swimming pool and excellent bakery and deli. $$$
Saphir Yogyakarta: Jl. Laksda Adisucipto No. 38. Tel: (0274) 566-222, Fax: 566-220, www.saphir-hotels.com. A four-star international standard hotel centrally located and within easy reach of all major attractions. Offers reasonably priced packages. $$$
Sheraton Mustika Yogyakarta: Jl. Laksda Adisucipto Km. 8.7. Tel: (0274) 488-588, Fax: 489-589, www.sheraton.com. This five-star hotel is just 10 minutes from the airport. Enormous spa offers Javanese massage as well as a wide range of other beauty and body treatments in the tradition of royalty. $$$
Indraloka Family Homestay: Jl. Cikditiro 18. Tel: (0274) 564-341, 580-893, Fax: 569-341, 580-897, e-mail: manuggal@yogya.wasantara.net.id, www.vocal.net/indraloka. A home away from home in a small and friendly hotel. Near Gadjah Mada University, this homestay is popular with foreign students. $

Where to Eat
The Jogja speciality is *gudeg* – a combination plate consisting of rice

with boiled *nangka muda* (young jackfruit), chicken, egg, coconut gravy and spicy sauce with boiled *sambal kulit* (spicy buffalo hide). As Jogja's large student population continues to grow, fine dining restaurants have begun to appear, much to the delight of local residents. Favoured are:
Gabah: Jl. Dewi Sartika 11-A. Tel: (0274) 515-626. A modern restaurant in a colonial house which combines great food with a comfortable atmosphere and excellent service. Located in a tree-lined neighbourhood near Gadjah Mada University. Open lunch and dinner. *Moderate*
Gadjah Wong: Jl. Gejayan. Tel: (0274) 588-294, Fax: 885-306. Three different dining areas offer guests a choice of ambience, accompanied by Javanese, jazz or Western music. Remarkably good food in a friendly, up-market setting surrounded by tropical gardens. *Moderate*

Restaurant Price Guide

Price categories for a three-course meal (Asian or Western), without drinks:
Expensive = US$26–50
Moderate = US$11–25
Inexpensive = under US$10

Hani's Bakery & Coffee Shop: Jl. Suryodiningratan 194. Tel: (0274) 371-093. Has a large expatriate following, thanks to its freshly baked wheat and grain breads, croissants, expresso coffee and congenial atmosphere. Also serves deli-style sandwiches, using imported ingredients rarely found elsewhere in Jogja. *Inexpensive*
Milas Vegetarian Restaurant: Jl. Mantrijeron Mj III 897A. Serves freshly prepared Indonesian and Western vegetarian food, sans msg. Milas also holds activities and programmes to support local artists, children and street youth. *Inexpensive*
Omah Dhuwur: Jl. Mondorakan 252, Kota Gede. Tel: (0274) 374-952. In Kota Gede, the centre of the silver industry, the buildings merge Arabic and Dutch styles, adding to the enchantment of this restaurant. Open for lunch and dinner. *Moderate*
Via Via Café: Jl. Prawirotaman 24B. Tel: (0274) 386-557. Serves Indonesian and Western food, both vegetarian and non-vegetarian, and is popular with budget travellers. Offers excellent travel information and alternative tours, such as bicycle trips and caving, and courses such as batik and Indonesian language. *Inexpensive*

Where to Shop

Kota Gede, to the southeast of Jogja, is the centre of the silver industry. There are two major workshops, **M.D. Silver** and **Tom's Silver**, and a number of small shops where one can watching the filigree-making process.

There are many shops on **Jl. Malioboro** selling leather goods and one of the better ones is Toko Setia. For slightly better quality, try **Kusuma**, just off Malioboro, or **Moeljosoehardjo's**, near Taman Sari.

Yakkum Craft, Jl. Kaliurang Km. 13.5. Tel: (0274) 895-386, Fax: 896-631, 895-181, www.yakkumcraft.com, a rehab centre for disabled people, carries an excellent range of quality leather wallets; also wood carvings, paintings and handicrafts.

The process of making *wayang kulit* puppets starts with buffalo hide, even if the thin, translucent *kulit* used is not tanned and could more accurately be described as parchment. For the best-quality puppets, try **Ledgar** and **Swasthigita** or **Aris Handicraft** at Jl. Kauman.

If antiques are your passion, head for the many shops that line Jl. Malioboro. Also check out the streets to the south and west of the Keraton, and the handful of small shops near the Ambarrukmo Palace Hotel and most of the batik galleries. Among the choice picks are carved and gilded chests for herbal medicines or a pair of *loro blonyo* (seated wedding figures) – traditionally kept in the ceremonial chamber of aristocratic Javanese homes. Elaborately-carved Dutch and Chinese teakwood furniture is also interesting, along with covered wedding beds, gilded panels, wicker chairs, massive chests and vanity tables with delicate carvings.

For fine art objects, visit **Affandi** on Jl. Laksda Adisucipto, a large studio-cum-gallery overlooking the river. At the **Indonesia Arts Institute** (ISI) on Jl. Parangtritis, view works by up-and-coming Indonesian artists: paintings, sculptures and handicrafts. ISI is regarded as one of the top art academies in the country.

Several galleries offer interesting programmes open to the public. Hours are usually 9am to noon and 5 to 9pm. Exhibitions and discussions are generally free, but there may be a small charge for films. As exhibitions and opening times are continually changing, call for current schedules.
Bentara Budaya: Jl. Suroto 2, Kota Baru. Tel: (0274) 560-404. Art exhibitions, movies, book discussions.
Cemeti Art House: Jl. D. I. Panjaitan 41. Tel: (0274) 371-105, e-mail: cemetiah@indosat.net.id. Fine art and modern art exhibitions, book discussions and performances.
French Cultural Centre: Jl. Sagan 3. Tel: (0274) 566-520. Art exhibitions, movies, book discussions and performances.
Kedai Kebun Forum's Gallery: Jl. Tirtodipuran 3. Tel: (0274) 376-114, e-mail: kkforum@indosat.net.id. Art exhibitions, performances, book discussions.

Hot Batik Spots in Jogja

Famous for its batik, Jogja is heaven for textile enthusiasts. Most shops are open from 9am to 8pm. There are several shops on Jl. Tirtodipuran. Recommended are **Winotosastro Batik** (Ibu Hani) and **Borneo Batik Textiles**. Other hot batik spots are:
Batik Museum: Boyong Kaliurang. Tel: (0274) 89-161. This museum displays the *keraton* (royal palace) batik style through contemporary fashion.
Batik Museum: Jl. Sutomo No. 13. Open 9am to 3pm, entrance fee. Owned by a Jogja family, a small museum with two sections, one dedicated to batik, the other to *sulaman*, the embroidery fancied by Javanese ladies for their formal wear.
Bixa Batik Studio: Pengok PJKA GK 1/7/43F, Tel: (0274) 546-545, Fax: 542-405, www.batikbixa.com. Well known for its natural dyed batiks.
Brahma Tirta Sari: Desa Tegal Cerme Kd. V, RT 08/RW14, Banguntapan. Tel: (0274) 377-881, www.brahmatirtasari.com. Open 8am from 4pm. An art studio and gallery focusing on its unique batik style using traditional spiritual motifs in contemporary designs. Holds cultural exchanges, seminars and workshops and also teaches batik courses and gives demonstrations by appointment. Located in a village south of Jogja. Call for directions.
Galeri Ardiyanto, Jl. Magelang Km. 5.8. Tel: (0274) 562-777, Fax: 563-280. Batik is only one of the offerings at Ardiyanto, which also stocks home decor and accessories in its villa-style showroom. A must-visit for serious shoppers.
Giriloyo Batik Village: Located in Giriloyo, Bantul, this isn't a shop, but the home of a craftswoman who sells batiks to aid the village. Prices are from Rp. 200,000 for a cotton scarf to Rp. 500,000 for a *kain panjang* (batik cloth).
Pasar Beringharjo, Jl. Malioboro, is Jogja's largest traditional market and a fun place to buy new and "antique" (used) batik.

Culture

The following performances are held at the **Keraton** from 10am–noon: *gamelan* music (Mon, Tue, Fri), dance (Sun, Thu), and puppetry (Wed, Sat). Traditional *wayang kulit* (shadow puppet) performances in the villages go on through the night, beginning at 9pm and ending at dawn; otherwise, the **Agastya Art Institute** (Jl. Gedong Kiwo III No. 237) – a private *dalang* school – stages rehearsal excerpts for tourists (daily except Sat, 3–5pm) and *wayang golek* (rod-puppets) on Saturdays. Other venues to watch *wayang kulit* follow:

Ambar Budaya in the Yogyakarta Craft Centre, near the Ambarrukmo Palace Hotel: Monday, Wednesday, Friday, 9.30am–10.30pm.

Sasana Hinggil at Alun Alun Selatan (South Palace Square): Every second Saturday of the month, 9pm–5.30am.

Museum Budoyo Archaeological at Jl. Trikora: Daily except Saturday, 11am–1pm.

The most magical time to experience the beauty of traditional Javanese dance is evenings at **Prambanan** temple, where the epic *Ramayana* is performed between 7–9pm. The season lasts May––October, a period when the weather is dry and favourable for outdoor performances. Other places to watch the *Ramayana* are: **Puruwisata Theatre**, at Jl. Brigjen Katamso, where there is an introduction in English (daily 8–10pm), and **Dalem Pujokusuman Theatre** at Jl. Brigjen Katamso (Mon and Fri, 8–10pm).

To watch innovative Javanese dancing in Yogyakarta, visit the **Indonesia Arts Institute** (ISI) on Jl. Parangtritis. One of Indonesia's five government tertiary-level schools, it has the most promising Yogya dancers.

Note: A detailed schedule of cultural events, including abovementioned performances by schools and cultural centres, are available from Provincial Tourist Services (tel: (0274) 566-000) or from travel agents. Pick up a copy of the Jogja Calendar of Events as well.

Other Activities

For those wishing to experience Javanese life on more personal level, several traditional villages have opened their doors and their lives to guests: **Brayut**, **Sambi** and **Tanjung** villages in Sleman regency, north of Jogja, and **Parangrejo** village in Bantul, south of Jogja. Visits can be arranged for day trips or overnight stays and include Javanese cooking classes, courses in handicraft making, Indonesian or Javanese language instruction, and trekking through surrounding hills and agricultural plantations. See www.sleman.go.id for more information on Sleman's traditional villages.

SOLO

Surakarta – or Solo, as it is better known – is an easy hour's drive from Yogyakarta (Jogja). Partly as a result of aristocratic emphasis on Javanese tradition and propriety, Solo is very different from Jogja. It is more sedate and refined, absent of the latter's youthful, revolutionary undercurrents.

Solo is quieter and smaller (in area if not in population), has less traffic, and also fewer tourists.

Getting There

From Jogja, the easiest way is by express mini-bus; book a seat at one of the travel offices on Jl. Diponegoro, just west of the Tugu monument. There are services running throughout the day that leave every 30 minutes, and will drop you anywhere in Solo.

You can also flag down a bus or mini-bus heading east, from Jogja's Jl. Jend. Sudirman or Jl. Solo; they will take you to Solo for about half the price, but the ride will take a good bit longer and the vehicle is usually packed.

Another alternative is to charter your own taxi or mini-van from Jogja and share the cost with other passengers.

It is also possible to go to Solo by train. The **Prambanan Express** runs from Jogja to Solo five times daily.

Solo has an airport, with daily flights to and from Jakarta and Surabaya. SilkAir flies direct to Solo from Singapore twice a week.

Tourist Office

Provincial Tourist Services: Jl. Slamet Riyadi. Tel: (0271) 711-435, www.solotouroff.go.id.

Hotel Price Guide

Price categories for standard rooms, usually without breakfast:
$$$$$ = above US$150
$$$$ = US$101–150
$$$ = US$51–100
$$ = US$30–50
$ = under US$30

Where to Stay

Lor-In Solo: Jl. Adisucipto No. 47. Tel: (0271) 724-500, Fax: 724-400, e-mail: solo@lor-in.com, www.lor-in.com. An oasis surrounded by sparkling lagoons, garden sanctuaries and pools, the Lor-In has 114 luxury rooms, swimming pool, health club, restaurants and bar. $$$$

Sahid Kusuma Raya Solo: Jl. Sugiyopranoto 22. Tel: (0271) 646-356, Fax: 644-788, www.sahidhotels.com. Converted from a palace, the present 120-room hotel still has a few of the original details. It has a nice ambience, with *gamelan* music in the lobby, shops and a restaurant on the hotel premises. $$$$

Cakra Hotel: Jl. Slamet Riyadi 171. Tel: (0271) 645-847, Fax: 648-334. This hotel is located in the centre of town and has nicely-landscaped gardens. The staff is friendly and helpful. $$$

Sahid Raya Solo: Jl. Gajah Mada 82. Tel: (0271) 644-144, Fax: 644-133, www.sahidhotels.com. Four-star business hotel close to the airport. 160 rooms, café, fitness centre and pool. $$$

Where to Eat

Sari: Jl. Slamet Riyadi No. 351. The overall best Javanese restaurant in Solo. Specialities here are *nasi liwet* (a Solo speciality consisting of rice cooked in coconut cream and with garnishing), fried chicken and various types of *pepes* (steamed or grilled seafood or mushrooms wrapped in banana leaf). *Moderate*

Ramayana: Jl. Ronggowarsito No. 2. In addition to great chicken and mutton *sate*, Ramayana also has excellent Chinese dishes such as fried water spinach (*kangkung*) and deep-fried pigeon (*burung dara goreng*). *Inexpensive*

Segar Ayam: Jl. Secoyudan (opposite Pasar Klewer, the central batik market, and within walking distance of the Keraton). The iced fruit drinks are excellent, meant to accompany the simple Javanese dishes like *gado-gado*, *pecel* (boiled vegetables with peanut sauce) and *nasi rames*. *Inexpensive*

Timlo Solo: Jl. Urip Sumoharjo No. 106. Other than its excellent daily specials, there are Javanese fried chicken, *pecel*, *gudeg* and *nasi kuning* (turmeric rice). *Inexpensive*

Tojoyo: Jl. Kepunton Kulon No. 77. Here, you get the best Javanese fried chicken in town, but only at dinner (between 6–9pm). Arrive early or you will be disappointed. *Inexpensive*

Where to Shop

Solo is known as Batik City, and the three largest producers, all with showrooms, are based here. **Batik Danar Hadi** has good-quality *kain* and batik shirts and also has a museum

(**Museum Batik Wuryoningratan**, Jl. Slamet Riyadi, east of Hotel Sri Wedari, near Novotel Hotel, Tel: (0271) 713-140) which displays batiks according to their place of origins and is a very informative venue. **Batik Semar** caters to the mass market with its printed batik dresses and shirts; and **Batik Keris** is somewhere in-between.

Bapak Gunawan (Jl. Cakra 21, Kauman. Tel: (0271) 632-214) is an important and elderly traditional batik master. **Hardjonagoro** (Jl. Yos Sudarso 176 and Jl. Kratonan No. 101. Tel: (0271) 643-289) is one of Indonesia's national treasures. He gained acclaim during the Sukarno era when he introduced different colours to traditional batiks. His studio is quite interesting. Make an appointment before visiting. For the best in Solonese *tulis* work, visit **Ibu Bei Siswosugiarto** (Sidomulyo label). **Pasar Klewer** market is worth a wander, as are the side streets near it, behind the Mesjid Agung.

For an idea of what's available in the local antiques market, visit **Pasar Triwindu** market on Jl. Diponegoro: antique brass oil lamps, round marble-top tables with matching chairs, and Chinese wedding beds. Then visit the established shops on **Jl. Slamet Riyadi** and **Jl. Urip Sumarharjo**, where there are all sorts of treasures. These shops are reputable, but do chose carefully and bargain hard. Look in **Eka Hartono** (Jl. Dawung Tengah No. 11/38) or **Mertojo** "Sing Pellet" (Jl. Kepatihan No. 31).

To buy an antique *keris* dagger, visit **Pak Suranto Atmosaputro** at his home just down a narrow alley across the RRI radio studios at Jl. Kestalan No. III/21. Pak Suranto, a university lecturer who teaches English, is a *keris* aficionado and a member of the Keris Lovers Association of Solo. He always has pieces for sale, or at least a selection for your examination.

The acknowledged centre for *wayang kulit* production in Java is **Manyaran** village, about 35 km (2¼ miles) to the south-west of Solo. Wares by its craftsmen are organised by the village head and sold for reasonable, fixed prices.

You can also go directly to the *dalang*, most of whom make their own puppets in their spare time. **Pak Soetrisno** is descended from a well-known court *dalang* family and now teaches *wayang kulit* at Indonesia Arts College (STSI) (tel: (0271) 52601). Ask for his office and leave a message; Pak Soetrisno speaks good English.

To buy a *gamelan* instrument or a whole orchestral set, or to just observe these beautiful bronze instruments being forged the way they have been for thousands of years, visit **Pak Tentrem Sarwanto**. Using hand-operated bellows, teakwood charcoal and simple tools, his family has made *gamelan* instruments for the royalty for generations. Pak's workshop is located south-east of the town at Jalan Ngepung RT 2/RK I, Semanggi.

Culture

Taman Sriwedari, on Jl. Slamet Riyadi, prides itself on having the most accomplished *wayang orang* (dance-drama) troupe in Java. The amusement park complex houses two theatres, several open-air restaurants and a billiards hall. One theatre puts on slapstick comedy routines, while the other offers more serious *ketoprak* drama in enactments of folktales and legends. There are evening shows from Monday to Saturday and a matinee on Sunday.

MAGELANG

Most visitors encounter Magelang the first time when visiting Borobudur, but this cool mountain town is also a crossroads connecting Jogja, Purworejo and Semarang. Coming from Jogja, you pass the turnoff to Borobudur on the left (to the west) before reaching Magelang, but if you're coming from Solo, you can take the scenic Selo Pass with breathtaking panoramas through mountainside rural areas and the beautiful waterfall, Kedung Kayang.

Getting There

There is no airport in Magelang, so the only way to get there is by bus, car or taxi. It is less than one hour north of Jogja or two hours south of Semarang. Local travel agents can help you arrange your trip.

Hotel Price Guide

Price categories for standard rooms, usually without breakfast:
- **$$$$$** = above US$150
- **$$$$** = US$101–150
- **$$$** = US$51–100
- **$$** = US$30–50
- **$** = under US$30

Where to Stay

In Magelang regency are two five-star resorts, each with its own special ambience, and a four-star getaway ideal for the family.
Amanjiwo Resort: Borobudur, Magelang. Tel: (0293) 788-333, Fax: 788-355, www.amanresorts.com. One hour from Jogja airport, the Amanjiwo is the ultimate in opulence, surrounded by four volcanoes and overlooking Borobudur in the distance. This excellent resort promises to immerse guests in the elegance of Javanese culture. $$$$$
Losari Coffee Plantation Resort & Spa: Desa Losari Grabag, Magelang. Tel: (0298) 596-333, Fax: 592-696, www.losaricoffeeplantation.com. A lovely boutique resort situated on 22 hectares of a working coffee plantation nestled in the highlands 900 metres (2,953 ft) above sea level. Approximately 1½ hour drive from Jogja, Solo and Semarang, it has 26 restored *joglo* villas, a spa, octagonal infinity-edge swimming pool, delicious food and of course great coffee. $$$$$
Puri Asri Hotel: Jl. Cempaka No. 9. Tel: (0293) 365-115, Fax: 364-400, www.hotelpuriasri.com. A four-star hotel amid lush greenery and cool mountain air. Its 160 rooms and suites have their own private terraces. Equipped with a swimming pool. River rafting trips start from here. Only 20 minutes to Borobudur. $

East Java

SURABAYA

The capital city of East Java, Surabaya is also Indonesia's second-largest city after Jakarta. It is an important commercial centre and port, but doesn't offer much in terms of tourist sights. For Indonesians, the city is historically significant as the place where the battle for Independence originated.

Getting There

Convenient domestic air services connect Surabaya with many cities in Indonesia, with regular shuttles to and from Jakarta. Many flights heading for the northern and eastern islands stop over at Surabaya.

Being an important commercial hub, there are also direct services from Singapore, Kuala Lumpur, Bangkok and Hong Kong.

A large number of trans-Java express trains and buses terminate or originate in Surabaya, with many immediate onward connections. As an important port of call, PELNI ferries connect Surabaya with Sulawesi and Kalimantan, and a weekly 925-passenger ferry service from Benoa Harbour (Bali) to Surabaya takes 7 hours. Contact Gama Dewata Bali Tours in Bali (Tel: (0361) 263-568, 232-704, Fax: 263-569).

Tourist Office
Provincial Tourist Services: Jl. Wisata Menanggal. Tel: (031) 853-1814/ 1816/1820/1821, Fax: 853-1822.

Travel Operators
Discover Hotel Reservations: Ruko Mangga Dua Blok B9-05, Jl. Jagir Wonokromo. Tel: (031) 847-0174; 847-0176; Fax: 847-0178, e-mail: discover@sby.dnet.net.id. Provides hotel reservation services, ticketing and tours.

Where to Stay
Surabaya hotels tend to be pricey but are not very well-maintained. East Java has high humidity, so air-con will be welcomed.

Hyatt Regency Surabaya: Jl. Basuki Rachmat 106–128. Tel: (031) 531-1234, Fax: 532-6420, 532-6405, e-mail: surabaya.reservations@hyattintl.com, www.hyatt.com. This luxury hotel (rated five stars) is conveniently located, and has a popular pub and a good *dim sum* restaurant. $$$$$

Hotel Majapahit Mandarin Oriental: Jl. Tunjungan No. 65. Tel: (031) 545-4333, Fax: 545-4111, e-mail: mosub-reservations@mohg-com, www.mandarinoriental.com. Built in 1910 by one of the Sarkies brothers (architects of Singapore's famous Raffles Hotel), this landmark hotel exudes colonial charm and elegance. A quiet haven in the city's centre. $$$$

Surabaya Hilton International: Jl. Gunungsari. Tel: (031) 568-2703, Fax: 568-2081, www.hilton indonesia.com. Located on the southern edge of town, near the airport and zoo and next to Yani Golf course is this delightful and quiet low-rise resort. It has Surabaya's largest swimming pool. $$$

Surabaya Plaza: Jl. Pemuda No. 31. Tel: (031) 531-6833, Fax: 531-6393, www.prlmeplaza.com. This international chain hotel is centrally-located downtown, next to the World Trade Centre. A bonus is its Café Soerabaia, a great place to try inexpensive local fare. $$$

Where to Eat
Coffee Garden: Shangri-la Hotel. The best place in town for a Western breakfast, it also offers a good-value buffet dinner. *Moderate*

Sea Master: Jl. May Jend. Sungkono. Choose fresh seafood from a range of vendors, and have it prepared the way you like it. *Moderate*

Kowloon Restaurant: Plaza Surabaya. A large assortment of good Indonesian and Chinese dishes served food-court style. *Inexpensive*

Where to Shop
For local items, including batik from Madura, brass lamps, bamboo decorations, stone statues, bronze figurines, basketry and paintings, try the large shopping complex on **Jalan Tunjungan**, not far from the Hotel Majapahit. There are a string of antique and curio shops near the Hyatt on **Jalan Basuki Rachmad** and **Jalan Tunjungan**.

For batik and hand-woven cotton textiles, the area around the Mesjid Sunan Ampel in the middle of the Arab quarter is best. There are daily exhibitions of metal and leather handicrafts and embroidery and textiles at the People's Amusement Park, or **Taman Hiburan Rakyat**, at Surabaya Mall on Jalan Kusuna Bangsa.

Culture
Javanese *wayang orang*, *ludruk* and *ketoprak* folk drama are performed nightly at two theatres in the **People's Amusement Park** (THR), in Surabaya Mall.

From June to November, there are fortnightly (first and third Saturdays of each month) *sendratari* classical Javanese dance-drama performances at the open-air **Candra Wilwatikta** amphitheatre in Pandaan, 45 km (30 miles) south of Surabaya.

The tourist office can arrange East Javanese *kuda kepang* "hobby-horse" trance dance performances; book three days in advance.

Regular bull races are held from August to October at the new stadium in **Bangkalan**, in Madura. Look up the schedules at the tourist office.

BALURAN NATIONAL PARK
Where to Stay
Rosa's Ecolodge: Ds. Sidomulyo, RT 03/03, Sumberwaru, Kecamatan Banyuputih, Situbondo 68374. Tel: (0338) 453-005, Fax: 453-191, e-mail: bineka@telkom.net. Located in a traditional village at the edge of Baluran National Park, there are five cottages and a main lodge and restaurant built in Madurese style. All cottages have air-con and Western-style toilets. The staff can arrange mountain and savannah hiking, birdwatching treks and excursions to Baluran beaches with Dutch or English speaking guides. Guest fees at the lodge help finance environmental education for villagers.

IJEN NATIONAL PARK
Where to Stay
Ijen Resort and Villas: Randu Agung, Banyuwangi. Tel: (333) 429-000, Fax: 420-800, e-mail: retreat@ijenresort.com, www.ijenresort.com. A new luxury hotel at the edge of the park. Overlooking terraced rice fields with a backdrop of volcanoes, the resort's 30 rooms and bungalows have standard, superior and suite accommodations, all with modern bath facilities including hot water. The hotel can arrange hikes, scenic drives and inspirational spots for meditation.

MALANG
Malang lies 90 km (55 miles) south of Surabaya via the new highway. Located in the foothills, the town offers a cool climate and has several golf courses.

Magical Gunung Bromo

For a memorable visit to the volcanic Gunung Bromo, spend a few days in Cemoro Lawang. A 46-km (28½-mile) mini-bus ride from Probolinggo, the village is a convenient starting point for the ascent to Bromo and a good place to take in the stunning views all around. Start at 2–3am if you want to catch an incredible sunrise at the peak. The best time to visit is during the dry season in April–October. At night, temperatures can drop below zero, so be sure to have warm clothing with you. Consider:

Grand Bromo Hotel: Desa Suleapura, Probolinggo. Tel: (0339) 981-103/4, Fax: 581-142. Set amidst lush, tropical vegetation only minutes from Mt. Bromo. Panoramic views. Deluxe rooms and cottages, hot water, swimming pool and Jacuzzi. $$

Yoschi's Guesthouse: Jl. Wonokerto No. 1, Wonokerto (2 km/1¼ miles downhill from Ngadisari). Tel: (0335) 541-018, Fax: 541-046. An excellent choice: options include clean, basic rooms or comfortable cottages, with hot water. Yoschi's also functions as an informal travel agent. Here, you can buy bus tickets, arrange for guides and buy trekking maps. It also has a garden and a good restaurant. $$–$

Lava View Lodge: (500 metres/547 yards left from town centre, follow the track between the shops and Hotel Bromo Permai). Tel: (0335) 541-009. Wonderful views due to its location on the edge of the crater. Rooms with hot water are available and there is a decent restaurant. $

Surfing Paradise

G-Land is on the south-easternmost tip of East Java off the coast of Alas Purwo National Park. Its perfect waves, said to be second only to the famous Pipeline in Hawaii, attracts internationally acclaimed professional surfers lured by reef names such as Speedies and Grajagan. Nomadic wave seekers follow Indonesia's south seas surfing trail from Sumatra in the west to Roti in the east seasonally. Primitive accommodations only. For further information, check www.g-land.com.

Unlike many Javanese towns in which activity is confined to a dreary main street, Malang sweeps over gentle ridges and gullies along the banks of the Sungai Brantas river, offering unexpected views and quiet backstreets that beg to be explored. It has escaped the explosive growth of other large Javanese cities and has remained a small, quiet town. A good base for exploring the rest of East Java.

Getting There

From Surabaya, express buses leave regularly from the Purabaya bus terminal for the 2-hour ride to Malang's Arjosari station, 5 km (3 miles) north of the town. The morning Jatayu train leaves Surabaya's Gubeng station and arrives at Malang after 90 minutes. Get your hotel to book train or bus seats.

Where to Stay

Hotel Tugu Malang: Jl. Tugu No. 3. Tel: (0341) 363-891, Fax: 362-747, www.tuguhotels.com. This award-winning boutique hotel has unique rooms, each splendidly appointed. The luxuriously cosy ambience of the museum hotel is punctuated by superb Javanese and Chinese antiques. $$$$
Regent's Park: Jl. Jaksa Agung Suprapto No. 12. Tel: (0341) 363-388, Fax: 362-966. A pleasant hotel with nice rooms: comfortable, has good views and hot tubs. $$$
Kartika Graha: Jl. Jaksa Agung Suprapto No. 17. Tel: (0341) 361-900, Fax: 361-911. This good-value hotel is bright and cheerful, with rooms that are very comfortable. Facilities include a 24-hour café and two pools. $$

Where to Eat

Melati Pavilion: Hotel Tugu Malang, Jl. Tugu No. 3, Tel: (0341) 363-891. This beautiful garden restaurant serves delicious Indo-Dutch food. *Moderate*
New Hong Kong: Jl. A.R. Hakim. If you want a break from Indonesian fare, and are in the mood for a taste of Chinese, this is your best choice. *Moderate*
Minang Jaya: Jl. Jend. Basuki Rakhmat No. 111. Here is the place to sample delicious Padang cuisine. *Inexpensive*
Toko Oen: Jl. Basuki Rachmat. Tel: (0341) 364-052. In an old Dutch building, this restaurant serves Indonesian and Dutch food, delicious desserts and bakery items.

Restaurant Price Guide

Price categories for a three-course meal (Asian or Western), without drinks:
Expensive = US$26–50
Moderate = US$11–25
Inexpensive = under US$10

Sumatra

North Sumatra

MEDAN

If you are starting your Indonesia trip in North Sumatra, Medan is a natural choice. The capital of North Sumatra, it is the jump-off point to attractions such as Danau Toba and Gunung Leuser National Park.

Getting There

By Air
Medan's Polonia International airport has daily flights not only from Jakarta but also from Singapore (SilkAir) and Malaysia (MAS). In terms of distance, Singapore and the Malaysian cities of Kuala Lumpur and Penang are closer to Medan than Jakarta. Garuda flies from Medan to Jakarta three times a day.
Garuda: Jl. Dr. Mongonsidi No. 34A. Tel: (061) 455-6777, Fax: 455-7747; Dharma Deli Hotel, Jl. Balai Kota No. 2. Tel: 453-7844.
Malaysia Airlines (MAS): Jl. Iman Bonjol 17. Tel: (061) 519-333.
Mandala: Jl. Brigjen Katamso No. 37E. Tel: (061) 513-309.
Merpati: Jl. Brigjien Katamso 219. Tel: (061) 321-888, 542-552.
SilkAir: Tiara Convention Centre, Jl. Cut Meutiah. Tel: (061) 537-744.
SMAC: Jl. Imam Bonjol 59. Tel: (061) 516-934.

By Sea
It is also possible to travel by ferry from Singapore to Batam island in the Riau archipelago and then fly direct to Medan. Between Medan and Penang, there are fast hydrofoil boats that make the twice-weekly crossing in 5 hours. Contact the office in Medan at Jl. Brigjen Katamso 62A. Tel: (061) 515-562.

Tour Operator

Tri Jaya Tour and Travel: Hotel Deli River, Jl. Raya Namorambe 129 (P.O. Box 1223). Tel: (061) 703-2967, Fax: 703-2965, e-mail: trijaya@attglobal.net, www.trijaya-travel.com. Tri Jaya does tailor-made tours throughout Sumatra, specialising in eco, cultural and historical tours.

Tourist Office
Provincial Tourist Services: Sumatra Utara, Jl. Jend. A. Yani No. 107, Medan. Tel: (061) 453-8101, Fax: 452-8436.

Hotel Price Guide
Price categories for standard rooms, usually without breakfast:
- $$$$$ = above US$150
- $$$$ = US$101–150
- $$$ = US$51–100
- $$ = US$30–50
- $ = under US$30

Where to Stay
Danau Toba International: Jl. Iman Bonjol No. 17. Tel: (061) 415-7000, 453-0553, www.hoteldanautoba.com. This lively hotel has international-class facilities including a health centre and an excellent pool. There is also a pub and a disco on the premises, as well as several restaurants. Good value. $$$

Tiara Medan: Jl. Cut Mutiah. Tel: (061) 457-4000, Fax: 451-0176, www.tiarahotel.com. This is Medan's best hotel. There are more than 200 well-furnished rooms and a Clark Hatch health centre on the premises. There is also a popular bar and lounge with live entertainment. $$$

Natour Dharma Deli: Jl. Balai Kota No. 2. Tel: (061) 415-1258, Fax: 414-4477. This charming colonial-style hotel restored from the former Hotel De Boer offers good value in this price range. The comfortable air-con rooms have garden views and there is a swimming pool and a good bakery. $$

Where to Eat
Medan offers a great variety in cuisines, from Padang and Chinese, to Indian and European. A local speciality is *kambing kurma* (lamb in curry sauce), and the most distinctive of local Batak dishes is *saksan* (an entire roast pig served with a spicy sauce made with pig's blood). Restaurants in Kutacane serve *cicang anjing* (dog curry) and *tuak* (palm wine).

Good coffee is available everywhere in North Sumatra, brewed with beans grown in the Gayo highlands.

Lyn's Restaurant: Jl. Yani 98A. A good place for Western food, not least because of its lively bar. A favourite place with the expat community. *Moderate*

Omlandia Restaurant: Deli River Resort, Jl. Raya Namorambe Pasar 4 No. 129. Tel: (061) 703-2964, A unique restaurant with beautiful architecture in the middle of unspoilt Sumatran nature on the banks of the Deli River. Serves traditional Indonesian and European cuisines. *Moderate*

Restaurant Garuda: Jl. Pemuda 20 (next to the textile market). Tel: (061) 327-692. Everything on the menu in this 24-hour eatery is good. Don't leave out their freshly-squeezed fruit juices. *Inexpensive*

Night market: Jl. Selat Pangang. The roadside stalls are a must-try, providing a fun (and delicious) way to soak up the local culture. There is a range of low-priced local fare and fresh seafood, including the finger-licking chilli crab.

Where to Shop
Medan is a large trading town with several markets offering handicrafts from all over Sumatra and Java. The best place to look for antiques are in the shops along **Jalan Yani**.

You will find a wide selection of Batak art pieces and curiosities, such as rice storage containers, *kain ulos* textiles, masks and carved wooden statues. Be ready to bargain hard.

Batak calendars and buffalo-horn medicine pouches are popular purchases. *Tungkat* (carved magic wands) – the genuine ones – are gruesome objects said to be very powerful as they contain the flesh of a sacrificed child.

Culture
Taman Budaya (Jl. Perintis Kemerdekaan) holds regular performances of dance and music from the regions outside the city. Check with your hotel or the tourist office for schedules.

BANDA ACEH

Banda Aceh is the gateway to and the capital of Aceh province. It is an area that has been plagued by turmoil since the Dutch occupied it in the late 19th century. Aceh is staunchly Islamic and women who travel there should be modest in both clothing and behaviour.

Note: At press time, the area has seen a resurgence of activity by the Islamic Free Aceh Movement (GAM) and travel to the area is not recommended.

Foreigners must report to the military to get a special permit and *surat jalan* (traveling papers) to enter Aceh. Check upon arrival in Indonesia to determine advisability of travel to Aceh.

Getting There
The 2,500-km (1,550-mile) Trans-Sumatran Highway runs from the ferry terminal in Bakauheni in the south to Banda Aceh in the north. Banda can be reached by a 12-hour express bus ride from Medan, but there are direct flights on Garuda from Jakarta and Medan. In addition, in northern Sumatra, a railway line runs from north Medan to Banda Aceh.

Where to Stay
Kuala Tripa: Jl. Mesjid Raya No. 24. Tel: (0651) 21108, Fax: 24535. Situated within walking distance of the Mesjid Raya (Mesjid Grand), this hotel has 40 spacious rooms with a good range of facilities including a swimming pool. The only bar and disco in town are on its premises. $$$

Hotel Sultan: Jl. Panglima Polim. Tel: (0651) 22469, Fax: 31770. Centrally located on a quiet street near a shopping complex. The rooms all have air-con and TV. The staff is friendly, and the restaurant serves decent Asian and Western food. $$

Where to Eat
The cuisine of the Aceh region contains distinct Arab and Indian influences. For example, one favourite local dish is *gulai itik Aceh* (duck in curry sauce), served with steamed rice. Other specialities include *sambal bunga kates* (papaya flower salad), *sayur bayam* (egg cooked in spinach) and the popular dessert *pulot hitam dua masak* (double-boiled black rice). A usual local breakfast is *teluar setengah matang* (a half-boiled egg taken with coffee).

The streets come alive every evening when the night market at Jalan Yani and Jalan Chairil Anwar is set up by numerous stalls hawking local treats such as *sate* (grilled meat on skewers), *mie goreng* (fried noodles) and *pisang goreng* (fried bananas).

Aroma: Jl. Cut Nyak Dhien. Indonesian and Chinese food is served in a simple and casual atmosphere. One of the few places that also serves Western food. *Inexpensive*

Where to Shop
Special items to look for in Banda Aceh include *rencong* (traditional Acehnese daggers) and delicate filigree jewellery. Antique lovers can try **Daud's** (Tel: (0651) 22794. The goldsmith shops are along **Jalan Perdagangan**, near the Mesjid Raya mosque. Pasar Aceh is a good place to look for local handicrafts such as baskets and Gayo *kerawang* embroidery.

PRAPAT/SAMOSIR ISLAND

This picturesque lakeside town is a favourite weekend getaway for residents of Medan. Located 175 km (109 miles) north of Medan, Prapat is a good place to buy Batak handicrafts. It is also the jump-off point to Samosir island, reached by a 30-minute boat ride. The island sits in the centre of the massive volcanic crater lake, Danau Toba.

Getting There
Scheduled bus services from Medan make the trip to Prapat within 4 hours. Alternatively, rent a mini-van and hire a driver.

Hotel Price Guide

Price categories for standard rooms, usually without breakfast:
$$$$$ = above US$150
$$$$ = US$101–150
$$$ = US$51–100
$$ = US$30–50
$ = under US$30

Where to Stay
Prapat
Natour Prapat Hotel: Jl. Marihat 1. Tel: (0625) 41012, 41018, Fax: 41019. This 85-room hotel on the lakefront has its own private beach. Built by the Dutch in 1911, it charms with its old-world ambience and clean, spacious rooms. The restaurant serves Asian food and, occasionally, there is Batak entertainment in the evenings. **$$$**
Niagara: Jl. Pembangunan No. 1. Tel: (0625) 41028, 41068; Fax: 41233, www.niagaralaketoba.com. Medan booking office: (061) 415-877, Fax: 415-5880. One of the newest hotels in the area, it sits on a hilltop offering expansive views of the lake and Samosir island. The rooms are tastefully furnished. There is a golf course and a 24-hour café. **$$$**

Samosir
Lodgings on the island remain modest by international standards, despite it being developed as a major tourist destination. Most hotels are located on the scenic Tuktuk peninsula situated midway between the main tourist attractions in Tomok and Ambarita.
Toba Beach Hotel: Pangembatan. Located in Parambatan village, 2 km (1 mile) south of Tomok. Tel: (0625) 41275, Fax: 732-0954. Medan office: (061) 734-4073. This hotel is hidden away from the others on the lakefront. It has a restaurant that offers good Indonesian food and a lake view. **$$**

Carolina Hotel: Tuktuk Sindong. Tel: (0625) 41520, Fax: 41521. A Tuktuk favourite located on the lakefront with a private swimming beach and superb views. The rooms range widely – from basic ones to traditional Batak-style bungalows. The open-air restaurant is the best on the island, serving freshly-baked bread. Dance performances feature every Saturday night. This place is popular, so be sure to book ahead. **$**
Silintong: Jl. Durian No. 5. Tel: (0625) 41345. Medan office: (061) 529-265. A modern hotel with bright, comfortable rooms and a cool, pleasant garden shaded by a canopy of tall pine trees. The restaurant is small but good. **$**
Tabo Cottages, Tuk Tuk, Lake Toba. Tel/Fax: (0625) 451-318, e-mail: tabors@indo.net.id, www.tabo-cottages.com. Situated on the shore of Lake Toba, surrounded by rice fields and plantations, Tabo Cottages offers rooms, a restaurant and wellness programmes in lush tropical gardens. **$**
Tao Cottages island: Tao Island. P.O. Box 4, Pematang Sianter (no phone). Tao Island is located off the north-eastern coast of Samosir Island; from Simanindo, it is a five-minute boat ride. The resort on this tiny island comprises 20 private cottages. Quiet and lovely. **$**
Toledo Inn: Tuktuk Sindong. Tel: (0625) 41181, Fax: 451-094. The oldest hotel on the island, it has the best swimming beach and is still the top choice with international groups. The rooms are comfortable and there is a large open restaurant that serves local and Western cuisine. **$**

Where to Eat
Prapat
Restaurant Hong Kong: Jl. Haranggaol No. 9. A popular family-style Chinese restaurant that also serves good Indonesian food. *Moderate*
Trogadero: Jl. Haranggaol No. 110. Good Indonesian food in pleasant surroundings. You can also get decent steaks and salads here. *Moderate*
Brastagi: Jl. Sisingamangaraja No. 55. Located along a stretch of eateries frequented by locals, Brastagi is a good place to go local. *Inexpensive*

Samosir
Almost every hotel on Samosir island has a small restaurant serving basic local fare and some Western food.
Carolina Restaurant: Carolina Hotel. Tel: (0645) 41520. By far, the best place on the island to eat: good food, good prices and a wonderful lakeside setting. Batak dances add excitement on Saturday evenings. *Inexpensive*

Rumba: Southern end of Tuktuk. The food here is very decent, and the pizzas are good. *Inexpensive*

Culture
In music, the Batak people are known for two kinds of ensembles. The larger, more dramatic *gondang sabangunan* is performed outdoors during traditional ceremonies. Drums and reed instruments are used to make lively and entertaining music. Daily shows take place at Simanindo (23 km/14¼ miles north of Tuktuk) from 10.30am–12.30pm. More informal *gondang hasapi* ensembles with flutes, guitars and percussion perform indoors and can be heard in most hotels and on Saturday night at Carolina Hotel.

West Sumatra

PADANG

The capital and gateway to West Sumatra, Padang is a thriving commercial centre regarded by most travellers as a stopover to the Minang Highlands or the west-coast islands. There is a semblance of old-world charm in the colonial homes and shop houses lining the wide avenues around Chinatown and Pasar Raya (Central Market). The city is best explored by walking or in a horse-drawn cart.

Getting There
By Air
Padang has the largest airport on the west coast and it services mainly domestic flights: Garuda flies to Jakarta twice daily and to Medan four times a day. Both Garuda and Singapore's SilkAir fly direct from Singapore to Padang while Malaysia Airlines flies in from Kuala Lumpur and Penang.
Garuda: Jl. Jend. Sudirman No. 2. Tel: (0751) 30173, 30737.
Merpati: Jl. Gerlja, Natour Muara Hotel. Tel: (0751) 38314, 31852.
SilkAir: Hotel Sedona Bumi Minang, Jl. Bundo Kandung No. 20. Tel: (0751) 38120/1.

Tourist Office
Provincial Tourist Services: Sumatra Barat, Jl. Jend. Sudirman No. 43. Tel: (0751) 34231.

Where to Stay
Accommodation choices range from international-standard hotels to budget lodgings.
Hotel Bumi Minang: Jl. Bundo Kandung 20. Tel: (0751) 37555, Fax: 37567, www.bumiminang.com. This large Minangkabau-style luxury hotel

is well-located in the centre of town. Aside from spacious rooms, it has decent facilities, including a business centre and a good restaurant. **$$$$**
Pangeran's: Jl. Dobi No. 3. Tel: (0751) 31233, Fax: 27180. This is a good choice if you're looking for a mid-range hotel. It is rather popular with tourists, perhaps due to the good service. **$$**
Mariani: Jl. Bundo Kandung No. 35. Tel: (0751) 34134, Fax: 25410. The decor is a little fussy but the place is airy, and the rooms are spacious. Good location. **$**

Where to Eat

This is the home of *nasi padang*, which consists of 20–25 small dishes of spicy vegetables or meat prepared beforehand and laid out on the table. It is the ultimate fast food – there is no waiting at all – and is nutritious too. Each diner pays for the portion he eats. The popularity of *nasi padang* has spread throughout Indonesia, and to Southeast Asia as well. Most of the dishes are hot, and a few favourites are *rendang* (curried beef), *dendeng* (beef with red chillies) and boiled egg in curry.
Simpang Raya: Jl. Bagindo Aziz Chan. This is the best place to sample *nasi padang*. The eatery has a branch on Jl. Bundo Kanduan. *Inexpensive*
Taman Sari: Jl. Yani. Good Javanese and Chinese food is served here. Try the *kway teow goreng* (fried flat noodles). *Inexpensive*

BUKITTINGGI

The cool, picturesque hilltop town of Bukittinggi, the heart of Minangkabau culture and the best base from which to explore the surrounding Minang Highlands, stands at 930 metres (3,050 ft). From here, travellers can head for the volcanic peaks of Gunung Agam, Gunung Singgalang and Gunung Merapi.

Getting There

Bukittinggi (Tall Hill) is a 3-hour bus ride from Padang. From Medan, the journey may take more than 18 hours. Bukittingi is also a major stop for buses traversing the Trans-Sumatran Highway.

Where to Stay

Most hotels are within walking distance of the city sights, except the newer luxury ones, which tend to be sited in the quieter outskirts. Backpacker lodgings are along Jl. Yani, though most offer only cold-water baths. Bring a jacket.
Novotel Coralia Bukittinggi: Jl. Laras Datuk Bandaro. Tel: (0752) 35000, Fax: 23800, www.novotel.com. The newest luxury hotel in the area, it is also the most elegant. Aside from the swanky decor, a big plus is the heated pool. **$$$$**
Dymen's: Jl. Nawawi No. 3. Tel: (0752) 21015, 23440, Fax: 21613. A favourite for tour groups, this luxury hotel with a good range of facilities is located in a quiet area south of the city centre. Holds regular traditional dance performances. **$$$**
Pusako: Jl. Sukarno-Hatta No. 7. Tel: (0752) 22111, 223-111, Fax: 32667. This is a 15-minute walk to the city centre, though a shuttle service is provided. The rooms are large with full facilities, the staff is friendly and helpful and, best of all, it has nice views. **$$$**
Denai's: Jl. Rivai No. 26. Tel: (0752) 21466, 21511. Of Minangkabau design, the hotel's main wing is flanked by comfortable cottages with TV and hot water. The hotel is clean and well-run and it has a restaurant. **$$**
Benteng: Jl. Benteng No. 1. Tel: (0752) 21115, 22128, Fax: 22596. Located on a quiet street, it has views of Gunung Merapi. The rooms come with hot water and TV and there is a restaurant. **$**

Where to Eat

Famili: Jl. Benteng No. 1. Situated on the Benteng de Kock hilltop, so you get a nice view and pleasant breezes. Serves good Padang and Western fare. *Inexpensive*
Mexico: Jl. Yani. A popular meeting spot, it serves steaks and ice-cold beer. *Inexpensive*
The Coffee Shop: Jl. Yani No. 105. A Bukittinggi institution and a favourite meeting point for travellers, the eatery serves a wide range of Western food, including delicious pancakes. Very crowded in the evenings. *Inexpensive*

Where to Shop

West Sumatra is renowned for its beautiful hand-loomed *songket* cloth and fine embroidery, silverwork and woodcarvings.

The weaving of silk *songket* brocade is carried out in several communities, the best known of which is **Silungkang**, a small town on the Agam plateau. Another popular centre is **Pandai Sikat**, which lies on the main road from Padang to Bukittinggi. Women working in these cottage industries require a long time – up to several months – to produce a two-piece *sarong* and *selendang* (scarf) set. **Pandai Sikat** is also renowned for its embroidery and woodcarvings. Silversmiths in the hilltop village of **Kota Gadang** produce fine filigree.

Most of Bukittinggi's antique shops are found along **Jalan Minangkabau**, where there're also ceramics, textiles and Dutch antiques, Batak woodcarvings and local handicrafts. Visit Crystal Art Shop or Aladin Art and Antique Shop at Jalan Yani No. 14.

Culture

Dance performances are held every evening at **Saayun Salangkah**, on Jalan Yamin. Local entertainment favourites are *pencak silat*, a dance that incorporates martial arts movements, and plate dance, in which plates are tossed onto the ground to form a carpet of broken shards over which the dancers perform.

NIAS ISLAND

Nias island, the largest of the west-coast islands, has a most unusual ancient culture which revolves around stone. The villages are veritable fortresses, with great stone-paved central walkways. In the remote centre of the island stands mysterious gigantic megaliths.

Getting There

There are daily flights on SMAC charter airlines to Nias Island from Sibolga, on the western coast of Sumatra. Sibolga can be reached by road from either Medan (in 9 hours) or Padang (10 hours). You can also take a boat from there; daily ferries make the 12- to 14-hour crossing to the Nias capital of Gunung Sitoli. Note: Storms are frequent and the waves can be quite dangerous.

Where to Stay

Most of the tourist attractions – the traditional villages and surfing beaches – are in the south, a 4–7 hour journey on poor roads from Gunung Sitoli. Lodgings are mostly simple *losmen*, with the exception of one new luxury resort. There are plans for more to be built.

Nias Stone Jumping

A Nias stone-jumping ceremony has men leaping over megaliths which are more than 2 metres (6-ft) high. Originally, the ritual was performed by Niah warriors, who had to negotiate dangerous spikes on top of the columns. Today, the barbs are absent and the performance is for the benefit of tourists. Arranging a private performance is costly; try to join a tour group that already has one lined up.

Sorake Beach Resort: Tel: (0630) 21364/21195. Catering to the high-end customer, this luxury hotel has 75 traditional cottages spread over 6 hectares (15 acres) of land on the beachfront. The interiors feature recreated Nias artefacts. There is a daily buffet but the menu is limited, serving mostly fresh seafood. $$$

SIBERUT ISLAND

Siberut island is the largest of the Mentawai island chain off Sumatra's west coast. Covered in dense rainforest with isolated farming settlements, it was until recently home to tribes who lived according to archaic traditions.

Trek inland from Rokdok or Madobat village into the interior for an unusual experience.

Getting There

By Sea
The trip from Padang to the island takes 12 hours and covers 150 km (90 miles). From Padang's Teluk Bayur Harbour, small passenger ferries depart twice a week for Muara Padang on Siberut. The boats can be very crowded, so book in advance (Tel: (0759) 21064; Siberut office, Jl. B.T. Arua No. 31, Teluk Bayar. Tel: (0725) 21941) or with a travel agent. If you are travelling independently, you should approach the Siberut Guide Association (Tel: (0759) 21064) to arrange for a guide; a travel permit (*surat jalan*) is required. Or arrange with a travel agent.

Where to Stay/Eat

Accommodation is very basic on Siberut. There is only one *losmen* in the town of Muarasiberut. Elsewhere, you have to stay either with the families or Christian missionaries. Malaria is endemic, so take precautions (see pages 348–9).
Syahruddin: At the mouth of the river, Tel: (0759) 21014. Very basic lodgings with common bath stalls. Bring your own mosquito net. A good coffee shop across the road serves rice dishes and grilled fish. $

South Sumatra & Riau

PALEMBANG

For well over 1,200 years a major trading port and the heart of the Buddhist Srivijaya kingdom, Palembang's wealth today comes from its oil deposits.

Getting There

Merpati flies from Jakarta, with additional services originating from cities in Sumatra, such as Medan, Pekanbaru and Batam island. There are bus and train services from Bengkulu and Bandar Lampung.

Tourist Office

Provincial Tourist Services: Jl. PON IX (Taman Budaya). Tel: (0711) 357-348.

> ### Hotel Price Guide
> Price categories for standard rooms, usually without breakfast:
> $$$$$ = above US$150
> $$$$ = US$101–150
> $$$ = US$51–100
> $$ = US$30–50
> $ = under US$30

Where to Stay

Swarna Dwipa: Jl. Tasik No. 2. Tel: (0711) 313-322; Fax: 362-992. This old colonial building in a quiet residential area 2 km (1 mile) west of the city centre overlooks a park. You can choose between a room in the new modern wing, or a restored deluxe one in the old wing. The service is friendly and there is a fitness centre. $$–$$$
Sriwijaya: Jl. Letkol Iskander No. 31. Tel: (0711) 355-555, Fax: 364-565. Sited in a convenient and quiet location, the hotel offers rooms with either fan or air-con and pleasant balconies. $$

Where to Eat

King's Palace: Kings Hotel. Serves the best Chinese food in town. There is live music and disco dancing after 9pm. *Inexpensive*
Sudi Mampir: Jl. Merdeka. This is one of the best places to try the local cuisine. *Inexpensive*

Where to Shop

Palembang is acclaimed for its rich *kain songket* textiles (hand-loomed silk cloths with gold or silver threads), *kain jumputan pelangi* (tie-dyed cloths, usually of silk) and unique red-and-black or gold-and-black lacquerware.

For textiles, the best known shops are **Cek Ipar** (Jl. Ki Gede Ing Suro No. 141) and **Songket Husin Rahman**. For lower prices (and quality), head for the local market, **Pasar Ilir 16**.

For lacquerware, try any of the antique shops in the **Serlo** area. There are more antique shops along **Jalan Faqih Jalauddin**. It is imperative that you bargain hard – it's part of the game.

Culture

At the Museum Sultan Machmud Badaruddin, daily dance performances are held in an open-air theatre. Traditional dancers wear beautiful costumes made of thick *songket* textiles. Check with the tourist office or the museum for performance times.

BENGKULU

The seaport town of Bengkulu (originally Bencoolen) was founded in the 17th century by the British. Sir Thomas Stamford Raffles, who later founded Singapore, was Bengkulu's lieutenant-governor for five years in the early 1800s.

Getting There

Merpati flies direct from Jakarta. Its office is at Jl. Jend. Sudirman No. 246. Tel: (0736) 27222, 27111.

Tourist Office

Provincial Tourist Services: Jl. Pembangunan No. 14. Tel: (0736) 21272.

Where to Stay

Nala Seaside Cottages: Jl. Pariwisata No. 2. Tel: (0736) 344-885, Fax: 344-282. The resort, which rests on the beach just 5 minutes from town, has air-con cottages but with cold showers. The restaurant overlooks the Indian Ocean. $

Where to Eat

Rumah Makan Srikandi: Jl. Ahmad Yani No. 331. Everything on the menu is good. Try the vegetable soup and *ayam goreng kalasan* (fried chicken). *Inexpensive*

BANDAR LAMPUNG

The main interest in this impoverished harbour town is that part of it was once destroyed by the Krakatau eruption in 1883. Today, it is the main bus and train terminus for travellers heading north.

Getting There

Merpati flies direct from Jakarta. The airline office is at Jl. A. Yani No. 88. Tel: (0721) 258-046, 263-226. There are also bus and train services to Palembang.

Tourist Office

Provincial Tourist Services: Jl. W.R. Supratman No. 39, Gunung Mas. Tel: (0721) 482-565, Fax: 482-081.

Where to Stay

Marcopolo: Jl. Dr. Susilo 4. Tel: (0721) 262-511, Fax: 254-419. The hotel sits on a hillside and has a wonderful view of the bay. The rooms are clean and comfortable, with a pool on the grounds. There is also a restaurant. **$$**

Sahid Krakatau: Jl. Yos Sudarso No. 294. Tel: (0721) 448-888, Fax: 486-589, www.sahidhotels.com. Located right on the bay with a large swimming pool, it caters largely to business travellers. **$$**

Where to Eat

Cookies Corner: Jl. Kartini No. 29. Everything is good on the extensive menu. The house specialities are salads, burgers and steaks. *Inexpensive*

Where to Shop

Lampung is known primarily for its hand-woven *kain tampan*, or ship cloths. It's very difficult – if not impossible – to come across genuine antique pieces. You can buy new ones at **Lampung Art Shop** (Jl. Kartini No. 12). Go upstairs to watch new pieces being woven by the skilled craftswomen.

PEKANBARU

Pekanbaru, the provincial capital and the largest city in mainland Riau, is a thriving oil production centre.

Getting There

Garuda and SilkAir fly daily directly from Singapore. Malaysia's Pelangi Air flies three times a week from Kuala Lumpur. Garuda, Merpati and Mandala fly from Jakarta to Pekanbaru, while Merpati also flies from Medan. In the last few years, Sumatra's forest fires have created poor visibility and halted air travel in the region during the dry season (July–October). Check schedules.

Tourist Office

Provincial Tourist Services: Jl. Diponegoro No. 24A. Tel: (0761) 31562, Fax: 31565.

Where to Stay

The region's proximity to Jakarta as well as its lucrative oil industry have driven development. As part of the "Golden Triangle" joint venture with Singapore and Malaysia, the Riau islands is one of the fastest growth areas in Indonesia. This accounts for the presence of many international-standard hotels.

Mutiara Panghegar: Jl. Yos Sudarso No. 12A. Tel: (0761) 23102,

Fax: 233-380. This is the best hotel in town, with comfortable rooms and good views of the Sungai Siak. A big plus is a restaurant that serves excellent Asian and Western food. **$$$**

Linda: Jl. Nangka No. 133. Tel: (0761) 36915. Conveniently located opposite the bus station, the place is clean and you have a choice of rooms with fan or with air-con, TV and hot water. **$**

Where to Eat

Other than restaurants listed below, you can also take your chances with cheaper eateries along Jl. Jend. Sudirman, in the vicinity of the central market.

Indrapura: Jl. Dr Sutomo. A good hotel restaurant that serves a wide choice of cuisines. You can get Indonesian, Chinese as well as Western dishes. *Moderate*

Medan: Jl. Juanda. Have a culinary experience at this Szechuan- speciality restaurant, which offers an incredibly wide choice of dishes, including Western fare. *Moderate*

BATAM ISLAND

Batam has become a major industrial satellite of nearby Singapore and is popular with weekend visitors from there, who come for its golf courses, beaches, duty-free shopping and seafood.

Getting There

By Air

Batam has a modern airport with direct services to several destinations in Sumatra. You can get to the other parts of Indonesia via Jakarta. Garuda offers a daily flight to Medan and to Pekanbaru.

By Sea

From Singapore's World Trade Centre ferry terminal, Batam is only 45 minutes away by hydrofoil, which arrives at Sekupang, Batu Ampar and Waterfront City. Contact Dino Shipping in Singapore (Tel: (65) 6276-0668). The same company operates a ferry service to Nongsa from Singapore's Tanah Merah Ferry Terminal (Tel: (65) 6276-9722). From Sekupang, there are ferry connections to Pekanbaru and other Sumatran cities.

Where to Stay

Most accommodation comprises full-facility beach resorts with a fancy pool, disco and sports facilities. Travel agents in Singapore usually offer discount packages and will arrange the ferry, transfer and a tour. Batam's largest town is Nagoya.

Budget *losmen* are 2 km (1 mile) out of town on Jl. Tenku Umar.

Batam View Beach Resort: Jl. Hang Lekir, Nongsa. Tel: (0778) 761-740, Fax: 761-747, www.batamview.com. Singapore office: (65) 235-4366. This lies next-door to a 36-hole golf course. In-house dining options includes a poolside barbeque and several restaurants. **$$$**

Meliá Panorama Batam: Komplek Tanjung Pantun, Sei Jodoh 29432. Tel: (0778) 452-888, Fax: (0778) 452-555, www.solmelia.com. Meliá Panorama, located just across the waters from Singapore in the heart of Batam city offers the services and facilities of an international four-star hotel, including 190 guestrooms and suites. For leisure, several 18-hole golf courses, shopping centres and beaches are within easy reach of the hotel, which provides a limousine service upon request. **$$$**

Turi Beach Resort: Nongsa. Tel: (0778) 310-078, www.nongsaresorts.com. Singapore office: (65) 6235-5544. This lovely, relaxed and well-run resort is situated on a tranquil beach with charming Balinese-style thatched-roof bungalows. A few rooms have balconies that look out to the sea. **$$$**

> **Restaurant Price Guide**
>
> Price categories for a three-course meal (Asian or Western), without drinks:
> *Expensive* = US$26–50
> *Moderate* = US$11–25
> *Inexpensive* = under US$10

Where to Eat

The quality varies greatly among the countless eateries on the island, from fast-food joints in malls to restaurants in the major hotels. There is some good-value seafood.

Lucy's Oar House: Nagoya. The liveliest place in town, Lucy's is frequented by locals and expats alike. Internet facilities also allow you to check your e-mail. *Moderate*

Selera Wisata: Batu Besar. A casual, busy set-up located right on the beachfront. It is not easy to get a table, but the very good food makes up for this. The pepper crab is excellent. *Moderate*

BINTAN ISLAND

Larger and more interesting than its neighbour Batam, Bintan also has better resorts, including a Club Med. Although it has several industrial projects in progress with more being developed, the island's expanse of jungle, swamp and mountain lies largely undisturbed. Pasir Panjang, the powdery-sand northern shore, is a mega resort area developed by Singaporeans. There have been isolated cases of malaria so take precautions (see pages 348–9).

Getting There

With the airport recently closed, boats are the only way to get to Bintan. Tanjung Pinang, the ancient capital of Riau on the south-west coast, is serviced by ferries from Batam and other Riau islands. From Singapore's Tanah Merah Ferry Terminal, high-speed catamarans take you there in 45 minutes. Contact Bintan Resort Ferries (Tel: (65) 6542-4369).

Hotel Price Guide

Price categories for standard rooms, usually without breakfast:
$$$$$ = above US$150
$$$$ = US$101–150
$$$ = US$51–100
$$ = US$30–50
$ = under US$30

Where to Stay

There are several modest hotels in Tanjung Pinang while the north-coast resort area has both mid-range as well as luxury accommodation. Ask your Singapore travel agent about promotion packages.
Banyan Tree Bintan: North Bintan. Tel: (0770) 693-100, Fax: 693-200, www.banyantree.com. This quietly luxurious and ecologically-minded resort has 74 secluded villas hugging a rainforest-clad cliff which look out over the sea. A few villas have their own private pool and jacuzzi. The spa facilities are extensive and a big plus is an in-house Italian restaurant that serves up innovative dishes. $$$$$
Angsana Resort & Spa: North Bintan. Tel: (0770) 693-111, Fax: 693-222, www.angsana.com. A new resort located next to the upscale Banyan Tree. Built on the beachfront, all rooms face either the sea or swimming pool. There is an 18-hole Greg Norman-designed golf course next-door. The Balinese massage is a must-try. $$$$
Club Med Ria Bintan: North Bintan. Tel: (0770) 692-801, Fax: 692-829, www.clubmed.com. In addition to the usual Club Med features of parties, courses and lavish meals, there is an in-house circus school. $$$$
Hotel Sedona Bintan Lagoon: North Bintan. Tel: (0770) 691-388, Fax: 691-300, www.bintanlagoon.com. This sprawling 300-hectare (740-acre) resort has two 18-hole golf courses designed by Greg Norman and Ian Baker-Finch. There is also a diving school. $$$$
Mana Mana Cabanas: North Bintan. Tel: (0770) 692-555, Fax: 692-577, www.manamana.com. These hill-side bungalows have wonderful views. There is an excellent watersports centre for diving, windsurfing and kayaking. $$$
Hotel Kartika: Jl. M.T. Harryono Km 3.5. Tanjung Pinang. Tel: (0771) 22446. A comfortable hotel in Tanjung Pinang with a pool and its own restaurant. $$

Restaurant Price Guide

Price categories for a three-course meal (Asian or Western), without drinks:
Expensive = US$26–50
Moderate = US$11–25
Inexpensive = under US$10

Where to Eat

Every evening at sunset near Tanjung Pinang's main square along Jalan Hang Tuah, a night market comes alive with stalls offering *sate* (grilled meat on skewers) and other local favourites. The major hotels have decent restaurants serving Asian and European food. Inexpensive, fresh seafood – fish, crab, lobster or shark – served grilled or steamed in a curry sauce are always good choices.

Bali

GETTING THERE

By Air

Bali's Ngurah Rai International Airport is well served with daily flights from major Indonesian cities and from around the world. A few international airlines fly only to Jakarta, from where there are daily flights to Bali. At the airport, fixed rates for air-conditioned taxis are posted at the counter just outside the baggage claim area; payment is by coupon, which is purchased from the cashier. Don't accept offers from the unauthorised "guides" loitering about.

Airport Departure/Arrival Info-line: Tel: (0361) 751-011. Press 0 for operator.

International Airline Offices
At Grand Bali Beach Hotel, Sanur:
Northwest Airlines: Tel: (0361) 287-841
Qantas: Tel: (0361) 288-331
Thai Airways: Tel: (0361) 288-141

At Ngurah Rai International Airport:
Air France: Tel: (0361) 768-310
Cathay Pacific: Tel: (0361) 766-937
China Airlines: Tel: (0361) 757-298
Continental Airlines: Tel: (0361) 752-107
Eva Air: Tel: (0361) 759-773
Japan Airlines: Tel: (0361) 756-123
Lufthansa: Tel: (0361) 759-756
Malaysia Airlines: Tel: (0361) 764-995
Royal Brunei: Tel: (0361) 755-748
Singapore Airlines: Tel: (0361) 768-388

At other locations:
Air Paradise International: Kuta Megah I-J, Jl. ByPass Ngurah Rai. Tel: (0361) 768-104, Fax: 750-100, www.airparadise.co.id.
Garuda: Ngurah Rai Airport, Tel: (0361) 751-011 ext. 5204. www.garuda-indonesia.com; Ticketing and Reservations (7am–10pm). Tel: 227-824; Natour Kuta Beach Hotel, Kuta. Tel: 751-179; Sanur Beach Hotel, Sanur. Tel: 278-915; Jl. Melati No. 61, Denpasar. Tel: 254-7478.

Domestic Airline Offices
Air Bali: Dewa Ruci Building, Jl. ByPass Ngurah Rai, Kuta. Tel: (0361) 767-466, 766-582 Fax: 766-581, www.airbali.com. For helicopter tours and transfers around the island.
Bouraq Airlines: Ngurah Rai Aiport, Tel: (0361) 766-929; Jl. Sudirman No. 7A, Denpasar. Tel: 241-391.
Merpati Nusantara Airlines: Jl. Melati No. 51, Denpasar. Tel: (0361) 235-358; Ngurah Rai Aiport, Tel: 751-011 ext. 5242, www.merpati.co.id.
Star Air: Ramada Bintang Bali Hotel, Kuta. Tel: (0361) 753-775, Fax: 753-930, www.starair-online.com. A new entrant in Indonesia's local airline scene.
Travira Air: Bali Operations, Ngurah Rai Airport. Tel: (0361) 768-353, Fax: 768-354, www.travira-air.com. A luxurious sea plane that can take nine people to hard-to-reach places, even on water.

By Road
With improved roads, the *bis malam* (night bus) from Java to Bali now travels faster than the train, but drivers can be reckless. Buses leave Jakarta three times daily; from there, connect with the ferry which arrives in Denpasar within 24 hours, after stopping at Semarang, Surabaya and Malang. To break the journey, stop over at Yogyakarta; from there it's 15–16 hours to Bali, or from Surabaya, 11 hours. There are travel agents along Jl. Hasanudin and Jl. Diponegoro in Denpasar.

A safer and more comfortable alternative to the Jakarta–Bali service is the costlier Lorena Bus ride, which has better services and a toilet. Contact the company at (Jakarta) Jl. K.H. Hasyim Ashhari No. 15 C2/3. Tel: (021) 231-3166, 345-8111, Fax: 350-0066, or at (Bali) Jl. Hasanudin No. 6 or Jl. Diponegoro No. 100/A12. Tel: 237-660, 221-937, 235-010.

By Sea
There are both private and state-run ferry services that operate between Ketapang in Java and Gilimanuk in Bali, a 30-minute trip that runs frequently. The ferry from Padang Bai Harbour in East Bali also runs every two hours 24 hours a day to Lembar Harbour in Lombok. The trip takes around 2 hours.

Longer-haul PELNI ferries connect Bali with other parts of Indonesia. The Bali office is at Benoa Harbour. Call: (0361) 723-4833, 720-962. **PELNI** ships go from Benoa harbour to Bima in Sumbawa, Makassar in Sulawesi, Manado and as far as Sorong and Timika in Papua. The Bali office is at Benoa Harbour. Tel: (0361) 723-689, www.pelni.co.id.

GETTING AROUND

Balinese roads double up as parade grounds for festival processions. They are becoming increasingly crowded, and traffic jams are frequent.

Public Transport
Minivans
Minivans (*bemo*) operate on fixed routes from terminals or marketplaces in cities and major towns. Some transfer points are at important crossroads. There are no marked places to get off and on; just flag them down and call out "stop" when you want to get out. Fares are based on distance travelled. As passengers and products of all sorts get loaded off and on, things can get hot and crowded. This mode of transport does take time but allows you to meet the locals; beware of pickpockets, though.

Buses
Major bus terminals are at Tegal in Denpasar (services to Kuta); Kereneng in Denpasar (services to places in the city, Batubulan and Sanur); Ubung (services to Tabanan, Singaraja and Jembrana); Batubulan (services to Gianyar, Singaraja, Bangli, Klungkung and Karangasem) and in Singaraja (services to Jembrana, Tabanan, Denpasar and Karangasem).

Taxis
Taxis are metered or have fixed rates from the airport to the major hotels. Check with the driver before you board the taxi as many drivers prefer to charge a flat rate instead of using the meter. Ask your hotel concierge on what the going rate is for the destination you want to get to. Few taxis, outside of the Kuta-Legian-Seminyak area, cruise the streets for passengers, so call one of the numbers below (or ask your hotel concierge to call a taxi for you).
Bali Taxi: Tel: (0361) 701-111
Bali Van: Tel: (0361) 228-271
Komotra: Tel: (0361) 499-449
Praja Taxi: Tel: (0361) 289-090

Motorcycle Taxis
Young men operate motorcycle taxis known as *ojek*; they wait at designated places and take you wherever you want to go. This is very convenient for locations not serviced by public transport. Agree on the price beforehand, and make sure you wear the extra helmet that the driver provides, as it's required by law. The drivers do weave in and out of heavy traffic but are very experienced.

Private Transport
Vehicle with Driver
Chartering a car or minivan with driver can be done by the half-day or full-day. Tip: Rates are cheaper if negotiated on the street rather than from your hotel; look out for young men who call out "transpor" and move their hands as if driving a car.

Rates vary according to the kind of vehicle, its condition, actual travel time, and total number of hours. This amount should include fuel. One way to calculate the rate is to start from a base of US$5 per hour. Add another US$3 for each hour of actual driving time. For example, if you take a 4-hour trip in an air-conditioned minivan from Kuta to Ubud (2 hours of travel time), the rate would be at least US$26.

It is courteous to give your driver money for a meal if you pause for lunch or dinner, or you may even invite him to dine with you (although some drivers may feel shy about doing this). If you are pleased with the driver, a tip of Rp 20,000 is appropriate. You will usually get a better rate if you arrange to use the same driver for all the trips during your stay.

It is easy to charter a minivan with a driver (and a guide if arranged through a tour agency or hotel) for an hour, day or month. Check with:
Ganda Sari Transport, Jl. Raya Ubud 33X, Ubud, tel: (0361) 975-520.
Perama Tourist Service, Jl. Legian 39, Kuta, tel: (0361) 751-551.

Car Hire
Driving in Bali can be dangerous. Generally, drivers do not drive defensively, the roads are narrow and poorly maintained, and stray dogs and chickens frequently dart into the road. If you collide with anything, you are responsible for all costs. It's safer to hire a driver while you relax and enjoy the sights.

Self-drive cars are available in Sanur, Kuta and Ubud, for which you must have a valid Indonesian or international driving licence. It's also advisable to pay the extra costs to ensure you have full insurance coverage. Petrol is not included in the price. You can book a car through your hotel or from any of the companies listed below – they will deliver the car to you and pick it up at the end of the rental period. Always test-drive the car before paying. Note: Drive on the left side of the road.

Prices (per day) range from US$35 for a Suzuki Jeep to US$45 for a larger Toyota Kijang. These rates should include collision insurance, unlimited mileage and pick-up and delivery service.

The following are recommended:

Kuta:
Bali Baru Wisata, Jl. Legian, Kuta, tel: (0361) 761-153.
Hertz, Hotel Patra Jasa Bali, Kuta, tel: (0361) 751-161.
Toyota Rent Car and Leasing, Ngurah Rai Airport, tel: (0361) 753-744.
Jimbaran:
Avis, Jl. Uluwatu 84, Jimbaran, tel: (0361) 701-770.
Toyota Rent Car and Leasing, Jl. Bypass Ngurah Rai, Jimbaran, tel: (0361) 701-747.
Nusa Dua:
CV Agung Rent Car, Jl. Pratama, Nusa Dua, tel: (0361) 771-275.
Golden Bird Bali, Jl. Bypass Ngurah Rai, Nusa Dua, tel: (0361) 756-170.
Hertz, Hotel Putri Bali, Nusa Dua, tel: (0361) 771-010.
Nusa Dua Rent a Car, Jl. Pantai Mengiat 23, Nusa Dua, tel: (0361) 771-905, fax: 772-432.
Sanur:
Bagus Car Rental, Jl. Duyung 1, Sanur, tel: (0361) 287-794.
Bali Car Rental, Jl. Bypass Ngurah Rai 17, Sanur, tel: (0361) 288-550, fax: 282-384.
Norman's Rent a Car, Holiday's Art Shop, Jl. Danau Tamblingan, Sanur, tel: (0361) 288-328, 288-830.
Ubud:
Dwi Tunggal, Padangtegal, Ubud, tel: (0361) 976-301.

Motorcycle Hire

Motorcycles are a convenient and inexpensive way to get around the island, but there are risks due to heavy traffic and poor roads. Helmets are required by law but the cheap ones provided by rental agencies offer little protection, so bring your own or buy a good one from a local shop, especially one with a face shield for protection from sun, rain, bugs and dust. Drive slowly and defensively, as locals and tourists are injured or killed every year in accidents.

The cost of motorbike hire varies according to the model, condition of the machine, length of rental, and time of year. Petrol is not included. Buy full insurance so that you are not responsible for any damage. Be sure to test drive it to check that everything is in working order, especially brakes and lights.

You should have an international driving permit valid for motorcycles, or else go to the Denpasar Police Office to obtain a temporary permit, valid for three months on Bali only. Normally the person who rents you the motorbike will accompany you to the police office. Bring your passport, driving licence from your home country, and three passport-sized photos.

Bicycles

Mountain bikes are available for rent everywhere, but before you pay for one make sure the wheels are properly aligned, the brakes work well, and that there is a working light. Then be selective about where you ride. The main roads of Bali are congested and full of potholes, and motor vehicles spew exhaust fumes into your face, so stick to the quieter country roads. Wear a helmet for extra safety, and try not to ride at night because roads are very poorly lit, or not lit at all.

TOURIST OFFICES

Denpasar Government Tourist Office: Jl. Surapati No. 7, Denpasar. Tel: (0361) 223-602.
Provincial Tourist Services: Jl. S. Parman Niti Mandala, Denpasar. Tel: (0361) 222-387.
Tourist Information Office: Singaraja: Jl. Gajah Mada No. 117, Tel: (0362) 23332. Lovina: Perama Anturan, Tel: (0362) 41161.
Ubud Tourist Information Service: Jl. Raya Ubud, Ubud. Tel: (0361) 973-285, www.ubudvillage.com.

Helpful tourist information can also be found at www.baliandbeyond.co.id.

TOUR OPERATORS

Other than travel agents, major hotels can also arrange tours, car hire, guides, airline tickets and hotel reservation.
Bali Discovery Tours: Komplek Pertokoan, Sanur Raya No. 27, Jl. Bypass Ngurah Rai, Sanur, tel: (0361) 286-283, fax: 286 284, www.balidiscovery.com.
Floressa Bali Tours: Jl. Gandapura III K. No. 16 Tohpati, Denpasar. Tel: (0361) 467-625, Fax: 467-347, e-mail: paultalo@indosat.net.id, www.floressa-bali.com. Specialises in Nusa Tenggara and onward to Kalimantan, Sulawesi and Papua (Irian Jaya). Has branch offices in Jakarta, Maumere (Flores) and Kupang (West Timor).
Golden Kris Tour: Jl. Bypass Ngurah Rai 7, Sanur, tel: (0361) 289-225, fax: 289-228, www.goldenkrisbali.com.
Pacto: Jl. Bypass, Sanur, tel: (0361) 288-247, fax: 288-240.
Satriavi: Jl. Bypass Ngurah Rai 11A, Kuta, tel: (0361) 756-769, fax: 756-768.
Tunas Indonesia: Jl. Danau Tamblingan 107, Sanur, tel: (0361) 288-056, fax: 288-727.
Vayatour: Jl. Bypass Ngurah Rai 107, Sanur, tel: (0361) 285-555, 289-339, fax: 281-144, www.vayatour.com/bali.

MEDICAL SERVICES

Bali International Medical Centre: Jl. Ngurah Rai No. 100X. Tel: (0361) 761-263; Fax: 764-345, e-mail: info@bimcbali.com. It provides 24-hour general medical treatment and emergency evacuation, under supervision by Australian medical personnel.
Klinik SOS Medika: Jl. Bypass Ngurah Rai No. 24X, Kuta 80361. Emergency hotline: (0361) 755-768, Injuries: 764-555, Fax: 764-530, e-mail: jwintsos@indosat.net.id. This clinic opens 8am–10pm and provides international-standard emergency medical care, including specialist and ambulance services.

ACTIVITIES

Multisports

A range of interesting outdoor activities are available, allowing visitors to enjoy the "real Bali". Cycling through villages or walking through rice fields to view flora, fauna and village life is relaxing and informative. Whitewater rafting takes places at either the Ayung or Telaga Waja rivers.
Bali Adventure Tours: Jl. Diponegoro 150 B-29, Denpasar. Tel: (0361) 238-759; Jl. Bypass Ngurah Rai, Kuta. Tel: (0361) 721-480, Fax: 721-481, www.baliadventuretours.com. For rafting, paragliding, rice paddy or jungle treks, mountain biking and elephant safaris. They also package two or three activities together to provide a full day outdoors. Fees include transfers, insurance, equipment, tuition and a meal.
Bali Bird Walks: Beggar's Bush Bar, Campuhan, Ubud. Tel: (0361) 975-009. See some of the many species of birds in Bali with experienced Balinese guides. Easy walk along trails, across rice fields and rivers, and through coconut groves. Fee includes drinking water, binoculars, lunch, tea, coffee and a bird list.
Sobek Bali Adventures: Jl. Tirta Ening 9, Sanur. Tel: (0361) 287-059, Fax: 289-448, www.sobekbali.com. Reputable operator offering a wide range of activities from sea kayaking, bird-watching, jungle trekking, whitewater rafting and mountain cycling. Both half and full days tours with meals and refreshments are offered.

Bungee Jumping

Bali Bungy: Jl. Pura Puseh, Legian. Tel: (0361) 752-658, Fax: 755-425.
A.J. Hackett: Jl. Double Six, Legian. Tel: (0361) 731-144.

Cooking Classes

Be sure to visit Bumbu Bali restaurant, located in Tanjung Benoa, close to the Nusa Dua area. Here you'll find superlative Balinese food served in an ambience-filled restaurant. Bumbu Bali also conducts cooking lessons at its premises. Led by Chef Heinz von Holzen, who has written a cookbook *The Food of Bali*, classes are limited to 12 persons at this hands-on full-day session. Inquiries at tel: 361 774502, fax: 771728, e-mail: hvhfood@balifoods.com; www.balifoods.com.

Golf

Bali Golf and Country Club: Nusa Dua. Tel: (0361) 771-791. Within walking distance of Nusa Dua's main hotels. Exquisite course with 9 holes by the sea and 9 holes on the edge of the hill.
Bali Handara Country Club: Pancasari, Bedugul. Tel: (0368) 288-944. The serious golfer will want to visit this 18-hole championship course, designed by Peter Thompson. The only course in the world set inside a volcano, it is also gazetted among the world's top 50 most beautiful courses. If you stay at the adjoining hotel, there is a 30 percent discount on the green fees.
Bali Hilton: Nusa Dua. Tel: (0361) 771-102. Nine-hole mini-golf course in landscaped gardens.
Grand Bali Beach Hotel: Sanur. Tel: (0361) 288-511. A small 9-hole course that can be used for 18 holes. Guests of the hotel can play for half price. Equipment and caddies are available. An 18-hole miniature golf course is also available.
Le Meridien Nirwana Golf Club and Resort: Tanah Lot, Tabanan. Tel: (0361) 815-960. Greg Norman's challenging course, set amidst rice terraces. Spectacular greens overlook the Pura Tanah Lot temple and the Indian Ocean.

Sailing

Bali Hai Cruises: Benoa Harbour. Tel: (0361) 720-331, Fax: 720-334, www.balihaicruises.com. Day cruises to Lembongan Island and sunset harbour/dinner cruises aboard luxury catamarans. Day cruises include hotel transfers, morning and afternoon tea, lunch, watersports, snorkel equipment, beach club or sea pontoon activities; island tours and diving are optional. Dinner cruise comes with hotel transfers, buffet and entertainment.

Bounty Cruises: Benoa Harbour. Tel: (0361) 733-333, 726-666, Fax: 730-404, www.balibountygroup.com. Offers transfers to and from Lombok and the Gili Meno island, day cruises to Nusa Lembongan island, and evening dinner cruises.
Sail Sensations: Benoa Harbour. Tel: (0361) 725-864, www.sailsensations.com. Offers day sailing to Nusa Lembongan and twilight dining on board its 26-metre (87-ft) yacht. Charters are also available.
Waka Louka Cruises: Benoa Harbour. Tel: (0361) 723-629, 723-659, Fax: 722-077, www.wakaexperience.com. Day cruise to Nusa Lembongan on its luxury sailing catamaran. Meals and refreshments included plus a tour of Lembongan island. The company also organises two interesting land trips – one to Mt. Batukaru and the other to Bukit Tedung.

Surfing

Surfing is reasonably good throughout the year, especially from June to August. The best places for beginners are Kuta, Legian and Seminyak. Intermediate surfers should go to Bingin to the south of the airport, and Canggu to the northwest of Legian. Much further west are Soka Beach at Lalang Linggah in Tabanan and Medewi Beach in Jembrana. For expert surfers there is Kuta Reef (accessible only by boat, from in front of the Sunset Club), Suluban and Padang-Padang. There is great surfing at Nusa Lembongan as well. The following places in Kuta sell and rent equipment:
Tubes: Gang Poppies II, Kuta. Tel: (0361) 753-510. This is the best source of information to find out about surfing conditions.
Dream Land Surf Shop: Kuta Square Block D-24. Tel: (0361) 755-159.
MCD Shop: Jl. Nyangnyang Sari 17, Kuta. Tel: (0361) 735-155; Jl. Legian, Kuta. Tel: (0361) 754-583.
Quiksilver: Jl. Raya Kuta 69X. Tel: (0361) 751-214.
Surfer Girl: Jl. Legian 318, Legian. Tel: (0361) 752-693.

Surfing School

The **School of Surf** run by champion surfer Cheyne Horan (tel: (0361) 735 858, www.schoolofsurf.com) has lessons ranging from half-a-day to five days and caters for different levels.

Diving

The following are good sources of information on where to dive in Bali:

Bali Diving Perdana: Jl. Duyung No. 10, Sanur. Tel: (0361) 286-493, 288-871.
Bali Hai Diving Adventures: Benoa Harbour and Gili Trawangan (Lombok). Tel: (0361) 724-062.
Dive 'n' Dives: Jl. Bypass Ngurah Rai No. 198, Sanur. Tel: (0361) 288-052.
Reef Seen Aquatics Dive Centre: Desa Pemuteran, Gerokgak, Singaraja. Tel/Fax: (0362) 92339, e-mail: reefseen@denpasar. wasantara.net.id. This place has Australian and American PADI instructors.

Other Watersports

Snorkelling, spearfishing, windsurfing and deep-sea fishing are also popular in Bali. Group charters and safari tours are available, along with equipment and instruction.
Baruna Water Sports: Jl. Bypass Ngurah Rai No. 300B, Tuban. Tel: (0361) 753-820. Arrangements can be made for diving, parasailing, jetskiing, waterscooter, windsurfing, canoe and paddleboard, glass-bottom boat, waterskiing and deep-sea fishing.
Blue Oasis Beach Club: Sanur Beach Hotel. Tel: (0361) 288-011 ext. 1792, www.blueoasisbc.com. Sanur's legendary 1998 Asian Windsurfing Champion Oka Sulaksana and his crew run this outfit.

WHERE TO SHOP

While Kuta has the best shopping choices, the entire island is given to thousands of artisans, craftspeople, seamstresses, woodcarvers and painters well-engaged in supplying the tourist demand. Kuta is filled with vendors who crowd the beaches and streets offering friendship bracelets, necklaces and watches. For handicrafts and paintings, head for Kumbasari market in Denpasar, Sukawati market, and Ubud.

Antiques

Be careful when buying antiques: there's no guarantee of the actual age of the items: intricately-carved doors, ornate wedding beds, ceremonial daggers, colonial-style lamps, masks and textiles. Chinese ceramics and sculptures from many parts of Indonesia and China are also available to the discriminating buyer. The antique shops adjacent to the Kerta Gosa in Klungkung house collections of rare Chinese porcelain pieces, with old Kamasan *wayang*-style paintings, antique jewellery and Balinese weavings. Prices are reasonable. On the main streets of Singaraja are a few of the best

> ### Bargain Sensibly
>
> There are many good buys to be found in Bali, especially in Kuta and Legian. In the tourist places, prices are always inflated, so it's worth your while to bargain down to around half of the asking price. In the villages, however, the difference of a few rupiah may mean a day's meals, so exercise common sense. Don't start haggling if you have no intention of buying.

antique shops in Bali. There are also innumerable shops in the areas surrounding Kuta, Legian, Seminyak, Kerobokan, Sanur and Ubud.

Ceramics

Jenggala Ceramic: Jl. Uluwatu, Jimbaran. Tel: (0361) 703-310, www.jenggala-bali.com. A good source for tea sets, dinnerware, vases and anything else you can think of that are made of ceramic, sometimes combined with wood. It also has an excellent café and ceramic-making classes for kids and adults. In Sanur, **Pesamuan Studio** has outlets at One World Gallery on Jalan Hanoman in Ubud, Warung Made II on Jalan Raya Seminyak, and at its factory at Jalan Pungutan No. 25, Sanur.

Gold, Silver Jewellery

Inventive Balinese jewellers forge delicate flowers, bowls and images of demons studded with semi-precious stones. The centres for metalworking are Celuk, Kamasan in Klungkung and Bratan in Buleleng, where such ornaments may be purchased at reasonable prices. Pieces and settings may also be made to order.

To buy gold jewellery, visit the shops on Jalan Hasanudin and Jalan Sulawesi. **Melati** is a reputable establishment that retails mostly 22–24K gold. One of the best goldsmiths is **Nyoman Sadia**, at Jalan Sersan Wayan Pugig No. 5 in Sukawati. The prices here are high but the workmanship is exquisite. **Treasures** (Jl. Ubud Raya next to Ary's Warung, Ubud. Tel: (0361) 976-697) features pricey but exquisitely designed jewellery.

For silver, go to one of the **Putra's** branches: in Ubud on Monkey Forest Road, across from Griya Restaurant on the main road; and there is a wholesale outlet in Puri Agung in Peliatan. Putra's prices are fixed and not inflated. There are also two branches in Kuta featuring modern and contemporary designs. Also try **Jonathan** (Jl. Majapahit No. 81, Jalan Legian, **Mirah**, tel: (0361) 757-780, **Mario's** (Jl. Raya Seminyak No. 19, tel: (0361) 730-977) and **Jusuf's** (Jl. Legian No. 182, tel: (0361) 758-442).

Suarti Silver Works (Tel: (0361) 751-660) has its headquarters on the main road in Celuk. Factory visits and direct orders are welcomed. They also have a large number of outlets dotted around the island, including the major shopping centres in Sanur, Kuta and Ubud. For jewellery par excellence try **Zoein Jewels**, Jl. Duyung Gang 1 No. 13, Sanur. Tel: (0361) 289-420, www.zoeinjewels.com.

Paintings

Bali's classical *wayang*-style paintings have their origins in Kamasan, Klungkung. Cheap renditions can be bought in the parking lot across from Kerta Gosa in Klungkung. For traditional paintings, go to Batuan, Pengosekan (specialises in fish and birds) and Peliatan, Ubud and Penestanan (the Young Artist-style). A good way to start is to visit **Museum Neka**, about 1 km up the road from Campuan, Ubud or **Arma Gallery** in Pengosekan, Ubud, pick out an artist you like, and seek him out at his home.

Stone Carvings

For traditional stone carvings, stop in at the workshops in Batubulan. **Wayan Cemul**, an Ubud stone carver with an international following, has a house full of his weird and wonderful creations at Jalan Kajeng No. 28. Tel: (0361) 973-449.

Textiles

The spiralling designs and geometric patterns of Javanese batik constitute Balinese daily wear. Most of what is sold on the streets is not hand-dyed batik, but printed. A good starting point for "temple clothing" is **Batik Populer** (Tel: (0361) 461-489), the small shops west of the river on Jalan Gajah Mada in Denpasar, or at Jalan Supratman No. 306. There is a wide choice of designs, from simple *cap* (stamped) to the glorious *tulis* batik (individually-waxed designs).

There are a number of spots from where you can purchase Balinese *endek* material. Parts of the island specialise in certain motifs, though the most accessible and well-known are those found in Gianyar. **Cap Togog** (Tel: (0361) 93046) and **Cap Cili** are two showrooms which organise tours to watch the process. Other *ikat* centres are **Sidemen** in Karangasem, **Gelgel** in Klungkung and **Singaraja** in the north.

For a display of *ikat* techniques and a gallery of weavings from throughout Indonesia, visit **Threads of Life Indonesian Textile Arts Centre**, Jl. Kajeng 24, Ubud. Tel: (0361) 972-187, Fax: 976-582, e-mail: tac@threadsoflife.com, www.threadsoflife.com. Threads of Life is a non-profit organisation which supports weavers of traditional cloths in remote villages while simultaneously creating a market for their textiles through education. Demonstrations, classes and workshops are offered.

Songket, another traditional Balinese cloth with gold and silver threads in the weft, is ritual wear for both men and women. The villages of Blayu, Sidemen, and Singaraja are known for *songket*.

Other types of weaving, such as *selendang* (temple sashes) are made in Batuan, Ubud, and Mengwi. The famous *geringsing* (double *ikat*) is made only in Tenganan, from where you can also buy *ikat* cloths from all over the archipelago. For more choices in weavings made elsewhere in Indonesia, try **Arts of Asia** (Jl. Thamrin, Tel: (0361) 423-350) which has the highest quality materials. **Batik Keris** outlets at Nusa Dua Galeria (Tel: (0361) 771-303) and the airport stock quality selections.

Woodcarvings

Good woodcarvings can be found in the shops along the main road in Mas. Particularly well-known is **Ida Bagus Tilem's Gallery and Museum** (Tel: 975-099). The prices are high, but the work is beautiful. You can also seek out woodcarvers in Kemenuh village. For masks, try **Ida Bagus Anom** in Mas, **I Wayan Tangguh** in Singapadu and **I Wayan Regog** in Lantanghidung near Batuan. **Kemenuh**, on the way to Gianyar, also has fine woodcarvings. **Pujung** (past Tegalalang, north of Ubud) is the centre for wooden fruits and flowers.

For exquisite work carved onto delicate tree root, **Muja** in Singapadu is unsurpassable.

South Bali

WHERE TO STAY

Denpasar

There really is no reason to stay in Denpasar unless you have business that can't await your commuting to the resort areas. There are scores of cheap and clean hotels catering to domestic tourists, many of which are found on Jalan Diponegoro, Jalan Suli and Jalan Trijata.

INNA Bali: Jl. Veteran No. 3. Tel: (0361) 225-681, Fax: 235-347. This 1930s resort was once Bali's colonial oasis and its historical charm is still evident in the recently-upgraded

executive rooms across Jalan Veteran. It has a good central location just a block from the town square. There is a good restaurant and bar. **$$**
Hotel Pemecutan Palace: Jl. M.H. Thamrin No. 2. Tel: (0361) 423-491. Situated in Badung palace grounds, this place has royal charm, but not much else. Day-to-day palace life continues in the compound. There is a restaurant on-site. **$$**

Hotel Price Guide

Price categories for standard rooms, usually without breakfast:
$$$$$ = above US$150
$$$$ = US$101–150
$$$ = US$51–100
$$ = US$30–50
$ = under US$30

Sanur

Sanur is peaceful and quiet. The main choice is between the convenience and luxury of the large five-star establishments or the quietude of a private bungalow by the sea. There is a nice shallow beach with a minimal number of beach hawkers, and lots of space for everyone.
Bali Hyatt: Jl. Danau Tamblingan. Tel: (0361) 281-234, 288-271/2, 288-360, Fax: 287-693, www.hyatt.com. A big hotel with almost 400 rooms, including suites overlooking the sea. It is remarkably breezy and public areas are spacious. Pluses are the clay tennis courts, fabulous gardens and a luxury spa. There are several restaurants and boutiques on the grounds. **$$$$**
Besakih Beach Resort: Jl. Danau Tamblingan No. 45. Tel: (0361) 288-423, Fax: 288-426, e-mail: besakih@indosat.net.id. The rooms are set along a meandering garden path that winds gracefully to the sea. **$$$**
La Taverna Bali: Jl. Danau Tamblingan No. 29. Tel: (0361) 288-387, 288-497, Fax: 287-126, www.latavernahotel.com. It has 34 delightful thatched bungalows with Italian stucco walls and elegantly-styled rooms set in a Balinese garden. The resort has its own private beach. **$$$**
Segara Village: Jl. Segara Ayu. Tel: (0361) 288-407, Fax: 287-242, www.segaravillage.com. More than 100 private bungalows, a few patterned after traditional rice granaries, arranged in tiny "villages" bordering the sea. There are three swimming pools, and for families, there is a children's recreation room. The hotel holds classes in traditional Balinese dance, music, painting, woodcarving and batik. **$$$**

Parigata Resort & Spa: Jl. D. Tamblingan 87. Tel: (0361) 286-286, Fax: 286-288, www.parigata.com. A small boutique hotel near the Hyatt with a nice pools and large standard rooms. **$$**
Swastika: Jl. Danau Tamblingan No. 128. Tel: (0361) 288-693, Fax: 287-526. Simple and good value with two pools; breakfast is included. **$**

Kuta and Tuban

Kuta has the best seafront on the island, although it is rather frenetic, catering to budget travellers who like to be in the thick of things. The Legian-Seminyak end of the beach is quieter and better for a prolonged stay. South of Kuta, Tuban is peaceful and good for families, as the surf here is safer.
Hard Rock Beach Hotel: Jl. Kuta Beach, Kuta. Tel: (0361) 761-869, Fax: 761-868, www.hardrockhotels.com. The hotel has more than 400 rooms and suites along the beach and has Bali's largest free-form pool, a children's club, and retail outlets. Dining options include Hard Rock Café of course. A great place for families. **$$$**
Poppies Cottages I: Gang Poppies I, Kuta. Tel: (0361) 751-059, Fax: 752-364, www.poppies.net. A selection of well-designed cottages in a beautiful garden that is only 300 metres (328 yards) from the beach. Very popular, so reservations are essential. **$$$**
Santika Beach Hotel: Jl. Kartika Plaza, Tuban. Tel: (0361) 751-267, Fax: 751-260, www.santikabali.com. An exquisite 170-room hotel situated on the beach with villa-style rooms and three swimming pools. **$$$**
Melasti Beach Bungalows: Jl. Kartika Plaza, Tuban. Tel: (0361) 751-860, Fax: 751-563, e-mail: melasti@indo.net.id. The hotel is located close to the beach and has a swimming pool. **$**

Legian, Seminyak, Petitenget and Canggu

Legian and Seminyak are north of the Kuta beach strip. Further north are Petitenget and Canggu. Located just 15–20 minutes from the centre of Kuta, yet free of the hype, these villages are perfect for extended holidays. Find what suits you best by shopping around.
Alu Bali: Gang Alu, off Jl. Raya Petitenget. Tel: (0361) 736-445, www.alubali.com. Seven 1, 2 and 3 bedroom villas with private swimming pool and a living pavilion in a very chic and contemporary style. Short walk to the beach and popular restaurants La Luciola, Hu'u, Ku De Ta and the Living Room. **$$$$$**

The Legian: Jl. Laksmana, Seminyak. Tel: (0361) 730-622, Fax: 731-291, www.ghmhotels.com. An upscale resort with luxury suites in a low-rise building along a wide beach. Architecture combines Balinese design with modern minimalist touches. Also has an excellent fine dining restaurant and a spa. The hotel provides guests with a complimentary shuttle service to Kuta. **$$$$$**
Oberoi Bali: Jl. Laksmana, Seminyak. Tel: (0361) 730-361, Fax: 730-791, www.oberoihotels.com. Located right on the beach, these luxurious rooms and villas have either a sea or garden view and are equipped with satellite TV and stereo systems. A few villas include a private pool. The hotel's coral-rock verandas and villas are adaptations of classic Balinese palace designs. **$$$$$**
Hotel Tugu Bali: Jl. Pantai Batu Bolong, Desa Canggu, North Kerobokan. Tel: (0361) 731-701, www.tuguhotels.com. An exquisite boutique hotel located in Canggu. Beautiful local décor and furniture, a replica of the Jogja home of the late painter Walter Spies. Ideal for honeymooners. **$$$$$**
Legian Beach Hotel: Jl. Melasti, Legian. Tel: (0361) 751-711, Fax: 752-652, www.legianbeachbali.com. 217 rooms in a large complex wrapped in a relaxed atmosphere near the beach. **$$$**
Resor Seminyak: Jl. Laksmana, Seminyak. Tel: (0361) 730-814, Fax: 730-815, www.resorseminyak.com. The rooms are near the beach and far from the crowds. There is a quaint spa, and beachside dining. **$$$**
The Sura: Jl. Kayu Cendana 1, Seminyak. Tel: (0361) 730-986, www.thesura.com. A small haven in the Seminyak area. 3 units with 7 rooms, each with their own kitchenettes, a very nice swimming pool and lots of green space. A 10-minute walk to the beach. **$$$**

Villa Rental

If the impersonality of a large hotel does not appeal, plump for a stay at a private villa instead. Many wealthy foreigners and Indonesians have built luxury homes in Bali which they rent out to visitors on a daily or weekly basis (or for longer extended periods). Villa accommodations range from 2–10 people and come equipped with kitchen and dining facilities plus a full complement of staff, from driver, cook and gardener.
Contact **Elite Havens**, tel: (0361) 731-074, fax: 736-391, www.elitehavens.com

Hotel Price Guide

Price categories for standard rooms, usually without breakfast:
$$$$$ = above US$150
$$$$ = US$101–150
$$$ = US$51–100
$$ = US$30–50
$ = under US$30

Jimbaran

This is the latest area to emerge as a luxury destination. The calibre of its hotels attract jet-setters who come for hideaway holidays. International-chain hotels are situated around a white-sand bay.

Four Seasons Resort: Jimbaran. Tel: (0361) 701-010, Fax: 701-020, www.fourseasons.com. Built on a terraced hillside amid landscaped gardens, this award-winning resort has a spectacular view of the bay and Gunung Agung. An all-villa resort, each with its own plunge pools. $$$$$
Bali Inter-Continental: Jl. Uluwatu, Jimbaran. Tel: (0361) 701-888, Fax: 701-777, www.interconti.com. The resort has more than 400 rooms set on 14 hectares (35 acres) of landscaped Balinese gardens and pools on a beautiful beach. An ideal viewing spot for Bali's sunsets. $$$$
Ritz-Carlton Resort & Spa: Jl. Karang Mas Sejahtera, Jimbaran. Tel: (0361) 702-222, Fax: 701-555, www.ritz-carlton-bali.com. This four-storey resort has club rooms and villas and sits perched on a bluff overlooking the Indian Ocean. Its Thalasso and Spa features a large seawater therapy pool and offers beauty and body treatments from Asia and from Europe. $$$$

Nusa Dua

If you want isolation from the rest of Bali, this is it. Unfortunately, this exclusive resort area with its white-sand beaches, is also quite sterile.

Grand Hyatt Bali: P.O. Box 53, Nusa Dua. Tel: (0361) 771-234, Fax: 772-038, www.hyatt.com. One of the most spectacular resorts in Asia. There are four Balinese-style villages with five swimming pools. Huge range of facilities. $$$$$
Meliá Bali: P.O. Box 88, Nusa Dua. Tel: (0361) 771-510, Fax: 775-208, www.solmelia.com. The newly-renovated rooms are set in lush landscaped gardens. There are also club villas. Facilities include a gym and watersports options and five restaurants. $$$$$
Nusa Dua Beach Hotel: P.O. Box 1028, Denpasar. Tel: (0361) 771-210, Fax: 771-229, www.nusaduahotel.com. The grandeur of this 380-room hotel is on par with the palaces of Bali's *raja*s. Owned by the sultan of Brunei, it is the top choice for visiting heads of state. There is a huge pool, a well-designed spa and an expansive beachfront. $$$$$
Sheraton Laguna: P.O. Box 77 Kuta, Nusa Dua. Tel: (0361) 771-327, Fax: 771-326, www.sheraton.com. Rooms come with butler service and are set amidst cascading waterfalls and swimming lagoons. $$$$$
The Bale: P.O. Box 76, Nusa Dua 80363. Tel: (0361)775 111, www.thebale-bali.com. This exclusive boutique property has only 20 oversized pavilions, all with individual lap pools. Combines ethnic Balinese materials with chic minimalist architecture. In-house Faces restaurant, led by Swiss chef, serves excellent fare. $$$$$

Tanjung Benoa

Tanjung Benoa, north of Nusa Dua Beach, is lined with hotels and watersports operations.

Novotel Benoa: Jl. Pratama, Tanjung Benoa. Tel: (0361) 772-239, Fax: 772-237, www.novotelbali.com. Lovely rooms furnished in coconut wood. The facilities include satellite TV, a boutique and drugstore, children's programmes, and a shuttle bus to Nusa Dua. $$$$
Club Bali Mirage: Jl. Pratama No. 72, Tanjung Benoa. Tel: (0361) 772-147, Fax: 772-156, www.grandmirage.com. This is an all-in-one club. The price includes all meals, beverages, entertainment and non-motorised watersports. A nice Balinese atmosphere. $$$
Rumah Bali: Jl. Pratama. Tel: (0361) 771-256, www.balifoods.com. Inspired by traditional Balinese compound-style houses, this resort has 1, 2 and 3 bedroom villas and is owned and managed by chef Heinz Von Holzen (see Cooking Classes on page 375). $$$

WHERE TO EAT

That every hotel will have at least one restaurant is a given. Listed below are some culinary experiences beyond hotel confines.

Denpasar

Ayam Bakar Taliwang and **Rumah Makan Taliwang Baru** on Jl. Teuku Umar No. 8, near Simpang Enam, specialise in the Lombok dish, Taliwang chicken. *Inexpensive*
Depot Mie 88: Jl. Sumatra No. 88. Chinese and Indonesian food in a clean setting and at good prices. *Inexpensive*
Rumah Makan Betty: Jl. Sumatra No. 56. Tel: (0361) 224-502. Serves a not-so-spicy menu of Javanese and Chinese dishes. Try the *tauhu goreng telur* (tofu and egg curry), *bubur ayam* (rice porridge with chicken) and *nasi campur*. *Inexpensive*
Warung Wardani: Jl. Yudistira No. 2. Tel: (0361) 224-398. To get there, turn north at Bank Indonesia 1946 (past the popular Chinese eatery Siefu) and continue for a couple of blocks. The best place to try local food, it is also frequented by the Balinese. *Inexpensive*

Sanur

Telaga Naga Restaurant: Jl. Danau Tamblingan (in front of the Bali Hyatt). Tel: (0361) 288-271, 281-234. Managed by Bali Hyatt, this elegant restaurant serves the best Chinese food in Sanur. *Expensive*
Café Batu Jimbar: Jl. Danau Tamblingan. Tel: (0361) 287-374. Popular with local expats and the business lunch crowd. *Moderate*
Kafe Wayang (Tel: (0361) 287-591) and **Jazz Grill** are side-by-side diners in Kompleks Sanur Raya, at the corner of Jalan Bypass Ngurah Rai and Jalan Raya Sanur. Both have consistently good food and a nice atmosphere. *Moderate*
Lumut Restaurant: Jl. Danau Tamblingan. Tel: (0361) 270-009. Has an elegant bar and serves good Western, Indonesian and Chinese cuisine in a garden pavilion. *Moderate*
Mezzanine: Jl. Danau Tamblingan No. 63. Tel: (0361) 270-624. A popular

Hitting the Nightspots

Most of Kuta's nightspots (like **Hard Rock Café** and **Peanuts**) have been overshadowed by newer offerings in **Seminyak**. Popular **Double Six** (tel: (0361) 755-661) recently opened after major renovations. It opens its doors around 10pm but really starts swinging around 2am and lasts until dawn. On Friday and Saturday nights bungy jumping takes place here as well. **Jalan Dhyana Pura** in Seminyak is another hot and happening street that has a string of trendy bars and clubs. Especially popular are **A Bar** (tel: (0361) 733-270), **Spy Bar** (0361) 730-600) and **Oxygen** (0361) 730-885). Two other places along this street, **Kudos Bar and Lounge** (0361) 738-696) and **Q Bar** (0361) 730-927), are popular with the gay crowd.

restaurant serving delicious Asian and international fare, along with scrumptious desserts in a two-level thatched restaurant that features terrace dining. *Moderate*
Swastika Gardens: Jl. Danau Tamblingan. Tel: (0361) 288-573. For those who are tired of paying hotel prices, here is good food from a varied menu. Order in advance to taste the Balinese speciality, smoked duck (*bebek tutu*). *Moderate*

Restaurant Price Guide

Price categories for a three-course meal (Asian or Western), without drinks:
Expensive = US$26–50
Moderate = US$11–25
Inexpensive = under US$10

Kuta and Legian

Kori: Gang Poppies 2, Kuta. Tel: (0361) 758-605, www.korirestaurant.com. Delicious international and local dishes, friendly staff and a nice laidback ambience. Live music on Wednesdays and Fridays; good wine selection, a cigar bar and pool table. *Moderate*
Made's Warung 1: Jl. Pantai Kuta. Tel: (0361) 755-297. Tasty food, drinks and desserts – and a fabulous Indonesian buffet on Saturday night – along with great music, always attracts a host of young Balinese. This place has been around for years, but still maintains its standards. *Moderate*
Poppies Restaurant: Gang Poppies I, Kuta. Tel: (0361) 751-059. Enjoy tasty salads, grilled seafood and steaks in this cosy garden idyll. The food isn't as great as most guidebooks make it out to be – it's not that standards have fallen but newer (and better) restaurants have appeared on the scene. *Moderate*
TJ's Mexican Restaurant: Gang Poppies I. Tel: (0361) 751-093. Serves the best enchiladas, tacos, tostadas, nachos and margaritas this side of the Pacific. Try the eggplant or tofu dip with chips – goes well with a cold beer. *Moderate*
Warung Kopi: Jl. Legian Tengah 427, Kuta. Tel: (0361) 753-602. Come here for great Indian curries, Mediterranean dishes, vegetarian food and all sorts of delectable desserts. *Moderate*

Seminyak

Gado Gado: Jl. Dyanapura 99. Tel: (0361) 730-955. Trendy restaurant serving both Western fare and local dishes. Excellent view of the ocean and lots of shade under the large trees. Open for lunch and dinner seven days a week. *Expensive*

Kafe Warisan: Jl. Kerobokan Banjar Taman No. 68. Tel: (0361) 731-1175. Widely featured in the international press, French and Algerian restaurateurs dish up fresh, light and tasty fare that leans towards French cuisine: pasta, salmon, salads and steaks. The prices are higher than in Kuta restaurants but fair for the quality. Reservations are essential. *Expensive*
Ku dé Ta: Jl. Laksmana, Seminyak. Tel: (0361) 736-969. This upmarket restaurant has received rave reviews since its opening in December 2000. Beautiful beachside location and spiffy waiters dressed in black bring sophistication to the Seminyak dining scene. *Expensive*
Café Moka: Jl. Raya Seminyak. Tel: (0361) 738-721. Great sandwiches, cakes, pasta and pizza in an air-conditioned setting. *Moderate*
Khaima: Jl. Laksmana. Authentic Moroccan food in a delightful setting. In the back is a tent-style room complete with hookah and other paraphernalia of eclectic Moroccan design. *Moderate*
La Lucciola: Jl. Laksmana, Seminyak. Tel: (0361) 261-047. The best Mediterranean food served in a big, two-level thatched structure that overlooks the sea. Great for sunset cocktails. Reservations are essential. *Moderate*
Living Room: Jl. Petitenget No. 200X, Kerobokan. Tel: (0361) 735-735. Good international food with outside seating amidst candles or inside an open-sided pavilion. *Moderate*
Made's Warung II: Jl. Raya Seminyak. Tel: (0361) 732-130. An upscale version of its Jl. Pantai sister located in the quieter suburbs of Seminyak. *Moderate*
Mykonos Taverna: Jl. Laksmana No. 52. Tel: (0361) 733-253. A big hit since it opening in 2001. Authentic Greek food and hearty portions. *Moderate*
Paul's Place: Jl. Laksmana No. 4A. Tel: (0361) 736-715. The newest place in Seminyak. A large complex serving a pan Asian fusion menu. *Moderate*
Trattoria Cucina Italiana: Jl. Laksmana. Tel: (0361) 737-082. Packed almost every night of the week, which says a lot about the food (and the reasonable prices) here. Fantastic pastas, pizzas and salads as well as beef and seafood dishes, but be prepared to wait if you havent made reservations. Tables are packed tight together in this smallish restaurant with a lively atmosphere. *Moderate*
Gateway of India: Jl. Abimanyu No. 10, Legian. Tel: (0361) 732-940. Authentic Indian fare with wonderful *tandoori* dishes. *Inexpensive*

Nusa Dua and Jimbaran

There are not many options outside of hotel eateries. In **Nusa Dua**, the **Galeria Nusa Dua** shopping complex has a wide range of cafés serving a mix of food from Indonesian to Mediterranean. In **Jimbaran**, beachside dining under the stars is a favourite indulgence. Scores of *warung*-style restaurants offer barbecued seafood.
Faces: The Bale, Nusa Dua. Tel: (0361) 775-111. Located in the exclusive all-villa The Bale resort, save this restaurant for a special night out. Creative modern European fare with Asian influences is the perfect foil for the restaurant's starkly minimalist setting. Reservations advised. *Expensive*
Bumbu Bali: Tanjung Benoa. Tel: (0361) 774-502, www.balifoods.com. "Bumbu" means spice paste, and this restaurant is famous for its large menu of authentic, beautifully presented Balinese dishes. Seafood and duck in banana leaf lead the specialities. You can also sign up for cooking classes *(see page 375)*, and free transport is provided from hotels in the area. Traditional Balinese dances on some nights. *Moderate*

Central Bali

WHERE TO STAY

Ubud

Alila Ubud: Desa Melinggih Kelod, Payangan. Tel: (0361) 975-963, Fax: 975-968, www.alilahotels.com. About 15 minutes' north of Ubud town, the rooms and villas are spectacularly situated against a backdrop of mountains, rice terraces and river valleys. $$$$$
Amandari: Sayan. Tel: (0361) 975-333, Fax: 975-335, www.amanresorts.com. Luxurious isolation within the resort's 30 villas that overlook Sungai Ayung. The main swimming pool (filtered with salt, not chlorine) is modelled after a Balinese rice paddy. Out of this world. $$$$$
Campuhan Hotel: Jl. Raya Campuhan. Tel: (0361) 975-368/9, Fax: 975-137, www.tjampuhan.com. The former home of German artist Walter Spies, a major influence among Balinese painters, now comprises 64 bungalows with spectacular views. There is a large spring-fed swimming pool. A 10-minute walk to the centre of Ubud. $$$
Four Seasons Resort: Sayan. Tel: (0361) 977-577, Fax: 977-588, www.fourseasons.com. Spectacular resort overlooking the Ayung River and occupying 7 hectares of terraced rice slopes. The luxuriously appointed

suites and villas (many with private plunge pools and outdoor showers) and the decadent spa facilities promise a sublime experience. $$$$$
Komaneka Resort: Jl. Monkey Forest. Tel: (0361) 976-090, Fax: 977-140, www.komaneka.com. Very central location but set back from main road so very quiet. Charming bungalows, gardens, pool, restaurant, spa, art gallery and boutique. $$$
Ulun Ubud: Jl. Sanggingan. Tel: (0361) 975-024, 975-762, Fax: 975-524, www.ulunubud.com. A gem of a hotel with 23 rooms carved out of the hillside. The grounds are filled with art pieces. One of the lower-level pools has stunning views of the paddy fields. It may be some distance from the Ubud town centre but the hotel provides transport. $$$
Villa Indah: Kedewatan, 4 km (3 miles) from Ubud town. Tel/Fax: (0361) 975-490, Fax: 975-490. Six suites with kitchen and private staff. Your meals are prepared-to-order and served on a wrap-around terrace. Soak in the peaceful view over Sungai Sayan valley. $$$
Nirwana Pension: Padang Tegal Kaja. Tel: (0361) 975-415, e-mail: rodanet@denpasar.wasantara.net.id. Six screened rooms run by batik artist Nyoman Suradnya and his wife Rai; the range includes smaller, simple rooms to larger ones with fans and hot water. The couple run a batik studio and gallery on the premises. Nyoman speaks fluent English and holds batik classes. $

Kintamani Area

Most of the accommodation in Gunung Batur is basic, with very cold mountain-spring water and magnificent views. All room prices are subject to negotiation (most cost under US$20) and generally reflect the market demand. Penelokan has the views and Kintamani is quieter while Toya Bungkah, down at the lake, has good sunrise and sunset views.
Hotel Puri Bening Hayato: Tel: (0366) 51234, Fax: 51248. An international-standard block of 30 rooms and eight bungalows located at the foot of the volcano. Friendly staff. $$$
Lakeview Restaurant & Hotel: Penelokan, Kintamani, Bangli. Tel/Fax: (0361) 975-742, Fax: 975-443. The tiny rooms without private baths are overpriced, but the hotel is popular because it is a stop-over point and has a restaurant with a nice view. $

WHERE TO EAT

Ubud

Ubud's eateries are almost as varied as Kuta's. There is egg *lawar* and yogurt shakes, feta salads and brown bread, and some of the best *nasi campur* on the island.
Ary's Warung: Jl. Raya Ubud. Tel: (0361) 975-053. This place used to serve superlative food at down-to-earth prices. After major refurbishment, however, prices have sky-rocketed while food quality has not always kept par. This was the situation at time of press, but it's possible that the restaurant may have improved over time. Mainly Western fare with Asian inflections. *Expensive*
Mozaic: Jl. Raya Sanggingan. Tel: (0361) 975-768. Highly recommended for those who appreciate fine cuisine and top class presentation and service, rare elsewhere on the island. Reasonably priced for such a high standard. Established by chef and owner Chris Salans in 2001, you have to reserve in advance. *Expensive*

Ubud Hotel Localities

Ubud Proper is quite large. The following is an indication of what to expect in the area where your hotel is located:
Andong: North of town, with views of rice fields. A little noisy.
Tebesaya: Close to town, mostly quiet, cosy family inns.
Padang Tegal Kelod: Within walking distance from town, quite close to rice fields, quiet.
Padang Tegal Kaja: Central but off the main road. Can be noisy.
Monkey Forest Road: Central, many hotels have views of rice fields, some noise if the hotel is not set back from the road.
Ubud Kaja: Central, noisy but convenient.
Campuhan: 5-minute walk west of the town. Restful and expensive.
Penestanan: Up a hill, rural and very quiet, with views of rice fields.
Sanggingan: Up the hill from Campuhan, tranquil and remote.
Sayan, Kedewatan and **Payangan**: 10–15 minutes from Ubud, on a ridge overlooking Ayung River. Quiet and pricey.
Pengosekan: 10–15 minutes south of Ubud, quiet, views of rice fields, lower prices.
Peliatan: South of Ubud and a 20-minute walk from it, centre of the music, dance and painting industries. Noisy and congested.

Restaurant Price Guide

Price categories for a three-course meal (Asian or Western), without drinks:
Expensive = US$26–50
Moderate = US$11–25
Inexpensive = under US$10

Batan Waru Kafe: Jl. Dewi Sita (near the football field). Tel: (0361) 977-528. Excellent food, nice atmosphere and great service. Also a great spot for people watching. Try the *tum tahu ayam* (ground chicken with soya bean curd and basil, wrapped in banana leaf) with a bowl of *soto ayam* and wash it down with a glass of ginger fizz. *Moderate*
Bebek Bengil (Dirty Duck): Jl. Raya Hanoman. Tel: (0361) 975-489. An old favourite, the decor is pure Balinese. *Bales* (pavilions) are scattered amongst ponds and gardens overlooking rice paddies. The menu caters to many tastes: Western, traditional Indonesian and Balinese, including local specialities like the *bebek betutu*, fried crispy duck. *Moderate*
Café Wayan: Jl. Wanara Wana (Monkey Forest Road). Tel: (0361) 975-447. The most famous eatery in Ubud, it is run by Ibu Wayan and her ever-smiling family. The Wayan Special Salad is delicious with a bowl of soup and garlic toast. The seafood and pizza are scrumptious. Ask for a table at the back where you can gaze at rice fields. *Moderate*
Casa Luna: Jl. Raya Ubud. Tel: (0361) 977-409. Good Balinese and vegetarian food, and has a children's menu. Jungle chicken is a speciality dish, as is the smoked duck, which has to be ordered a day ahead. The café also conducts Balinese cooking classes, with a minimum of five students. *Moderate*
Griya Barbecue: Jl. Raya Ubud. Tel: (0361) 975-428. There is mouth-watering grilled tuna, chicken and beef. The dining room overlooking the gorge at the back has a view. *Moderate*
Lotus Café: Jl. Ubud Raya. Tel: (0361) 975-660. Set in an open-air courtyard with a lotus pond, the café's menu includes good home-made pasta, cheesecake and brownies. Dance performances some evenings. *Moderate*
Mumbul Garden Terrace: Jl. Raya Ubud (near Museum Puri Lukisan Art). Tel: (0361) 975-364. A small, intimate café with an extensive menu and the best ice cream on the island. The cooks have published a cook book of their favourite recipes. *Moderate*

Murni's: Jl. Raya Ubud (near the old suspension bridge). Tel: (0361) 975-233. With seating on three levels with great views, this café serves consistently good food, especially grilled fish, prawns and chicken. Try their delicious milk shakes. *Moderate*
Terazo: Jl. Suweta. Tel: (0361) 978-941. A stylish restaurant with good quality international cuisine as well as Asian dishes in big portions. Ask to see the daily specials on the board, which are usually worth trying. The food is good here so save some space for its delicious desserts. *Moderate*

Hotel Price Guide

Price categories for standard rooms, usually without breakfast:
$$$$$ = above US$150
$$$$ = US$101–150
$$$ = US$51–100
$$ = US$30–50
$ = under US$30

East Bali

WHERE TO STAY

Nusa Penida, Nusa Lembongan
Arid Nusa Penida island has only one place to stay in the government-run *losmen* in Sampalan, while Nusa Lembongan, which attracts surfers, divers and snorkellers, has a number of *losmen* and three hotels, and is accessible by catamaran from Benoa.
Nusa Lembongan Resort: Nusa Lembongan. Tel: (0366) 725-864, Fax: 725-866, www.nusa-lembongan.com. There are 12 villas with private terrace dining. Facilities include a spa and a restaurant. $$$$
Wakanusa: Nusa Lembongan. Tel: (0366) 723-629, Fax: 722-077, www.wakanusa.com. Ten bungalows laid out in a cozy compound, with a restaurant and watersports facilities. $$$

Balina Beach, Manggis
One of the major diving centres in Bali, Balina is a wide, white-sand beach 5 km (3 miles) from Candidasa, with a few hotels.
Alila Manggis: Desa Buitan, P.O. Box 13, Manggis, Karangasem. Tel: (0363) 41011, Fax: 41015, www.alilahotels.com. With rooms in elegant coconut-wood furnishing that face both pool and beach, the hotel has a restful air. There is a very nice restaurant set on a beautiful water garden. Cooking-classes run by the hotel chef are a popular diversion. $$$–$$$$
Puri Bagus Manggis: Jl. Candidasa, Puri Bagus Manggis, Karangasem. Tel: (0363) 41304, Fax: 41305, www.bagus-discovery.com. This former Balinese house has teak-furnished rooms with hill or paddy views and garden baths. Private dining. $$$

Candidasa
A string of hotels, restaurants and shops make Candidasa a veritable tourist area, but one that thankfully has a low profile. Due to overdevelopment, the beach has completely disappeared and is visible only at low tide.
Puri Bagus Candidasa: P.O. Box 129, Candidasa, Karangasem. Tel: (0363) 41131, Fax: 41290, www.bagus-discovery.com. The traditional Balinese villas have either a sea or garden view. Activities include sailing and scuba diving. $$$
The Water Garden: P.O. Box 39, Amlapura. Tel: (0363) 41540, Fax: 41290, www.watergardenhotel.com. An elegant hotel built of teak with 14 rooms set amid pools and gardens. $$$

WHERE TO EAT

Candidasa
The food in Candidasa primarily emphasizes fish dishes, with Asian and Western cuisines complementing the local traditional rice dishes like *nasi campur* and *nasi goreng*.
The Kedai: Jl. Raya Candidasa. Serves contemporary Asian and Western food combined with traditional food, primarily fish. The setting is a large open-air pavilion with a cone-shaped *alang alang* (grass) roof. Very stylish. *Moderate*
Lotus Restaurant Candidasa: Jl. Raya Candidasa. Food is similar to the other Lotus Cafés around Bali; consistently good. Great location, right by the beach. *Moderate*
TJ's Café: Tel: (0363) 41540. A branch of the famous Kuta café, this TJ's serves not Mexican meals but excellent salads and desserts in an elegant atmosphere, with prices to match. *Moderate*
Pandan Restaurant: On the beach. Tel: (0363) 41541. Serves Balinese food on Tuesday and Friday, including fruit and a cocktail. *Inexpensive*
Pondok Bamboo: Tel: 41534. Excellent grilled fish and iced juices. *Inexpensive*

North Bali

WHERE TO STAY

Lovina Beach
A northern beachfront alternative, Lovina is 10 km (6 miles) west of Singaraja. Serene, black-sand beaches are protected by extensive coral reefs. The snorkelling is superb, with the reef close enough even for beginner swimmers.
Damai Lovina Villas: Jl. Damai, Kayuputih. Tel: (0362) 41008, Fax: (0362) 41009, www.damai.com. These luxurious villas are set on a mountain slope and surrounded by rice fields, spice plantations and tropical jungle. It's a quiet and peaceful getaway with an excellent restaurant. 8 villas. $$$$
Puri Bagus Lovina: P.O. Box 22627, Lovina, Singaraja. Tel: (0362) 21430, Fax: 22627, www.bagus-discovery.com. The best in Lovina, several of the 40 air-con villas come with two bedrooms and a private pool. Friendly staff. $$$
Sol Lovina: Jl. Raya Lovina Singaraja. Tel: (362) 41755, Fax: 41659, www.solmelia.com. Located in Lovina beach, it features resort style accommodations. Popular with dive enthusiasts. $$$
Jati Reef Bungalows: Desa Tukad Mungga, Pantai Hepi Singaraja. Tel: (0362) 41052, Fax: 41160. Ideally located behind rice fields, near the beach. The rooms have well-thought out details such outdoor showers and safe deposit lockers. There are also four fan-cooled bungalows with large garden bathrooms. $$

Pemuteran, Menjangan
Part of the Bali Barat National Park, this is a haven for all-season diving and snorkelling. Many visitors stay at Pemuteran on the north shore, which has professional diving facilities, and take a 30-minute boat ride to Menjangan island.
Puri Ganesha: Desa Pemuteran, Gerogak, Buleleng. Tel: (0362) 93433, www.puriganesha.com. The ultimate resort in Pemuteran for people who are seeking privacy, quality and personal service. Gorgeous villas each have their own private beachfront. $$$$–$$$$$
Matahari Beach Resort: Desa Pemuteran, Kecamatan Gerogak, Buleleng. Tel: (0362) 92312, Fax: 92313, www.matahari.com. Luxurious Balinese-style bungalows with garden showers, located 200 metres (220 yards) from the beach. There is a dive centre, restaurant and a luxurious spa. $$$$

WHERE TO EAT

In Singaraja, good eateries are few and far between. One of the most popular is the **Chinese Gandhi Restaurant** (Tel: (0362) 21163) with an extensive menu. *Inexpensive*

In the Lovina area, fresh seafood is the best meal while most restaurants offer a variety of Indonesian dishes. The food is like the lifestyle: simple and satisfying.
Badai Restaurant: On the main road. A very popular tourist hang-out that serves delicious fish dishes. Vegetarian fare is also available. *Inexpensive*
Dhyana Bar and Restaurant: On the ocean side of the main road. A well-managed place that offers home-cooked food. The mixed seafood grill and yogurt *lasis* are house specialities. *Inexpensive*

Hotel Price Guide

Price categories for standard rooms, usually without breakfast:
$$$$$ = above US$150
$$$$ = US$101–150
$$$ = US$51–100
$$ = US$30–50
$ = under US$30

West Bali

WHERE TO STAY

Along the coast north of Kuta and Legian lies a stretch of black-sand beach known only to surfers. With a dangerous reef and heavy undertow, the waters are not safe for swimmers or beginner surfers.
Dewi Sinta Cottage: Jl. Tanah Lot, Kediri, Tabanan. Tel: (0361) 812-933, Fax: 813-956. There are standard rooms with terraces as well as spacious new suites with bathtub and TV. Lovely pool and views of golf courses. Clean place with friendly staff and a nice restaurant. $$
Medewi Beach Cottages: Medewi Beach, Pekutatan, Jembrana, Negara. Tel: (0365) 40029/30, Fax: 41555, 40034. The best surf beach in the area. The 20 cottages – with either garden or ocean views – come with a large bath, satellite TV, refrigerator and private terrace. Seven standard rooms have fans. $$

Nusa Tenggara

Lombok

GETTING THERE

By Air

According to long-delayed plans that have been resurrected, Lombok will have a new international airport by 2006. In the meantime, SilkAir flies from Singapore six times a week, while the reliable AirMark Indonesia Aviation operates several daily flights from Bali. Garuda runs flights from Lombok to Yogyakarta, that continue on to Jakarta and Surabaya. Merpati flies daily between Denpasar and Lombok; and to Sumbawa Besar and Bima in Sumbawa, and Surabaya in Java.

Lombok's Selaparang Airport is in the capital, Mataram, only 3 km (2 miles) from the city. Most visitors head straight for the main tourist area of Senggigi, north of Mataram.
AirMark: Tel: (0370) 631-550, (Selaparang Airport), Tel/Fax: (0370) 646-847. Bali office: Putri Mandalika, Jl. Hang Tuah, Sanur, Tel: (0361) 287-450, Fax: 285-330.
Garuda: Jl. Panca Usaha No. 11, Mataram. Tel: (0370) 637-950, 638-259.
Merpati: Jl. Pejanggik No. 69, Mataram. Tel: (0370) 636-745, 632-226.
SilkAir: Jl. Senggigi Raya, Komplek Pasifik Supermarket. Tel: (0370) 693-877, Fax: 693-822.

By Sea

The public ferry departs every 2 hours from Padang Bai in Bali to Lombok's Lembar Harbour, which is 20 km (12 miles) south of Mataram. Travel time is about 4 hours and the waters can be rough. High-speed catamarans which depart from Bali's Benoa Harbour *(see below)* take 2½–3 hours to make the same journey.

Transfer to your hotel by unmetered taxi (it's about US$5 to Senggigi, less to go to Mataram).
Bounty Cruises: Lembar Harbour. Tel: (0370) 693-666, Fax: 641-177. Bali office: Jl. Nakula No. 18, Seminyak, Tel: (0361) 733-333, 726-666, Fax: 730-404, e-mail: reserv@bounty.famili.com. Daily departures from Bali to Senggigi, and on to Gili Meno.
Mabua Intan Express: Lembar Harbour. Tel: (0370) 81195, 81125, Fax: 81124. Bali office (Benoa Harbour) Tel: (0361) 721-212, Fax: 723-615, e-mail: mabuaexp@indosat.net.id. Daily departures, but these depend on weather and sea conditions (as well as tourist demand). Call first before going to the harbour.

GETTING AROUND

Motorcycles

Motorbike rental is available in Ampenan, Mataram and Senggigi for US$7–8 a day. Enquire at your hotel or any motorcycle shop.

Taxis

Lombok Taxi: Tel: (0370) 27000, Fax: 23972. Metered taxis with courteous drivers. Flag one down on the street, or phone ahead to book one. Hourly or day-rate charter also available.

Bemo and Buses

Bemo (mini-vans) and buses service all the towns on the island, but they are slow and uncomfortable. The central terminal is at the crossroads at Sweta, just to the east of Cakranegara – there is a signboard displaying the fares to all destinations. *Bemo* can also be chartered for the day at US$25–30.

Car Rental

It is worth paying a bit more for a taxi or rented car with an English-speaking driver.
Rinjani Rent-a-Car: Jl. Bung Karno No. 6B. Tel: (0370) 645-183.
Toyoto Rent-a-Car: Tel: (0370) 626-363, Fax: 627-071, e-mail: lombok@trac.astra.co.id.

TOURIST OFFICES

Department of Tourism, Art & Culture: (Regional office) West Nusa Tenggara Province, Jl. Singosari No. 2, Mataram 83127. Tel: (0370) 634-800, 632-723, 635-308/874, Fax: 637-233.
Lombok-Sumbawa Tourism Promotion Board: Lombok Raya Hotel, Jl. Panca Usaha No. 11, Mataram. Tel: (0370) 641-220, Fax: 634-224, www.visitlombok.com.

TOUR OPERATORS

A&T Holidays: Jl. Gelatik No. 7D, Cakranegara. Tel: (0370) 640-107/8, Fax: 34533, www.lombok.bali.net. This rapidly-expanding agency offers innovative tours. Try its Jalan-jalan city tour or mountain biking, sailing or golfing trips.
Bidy Tour: Jl. Ragi Genep No. 17, Ampenan. Tel: (0370) 632-127, 634-095, Fax: 631-821, 637-307, www.bidytour@indo.net.id. The largest agency in Lombok offers city tours and trips to pottery, weaving and handicraft villages. It also arranges surfing, windsurfing, snorkelling and fishing trips, as well as trekking excursions.

WHERE TO STAY

International-standard hotels and budget *losmen* abound along Senggigi beach.

Senggigi

Pool Villa Club: Jl. Raya Senggigi. Tel: (0370) 693-210/9, Fax: 693-200/229, www.aerowisata.com. 16 luxury villas in exotic furnishings come with a private sun-deck and jacuzzi. There is a swimming lagoon and a spa, and the club house provides books, music and videos. Good for families, with baby-sitting services. French, Continental and Asian restaurants. $$$$$
Sheraton Senggigi Beach Resort: Jl. Raya Senggigi Km 8. Tel: (0370) 693-333, Fax: 693-140, www.sheraton.com/senggigi. This five-star resort with rooms and luxury suites is set among inviting pools. There is a spa and a fitness centre. $$$$$
Holiday Inn Resort Lombok: Jl. Raya Mangsit. Tel: (0370) 693-444, Fax: 693-092/206, www.holidayinn.com. A selection of rooms, chalets and villas with satellite TV. There is a health club, restaurants and a clinic on the premises. $$$$

The Hilberon Resort: Jl. Raya Mangsit Senggigi. Tel: (0370) 693-898, Fax: 693-252, www.hilberon.com. European-style bungalows set among landscaped gardens. $$$$
Alang-Alang Boutique Beach Resort: Jl. Raya Mangsit No. 888, Senggigi. Tel: (0370) 693-518, Fax: 693-194, www.alang-alang-villas.com. There are 18 bungalows and a palatial villa nestled in a private cove. A nice touch is the free-form swimming pool. $$$

Mataram

Hotel Lombok Raya: Jl. Panca Usaha No. 11, Mataram. Tel: (0370) 632-305, Fax: 636-478. A three-star hotel with large, air-con rooms with TV. There is a pool and a restaurant. $$
Hotel Sahid Legi Mataram: Jl. Sriwijaya No. 81, Mataram. Tel: (0370) 636-276, Fax: 636-281, www.sahidhotels.com. Conveniently-located downtown, the hotel has rooms with TVs, a business centre and a free-form swimming pool. $$

How to Tackle Nusa Tenggara

Tips

Travel to these south-eastern islands requires a spirit of adventure, a willingness to endure minor discomforts, and plenty of time. Even though flights to remote islands appear on Merpati schedules, they are often cancelled. PELNI ships servicing the islands are infrequent and rarely comfortable. Delays, cancellation and overbookings are common.

There are a few hotels in the district capitals; elsewhere, there are the *losmen* (homestays) with only basic amenities.

Conservative and modest dress is very important in Nusa Tenggara. Women should be conscious of Muslim sensitivities, and remember to keep shoulders, midriffs and thighs covered.

It is best to carry all the cash you will need before setting out, as money-changers, banks and ATM machines are few and far between.

Tours

Several tour operators in Bali offer Nusa Tenggara sailing or dive itineraries. Recommended is:
Dian N. Gafar: Perum Kedua Permai A1, Banjar Cengkilung, Peguyangan Kangin. Mobile: 0812-3687-188, e-mail: balibugis@yahoo.com. Organises a few charters a year to the eastern Indonesian islands, primarily the Lesser Sundas (Nusa Tenggara), Maluku and the Banda Sea. Also combines Maluku and Banda expeditions with Papua, including the Rajah Ampat islands and down the south coast to Timika to visit the Asmat people living in the longest stretch of mangrove forest in the world. Also arranges customised expeditions and accompanies passengers onboard as expedition leader, and snorkel or dive master. Guest lecturers can also be provided on board.

Sailing

The best way to tour the islands is the same way merchants of yore saw them — by sea. There are several vessels plying the waters between Bali and points east: basic live-aboard dive boats, *(see page 386 for recommendations)*, a few traditional *pinisi* (schooners), and a luxurious tall ship. Some are available only by charter, others have regular runs. Most go to Komodo National Park, the primary tourist destination in Nusa Tenggara.
S/S Adelaar Tall Ship Adventures: Bali International Marina, Benoa Harbour, Bali, Tel (mobile): (081) 835-4277, Fax: (0361) 723-604, www.adelaar-cruises.com. By charter only. Sail on a well-restored 1902 Dutch schooner. It sleeps 16 in seven air-con cabins with common facilities. The main salon has a library where you can watch videos. Friendly, helpful crew and excellent cook. The charter rate is about US$2,000 per day.
Mona Lisa Cruises: Jl. Mertasari 2, Sanur, Bali. Tel: (0361) 289-388, Mobile: 0812 3829 690, e-mail: lheureux@indo.net.id, www.mlcruise.com. Charter a traditional *pinisi*, sailing to Nusa Tenggara, Maluku and Papua (Irian Jaya). There are six air-con double cabins, with common facilities. Equipped with safety equipment and water separator. The rate is US$1,800 per day, depending on the itinerary.
Ombak Putih Cruises: P.O. Box 3356, Denpasar 80000, Bali. Tel: (0361) 730-191, Fax: 733-942, www.indonesiacruises.com. Sail on a Bugis *pinisi* on one of its scheduled runs to Komodo, Lombok, Sumbawa, Sumba and South Sulawesi. There are 12 air-con cabins, each with attached bathroom. You can waterski, snorkel or canoe. An eight-day cruise costs US$1,320 per person.
Sea Trek Sailing Adventures: Jl. Danau Tamblingan No. 77, Sanur 80228, Bali. Tel: (0361) 283-192, Fax: 285-440, www.seatrekindonesia.com. Travel on a wooden *pinisi* with eight air-con cabins, each with attached bathroom. Activities include snorkelling and fishing. There are scheduled cruises to Nusa Tenggara and Papua (Irian Jaya) for US$550–2,220 per person, depending on itinerary.

Getting to the Gilis

Public boats from Bengsal beach to Gili Air cost about US$1 per trip, and a bit more to go to Gili Trawangan. You have to wait until they fill up. It costs about US$4 to charter a boat at a new ticket office on the beach, on the left. Ignore the touts who try to convince you that the office is closed. Check it out yourself.

Gili Islands

Gili Meno
The smallest and least developed of the Gili Islands, it allows the illusion of a real island escape.
Bounty Beach Bungalows: Tel: (0370) 649-090, 642-361, Fax: 641-177, www.balibountygroup.com. Affiliated with Bounty Cruises, the resort's 17 air-con bungalows have open-air baths and private balconies. There is swimming pool and a restaurant. Watersports are available, including glass-bottom boat rides and snorkelling. $$$

Gili Trawangan
The many *losmen* on this party island are generally fully-booked in July and August. Trawangan has beachfront restaurants, bars, money-changers, Internet cafés – the works. After dinner, the centre of the island turns into a disco scene.
Vila Ombak: Tel: (0370) 642-336, Fax: 642-337. Bali office: Tel: (0361) 730-204, Fax: 731-106, www.vilaombak.com. Traditional, air-con Sasak-inspired huts and bungalows. An interesting feature is the two-level swimming pool with whirlpool. It has a seaside pizzeria, a spa and a diving school. $$

Gili Air
This island has the largest local population and is a great place for families. There are a few bars.
Hotel Gili Air: Office: Jl. Pemenang, Mataram. Tel: (0370) 634-435. It has rooms with air-con or fans, private showers and hot water. There is a bar and a restaurant. $

Other Areas

There are alternatives to the usual tourist destinations. In the south, the Novotel Lombok Coralia rules in luxurious isolation. In the north-west, The Oberoi is a draw for the rich and famous. In Central Lombok, there's a haven near the Balinese water palace garden. New on the luxury scene are unique floating villas near Sekotong Barat, on Lombok's south-westernmost peninsula.

The Oberoi Lombok: Medana Beach, Tanjung. Tel: (0370) 638-444, Fax: 632-496, www.oberoihotels.com. This luxurious resort has 20 villas and 30 terrace rooms along a remote beach; they feature sunken baths, satellite TV and CD sound systems. Most villas have a garden shower and private pool. The resort has restaurants, a health club and a spa. $$$$$
Nirvana Roemah Air: Jl. Raya Medang, Sekotong Barat. Tel: (0370) 640-107, Fax: 634-533, e-mail: balisales@lombokandbeyond.com. This is Lombok's first and only floating village resort. Constructed on double-hull fishing platforms known as *bagan*, these villas offer both tranquility and luxury. $$$$
Novotel Lombok Coralia: Mandalika Resort, Pantai Putri Nyale, Kuta. Tel: (0370) 653-333, Fax: 653-555, www.novotel-lombok.com. A delightfully unusual resort that is a re-creation of an ancient Sasak village. Thatched bungalows on the beachfront surround water-garden pools and statuary. There are three pools, a spa and several restaurants. $$$$
Suranadi Hotel: Jl. Raya Suranadi No. 1, Narmada. Tel: (0370) 633-686, 636-411, Fax: 635-630, www.suranadihotel.com. Dating from the colonial era, this hotel is set in a nature reserve 300 metres (1,000 ft) above sea level. It offers spectacular views from its 18 cottages lining a spring-fed swimming pool. $$
Matahari Inn: Kuta. Tel: (0370) 655-000, 654-832, Fax: 654-909, www.lombokonline.com/matahari. Owned by a Swiss lady and her Sasak husband, this clean place offers a range of rooms and bungalows. There is a swimming pool, and free transport to nearby beaches is provided. $

Restaurant Price Guide

Price categories for a three-course meal (Asian or Western), without drinks:
Expensive   = US$26–50
Moderate   = US$11–25
Inexpensive = under US$10

WHERE TO EAT

Ayam pelicing, searing hot curry chicken, is Lombok's speciality. Balinese roast suckling pig, *babi guling*, prepared by the Lombok Balinese beats anything on the mother island. Outside of the areas listed below (where the food is cheap), it is safer to eat in hotel restaurants.

Mataram, Ampenan, Cakranegara

Arab restaurants in Mataram often serve both Yemeni and Lombok dishes. **Taliwang**, in the shopping centre on Jl. Pejanggik, specialises in *ayam pelecing* (fried chicken), as does **Restaurant Taliwang** (Jl. A.A. Gede Ngurah. Tel: (0370) 682-530/15). The **Garden House** (Jl. Pusat Pertokoan. Tel: (0370) 632-233) serves Indonesian and Chinese food.

Tjirebon and **Pabean**, two old Chinese restaurants on Jalan Pabean in Ampenan and favourite hang-outs of backpackers, are centrally-located and serve good food. Tjirebon has cold beer and steak with fries.

In Cakranegara, there are many restaurants along Jalan Selaparang. **Asia** and **Harum** serve Chinese food, while **Minang** has West Sumatran *nasi padang*.

Senggigi

The main road to Senggigi is lined with a good number of restaurants. Recommended are the following:
Café Wayan: Tel: (0370) 693-098. A sister restaurant of the famous Café Wayan in Ubud, Bali, though not quite as good. Western fare, local dishes and delicious cakes and pastries. *Moderate*
Kafe Alberto: 4 miles (6 km) from Senggigi towards Ampenan. Tel: (0370) 693-039/313. Serves grilled seafood, home-made pasta and pizza from a wood-fired oven. *Moderate*
Marina Pub: Tel: (0370) 693-136. On the menu is Western food, burgers and steaks. *Moderate*
Alang-Alang: Adjacent to Puri Mas. Seafood is served in a beautiful garden setting. *Inexpensive*
Kafe Espresso: Tel: (0370) 693-148. Serves sandwiches, soup and pasta, but an Indonesia menu is also available. *Inexpensive*
Lombok Coconut: North of Senggigi on a hillside. A nice environment with spectacular sunset views across the Lombok Strait. *Inexpensive*
Pasifik Restaurant: Pasifik Supermarket. Serves a range of cuisines, including Indonesian, Chinese and Italian. The **Blue Ocean** bar is upstairs. *Inexpensive*
Putri Lombok: Central Senggigi. Tel. (0370) 693-011. Serves Mexican food, steaks and barbecued food and superb margaritas. The downstairs bar has the coldest draught beer around and an extensive drinks list. *Moderate*

On the beachfront at Senggigi Art Market (*Pasar Seni*), **Café Coco Loco** serves Western and local dishes, **Warung Lino** has grilled seafood, while **Kafe Senggigi Indah** serves Italian, Indonesian and barbecued food.

NIGHTLIFE

The **Tropicana Club & Restaurant** (Jl. Raya Senggigi. Tel: (0370) 693-432) is the hottest spot in town, transforming itself into a disco after dinner. Or head for **Indigo** (Jl. Raya Senggigi), a sophisticated place for cocktails, either before or after dinner.

WHERE TO SHOP

Textiles
In these villages, traditional textiles are woven by hand: **Sukarare** (*tenun Lombok*), **Pujung** (*kain lambung*), **Purbasari** (*kain Purbasari*) and **Balimurti** (sacred *beberut* cloth). **Labuhan Lombok** also produces fine blankets.

Pottery
The **Lombok Pottery Centre** (Jl. Sriwijaya No. IIIA. Tel: (0370) 640-350) offers high-grade earthenware. Lombok clay is also crafted into contemporary ceramic tableware at **Citra Lombok Ceramics**, at Jalan Brawijaya No. 26 in Cakranegara. Tel/Fax: (0370) 634-502. The villages of **Banyumulek**, **Masbagik** and **Penujak** all produce pottery and sell them as well.

Baskets
Lombok's rattan and grass baskets are extremely fine and sturdy and many of these are produced in the eastern villages of **Kotaraja** and **Loyok**. Baskets, pots and handicrafts are cheap and plentiful at the **Mandalika Market** by the bus terminal in Sweta, or at the **Cakranegara Market** to the west of the Pura Meru temple.

Antiques
Visit **Sudirman's Antiques**, located a few hundred metres down a side lane from Jalan Pabean in Ampenan (the entrance is opposite the *bemo* station). A second outlet is on Jalan Raya Senggigi.

Parmour Antiques has two outlets: One at Jalan Montong Buwuh, Km 13, Ampenan (Tel: (0370) 693-692), and the other, a large gallery, at Jalan Raya Senggigi (Tel: (0370) 693-104). The gallery features fine antiques and furniture collected by its owner Agus Heri Gomanthy, who is a good source of information on the subject.

ACTIVITIES

Rafting
Lombok Inter Rafting: Jl. Raya Senggigi. Tel: (0370) 693-202. It arranges rafting trips led by experienced river guides to the Sungai Segara on the slopes of Gunung Rinjani.

Trekking
Rinjani Trek Ecotourism Programme: Hotel Lombok Raya, Mataram. Tel: (0370) 641-124, 632-305, e-mail: rinjani@indo.net.id, www.lomboksumbawa.com offers guides, maps, tourist information and Mt. Rinjani climbing, plus wildflower, village and waterfall walks for the less adventurous. Established with the assistance of New Zealand aid, this programme is a role model for national park management throughout Indonesia.

Golf
Rinjani Country Club Golf & Resort: Golong, Narmada, 20 km (12 miles) east of Mataram. Office: Jl. Sriwijaya No. 396, Mataram, Tel: (0370) 637-316, Fax: 627-396. The resort is a joint venture with the Japanese and features an 18-hole course. There is a Japanese golf professional in residence. Non-guests may use the pool for a small fee. $$$

Diving
There are more than 15 dive sites mapped around the Gili islands. Certified foreign and Indonesian dive instructors offer courses in several languages.
Dream Divers: Gili Air: Tel: (0370) 634-547. Gili Trawangan: Tel: (0370) 634-496. Senggigi office: Tel: (0370) 693-738, www.dreamdivers.com. This is a German-run diving school offering instruction by PADI-certified instructors and dive-masters.
Reefseekers Dive Centre and Turtle Nursery: Gili Air. Tel: (0370) 641-008, Fax: 641-005, www.reefseekers.net. An ecologically-minded PADI diving centre that also arranges tours and airport transfers. Proceeds go towards the care of turtle hatchlings, which the centre works toward returning to the sea.

Sumbawa

GETTING THERE

By Air
Merpati flies to Sumbawa Besar from Denpasar via Lombok, and between Bima and Denpasar, Mataram, Labuhanbajo, Maumere, Ende, Tambulaka and Kupang. Merpati also flies daily from Denpasar to Maluk via Lombok. Opened in February 2004 is a new airstrip at Sekongkang, with Merpati flights from Denpasar, stopping in Mataram. For further information see the Merpati website: www.merpati.co.id.

Sumbawa Besar office: Jl. Yos Sudarso, Tel: (0371) 22002, Fax: 21991.
Bima office: Jl. Soekarno Hatta 60, Tel: (0374) 45114, Fax: 44074.
Maluk office: Trophy Hotel, Jl. Raya Maluk, Tel: (0367) 35116/8/9, 35130.

By Sea
Daily ferries take 3 hours from Lombok to Poto Tana in West Sumbawa. *Bemo* meet the ferries to take passengers to either Sumbawa Besar (another 3 hours) or to Bima (9 hours). A weekly 925-passenger fast-ferry service travels direct from Benoa (in Bali) to Bima and then on to Kupang, in East Timor.

Contact **Gama Dewata Bali Tours** in Bali: Tel: (0361) 263-568, 232-704, Fax: 263-569.

TOUR OPERATORS

Sumbawa Besar
Tambora Duta Wisata Tours & Travel: Jl. Kebayan No. 2. Tel: (0371) 22111, 21555, 22555, Fax: 22624, e-mail: tambora_hotel@hotmail.com. Arranges city tours, buffalo races, fishing, trekking and tailor made tours. Also safari adventure tours and scuba diving to Moyo Island, snorkelling and scuba diving tours to Pulau Satonda, and trekking tours to Gunung Tambora. For diving tours see www.divenet.info or e-mail: sumbawa_kencanabeach@hotmail.com.

Bima
Ora Tours & Travel: Jl. Manggemaci No. 10. Tel: (0374) 43339, 42810, Fax: 42426, e-mail: oratravel@plasa.com. Can arrange a boat that sleeps 18 people for trips to Komodo and Flores.

WHERE TO STAY

Sumbawa Besar
Kencana Beach Safari Resort: Jl. Raya Tano, 11 km, Badas. Tel: (0371) 22555, Fax: 22439, e-mail: sumbawa_kencanabeach@hotmail.com. Attractive beachfront cottages with fan or air-conditioning located on

Hotel Price Guide

Price categories for standard rooms, usually without breakfast:
$$$$$ = above US$150
$$$$ = US$101–150
$$$ = US$51–100
$$ = US$30–50
$ = under US$30

a quiet little bay just west of Badas Harbour looking out to Moyo Island. An open-air restaurant serves a mixture of Indonesian and European food, and the swimming pool is surrounded by tropical gardens. Diving and fishing tours to Moyo and Satonda Island depart from here. $
Tambora Hotel: Jl. Kebayan No. 2, Sumbawa Besar. Tel: (0371) 21555, Fax: 22624, e-mail: tambora_hotel@hotmail.com. Located in the heart of Sumbawa Besar just 5 minutes from the airport, Tambora Hotel's 60 rooms offer a range of accommodation from basic to suites with air-con and hot water. There is a restaurant and a mini-market next door. $

Hu'u

Amangati: Jl. Raya Hu'u, Nangadoro, Dompu. Booking office: Kuta Amangati, Jl. Bakung Sari, Kuta, Bali. Tel: (0361) 753-052, www.amangati.com. Popular with surfers, Amangati has the best budget bungalows. Its restaurant has a big-screen TV showing non-stop surfing videos and serves good European and Indonesian food. $

Maluk

Trophy Bar & Hotel: Jl. Raya Muluk. Tel: (0376) 35116/8/9, 35130. This new establishment caters mainly to the expanding mining population. $

Moyo Island

Amanwana: Office: P.O. Box 33, Sumbawa Besar 83401. Tel: (0371) 22233, Fax: 22288, www.amanresorts.com. Access to this secluded Aman hideaway is by the resort's private yacht. The almost undeveloped Moyo island, 15 km (9 miles) off the coast of Sumbawa, also has a wildlife sanctuary. Accommodation at the resort is in 20 ultra-luxurious "tents". There is open-air dining and a bar and lounge area. $$$$$

Bima

Bima has several *losmen*, a few cleaner and more popular than others, to accommodate backpackers en route to Komodo.
Lambitu Hotel: Jl. Sumbawa No. 4. Tel: (0374) 42222, 43333, Fax: 42304. The best hotel downtown, it has standard rooms with a fan and shower, as well as air-con suites with hot water. $

WHERE TO EAT

In Sumbawa Besar try **Aneka Rasa**, Jl. Hasanuddin No. 14, for good Chinese food and the restaurant in **Tambora** Hotel, Jl. 8 Kebayan, serving good Indonesian food. For a nice beach front meal outside of town, there's **Santoana Restaurant** at Kencana Beach Safari Resort, just 15 minutes out of town.

Komodo & Rinca

Visitors to **Komodo National Park** must pay an entrance fee of Rp 25,000 per person, valid for three days and easily extendable. Entrance fees may be paid at the ranger station at either Loh Liang, Komodo or Loah Buaya on Rinca. The three-day pass is good for both islands.

GETTING THERE

By Air and Land

Komodo National Park can only be reached by sea. There are two entry points to the park. Merpati flies from Denpasar to Bima, on Sumbawa, and to Labuhanbajo, western Flores. From Bima, travel overland to Sape by public bus or hired vehicle. For groups of 15 or more, the ferry will land at Komodo for an extra fee per person. Obtain confirmation from the captain before sailing to ascertain this.

By Sea

At the harbours at both Sape and Labuhanbajo are local boats (bargain for reasonable fares) and a scheduled ferry service (buy a ticket at the ferry terminal). The crossing from Sape to Komodo takes 8 hours in calm seas, longer if the waves are strong. Service is usually suspended in bad weather. From Labuhanbajo, it's about 3 hours to Komodo and it's a far more scenic crossing. However, flights entering and exiting Bima are more frequent and generally more reliable. From either direction, ferries will stop near Komodo island, where small, local boats will take you to land for a nominal fee. Be sure to inspect the vessel before paying. The currents are strong in these seas, and although boatmen don't take unnecessary risks, boats do sink with alarming regularity. Departure times depend entirely upon the tides and currents.

Alternatively, chartered boats from either Sape or Labuhanbajo may be pre-arranged through travel agents in Jakarta, Bali or Lombok or chartered through tour operators in Bima, Sape or Labuhanbajo.

Alternatively, you may choose to cruise in comfort on one of the tourist boats listed on page 383.

Komodo National Park Conservation Groups

The Komodo Foundation (Yayasan Kawan Komodo): www.komodofoundation.org is an independent, non-profit and non-governmental organisation working in the fields of education and environmental awareness. Programmes target the coastal and maritime peoples of Komodo, Flores and Nusa Tenggara and aim to foster changes in attitudes and livelihoods by promoting responsible action regarding the natural environment. Projects include environmental educational programmes (including solid waste management, turtle conservation and coral regeneration) and rehabilitation of classrooms and toilet blocks in Labuhanbajo schools.

PKA Balai Taman Nasional Komodo: www.komodonationalpark.org is a cooperative effort of the Indonesian Department of Forestry, the Nature Conservancy and a private consortium, working together to protect the biodiversity (both marine and terrestrial) of Komodo National Park. It also breeds stocks of commercial fishes for replenishment of surrounding fishing grounds. Its goal is to reduce threats to resources and solve conflicts between destructive fishing practices and conservation.

Komodo Dive Boats

Baruna: PT Wisata Tirta Baruna, Jl. ByPass Ngurah Rai 300-B. Tel: (0361) 753-820, Fax: 753-809, e-mail: baruna@denpasar.wasantara.net.id, www.komodo-divencruise.com. One of the oldest cruising and diving operations in Bali and Nusa Tenggara.

Grand Komodo Tours: Jl. Hang Tuah No. 26, Sanur. Tel: (0361) 287-166, Fax: 387-165, e-mail: gkomodot@indosat.net.id. The agency has several basic boats with shared facilities for trips to Komodo. Dive packages include the boat, all diving equipment, the park entrance fee and meals. A package for eight days costs US$900 per person.

S.M.Y. Ondina: www.thebestdivingintheworld.com. A 34 metre *pinisi* (schooner) with eight air-conditioned cabins, all with en suite baths. Equipment includes two powerful compressors, all dive gear and onboard slide-film processing room. Operated by a Spanish owner, this is a very professionally run outfit.

Hotel Price Guide

Price categories for standard rooms, usually without breakfast:
- $$$$$ = above US$150
- $$$$ = US$101–150
- $$$ = US$51–100
- $$ = US$30–50
- $ = under US$30

WHERE TO STAY

Basic accommodations and cheap meals are available at the ranger stations at both Loh Liang on Komodo and Loh Buaya on Rinca. Charges are minimal. Upon arrival at either island, register and pay the fee at the ranger station. Visitors leaving the compound must be accompanied by a ranger, who charges a nominal daily fee.

Flores

GETTING THERE

By Air

Merpati flies to Labuhanbajo and Maumere in Flores from Denpasar, (Bali) and Bima (Sumbawa). Buy your tickets in the departure town itself, as there is no connection to a central reservation computer system and bookings made outside the area may not be recognised.

There are landing strips at Bajawa, Ruteng, Ende and Larantuka. Check with a local travel agent for schedules.

Merpati's Maumere office: Jl. Don Thomas No. 19. Tel: (0382) 21342 and at Jl. Sudirman, Tel: (0381) 21342, Fax: 22791. Labuhanbajo office: Jl. Eltari No. 6. Tel: (0385) 21147.

By Sea

PELNI ships have several routes to Labuhanbajo. Check their website for detailed information: www.pelni.co.id

GETTING AROUND

Of the major islands in Nusa Tenggara, Flores has the worst road network because of its rugged terrain. Mountains and 14 active volcanoes make for beautiful scenery, but also constitute an engineering headache.

You can travel the length of Flores by public transport, but be aware that the 670-km (400-mile) road running the length of the island will take a good four to five days to complete, as transport seldom runs at night.

During the rainy season (November–May), travel between the principal towns could be shut down for hours or days due to landslides.

TOURIST OFFICE

Manggarai Regency Tourist Office: Labuhanbajo. Tel: (0385) 41107.

TOUR OPERATOR

Maumere

Floressa Tours: Jl. Jendral Ahmad Yani No. 11. Tel/Fax: (0382) 22281. A branch office of Floressa Tours in Bali, it offers tours to Kelimutu on the south coast of Flores, volcano trekking and trips to crafts villages.

WHERE TO STAY

The lodgings in Flores are basic at best and none provides hot water. Bring a *sarong* along to double up as a top sheet or bath towel, and if intending to stay over in one of the mountain areas, bring a jacket or sweater. Buy toilet paper and soap at the shops when you arrive, as most *losmen* don't provide these items.

Labuhanbajo

Chez Felix: Jl. Prof. W.Z. Johanes. Tel: (0385) 41032. Located up on a hill overlooking the harbour. A clean place with a nice view from the restaurant. **$**
Gardena Bungalows & Restaurant: Jl. Sukarno-Hatta. Basic bungalows with fan (no hot water) and lovely views overlooking Labuhanbajo bay. Fabulous sunsets. **$**

Ruteng

Hotel Dahlia: Jl. Bhayangkara No. 18. Tel: (0385) 21377. A few rooms have TVs and spring mattresses rather than the hard cotton ones. Well-kept. **$**

Bajawa

Ariesta: Jl. Diponegoro. Tel: (0384) 21292. Next door to the hospital and away from the main bustle of town. A clean and quiet establishment. **$**

Ende

Dwi Putra Hotel: Jl. Yos Soedarso No. 27. Tel: (0381) 21685. The most upmarket hotel here, it is also one of the few that has hot water. A few rooms have air-con. **$**
Hotel Ikhlas: Jl. Ahmad Yani No. 69. Tel: (0381) 21695, Fax: 22555. Owner Djamal Alhadad speaks English and German and arranges tours with an English-speaking guide. Go for one of the new rooms with a small balcony. The restaurant serves simple fare. **$**

Maumere

Flores Sao Resort: Jl. Sawita. Tel: (0382) 21555, Fax: 21666. Located some distance from town. It has a swimming pool that overlooks the sea and arranges diving tours. A restaurant serves local food. **$$**

Restaurant Price Guide

Price categories for a three-course meal (Asian or Western), without drinks:
- *Expensive* = US$26–50
- *Moderate* = US$11–25
- *Inexpensive* = under US$10

WHERE TO EAT

Labuhanbajo

Borobudur Restaurant: Jl. Sukarno-Hatta. The restaurant serves Schnitzel, prawns, and Thai dishes such as ginger chicken. Overlooks the sea. *Inexpensive*

Ruteng

Merlin Restaurant: Jl. Bhayangkara No. 32B. Tel: (0385) 22475. The plain façade belies its excellent Chinese and Indonesian dishes, more exciting that the usual fare. Try the *mie kwantong ayam* (Cantonese noodles with chicken and spinach). *Inexpensive*

Bajawa

Camellia Restaurant: Jl. A. Yani No. 74. Tel: (0384) 21458. The best restaurant in town, it serves Chinese food, with a surprisingly good Swiss rosti. Try the guacamole with prawn crackers. *Inexpensive*
Lukas Café: Jl. A. Yani No. 71. Serves both Western food and local cuisine.

Ende

Merlyn: Jl. Gatot Subroto (near Hotel Iklas). Tel: (0381) 21667. Excellent Chinese food; try the prawns, squid, crab and grilled lobster at market prices. *Inexpensive*

Maumere

Sumber Indah: Jl. Raja Centis No. 31. Tel: (0382) 21375. A simple little restaurant in the busy section of Maumere, serving possibly the best food on the island. The *ikan asam manis* (sweet and sour fish) and the *cah sayur ijo udang* (water spinach with prawns) are tasty. *Inexpensive*

WHERE TO SHOP

Maumere

Kota Pena: Jl. Gajah Mada No. 11. Tel: (0382) 21032. Interesting artefacts from Indonesia's other islands at good prices – bargaining is acceptable. **Harapan Jaya** has fixed-price weavings from all across eastern Nusa Tenggara. A little expensive.

Solor & Alor Archipelagos

GETTING THERE

Boats leave daily from Larantuka in Flores to Lewoleba (Lembata) and Solor. The trip from Larantuka to Lewoleba takes 4 hours, stopping at Waiwerang on Adonara island en route. A ferry service links Larantuka and Kalabahi (Alor). Alor is also accessible via PELNI ferry line from Kupang in West Timor.

TOUR OPERATOR

CV Latour: Jl. Podor Lewolere, Larantuka. Tel: (0383) 21388, Fax: 21452. Arranges tours to Solor and Lembata, including the Lamalera whaling village, as well as traditional villages in eastern Flores.

Hotel Price Guide

Price categories for standard rooms, usually without breakfast:
- $$$$$ = above US$150
- $$$$ = US$101–150
- $$$ = US$51–100
- $$ = US$30–50
- $ = under US$30

WHERE TO STAY

Lembata
Lamalera
There are two places to stay in Lamalera, one in the village square beyond the beach and the other at Guru Ben's house on the hillside looking down on the beach. Guru Ben was a great source of information to visitors of Lamalera. He died in 2003 of malaria, and his wife, Yudis, continues to run the small homestay.
Guru Ben Homestay: Located on the hillside overlooking Lamalera Bay. Two private rooms and one communal room, shared family bath. Meals are meagre so you might want to bring your own snacks. $

Lewoleba
Hotel Lewoleba near Bank BNI just on the east side of the market has simple rooms.
Lile Ile: Tel: (0383) 41250. About 400 metres east of the harbour is Lile Ile, a clean, friendly homestay with only four rooms and a common bath. The front porch looks out to Ile Ape and has lovely breezes coming off the bay. The owners, Jim and Kalis, are helpful guides as Jim has led tours throughout Indonesia for many years. Delicious local dishes are served with lots of vegetables and fish, tempe or tofu. $
Rejeki 1: Jl. Lembata No. 1193, Lewoleba. Tel (0383) 41028. Simple rooms run by the owner, Pak Alex, who also provides maps and helps with travel arrangements. Businessmen and government employees mostly stay here. Common or private bathrooms are available. $

Alor
Pelangi Indah: Jl. Diponegoro No. 34. Tel: (0397) 21251. The newest hotel in Alor, it has good standard rooms and facilities. There is no restaurant, but meals can be provided with advance notice. $

WHERE TO EAT

As there are only small *warung* in these remote areas, it's a relief that the *losmen* can prepare simple meals as well. Bring snacks with you to supplement an unvarying diet of *nasi* or *mie goreng* (fried rice or noodles).

SHOPPING

The Solor and Alor archipelagos are heaven for textile lovers. The central markets are vibrant places to shop for local weavings. Better yet, check with your hotel which villages welcome foreign shoppers.

Sumba

GETTING THERE

By Air
Tambolaka airport, near Waikabubak in West Sumba, stands idle most of the time, as flights are few. Merpati operates several weekly services between Bali and Java, and Waingapu, in East Sumba.

By Sea
West Sumba has a small harbour on the north coast at Waikelo, about 50 km (30 miles) from Waikabubak. East Sumba has a better and busier harbour at Waingapu. Unscheduled freighters that call at either of the two ports will usually take on passengers. Larger ships call twice a month at the ports along the way between Surabaya (Java) and Kupang (Timor). As these ships also call at the harbours of several neighbouring islands, this mode of travel is an excellent way to island hop. PELNI (Jl. Hasanudin No. 1, Waingapu. Tel: (0387) 61665) also does runs between the islands.

GETTING AROUND

The two district capitals, Waikabubak and Waingapu, are linked by a 140-km (80-mile) road, and two daily bus services which cover the 5-hour trip. *Bemo* ply smaller roads, mainly unpaved, to small towns and villages.

TOUR OPERATORS

The larger hotels in each city can arrange tours and English-speaking guides. Prices vary according to the destination and whether a dance performance is included.

WHERE TO STAY

West Sumba
Nihiwatu Resort: Bali office: Jl. Raya Seminyak No. 12, Seminyak. Tel/Fax: (0361) 752-374, Fax: 731-172, www.nihiwatu.com. Set on a secluded bay on the south-western coast, the resort is surrounded by tropical forest and rice terraces. There are six cottages and a two-bedroom family villa with views of the sea and sunset. There is a pool and a restaurant, and you can go deep-sea fishing, boating, diving or horse riding. $$$$
Newa Sumba Resort: Newa, Sumba. Jakarta office: Tel: (021) 522-9117/8, Fax: 522-9109, www.newasumbaresort.com. The resort's peaked-roof villas in coconut wood have living rooms and private balconies. It sits on 100 hectares (247 acres) of land fringed by a white-sand beach. The extensive grounds also encompass a nature reserve. $

Waikabubak
Manandang: Jl. Pemuda No. 4. Tel: (0387) 21197, 21292, Fax: 21634. The nicest place in town, with an excellent restaurant. Vehicle hire available. $

Waingapu
Elvin: Jl. A. Yani No. 73. Tel: (0386) 62097. Formerly the Elim Hotel, the rooms here have private showers. Meals are available. $

WHERE TO EAT

The best restaurants are in the hotels.

WEST TIMOR/ROTI/SAVU ◆ 389

WHERE TO SHOP

Purchasing traditional Sumbanese *ikat* textiles is the top priority for most visitors. Shop carefully, as much inferior work appears on the market. Bargain hard, as the final price could well be one-third of the first asking price. **Prailiu** and **Mangili** villages, outside Waingapu, are the centres of the weaving industry. **Melolo** (on the south-east coast) is also a good source of old Sumbanese hand-woven fabrics.

West Timor

GETTING THERE

By Air

Flights from Darwin to Kupang are scheduled to be reinstated for the first time since their 2000 hiatus. Domestically, there are flights to Kupang, the capital of West Timor, from Surabaya (Java), Denpasar (Bali), Maumere (Flores), or Waingapu (Sumba). It is cheaper to buy tickets within Indonesia, and there are four airlines to choose from:
Batavia Air: Jl. A. Yani No. 73, Tel: (0380) 830-555.
Merpati: Jl. A. Yani No. 66, Cell phone: (0380) 833-833.
Pelita Air: Jl. Jend. Sudirman No. 68. Tel: (0380) 832-573, 831-763, Fax: 833-121.
Star Air: Kupang Airport, Tel: (0380) 882-040.

By Sea

PELNI has several routes to Kupang. For more information, see www.pelni.co.id.

TOURIST OFFICE

Provincial Tourist Services: Jl. Jend. Basuki Rahmat 1, Kupang. Tel: (0380) 21540, 21824.

WHERE TO STAY

Kupang

There are several decent hotels in Kupang, as it is the regional capital of Nusa Tenggara Timur, regularly hosting government and business conventions and conferences.
Hotel Kristal: Jl. Timor Raya No. 59. Tel: (0380) 825-100, Fax: 825-104. Large beachfront hotel with its own restaurant, swimming pool and conference facilities. $$$
Sasando International: Jl. Kartini No. 1. Tel: (0380) 833-334, Fax: 833-338. This hilltop hotel is a 15-minute taxi ride from town. It has good views over Kupang Bay, a swimming pool and an in-house travel agency which can book airline tickets. $$$
Hotel Maya: Jl. Sumatra No. 31. Tel: (0380) 832-169. Good mid-range hotel in central Kupang, close to banks, shops, and overlooking the sea. $
Hotel Pantai Timor: Jl. Sumatra. Tel: (0380) 831-651. Good mid-range hotel in central Kupang, on the seafront, with its own restaurant serving Indonesian, Chinese & European meals. $

WHERE TO EAT

Kupang

Palembang International: Jl. Moh Hatta, Koinino. Excellent Chinese and Indonesian food. *Moderate*
Restoran Nelayan: Jl. Timor Raya, Pasir Panjang. Good Chinese and Indonesian food in outdoor setting by the sea. *Moderate*
Restoran Teluk Kupang: Jl. Timor Raya. Delicious Indonesian and Chinese fare, specialising in seafood. One of the best restaurants in town. *Moderate*
Lima Jaya Raya: Jl. Sukarno No. 15A. Good Indonesian, Chinese and European food. *Inexpensive*

WHERE TO STOP

Kupang

Beautiful hand woven textiles are to be found everywhere in West Timor if you travel out to the villages. The markets at Niki-Niki, Oinlasi and Maubesi are also good sources for textiles, silver jewellery and woven betelnut containers. A very good dealer specialising in West Timorese textiles and antiques is **Pak Alfred Makh**, Jl. Bill Nope No. 17, So'e. Tel: (0388) 21419.

Textile Tour

Timorese-Australian couple, **Willy and Ruth Daos Kadati**: P.O. Box 1196, Kupang, Tel: (0380) 839-313, e-mail: willydaoskadati@yahoo.com offer specialised textile tours around West Timor covering the techniques of *futus* (ikat weaving), *buna* (supplementary weft) and *sotis* (warp-faced float or pick-up weave) and also indigo and *morinda* dyeing. West Timorese hand woven textiles are regionally specific, varying greatly from one region to another. Visits to markets, to weavers in traditional villages, and the NTT (East Nusa Tenggara) Museum in Kupang are included.

Roti

GETTING THERE

By Sea

There is daily ferry service to Roti from Pelabuhan Bolok, Kupang's main harbour. Information on schedules and prices is available from:
Japindo Tour & Travel: Jl. A. Yani No. 83. Tel: (0380) 827-450.

WHERE TO STAY

Roti has become a hot spot for international surfers, so there are plenty of basic accommodations. Recommended are:
Hotel Gress: Jl. Pabean, Roti.
Hotel Ricky: Jl. Gereja, Roti.

Savu

GETTING THERE

By Air

There is one flight per week (usually on Monday morning) from Kupang to Savu, returning to Kupang. As it is a small plane, tickets must be booked 2 to 3 weeks in advance at the Merpati office in Kupang, Tel: (0380) 833-833 or through Kupang travel agents.

By Sea

There is a ferry from Kupang every Monday afternoon, arriving at Seba harbour on Savu on Tuesday morning. Note that the seas are rough in January and February and ferries often don't run. Travellers should avoid visiting Savu by sea during these months.

GETTING AROUND

On the island, transportation is by foot, horseback or motorcycle. There are a few *bemos* (mini-vans) linking the harbour to east and west Savu on the days the ferry arrives. There are also a few trucks, mainly for road works or for the transportation of sea grasses; these can also transport people.

WHERE TO STAY

Savu has no accommodations of international standard. In **Seba**, there are two homestays and one *losmen*. All offer basic accommodation. **Pak Octo Jo Naga**, opposite the Telkom office, Tel: (0380) 861-022 or 861-002, offers a quiet homestay, and the hostess is a good cook. **David Kido** offers a homestay near the harbour and beach, Tel: (0380) 861-006.

Kalimantan

East Kalimantan

BALIKPAPAN

The busy oil and timber town of Balikpapan holds little interest for travellers and sees mostly business visitors. Independent travellers head straight for Samarinda – the gateway to Dayak country – by air, or up a 115-km (70-mile) paved road to begin their journey up the great Sungai Mahakam into the interior.

Getting There

There is no single entry point into Kalimantan; travellers to the east enter via Balikpapan and on to South Kalimantan through Banjarmasin. Visitors seeking orangutan in Central Kalimantan choose between Palangkaraya or Pangkalanbun, while the West Kalimantan gateway is Pontianak.

By Air

Silk Air has daily flights from Singapore, and Malaysian Airlines has twice weekly flights from Kota Kinabalu. Domestic flights between Jakarta, Surabaya (Java), Makassar (Sulawesi) and other points in Balikpapan are serviced by Bouraq, Garuda and Merpati.

As schedules change frequently, it's best to contact the airlines directly or local travel agents for current itineraries.

Passengers flying to the more remote parts of Kalimantan may experience frequent delays, cancellations or overbooking.
Bouraq: Sepinggan Airport, Balikpapan. Tel: (0542) 731-475.
Garuda: Hotel Bahtera, Jl. Jend. Sudirman, Tel: (0542) 422-300/1.
Malaysian Airlines: Benakutai Hotel, Tel: (0542) 396-939.
Merpati: Jl. Jend. Sudirman Blok B2 No. 32. Tel: (0542) 424-452.
SilkAir: Hotel Grand Senyuir, Jl. Mohammad 7, Tel: (0542) 730-800.

By Sea

There are three PELNI ferry services to Balikpapan. One connects to Surabaya in Java, the other to Makassar in Sulawesi and the third is to Tarakan in East Kalimantan, close to the Sabah border.
PELNI: Jl. Yos Sudarso No. 1. Tel: (0542) 737-774.

Getting Around

The Trans-Kalimantan Highway extends from Batakan, south of Banjarmasin, to Balikpapan and then to Samarinda. It eventually connects to Bontang and Tarakan. Buses run on a regular schedule from Banjarmasin to Balikpapan and Samarinda. Because of the thick forest, water transport is the key means of getting around in Kalimantan. River boats and ferries – *taksi sungai* (river taxi) or *bis air* (water bus) – are popular forms of transport.

Tour Operator

Bayu Buana Travel: Balikpapan. Tel: (0542) 422-751, 422-747; Fax: 433-683. Jakarta office: Tel: (021) 380-1705; Fax: 386-1955. Formerly Tomaco Tours, the agency offers tours lasting 3–10 days on the Sungai Mahakam aboard its own boat.

Where to Stay

Along with the airport expansion is the growth of hotels to cater to the developing oil and timber industries. Accommodation ranges from three-star hotels to *losmen*.

Note that many of Balikpapan's street names have changed recently, which could cause confusion if navigating the city using an old map.
Dusit Inn: Jl. Jenderal Sudirman. Tel: (0542) 420-155, Fax: 420-150, www.dusit.com. The hotel combines an attractive setting with first-class facilities. It sits amid extensive gardens adjoining a beautiful sandy beach overlooking the Makassar Strait. There is a Cantonese restaurant and a café, with adult and children's pools. $$$$
Benakutai: Jl. Jend. A. Yani. Tel: (0542) 731-896, Fax: 731-823, www.benakutai.co.id. This has all the comfort and facilities of a top-class hotel, with a business centre, delicatessen and health club. $$$
Blue Sky (Bahana Surya): Jl. Letjen. Suprapto No. 1, Tel: (0542) 735-845, email: bluesky1@indo.net.id. The rooms have in-house videos and satellite TV, and the hotel has a good range of facilities, including a gym and a sauna. $$$

Where to Eat

Bondy: Jl. Pulau Antarsari 137A (near the Benakutai Hotel). Tel: (0542) 424-438. Fronted by an ice cream and pastry parlour is an open-air restaurant specialising in grilled fish. Local and imported steaks are also on the menu. *Moderate*
Jack's Place: Jl. Mulawarman No. 56. Tel: (0542) 760-120, e-mail: ed-jack@indo.net.id. This beachside restaurant has a profusion of plants so you could be forgiven for thinking you were eating in a forest. There is an extensive menu listing home-cooked Western fare: steaks, gumbo, beef brisket, stews and meatloaf. Top off a satisfying meal with apple pie and coffee. Drink choices include wine. *Moderate*
Dynasty: Jl. Jend. Ahmad Yani 117. Tel: (0542) 424-086. This place offers hearty Chinese seafood. Recommended. *Inexpensive*
New Shangrila: Jl. Jend. Ahmad Yani 250 (about 15 minutes' walk from Benakutai Hotel). Tel: (0542) 423-124. The house special is hot plate meat (either chicken, prawns or beef) with vegetables and pigeon eggs. *Inexpensive*

Where to Shop

Balikpapan
Kalimantan Art Shop: Located on Jalan Sutoyo, the shop retails Dayak crafts, including antique and new carvings, as well as Chinese ceramics and old glass beads.

Dayak Arts and Crafts

Dayak arts and crafts display extraordinary and vibrant design. The characteristic flowing geometrical patterns used in portraying scenes of jungle life come from Chinese and Vietnamese Dong Son influences. More than any other ethnic group in Indonesia, the Dayak are famed for their beadwork. They use thousands of tiny glass beads to decorate purses, tobacco pouches, scabbards, baby carriages, basket lids, dress hems, caps and headbands.

Another craft is basketry, in a wide variety of types in characteristic two-tone patterns. Weaving had almost died out until it was revived for the tourist trade in Tanjung Isuy village in East Kalimantan. *Ikat* is the common technique in weaving, originally using bark fibre and natural dyes. Now, commercial yarn and dyes are common.

Gender roles differentiate most of the Dayak crafts. Men are more at home carving wood and working metal, while the women tend towards plaiting, weaving and beadwork.

SAMARINDA

Samarinda, the capital of Kalimantan Timur province (or Kaltim), is the jump-off point to the Dayak homelands in the interior. Tours include overnight stays on tourist houseboats or longhouses.

New roads are under construction or in the planning stage and a government-owned air service, Perusahaan Daerah (PRUSDA), has begun flights to the hinterland. An international airport will soon be built between Samarinda and Tenggarong, and five new hotels are currently under construction in Samarinda.

Getting There

Buses from Balikpapan make the journey to Samarinda in about 2 hours. Chartered taxis are more expensive but quicker. Speedboats depart Samarinda daily and arrive in Bontang about 5 hours later. Water taxis take about twice as long. Local airlines and flight schedules are continually being added to connect the provincial capital with the hinterland. Check with local travel agencies upon arrival for the latest information, or try to catch a ride with MAF (Missionary Aviation Fellowship) in small Cessna planes to reach the inaccessible places. MAF has no fixed schedules and operate strictly on a seat-available basis. MAF **Mission Aviation Fellowship**, Complex Universitas Unmul, Tel: (0541) 203-779 in Samarinda flies to Long Sulei or Long Lebusan.

Tourist Office

Provincial Tourist Services: Jl. Sudirman 22. Tel: (0541) 736-850.

Tour Operator

Mesra Tours: Jl. Pahlawan No. 1. Tel: (0541) 738-787, Fax: (0541) 741-017, e-mail: mesratours@mesra.com, www.mesra.com. In addition to the usual tours to Tanjung Isuy, Sungai Mahakam, the Apokaya hinterland, rainforest trekking and bamboo rafting, it arranges unusual trips such as hunting with a Dayak tribe.

Where to Stay

Mesra International: Jl. Pahlawan No. 1. Tel: (0541) 732-772, Fax: 741-017, e-mail: hotelmesra@mesra.com, www.mesra.com. A hill-top business and resort hotel in the heart of Samarinda sitting on 10 hectares (25 acres) of tranquil greenery. There is a business centre and dining options include a restaurant and a 24-hour café. The hotel doubles up as a tour agency. **$$$**

Restaurant Price Guide

Price categories for a three-course meal (Asian or Western), without drinks:
Expensive = US$26–50
Moderate = US$11–25
Inexpensive = under US$10

Where to Eat

Lezat: Jl. Mulawarman. Excellent Chinese dishes such as squid, oysters, prawns, frog and crab as well as pork and chicken. *Moderate*
Sari Pacific: Jl. Panglimabatur 5-7, Tel: (0541) 743-289. Javanese cuisine and European steaks. *Moderate*
Sari Rasa: Jl. Agus Salim No. 26. Tel: (0541) 222-771. It specialises in Chinese and Western dishes from a large menu. Apart from the usual frog, prawn and crab dishes, there are imported beef and Japanese dishes. A little pricey, but recommended. *Moderate*

South Kalimantan

BANJARMASIN

The small, swampy province of South Kalimantan is known as Kalimantan Selatan (or Kalsel) – the Land of a Thousand Rivers. Banjarmasin, the capital city, is famous for its colourful floating markets and bustling canals. The Banjarese are strict Muslims. Dress modestly while travelling here.

Kalsel grows rice for export to other parts of Indonesia, but its major export is timber. It also exports rubber and rattan, and diamonds, gold, coal and granite.

Getting There

By Air
In addition to the commercial airlines, the privately-owned Dirgantara Air Service (DAS) also flies to Banjarmasin. Check with an Indonesian travel agent for schedules.
Bouraq: Sjamsudin Noor Airport. Tel: (0511) 95065/6. City office: Tel: 252-445/285.
Garuda: Hotel Istana Barito, Jl. Letjen. M.T. Haryono No. 16. Tel: (0511) 59064/5/6.
Merpati: Jl. Armad Yani No. 1470, Km 3.5. Tel: (011) 268-462.

By Sea
PELNI's Kelimutu line calls at Banjarmasin on the run between Surabaya and Semarang in Java. *Marina Nusantara* sails to Banjarmasin from Surabaya in 16 hours. Contact a Banjarmasin travel agent to make a booking.

PELNI: Jl. Laks. R.E. Martadinata No. 10. Tel: (0511) 53077, 54120.

By Bus
From Balikpapan and Samarinda, overnight buses make the journey to Banjarmasin in 12 and 14 hours, respectively.

Getting Around

Boats are the main mode of travel in this land of rivers. From Banjarmasin, you can go northwards via Sungai Barito to its headwater. If you have a couple of weeks, you can explore the whole river. Boats can be chartered upriver as far as Mauratewe. From there, switch to a canoe as you approach the headwater.

A long trek north-east (you can shorten the journey by road) over swamps leads to Intu and finally to Long Iram on Sungai Mahakam. Samarinda is 36 hours away down the Mahakam River.

But if you are game for more river travel, on arrival in Long Iram, boat up the Mahakam to the Dayak villages of Longbangun, through the rapids to Long Pahangai, Tiong Ohang and further.

Tourist Office

Provincial Tourist Services: Jl. Majend. D.I. Panjaitan No. 23, Banjarmasin 70114. Tel: (0511) 52982, Fax: 584-119.

Tour Operator

Bagus Travel: Jl. Sulawesi No. 17, Banjarmasin 70115. Tel: (0511) 59979, Fax: 54878. Well-thought out itineraries ranging from city tours and three-day diamond-mining, bamboo-rafting or trekking trips, to 10-day Dayak expeditions. There is also an itinerary for Tanjung Puting National Park.

Hotel Price Guide

Price categories for standard rooms, usually without breakfast:
$$$$$ = above US$150
$$$$ = US$101–150
$$$ = US$51–100
$$ = US$30–50
$ = under US$30

Where to Stay

Hotel Istana Barito: Jl. Haryono M.T. No. 16. Tel: (0511) 67300, Fax: 52240, e-mail: baritohotel@banjarmasin.wasantara.net.id. A standard hotel with an excellent restaurant serving seafood and steaks. **$$$**
Hotel Arum Kalimantan: Jl. Lambung Mangkurat. Tel: (0511) 66818, Fax: 67345, e-mail: arum@bjm.mega.net.id.

This hotel is well-equipped with facilities that include a business centre, a gym and a pool. $$
Hotel Batung Batulis: Jl. Jend. Soedirman No. 1. Tel: (0511) 66269, Fax: 66270. Located in the centre of town, it has air-con rooms with bathroom and TV. $$
Hotel Mentari: Jl. Lambung Mangkurat No. 32. Tel: (0511) 68944, Fax 53350. Centrally located in town, the hotel has an in-house disco and also handles ticketing. $$
Swiss-Belhotel Borneo: Jl. Pangeran Antasari No. 86A, Tel: (0511) 271-111, www.swiss-belhotel.com. Located in centre of Banjarmasin overlooking the Martapura River and opposite Mitra Plaza, Banjarmasin's largest shopping complex. A variety of restaurants are within walking distance. $$

Where to Eat

Jorong Steak House: Jl. S. Parman. An extensive, out-of-the-ordinary menu with everything from grilled lobster at the high end to burgers, hot dogs and fries. The eatery also serves ox tongue, lamb chops and venison. *Moderate*
Shinta Restaurant: Jl. Lambung Mangkurat No. 62. Housed in the Arjuna Plaza complex, this Chinese restaurant is the city's nicest eatery. On offer are shark's fin or bird's nest soup, and pigeon, chicken, pork, seafood, beef and frog entrees. It is quiet in the day and very busy at dinner. *Moderate*
Jayakarta: Jl. Haryono M.T. The Chinese dishes on the menu include crab, chicken, fish, prawns and frog's legs. *Inexpensive*
Lezat Baru: Jl. Samudra No. 22. Tel: (0511) 53191. Excellent Chinese food and service at reasonable prices. *Inexpensive*

Where to Shop

The traditional South Kalimantan batik, *sasirangan*, was once used by the nobles to protect themselves against evil spirits. Visitors can watch the hand-made cloth being produced at several shops along Jalan A. Yani.

Central Kalimantan

PALANGKARAYA

Palangkaraya is the capital of Kalimantan Tengah (Central Kalimantan), or Kalteng – the Dayak province par excellence. For centuries dominated by the Muslim Banjarmasin, the local Dayak tribes fought to obtain separate provincial status, which was granted in 1957.

Getting There

There are several ways to reach Palangkaraya from Banjarmasin. By bus or car across a new road takes about 8 hours or travel the way the local people do, by *bis air* (water bus) or speedboat. There is an airport at the edge of town, but flights are unreliable. Or fly to Pangkalanbun and travel by road to Palangkaraya.

Tourist Office

Provincial Tourist Services: Jl. Tjilik Riwut Km 5, Palangkaraya 73112. Tel: (0536) 31110, 31007.

Where to Stay

Hotel Dandang Tingang: Jl. Yos Sudarso No. 13. Tel: (0536) 21805, Fax: 21254. The high-end rooms have air-con, TV and hot water, and a private dining room. The restaurant serves Indonesian, Chinese and European food, and turns into a disco in the evening, fuelled by a live band. $$
Yanti: Jl. A. Yani No. 82A. Tel: (0536) 21634. Clean and modest, and options include air-con rooms with bathroom and hot water. $

PANGKALANBUN

The main reason anyone comes to Pangkalanbun is that it's on the way to Tanjung Puting National Park, where orangutans are the star attraction.

Getting There

Unlike in the past, there are now at least five arrivals and departures daily, connecting Pangkalanbun with Pontianak, Banjarmasin and Palangkaraya (Kalimantan), and Jakarta, Semarang and Yogyakarta (Java).
Deraya Airlines: Jl. Pakanegara 50. Tel: (0532) 21224.
KalStar/Trigana Air: Jl. Hasanuddin No. 2. Tel: (0532) 22824, Fax: 27509.
DAS: Jl Hasanuddin No. 35. Tel/Fax: (0532) 21177.

Where to Stay

Abadi Hotel: Jl. P. Antasari, No. 150. Tel: (0532) 21021. Fairly new, clean and comfortable, well located near shopping, food, banks and transport.

Hotel Price Guide

Price categories for standard rooms, usually without breakfast:
$$$$$ = above US$150
$$$$ = US$101–150
$$$ = US$51–100
$$ = US$30–50
$ = under US$30

Three floors, each with a common lounge area. Rooms range from economy with fan to standard rooms with air-con, telephone, TV and fridge. All have private bathrooms. $
Blue Kecubung Hotel: Jl. Domba. Tel: (0532) 21211, Fax: 21513. The poshest hotel in town, though it's seen better days, and the only one to offer a bar with live music on most nights. Good Chinese restaurant. Large, airy single rooms, most with nice views. Breakfast and snacks included in the price. $
Hotel Bone: Jl. Domba No. 21. Tel: (0532) 21213. Budget hotel with basic rooms. Shared bathrooms are basic but clean. $
Purnama Indah Hotel: Jl. A. Yani. Tel: (0532) 24990. Large hotel built around 1998, unfortunately located away from shopping and transport and next to bad roads. Standard rooms have fan, some with shower, air-con, TV and small fridge. $
Hotel Tiara: Jl. P. Antasari, No. 26. Tel: (0532) 22721, 22717, Fax: 25151. Possibly the best value hotel in town. Very clean and new (built in 2002), well located centrally near shopping, food, banks and transport. Standard rooms come with TV, fans and decent ensuite bathroom. For slightly more, upgrade to a more spacious and comfortable deluxe room with air-con, shower, fridge, TV and phone. Some English spoken. $

TANJUNG PUTING NATIONAL PARK

Getting There

Visitors must register with the PHPA (Forestry Department) office in Pangkalanbun to obtain a permit to go into the park. You'll need a photocopy of your passport (including the white embarkation card you received when you entered Indonesia). Current registration fee is about US$5.

From Pangkalanbun, it's 20 minutes by taxi to Kumai, the riverside village that is the entry point into Tanjung Puting National Park. At Kumai harbour, rent a *klotok* (motorised local boat) for about US$35 per day for one to four people. If you plan to eat and sleep on the boat, you'll pay extra for a cook. Be sure to buy food and water in Kumai before heading upriver.

Where to Stay

There are two lodges on the Sekonyer River in the park, **Rimba Lodge** and **Sekonyer Ecolodge**. As the food in both isn't the tastiest on the planet, visitors are advised to bring snacks and fruit from Kumai.

Friends of the National Parks Foundation (FNPF) runs a small **guest house** at Tanjung Harapan, the first park post encountered upriver. The room rate of about US$10 per night includes all meals. FNPF can also arrange boat hire from Tanjung Harapan post to various points along the river. All money received from the guest house or boat hire helps support FNPF's conservation and village projects in the park. FNPF can also arrange homestays in Tanjung Harapan village, which start from about US$12 per night, inclusive of meals.
Tanjung Harapan Guest House & Village Homestay, c/o Friends of the National Parks Foundation (FNPF), Jl. Harimau No. 74, Pangkalanbun 74111, KalTeng. Tel/fax: (0532) 23369, e-mail: fnpf@dps.centrin.net.id.
Sekonyer River Ecolodge, Jakarta reservations office: Kalpataru Adventures, Jl. Kenaga II/2, Jaka Permai Kompleks, Bekasi, Jakarta. Tel: (021) 889-1183, 889-1184, Fax: 885-1914, e-mail: kalpaadv@idola.net.id. Kalpataru agency owns the lodge and also organises tours to Tanjung Puting and Dayak country.

Tour Operator
Wanaprasta Tours: Fax: (0361) 811-111, e-mail: pkaler@dps.centrin.net.id. Operational office in Pangkalanbun: Tel: (0532) 21611. Specialises in Tanjung Puting and the surrounding area, working very closely with FNPF and other conservation organisations.

West Kalimantan

PONTIANAK

The provincial capital, Pontianak (the name refers to the ghost of a woman who dies in childbirth) lies near the sea at the juncture of the Kapuas and Landak rivers. This bustling and relatively well-off town – satellite TV is common – is populated by Chinese, Malays and Bugis, with just a handful of the indigenous Dayak. Commerce lies mainly in timber production, and the export of Siamese oranges.

Travel Advisory

Inter-ethnic conflict has led to grisly violence (beheadings) in West Kalimantan recent years. Keep informed of events in the area and exercise extreme caution when travelling.

Getting There
By Air
Malaysia Airlines flies here from Kuching (Sarawak), where there are international connections from Singapore and Kuala Lumpur. Domestic airlines servicing Pontianak are Garuda and Merpati and newcomer P.T. Lion Mentari Air (Lion Airlines), which commenced operations in June 2000. Contact an Indonesian travel agent for schedules.

The trip from the airport into town takes about 20 minutes, depending on traffic conditions. Taxis are available.
Deraya Airlines: Jl. Wahid Hasyim 227, Tel: (0561) 723-865.
Garuda: Jl. Rahadi Usman No. 8A. Tel: (0561) 741-441.
Malaysian Airlines: Airport office, Tel: (0561) 737-327.
Merpati: Jl. Tanjung Pura No. 7. Tel: (0561) 736-625.

By Sea
Three PELNI ferries stop at Pontianak, and connect to Surabaya, Semarang and Jakarta. Contact the **PELNI** office at Jalan S. Abdurrakman in Java. Tel: (0561) 748-124/132.

Getting Around
The ride by road from Pontianak to Sambas takes 5 hours. To go to Sintang, you can fly there in 45 minutes on a nine-seater DAS plane, or ride 12 hours by bus, or two days by houseboat up the Sungai Kapuas.

From Pontianak, a serviceable road runs north and forks at Seipenyu village. If you take the road on the left, you will head northwards towards the border with Sarawak, passing an area well-known for excellent hand-woven cloth. (You need a visa to cross the border.) The road on the right heads east to Sintang.

Logging roads provide a crude path for sturdy vehicles in a few areas. Bridges are often made with rotting logs, and erosion and mud-slides create common obstacles. In dry weather, it is possible to travel by jeep.

Tourist Office
Provincial Tourist Services: Jl. Achmad Sood No. 25, Pontianak 78121. Tel: (0561) 736-712, Fax: 743-104.

Tour Operator
Ateng Tour: Jl. Gajah Mada No. 201, Pontianak. Tel: (0561) 732-683, Fax: 736-620, e-mail: ateng.tour@mailcity.com. Offers tours to Dayak country near Singkawang and Sambas, and a Serimbu rapids adventure with local boats. Other itineraries include expeditions to Mount Kelam and to Gunung Palung National Park, as well as to Mulu Caves in Sarawak.

Where to Stay
Kartika: Jl. Rahadi Usman. Tel: (0561) 34401, 32012, 32423, Fax: 38457. Located by the Kapuas River across from the City Hall, it has a coffee shop and a restaurant. **$$**
Kapuas Palace: Jl. Imam Bonjol. Tel: (0561) 36122, Fax: 34374. Not so conveniently located, but the hotel has a good range of amenities: a convention hall, a fitness centre, indoor tennis courts, a pool; and for dining, there is a *dim sum* restaurant and a 24-hour café. **$$**
Mahkota Kapuas: Jl. Sidas No. 8. Tel: (0561) 36022, 36023. Aside from easy access in the centre of town, this high-rise hotel has an excellent restaurant. A buffet breakfast is included in the room price. **$$**
Santika Pontianak: Jl. Diponogoro 46. Tel: (0561) 733-777, www.santika.com. The city's newest 3-star hotel. Located within the central business district and only 20 minutes from the airport. Caters to both business and leisure travellers. **$$**

Where to Eat
The hotels have the best restaurants, or take your pick of the local delicacies and simple rice meals at the many *warung* at the night market on Jalan Diponogoro.

Restaurant Price Guide

Price categories for a three-course meal (Asian or Western), without drinks:
Expensive = US$26–50
Moderate = US$11–25
Inexpensive = under US$10

Sulawesi

South Sulawesi

MAKASSAR (UJUNG PANDANG)

Once the port and trading centre for the mediaeval kingdom of Goa, Makassar is today a big, modern business city and the capital of South Sulawesi province. Following Independence, the city was renamed Ujung Pandang but, in 1999, officially reverted to its colonial name of Makassar. Oddly, some flight schedules still often refer to it as Ujung Pandang.

Getting There

By Air
Several airlines originating in Jakarta and Surabaya service Makassar. See an Indonesian travel agent for details.
From the airport, it is about 40 minutes to town. To ride in an authorised taxi, purchase a coupon at the taxi counter outside the arrival hall.
Bouraq Airlines: Jl. Veteran Selatan No. 1. Tel: (0411) 452-506.
Expres Air: Jl. Awakaraeng. Tel: (0411) 326-333.
Garuda Indonesia: Jl. Andi Pangerang Pettarrani No. 18B. Tel: (0411) 433-737.
Lion Air: Jl. Balai Kota No. 11. Tel: (0411) 327-217.
Mandala Airlines: Jl. S. Saddang Komplex. Tel: (0411) 314-888.
Merpati Nusantara: Jl. Bawakaraeng No. 109. Tel: (0411) 442-471.
Pelita Air: Jl. Pasar Ikan. Tel: (0411) 319-222.

By Sea
PELNI stops in Makassar via Balikpapan, Bau Bau and points in Java and Flores. Office: Jl. Jendral Sudirman No. 38. Tel: (0411) 331-395/7/8.

Tourist Office

Provincial Tourist Office: Jl. Jend Urip Sumoharjo No. 269, Gedung J. Lt. III & IV. Tel: (0411) 453-616, Fax: 451-383. There is also a tourist information office (closed Monday) inside Benteng Rotterdam. You can pick up multi-lingual brochures here.

Tour Operators

Caraka Travelindo: Jl. Samalona No. 12. Tel: (0411) 318-889, e-mail: trvlindo@upg.mega.net.id. Under Dutch management, this efficient and professional agency arranges everything from car and driver hire to customised itineraries for trips to remote corners of eastern Indonesia.
Cendana Tours: Griya Alam Permai A/10 and at arrival hall at Hasanudin Makassar Airport. Tel: (0411) 585-182, Fax: 585-182, e-mail: bida@indosat.net.id. Locally owned, this efficient agency organises tours, trekking, car hire with or without driver and hotel reservations. Also has an office in Rantepao.

Getting Around

For short distances, *becak* (pedicabs) are an environmentally friendly way to get around. To travel by air-con metered taxis, either hail one on the street or call one by phone (**Bosowa Taxi**: (Tel: (0411) 445-541).
Boats to Samalona Island or other places can be chartered from **Pantai Benteng** (across from Benteng Rotterdam) for about US$6 for a round trip.

Hotel Price Guide

Price categories for standard rooms, usually without breakfast:
$$$$$	= above US$150
$$$$	= US$101–150
$$$	= US$51–100
$$	= US$30–50
$	= under US$30

Where to Stay

Makassar has a glut of deluxe hotels; discounts for rooms can be easily negotiated outside of the busy season of June–August.
Hotel Imperial: Jl. Somba Opu No. 297. Tel: (0411) 870-555, Fax: 870-222, e-mail: imperialmks@meganet.com. The best hotel in Makassar (formerly the Sedona) for business or holiday. Air-con rooms with ensuite bathrooms and good range of facilities. $$$$
Hotel Pantai Gapura: Jl. Pasar Ikan No. 10. Tel: (0411) 325-791, e-mail: hotelpg@upg.mega.net.id. The resort has lovely deluxe cottages over the water, and a plus is the remarkable swimming pool. $$$$
Bira View Inn: Tel: (0413) 82043, Fax: 81515. Bugis-inspired cottages perched on a cliff offer stupendous views overlooking the sea. $
Resort Celebes: Jl. Hasanuddin I. Tel: (0417) 21134. The rooms are nicely furnished and set in a garden. $

Where to Eat

Every evening, the Pantai Losari strip along the Makassar waterfront comes alive with tented foodstalls dishing up a range of declicious Indonesian fare.
Surya Super Crab: Jl. Nusa Kambangan No. 16. The extensive seafood menu includes giant tiger prawns and spicy crab-in-the-shell. *Moderate*
Kios Semarang: Jl. Penghibur No. 73. The third floor of the multi-storey restaurant is a long-time favourite of expats, who go for the cheap beer, decent Chinese-Indonesian food and the view over Losari beach. *Inexpensive*

Where to Shop

Along the length of **Jalan Sombu Opu**, look for shops selling gold and silver filigree statues, Torajan handicrafts, Chinese porcelain artefacts and Bugis silk *sarong*. **Sutra Alam**, at Jalan Onta Lama No. 417, has local textiles and also puts on demonstrations of Bugis silk processing and weaving.
Aneka Textil, on Jalan Gunung Latimojong No. 120, sells bolts of silk with Bugis motifs.

RANTEPAO

Amid the rugged peaks and fertile plateaus of inland South Sulawesi live many isolated tribes known collectively as the Torajan, one of the world's most unique cultures.. Rantepao serves as the centre of the tourist trade in the Toraja area.

Getting There

By Land
Travel agents can arrange chartered vehicles for 7–8 hour trips from Makassar to Rantepao via Parepare. Or book a seat on an express bus a day in advance with any of the operators along Jalan Ikhwan in Makassar.

Tourist Offices

Government Tourist Office: Jl. A. Yani No. 62. Tel: (0423) 21277.

Tour Operator

Cedana Tours: Jl. Pongtiku No. 1. Tel: (0423) 21007, Fax: 23400. With headquarters in Makassar, this locally owned agency organises tours, trekking, car hire with or without driver and hotel reservations.

Activities

Scenic one- or three-day rafting trips are particularly exciting during the rainy season from November to March. Tour operators provide pickup from the hotel, and excursions include guides, equipment and meals.

Sobek (Torango Buaya): Jl. Pongtiku. Tel: (0423) 21336. Good for white-water rafting trips.
Indo Sella: Jl. Suloara No. 113. Tel: (0423) 25210, Fax: 23605. Excursions include rafting, kayaking, mountain biking, trekking and paragliding.

Getting Around

Rantepao is small enough to explore on foot. You can also hop into a *becak* or ride around on a rented bicycle. *Kijang* vehicles make the 20-minute run between Rantepao and Makale several times throughout the day. All *pete-pete* (mini-vans) start their trip from **Terminal Bolu** and can be flagged down anywhere along Jalan A. Yani for travel to nearby destinations.

Hiking is often the best way to explore Tana Toraja. One-day walks can be made around the area, but several days are needed to see remote areas such as Mamasa valley. May–October is the best time, otherwise your hike may well end up to be just a long slog in the mud.

Where to Stay

Rooms providing hot-water baths will be appreciated in Toraja's cooler climate. Reservations are advised during the high season in June–August. Prices also peak during this time.
Novotel Toraja Coralia: Tel: (0423) 21192, Fax: (0423) 21666, www.novotel.com. Luxurious Torajan-style structure in a beautiful mountain setting. The finest of the lot. **$$$$**
Toraja Prince: Tel: (0423) 214-304, Fax: 21304. Luxury hotel with a quiet atmosphere. Torajan architecture, nice garden and swimming pool. **$$$**
Rantepao Lodge: Tel: (0423) 23717, Fax (0423) 21248. Traditional buildings, with a pleasant garden and a swimming pool. **$$**
Hotel Pison: Jl. Pongtiku No. 38. Tel/Fax: (0423) 21344. Standard hotel with three categories of rooms, some with hot water. **$**
Pondok Torina: Jl. Paorura 37, Tel: (0423) 21293, Fax: 27048. About 1.5 km from the city centre. Rooms have hot water and nice views. Torajan architecture, swimming pool. **$**

Where to Eat

Torajan specialities such as *papiong* (meat cooked in a bamboo tube) and *balu tongkonan* (fish wrapped in banana leaf) can be ordered in advance from restaurants catering to tourists along **Jalan A. Yani** and **Jalan Andi Mapanyukki**.
Mart's Café: Jl. Ratulangi No. 44A. Owned by a local guide, Mart's Café features Torajan food. *Inexpensive*

Rima: Jl. Andi Mapanyukki No. 115 Good Torajan food. *Inexpensive*

Where to Shop

Look for Torajan handicrafts in shops along **Jalan Andi Mapanyukki**; they stock a wide range of quality merchandise. Torajan woven cloths are not plentiful (and are expensive) but may be purchased in **Sa'dan Sangkombong** and **Sa'dan Tobarana** villages. The more popular tourist stops and villages around Rantepao sell souvenirs. Vendors can be persistent.

Central Sulawesi

PALU

The pleasant port town of Palu – the capital of Central Sulawesi – is surrounded by grassy hills and located at a bottleneck of land between Tomini Bay and the Makassar Strait.

South-east of Palu is the Lore Lindu National Park, which hosts incredibly diverse plant and animal life: hornbills, hordes of unusual butterflies, and elusive mammals such as the anoa (dwarf buffalo), babirusa (deer-pig) and the nocturnal Sulawesi palm civet.

Getting There
By Air
Bouraq and Merpati fly daily from Makassar and Manado, respectively.
Bouraq: Jl. Juanda No. 87. Tel: (0451) 28470. Mutiara Airport office: Tel: 22112.
Lion Air: Palu Golden Hotel. Tel: (0451) 428-775.
Merpati: Jl. Kartini No. 33. Tel: (0451) 423-341, 453-821.

By Sea
PELNI passenger ships travel overnight from Balikpapan, Bitung, Makassar and Parepare. Office: Jl. Kartini, Tel: (0451) 23237.

Getting Around
To get to most of Central Sulawesi, you have to employ a combination of trekking, taxis, four-wheel-drive vehicles, buses and boats. For a hassle-free holiday, use a tour agent.

Tourist Office
Provincial Tourist Services: Jl. Raya Moili No. 103. Tel: (0451) 21715, 26810.

Tour Operator
Uedatu Tour and Travel: Jl. Raden Saheh No. 1, Palu Golden Hotel. Tel/Fax: (0451) 429-850, e-mail: uedatu@palu.wasantara.net.id. The helpful, English-speaking staff can arrange treks to Lore Lindu National Park and Morawali Reserve.

Rafting Operator
P.T. Toranggo Buya: P.O. Box 107, Makassar 90131. Tel: (0411) 858-836, 871-791, Fax: 853-665, 873-676. Tana Toraja office: Tel: (0423) 21336. Arranges trips that include Class II–V rapids in Lore Lindu park.

Where to Stay
Palu Golden: Jl. Raden Saleh No. 1. Tel: (0451) 21126, Fax: 23230. Popular with tour groups, the hotel is set on the waterfront and located north of the town centre. Some rooms have balconies with nice views. The place has a good range of facilities, including a fine swimming pool. **$$**
Hasanah: Jl. Cut Nyak Dien No. 19C. Tel: (0451) 22225. This small, family-run place has spacious double rooms. Friendly staff. **$**

Where to Eat
A good, breezy spot to have an enjoyable open-air meal is at the stalls set up on the beach along Jalan Raja Moili, close to the Palu Golden Hotel. Mostly local food.
New Oriental: Jl. Hassanuddin II. Large higher-end restaurant with a wide selection of fine Chinese food. *Inexpensive*
Andalas: Jl. Raden Saleh No. 50. You can get good Padang food here. *Inexpensive*

Travel Advisory

Inter-religious conflict has claimed many victims in recent years in the Poso area. Keep informed of events in the area and exercise extreme caution if travelling in the region.

POSO/TENTENA

Most visitors head on to either Pendolo, on the southern shore of Lake Poso, or to Tentena on the northern shore. Facilities are much better at Tentena where it is also possible to organise treks to Lore Lindu National Park and Morawali Nature Reserve. You can also travel by boat across Lake Poso from Tentena to Pendolo.

Getting There
Buses make the journey from Palu to Poso in about 6 hours, but as the roads are rough, the journey is a tedious one. From Poso, there are regular mini-buses to Tentena (a 2-hour trip). A chartered taxi is a more comfortable option and can take you direct to Tentena.

Hotel Price Guide

Price categories for standard rooms, usually without breakfast:
$$$$$ = above US$150
$$$$ = US$101–150
$$$ = US$51–100
$$ = US$30–50
$ = under US$30

Where to Stay
Hotel Victory: Jl. Diponegoro No. 18, Tentena. Tel: (0458) 21392. Airy rooms, helpful management in a hotel with the cleanest kitchen in town. Tour information available on Morowali, Togian islands and Lore Lindu. $
Hotel Intim Danau Poso: Jl. Yos Sudarso, Tentena. Tel: (0458) 21345, Fax: 21488. The rooms are spacious. A plus is the lovely sea and mountain views. $
Wisata: Jl. Pattimura No. 19, Poso. Tel: (0452) 21379. Located close to the port, this small hotel with spacious rooms is nice and quiet. There is a pleasant garden at the back and views across the bay. $

Where to Eat
Lalanga: Jl. Komodor, Poso. Good seafood at this tiny restaurant on stilts located near the port. Friendly staff. *Inexpensive*
Pamona Indah Inn: Jl. Yos Sudarso, Tentana. This hotel restaurant on the lakeside serves good-value Chinese and Indonesian food. *Inexpensive*

TOGIAN ISLANDS

This remote forest-capped island cluster in the azure Bay of Tomini has much to offer the jaded tourist: stunning limestone cliffs, secluded white-sand beaches, and wonderful snorkelling and diving.

Getting There
Getting to the Togian Islands is rough, especially during the wet season. It is best to arrange the trip with a travel agent. At Ampana, the jump-off point on the mainland, contact the Togian information centre at (0464) 21250.

Where to Stay
Kadadiri Paradise Bungalows: Kadadiri island, Togians. Office: Tel: (0464) 21058. Simple bamboo bungalows on a nice beach with diving facilities. **Wakai Cottages** on Wakai island and secluded cabins on lovely **Taipi** island are run by the same owner. Meals included. $
Walea Dive Centre Resort: Walea Bahi island. Booking office (in Italy): Tel/Fax: (39-52) 1233-628, www.walea.com. This Italian-run upscale resort is located near a number of excellent dive sites. There are 11 simple cottages. Note that the price includes all meals and three dives a day. $$$$

Southeast Sulawesi

KENDARI

Kendari, the capital of South-east Sulawesi, is a port town whose craftsmen are renowned for their intricate silver filigree work.

A good place to break a journey because of its decent range of lodgings. Spend a day soaking and swimming at the spectacular seven-tiered waterfall at Morame.

Getting There
By Air
Merpati and Pelita fly to Kendari daily from Makassar.
Merpati: Jl. Sukarno No. 85. Tel: (0401) 21896.
Pelita Air: Kendari airport and in Hotel Makassar Golden.

By Sea
PELNI ferries sail overnight to Bau Bau and Rahu en route from Makassar, Kendari, Luwuk, Kolonodale and Ambon. Office: Jl. Pahlawan No. 1, Bau Bau. Tel: (0402) 21905.
There is also a daily Andhika Express "super jet" ferry service from Kendari to Bau Bau in 5 hours. Purchase your tickets at the harbour. Office: Jl. Sukowati No. 8, Kendari. Tel: (0401) 24514.

Getting Around
As Kendari has only one main road, you can't get lost. *Pete-pete* run frequently, stopping anywhere along the way for a low fixed fare; they can also be chartered to any destination in the city. There are also metered taxis and *becak* for shorter distances.

Tourist Office
Provincial Tourist Services: Jl. Lakidende No. 9. Tel: (0401) 21764.

Where to Stay
Kendari Beach Hotel: Jl. Hasanuddin No. 44. Tel: (0401) 21988. Good standard rooms with air-con. A bit way out, but a nice location once you're there. Lovely views of the bay and nice gardens too. $$$
Kartika: Jl. S. Parman No. 84. Tel: (0401) 21088. Decent rooms, a few with air-con, and attached bathrooms. $$

Where to Eat
Many food vendors line the streets of Kendari, serving traditional Indonesian fast food such as *mie goreng*, *bakso* and *martabak*.
Kendari Beach Hotel: Jl. Sultan Hasanuddin No. 44. Tel: (0401) 21988. Serves Chinese and Indonesian food in an open-air terrace overlooking the bay. *Moderate*

Restaurant Price Guide

Price categories for a three-course meal (Asian or Western), without drinks:
Expensive = US$26–50
Moderate = US$11–25
Inexpensive = under US$10

Where to Shop
Pusat Kerajinan: Jl. A. Yani. This government-run handicraft centre sells a good selection of local textiles, baskets, silver jewellery and woodcarvings.
Kampung Gembol: Several shops line the streets selling furniture, clocks and teak-stump items.

BAU BAU

Bau Bau is quite modern and the main town on Buton, the largest island in Sulawesi and once the seat of a powerful sultan.

Bau Bau is the nearest town to Lasalimu on the eastern coast, the jump-off point to the Tukang Besi islands.

Getting There
Fast boats departing Kendari at 7am arrive in Bau Bau within 5 hours. The airport has been closed indefinitely.

Getting Around
Bau Bau is so small, you can walk to most places. Otherwise, *pete-pete*, *ojek* and *becak* are available.

Tourist Office
Buton Tourist Office: Tel: (0402) 23588.

Where to Stay
Highland Resort: Tel: (0402) 21189; e-mail: trvlindo@upg.mega.net.id. Features a hill-top location 7 km (4 miles) from town, with a beautiful view of the bay and mountains. Common bath, and meals are included in the room price. $
Wakatobi Dive Resort: Tomea Island. www.wakatobi.com. This remote diving resort has a guest lodge and bungalows based loosely on traditional architecture. The prices for diving packages include meals and dives. $$$$$

Where to Eat

Warung Pangkep: This is the largest and busiest of the many eating houses serving grilled fish. *Inexpensive*

North Sulawesi

MANADO

Manado is the provincial capital and lies at the foot of the lovely mountainous Minahasa region, which is dotted with active volcanoes, clear highland lakes and hot water springs. North Sulawesi exports enough coffee and cloves to afford a relatively high standard of living for its people, who survived relatively unscathed during the 1997–9 Asian economic crisis.

Getting There

By Air

SilkAir flies from Singapore twice a week, while Garuda flies daily from Denpasar and Jakarta via Makassar. Bouraq flies from Makassar five times a week. Lion Air flies to Manado three times daily. Merpati flies from Palu and Luwuk three times a week, but the flights are sometimes cancelled with short notice.
Bouraq: Jl. Sarapung No. 27, Tel: (0431) 841-470. Sam Ratulangi Airport: Tel: 60449.
Garuda: Jl. Diponegoro No. 15. Tel: (0431) 851-544, 852-154.
Lion Air: Ruko Mega Mas Lok 1 No. 8. Tel: (0431) 847-000.
Merpati: Jl. Diponegoro No. 119. Tel: (0431) 853-213.
Mandala: Jl. Sam Ratulangi No. 206. Tel: (0431) 851-743.
SilkAir: Jl. Sarapung No. 5. Tel: (0431) 863-744/844.

By Sea
Because domestic flights to Manado have unreliable schedules, ferries are sometimes more dependable. PELNI ships from Ambon, Talaud, Sorong, Ternate, Bau Bau and Banggai Islands sail overnight to arrive in Bitung Harbour, an hour east of Manado city.
Manado office: Jl. Sam Ratulangi No. 7. Tel: (0431) 862-844.
Bitung office: Jl. D.S. Sumolang. Tel: (0438) 21167.

Getting Around

Most metered taxis in Manado are ramshackled affairs. Some drivers ask for outrageous fares and will refuse service to areas that are prone to congestion.

One company, **Dian Taxi** (Tel: (0431) 851-010) is fairly efficient. Otherwise, take a *microlet* (mini-bus) which travels along fixed routes. Or charter by the hour comfortable, air-con *taxi gelap* (non-official taxi with driver included) at the *taman* (park) in **Pasar 45**.

Tourist Offices

Provincial Tourist Office: Jl. Augustus No. 17. Tel: (0431) 865-604.
Regional Department of Tourism: Jl. Diponegoro No. 111. Tel: (0431) 851-723, 851-835.

Tour Operator

Maya Express: Jl. Sudirman No. 15. Tel: (0431) 870-111; e-mail: mayaexp@mdo.mega.net.id. One of the best travel agents in town that cater to foreign visitors.

Rafting Operator

Waraney: Jl. Sam Ratulangi No. 199. Tel: (0431) 850-363; e-mail: waraney@manado.wasantara.net.id. Arranges one- and two-day rafting trips on Class II–IV rapids. Attentive and experienced crew.

Where to Stay

Manado offers a variety of clean, well-run hotels in a range of prices. Dive resorts are often the nicest, breeziest places to stay due to their waterfront locations. On **Bunaken Island**, there are no air-con rooms nor is there hot water, and electricity is only available during 6pm–6am. Check that your room has a mosquito net and a fan to ensure a restful sleep. In **Minihasa**, temperatures can plummet at night. Long pants and a sweater are recommended.

Manado

Santika Manado: Desa Tongkaina. Tel: (0431) 858-222; www.santika.com. A resort set on lovely landscaped grounds with a swimming pool. There is a free boat shuttle service to Bunaken and Siladen islands. **$$$$**
Hotel Kawanua: Jl. Sam Ratulangi No. 1. Tel: (0431) 52222, Fax: 65220. Located in the city centre, this is the oldest 4-star hotel in Manado. Large building with more than 100 rooms, swimming pool and restaurant. **$$**
Hotel Minahasa: Jl. Sam Ratulangi No. 199. Tel: (0431) 862-559. This colonial-design hotel is conveniently located and offers rooms with air-con and hot water. Breakfast is included in the price. A pleasant place. **$**
Hotel New Queen: Jl. Wakaba 14. Tel: (0431) 65979, Fax: 65748. A 35-room deluxe hotel. Very clean. **$**

Bunaken Island

Seabreeze Bungalows: Pangalisang Beach. Tel: (0431) 859-379. The newly-built, simple wooden cottages feature terraces and waterfront views. Meals are included in the price. **$**

Where to Eat

Minahasans love chillies, and variations of *dabu-dabu*, a tangy but

Dive Operators in Manado

Dive operators who are members of **North Sulawesi Watersports Association (NSWA)** maintain a high standard of safety, and support marine conservation by adhering to environmentally responsible practices. NSWA is currently working together with villagers from Manado Tua island to become the world's first demonstration site for new EcoReef rehabilitation technology. In February 2004, 620 EcoReef modules were transported, assembled and installed. See www.bunaken.info or contact NSWA at e-mail: nswa@bunaken.info for further information. NSWA member groups are as follows:

Bastiano's Cottages and Diving: e-mail: info@bastianos.com.
Celebes Divers: e-mail: celebes@kudalaut.com.
ChaCha Dive Resort: e-mail: cha2@indosat.net.id.
Dive Center Thalassa: e-mail: info@thalassa.net.
EcoDivers: e-mail: info@eco-divers.com.
Froggies Divers: e-mail: christiane@divefroggies.com.
Gangga Island Resort: e-mail: ganggais@indosat.net.id.
Kungkungan Bay Resort: e-mail: info@kungkungan.com.
Living Colours Diving: e-mail: info@livingcoloursdiving.com.
LumbaLumba Diving: e-mail: lumbalumba@manado.wasantara.net.id.
Minahasa Lagoon Resort and Diving: e-mail: resort@minahasalagoon.com.
Murex Dive Resort and Liveaboards: e-mail: info@murexdive.com.
Murex/Lembeh Resort: e-mail: info@lembehresort.com, moore@indosat.net.id.
Nusantara Dive Centre: e-mail: info@ndc-manado.com.
Two Fish Divers: e-mail: diving@twofishdivers.com.

fiery condiment, accompany nearly every meal.

For the adventurous palate, Minahasan restaurants serve a spread of fruit bat on the spit, chopped forest rat and spicy wild pig with generous chunks of fat.

Xanadu: Jl. Sam Ratulangi. Tel: (0431) 863-022. Good upscale Chinese food and live entertainment. *Moderate*

Dolpin Donuts: Jl. Sam Ratulangi No. 51. Tel: (0431) 859-840. A large menu lists Western and Indonesian dishes and fruit juices. Open for breakfast. *Inexpensive*

Green Garden: Jl. Sam Ratulangi, No. 52. Tel: (0431) 870-089. Serves Chinese and Indonesian dishes, with consistently good food and efficient service. *Ayam goreng* and *babi merah* are winners. *Inexpensive*

Where to Shop

Local art includes figures of local animals carved out of wood, coconut shell and bamboo. Other purchases are embroidered fabric from the Gorontalo area, and candy made from coconut, *kenari* nut or sago.

Maleo Art Shop: Jl. Walanda Maramis No. 34. Tel: (0431) 851-801. The best selection of local souvenirs and handicrafts.

Matahari Department Store: Jl. Sam Ratulangi. You can probably do all your shopping here, including handicrafts on the third floor.

Maluku

Travel Advisory

In early 2004 flights, suspended in 2000 due to the escalating Christian-Muslim conflict, were restored. However, Maluku's tourism infrastructure – including hotels, dive resorts and restaurants – is practically non-existent, as many owners and workers fled the islands during the conflict. Check with a reputable travel agent in Indonesia who is familiar with the situation for the latest information on travel to Maluku.

Papua (Irian Jaya)

Jayapura/Sentani

Jayapura, the capital of Papua (Irian Jaya) province, lies on Yos Sudarso Bay and its backdrop of steep-walled coves easily makes it the most gorgeous provincial capital in Indonesia. Those who want to visit the interior of Papua must obtain a *surat jalan* (travel permit) from Jayapura, Biak or Sorong.

GETTING THERE

By Air

Flights to Jayapura actually land at Sentani, a 45-minute drive from Jayapura. Garuda and Merpati both have daily services. The Garuda flight goes via Makassar (formerly Ujung Pandang) in Sulawesi and Biak. The Merpati flight goes via Surabaya (Java), Makassar (Sulawesi), Ambon (Maluku) and either Biak or Timika. Garuda flies from Denpasar (Bali) to Jayapura, with an overnight transit in Makassar, and connects with a Merpati flight from there.

Garuda: Jl. Percetakan No. 4. Tel: (0967) 536-218.
Merpati: Jl. A. Yani No. 15. Tel: (0967) 33111, 33220/7.

By Sea

It's worth trying to hitch free rides on one of the coastal steamers as the oil industry in Papua is served by a number of sea-going vessels. On the south coast, Merauke is the major port.

Other boats carry passengers, but for a fee. If you're in no hurry, the PELNI ferry sails from Jakarta to Jayapura and other points in Papua.

TOURIST OFFICE

Provincial Tourist Services: Jl. Sau Siau Dok II, P.O. Box 499, Jayapura. Tel: (0967) 2138 ext. 263.

TOUR OPERATORS

Dani Sangrila Tours and Travel: Jl. Pembangunal No. 19, Jayapura.

Tel: (0967) 31060, Fax: 31529. Has a good reputation.
Insatra Exclusive Tours: Jl. Pembangunan no. No. 19, Jayapura. Tel: (0967) 31060, Fax: 31529. Insatra has much experience in Wamena and Asmat tours; reputable and knowledgeable.
Remote Destinations Indonesia: Head office: Jl. Rimba Buntu No. 46, Jakarta. Tel/Fax: (021) 726-0940, e-mail: dani@jayapura.wasantara.net.id. Owner Leksmono Santoso places emphasis on responsible cultural excursions.

Travel Permit

A *surat jalan* (travel permit) is required for visits to the interior of the island. After landing in Sentani, hire a car at the airport and go directly to the police station in Jayapura (a 45-minute drive), where travel permits are processed. Have on hand 2–4 passport-sized photos (depending on the number of places you plan to visit), photocopies of the first two pages of your passport, and your embarkation card. (Expatriate residents need a copy of the KITAS or KIMS instead of the embarkation card.)

When applying for the *surat jalan*, be certain to list all of the places you plan to visit in the interior – Baliem Valley, Asmat, Wasur, for example – and have photocopies made of it. You will have to leave one copy at each area visited, as police check points often ask for it, even in non-restricted areas.

WHERE TO STAY

Except for the deluxe Sheraton Hotel in Timika, most places in Papua are extremely basic and lack atmosphere. Ask for air-con rooms everywhere except in Wamena, where the weather may be warm during the day but turns chilly in the night.

Sentani

Sentani Indah: Jl. Raya Hawai. Tel: (0967) 592-828. Located 10 minutes from Sentani airport, this standard hotel has a nice pool and a good restaurant specialising in grilled fish. There is disco dancing on weekends. The rooms at the back offer a good view of the Cyclops Mountains. **$$$**
Hotel Semeru: Jl. Yabasco. Tel: (0967) 91447. Very basic but clean air-con rooms. A 5-minute walk from the airport. There is no restaurant, but a simple breakfast of hard-boiled egg and bread is included in the price. **$**

Jayapura

Matoa Hotel: Jl. Jend. A. Yeni No. 14. Tel: (0967) 531-633, Fax: 531-437. Near the police station and Merpati offices in downtown Jayapura. Clean air-con rooms, but rather lacking in atmosphere. The food in the restaurant is passable. **$$$**
Yasmin Hotel: Jl. Pereetakan Negara No. 8. Tel: (0967) 533-2222, Fax: 536-027, e-mail: yasmin-jyp@jakweb.com. Located in downtown Jayapura, the rooms here are clean, but small. There is a good restaurant with the best iced coffee in town. The Garuda office is next door. **$$**

Restaurant Price Guide

Price categories for a three-course meal (Asian or Western), without drinks:
Expensive = US$26–50
Moderate = US$11–25
Inexpensive = under US$10

WHERE TO EAT

Meals available all over Papua are generally decent but simple – fried rice, fresh fish and vegetables. Various fruits are available in certain areas seasonally It is a good idea to carry a jar of peanut butter and some granola bars when travelling to the more remote areas, such as Asmat.

Sentani

Pondok Wisata Younywa: Lake Sentani. This pleasant, open-air restaurant has great grilled fish, especially the *gabus*, a local lake fish. The *kangkung* (water spinach) is also good. *Inexpensive*
Restoran Mickey: Main street, Sentani. One of the old stand-bys in Sentani, it serves good Chinese and Indonesian food. *Inexpensive*

Jayapura

Jaya Grill: Jl. Koti No. 5. Tel: (0967) 23436, 22783. Located at the harbour, this restaurant opens only in the evenings. The specialities are grilled fish and Chinese food. *Inexpensive*
Pondok Ria Wisata: Jl. Soa Sin Dor II. Tel: (0967) 32011. One of those restaurants that allows diners to pick out their own fish before cooking. An open-air setting not far from downtown with a nice view of Jayapura bay. Open all day. *Inexpensive*

WHERE TO SHOP

The demand for Asmat carvings has increased over the years. Simple colours – red, black and white – are an Asmat trademark. There are several shops in Hamadi, a suburb of Jayapura, which have good selections of pieces from Asmat and Sentani.

Wamena

Wamena is the only urban centre in the Baliem Valley. Most of the town's inhabitants are immigrants; the indigenous people of the valley are the Dani, Lani and Yali, a neolithic race with unknown origins who prefer to remain in the hills. Until the 1960s when steel was introduced to them, they used wood, flint and stone for weapons and tools.

Getting There

Merpati has daily flights from Jayapura to Wamena. It is also possible to stand by for one of the Trigana cargo flights (Tel: (0969) 31611), which leaves almost hourly, but sometimes has no room for passengers.
Merpati office: Jl. Trikora No. 41. Tel: (0969) 31080.

Hotel Price Guide

Price categories for standard rooms, usually without breakfast:
$$$$$ = above US$150
$$$$ = US$101–150
$$$ = US$51–100
$$ = US$30–50
$ = under US$30

WHERE TO STAY

Honai Resort: Jl. Hom-Hom-Pikhe. Tel: (0969) 31515, 31516, Fax: 31513. A 30-minute drive north of Wamena, this hotel was built by the owners of Lymbunan Tours. Over-priced. **$$$**
Baliem Pilamo: Jl. Trikora. Tel: (0969) 31043, Fax: 31798. Located on the main street, it offers a range of rooms from basic to standard. The water supply is always a problem. The restaurant offers basic but good food. **$**
Nayak Hotel: Jl. Gatot Subroto. Tel: (0969) 31067, Fax: 32641. A favourite with budget travellers, the Nayak is a 2-minute walk from the airport. Standard rooms and a small restaurant with simple fare. **$**
Sinakma Elok: Jl. Raya Habema, Sinakma. Tel: (0969) 33025. Jakarta office: Fax: (021) 726-094, e-mail: dani@jayapura.wasantara.net.id. A 10-minute drive west of Wamena and a 5-minute walk from several Lani villages, the establishment has seven traditional cottages with thatched roofs and modern tiled bathrooms

with hot water. Native ambience, with hand-made furniture and traditional handicrafts. There is an open-air restaurant. **$**

WHERE TO EAT

Mas Budi Restaurant: Jl. Trikora No. 106. Tel: (0969) 31214. Located on the north fringe of Wamena, this place has very friendly staff and serves good food. *Inexpensive*

Mentari Restaurant: Jl. Yos Sudarso No. 47. Tel: (0969) 31771. A 10-minute walk from Wamena's main street, Mentari has a pleasant atmosphere and good food at reasonable prices. Try the *udang sungai* (crayfish) from the Sungai Baliem. The Chinese dishes are also good. *Inexpensive*

Sinta Prima: Jl. Trikora. A small restaurant serving very decent, basic food. Good value. *Inexpensive*

WHERE TO SHOP

Wamena has three handicraft shops on its main street, Jl. Trikora, with selections of Dani, Lani and Yali pieces. Items of interest are stone axes, penis gourds, orchid fibre skirts, shell necklaces, slate "bride stones", and bows and arrows.

Such items may also be purchased directly from the Dani and Lani when visiting their villages.

Timika

Timika is the jump-off point to Agats, the only town in Asmat (the land as well as the people share this name).

GETTING THERE

Only Merpati flies to Timika. The flights leave Jayapura in the morning and return from Timika in the afternoon. There are flights daily except on Wednesdays.

Merpati office: Jl. Rayangkara No. 2. Tel: (0901) 321-745.

WHERE TO STAY

Sheraton Timika: P.O. Box 3. Tel: (0901) 549-5959, Fax: 549-4950, www.sheraton.com. Beautiful and expensive, but well worth the price. Located 10 minutes from the airport, the resort has the full range of deluxe facilities including a beautiful pool, and a nature walk. Another plus is the excellent restaurant right on the premises. **$$$$**

Hotel Serayu: Timika. Tel: (0901) 21096, 21345. Located in downtown Timika, the rooms are basic with air-con. There is a restaurant serving passable food. **$$$**

WHERE TO EAT

Sheraton Timika: Tel: (0901) 549-5959. This is the only restaurant in Timika. The hotel is four-star, and the restaurant also deserves that rating. *Moderate*

Agats

Agats is the main town in Asmat. The Asmat, once feared headhunters and cannibals, are now fishermen and carvers who live in the harsh environment of an alluvial swamp on the south coast of Papua.

GETTING THERE

By Air

MAF – Missionary Aviation Fellowship – operates private flights. It sometimes charters out an entire flight, but this must be arranged in advance and is an expensive option. Check with a local travel agent for details.

By Sea

On arrival in Timika, it takes a day or two to arrange onward travel to Agats. There is a private wooden ship which acts as a ferry and leaves Timika for Agats about once in two weeks, but the schedule is haphazard.

Another alternative is to hire a speedboat, which takes about 6 hours on the open Arafura Sea, or a motorised Asmat longboat (hollowed out of a tree trunk), for an 8–12 hour ride. Such arrangements can usually be made at any of the local hotels.

WHERE TO STAY

Asmat Inn: Very basic rooms, no restaurant. Meals have to be pre-ordered. Water is rationed during the dry season. **$**

Losmen Pada Elo: A two-storey place offering very basic rooms. The second floor is cooler and a little nicer. Standing fans are available on request. A simple breakfast is served, as well as coffee or tea on request. Meals may be ordered in advance. Water is rationed during the dry season, but at other times, it is collected in converted fuel barrels which sit in the bathroom under the eaves. **$**

WHERE TO EAT

Buetkawer: This tiny stall next to the dock serves simple food and beer. *Inexpensive*

Daliah: A stall dishing up very basic food. *Inexpensive*

WHERE TO SHOP

Agats has four shops offering a wide variety of Asmat pieces, but it is easy to purchase pieces directly from the villages nearby. The quality varies considerably and it is becoming difficult to find older pieces. Two of the shops – **Kios Asmat** and **Toko Anda** – are owned by immigrants from other islands. Better yet, enquire at one of the two small hotels how you can buy art pieces. In a matter of hours, you will find Asmat villagers turning up with a few pieces for sale.

Biak

Boot-shaped Biak island, lying one degree off the equator on Papua's north coast, is known for its spectacular diving spots. The tiny island, the scene of World War II battles, is extremely hot and humid.

GETTING THERE

Garuda and Merpati fly into Biak several times weekly.

Diving at Raja Ampat

The hottest new destination in Indonesia's dive scene is the Raja Ampat ("Four Kings") group of islands. (Note: The Indonesian word for "four" – *empat* – is spelled *ampat* here.) Located west of the Bird's Head Peninsula, most of the islands are uninhabited except for an occasional village, leaving them pristine. Ecosystems from rainforests with rich flora and fauna to remarkable coral reefs make these islands a haven for naturalists and water enthusiasts. Limestone islands, cathedral-like caves, tranquil lagoons and pure white sand beaches complete the picture.

Several Indonesia-based tourist and dive boats now include the Raja Ampat islands on their itineraries. See page 383, "How to Tackle Nusa Tenggara" and page 386 "Komodo Dive Boats" for boats and their websites.

LANGUAGE ♦ 401

Tribal Guides

Experienced Dani and Lani guides who speak English can be hired in Wamena to accompany tourists on treks. Hiring experienced, English-speaking guides in both the Baliem Valley and Agats is expensive.

Expect to pay US$15–20 per day for a guide and US$3–5 per day for a porter or helper. There are more guides in the Baliem Valley than in Asmat. They are supposed to be licensed, but most are not.

It is a good idea to check with the local police to see if any complaints have been filed by previous tourists. There have been reported incidents of night thefts and the subsequent disappearance of guides.

Longer treks are best organised through one of the local tour operators.

Garuda: Jl. Sudirman No. 3. Tel: (0981) 25737/47.
Merpati: Jl. Moh. Yamin No. 1. Tel: (0981) 21213, 21251.

TOUR OPERATOR

PT. Biak Irian Wisata Tours & Travel: Arumbai Hotel, Jl. Selat Makassar No. 3. Tel: (0981) 23196, Fax: 22501, e-mail: paradise@biak.wasantara.net.id. This small company specialises in tours to see the bird-of-paradise on Yapen island. It also organises diving and snorkelling trips to the Biak/Sorong area.

WHERE TO STAY

Hotel Arumbai: Jl. Selat Makassar No. 3. Tel: (0981) 21835, Fax: 22372. Located in the centre of Biak town, Arumbai has clean air-con rooms but no view. The restaurant is small, but the food is good. **$$$**
Irian Hotel: Jl. Professor Moch Yamin. Tel: (0981) 21139, 21939, Fax: 21458. Decent basic air-con rooms and food. Good value. **$**

WHERE TO EAT

Arumbai Restoran: Jl. Selat Makassar No. 03. Tel: (0981) 22159, 21835. Very good Chinese and Western food at reasonable prices. *Inexpensive*
Restoran 99: Jl. Imam Bonjol No. 32. Tel: (0981) 21450. A simple restaurant with good Chinese food. *Inexpensive*

WHERE TO SHOP

The best place to find local art is the **Iriani Art Shop** on Jl. Imam Bonjol.

Merauke

Merauke, the easternmost town in Indonesia, is the entry point to southern Papua. The town is virtually one long street – Jl. Raya Mandala. Here, you can obtain a permit to Wasur National Park.

GETTING THERE

Merpati flies between Jayapura and Merauke. Office: Jl. Raya Mandala No. 226. Tel: (0971) 321-182.

WHERE TO STAY

Megaria Hotel: Jl. Raya Mandala No. 166. Tel: (0971) 21932. Rooms include a few with Western-style bathrooms and hot water. Breakfast is included; other meals have to be pre-ordered. The reception desk stocks cold beer. **$**
Nirmala Hotel: Jl. Raya Mandala No. 66. Tel: (0971) 21849. A very basic hotel with a huge restaurant that serves good food. The economy rooms come with a fan and use of a common bathroom, the mid-priced rooms have air-con but no hot water, while the deluxe rooms have both air-con and hot water. **$**

WHERE TO EAT

Café Jaya: Across from the Nirmala Hotel. Good Padang food that is very spicy. *Inexpensive*
Sari Laut: Opposite the Megaria Hotel. Good food, good value. *Inexpensive*

Wasur

It takes 30 minutes by car from Merauke to the entrance of Wasur National Park, and another hour to Yanggandur, within park boundaries. Taxi drivers may only agree to take you there during the dry season. It is also possible to hire four-wheel-drive vehicles in Merauke.

The **World Wildlife Fund** (WWF) (P.O. Box 284, Merauke, Tel/Fax: (0971) 21397) can arrange guides and transport to Wasur.

Language

General

Indonesia's motto, *Bhinneka Tunggal Ika* (unity in diversity) is seen in its most potent form in language. Although there are over 350 languages and dialects spoken in the archipelago, the one national tongue, Bahasa Indonesia, will carry you from the northernmost tip of Sumatra to Java and across the string of islands to Papua.

Bahasa Indonesia is both an old and a new language, and is based on Malay, which has been the lingua franca throughout much of Southeast Asia for centuries, but has changed rapidly in the past few decades to meet the needs of a modern nation.

Although Bahasa Indonesia is a complex language demanding serious study, the construction of basic Indonesian sentences is relatively easy. Indonesian is written in the Roman alphabet and, unlike some other Asian languages, is not tonal.

Indonesians always use language to show respect when speaking to others, especially when a younger person addresses his elders. The custom is to address an elder man as *bapak* or *pak* (father or Sir) and an elder woman as *ibu* (mother or Madam), and in the case of slightly younger people who are VIPs, this form of address is also suitable and correct.

Bung (in West Java) and *mas* (in Central and East Java) roughly translate as "brother" and are used to address your equals, people of your own age whom you don't know all that well. You can also use it to address strangers, even service personnel such as hotel clerks, taxi drivers, tour guides and waiters (it's friendly, and a few notches above "buddy" or "mate").

a short as in 'father'
 (*apa* = what, *ada* = there is)
ai rather like the 'i' in 'mine'
 (*kain* = material, *sampai* = to arrive)
k hard at the beginning of a word as in 'king', but hardly audible at the end of a word.

(*kamus* = dictionary, *cantik* = beautiful)
kh (*ch*) slightly aspirated, as in 'khan' or the Scottish 'ch' in 'loch'
(*khusus* = special, *khabar* = news)
ng as in 'singer', never as in 'danger' or 'Ringo'
(*bunga* = flower, *penginapan* = cheap hotel)
ngg like the 'ng' in 'Ringo'
(*minggu* = week, *tinggi* = high)
r always rolled
(*rokok* = cigarette, *pertama* = first)
u (*oe*) as in 'flute', never as in 'bucket'
(*umum* = public, *belum* = not yet)
y (*j*) as in 'you'
(*saya* = I or me, *kaya* = rich)
c (*tj*) like the 'ch' in 'church'
(*candi* = temple, *kacang* = nut)
e 1. often unstressed as in 'open'
(*berapa* sounds like *b'rapa* = how much?)
2. sometimes stressed, somewhere between the 'e' in 'bed' and 'a' in 'bad'
(*boleh* = may, *lebar* = wide)
g hard as in 'golf', never as in 'ginger'
(*guntur* = thunder, *bagus* = good)
h generally lightly aspirated
(*hitam* = black, *lihat* = to see)
i either short as in 'pin', or longer, like 'ee' in 'meet'
(*minta* = to ask for, *ibu* = mother)
j (*dj*) as in 'John'
(*jalan* = road or street, *jahit* = to sew)

Two minor points about spelling. Despite the new rules, you will find many instances where the names of people continue to be spelled with the old 'oe' rather than the current 'u'. Some may change, but most stick to their birthright. For example, the former president, whose name is Suharto, is spelt by the local press as Soeharto.

Less important are the subtle distinctions in Central Java between the two forms of 'o' and the liquid sounds of 'l' or 'r'; the niceties are of interest only to experts in phonetics, but in practical terms, it means that the city of Solo may also appear as Sala, and that the Siva temple at Prambanan may be written (in its popular form) as Lara Janggrang, Loro Jonggrong or Roro Jonggrang ... and they are all correct.

GREETINGS & CIVILITIES

Thank you	Terima kasih
Good morning	Selamat pagi
Good day	Selamat siang
Good afternoon/ good evening	Selamat sore (pronounced soray)
Good night	Selamat malam
Goodbye (to person going)	Selamat jalan
Goodbye (to person staying)	Selamat tinggal
I'm sorry	Ma'af
Welcome	Selamat datang
Please come in	Silakan masuk
Please sit down	Silakan duduk
What is your name?	Siapa nama Anda
My name is...	Nama saya...
Where do you come from?	Saudara datang dari mana?
I come from...	Saya datang dari...

PRONOUNS/ FORMS OF ADDRESS

I	Saya
You (singular)	Anda
He, she	Dia
We (excluding the listener)	Kami
We (including the listener)	Kita
You (plural)	Anda semua
Mr	Pak/bapak
Mrs	Ibu/bu
Miss	Nona

DIRECTIONS/TRANSPORT

left	kiri
right	kanan
straight	terus
near	dekat
far	jauh
from	dari
to	ke
inside	di dalam
outside of	di luar
here	di sini
there	di sana
in front of	di depan/muka
at the back	di belakang
next to	di sebelah
pedicab	becak
car	mobil, motor
bus	bis
train	kereta api
bicycle	sepeda
motorcycle	sepeda motor
Where do you want to go?	Mau kemana?
I want to go to...	Saya mau ke...
Stop here	Berhenti di sini
bank	bank
post office	kantor pos
Immigration department	Departemen immigrasi
tourist office	kantor pariwisata
embassy	kedutaan

RESTAURANTS

restaurant	restoran/rumah makan
food	makanan
drink	minuman
breakfast	makan pagi
lunch	makan siang
dinner	makan malam
boiled water	air putih/ air matang
iced water	air es
tea	teh
coffee	kopi
milk	susu
rice	nasi
noodles	mie/bihun
fish	ikan
prawns	udang
vegetables	sayur
fruit	buah
egg	telur
sugar	gula
salt	garam
pepper	merica, lada
cup	cangkir
plate	piring
glass	gelas
spoon	sendok
knife	pisau
fork	garpu

SHOPPING

shop	toko
money	uang
change (from a bill)	uang kembali
to buy	beli
price	harga
expensive	mahal
cheap	murah
fixed price	harga pas
How much is it?	Berapa?/Berapa harganya?

SIGNS

open	buka, dibuka
cashier	kasir, kassa
closed	tutup, ditutup
entrance	masuk
exit	keluar
don't touch	jangan pegang
no smoking	dilarang merokok
push	dorong
pull	tarik
gate	pintu
ticket window	loket
ticket	karcis
information	keterangan
city	kota
market	pasar

Further Reading

History

A History of Modern Indonesia by M.C. Ricklefs. *MacMillan, London, 1981.*
Bali: A Paradise Created by Adrian Vickers. *Periplus, Singapore, 1989.*
Banda by Willard A. Hanna & Nigel Simmonds. *Yayasan Warisan dan Budaya Banda, Banda Neira (Maluku), 1997.*
Forgotten Kingdoms in Sumatra by F.M. Schnitger. *Oxford University, 1989.*
Indonesian National Revolution 1945–1950 by Anthony Ried. *Longman, Hawthorn, 1974.*
Jogjakarta Under Sultan Mangkubumi 1749–1792: A History of the Division of Java by M.C. Ricklefs. *Oxford, London, 1974.*
Sumatra: Its History and People by Edwin Loeb. *Oxford University Press, Singapore, 1989.*
The Policy and Administration of the Dutch in Java by Clive Day. *Oxford, Kuala Lumpur, 1966.*
The Stone Age of Indonesia by Van Heekeren. *H.R. Martinus Nijhoff, The Hague, 1972.*

Geography & Natural History

A Visitor's Guide to Lore Lindu National Park by C. Ellis. *The Nature Conservancy, Jakarta, 1998.*
The Malay Archipelago: The Land of the Orangutan and the Bird of Paradise by Alfred Russel Wallace. *Reprint, Graham Brash, Singapore, 1983.*
Zoo Quest for a Dragon by D. Attenborough. *Lutterworth Press, London, 1957.*

Society & Religion

A Little Bit One O'clock: Living with a Balinese Family by William Ingram. *Ersania Books, Ubud, Bali, 1998.*
Indonesia: Its People, Its Society, Its Culture edited by Ruth McVey. *HRAF Press, New Haven, 1963.*
Indonesia: The Making of a Culture by J.J. Fox. *Australian National University, Canberra, 1980.*
Offerings: The Ritual Art of Bali by Francine Brinkgreve & David Stuart-Fox. *Image Network Indonesia, Bali, 1992.*
State and Civil Society in Indonesia edited by Arief Budiman. *Monash University, Australia, 1990.*
The Batak by Achim Sibeth. *Thames and Hudson, London, 1991.*
The Island of Bali by Miguel Covarrubias. *Periplus, Singapore, 1999.*
The Rope of God by James Siegel. *University of California Press, Berkeley, 1969.*
Tragedy in Bali (A Personal Account of the Bali Bombing) by Alan Atkinson. *ABC Books, Sydney. 2002.*
Ubud is a Mood by 14 contributing writers and photographers. *Yayasan Bali Purnati, Bali, 2004.*

Textiles

Contemporary Tie and Dye Textiles of Indonesia by Kim Jane Saunders. *Oxford University Press. Kuala Lumpur, 1997.*
Indonesian Textiles by Michael Hitchcock. *Periplus, Singapore, 1991.*
Splendid Symbols: Textiles and Tradition in Indonesia by Mattiebelle Gittinger. *The Textile Museum, Washington D.C., 1979.*

The Arts

Ancient Indonesian Art by A.J. Bernett. *Harvard University Press, Cambridge, 1959.*
Art in Indonesia: Continuities and Change by Claire Holt. *Cornell University Press, New York, 1967.*
Beyond the Java Sea: Art of Indonesian's Outer Islands by Paul Michael Taylor & Lorraine Aragon. *Harry Abrams, New York, 1991.*
Court Arts of Indonesia by Helen Ibbitson Jessup. *Harry Abrams, New York, 1990.*
Dance and Drama in Bali by Beryl de Zoete and Walter Spies. *Faber and Faber, London, 1938.*
Dances in Indonesia by Soedarsono. *Gunung Agung, Jakarta, 1974.*
Indonesia: The Art of an Island Group by Frits Wagner. *Greystone, New York, 1967.*
Music in Java by Jaap Kunst. *Martinus Nijhoff, The Hague, 1973, 2 vols (3rd edition).*
The Sculpture of Indonesia by Jan Fontein. *Harry Abrams, New York, 1990.*

Art & Photo Credits

Angsana Resorts & Spa 194
Apa archives 16/17, 21, 24, 26, 28, 31, 165, 263
Archives of the Royal Tropical 38, 141
Paul Beiboer 124T, 136T, 226, 227, 335, 335T, 336T
H. Berbar/HBL spine top, 5B, 43, 44, 52R, 55, 56, 91, 123, 126, 138, 147, 148T, 155, 180, 283, 292
Peter Bruechman 101, 266, 267, 270, 295, 298, 301, 304, 305, 317, 325, 327
Debe Campbell 272, 211
Christiana Carvalho 338
Frank Castle 27, 29, 37, 279
Alain Compost 105, 193, 342T
Gerald Cubitt 104, 175, 184, 190, 250, 274/275, 281T, 285, 287, 290T, 291, 303, 308, 310, 322, 327T, 333, 337, 343
Suzanne D'Angelo 59
Steve Davey/La Belle Aurore 149
Mark Erdmann 249T, 261, 316
Alain Evrard 159, 160T
M. Fornari/HBL 45
Jill Gocher 131
Tim Graham/Colorific 3B
Linda Hahn 338T, 339, 340
Linda Hoffman 61
Kevin Hamdorf 163, 164R
Blaine Harrington front flap top, 116/117
HBL 68, 182
Tony Hillhouse 342
Hans Höfer 51, 52L, 53, 58, 66L, 102, 136, 145, 151L, 158, 164L, 178, 191, 213, 286, 288, 289, 290, 344
Jack Hollingsworth back flap top, back cover centre bottom, 2/3, 4B, 8/9, 48/49, 57, 63, 69, 71, 72, 73, 75, 78, 80, 83, 89, 94, 95, 96, 182T, 186T, 193T, 200, 201, 202, 202T, 203, 204, 205, 205T, 206, 207, 208, 208T, 209, 210, 210T, 212, 214, 215, 216, 216T, 217, 218, 219, 220T, 222, 222T, 223, 228, 229, 229T, 230, 231,

232, 233, 234, 234T, 235, 236, 236T, 237, 238, 239, 246, 246T, 248, 249, 251, 252, 252T, 253, 261T, 264, 292T, 315
J. Houyvet/HBL 186
R. Humphries/HBL 84, 125T, 128T, 155T, 170, 172T
Indonesian Department of Information 19, 36, 39, 40
Luca Invernizzi Tettoni 1, 18, 20, 30, 33, 34L, 35, 41, 46/47, 62, 66R, 79, 81, 86, 100, 110/111, 124, 126T, 130, 132, 137, 139, 139T, 140, 143, 144, 146, 148, 150, 150T, 152, 154
Jakarta History Museum 32
Ingo Jezierski 133T, 135
Lyle Lawson 108/109
Frederic Lontcho 187
Patrick Lucero 174
Minassio/Globe Press 4/5, 97, 214T, 221, 245
Kal Müller 67, 87, 171, 172, 179, 242, 268, 269, 271
Eric M. Oey 22, 23, 25, 64, 85, 160, 161, 162
Photobank front cover, back flap bottom, back cover left, 4R, 12/13, 34R, 42, 50, 60, 65, 77, 82, 103, 166/167, 168, 177, 192, 195, 196/197, 238T, 254, 255, 257, 258, 259, 260, 262, 269T, 278, 280, 282, 283T, 284, 293, 294, 296/297, 303T 309, 318/319, 320, 323, 329, 330, 332, 334, 341
Private archives 99
L. Rebmann/HBL 306
Simon Rowe 306T, 307, 311T, 330T, 331
D. Saulnier/HBL 121, 125, 128
Morten Strange 231T

Cartographic Editor Zoë Goodwin
Production Caroline Low
Design Consultants
Carlotta Junger, Graham Mitchener
Picture Research Hilary Genin

Arthur Teng back cover right, 54, 112/113, 244
Wim Verheugt 311
Goradz Vilhar 143T, 151R
Bill Wassman 74
Christopher Wee 162T
Martin Westlake front flap bottom, 2B, 6/7, 10/11, 14, 70, 76, 88, 90, 98, 120, 123T, 127, 129, 133, 134, 156, 157, 165T, 177T, 181, 183, 185, 188, 189, 220, 240/241, 265, 265T, 273, 273T, 314, 324T, 326, 328
Joseph Yogerst 276

Picture Spreads

Pages 92/93: *Top row, left to right*: Suzanne D'Angelo, Suzanne D'Angelo, Photobank, Suzanne D'Angelo. *Bottom row, left to right*: Photobank, Suzanne D'Angelo, Suzanne D'Angelo, Suzanne D'Angelo, Suzanne D'Angelo, Dipika Rai.
Pages 106/107: *Top row, left to right*: Gerald Cubitt, Photobank, Paul Beiboer, Debe Campbell. *Centre row, left to right*: Gerald Cubitt, Jean-Luc Petit/HBL. *Bottom row, left to right*: Gerald Cubitt, Gerald Cubitt, Gerald Cubitt, Gerald Cubitt, Debe Campbell.
Pages 224/225: *Top row, left to right*: Andrea Pistolesi, Andrea Pistolesi, Andrea Pistolesi. *Centre row, left to right*: both Rio Helm/Auscape. *Bottom row, left to right*: Rio Helmi/Auscape, Jim Holmes/Axiom.
Pages 312/313: *Top row, left to right*: Gerald Cubitt, R. Margaillan/HBL, Gerald Cubitt, Mark Erdmann. *Bottom row, left to right*: Gerald Cubitt, Mark Erdmann, Gerald Cubitt, Gerald Cubitt, Mark Erdmann, Gerald Cubitt.

Map Production Cosmographics
© 2004 Apa Publications GmbH & Co.
Verlag KG (Singapore branch)

Index

Numbers in italics refer to illustrations

a

Aceh 169, 171–4, 177
  see also **Banda Aceh**
  Free Aceh Movement (GAM) *170*, 171, 172
  independence movement 45
  Islam in 28, 29, 35, 45, 52–3, 60
  Kampung Kuala Aceh 172
  political unrest 56
  Weh island 172
Agung, Sultan 32–3, 77, 159
Ai Bari 256
Ai island 328
Alor 269
Ambon 51, 54, 59, 321, 324–6, *325*, 327
  Australian War Cemetery 325–6
  Benteng Victoria 325
  Dutch control 31, 32, 324–5
  Museum Siwalima 325
Anak Krakatau (Child of Krakatau) *100*, *106*, 133, 193, 194
animism 55, 59, 95, 243, 263, 339
antiques, Solo 156
Apayo island 334
art 99
  Asmat 338–40
  Sanur (South Bali) 204–5
  Tanimbar 329
  Ubud (Bali) 99, 215, 217–8, 220
arts academies (ASTI) 80, 155
arts and crafts 95–9, *96*, 211
  basketry 98, 101
  beadwork 98–9
  Celuk (Bali) 213
  Denpasar (South Bali) *203*
  and gender 95
  gold and silver smithery 97–8, 183
  jewellery 97–8
  Kudus teakwood houses *139*
  local *pasar* (markets) 95
  Mas (Bali) *215*, 215–6
  metalwork 96–7
  wayang kulit (shadow puppets) 95
  Papua 91, 337
  woodcarvings 96
  Yogyakarta and area 146
Aru islands 329
Arumbai 342

Asmat (Papua) 96, 321, 337–40, *338*, *340*, 341
Auki 342

b

Badui people 119
Badung 199
  see also **Denpasar (South Bali)**
Balaputra 151
Bali 25, 26, *112–3*, 115, 199
  see also **Central Bali**; **East Bali**; **North and West Bali**; **South Bali**
  art 99, 217–8, 220
  arts and crafts 96, *97*, *215*, 215–6
  Brahmans 55, 216
  dance *8–9*, *74*, 75–6, 77–9, *78*, 80, *212*, 213, 214
  Dutch colonial period 31, 35
  farming 102, 104
  feasts and festivals 62, 64–5, *224–5*
  food 69, 70, 71
  funerary rites *67*, 224, *225*, 227, 248
  gamelan music 84, 85, *214*, 216
  Hinduism 55, 59, 62–3, 81
  legong dancers *8–9*, *74*, 78, 215, 220
  mask plays 79
  popular unrest 41
  population 15, 42, 54, 55, 56, 104, 199
  religious conversion 64
  rice cultivation 56, 101
  social structure 199
  temples to Dewi Sri 66
  textiles 88, *89*, 90, 91, *92*, 216, 234, *238*, 239
  and tourism 211
  volcanic eruptions 102, 104
  wayang puppet theatre 79
Banda Aceh *170*, 171–2
  see also **mosques (mesjid)**; **museums**
  Gunongan 171
  Jalan Iskandar Muda: cemetery 172
  Jalan Teuka Umar 171
  Kampung Kuala Aceh 172
Banda Besar 328
Banda islands (Kepulauan Banda) 32, 321, 323, 328–9, *329*
Bandaneira 328–9
  Istana Mini 329
Bandung Study Club 38

Bandung (Western Java) *14*, *52*, 131, 135–6
  Gedung Sate 136
  Institute of Technology (ITB) 136
  Jalan Braga 136
  Jalan Cihampelas 136
  Museum Geologi (Geological Museum) 21, 136
  new art 99
Bangka island 91, 104, 192
Banjarese 53, 283
Banjarmasin (Kalimantan) 283–4, 285
Baranusa 269
Batak 53, 59, 75, 88, 90, 96, 169, *176*, 176–8, *177*, 179
  Barus Jahe (village) 176
  Lingga (village) 176
Batam island (Riau), Nagoya 195
Batavia 121–3, 124–5
  see also **Jakarta**
  Dutch colonial period *32*, 32–3, 34
  Kota 124
  massacre of Chinese 57
  Taman Fatahillah 124
Batubulan (Central Bali) 96, 213–4
  Taman Burung Bali Bird Park 213
Bengkulu (South Sumatra) 191, 192–3, *193*
  Dendam Taksuda Botanical Gardens 193
Benteng Amsterdam (Maluku) 327
Benteng Belgica (Maluku) 328
Benteng Budaya (Fort Vredebug) (Yogyakarta) 145–6
Benteng Bukit Kursi (Riau) 195
Benteng de Kock (Bukittinggi) 183
Benteng Duurstede (Maluku) 327
Benteng Kayu Merah (Ternate) *322*
Benteng Keraton (Buton) 311
Benteng Marlborough (Sumatra) 192, *193*
Benteng Nassau (Maluku) 328
Benteng Oranje (Ternate) 330
Benteng Rotterdam (Makassar) 302, *303*
Benteng Toloko (Ternate) *330*, 331
Benteng Victoria (Ambon) 325
Biak island *332*, 333, *341*, 341–2
Bintan island (Riau) *194*, *195*
  Angsana Resort & Spa *194*
  Banyan Temple 195
  Benteng Bukit Kursi 195
  Istana Raja Ali Marhum 195
  Mesjid Sultan 195
  Pasir Panjang beach 195
  Penyengat 195
  Senggarang 195

Tanjung Pinang 195
Trikora 195
Blambangan (Java) 159, 164
Bogor
  Istana Bogor (Presidential Palace) 134
  Kebun Raya (Botanical Gardens) 134
  PHPA headquarters 105
Bonnet, Rudolph 99, 203
Borneo 53, 277, *279*
  see also **Kalimantan**
Borobudur 23, 24, 77, *106–7*, 119, 141, *147–50*, 147–50
  Candi Mendut 150
  Candi Pawon 149–50
Bosnik 342
Brooke, James ("White Raja") 293
Buddhism 59, 63, 64
  early history 23, 24, 25
  and Islam 61
  in Java 63
  Srivijaya kingdom (Palembang) 23–5, 27, 53
  in Sumatra 63
  Tantric Bhairawa sect 25
Bugis (Buginese) 51, 53, 123, 231, 253, 284, 299, *300*, 301, *304*, 305, 311
Bukittinggi 182–4, *183*
  Benteng de Kock 183
  Pasar Raya (Central Market) 183
Buru 323
Buton island 311

c

candi **stone monuments** *147*
  see also **Borobudur**
  Bali 222–3
Cemara Lwang (East Java) 165
Central Bali 199, 213–23
  see also **Batubulan; museums; temples; Ubud**
  Bangli 223
  Batuan 215
  Bedulu *78*, 221
  Blahbatuh 216
  Bona 216
  Bukit Demulih 223
  Celuk 97, 213
  Gianyar 216
  Goa Gajah *221*
  Kedewatan 219–20
  Mas *215*, 215–6
  Pejeng 221–2
  Peliatan 220, 221
  Penestanan 220
  Sangeh 220
  Singapadu 213–4
  Sukawati 214–5
  Sungai Ayung *220*
  Yeh Puluh 221
Central Java 141–56
  see also **Borobudur; Mataram empires; Prambanan; Sangiran; Solo (Surakarta); Yogyakarta (Jogja)**
  arts and crafts 89, 96
  dance and drama 75, *76*, 76–7, 78, 79, 141, *142*, 144
  Dieng Plateau 24, *153*
  early history 24
  gamelan music 83
  Java Man *21*, 21–2, *107*, 119, 136
  Kasongan 146
  Kota Gede 98, 141, 146
  loro blonyo (painted wood statues) 95
  Parangtritis 147
  population 141
  Telaga Warna (Coloured Lake) 153
Chinese 15, 34, 57, 63, 125, 139, 160, 294
Christianity 45, 59, 61, 64
  Batak people 53, 59, 169, 177, 178
  Catholicism in Flores 55, *262*, *263*, 267
  conversion to 29
  Dayak people *283*
  and Islam 60, 61
  in Java 51, 52
  in Maluku 54, 321, 323, 324
  in Sulawesi 53–4
  in Sumatra 53, 59
  in Papua (Irian Jaya) 55, 59
churches
  Catholic Cathedral (Jakarta) *126*
  Immanuel Church (Jakarta) 127
  Immanuel Church (Maluku) 327
  Immanuel Protestant Church (Medan) 174
  old Dutch Church (Gereja Blenduk) (Semarang) 139
Cirebon (Western Java) *6–7*, *137*, 137–8
  batik 86, *92*, 137, 138
  ceremonial masks 96
  Keraton Kanoman 138
  Keraton Kesepuhan 137, 138
  Mesjid Agung (Grand Mosque) 137
  Taman Arum Sunyaragi 138
  Tomb of Sunan Gunung Jati 138
climate 101

Coen, Jan Pieterszoon *31*, 31–2, 33, 121, 328
communism 37–8, 41
Confucianism 57, 63
Conrad, Joseph 159
Cook, James 132, 272, 338
Cornelius, H.C.C. 148
customs and rituals 53, 64–7, *224–5*
  see also **feasts/festivals; *keris* daggers**
  adat 53, 64, 118, 177
  funerary rituals 67, 95, 224, *225*, 227, 248, 281, 289, *306*, 307, 339–40
  life cycle and the arts 95
  jiwa 65–7
  and textiles 90, 91, *92*

d

Danau Batur *227*
Danau Bratan *228*, 229
Danau Buyan 228–9
Danau Habbena *318–9*
Danau Jempang 280–81
Danau Laguna 331
Danau Riam Kanan 286
Danau Segara Anak 250
Danau Sentani 334
Danau Tamblingan 229
Danau Tempe 305
Danau Toba 96, *168*, 169, *176*, 177, *178*
Danau Tolire 331
Danau Tondano 317
Danau Unggi 342
dance and theatre 75–81
  Balinese 77–9, 211
  Balinese *barong* 75, 75–6, 80, *212*, 213, 214
  Balinese *kecak* 78, *196–8*
  Balinese *legong* dancers *74*, 78, 215, 220
  Balinese trance dances 76, 216
  Indonesian Arts College (STSI) (Solo) 155
  Java dance and drama 75, *76*, 76–7
  kebyar 8–9, 79
  Mahabharata epics 26, 62, 79, 81, 95, 153, 163
  Nias island 187
  Purawisata (Ramayana Dance School) (Yogyakarta) 146
  Ramayana Ballet (Yogyakarta) *146*
  Ramayana epics 26, 62, 79, 81, 95, 139, 153, 220

sendratari 80
serimpi dance *140*
Trimurti Theatre (Prambanan) 153
wayang puppet theatre 52, 64, *79*, 79–80, 85, *93*, 95, 118, 125, 131, 139, 142, *146*, 155, 156, 163, 214–5, 246
Dani people 65, 321, *334*, *335*, 336, 337
Dayak peoples *53*, 65, 77, 97, 277, *278*, 279, *280*, 282, *283*, 286, *288*, *289*, 290, 295
arts and crafts 96, 97, 99, 101, *294*
customs and rituals 281, 289, 290
food 71–2
longhouses *280*, 281, 290, 295
De Houtman, Cornelis 31, 201
Demak, Islamic kingdom of 25, 27, 29, 121, 139
Demak (Western Java) 139
Mesjid Besar (Grand Mosque) 139
Denpasar (South Bali) 201–3, 211, 213
see also **markets; temples**
Catur Mukha 202
Gedung Buleleng 202
Hotel Puri Pemecutan 202
Lapangan Puputan *201*, 201–2
Museum Bali 202
Pusat Dokumentasi 203
Sekolah Tinggi Seni Indonesia (STSI) 203
Werdi Budaya Art Centre *203*
Dharmawangsa, King 25
Diponegoro, Pangeran *35*, 141, 317
Tomb of (Sulawesi) 302
Dobo (Maluku) 329
Dong Son Bronze Age 22–3, *23*, 82, 96, 221
Doyo Lama 334
Dubois, Eugene 107
Dullah island, Tual 329
Dutch
collapse of rule 39, 41
colonial period 28, 29, 31–5, 53, 54, 55, 119, 131, 324–5, 338
Cultuurstelsel (forced labour system) 131
and rise of nationalism 37, 38, 39
Dutch East India Company (VOC) 31, 34, 121, 123, 125, 126, 154, 329, 338

e

East Bali 233–9
see also **Klungkung; museums; temples**
Amed *239*
Amlapura ("Karangasem") 239
Bugbug 238
Candidasa *237*, 237–8
Gandhi Ashram 238
Gelgel 237
Goa Lawah 237
Kamasan 97, 234
Kusamba 96, 237
Manggis 237
Muncan 235
Nusa Lembongan 237
Nusa Penida 237
Padang Bai 237
Puri Agung Karangasem 239
Puri Kanginan 239
Sidemen *234*, 234–5
Tenganan 91, *92*, *238*, 238–9
Tirtagangga 239
Tulamben 239
Ujung 239
East Java 33, 141, *158*, 159–65
see also **Kediri; Madura island; Malang; Surabaya**
Alas Purwo National Park 165
arts and crafts 96
Baluran National Park *165*
Belahan bathing pool *162*
Bromo-Tengger-Semeru National Park, 164
Candi Bajang Ratu 162
Candi Jawi 162
Candi Panataran 163
Candi Tikus 162
early history 24, 25
Ijen National Park, 165
ikat textiles 88, 90
Islam 159
Meru Betiri National Park 165
music 82
Selekta 163
Sukarno's mausoleum 163
Sungai Brantas 25, 159
Tengger highlands 164–5
Tenggerese people 52, 119, 164
Tralaya cemetery 162
Tretes 162
Trowulan 25, 162
wayang puppet theatre 79
Wringin Lawang 162
East Timor (Timor Leste) 15, 22, 39, 43, 45, 54, 56, 272–3
El Nino drought 102
Empu Kuturan 201

f

Fa Hsien (monk) 23
Fahnestock brothers 85
farming 22, 24, 42, 56, 119
see also **rice**
and volcanic ejecta 102, 104
feasts/festivals 64–5
Bali 62, 64–5, *224–5*
Kasodo 164
Lombok 247, 253
Sekatan 85
selamatan 64, 146
Sulawesi 315–6
Torajan death feasts 307
film, *Trance and Dance in Bali* (Margaret Mead) 75–6
flora and fauna *101*, 102, 103–5, *104*, *105*, 106
see also **forests; national parks and nature reserves; rainforests**
Bali 213
Kepulauan Seribu 131
Komodo dragons *259–60*, 266
Lombok 248, 251
Maluku *105*, 323–4
monkey forests *219*, 220–21, 251
orangutan *175*, *276*, 277, 283, 287, 290, 291–2, *292*
Rafflesia Sanctuary (West Sumatra) 184
Raya Pasi (Kalimantan) 294
Sangeh (Bali) 220–21
Sulawesi *105*, 299, *312–3*, 315
Sumatra *105*, 169, 181, 184, 186, 188
Wallacea *105*, 246
Flores 35, 55, 59, 243, 259, 261, *262*, *263*, 263–7
Bajawa 265
bark cloth 91
Batu Cermin 264
Bena 265, 266
Boloji 265
Boripo 265
Cancar 264
Dintor 265
Ende 263, 266, 267
forests 104, 264
Golo Curu 264
Japo 267
Kampung Ruteng 265
Labuhanbajo *264*
Langa 265, 266
Larantuka 263, 267
Likowali 265
Manggarai 264–5

Maumere 267
Moni 267
Nggela 267
Rana Mese 265
Riung 266
Ruteng 264
Seventeen Islands Nature Reserve 266
So'a 266
Todo 265
Warusoba 265
Watujaji 265
Welo 265
Wogo Tua 265
Wolowaru 267
food and drink 69–73
  bananas 69, 70–71, 72
  Bintang beer *72*
  chicken 71, 72
  chillies 70
  Chinese influences 69
  coconut/coconut products 69, 70, 72, 73
  desserts 72–3, *73*
  es campur 73
  five pillars 69–71
  fruit 72, 73
  kitchens 73
  meat and animal parts 71–2
  mi (noodles) 70
  nasi campur 72
  Padang cuisine 70, 72, 181, *182*, 189
  peanuts 69, 71
  religious offerings 59, 222
  rijstaffel (rice table) *69*
  sate 69, *71*
  seafood 71, 137
  soya beans 69, 71
  spices 70
  standards of hygiene 73
  tea 72
  vegetables 71, 72
  vegetarian cuisine 72
  warung (eating houses) 73
  western fast food 73, *121*
forests 103–4, 264
  see also **rainforests**
  Bangko-Bangko 247
  fires 104, 184, 194
  Hutan Wisata Suranadi (Lombok) 248
  illegal logging 102
  Kalimantan 277
  Maluku 321
  reforestation 104– 5
fossils 21–2, *107*

g

Galdikas, Birute 287, 292
gamelan music 65, 79, *80*, *82*, 82–5, *85*, 118, 131, 141, 142, 144, 155, *156*, *214*, 216
geology 101–2
Gili Air 248, *249*
Gili Meno 249
Gili Trawangan 248–9
Goa, kingdom of (Sulawesi) 301, 302, 303
Goa Mabolu 311
gold 255, 277, *285*, 294, 337
Gresik, *ikat* textiles 90
Gujarat 26
Gunawan, Hendra *99*
Gunung Agam 183
Gunung Agung 199, 227, 233, 236, 248
Gunung Api *328*, 329
Gunung Ara 261
Gunung Arjuna 162
Gunung Batukau 199, 228
Gunung Batur 199, *227*
Gunung Bromo *108–9*, *164*, 165
Gunung Catur 228
Gunung Dempo 192
Gunung Ebulobo 266
Gunung Gamalama 330, 331
Gunung Gede 135
Gunung Ifar 334
Gunung Ile Ape 268–9
Gunung Inerie 266
Gunung Kelam (Dark Mountain) 295
Gunung Kelimutu *266*, 266–7
Gunung Kerinci 181, 186
Gunung Kiematubu 331
Gunung Mahawu 317
Gunung Merapi (Java) 24, 148, 153
Gunung Merapi (Sumatra) 183, 185
Gunung Muller 295
Gunung Nona 325
Gunung Pangrango 135
Gunung Penanggungan 162
Gunung Penanjakan 165
Gunung Prapat Agung 231
Gunung Puncak Jaya 186
Gunung Ranaka 264
Gunung Rinjani 245, 248, *250*, 251
Gunung Satalibo 261
Gunung Seblat 186
Gunung Semeru 164–5
Gunung Singgalang 183
Gunung Sirung 269
Gunung Tambora 103, 255, 257
Gunung Tangkuban Perahu *136*
Gunung Tiranggang Hulu 286
Gunung Tujuh 186
Gunung Welirang 162
Gus Dur *see* **Wahid, Abdurrahman**

h

Habibie, B.J. 43, 44, 45, 51, 53, 304
Halmahera island 321, 323
  Daru 331
  funerary rites 67
  Tobelo 331
Hamengkubuwono I 143, 144
Hamengkubuwono VIII *30*
Hamengkubuwono IX 142
Hamengkubuwono X *46–47*
Hari island 311
Hatta, Mohammad 39, 53, 329
Hayam Wuruk 25
Hindu-Dharma religion 199, 222
Hinduism 64
  in Bali 55, 59, 62–3, 81
  early history 24, 27
  and Islam 61
  in Java 52, 81
  in Lombok 59
Hiri 331
history 18–44
hotels
  Borobudur Hotel (Jakarta) 126
  Grand Bali Beach Hotel (Sanur, South Bali) 204, 205
  Grand Hyatt (Jakarta) 128
  Hilton Hotel (Jakarta) *82*, 128
  Hotel Indonesia (Jakarta) 128
  Hotel Tugu Malang (Malang) 163
  Mandarin Oriental Hotel Majapahit (Surabaya) 160

i

independence movement *159*
Indianised kingdoms 23, 24
International Monetary Fund 43
Irian Jaya *see* **Papua (Irian Jaya)**
Iskandar Muda, Sultan 171
Islam *58*, 59, 60–2, 64, 243
  see also **Aceh**
  conversion to 119
  Demak, kingdom of 25, 27, *29*, 121, 139
  five "pillars" 61
  in Flores 263
  in Java 26, 51–2, 60, 76, 77, 137, 159
  in Kalimantan 53, 60

Koran 58, 60, *61*, 62
in Lombok 55, 245, *248*, 250–51
Malacca 25, 27–8, 60
in Maluku 54, 321, 323
and nationalism 37–8
in Nusa Tenggara 60
rise of 26–9
Sekatan festival 85
Sharia 62
in Sulawesi 53, 54
in Sumatra 52–3, 60
in Sumbawa *254*, 255
Sunna 60
Wahid and Nahdlatul Ulama (NU) 44
in Papua (Irian Jaya) 55

j

Jakarta 15, 114, 118–9, 131
see also **Batavia; hotels; museums**
Ancol Dreamland 124
Ancol Marina 124
Benteng Noordwijk 126
Bharata *wayang wong* company 80
Blok M 128
Café Batavia 125
Catholic Cathedral *126*
Central Business District 121
Chinatown (Glodok) *125*
Dunia Fantasi *124*
Dutch lookout tower (Uitkik) 123
Gedung Pancasila 126–7
Immanuel Church 127
Irian Jaya Freedom Memorial 126
Istana Merdeka 126
Istana Negara 126
Jakarta Convention Centre 128
Jalan Sudirman *120*
Jalan Surabaya 127
Jalan Thamrin *116–7*, 121, 128
Jl. Kali Besar Barat No. 11 (town house) 125
kampung (village) dwellings 121
Lapangan Banteng 123, 126
Medan Merdeka (Freedom Square) 123, 126
Mesjid Istiqlal 126
Monas (National Monument) *126*
mosques and Islam 61
National Archives 126
nationhood 39
Pasar Ikan (fish market) 124
Pasaraya department store 128, 129
Plaza Indonesia 128
Pondok Indah 128
population 121
Presidential Palace 126
Ragunan Zoo 129
riots and unrest 42, *43*, *56*, 57, 125
Sea World 124
Senayan Plaza *128*
Si Jagur *125*
Sunda Kelapa Harbour *123*
Taman Ismail Marzuki 127
Taman Mini Indonesia 129
Taman Ria 128
Tanjung Priok 121
Trisakti University 43
Welcome Statue (Menteng) *127*, 127–8
Jambi (South Sumatra) 88, 191
Candi Muara 191
Pasar Raya (main market) 191
Tiangko Caves 191
Janggala 25
Japan
Japanese War Memorial (West Papua) 342
World War II occupation 38–9, 55, 123, 160, 174, 325, 329, 341
Japanese *samurai* 32
Java 26, 27, 28–9, 31, 101, 118–9
see also **Central Java; East Java; Jakarta; West Java**
batik textiles *86*, 88–9, *92–3*
Buddhism 63
communism in 38
cuisine 69, 71
Dutch colonial period 32–4
early history 23, 24–5
effects of volcanic eruptions 102, 104
English invasion of 34–5
European influences 37
farming 102, 104
forest fires 102
gamelan music 82–3, 84, 85
Gunung Ungaran 24
Hinduism 52, 81
Islam 26, 51–2, 60, 76, 77
new art 99
and Outer Islands 56
pan-Islamic movement 37
popular unrest 41
population 15, 42, 51–2, 56, 104, 114, 119
reforestation 104
rice cultivation 56, 101
trance dances *76*
transmigration 54
wayang puppet theatre 52, 64, 79, 79–80, *93*, 118, 125, 139, 142
Java Man *21*, 21–2, *107*, 119, 136
Java War (1825–30) 35, 141
Javanese
arts and crafts 96
culture and customs 64, 67
language 51
transmigration 54, 55
Jayabaya (Joyoboyo), King 38
Jayakarta 32, 121, 123
see also **Jakarta**
Jesuits 29
jiwa 65–7
Johor 28

k

Kaget island 284
see also page 414
Kai Besar island 329
Kalabahi (Alor) 269
Kalimantan 23, 115, 277
see also **Dayak peoples; flora and fauna**
animism 59
arts and crafts 91, 97, 98
Banjarese 53, 283
Christianity 59
exports 104
forest 101, 102, 103, 277
funerary rites 67
Islam 53, 60
population 42, 53, 54, 277
tensions with Jakarta 45
Kalimantan Barat (West Kalimantan) 292–5
see also **Pontianak; Sambas; Singkawang**
Gunung Palung National Park 287, 295
Gunung Poteng 294
Juang Mandor Cemetery 294
Kampung Saham 293–4
Ketapang 295
Nanga Pinoh 295
Pasir Panjang 294
Putussibau 295
Raya Pasi 294
Sanggau 295
Sintang 295
Tugu Khatulistiwa (Equator Monument) 294
Kalimantan Selatan (South Kalimantan) 283–6
Banjarmasin 283–4, 285
Batu Laki 285
Cempaka 284–5, *285*
Gunung Tiranggang Hulu 286

Kahung Valley 286
Kentawan Nature Reserve 286
Loksado 285–6
Martapura 285
Muara Hatip 285
Pelaihari 285
Pelaihari Martapura Nature Reserve 286
Kalimantan Tengah (Central Kalimantan) 289–92
Camp Leakey 287, *291*, 291–2
Kumai 290
Museum Balanga 289
Palangkaraya 289, 290
Pangkalanbun 290
Penda Tangaring 290
Tanjung Puting National Park 274–5, 287, 291–2, *292*
Tewah 290
Tumbang Maharoi 290
Tumbang Samba 290
Kalimantan Timur (East Kalimantan) 279–83
Apokayan region 282–3
Balikpapan 279
Barong Tongkok 281
Bontang 279, 283
Data Dawai 282
Kersik Luwai orchid reserve 281
Kota Bangun 280
Kutai National Park *283*
Long Ampung 282, 283
Long Bagun *282*
Long Iram 281–2
Long Lindung Payau 283
Long Sungai Barang 283
Long Uro 283
Mancong 281
Melak 281
Muara Muntai 280
Samarinda 279
Tanjung Isuy *280*
Tenggarong 279–80
Wanariset 287
Kao 331
Karowai ("tree people") 341
Kediri (East Java) 25, 159, 301
Kembang island (Flower Island) 284
Ken Arok 25
Ken Dedes 25
Kepulauan Banda (Banda islands) 32, 321, 323, 328–9, *329*
Kepulauan Seribu (Thousand Islands) 124, *131*, 131–2
Kepulauan Tanimbar 329
Kepulauan Togian islands 311
Kepulauan Tukang Besi (Wakatobi) 311

Kerambitan (South Bali) 209–10
Puri Agung Wisata 209
Puri Anyar 209, 210
Keraton (Sultan's Palace) (Yogyakarta) 142–4
Keraton Kadariah (Istana Qadariyah) (Pontianak) 293
Keraton Kanoman (Cirebon) 138
Keraton Kasunanan (Solo) 154
Keraton Mangkunegaran (Solo) 85, 155–6
keris daggers *66*, 76, 96, 156, 157, 201, 225
Kertanegara, King 25, 162
Klungkung (East Bali) 233–4, 237
Bale Kambang *232*, 234
Kerta Gosa 233
Puri Semarapura *233*
Taman Gili 233
Komara, Josephine 93
Komodo *see* **national parks**
Kota Biak 341, 342
Kota Kembang (City of Flowers) *see* **Bandung**
Krakatau 100, 102–3, *106*, 133, 169, 193, 194
Kublai Khan 25
Kunst, Jaap 82
Kupang (West Timor) 273
Kuta (Bali) 201, *205*, 205–6, 211
Kuta (Lombok) 253

l

language 15, 51
  Alor 269
  Bima 255
  Chinese 57
  Dani/Lali peoples 335
  Javanese 51
  kedaton 51
  Madurese 51, 52
  Malay 51, 53, 55
  and nationalism 37, 39
  Sundanese 51, 52
Lani people 335, 336, 337
Lembata (Lomblen) 268–9, *269*
Lesser Sundas *see* **Nusa Tenggara**
Leweloba (Lembata) 268
Lombok 79, 103, 115, *242*, 245–53
  see also **Islam**; **Mataram**; **temples**
  Air Nyet 248
  Ampenan 246
  Bangko-Bangko 247
  Bangsal 248
  Batu Rintang 253
  Batulayar 248

Bayan 249–50
Bonjeruk 251
Cakranegara 247
dance traditions 77
Dutch colonial period 35
eastern and central 250–51
Gerung 246
Gerupuk 253
Getap 251
Gili Nanggu 247
Gondang 249
Hinduism 59
Hutan Wisata Suranadi 248
Jukut 251
Kerurak 249
Kuta 253
Labuan Lembar 246
Lendang Nangka 251
Lenek 250
Lingsar 248
Mandalika 253
Mawun 253
Mesjid Kuno 252
Museum Nusa Tenggara Barat (Mataram) 245–6
northern 248–50
Pemenang 248
Penujak *251*, 251–2
popular unrest 41
population 55
pottery *98*, *244*, *251*, 251–2
Praya 251
Rambitan *252*
Sade 252
Sedang Gile 250
Segenter 249
Selong Blanak *253*
Sembalun Bumbung 250
Sembalun Lawang 250
Senaru 250
Senggigi 248
Sesaot 248
Sira 249
Suranadi 248
Tanjung Aan 253
Tanjung Luar 253
Tetebatu 251
Tiu Pupas 249
western 88, 245–8
Lorentz mountains (Papua) 103

m

MacArthur, Gen. Douglas 331, 333, 334
McPhee, Colin 82
Madura island 52, 159, 161–2
  batik 88
  bull races *161*

INDEX ◆ 411

Mesjid Jamiq 162
Pamekasan 161
Sumenep 162
Madurese people 51, 52, 53, 119
Majapahit empire 25, 27, 29, 51, 119, 159, 162, 163, 164, 227, 243, 263, 301
Makassar (South Sulawesi) 28, 29, 88, 299, 301–3, 304, 305
Benteng Rotterdam 302, *303*
C.L. Bundt's residence 303
Pantai Losari 303
Pelabuhan Paotere 303
port 32, 33
Makassarese 29, 51, 53, 299, 301, 311
Malacca
Islamic 25, 27–8, 60
Portuguese 27, 29
Malang (East Java) 25, 162–3, *163*
Candi Jago 163
Candi Singosari 163
Hotel Tugu Malang 163
Malay language 51, 53, 55
Malays 15, 53, 64, 195, 290
Malaysia 41
Malukans 323
Maluku 19, *26*, *28*, 29, 54, *70*, 115, 121, 292–3, 323–31
  see also **Ambon**; **Banda islands**; **Halmahera**; **Ternate**; **Tidore**
Amahusa 326
Bacan 321
Benteng Amsterdam 327
flora and fauna *105*, 323–4
forests 101, 321
Hila 327
Honimua 326
Immanuel Church 327
Makian 321
Masohi 327
Mesjid Wapauwe 327
Moti 321
Namalatu *326*
Natsepa 326
population 54
separatism 45
Soya Atas 326
Tanimbar islands *320*
Waai 326
Manado (North Sulawesi) 315–6
Bunaken National Marine Park *314*, *316*
Mandarese 305
Marco Polo 26, 176
markets
Bukit Munggu (Candi Kuning) (Bali) 228

Kuta Art Market (Bali) 206
Pasar Badung (Denpasar) *202*
Pasar Beringharjo (central market) (Yogyakarta) 146
Pasar G.B. Wenas (Papua) 336
Pasar Ikan (fish market) (Jakarta) 124
Pasar Kumbasari (Denpasar) 202
Pasar Ngasem (Bird Market) (Yogyakarta) 144
Pasar Ubud (Central Bali) 219
Pasar Raya (Central Market) (Bukittinggi) 183
Pasar Raya (Central Market) (Padang) 182
Pasar Raya (Central Market) (Jambi) 191
Pasar Seni (Central Bali) 215
Pasar Terapung (Banjarmasin, Kalimantan) *284*
Pasar Triwindu (Solo) 156
Pelabuhan Ratu fish market 135
Sukawati (Central Bali) 215
Tomohon (North Sulawesi) 317
Mataram empires 28–9, 32–3, 34, 77, 141, 144, 153, 159
Mataram (Lombok) 245–6
Matulessy, Thomas (Pattimura) 326, 327
Medan 174–5, 176
  see also **churches**; **mosques**; **temples**
Istana Maimoon 174
Jalan Jendral A. Yani 174
Medan Fair 174
Merdeka Square 174
Museum Sumatera Utara 174–5
Taman Margasatwa zoo 174
Tjong A. Fie's mansion 174
Megawati Sukarnoputri 42, 44, 45
Melanesians 15, 45
Melayu Kingdom 191
Menadonese *see* **Minahasans**
merdeka proclamation 39
Minahasans 51, 54, 299, 315, *317*
Minangkabau 35, 51, 53, *91*, *166*–7, 169, 177, *180*, *181*, 182–3
matrilineal society 181, 189
songket textiles *91*, 185, 189
minerals 42, 104, 171, 255, 277, 321, *337*
Moluccas *see* **Maluku**
Morotai island 331
mosques (mesjid) *60*, 61
Baiturrahman Mesjid Raya (Banda Aceh) *172*
Mesjid Agung (Grand Mosque) (Banten) 29, *132*

Mesjid Agung (Grand Mosque) (Cirebon) 137
Mesjid Al Fatah (Ambon) 325
Mesjid Besar (Grand Mosque) (Demak) 139
Mesjid Besar (Grand Mosque) (Yogyakarta) 145
Mesjid Hatta-Syahrir (Bandaneira) 329
Mesjid Istiqlal (Jakarta) 126
Mesjid Jame (Ambon) 325
Mesjid Jami (Abdurrahman Mosque) (Pontianak) 293
Mesjid Jamik (Madura) 162
Mesjid Kuno (Lombok) 252
Mesjid Raya (Grand Mosque) (Medan) 174
Mesjid Raya Sabilal Muhtadin (Grand Mosque) (Kalimantan) 284
Mesjid Sultan (Riau) 195
Mesjid Wapauwe (Ambon) 327
Moyo island 256
Muna island 311
museums and galleries
Agung Rai Museum of Art (Ubud) 218
Antonio Blanco Museum 217
Asmat Museum of Culture and Progress *339*
Museum Adityawarman (Padang) 182
Museum Bahari (Jakarta) 123–4
Museum Balanga (Kalimantan) 289
Museum Bali (Denpasar) 202
Museum Ballompoa (Sungguminasa) 303
Museum Belawang (Dullah) 329
Museum Captain Cole (Bandaneira) 329
Museum Cendrewasih (Biak) 341
Museum Geologi (Geological Museum) (Bandung) 21, 136
Museum Indonesia (Jakarta) 129
Museum Lapawawoi (Watampone) (Bone) 305
Museum Le Mayeur (Sanur) 205
Museum Loka Budaya (Papua) 333
Museum Mohammed Hatta (Bandaneira) 329
Museum Negeri Aceh (Banda Aceh) 171
Museum Negeri Kupang (West Timor) 273
Museum Negeri (Pontianak) 293
Museum Negeri Propinsi

Sulawesi Tengah (Palu) 309
Museum Negeri Propinsi Sulawesi Utara (Manado) 316
Museum Negeri (Papua) 333–4
Museum Neka (Ubud) *217*
Museum Nusa Tenggara Barat (Mataram) 245–6
Museum Provincial Lampung (Bandar Lampung) 193
Museum Provincial Makassar 302
Museum Purbakala (Central Bali) 221
Museum Puri Lukisan (Ubud) 217
Museum Purna Bhakti Pertiwi (Presidential Palace Museum) (Jakarta) 129
Museum Riau (Tanjung Pinang, Bintan) 195
Museum Rudana (Ubud) 218
Museum Rumah Aceh Awe Gentah (Banda Aceh) 171–2
Museum Rumah Bari (Palembang) 192
Museum Rumah Budaya (Bandaneira) 328
Museum Sejarah Jakarta (History Museum) *124*, 124–5
Museum Seni Lukis Klasik Bali (East Bali) 234
Museum Seni Rupa (Fine Arts Museum) (Jakarta) 125
Museum Simalungun (Pematangsiantar) 176
Museum Siwalima (Ambon) 325
Museum Sjahrir (Bandaneira) 329
Museum Sono Budoyo (Yogyakarta) 85, 145
Museum Sumatera Utara (Medan) 174–5
Museum Trinil (Sangiran) 21, 156
Museum Trowulan (East Java) 162
Museum Wamena (Papua) 336
Museum Wayang (Jakarta) 125
National Museum (Jakarta) 96, *107*, 127
Puri Lempad (Ubud) 218
Sangkar Agung (Bali) 231
Sawangan (North Sulawesi) 316
Seniwati Gallery (Ubud) 218
Taman Dundo Kanduang (Rumah Adat Baandjuang Museum) (Bukittinggi) 183
music
 see also **gamelan** music
 Fahnestock brothers 85

 karawitan 82
 traditional music (Sulawesi) 315
Muzakar, Kahar 53

n

Namata (Savu) 272
Napabale Lagoon 311
Nasution, A. H. 53
national parks and nature reserves 104–5
 Alas Purwo National Park 165
 Baluran National Park *165*
 Bogani Nani Wartabone National Park 317
 Bohorok Orangutan Rehabilitation Centre 175
 Bunaken National Marine Park *314*, *316*
 Gunung Ambang Nature Reserve 317
 Gunung Gede-Pangrango National Park 103, 134–5
 Gunung Leuser National Park 175–6, 287
 Gunung Palung National Park 287, 295
 Iboih National Park 172
 Ijen National Park 165
 Kakanauwe Nature Reserve 311
 Kentawan Nature Reserve 286
 Kerinci Seblat National Park 181, 186
 Kersik Luwai orchid reserve 281
 Komodo National Park 105, 106, *107*, *258*, 259–61, 264
 Kutai National Park *283*
 Lore Lindu National Park 309–10, *313*
 Lorentz National Park *106*, *107*, 343
 Manusela National Park 327
 Meru Betiri National Park 165
 Morawali Nature Reserve 310, 311
 Palau Supiori Reserve 342
 Pelaihari Martapura Nature Reserve 286
 Rawa Aopa National Park 311
 Rimba Panti Nature Reserve 184
 Seventeen Islands Nature Reserve 266
 Tangkoko-Dua Saudara Nature Reserve 316
 Tanjung Puting National Park 274–5, *287*, 291–2, *292*
 Ujung Kulon National Park *106*, *107*, 133–4

 Wasur National Park *343*
 Way Kambas National Park *190*, 193–4
 West Bali National Park 230, 231
nationalism 37–9, 41, 45, 55, 56, *159*
Naulu people 327
Ndao island 272
Nemoto, Naoko (Dewi Sukarno) 40
New Guinea 22, 39, 41, 101, 115, 321, 338, 341
Ngadisari (East Java) 165
Ngurah Rai, Col. 210
Ngurah Rai International Airport (South Bali) 206
Nias island 96, *186–8*
 Bawomataluwo 187
 Gunung Sitoli 187
 Hillisimaetano 187–8
 Lagundi 187
 Telukdalem 187
Nona island 316
North Sumatra 171–9
 see also **Aceh**; **Batak**; **Danau Toba**; **Medan**; **Pematangsiantar**; **Samosir island**
 Ambarita 178–9, *179*
 Berastagi 176
 Bireuen 173
 Bohorok Orangutan Rehabilitation Centre 175
 Bukit Lawang 175
 Cermin 176
 Danau Laut Tawar 173
 Gayo highlands 173–4
 Gunung Leuser National Park 175–6, 287
 Kabanjahe 176
 Kampong Balik 173
 Kampong Kibet 173–4
 Lamno 174
 Pangururan 179
 popular unrest 41
 Prapat 178
 Sialangbuah 176
 Sigli (Padri) 35, 173
 Simanindo 179
 Sipisopiso Waterfall 176
 Takengon 173
 Tao island 179
 Tomok 178
 Tongging Valley 176
 Tuk Tuk 178, 179
North and West Bali 199, 227–31
 see also **temples**
 Air Panas (Hot Springs) 230
 Air Sanih (Yeh Sanih) 230

Air Terjun Gitgit 229
Batukau Nature Reserve 231
Bedugul 228
Bukit Munggu (Candi Kuning) 228
Buleleng 229
Cekik 231
Gedong Kirtya (Singaraja) 229
Jagaraja 229
Jatiluwih 228
Kebun Raya Eka Karya Bali 228
Kedisan 227
Kintamani 227
Labuan Lalang 230–31
lakes *227*, 228–9
Loloan Timor 231
Lovina 230
Makam Jayaprana 231
Medewi 231
Menjangan (Deer Island) 230
Pekutatan 231
Pemuteran 230
Penelokan 227
Pengastulan 230
Perancak 231
Pulaki 230
Sangsit 229
Sawan 229
Singaraja 229
Taman Rekreasi Perancak 231
Toya Bungkah 227
Trunyan 227, 228
West Bali National Park 230, 231
Yeh Panas 228
Northmore, Mary 218
Numfor 342
Nusa Tenggara 55, 115, 243
arts and crafts 88, 97
East Nusa Tenggara *see* **Flores; Sumba; West Timor**
flora and fauna 101, 105
forests 103
Islam 60
Komodo National Park 105, 106, *107*, *258*, 259–61, 264
population 104
West Nusa Tenggara *see* **Lombok; Sumbawa**

o

oil *36*, 42, 104, 169, 171, *191*, 192, 194, 279
Onrust island 131, 132
Orang Laut 169, 195
Owi 342

p

Padaido islands 342
Padang (West Sumatra) *166–7*, 181–2
cuisine 70, 181, *182*, 189
Kampung Cina (Chinatown) 182
Museum Adityawarman 182
Pasar Raya (Central Market) 182
Sungai Muara 182
Teluk Bayur 182
Padri War 35, 173
Palembang (South Sumatra) 191–2, *192*
see also **Srivijaya kingdom**
Museum Rumah Bari 192
oil town *191*, 192
textiles 88, 90, 91
Pantar 269
Papua (Irian Jaya) 15, 39, 101, 115, *318*–9, 321, 333–43
see also **Asmat; museums; Timika**
Abepura 333
Agats 337, *338*, 339, 340
Akima 336
Amomoge 336
animism 55, 59, 339
Balai Latihan Kerja 336–7
Baliem Valley 334–7, *335*, 341
bark cloth 91
Bird's Head Peninsula 342
Christianity 55, 59
Cook's Bay 338
exports 104
flora and fauna *104*, 105
forest fires 102
Freeport-McMoRan Mine 255, 321, *337*
Gereja Koawi 342
Gunung Puncak Jaya 186
Hamadi 333
independence movement 45
Irian Jaya Freedom Memorial (Jakarta) 126
Japanese War Memorial 342
Jayapura *333*
Jiwika 336
Kabupaton Biak Numfor 341
Lorentz mountains 103
Lorentz National Park 106, *107*, 343
Manokwari 342
Merauke 343–4
political unrest 56
population 42, 54–5, 321
rainforests 103
Sentani 333, 334
Sorong 342–3
Tanjung Ria 333
transmigration 54
Wamena 335, 337
Wasur National Park *343*
parks and gardens
Bali Hyatt (Sanur) 204
Cibodas Botanical Gardens 134
Dendam Taksuda Botanical Gardens (Bengkulu) 193
Gunungan (Banda Aceh) 171
Hutan Wisata Suranadi (Lombok) 248
Kebun Raya (Botanical Gardens) (Bogor) 134
Kebun Raya Eka Karya Bali (Bali) 228
Pura Narmada (Lombok) 248
Taman Burung Bali Bird Park (Bali) 213
Taman Sari (Yogyakarta) 144
Pematangsiantar, Museum Simalungun 176
politics 15, 40–41
democracy 43–4
Golkar 42
"Guided Democracy" 40
"New Order" 42–3
"*Reformasi*" (Reform) 43–4
Pombo island 326
Pontianak (West Kalimantan) 293, 294, 295
Keraton Kadriah (Istana Qadariah) 293
Mesjid Jami (Abdurrahman Mosque) 293
Museum Negeri 293
population 15, 28, 40, 42, 51–7, 104
Bali 199
Jakarta 121
Java 114, 119, 131, 137, 141
Kalimantan 277
Lombok 245
Nusa Tenggara 243
Sulawesi 53–4, 299, 309, 315
Sumatra 52–3, 104
Sumbawa 255
Surabaya (East Java) 159
transmigration 54, 56, 280
'Unity in Diversity' 55–6
Papua (Irian Jaya) 321
Portuguese 27–8, 29, 31, 39, 45, 54, 55, 56, 121, 243, 299, 315, 323, 328
pottery 22, 98, *244*, *251*, 251–2, 337
porcelain 26
Prambanan 20, 23, *62*, 77, 106, *107*, 110–11, 141, 151–3

Candi Brahma 151, 152
Candi Sewu 151, 152
Candi Siva Mahadeva temple
(Candi Roro Jonggrang) 146,
151, *152*, 151–2
Candi Vishnu 151, 152
Trimurti Theatre 153
pusaka 66–7

r

Raffles, Sir Thomas Stamford *34*,
34–5, 118, 148, 192–3
rainforests 101, 102, 103, 104,
106, 169, 186, 188, 264, 286,
311
Rakai Pikatan 24, 151
religion 15, 59–63
see also **animism; Buddhism;
Christianity; customs and
rituals; Hinduism; Islam**
conversion 64
Kaharingan (Dayak faith) 289
Muslim/Christian violence:
Maluku, 61, 321, 323
Pancasila code 59, 62, 63,
126–7
restaurants
Café Batavia (Jakarta) 125
Rindu Alam Restaurant (Puncak)
135
Sumatra: *nasi padang*
restaurants 72
Riau 169, 191, 194–5
see also **Batam island; Bintan
island**
Pekanbaru 194
Siak Sri Indrapura 194
rice
cultivation 40, 101, 199, 283
early production of 26, 27
and *jiwa* 66
staple food *69*, 70
wet-rice cultivation 24, 56, 131,
245
Rijksen, Dr Herman 287
Rinca island 259, 261, 266
Rockefeller, Michael 339
Roti (Rote) 70, 272, *273*
Royal Dutch Shell 42

s

Sabang (Weh island) 172
Sailendra dynasty 24, 148, 151
Saleh, Raden 99
Samalona island (Sulawesi) 303
Sambas (West Kalimantan) 294–5
Istana Sambas 295

Samosir island 177, *178*, 178–9
sandalwood 243
Sangiran (early site), near Solo 21,
107
Sanglia Dol 329–30
Sanjaya rulers 24
Sanskrit 23, 25
Sanur 201, 203–5, *204*, 211
see also **temples**
Museum Le Mayeur 205
Pura Belanjong 205
Saparua 326, 327
Benteng Duurstede 327
Nusa Laut 327
Ouw village 327
Savu (Sawu) 70, *272*
sculpture 22, 23, 96, *97*, 192
see also **candi** stone
monuments
megaliths *255*, 256, 265, 270,
310
Semarang 138–9
Gedung Batu 139
Kampung Cina (Chinatown) 139
Ngesti Pandhawa *wayang wong*
company 80
old Dutch Church (Gereja
Blenduk) 139
Thay Kak Sie temple 139
separatism 40, 45, 56, 171
Seram 323, 327
Gesser 327
Manusela National Park 327
shops/shopping
Galerie Nusa Dua (South Bali) 208
Jakarta 127, 128, 129
Jalan Cihampelas (Bandung) 136
Kuta (Bali) 206
Surabaya 160
Tragia (Nusa Dua) 208
Yogyakarta 145
Siberut island 188
Siddhartha Gautama 63
Simatupang, T.B. 53
Singasari dynasty 25, 79, 159,
161, 162, 163
Singkawang (West Kalimantan)
293–4
Smit, Arie 99, 220
Smits, Dr Willie 287
Soedjojono 99
Solo (Surakarta) 34, 51, *65*, 77,
80, 141, 153–6
batik 155–6
Bengawan Solo 153
Keraton Kasunanan 153–4, *154*
Keraton Mangkunegaran 85,
154–5
Pasar Triwindu 155

puppet makers 95
Sasana Mulya 154
Solor island 243, 263, *268*
Sougb people 342
South Bali 201–10
see also **Denpasar; Kerambitan;
Kuta; Sanur; temples**
Badung 199
see also **Denpasar**
Belanjong 201
Bualu 208
Bukit Badung *207*, 207–8
Canggu 208
Garuda Wisnu Kencana cultural
complex 207
Jimbaran 206–7
Kapal 210
Kerobokan 201
Legian 206
Marga 210
Mengwi 209, 210
Nusa Dua 201, 207–8, *208*
Pecatu 208
Seminyak 206
Tabanan kingdom 209
Tanjung Benoa 208
Tuban 206
Waterbom Park 206
South Papua, forests 103
South Sumatra 191–5
see also **Bengkulu; Jambi;
Palembang; Riau**
Bandar Lampung 193, 194
Kalianda 193
Kubu people 191
Labuhan Meringgi 194
Lahat 192
Lampung 191, 193
Lingga island 191
Museum Provincial Lampung 193
Sungai Batanghari 191
Sungai Musi 191, 192
Tanjung Karang 193, 194
Way Kambas National Park *190*,
193–4
Spice Islands *see* **Maluku**
spice trade 29, 31, 32, 34, 243,
292–3
Spies, Walter 99, 203, 218
sport
see also **water sports**
Bali Golf & Country Club (Nusa
Dua, South Bali) 208
Tretes (East Java) 162
Srivijaya kingdom (Palembang)
23–5, 27, 53, 151, 301
storytelling 75
Strait of Malacca 26, 169
Sudirman, Gen. 39

Suharto *40*, *41*, *42*, 45, 243, 337
  anti-Chinese policy 57
  and Bali's tourism 211
  and Borobudur 149
  decline and fall 43
  rise to power 41, 42
  transmigration policy 54
Sukarno *40*, *41*, *42*, 44, 126, 128, 289
  arrest and death 134
  exile 266
  founds PNI 38
  mausoleum 163
  Pancasila code 59
  proclaims *merdeka* 39
Sukarno, Dewi 40
Sukarnoputri, Megawati *see* Megawati Sukarnoputri
Sulawesi 35, 101, 115, 299
  see also Bugis (Buginese); Makassarese; Torajan people
  ancient history 22
  arts and crafts 88, 91, 309
  flora and fauna 105, 299, *312–3*, *315*
  forest fires 102
  population 53–4, 299, 309, 315
  rainforests 101, 103
  separatist rising 40
  traditional music 315
  transmigration 54
Sulawesi Selatan (South Sulawesi) 53, 67, 71, 78, 123, *296–7*, 301–7
  see also Makassar; Sungguminasa; Watampone (Bone)
  Bantimurung 304
  Batu Tomanurung 303
  Bira 304
  Bulukumba Coast 304
  Buntu Kabobong (Erotic Hills) 306
  Camba 304
  Goa Leang-Leang (caves) 304
  Gua Mampu (caves) 305
  Ke'te *306*
  Lemo 306, 307
  Londa 306
  Malino 303
  Mamasa 307
  Palawa 306–7
  Palopo 305
  Pare Pare 304, 305, 306
  Rantepao 306
  Sangalla 307
  Sengkang 305
  Takapala Waterfall 303
  Tana Beru 304

Tana Toraja *298*, 305–6
  tau-tau 306–7
  Ujung Pandang *see* **Makassar**
  Watangsoppeng 305
Sulawesi Tengah (Central Sulawesi) 309–11
  Donggala 309
  Lore Lindu National Park 309–10, *313*
  Morawali Nature Reserve 310, 311
  Napu valley *308*, *310*
  Palu 309
  Poso 310
  Taman Angerek Bancea 310
  Tanjung Karang 309
  Towale 309
Sulawesi Tenggara (South-east Sulawesi) 309, 311
  Kendari 311
  Morame 311
  Rawa Aopa National Park 311
Sulawesi Utara (North Sulawesi) 299, 315–7
  see also **Manado**
  Airmadidi 316
  Amurang 317
  Bitung 316
  Bogani Nani Wartabone National Park 317
  Gorontalo 317
  Gunung Ambang Nature Reserve 317
  Kampung Java 317
  Kema 316
  Kolongan Kawangkoan 317
  Kotamobagu 317
  Kyai Maja mausoleum 316–7
  Lahendong 317
  Langowan 317
  Lembeh Strait 316
  Manado Tua *313*
  Minahasan Highlands 316–7
  Tangkoko-Dua Saudara Nature Reserve 316
  Tomohon 317
  Tondano 316, 317
Sumatra 32, 63, 72, 98, 101, 114–5, 169
  see also **North Sumatra**; **South Sumatra**; **West Sumatra**
  communism in 38
  cuisine 69, 70, 71
  flora and fauna 105, 169, 181, 184, 186, 188
  forest fires 102, 184, 194
  funerary rites 67
  Islam 52–3, 60
  oil *36*, 42, 194

Pasai 26
Pasemah highlands: stone sculptures 22, 192
Perlak 26
population 52–3, 104
rainforests 101, 103, 186, 188
Samudra: tomb of Sultan Malik al Saleh 26
separatism 40, 45
textiles 88, 90, 91
trade 26, 104
transmigration 54
Sumba *12–3*, 55, 95, *240–41*, *270*, 270–71
  forests 104
  Lai Tarung 270
  Pasunga 270
  Prai Goli 270
  Rende 271
  Sodan 270–71
  Tarung 270
  textiles *87*, 89–90, *90*, *270*, 270–71
  Waikabubak 270, 271
  Wanokaka 270, 271
Sumbawa 22, 55, 243, 245, 255–7, *257*
  see also **Gunung Tambora**; **Islam**
  Ai Bari 256
  Ai Beling 256
  Batutering 256
  Benete 256
  Bima 257
  Calabai 257
  forests 104
  Hu'u 257
  Jereweh 256
  Maluk 256
  Maria 257
  Poto 257
  Sape 257
  Tanjung Pasir 256
Sumbawa Besar 256
  Balai Kuning 255
  Dalam Loka 255
Sunan Kalijaga 139
Sundanese (West Java) 15, 51, 52, 119, 131
Sungai Amandit 285
Sungai Baliem 335, 336
Sungai Brantas 25, 159
Sungai Kahayan 289–90
Sungai Kapuas 292, *293*, 295
Sungai Mahakam *278*, 279–82
Sungai Martapura 284
Sungai Sekunir *274–5*
Sungguminasa (South Sulawesi) 302, 303
Supiori 342

Surabaya (East Java) 33, 159–61
  Centre Culturel Français 161
  Chinese quarter 160
  Governor's Mansion 160
  Heroes Monument 160
  Hok An Kiong Temple 160
  Hong Tik Hian Temple 160
  House of Sampoerna 160
  independence movement *159*
  Jalan K.H. Mas Mansyur 160
  Joko Dolog 160–61
  Kali Mas canal *160*
  Kebun Binatang 161
  Mandarin Oriental Hotel Majapahit 160
  population 159
  Red Bridge 160
  Surabaya Sue 160
  Tomb of Sunan Ampel 160
Surakarta see **Solo**
Syahrir, Sutan 53

t

Tanah Sunda (Sunda Lands) see **Western Java**
Taoism 63
temples
  see also **Borobudur; Prambanan**
  Banyan Temple (Bintan) 195
  Batuan (*pura puseh*) (Central Bali) 215
  Bin Hun Kiong (Manado) 316
  Candi Jago (Malang) 163
  Candi Jawi (East Java) 162
  Candi Muara (Jambi) 191
  Candi Panataran (East Java) 163
  Candi Singosari (Malang) 163
  Dieng Plateau (Central Java) 153
  Gedung Songo (Western Java) 139
  Gunung Pengsong Temple (Lombok) 246
  Hok An Kiong Temple (Surabaya) 160
  Hong Tik Hian Temple (Surabaya) 160
  Pelinggih Arjuna Metapa (Central Bali) 222
  Pulaki (Bali) 230
  Pura Batu Bolong (Lombok) 248
  Pura Beji (North Bali) 229
  Pura Belanjong (Sanur, South Bali) 205
  Pura Besakih (East Bali) *235–6*
  Pura Bukit Sari (Central Bali) 221
  Pura Dalem (North Bali) 229
  Pura Dalem Agung Padangtegal (Ubud) 219

  Pura Gunung Kawi (Central Bali) 222
  Pura Jagatnata (Denpasar) 202
  Pura Kebo Edan (Mad Bull Temple) (Central Bali) 221
  Pura Kehen (Central Bali) 223
  Pura Lingsar (Lombok) *248*
  Pura Luhur Batukau (North Bali) 228
  Pura Luhur Uluwatu (South Bali) 201, 207
  Pura Maospahit (Denpasar) 202–3
  Pura Mayura (Lombok) 247
  Pura Meduwe Karang (North Bali) 229
  Pura Mengening (Central Bali) 223
  Pura Meru (Lombok) *246*, 247
  Pura Narmada (Lombok) 247–8
  Pura Penataran Agung (East Bali) 236
  Pura Penataran Sasih (Pejeng, Central Bali) 222
  Pura Petitenget (South Bali) 201
  Pura Pusering Jagat (Central Bali) 222
  Pura Rambut Siwi (West Bali) 231
  Pura Sada (South Bali) 210
  Pura Sakenan (South Bali) 201
  Pura Samuan Tiga (Bedulu, Central Bali) 221
  Pura Segara (Lombok) 248
  Pura Segara (Sanur, South Bali) 205
  Pura Suranadi (Lombok) 248
  Pura Taman Ayun (South Bali) *63, 210*
  Pura Tanah Lot (South Bali) 208–9, *209*
  Pura Tegeh Koripan (North Bali) 227
  Pura Tirtha Empul (Central Bali) *223*
  Pura Ulun Danu Batur (North Bali) *226*, 227
  Pura Ulun Danu Bratan (North Bali) 228
  Sri Mariaman (Medan) *174*
  temples to Dewi Sri (Bali) 66
  Thay Kak Sie temple (Semarang) 139
  Vihara Gunung Timur (Medan) *174*
  Wan-De Yuan (Banten) 132
Tenggerese people 52, 119, 164
Ternate island *28*, 29, 32, 321, 330–31, *331*

  Batu Angus (Burnt Rock) 331
  Benteng Kayu Merah *322*
  Benteng Oranje 330
  Benteng Toloko *330*, 331
  Dufa-Dufa *330*, 331
  Kedaton 330
textiles 87–93, 98–9, 309
  bark cloth 91
  batik *86*, 88–9, *92–3*, 98, 137, *138*, 144–5, 146–7, 156
  beadwork 98–9
  geringsing 89, 91, *238*, 239
  hinggi 87, 89–90, *90*, 270–71
  ikat 88, 89, 89–91, 98, 234, 239, 267, 268, *270*, 271, 272, 273, 295
  kain endek (Bali) *216*
  kain sambas (Kalimantan) 294–5
  kain ulos (Sumatra) 178
  selimut (waist wrap) 90
  songket 91, 185, 189, 234, 257
  trade in 26
theatre see **dance and theatre**
Tidore island 32, 321, 331
Timika, Freeport-McMoRan Mine 255, 321, *337*
Timor 91, 104, 263, 272–3
  see also **East Timor; West Timor**
Tirta, Iwan 93
Toer, Pramoedya Ananta 41
Tolaki people 311
Tomekongga people 311
Torajan people 51, 53–4, 65, 67, 91, 98, 299, *305*, *306*, 305–7, *307*
trade 104, 121
  free trade 34–5
  and Islam 26–7
  Maluku 323
  Nusa Tenggara 243
  spice trade 29, 31, 32, 34, 182, 243, 292–3
  Srivijaya, kingdom of 23–4
  Sulawesi 299
  Sumatra 169
  under Dutch 31, 34
  Western Java 136–7
transmigration *54*, 56, 280
Trowulan 25, 162
Trunajaya, Prince 33–4

u

Ubud (Central Bali) 99, 211, *213*, 216–20
  see also **museums and galleries**
  art 215
  Campuhan 217
  Monkey Forest *219*

INDEX ◆ 417

Pengosekan 218
Pura Dalem Agung Padangtegal 219
Puri Saren Agung 219
Sayan 220
Ubud Market 219
Yayasan Bina Wisata 217
Una-una island 311
UNESCO
 and Borobudur 149
 Lore Lindu National Park 310
 World Heritage Sites *106–7*, 259, 343
United Nations 39, 41, 45, 273, 339

V

Van den Bosch, Johannes 35
VOC *see* **Dutch East India Company**
volcanoes 102–3, 104, 165
 see also **Krakatau**
 Bali 199
 East Java 159
 Gunung Agung 235–6
 Gunung Api *328*
 Gunung Batur 227
 Gunung Bromo *164*
 Gunung Ebulobo 266
 Gunung Inerie 266
 Gunung Kelimutu *266*, 266–7
 Gunung Kiematubu 331
 Gunung Mahawu 317
 Gunung Rinjani 245, *250*
 Gunung Semeru 164
 Gunung Sirung 269
 Gunung Tambora 103, 257
 Gunung Tangkuban Perahu *136*
 Sumatra *183*
 Una-una island 311
Von Koenigswald, G.H.R. 107

W

Wahid, Abdurrahman (Gus Dur) 44, 45
Wallace Line 245, 246
Wallace, Sir Alfred Russel 105, 245, 246, 261
Wallacea 105, 246, 327
Watampone (Bone) (South Sulawesi) 305
watersports
 Banda islands 329
 Biak island 341
 East Bali 237
 Flores 267
 Kepulauan Seribu (Thousand Islands) 132
 Kepulauan Tukang Besi (Wakatobi) 311
 Lombok 248, 249
 North Sulawesi *314*, 315, 316
 Pantai Merah (Komodo) 261
 Pombo island 326
 Saparua 327
 South Sulawesi 304
 Sumbawa 256
Weh island 172
West Java *93*, 131–9
 see also **Bandung**; **Bogor**; **Cirebon**; **Demak**; **mosques (mesjid)**; **Semarang**; **temples**
 Anyer 133
 Anyer Lighthouse 133
 Baduy 52
 Bandungan 139
 Banten *29*, 31, 33, 121, *130*, 132
 Carita *133*
 Ciater 136
 Cibeureum waterfall 135
 Cibodas Botanical Gardens 134
 Cilegon 132
 Cipanas 135
 dance and drama 79
 Dutch colonial period 31, 34, 131
 Gunung Gede-Pangrango National Park 103, 134–5
 Islam 60
 Jepara 139
 Karang Bolong 133
 Kota Batik (Batik City) 138
 Kudus ("Kota Kretek") *139*
 Lembang 136
 Merak 132
 Night Safari 134
 ornamental metalwork 96
 Parahyangan Highlands 134, 136
 Pekalongan *138*
 Pelabuhan Ratu *135*
 performing arts 131
 population 131, 137
 Puncak Pass *10–11*, *134*, 135
 separatism 40, 45
 Taman Safari 134
 Tarumanegara: stone inscription 23, *24*
 Ujung Kulon National Park *106*, *107*, 133–4
West Sumatra 181–9
 see also **Bukittinggi**; **Minangkabau**; **Nias island**; **Padang**; **Siberut island**
 Air Manis 182
 Batusangkar 185
 Bukit Barisan 181
 Danau Bentu 186
 Danau Maninjau 184, *185*
 Danau Singkarak 185
 Harau Canyon *184*
 Kerinci Seblat National Park 181, 186
 Kota Gadang 183
 Minang Highlands 182, 183
 Ngalau Kamang 184
 Ngarai Sianok Canyon 183
 Pandai Sikat 184–5
 Pariangan 185
 Payakumbuh 184
 Rafflesia Sanctuary 184
 Rimba Panti Nature Reserve 184
 Sibolga 187
 Solok 186
 Sungaipenuh 186
 Tabek 185
 Tanah Datar 185
West Timor 45, *88*, 90, 273
Wijaya 25
Wijayakrama, Prince 32
Wonosobo 153

Y

Yali people 335, 336, 337
Yamdena island, Saumlaki 329
Yapen island 342
Yogyakarta (Jogja) 34, 51, *140*, 141–7, 153
 ancient Mataram 141
 Balai Penyelidikan Batik 146
 batik painters' colony 144
 Benteng Budaya (Fort Vredeburg) 145–6
 Dalem Pujokusuman Theatre 146
 Jalan Malioboro 145–6
 Jalan Tirtodipuran 147
 Keraton (Sultan's Palace) *141*, 142–4, *143*, *144*, 146
 Mesjid Ageng (Grand Mosque) 145
 Museum Sono Budoya 85, 145
 new art 99
 Pasar Beringharjo (central market) 146
 Pasar Ngasem (Bird Market) 144
 Pesarean Pertapaan 144
 puppet makers 95
 Sasano Higgil 146
 Sekatan festival 85
 Sumur Gumuling (circular well) (Taman Sari) 144
 Taman Sari 144
 Water Castle (Taman Sari) 144
 wayang puppet theatre *146*
Yusuf, Gen. M. 53

INSIGHT GUIDES

The classic series that puts you in the picture

- **A**laska
- Amazon Wildlife
- American Southwest
- Amsterdam
- Argentina
- Arizona & Grand Canyon
- Asia's Best Hotels & Resorts
- Asia, East
- Asia, Southeast
- Australia
- Austria
- **B**ahamas
- Bali
- Baltic States
- Bangkok
- Barbados
- Barcelona
- Beijing
- Belgium
- Belize
- Berlin
- Bermuda
- Boston
- Brazil
- Brittany
- Brussels
- Buenos Aires
- Burgundy
- Burma (Myanmar)
- **C**airo
- California
- California, Southern
- Canada
- Caribbean
- Caribbean Cruises
- Channel Islands
- Chicago
- Chile
- China
- Colorado
- Continental Europe
- Corsica
- Costa Rica
- Crete
- Croatia
- Cuba
- Cyprus
- Czech & Slovak Republic
- **D**elhi, Jaipur & Agra
- Denmark
- Dominican Rep. & Haiti
- Dublin
- **E**ast African Wildlife
- Eastern Europe
- Ecuador
- Edinburgh
- Egypt
- England
- **F**inland
- Florence
- Florida
- France
- France, Southwest
- French Riviera
- **G**ambia & Senegal
- Germany
- Glasgow
- Gran Canaria
- Great Britain
- Great Gardens of Britain & Ireland
- Great Railway Journeys of Europe
- Greece
- Greek Islands
- Guatemala, Belize & Yucatán
- **H**awaii
- Hong Kong
- Hungary
- **I**celand
- India
- India, South
- Indonesia
- Ireland
- Israel
- Istanbul
- Italy
- Italy, Northern
- Italy, Southern
- **J**amaica
- Japan
- Jerusalem
- Jordan
- **K**enya
- Korea
- **L**aos & Cambodia
- Las Vegas
- Lisbon
- London
- Los Angeles
- **M**adeira
- Madrid
- Malaysia
- Mallorca & Ibiza
- Malta
- Mauritius Réunion & Seychelles
- Mediterranean Cruises
- Melbourne
- Mexico
- Miami
- Montreal
- Morocco
- Moscow
- **N**amibia
- Nepal
- Netherlands
- New England
- New Mexico
- New Orleans
- New York City
- New York State
- New Zealand
- Nile
- Normandy
- North American & Alaskan Cruises
- Norway
- **O**man & The UAE
- Oxford
- **P**acific Northwest
- Pakistan
- Paris
- Peru
- Philadelphia
- Philippines
- Poland
- Portugal
- Prague
- Provence
- Puerto Rico
- **R**ajasthan
- Rio de Janeiro
- Rome
- Russia
- **S**t Petersburg
- San Francisco
- Sardinia
- Scandinavia
- Scotland
- Seattle
- Shanghai
- Sicily
- Singapore
- South Africa
- South America
- Spain
- Spain, Northern
- Spain, Southern
- Sri Lanka
- Sweden
- Switzerland
- Sydney
- Syria & Lebanon
- **T**aiwan
- Tanzania & Zanzibar
- Tenerife
- Texas
- Thailand
- Tokyo
- Trinidad & Tobago
- Tunisia
- Turkey
- Tuscany
- **U**mbria
- USA: The New South
- USA: On The Road
- USA: Western States
- US National Parks: West
- **V**enezuela
- Venice
- Vienna
- Vietnam
- **W**ales
- Walt Disney World/Orlando

INSIGHT GUIDES
The world's largest collection of visual travel guides & maps

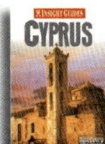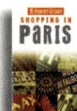